Colleges of Distinction

Go beyond the rankings of commercially-driven lists.
Discover the college that's right for you.

Student Horizons

KENDALL HUNT PROFESSIONAL

Published by Kendall/Hunt Publishing Company
4050 Westmark Drive
P.O. Box 1840
Dubuque, IA 52004

For bulk sales to schools, colleges, and universities, please contact Student Horizons at
info@studenthorizons.com or Kendall/Hunt Publishing Company at (800) 338-8290.

Printed in the United States of America
2008
10 9 8 7 6 5 4 3 2 1
Library of Congress Control Number: 2007940925
ISBN 13: 978-0-98001320-7

A special **Thank You** to all those that worked on this book and made it possible.

Editors: *Christine Kolaya, Stacy Downs, David Bushko, Ruth McClellan Nugent PhD*

Writers: *Ann McClellan, Alexis Andrews, Darrell Delamaide, Ellen Hirzy, Mason Smith, Rob Haulton, Ruth McClellan Nugent PhD*

Project Coordinators: *Julianne Salisbury, Lori Wilson, Kelly Lightfoot*

Cover Design: *Cinda Debbink*

Interior Page Design and Layout: *Cinda Debbink, Eric Petersen*

Special thanks to Chris Leahey, Lauren Clemence, Andrew Knap, Lisa Munns, Ruthanne Salisbury, Karianne Salisbury, Sarah Beck, Chris Lange, Howard Yoon, Gail Ross.

Contents

Northeast

Connecticut

Maine

Massachusetts

New Hampshire

New York

Rhode Island

Vermont

Mid-Atlantic

Maryland

New Jersey

Pennsylvania

West

What Are the
Colleges of Distinction?

Colleges of Distinction owes its origin to parents who accompanied their children through the college-search process, who were surprised at the difficulties they encountered trying to get beyond the "brand-name" institutions to find the colleges that offered the best undergraduate educations, and then—through the next four years and beyond—were pleased to see the growth their children experienced at the "hidden-gem colleges" they had discovered. In collaboration with academic professionals, these parents have created *Colleges of Distinction* as a way to help students and parents find colleges they might not have otherwise considered, but which might be exactly the right college for them.

Every featured college is unique, but they all share key characteristics:

• Their students are bright, motivated, and engaged.

• Their classrooms are interesting, exciting places to explore and learn.

• They offer their students vibrant campuses and communities.

• And, they turn good students into well rounded, successful citizens with the capacity to contribute to their communities, their nation, and their world.

If this sounds like what you are looking for in a college, then you are the student (or the parent of a prospective student) for whom we wrote this book.

Our goal, with *Colleges of Distinction*, is to help you get beyond the advertisements and the rankings to find colleges and universities that consistently provide a remarkable undergraduate college experience and produce successful graduates.

These are schools that get praise from high school guidance counselors across the country, as well as from college admissions officers, professors, students, and satisfied alumni. So why haven't you heard of them?

The truth is, many schools are famous for reasons that have nothing to do with the quality of their educational programs. They may have big-time football or basketball programs. They may be known for the path-breaking research conducted by scientists who never actually teach. Or, they may be recognized for the quality of their Ph.D. programs and medical schools.

The colleges in this book may not receive that kind of publicity, but employers and graduate schools know that *Colleges of Distinction* produce real winners.

How do they do this?

They welcome students who demonstrate both academic promise and community involvement. They keep classes small, so professors get to know their students as individuals, not numbers. They encourage athletics and a wide range of cultural, intellectual, and social activities, but they help students keep it all in balance with their studies. They encourage their students to get involved with their own communities, as well as exposing them to the global community.

Year after year, they do a great job. And, looking back, their graduates say, "This might not be the right college for everyone, but it was exactly right for me."

"The truth is, many schools are famous for reasons that have nothing to do with the quality of their educational programs."

You'll find many small, private, liberal arts colleges in this book. Schools of this kind have long been recognized for their focus on personal attention and student engagement. There are public universities in this guide as well, proving that these institutions can be just as personalized as their private counterparts. There are also single-gender schools, historically Black colleges, engineering schools, Christian colleges, and more.

Why do we call them Colleges of Distinction?

They may be modest about it, but these schools have just as much history and heritage as the better-known, brand-name colleges. What's more, they have a proven record in four key areas:

Engaged Students

GPAs and board scores are important, but *Colleges of Distinction* look for students who will be engaged outside the classroom, as well as inside it. These students compete in sports, do volunteer work, conduct independent research, and study abroad. They are not just thinkers, they are doers.

Great Teaching

Professors who teach in *Colleges of Distinction* know students by name and are committed to seeing them succeed. They're experts in their fields and they are dedicated to teaching. Their students learn in environments that encourage lots of reading, writing, research, and personal interaction. Their students learn to analyze problems, think creatively, work in teams, and communicate effectively.

Vibrant Communities

Colleges of Distinction provide a rich, exciting living-and-learning environment, both on and off-campus. They offer a variety of residential options, clubs and organizations to satisfy every interest, plenty of cultural and social opportunities, and avenues for leadership, character, and spiritual development. Whether they are in rural or urban settings, they provide ways for students to be involved in the life of the surrounding community.

Successful Outcomes

Colleges of Distinction have a long record of graduating satisfied, productive alumni who go on to make their mark in business, medicine, law, education, public service, and other fields. In terms of the return they offer on investment, these schools are outstanding educational values.

As different as these colleges may be from each other, among people "in the know" they all have outstanding national reputations. We hope you benefit from finding out more about the best-kept secrets in college education today.

Finding the right college is one of the biggest decisions you'll ever make. It ranks right up there with choosing a spouse and deciding on a career. Finding the right college can change your life; getting stuck at the wrong one can leave you frustrated and unhappy.

How do students choose? How can their parents help?

So, how do high school students select the right college? And, if you are the parent, how do you help your son or daughter make the right choice?

Let's be realistic. It's your junior or senior year of high school. You're busy with your schoolwork, concentrating on the SAT or ACT, fitting in school activities, and

trying to have a social life, too. Are you likely to devote a huge number of hours to carefully reading every college's marketing materials, pouring over piles of guidebooks, studying the characteristics of hundreds of colleges and universities, and eventually making a deliberate, well-considered decision? Of course not.

According to research by the College Board, the most important source of information for students deciding which colleges to apply to is *word-of-mouth information.* They listen to advice from teachers and guidance counselors, parents and other family members, and—often most compellingly—from their friends.

College guidebooks are another source of information, and many students and parents make good use of them.

Often, of course, this process will guide you to the right college. Yet there may be excellent schools— maybe the perfect school *for you*— that no one tells you about, that you haven't heard of, and that you

won't discover by scanning the top 10 colleges in an annual numerical ranking.

That's where *Colleges of Distinction* comes in.

College Guidebooks

It's the "best" college—or the second or third or twentieth best. It ranks at "the top of the list." It has an "excellent reputation."

Ever wonder what these phrases really mean? Can diverse institutions really be rank-ordered using statistics? How relevant are these measurements and rankings to what is going to be the ideal college experience *for you?*

The truth is, it's extremely difficult to quantify the quality of colleges and universities. For one thing, the very act of measuring colleges is based on the assumption that all students are alike, that they want and need the same things, and that it might be possible to create a single ideal college that would be perfect for everyone. Of course, that isn't true.

Unlike high school, college students spend their time studying vastly different subjects. They enter college with a huge variety of expectations, hopes, and dreams. There are no SAT's or ACT's to measure achievement, no national "standards of learning" to compare the quality of one college with that of another. There are no published statistical measures on how happy and satisfied students are at the over 3,000 colleges in the country.

So how do we judge quality?

The Rankings and Ratings Approach

A number of widely-read guidebooks make a game attempt at comparing schools. *U.S. News & World Report's* annual "Best Colleges" uses a statistical approach that considers many different factors, all of which, they claim, contribute to the overall quality of a college. Among the factors U.S. News plugs into their statistical formula are:

- *The college's overall faculty: student ratio*
- *The number of faculty members with Ph.D.s*
- *The size of the college's financial endowment*
- *Faculty salaries*
- *SAT and ACT scores of entering students*
- *Percentage of entering students in the top 10% of their high school class*
- *Level of alumni giving*
- *Percentage of applicants rejected*
- *Student retention and graduation rates*

But can you really find the "best" school—especially, the best school for you—from statistics alone? For example, selectivity is fairly easy to measure: divide the total number of applicants by the number of applicants rejected. But if a school is hard to get into, does that necessarily mean it is a better place to learn, live, and grow? Would it be the best place for you?

And exactly what does "high selectivity" mean, anyway? Some schools—in the Northeast, especially—receive so many applications just because of their location. Schools in other parts of the country may have equally tough

Photo: iStockphoto.com/TriggerPhoto

entrance requirements, but because fewer students choose to apply to them, they appear—statistically— less selective.

When guidebook editors decide which characteristics to measure, they are making value judgments that greatly affect the results—and they don't necessarily value the same things you do. For example, if ethnic diversity is important to you, does the guidebook use it as one of its statistical criteria? What about the safety of the campus (by Federal law, this information is available in the Campus Safety Office, but you won't find it in the college's marketing materials or in a college guidebook)?

And, when guidebook editors decide what to measure, they shy away from the hard-to-quantify intangibles—quality of life, actual classroom experience, friendliness of the campus—that are vitally important in each student's college experience.

Rankings-based guidebooks provide important information. But, as a smart consumer, you should be aware of their limitations. As you thumb through the rankings, we suggest you ask:

Other Approaches

▶ Is "the best college" really the best college for you? What facts and figures made it "the best"? Are these criteria that you value highly?

▶ Do you value something that can't be measured by statistics? Are spiritual identity, classroom excitement, and active residence life programs important to you?

▶ As a student at this particular college, will you be able to participate in all the activities in which you have an interest? Do you need to be a theatre major in order to audition for a role in a play, or are auditions open to all students? Are all interested athletes welcome to try out for the college's teams?

▶ How much learning actually goes on at the college you're considering? Who actually does the teaching? Are students excited about what goes on in the classroom and the lab?

▶ In addition to college guidebooks based on statistics, there are many kinds of guides, websites, and studies, which may or may not be useful in your college search.

You Will Find:

The Inside Scoop

Some guidebooks, like *The Princeton Insider's Guide*, emphasize surveys of students and faculty members. They usually deliver on what they promise: an "inside look," an informal and unauthorized view of the campus—things you definitely won't find in the college's marketing materials. On the down side, their editors may choose quotes for dramatic effect. One dissatisfied student's response has been known to give a false impression of an otherwise very fine school.

Expert Advice

Other guides give you "expert opinions" based on a lifetime of working in education or in education-related journalism. Loren Pope's *Colleges That Change Lives* and Jay Mathews' *Harvard Schmarvard* are excellent examples of these books. Both of these gentlemen have spent a lifetime as education journalists, and they are intimately acquainted with the college admission process. Interestingly, both writers avoid strict rankings, although both offer lists and comments on colleges they recommend.

Measuring Engagement

On the scholarly end of the scale, a few ongoing research projects attempt to do what *U.S. News* doesn't: measure the actual learning that takes place at various colleges. The National Survey of Student Engagement (NSSE), based at Indiana University, collects detailed survey information from students at many colleges and universities. Another is the Cooperative Institutional Research Program, an ongoing national study of 11 million students, 250,000 faculty and staff, and 1,600 higher education institutions. NSSE and CIRP provide interesting and valuable data about the experience of students at American colleges and universities. Unfortunately, they do not release results for individual schools.

There Must Be a Better Way!

With *Colleges of Distinction*, we are trying to do something a little different- give you a reliable, journalistic look at schools that may not have the biggest names in higher education, but that consistently do a great job educating undergraduate students.

Every one of these colleges excels in the four areas we have defined as most important in the college experience: attracting and supporting engaged students, promoting outstanding teaching, encouraging a vibrant campus life, and producing successful graduates. But every one of them does so in different ways.

So how did we identify the schools in this book?

First, we asked people "in the know" about colleges. We solicited recommendations from the heads of admissions at different colleges. We then sifted through this rather large list looking for certain characteristics:

1 **Evidence of schools looking for, and keeping, engaged students.** For the most part, we avoided schools that rejected more than 50% of their applicants, giving preference to those that consider factors beyond SATs and ACTs in admissions. We looked for schools that excelled in scores tabulated by the National Survey of Student Engagement. We considered retention and four-year graduation rates. We also considered each school's rate of study abroad, internship participation, and other "hands-on" learning opportunities.

2 **Evidence of schools that value good teaching.** We looked for schools with lots of chances for students to interact with professors and where faculty members are rewarded primarily for teaching, rather than research or publishing. Specifically, we looked for large proportions of full-time faculty, good student:teacher ratios (16:1 and below), small average class sizes, and programs that encouraged student/faculty interaction.

3 **Evidence of vibrant campus communities.** Although we decided to accept universities with as many as 8,000 undergraduates , we held such institutions up to close scrutiny, looking for evidence that they still managed to build a strong sense of community through their residence halls, campus activities, and opportunities for student involvement.

4 **Evidence of successful alumni.** We looked for schools with strong records of graduate school and professional school success and good results in employment after graduation. Where possible, we also considered alumni satisfaction, as measured by satisfaction surveys and rates of alumni giving.

That's why we don't rank the schools in this book. We explain how each of them commits itself to achieving the four elements of successful colleges, and we leave it up to you to determine the one that matches your talents and interests, that promises to be the place where you want to live and learn—the one that's best *for you*.

Finding the School that Fits Your Style

Next, we polled high school guidance counselors from across the country, asking them to tell us which schools belonged on our list and which ones did not.

Informally, we talked to parents, students, and professors at a variety of institutions around the country, seeking even more feedback on our list.

From this diverse community, common opinions began to emerge. Some schools came up again and again; others, we found, were deserving of the high reputation we had originally assigned them.

Having thoroughly polled the available opinions, we then began our own investigation of the institutions that remained on our list. We visited campuses ourselves,

interviewed a cross-section of the campus community, and sat in on classes. We dug into school records and spoke frankly with admissions directors.

The result is a book with colleges that we're convinced are terrific places to learn. Measured by both quantitative and qualitative data, these schools come out ahead. While we can't guarantee that you'll find a school you like in *Colleges of Distinction*, chances are you'll find a number that interest and intrigue you.

How This Book Is Structured

Chapters 2-through-5 talk in depth about the Four Distinctions that we believe distinguish those colleges and universities that offer great undergraduate educations: Engaged Students, Great Teaching, Vibrant Communities, and Successful Outcomes. Reading through these chapters will give you a better idea of what these qualities are, why they matter, how we measured them, and how you can judge a school in these areas.

In Chapter 6, high school guidance counselors discuss the "admissions

climate" among colleges in their own region of the country. You may want to look at all four regions, or you may only be interested in those areas closest to you. Wherever you decide to apply, this discussion should help you make the best possible application.

Later in the book, there is an entry describing each College of Distinction. You'll find Fast Facts about each college and a guide about how to read the first part of the entry (the facts and figures), what all the numbers mean, and what you might want to use them for. We'll describe the campus and fill you in on the general social, cultural, intellectual, and political character of the college.

Throughout this book, you'll find suggestions on how to use the information we've included, as well as questions to ask when visiting a campus, and positive and negative things to consider. While no book can ever substitute for a campus visit, *Colleges of Distinction* should help you decide which campuses you want to visit.

Good luck with your college search. We hope you find the campus that is truly the best for you!

Photo: © iStockphoto.com/ichaka

"Rather than wondering, 'What will I do with my college education?' the more important question to ask as you consider college is, 'Who will I be?' What kind of a person do I want to become? What kind of qualities do I want to nurture? What kind of contribution do I want to make to the world? Who will I be?"

—*Ronald R. Thomas, President, University of Puget Sound*

Chapter **2**

Engaged Students

Who Are You? (And How Do You Learn?)

"Different is good," proclaimed a recent fast-food advertising campaign, and most Americans would agree. We Americans pride ourselves on our diversity. We like to think of ourselves as unique individuals.

A Day at a College of Distinction

Every student is different and every college is different, on any given day, you might find yourself:

- Interviewing with Career Services for your-upcoming internship at the local police department.

- Working with your mechanical Engineering class to build a solar-powered car.

- Conducting a mock Salem witchcraft trial in a history class of 20 people.

- Meeting with your fraternity to plan a dunking booth for the campus fair, raising money for kids with cancer.

- Competing in an intramural football game.

- Bowling with a group of friends from your residence hall.

- Giving a presentation at the Study Abroad Office about your summer studying in Japan.

- Practicing with the varsity swim team.

- Presenting set designs for the upcoming production of "The Importance of Being Earnest" in a theater class of 10 people.

- Conducting research in the bio-chemistry lab for a professional article you're writing with a professor.

- Making travel arrangements for next weekend's Habitat for Humanity project.

- Editing your own weekly campus news program in a journalism class of 25 people.

- Meeting with your Spanish professor to go over some difficult homework.

When it comes to education, we often talk as if one size fits all. Students often figure that colleges are pretty much the same. If it's a "good school," it must be good for me. But educators know that different people learn in different ways.

If you're the kind of person who learns best from talking things through, you're not going to thrive in an environment where you sit in a crowd of 500 and listen to talking heads. If you learn by solving problems, tests or papers emphasizing rote memorization are going to turn you off.

One of the best ways to start figuring out how you like to learn is to think about situations where you have learned new information or skills most easily.

When someone gives you driving directions, do you need to see a map or can you listen to directions by ear? Does it help you to be told what landmarks to look for while driving, or do you prefer to think in terms of distance and direction?

How do you prefer to study for tests? Do you like to read over material alone, or does it help you to talk it over with a friend? Does it help you to actively write out material by hand, or to listen to someone repeat it to you?

What activities or hobbies give you pleasure? Are you a physical person who prefers sports or dance? Do you like other performance-based activities, such as singing or acting? Do you enjoy "hands-on" hobbies like carpentry or sculpture? Do you

enjoy the process of collecting and classifying items like stamps or dolls? Do you read or write for pleasure?

It's quite likely that you are unaware of your best learning-style. It may be that you've never had the chance to combine your hobbies and passions with your academic interests. Maybe some of your grades have even suffered as a result.

The good news is that college can give you a chance to be a hands-on learner. You can travel abroad to learn a language, or take an internship to try out a job. Your campus activities can teach you leadership skills or even academic knowledge while you have fun. The *Colleges of Distinction* offer you a wide range of ways to get engaged in learning.

Measuring Engagement: What is it, how can I find it?

The term "engagement" is more than a buzzword. It's a serious part of how good colleges teach their students. Hands-on learning gives you practical skills for the future, as well as making learning easier. Important forms of engaged learning include:

1 **Classroom experiences that emphasize reading, writing, and speaking.** Whether it's history, biology, Spanish, or engineering, you should be actively engaged in the skills of analysis and expression. Some lecture-based courses are inevitable at most (though not all!) colleges, but classes that emphasize active learning—learning in which you are actively involved in the learning process—help you develop the skills you'll need for success in the workplace and other aspects of your life.

2 **Collaborative learning in and outside the classroom.** Whether it's working on a group project in class or undertaking joint research with a professor, collaborative learning reflects the reality that most people do not work alone. Learn to work with others in college, and you'll be ahead in almost any field.

3 **Field experience.** Learning outside the classroom is especially important in research-based disciplines, but almost any course that involves field experience will give you a leg up on your resume. Internships, which let you try out a career, and service learning, which allows students to serve their community as part of a class, are good forms of field experience.

4 **Interacting with other cultures.** Whether through studying abroad or through a multicultural experience in the U.S., college students have more opportunities than ever to learn about different peoples, great preparation for a job market that is increasingly international and multicultural.

Words to the Wise: Are you Engageable?

"College and university admission officers at selective institutions typically have a broad definition of merit, as well as a deep commitment to fairness and equity. They know that the ability to contribute and succeed in college goes beyond grades and testing.

Typically, selective colleges consider:

- the quality of courses a student has chosen
- the student's involvement in the school or community
- the ability of the student to write effectively
- the student's character and ability to function in a community (as reflected by recommendations from teachers, employers and others)."

—*Carey Thompson, Dean of Admissions, Centre College of Kentucky*

"Standardized exams cannot measure heart (and neither can I, by the way), but we do have ways of getting a read on how much initiative or drive, or whatever you want to call it, plays in the process. Is the student involved outside of class? Is she a leader? Does he write well? How are her interpersonal skills? What do his peers and teachers think of him? All these elements contribute to the equation of whether or not a student is admitted to TCU. Our decisions are holistic in nature as we try to take into account everything we are able to discover about the student."

—*Ray Brown, Dean of Admissions, Texas Christian University*

Before You Visit

▶ Look over any materials you have received from the college. Are there any interesting opportunities that you would like to learn more about?

▶ When making the appointment for your visit, ask if you can meet with someone who knows more about the programs that interest you. For example, is it possible to visit the Study Abroad Office or meet with a professor who conducts research with students?

When You Are On Campus

▶ Ask an admissions counselor what the school values in an applicant. Does the description sound like a good match for you?

▶ How many students participate in study abroad, internships, student research, service learning, and other hands-on opportunities?

▶ Is there a time when students generally engage in these opportunities (the beginning of junior year, for example)?

▶ Do you need to qualify for any special programs (like an Honors College) in order to have these opportunities? If so, how well do your qualifications stack up?

▶ Talk with the admissions counselor about your current high school interests and activities. Are there groups on campus in these categories?

A Checklist for finding...
Engaged Students

Doing Your Homework

☑ If they do not use NSSE, does the college offer any other measures of how well students are learning?

☑ To what degree does the faculty subscribe to "active learning"? Ask for examples of professors who teach in this way.

☑ What percentage of students participate in study abroad, internships, and undergraduate research experiences? (More than one-third usually represents a significant part of the campus.)

☑ Does the school have short one-month terms? (Usually offered in January or May, these can make off-campus experiences easier to integrate into your regular course schedule.)

☑ What summer opportunities are available at the school?

☑ Do scholarships and other financial assistance cover off-campus study?

☑ What opportunities are there for students to build resumes?

☑ Does the school offer research opportunities? (This is especially important for science-oriented students or those considering graduate school in any field.)

☑ Does the school have programs for service learning?

☑ How well does the school work with local resources (businesses, philanthropies, government, museums, and artistic groups) to enrich student education?

Ask Students

▶ What kind of engaging experiences have they had? Study Abroad? Internships? Service? Do they have any planned?

▶ What are their favorite classes? What makes these classes interesting? Do they sound interesting to you?

▶ Have students had any "hands-on" learning experiences that they especially enjoyed?

▶ Have they been involved in any research projects, fieldwork, or special trips related to a class? Do these experiences sound interesting to you?

Great Teaching

It's common sense. Better teaching means more learning. But how do you define good teaching? Most prospective college students would like to find a school where they will enjoy the best teaching available. Unfortunately, teaching quality isn't as easy to measure as endowment dollars or the size of dorm rooms.

There are some widely accepted standards defining what "good teaching" is. Once you're familiar with them, it's easier to know which questions to ask.

Most colleges will promise you that they have "great faculty," but not every school delivers. Learning about good teaching can help you get beyond the promises to find the quality you're looking for at the colleges you're considering.

According to the American Association of Higher Education, there are **seven basic practices** in good undergraduate education. Good teaching should:

1 *Encourage contact between students and faculty.* It's easier for faculty to help students when they know each one by name. Likewise, when students feel comfortable approaching professors, they can ask more questions, get more involved, and get better help.

2 *Develop reciprocity and cooperation among students.* Good teachers help students learn from each other, not just from the teacher. Not only does this help students learn the subject matter, it also helps them learn valuable career skills like leadership, creativity, and working in teams.

3 *Use active learning techniques.* Students tend to learn more when they take an active role in their education, rather than just sitting back and waiting for the information to flow in. Active learning techniques include discussion seminars, independent research projects, field work, lab work, internships, and other "hands-on" opportunities.

4 *Give prompt feedback.* Students need more than a grade. They need to know what they're doing right, what they're doing wrong, and how to improve. The more

Profile:
The teaching scholar at a College of Distinction

Teaching at a College of Distinction is more than lecturing and the laboratory. Among the activities that might fill a professor's typical day are:

> **Giving a lecture to first-year students**

> **Participating in a student-faculty panel about current events**

> **Attending a departmental meeting on updating class offerings**

> **Calling prospective students to describe the program**

> **Moderating a discussion panel in an upper-division class**

> **Writing graduate school references for former students**

> **Eating lunch with a student service group in order to plan a weekend project**

> **Moderating a chat room discussion for an honors class**

> **Writing feedback for student essay projects**

> **Working with a student on a paper they are publishing together**

opportunities they have for feedback on assignments, the better students can improve and grow.

5 *Emphasize time on task.* Good learning requires time and effort; good teachers help students learn to manage their time by offering concrete guidelines for learning outside the classroom. Unlike high school learning (which emphasizes in-class activities), college learning requires a great deal of commitment outside of the classroom.

6 *Communicate high expectations.* Expect more from students, and they usually deliver. When professors let students know

how much they can strive for, students have more incentive to work harder and learn more.

7 *Respect diverse talents and ways of learning.* Different students learn in different ways. Good teaching is more than standing behind a podium; it engages students who learn from visuals, hands-on experience, reading, listening, speaking, and other ways of learning.

As you can imagine, there are many different ways to ensure good teaching practice; each of the *Colleges of Distinction* has its own approach.

Words to the Wise: The Importance of Teaching

"Knowledge germinates. Ideas are seedlings in need of nurturing. Left on their own, even with water and sun (or perhaps library books), they may die, or grow deformed. But with the right care from a skilled gardener, they will spread their leaves and reach towards the sun. In the end, good professors do more than enliven their material: they bring their students to life."

–Lisa Gilbert, Alumna, Truman State University

"Students are the real reasons I teach, students who grow and change in front of my eyes."

—Bruce Saulnier, Professor, Quinnipiac University

"My professors were friendly and approachable, and most of them told us to call them by their first name. It was the first time that I had been in an educational setting where I felt like I was part of a team with the teacher instead of being taught at by a teacher. I felt like the faculty loved what they were doing and that they wanted to see us succeed."

–Jeff Morton, Alumnus, St. Michael's College

Research and Teaching: A Better Relationship

What is a professor's job? Unlike a high school teacher, college professors are not trained teachers in most cases. They are hired as scholars, as experts in their fields. In most schools, that means they are expected to spend time researching and publishing as part of their duties. "Publish or perish" is true whether the field is biochemistry or political science. In addition, most professors are expected to take a hand in running their department or participating on a college committee. Whether that's helping to get books ordered for the library, deciding promotions for fellow faculty, or raising money for the school's annual appeal, service is an important part of the professor's job.

On some campuses, teaching comes far behind research and service in faculty priorities. To put it bluntly, not every school rewards good teaching. Many schools promise personal attention and a

A Checklist for finding...
Great Teaching

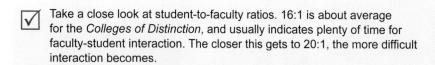

Doing Your Homework

☑ Take a close look at student-to-faculty ratios. 16:1 is about average for the *Colleges of Distinction*, and usually indicates plenty of time for faculty-student interaction. The closer this gets to 20:1, the more difficult interaction becomes.

☑ Take a close look at full-time versus part-time faculty. Also look to see how many faculty are tenured or tenure-track. These faculty will most likely be at the school from year to year, providing you continuity on your courses.

☑ Does the school use teaching assistants (T.A.s)? If so, how? Is it mostly the professors who grade and teach, or mostly the teaching assistants?

☑ Look at average class sizes. What percentage of classes are under 25 students? Under 35?

☑ If some classes are large, what does the school do to promote personal attention? Common ways to promote face-to-face interaction include freshman study groups and small labs in science classes.

☑ Is there a special freshmen-year experience that attempts to integrate the major areas of human knowledge and that stresses writing and speaking, instead of just requiring freshmen to take unrelated introductory courses in large (over 50 students) classes?

☑ What resources are available to help freshmen adjust academically? Is there a special office for students with learning disabilities?

☑ Does the school offer majors or programs that will help you achieve your career goals? (Even when a school does not offer the precise major you are looking for, it may well offer individualized study options that will make career preparation possible.) Does the college make an effort to relate courses in the humanities, sciences and social sciences to careers and vocations, perhaps through credit-bearing internships?

☑ If you are undecided about your career goals, how well will the school's curriculum help you find your way? Is there a Career Planning Office that works closely with the faculty?

Chapter 3

iStockphoto.com/TriggerPhoto

"Most colleges will promise you that they have "great faculty," but not every school delivers. Learning about good teaching can help you get beyond the promises to find the quality you're looking for at the colleges you're considering."

great classroom experience; not all of them deliver. At some, most instruction is done by graduate students working as teaching assistants.

Fortunately, many colleges are learning there's a better way to encourage both research (which helps keep academics up-to-date in their fields) and good teaching (which is what brought most undergraduates to the college). At the *Colleges of Distinction*, you will find classes that are deliberately kept smaller so faculty can give meaningful assignments and get to know their students. Furthermore, they are encouraged to involve students in their research.

Schools that are serious about teaching usually run teaching seminars, institutes, and other serious programs to help professors continue to develop as teachers and academics.

Finally, most teaching-centered schools recruit faculty who genuinely enjoy students. If the faculty at the schools you visit seem

happy to speak with their students and are genuinely interested in them—and if professors are happy to speak with you during your visit—chances are you've found a school that really values great teaching.

Before You Visit

Ask if it is possible to meet with a faculty member in your area of interest. Prepare some questions about the program's requirements, what jobs recent graduates are doing, and what activities and research projects are possible.

If it is not possible to meet with a faculty member, ask if you can e-mail your questions.

Arrange to visit a class, preferably one for freshmen. Don't worry too much about finding one in your proposed major; just ask for an interesting class that is popular with students. Is this a class that you would like to take?

When You Are On Campus

Ask your admissions counselor to clarify any questions you have about class sizes, student-faculty ratios, etc. If the school uses T.A.s, ask about their role and how often you will encounter them.

Ask your admissions counselor some specifics about student-faculty interaction. Will you have a faculty member as an advisor (helping you pick classes and chart an academic path)? What other opportunities will you have to work closely with faculty?

Ask students about their favorite professors, and why they are favorites.

If you eat in the cafeteria or take a campus tour, look at how professors and students interact outside the classroom. Do professors seem accessible? Do students want to talk to their professors?

Photo: © iStockphoto.com/alvarez

Vibrant Community

"Just Right": Where do you want to be?

As with other aspects of choosing a college, finding the right community can be tricky. You'd be surprised how many students transfer, not because of academic difficulty but because they are unhappy with their campus life. The big city that one student finds exciting may be too anonymous and distracting for another student. From athletic opportunities to religious atmosphere, from campus political opinion to cultural opportunities, from community service to residence life, there are a lot of variables to consider when looking at a college campus.

Some Self-Assessments on Campus Life

When you're thinking about campus communities, it's important to be honest with yourself about who you are and what you want. By using these three self-assessments, you can get an idea of what size college you might like, what kind of campus life interests you, and what setting you'd like to study in.

Self-Assessment #1: College Size

Pick A or B

I like...

(a) my teacher to know my name and understand my problems.

(b) to be somewhat anonymous in class.

When I go to a sporting event as a fan, I like to...

(a) know people in the crowd and on the team as I cheer them on.

(b) be part of a huge crowd in a huge stadium.

If I go to a party where I don't know anybody, I really like it when...

(a) someone introduces themselves and goes out of their way to make me feel welcome.

(b) people leave me alone and let me observe.

When I go to college, I think I would like to...

(a) know everything that's going on, and be able to try many different options.

(b) stick with one or two favorite activities.

Assessment #2: My Activity and Living Priorities

My dream campus would offer...
(check all that apply)

- ☐ A particular varsity sport
- ☐ A particular intramural or club sport
- ☐ A variety of intramural or club sports
- ☐ Cheerleading or other sport-booster activities
- ☐ Political or issue-oriented organizations
- ☐ Multicultural/ethnic organizations
- ☐ Camping or outdoors clubs
- ☐ Greek-letter fraternities/sororities
- ☐ ROTC or other military opportunities
- ☐ A particular religious affiliation with college-sponsored spiritual life
- ☐ No particular religious identity, but many spiritual/religious life groups

- ☐ Women's-interest organizations
- ☐ GLBT organizations
- ☐ Newspaper, radio, TV, or other media activities
- ☐ Film or literary clubs
- ☐ Specific hobby or interest clubs (gun club, anime club, etc.)
- ☐ A wide array of service-oriented groups
- ☐ Theatre opportunities for non-majors, both as performers and technicians
- ☐ Music opportunities for non-majors
- ☐ Other performance arts, such as dance or mime
- ☐ Clubs for a particular academic subject or career interest
- ☐ The chance to live in a "theme" house or residence (all French-speaking, for example, or a service-themed house)

- ☐ The chance to live in an apartment-style situation
- ☐ The chance to live in a fraternity or sorority house
- ☐ Women's-only or men's-only housing
- ☐ Another residence preference
- ☐ A wide range of weekend trips and off-campus fun for students
- ☐ A wide range of touring bands and other visiting performers

Assessment #3: Campus Identities

I would be open to exploring campuses that are…
(check all that apply)

☐ Public (state-supported)

☐ Private

☐ Private, where religion plays a strong role (specify religion[s])

☐ Single-sex (all women or all men)

☐ Military-style

☐ Historically Black

☐ Primarily undergraduate

☐ Largely graduate/professional

☐ Engineering-focused

☐ Arts-focused

☐ In a very large city or its suburbs

☐ In a smaller or medium-sized city (such as St. Louis, Cincinnati, Portland) or its suburbs

☐ In a large "college town"

☐ In a small "college town"

☐ In a rural or wilderness setting

Assessment Outcomes

Assessment #1: College Size

"A" answers are more typical of students at smaller schools; "B" are more typical of students at large universities. If you find you're somewhere in between, then "medium" may be just right for you.

Assessment #2: My Activity and Living Priorities

This exercise should help you sort out what you would like in a campus. You may find it helpful to update this list as you continue your college search and get a better idea about things you'd like.

Assessment #3: Campus Identities

Don't worry if some of these are contradictory—the more options you have at first, the better. You can re-visit this list as you learn more about various options.

Photo: © iStockphoto.com/dlewis33

Chapter **4**

Words to the Wise: About Getting Involved

"It was apparent to me early on that even though I was new to the university, I was in a place where I could contribute to my school, and affect my community in a way I thought was reserved for older, more seasoned veterans in the college arena."

–Byron Sanders, Alumnus, Southern Methodist University

"Some of the greatest lessons come from campus involvement. Currently, I am the president of the campus chapter of a national economics honor society, chair of elections/secretary for the Student Government Association, and a representative of the Office of Admissions on the Tower Council. Through these associations, I have gotten to really know the women I work closely with day in and day out. This does not just include members of the student body, but various deans, school administrators, and professors. They teach us by listening to us—students have a say in almost all decisions made on campus."

–Mary Frances Callis, Alumna, Agnes Scott College

"We hold our student-athletes in high regard as students and as athletes. We respect their contributions on the playing field because we insist that those contributions remain part of a larger undergraduate experience where the classroom comes first and out-of-class activities second….. Athletic competition can also be extremely fulfilling at our level. When everyone plays by the same rules, not only is competition spirited and intense, but great athletic traditions can develop."

–Baird Tipson, President of Washington College

Photo: © iStockphoto.com/digitalskillet

Involvement and Community

Colleges of Distinction schools offer opportunities inside as well as outside the classroom. Today, campus life is considered to be one of the most important elements in a college education. The Association of College Unions International (ACUI) states that campus life provides a "complement [to] the academic experience through an extensive variety of cultural, educational, social, and recreational programs. These programs provide the opportunity to balance course work and free time as cooperative factors in education."

They also make you a stronger student. Studies have shown that students who are involved in extracurricular activities graduate after four years or less at higher rates and do better academically.

In other words, a good campus life not only means doing better academically, but getting more out of your education: more exposure to activities, more chances to apply the ideas you learn in class, more personal growth and discovery, more fun and more friends. That "more" also means more opportunities after college, when being well-rounded really helps you stand out from the crowd of job applicants.

Some students persuade themselves that campus life really isn't all that important. They figure that college will be a lot like high school: go to class, go to a practice or a meeting, go home. But college is a 24-7 environment: It's your classroom, your social life, and your home wrapped into one package.

Other students assume that they have to attend a huge campus to have lots of opportunities. In fact, many discover that small- or medium-sized schools make it easier to get involved, whereas big schools may be so anonymous that it's difficult to meet people.

You may also want to think about schools with unique identities—church-affiliated colleges, historically Black colleges, single-gender colleges, and other special places. What activities are you interested in? Are you a big city or a small town person—or somewhere in between? Do you want to be recruited to a professional team—or just compete in the sport you love? The lists in this chapter can give you some places to get started, but don't be afraid to add your own personalized requirements for a college. The choices depend on you and your personality. Finding the right environment is important as you look ahead to a great college experience and a great future.

Before You Visit

▶ If you have a particular activity interest, arrange to visit these programs and their facilities. If possible, ask to speak with faculty or staff who work with the program.

▶ If you are interested in a sport, try to arrange to visit with a member of the coaching staff. If it's not possible to meet, try to get a name and an email address for an inquiry.

When You Are On Campus

▶ Ask students what they do on weekends and for fun. What campus events do they most enjoy?

▶ Drive or walk through the surrounding community/neighborhood. Is it an area that you like? Ask whether the college has a good relationship with the community or whether there are tensions.

▶ Visit residence options for freshmen. If possible, ask a resident assistant or hall assistant about the programs available to those living in the residence. Are they programs in which you would like to participate?

▶ Look at signs, posters, and announcements around campus. Are there many for activities and events that interest you? Does the political and social atmosphere of the campus seem to fit your personality and values? Reading the student newspaper should give you a sense of what is going on from a student perspective.

▶ Ask a student about his or her favorite campus activities and traditions. Do these sound fun and interesting to you?

A Checklist for finding...
Vibrant Community

Doing Your Homework

☑ What activities available on campus match your interests? Are most of the activities you enjoy open to non-majors? For example, if you are interested in theater but majoring in biology, will you still be able to participate in theatrical productions?

☑ What percentage of students are involved in campus activities?

☑ Are there campus activities that you have never tried but which sound interesting to you?

☑ If you are interested in athletics, does the college offer the sport you play? If you are interested in varsity competition, what are its policies regarding walk-ons? Is there an active intramural program for non-varsity athletes?

☑ What cultural and entertainment opportunities does the campus provide? How does it make use of facilities in the surrounding community?

☑ What special events or speakers were on campus in the last year?

☑ Is the college a suitcase campus? That is, what percentage of the students leave campus on the weekends? If there is a vibrant city nearby with a wide range of cultural and social opportunities, students going off campus during the weekend might be a good thing; but it is not a good thing when everyone is going home every weekend!

☑ What kind of residence options does the college offer? What programs are available to help you make friends, meet people, and settle in? How will your roommate be selected?

☑ Are there health facilities or programs on campus? What kind of counseling and crisis support does the campus offer? Does the college provide resources for students with physical or learning disabilities?

Chapter 5

Successful Outcomes

One of the problems with the *U.S. News & World Report* annual survey of colleges is that it measures a college's quality largely by SAT scores and high school grades. But if you think about it, these are indicators the college had nothing to do with.

Perhaps a better way of measuring a college's quality would be by studying "outcomes"—what happens after students graduate? Indicators of successful outcomes include the acceptance rate into graduate or professional schools and the percentage of seniors getting employment in their chosen fields soon after they graduate.

Ultimately, successful outcomes are linked to the alumni who, in a real sense, are the "product" of a college education: What kinds of professions did they enter? Have they distinguished themselves in these professions?

This is how *Colleges of Distinction* measures successful outcomes.

While entering students are not expected to know right away what their major will be or what they want to become in life—freshman and sophomore years should be largely reserved for experimentation and discovery—it is too often the case that by senior year, students still don't know what they want to do.

Colleges of Distinction are especially good at orienting students, right from the beginning, to what they might become in life. They often begin this process by introducing freshmen to the Career Services Office during orientation so that they know what resources are available to them.

Sophomores are then encouraged to consider employment-related internships and externships. Tied closely to these programs are career counseling seminars that help students orient themselves to career possibilities, workshops for resume writing and mock interviews, and career fairs where firms can meet future employees.

By senior year, students enrolled at *Colleges of Distinction* not only have

At most Colleges of Distinction, over 85% of those seeking employment after graduation will find well paying jobs with advancement potential within six months of graduating.

a fairly good idea of what they will do in their first job, but are well on their way to submitting resumes and having interviews.

For those who plan to go on to a graduate or professional school, the same Career Services Office, working with pre-professional advisors (especially pre-med and pre-law) will give advice about available scholarships and the various exams necessary to get into graduate, medical or law school. College professors, of course, having

all gone to graduate school, are an excellent source of advice on master's and doctoral programs.

At most *Colleges of Distinction*, more than 85% of those seeking employment after graduation will find well paying jobs with advancement potential within six months of graduating. Similarly, 20% or more of the graduating class will go directly to graduate or professional school. Sixty percent will have gone on for further education within six years of graduation.

Finally, the "product" of *Colleges of Distinction*—the ultimate outcome—are the alumni. Perhaps the major goal of these colleges is to prepare the future leaders of our society—the business leaders who keep our economy strong, the political leaders who govern us, the professional leaders who impact our lives in many ways and on a daily basis. *Colleges of Distinction* are especially strong in the number of these leaders who attended their institutions. These people not only give of themselves to society in general, but also support their institutions in various ways, including helping new graduates get their first job.

In the first place, a college education should not—indeed cannot—be seen as preparation for only one career. Because of the massive changes we are seeing in society, created in large part by advances in technology, current college graduates will have as many as six or seven entirely different jobs or careers before they retire! Therefore the best preparation for a rapidly changing and utterly unpredictable future is a liberal arts and sciences education. Why? Because liberal arts and sciences provide students with three basic and universal skills that are at the core of any successful career: intellectual flexibility, the ability to communicate effectively, and the skills to engage in life-long learning.

How is this done? *Colleges of Distinction* require students to take a wide variety of courses in the social sciences, humanities, and natural and mathematical sciences, in addition to majoring in a liberal arts or vocational discipline. The result is a graduate who has the intellectual tools to adapt to the shifts and changes we can expect in the 21st century.

Colleges of Distinction prepare their students not only for the first job, but also for the last job!

A Checklist for finding...
Successful Outcomes

Doing Your Homework

☑ What information does the school provide about employment-related internships and externships? How many internships can a typical student take?

☑ What professional development does the school offer students? Does the school offer resume support, mock interviews, career fairs, and other employment support?

☑ What are the employment rates for graduates within 6 months of graduation? Within one year?

☑ If you are considering graduate or law school, does the school provide information about rates of acceptance and give examples of schools to which graduates were accepted?

☑ What is the school's rate of alumni giving? Rates of 30% or more are generally considered fairly strong.

☑ If the school publishes an alumni magazine, ask for a copy with your admissions packet. How important and well-organized does the alumni association seem to be? Are alumni involved in student life? Do they provide a network for students seeking employment?

Before You Visit

▶ Arrange a visit to the Career Services Office. Make a list of questions to ask about internships and other career-exploration opportunities.

▶ Ask if there are recent alumni available in your area with whom you can speak about the school.

When You Are On Campus

▶ Ask your admissions counselor about graduation rates, employment rates, and similar issues.

▶ Ask students about their plans for the future. What is the school doing now to help them achieve their goals?

▶ Ask staff in the Career Services Office or the Alumni Office how alumni help current students.

Photo: © iStockphoto.com/keeweeboy

Admissions Climate and Financial Aid

If you feel that college admissions is a competitive game, you're not alone. College rankings have given the general public the idea that it's no longer enough to be admitted to college; students have to get into a top-ranked school. Different regions of the country experience this pressure in different ways, but the symptoms are universal.

These days, students and parents spend an enormous amount of time and money on guidebooks, SAT tutors, private admissions counselors, and other tools. In some cases, students may actually be missing out on valuable high school experiences and learning because they focus so much energy on getting into the "right" school.

Many college admissions personnel agree that the climate has become overly competitive, but there is no quick fix. What can you do?

First and foremost, decide which schools are really the best for you—not just a magazine's "best." Where will you be happiest? What schools offer the programs and development that are right for you? We urge you to worry less about what school is "the best," and instead ask, "Which school is the best for me?"

You are going to spend a lot of valuable time on the college admissions process. Having been through the process ourselves, we at *Colleges of Distinction* suggest you look past Big Name University, perhaps find the Hidden Gem College that's perfect for you, and tailor your strategy to what that school really wants, rather than wasting your resources on a "one-size-fits-all" approach to test prep and applications strategies.

Use the following checklist to prioritize what's important for you as you're looking at schools. You may also want to use our self-assessment in chapter 4 as one of your tools. Then, be sure to read the sections that discuss the admissions climate in the six regions of the country. They include additional information that will help you understand the specific challenges of your region. Good luck!

Narrowing the Field

Once you have finished this section, you should have a fairly complete picture of what you are looking for in a college. Think about the colleges you have visited. Look at the materials colleges have sent you. How many fit the bill? Knock off the ones that just do not match what you're looking for. You'll be left with a list of colleges that approach the ideal college for you.

How well do your SATs, ACTs, and GPA stack up against their average admissions? You can find some of this information in our book; for more up-to-date figures consult the school's website or other online resources that list this data. Do you score significantly above or below the average? This can give you a very rough estimate of how well you will stack up against other applicants. Don't be discouraged if your scores are lower than the college's average: remember, half of all students admitted to any given colleges have scores and grades below the mid-point, and many of those students have great careers in college and beyond.

Keep in mind, that *Colleges of Distinction* consider many other factors in their admission decisions. Among those you should consider:

▶ Do you have any special skills or interests that might interest one or more of these schools? Schools with extensive service programs or special service scholarships may be especially interested in your service activities. Every college needs a flute player in the band, an actor for the drama program, and a reporter for the school newspaper. Schools with competitive swim teams might be especially interested in recruiting a talented swimmer. Be sure to mention these interests and talents.

▶ Are you a member of a group that is under-represented at one of the colleges you are considering? Many schools have far fewer men than women in their student body and, though they won't admit it, are interested in recruiting men to help correct the inbalance. Some campuses have special programs to encourage first-generation students or members of certain ethnic and racial groups to apply. Still other campuses would like to recruit more "legacies," children or grandchildren of alumni.

▶ Do you have life experiences that make you stand out from the crowd? Have you lived abroad or participated in educational travel opportunities? Have you won any special awards or been recognized for your activities? Have you started clubs or programs in your community, at your school, or through your faith group?

Refine your list based on these questions and narrow your choices down to eight-to-ten colleges: four or five that closely match your interests and to which acceptance is likely; two, where the profile might be above yours ("stretches"); and two that have profiles below yours where admission is almost guaranteed ("safeties"). If you think you'll be unhappy at being accepted by any of the colleges on your list, cross it off right now.

The Facts about Financial Aid: Can you afford not to go to college?

One final issue needs to be discussed: the cost of a college education.

The cost of college is a big public policy issue in America. Parents are usually in shock when they see how expensive college can be,

especially private colleges and universities where tuitions have been skyrocketing at rates far beyond inflation.

The truth is, college is still very affordable. If you have financial need, there are federal, state and institutional grants to help pay for a college education. But even students who do not qualify for need-based financial aid can receive merit-based aid if their high school grades and extracurricular activities are noteworthy. So don't look at the so-called sticker price. After scholarships, campus jobs, and loans are taken into consideration, most colleges are quite affordable.

What about private colleges vs. public universities?

We all know that tuition at public universities is lower than tuition at private colleges. That's because taxpayers subsidize public

tuitions. The fact that the total four-year tuition, room and board costs at many flagship public universities is $50,000 or less, compared to $100,000 or more at private colleges and universities, discourages many parents from considering these institutions.

But things are not always as they seem!

In many states, large public universities are overcrowded. As a result, students often cannot get their first choice of a major. And since classes are frequently full, it often takes five or six years to graduate! Looking at the situation this way, the student attending a public university will not only pay a total of $65,000 in tuition, room and board for five years, but also forgo a year earning a salary (another $40,000+) for a total "real" cost of over $100,000. Now the $100,000+ paid to attend a

private college that graduates its students in four years or less doesn't look so bad. This fact, together with the scholarship support private colleges can offer, considerably levels the playing field. So you really do have a choice.

Finally, one might ask, "Why take on all those loans? Wouldn't I be better off just getting a job after high school?"

The fact is that college graduates, over a lifetime, earn $2 million more in income than high school graduates. Of course this should not be the major reason you go to college. College-educated people are usually happier in their jobs, healthier, and enjoy all the intangible benefits that a college education provides. Taking on $25,000 or more in college loans (scholarships are free gifts and don't have to be repaid) is insignificant in the long run compared to the earning power of a college degree.

Chapter 6

A Checklist for...
Schools

Location

☐ **I am looking for a school that is:**

☐ in my hometown

☐ within an easy drive of my hometown

☐ within a one-day drive of my hometown

☐ within a short flight of my hometown

☐ anywhere

☐ **Specifically, I am interested in schools in the following states:**

Hint: Are you looking for new experiences? Is climate a concern? Do you want to be close to your parents, siblings, or other relatives?

....

....

....

....

....

☐ **I am interested in a location that is:**

☐ a really big city

☐ a regionally important city

☐ a college town

☐ a very small town or a rural campus

Hint: What do you consider a "big" city or a "small" town? People from Los Angeles or New York City may consider cities like St. Louis or Alberquerque very small. If you are from a town of under 10,000, these same cities may seem very large.

Photo: © iStockphoto.com/gregobagel

Photo: © Shutterstock

Photo: © Shutterstock

Photo: © Jupiterimages

Photo: © iStockphoto.com/stevegeer

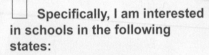

Photo: © Shutterstock

Academic

Hint: Most students change their majors at least once, so don't feel too concerned if you don't quite know what you want right now. Also, be aware that colleges offer majors that will help you achieve your goals under many different names. And be sure to look for opportunities to design your own curriculum!

Other goals for my life include:

Academic subjects that I think might help me achieve these goals are:

Learning experiences that I think I might enjoy include:

- ☐ A unified curriculum, all students take the same classes

- ☐ A core curriculum, where all students take some of the same classes

- ☐ Special freshmen seminars or other freshmen-only classes

- ☐ Classes under 10 people before my junior and senior year

- ☐ Classes under 25 people

- ☐ Classes over 100 people

- ☐ Living-and-learning communities where my roommates and neighbors are studying the same major, taking some of the same classes, or have other academic options in common

- ☐ Service-learning programs where my classroom experiences are connected to community service

- ☐ Studying abroad at a foreign university (specify institution if you know)

- ☐ Studying abroad at a program run by my college (specify country if you know)

- ☐ Studying off-campus in the United States

Chapter 6

Career and Life

I am looking for a college:

☐ Where I can explore my career through an internship

☐ Where I can explore more than one internship

☐ Where there are special resources for undecided majors

☐ With a multi-year professional/ career development program (begins before senior year)

☐ That has specific programs to support my career goals: (specify)

I am looking for a college that will:

☐ Help me get involved in service opportunities (specify your interests)

☐ Give me the chance to play a certain sport (specify)

☐ Help me deepen my spirituality (specify your interests)

☐ Let me pursue my hobbies and interests through co-curricular activities or groups (specify your interests)

Photo: © iStockphoto.com/rcinno

Other career resources that interest me include:

_____

_____

_____

Co-curricular programs that interest me include:

_____

_____

_____

Other programs that might be interesting to explore include:

_____

_____

_____

Help me pursue the following interests:

_____

_____

_____

IT'S AMAZING WHAT CAN
HAPPEN WHEN YOU GIVE YOURSELF
PERMISSION TO DREAM.

Whitney Wilding, '07 – French/International Relations

Bring yourself and your hopes and dreams to Bethany, and you'll experience a transformation. Surrounded by great courses, faculty, facilities, and most important, experiences, you'll learn how to make your dreams become reality.

Bethany stands apart as a small, liberal arts college of national distinction. Our graduates have won a Pulitzer Prize, Academy Award, been named Gates, Madison and Fulbright Scholars, and been elected Governor.

Our 1,300-acre wooded campus in the panhandle of West Virginia has attracted visits by five U.S. Presidents.

If these dreamers could make their way here, so can you.

Come to Bethany. And give yourself Permission to Dream.

 Bethany

Bethany College • Bethany, West Virginia 26032 • 800-922-7611 • www.bethanywv.edu

Student Horizons

providing resources to help find the college that's right for you!

Student Horizons, Inc. is a digital services company devoted to higher education. Founded by concerned parents and admissions professionals, Student Horizons, Inc.'s mission is to enable students to find colleges and universities that appeal to and complement their unique personalities and aspirations.

Our flagship initiative, **Colleges of Distinction** (www.collegesofdistinction.com), profiles approximately 200 schools that excel at engaging students, providing outstanding teaching, offering vibrant communities, and producing successful outcomes, the pillars of a strong and active undergraduate education. **College Student Athletes** (www.collegestudentathletes.com) is a free search tool for students looking to combine athletics with academics.

Student Horizons, Inc.'s newest initiative, **Beyond the Books**, will promote experiential learning opportunities in the United States and overseas. Student Horizons, Inc. also offers digital marketing solutions to colleges and universities through its suite of ASP applications, developed in partnership with leading technology providers.

Visit us online at **www.studenthorizons.com**

The *Guide to Service-Learning Colleges & Universities* will serve as an innovative resource to assist the college-bound community during the college application and search process.

To learn more about the Guide and its parallel website, visit www.beyondthebooks.org

Beyond the Books

Student Horizons, Inc. and Beyond the Books believe that the quality of the educational experience is enhanced by experiential learning: research projects, internships, community service and service-learning, study abroad, leadership programs, entrepreneurial training, and living learning communities.

These types of opportunities enhance classroom learning and help students develop transferable life skills that are needed after college. The best colleges are those that use the whole campus experience—in class and out—to promote the connection between knowledge and action.

Beyond the Books is committed to promoting experiential learning programs and colleges and universities that excel in providing these opportunities. Beyond the Books' mission is to fill the need for a comprehensive database of information about the plethora of experiential learning opportunities, making it easier for interested students to find programs that fill their individual interests.

Visit Beyond the Books on the Web!

www.beyondthebooks.org

32

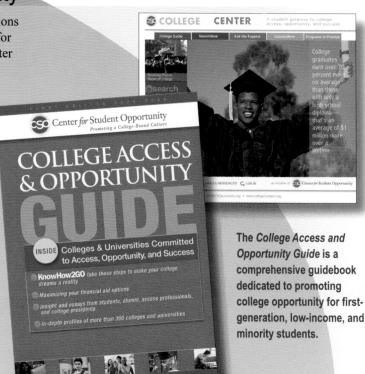
Center for Student Opportunity

Founded by a group of concerned parents, admissions professionals, and nonprofit practitioners, Center for Student Opportunity seeks to fill the need for greater college counseling and preparation resources for first-generation and other historically underserved college-bound students. An independent 501(c)(3) nonprofit organization, CSO is the realization of an idea put forth by the principals of Student Horizons, Inc.

Studying the national landscape of college access to first-generation and underserved populations, the principals discovered that while there are numerous local and sub-regional programs that effectively serve these populations, few if any of these organizations have the resources to expand their reach and fewer still, have the network to access many of the colleges and universities that have targeted these student populations for admission.

Visit the Center for Student Opportunity on the Web!

www.CSOpportunity.org

The *College Access and Opportunity Guide* is a comprehensive guidebook dedicated to promoting college opportunity for first-generation, low-income, and minority students.

CollegeStudentAthletes.com

CollegeStudentAthletes.com is a free college search website for students looking to combine sports and academics at a Division III (D3) college.

D3 athletic programs allow students to continue their athletic careers while attending a first-rate college. And *CollegeStudentAthletes.com* helps them find the right ones. Student athletes may search a comprehensive database of D3 schools to match their academic, athletic, and extracurricular needs.

CollegeStudentAthletes.com provides a library of information about D3 colleges, from the recruiting process to financial aid to in-depth testimonials from college coaches about individual schools. It also showcases current D3 student athletes and successful D3 alumni.

Visit College Student Athletes on the Web!

www.CollegeStudentAthletes.com

Colleges of Distinction Profiles

Read more to get the inside scoop about *Colleges of Distinction* and find the college that's right for **YOU!**

Colleges of Distinction
Northeast Region Schools

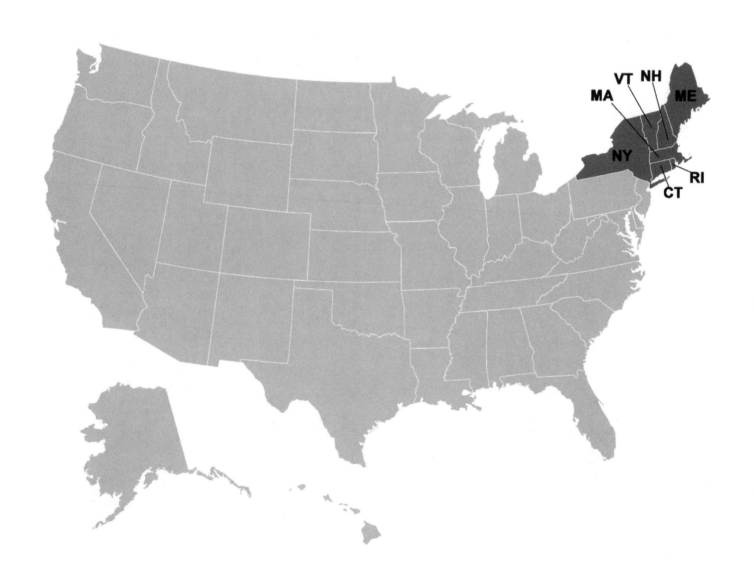

Photo: CiStockphoto.com/lisapics

Notes

_____

_____

_____

_____

_____

_____

_____

_____

_____

Eastern Connecticut State University

CONNECTICUT

Eastern Connecticut State University—a predominantly undergraduate, residential, public liberal arts university founded in 1889—is dedicated to preparing students from a variety of backgrounds for a lifetime of inquiry, discovery, and responsible citizenship.

Admissions Contact:

Eastern Connecticut State University
83 Windham Street
Willimantic, Connecticut 06226
(877) 353-ECSU
Ph: (860) 465-5286
Fax: (860) 465-5544
Email: admissions@easternct.edu
www.easternct.edu

The 4 Distinctions

Engaged Students

Dynamic class discussions, independent research, and a variety of out-of-class opportunities — field study, internships, study abroad, and campus activities — enable Eastern's community of learners to apply their education in practical, real-world settings and encourage their active participation in campus and community life.

Students can choose from 33 majors or select the Individualized Major option, which has allowed students to design such majors as Digital Multimedia, Psychology and Business Administration, Law and Society, Philosophical Methodology, Multimedia Writing/Production for the Deaf, Behavioral Biology, and French Women's Studies.

Fifty study abroad programs take students to such countries as Canada, Puerto Rico, Ghana, Japan, Poland, Uganda, Sweden, and Taiwan. Participation is encouraged in one of Eastern's active field studies, such as those in the Greater Caribbean's barrier reefs and rainforests where students have traveled each year since 1967. Communication students visited Veracruz, Mexico in June 2007 to produce a documentary about the rainforest environment and preservation of biodiversity. The Native American Cultural Study program explored the Navajo, Hopi, and Yavapai cultures in Arizona. And students from the departments of History, Communication, and Business Administration traveled to China in summer 2007 to experience its culture and learn more about its economy.

Hands-on learning is provided on campus in the university's planetarium, black-box theatre, Julius Akus Gallery, radio station, all-digital television studio, and many outstanding science labs. Eastern also places an emphasis on community engagement and service learning as part of its public liberal arts mission.

Great Teaching

Eastern's faculty is dedicated to teaching and focused on mentoring and facilitating students' learning. Students have the opportunity to get to know and learn one-on-one from professors who frequently win recognition for their own scholarship and research and who assume leadership and service roles in the local community.

Experts in their fields, professors bring the school's motto "Excellence that Inspires" to life by publishing poetry; producing award-winning documentaries; writing books; engaging in challenging field studies; traveling and teaching throughout the world; and accomplishing top-notch research. Several have won Fulbright Scholar awards, and an Eastern art professor designed the Connecticut quarter as part of the U.S. Mint series.

The liberal arts core curriculum uses innovative and interdisciplinary courses to expose students to a broad range of academic disciplines and develop their skills in critical thinking, communication, collaboration, and independent research.

Eastern's First-Year Program offers first-time, full-time college students a rich and comprehensive introduction to academics and campus life at Eastern, connecting them with some of the University's best teachers, involving them in innovative courses, and helping them to develop bonds with faculty members and peers from the day they arrive on campus.

Eastern's Honor Program promotes undergraduate scholarship and complements the university's liberal arts mission by providing academically talented students with opportunities to participate in specially designed courses that prepare them to conduct independent research and/or scholarly activity under the direction of a faculty mentor. Examples of such courses include Popular Music in a Global Context; Family in Film, Theatre, and TV; Native American and Ancient Cosmologies in Literature and Culture; and Mass Mediated Political Rhetoric.

Vibrant Community

The Eastern campus is a close-knit community of individuals who respect diverse opinions and backgrounds. Dynamic student organizations, intercollegiate and intramural athletic activities, and hundreds of guest lectures, artist performances, and other cultural and intellectual events each year enhance academic life.

More than 60 clubs and organizations cater to interests in print and broadcast media (including newspaper, yearbook, campus television and radio stations); culture; spirituality;

leadership and service; social activism; professional associations; academics; honors; community service; performing arts; government and politics; and others.

The Eastern Warriors, winners of nine national championships (four baseball and five softball) are in the Little East Conference and are affiliated with the NCAA's Division III. The University provides a well-rounded, broad-based athletic and recreational program, including club sports, recreational activities, intramurals, and intercollegiate competition. It sponsors 17 varsity sports— men's basketball, cross-country, lacrosse, soccer, indoor and outdoor track and field, baseball; and women's baseball, basketball, cross-country, lacrosse, soccer, indoor and outdoor track and field, softball, swimming, field hockey, and volleyball.

Eastern also has intramural sports such as basketball; volleyball; soccer; softball; and flag football, and club sports including rugby; cheerleading; dance team; and tae kwon do.

Trips ranging from shopping and theatre excursions in New York City and Boston to activities such as hiking and river rafting are sponsored by the student-run Campus Activity Board.

Eastern's new Student Center features a bookstore; wireless Internet access lounge; fitness center featuring the latest aerobic equipment; state-of-the-art meeting and conference rooms; and a food court offering diverse food and beverage selections.

Broadening the cultural and social perspectives of Eastern students is an important element of the university's liberal arts mission. The Arts and Lecture Series brings world-renowned authors, artists, and film personalities to campus to enrich the cultural perspectives of students, faculty, and staff as well as the local community. Previous guests have included basketball legend Bill Russell, Pulitzer Prize-winning historian David McCullough, noted author John Updike, CNN Anchor Soledad O'Brien, filmmaker Spike Lee, social activist Gloria Steinem, and actor James Earl Jones.

Successful Outcomes

Eastern graduates are prepared for a variety of professional careers and armed with the life skills necessary to succeed in today's changing world—able to think for themselves, work collaboratively, and serve as community leaders.

Eastern's placement rate (employment and graduate school) is 95 percent. The Office of Career Services provides comprehensive career counseling and job assistance to Eastern students and alumni, reviewing résumés; conducting mock interviews; and offering internship; co-op and full-time employment opportunities. Graduates attend top graduate programs at Harvard University, Yale University, Boston University, Wesleyan University, Tufts School of Veterinary Medicine, Georgetown School of Law, and Columbia University.

Distinguished alumni, who contribute in all sectors of society, include Connecticut State Senator Edith Prague ('65); nationally-recognized research neurobiologist Marc Freeman ('93), who received the Outstanding Doctoral Dissertation Award while earning his Ph.D. at Yale University; and Thomas P. Sweeney III ('83), chairman and CEO of Incentra Solutions, Inc. in Boulder, Colorado.

Fast Facts

Eastern Connecticut State University is a public residential liberal arts university, founded in 1889.

Web site

http://www.easternct.edu

Location

Willimantic, Connecticut—30 minutes from Hartford and midway between Boston and New York.

Student Profile

4,826 undergraduate students full- and part-time (55% female, 45% male); 26 states; 34 countries; 16% minority;

Faculty Profile

71% of faculty members teach full-time. 95% of full-time faculty hold doctorates or the highest degree in their field. 16:1 student/faculty ratio. Average class size is 24.

Residence Life

88% of freshman students live in college-owned, college-operated, or college–affiliated housing. Rooms for one to two students; suites for up to four students; apartment-style units for four to six students. High-speed access to the University's computer network and the Internet from residence halls. Residences have recreation and laundry facilities, lounges, and computer labs.

Athletics

NCAA Division III, Little East Conference. 17 varsity sports: men's basketball; cross-country; lacrosse; soccer; indoor and outdoor track and field; and baseball; women's basketball; cross-country; lacrosse; soccer; indoor and outdoor track and field; swimming; softball; field hockey; and volleyball. Numerous intramural and club teams.

Academic Programs

Majors include: Accounting, Biochemistry, Biology, Business Administration, Business Information Systems, Communication, Computer Science, Early Childhood Education, Economics, Elementary Education, English, English/American Studies, Environmental Earth Science, General Studies, History, History with American Studies, History and Social Sciences, Individualized Major, Mathematics, Performing Arts, Physical Education, Political Science, Psychology, Secondary Education, Social Work, Sociology and Applied Social Relations, Spanish, Sport and Leisure Management, and Visual Arts.

Costs and Aid

2007-2008: Full-time tuition and fees $6,961 (in-state); full-time tuition and fees $15,681 (out-of-state); housing $4,680 (in-state and out-of-state); Silver Meal Plan $3,700 (in-state and out-of-state). 81% of full-time undergraduates received financial aid in 2006-2007.

Endowment

$10.2 million.

More Distinctions

• Recently named as one of the Northeast's Top Colleges by *The Princeton Review*.

• Recently named to Colleges of Distinction.

Quinnipiac University

CONNECTICUT

A full-fledged university with a small college feel, Quinnipiac University makes a strong liberal arts education the foundation for career-focused programs in health sciences, business, communications, education, and law. Students are the priority, and Quinnipiac features a wide range of majors, dedicated faculty, excellent experiential programs, and a dazzling social scene.

Admissions Contact:

Quinnipiac University
275 Mount Carmel Ave.
Hamden, CT 06518-1908
(800) 462-1944
Email: admissions@quinnipiac.edu
www.quinnipiac.edu

The 4 Distinctions

Engaged Students

Quinnipiac challenges, supports, and prepares students for successful careers and lives. The National Survey of Student Engagement (NSSE), the standard for determining student satisfaction with their college, rates Quinnipiac highly compared to schools across the nation. Quinnipiac students tend to be better prepared for classes, spend more time outside of class with faculty, engage in more active-learning activities, and exceed their own academic expectations more often than students at other colleges. The survey also shows a very high rate of student satisfaction (94 percent report an excellent or good academic experience) and an above-average level of academic support.

Students are encouraged to broaden their education and gain real-world experience through internships. The university works closely with each student to find an internship opportunity that matches the student's interests and future goals. . Clinical placements for students in the health-care majors provide the link between classroom learning and patient care.

Quinnipiac provides several options for foreign study, including an arrangement with University College Cork in Ireland.. Through agreements with other universities and international programs, Quinnipiac offers study-abroad programs in a number of other countries.

Great Teaching

Quinnipiac's University Curriculum (UC) provides an introduction to the liberal arts, the humanities, and the sciences along with three seminar courses that explore the individual as a member of the local, national, and international community. The UC teaches students how to analyze ideas, think creatively, write clearly, and speak effectively by providing a solid background in a large number of disciplines. The Writing Across the Curriculum initiative stresses the importance of developing excellent writing skills in all disciplines.

State-of-the-art facilities enhance and enrich students' learning. Quinnipiac's academic buildings have won several awards for design; they offer students ample space for discussion, hands-on learning, and access to the latest technology. Labs are well equipped; the critical care unit in Buckman Center accurately simulates a fully equipped hospital setting; and the Ed McMahon Mass Communications Center gives students full access to a high-definition, fully-digital television production studio, digital editing suites, and a news technology center for journalism. The motion analysis lab provides support to the athletic training and physical therapy program as well as figure movement modeling for the interactive digital design major. The financial technology center is a high-tech simulated trading floor, providing students with an opportunity to access real-time financial data, conduct interactive trading simulations, and develop financial models preparing them for careers in finance. The university's Arnold Bernhard Library has multiple work areas for group and individual study, and is open 24/7 during the fall and spring semesters. All campus buildings and residence halls are supported by a wireless computer network.

Quinnipiac offers more than fifty major fields of study, including several unique and innovative programs. In several programs, including accounting, business, journalism, and education, students can spend one or two extra years in school and earn a master's degree in addition to their bachelor's. The university's health sciences programs in physical therapy, physician assistant, and occupational therapy graduate students with an advanced degree. The physical therapy program is a six and a half-year BS/Doctor of Physical Therapy degree, occupational therapy is a five and a half-year BS/MOT, and the physician assistant program is a six-year BS/MS. Interactive digital design combines computer science with artistic imagination in the context of the humanities.

Vibrant Community

Quinnipiac is located in Hamden, Connecticut, just eight miles north of New Haven, and midway between New York City and Boston on a beautiful five hundred-acre New England campus.

The residential life program at Quinnipiac University provides a safe, comfortable environment where every student can make the most of the college experience. The university strives to sustain a college community focused on the individual as it prepares students for productive lives and careers. Residence staff provides programming to help students grow intellectually, emotionally, and socially. Every hall hosts faculty members for discussion groups, as well as workshops on real-world skills.

Quinnipiac is expanding its residence halls in order to guarantee housing to undergraduate students for all four years. Currently, 3,300 students live on the Mount Carmel campus in traditional residence halls and suite-style housing, some with kitchens. Construction of an additional 1,800 beds is under way, along with a second student center on the nearby York Hill campus, home to the new TD Banknorth Sports Center with twin 3,200-seat arenas for ice hockey and basketball. The view from the top of York Hill is spectacular, looking out over greater New Haven to Long Island Sound. Although resident freshmen may not bring cars to campus, the university shuttle system transports student to area attractions, including shopping, eating, and sports events.

There's plenty to do on campus. The Carl Hansen Student Center is the hub of many student activities. The center is home to the student government office, the headquarters of several student clubs, and the editorial office of the student-produced Chronicle. Over seventy clubs and organizations provide an excellent forum for meeting students with similar interests. Greek life is also available through four national fraternities and sororities. Quinnipiac also schedules special events nearly every weekend, including Parents' Weekend, the Holiday Dinner, and award-winning productions by the theatre department. Recent productions have included *Dead Man Walking*, *The Laramie Project*, and *The Troubles of Romeo and Juliet*.

The Quinnipiac Bobcats play highly competitive NCAA Division I athletics in the Northeast Conference (NEC) in most sports, and in the prestigious ECAC in men's and women's ice hockey. Bobcat athletics involve the entire campus, from the Crazy Bobcat Club to student-athletes to fans in the stands. The university's teams have a tradition of excellence. The men's ice hockey team was ranked sixteenth nationally in 2007.

Quinnipiac students are active, sports-minded, and interested in physical fitness. The university provides a full range of activities to help students stay in shape. Students field teams in fourteen intramural sports for both casual and competitive play.. Other options include a well-equipped fitness center for strength training and cardiovascular exercise, as well as organized fitness classes like step aerobics, karate, and hip-hop dance.

Successful Outcomes

Quinnipiac offers first-rate preparation for both the workforce and advanced study. Within six months of graduation, 80 percent of Quinnipiac's graduates are employed or in graduate school, and 90 percent are within a year. Quinnipiac graduates are employed in business, communications, education, social services, hospitals and health-care centers. Graduates have taken jobs at companies such as Bristol-Myers Squibb, Johnson & Johnson, Dell Computers, JPMorgan Chase, and ESPN, as well as for the television program *48 Hours*.

Fast Facts

Quinnipiac University is a four-year, independent, comprehensive university founded in 1929.

Web site

http://www.quinnipiac.edu

Location

Hamden, Connecticut—8 miles north of New Haven and 2 hours each from New York City and Boston.

Student Profile

5,400 undergraduate students (40% male, 60% female); 26 states and territories; 10% minority, 1% international. Additional 2,000 graduate, law and part-time students.

Faculty Profile

290 full-time faculty. 15:1 student/faculty ratio. Average class size is 22.

Residence Life

95% of freshmen live on campus. Housing is guaranteed to all undergraduate full-time students.

Athletics

NCAA Division I, Northeast Conference (NEC), ECAC in ice hockey, and Great Western league for men's lacrosse.

Academic Programs

Accounting; advertising; athletic training/sports medicine; biochemistry; biology; biomedical marketing; biomedical sciences; bio products marketing; business BS/MBA program; chemistry; communications (media production or media studies); computer science; criminal justice; diagnostic imaging; economics; education (5 year program BA/MAT for elementary and secondary grades); English; entrepreneurship; finance; gerontology; health/science studies; information systems management journalism; history; independent major; interactive digital design; international business; journalism; legal studies; management; marketing; mathematics; microbiology/molecular biology; nursing; occupational therapy (5 ½ year BS/MOT); physical therapy (6 ½ year BS/DPT); physician assistant (6 year BS/MHS); political science; psychobiology; psychology; public relations; social services; sociology; Spanish language& literature; theater; veterinary technology.

Costs and Aid

2007-2008: $39,920 comprehensive ($28,720 tuition/fees). 70% of students receive some form of financial aid. Merit scholarships range from $5,000 to $16,000 based on high school rank in class and SAT or ACT scores.

Endowment

$210 million.

Sacred Heart University

CONNECTICUT

Distinguished by the personal attention it provides its students, Sacred Heart University (SHU) is known for its commitment to academic excellence, cutting-edge technology, and community service. With six thousand students enrolled in more than forty undergraduate, graduate, and doctoral programs, this dynamic, lay-led university is an innovative presence within Catholic higher education.

Admissions Contact:

Sacred Heart University
5151 Park Avenue
Fairfield, Connecticut 06825-1000
Ph: (203) 371-7880
Email: enroll@sacredheart.edu
www.sacredheart.edu

The 4 Distinctions

Engaged Students

Characterized by its mission and the Catholic Intellectual Tradition, Sacred Heart University is committed to the holistic development of its students. With endless opportunities for hands-on education through research, internships, clinical placements, independent study, service learning, work-study, and study abroad programs worldwide, Sacred Heart University students are consistently challenged to apply their skills and knowledge outside the classroom. The most recent evidence of this commitment to experiential learning lies in Sacred Heart University's new, innovative undergraduate Core Curriculum which features an academically rigorous, multidisciplinary centerpiece known as *The Common Core: The Human Journey*. This new Core Curriculum exemplifies distinctiveness in its emphasis on co-curricular activities including collaborative, team-taught classes, capstone experiences, and cultural learning opportunities beyond the customary classroom environment.

The University's dedication to social responsibility and service to those in need creates an ideal atmosphere for a dynamic service learning program on campus. Through the Office of Service Learning and Volunteer Programs (OSLVP), SHU students coordinate service learning experiences with members of the faculty to receive academic credits for community service-optioned courses. Each year, hundreds of Sacred Heart University students contribute their collective intellect and energy to community organizations locally, nationally, and internationally through an array of service learning and volunteer opportunities.

Student organizations on campus also provide diverse forums for experiential learning that are easily accessible to all students. Additionally, all students are taught research skills within the undergraduate curriculum, and opportunities for upper class students to conduct research with faculty are available in Sacred Heart University's three academic colleges: the College of Arts & Sciences, College of Education & Health Professions, and John F. Welch College of Business. Students in all majors are also encouraged to participate in one or more off-campus internships as undergraduates. Internships are facilitated through the Office of Career Development, where staff members personally connect students to internships through semi-annual Internship & Career Fairs as well as SHU's eRecruiting system, actively utilized by over 2,500 employers representing all career fields. These and many other experiential learning opportunities for SHU undergraduates not only challenge students to practically apply their knowledge, but also serve as outstanding preparation for students to enter top graduate schools and the workplace.

Great Teaching

Sacred Heart University fully embodies its motto, "where personal attention leads to personal achievement" inside the classroom. With a 13:1 student-faculty ratio and an average academic class size of 22 students, SHU students benefit from forming close relationships with faculty members across disciplines. Although research is of great importance to the dynamic faculty at SHU (75% of whom hold doctorate degrees), the University's highly accessible, student-focused professors are committed to their primary objective and passion, teaching. Given the importance of the first-year student experience, each freshman is assigned to a full-time, professional student affairs mentor as well as a faculty academic advisor to guide them through the course selection and registration process.

Sacred Heart University's consistently evolving curriculum features the aforementioned new undergraduate Core Curriculum developed and proposed by faculty in the College of Arts & Sciences. The innovative qualities of this new Core resulted in the University's invitation to become a member of the Association of American Colleges & Universities (AAC&U) Core Commitments Leadership Consortium. Comprised of just 25 institutions nationally, the Consortium provides leadership in making personal and social responsibility a central part of a high-quality undergraduate education for all students.

Vibrant Community

Sacred Heart University's experiential learning opportunities are complemented by a rich student life program offering over 80 student organizations including strong music programs, media groups, intramural and club sports, service organizations, leadership programs, and academic honor societies. SHU's 3,400 undergraduate students enjoy the University's beautiful 65-acre suburban campus which houses a vibrant residential life community, two state-of-the-art fitness centers, cafés, eateries, and lounges for study and relaxation. Cultural events abound on campus, including live entertainment and poetry nights featured weekly at the new Holy Grounds Café, the Student Affairs Lecture Series which brings renowned guest speakers to campus, and professional-quality theatrical, musical, and dance performances at the Edgerton Center for the Performing Arts. Drawing on the rich resources in New England and New York City (just 55 miles south of SHU), students are immersed in enriching activities including group events in NYC such as Broadway shows, and trips to historical Philadelphia and Washington, DC.

SHU's robust school spirit is characterized by the University's highly successful Division I Intercollegiate Athletics program. 32 varsity sports comprising more than 800 student-athletes create an electric atmosphere of Pioneer pride on game day. The student body demonstrates its school spirit at athletic events as fans, cheerleaders, dance team members, members of the pep and marching bands, and by joining the "Red Wave," SHU's unique Spirit Club. Frequent bus trips to away games and spirit contests between residence halls add to the exciting atmosphere of Pioneer spirit on campus.

Also among the University's most defining qualities is Sacred Heart's commitment to community service, which is evident in its award-winning recognition by the Connecticut Department of Higher Education. In twelve of the past fourteen years, SHU has received a Connecticut Department of Higher Education Service Award for its exceptional community service contributions.

Successful Outcomes

Sacred Heart University graduates are highly successful in their respective professional fields, and are quick to be hired by Fortune 500 and 1000 companies, school systems, non-profit agencies, and small and large businesses alike. The placement rate for graduating classes within the past five years has ranged from 94-98%. Most SHU graduates ultimately receive advanced degrees, with roughly 40% of each graduating class continuing directly on for Master of Arts, Master of Science, Master of Education, Law, and Doctoral degrees upon graduation. Pre-professional programs in Medicine, Dentistry, Law, Optometry, Pharmacy, Osteopathy, Physician's Assistant, and Veterinary Science prepare students for the rigorous application process to these respective graduate programs. In addition, all students interested in pursuing graduate studies receive advisement from their academic departments and the Office of Career Development.

Fast Facts

Sacred Heart University, founded in 1963, is an independent, comprehensive liberal arts university in the Catholic Intellectual Tradition that offers more than 50 academic programs to undergraduate, masters, and doctoral students in the arts and sciences, business, education, and health professions.

Web site

http://www.sacredheart.edu

Location

Fairfield, Connecticut— 55 miles north of New York City.

Student Profile

3,400 undergraduate students (40% male, 60% female); 31 states and territories, 42 countries, 68% out-of-state; 10% minority, 2% international.

Faculty Profile

189 full-time faculty members. 76% hold a terminal degree in their field. 13:1 student/faculty ratio. Average class size is 22.

Residence Life

Highly residential: 68% of students live on campus. 94% of freshmen live on campus; some students elect to move off campus as upperclassmen, however, campus housing is guaranteed for four years.

Athletics

NCAA Division I, Northeast Conference (Affiliate members of Atlantic Hockey Association and Colonial Athletic Association). 32 varsity sports (15 men's: baseball, basketball, bowling, cross-country, fencing, football, golf, ice hockey, lacrosse, soccer, tennis, track & field (indoor & outdoor), volleyball, wrestling; 17 women's: basketball, bowling, cross-country, equestrian, fencing, field hockey, golf, ice hockey, lacrosse, rowing, soccer, softball, swimming, tennis, track & field (indoor & outdoor), volleyball; 10 club sports, and 10 intramurals.

Academic Programs

Accounting; art; athletic training; biology; business administration; business economics; education*; exercise science; chemistry; communication & technology studies; computer science & information technology; criminal justice; English; finance; history; mathematics; media studies; nursing; occupational therapy (4+2 BA/BS/MSOT); philosophy; physical therapy (3+3 BS/DPT); political science; predental**; prelaw**; premedical**; preoptometry**; preosteopathy**; prepharmacy**; preveterinary**; psychology; religious studies; social work; sociology; Spanish; sport management. Graduate programs are available at the Master and Doctoral levels; post-bachelor and post-master certificate programs also available.

*Leads toward certification in the State of Connecticut with reciprocity in 39 additional states

**Special Advising Program

Costs and Aid

2007–2008: $37,966 comprehensive (27,150 tuition & fees). 67% of students receive some financial aid. Average award: $16,025.

Endowment

$53,921,426.

University of Maine at Farmington

MAINE

University of Maine at Farmington is a selective, residential, public liberal arts college nestled in western Maine's lakes and mountains region. Small classes, an emphasis on in-depth learning, a low student to faculty ratio, and valuable outside-the-classroom learning opportunities are keys to its success.

Admissions Contact:

University of Maine at Farmington
246 Main Street
Farmington, Maine 04938
Ph: (207) 778-7050
Email:
www.farmington.edu

The 4 Distinctions

Engaged Students

Farmington offers a number of opportunities to help students connect their classroom studies to what could be their future work. Many of UMF's students find that some of their most valuable learning experiences happen outside the classroom. These include internships, student teaching, class projects, and service learning. Last year, about 70 percent of all UMF students participated in a variety of practical, hands-on learning opportunities—from Maine-based science internships at Jackson Laboratories in Bar Harbor and Portland's Maine Medical Center, to geography internships and research projects in Lanai, Hawaii.

UMF intentionally limits its enrollment to two thousand students to provide the ideal size for a quality, student-centered academic experience. Whether involved with class work, internships, or community service, each day and every hour at UMF is constructed to be a part of a student's education. Students who are engaged with the campus and the surrounding community seven days a week are often the most successful throughout their college careers. UMF students are civic-minded, are an active part of the community, and help to make the Farmington area an even better place to live. Students volunteer as youth soccer coaches, help fill the local food pantries, organize blood drives, and distribute winter hats and mittens to area children. They are concerned about the environment and interested in the concept of sustainability. UMF students' strong drive to make a difference also expands globally and beyond graduation.

Farmington students are active and involved, participating in over sixty clubs and organizations. Opportunities for creative expression through music, dance, writing, art, and theater are complemented by participation in club sports, intramurals, and eleven NCAA Division III athletics.

Great Teaching

For the past ten years, U.S. News & World Report has consistently recognized UMF as a top public liberal arts college. The American Association for Higher Education recently cited UMF among twenty colleges and universities nationwide that best exemplify the creation of opportunities for student success.

UMF provides its students with high educational standards; strong academic programs in the arts and sciences, education, and human services; a committed, caring, and rigorous faculty; learning environments that stimulate creativity and critical thinking; and financial resources that make its excellence affordable.

Farmington offers a wide range of majors, opening the door to an almost limitless variety of careers or graduate-study opportunities. These degree programs prepare students for careers in business, education, medicine, science, government, law, industry, human services, social science, the arts, and countless other professions.

Because many students have multiple academic interests, Farmington offers a variety of interdisciplinary majors such as sociology/anthropology, music/arts, geology/geography, and environmental planning and policy. Students may also create their own program, referred to as an individualized studies major, in which they combine courses from at least two disciplines and have a faculty adviser from each discipline.

The UMF honors program is open to outstanding students who have shown exceptional motivation, creativity, and a strong interest in the world of ideas. Participants in the program take small, seminar-style interdisciplinary courses and attend a variety of specially planned lectures and field trips.

Farmington believes in the value of travel as a learning experience. Travel opportunities extend from a few days at professional conferences with faculty, to three-week courses over winter break and May terms, to a full semester at another college in the U.S. or abroad. In the past few years, students and faculty have traveled to Mount Saint Helens, Ireland, Scotland, and Newfoundland to study geology; England to shoot photography; Italy and Germany to study politics; Mexico and England to study special education; sites across Maine, Vermont, and New York to study archaeological digs; Costa Rica to study biology and engage in environmental writing; and Japan to study theater and architecture.

In addition, Farmington is a member of the National Student Exchange Program, which enables students to study for up to a year at 177 different institutions across the United

States and Canada, or at any of the programs abroad offered by those schools. Students can also participate in one of UMF's direct exchange programs in Russia, China, France, or England.

Vibrant Community

The quality of the people who make up the University of Maine at Farmington has enabled it to build a national reputation for academic excellence. Important to the university is its ongoing commitment to civic engagement across the curriculum and its shared interest in interdisciplinary approaches to sustainability and the study of natural and social systems.

UMF's location in the foothills of the spectacular lakes and mountains region of western Maine is itself a source of strength. UMF values both the close integration of the campus with the Farmington community and its proximity to a natural world, offering inspiring landscapes and opportunities for outdoor recreation such as skiing, snowboarding, hiking, and kayaking.

Over 50 percent of UMF students work on campus, which provides both income and opportunities to make connections with other students, faculty, and staff. Students can choose from a wide variety of jobs, including online research, campus photography, Web design, coordinating student events and activities, office work, lifeguarding, personal training, and much more.

One of the greatest experiences of attending college is living in a residence hall. At Farmington, typically 95 percent of first-year students, and over half of all students, live in on-campus housing. Farmington has recently made a significant commitment to enhancing the residential experience as evidenced by increased weekend programming, extended food-service hours, increased access to campus facilities, and the opening of a new "green" residence hall.

Farmington offers a summer experience program every June, intended to assist incoming first-year students with the transition from high school to college. The one-week academic program, for which the students receive credit, serves as an introduction to college-level work and expectations, and enables students to make connections with their classmates and the campus community.

Successful Outcomes

A growing number of students each year pursue graduate studies in fields such as creative writing, law, medicine, pharmacy, veterinary medicine, and optometry. Some jump right into the workforce. Other graduates are employed in nonprofit organizations, publishing houses, accounting firms, medical labs, different levels of government, and many other fields. Because of UMF's strong tradition of teacher preparation, UMF education graduates are regarded as leaders in their respective fields and are teaching in schools from New England to Florida, Istanbul to France.

Fast Facts

The University of Maine at Farmington is a four-year, public, liberal arts university founded in 1863.

Web site

http://www.farmington.edu/

Location

Farmington, Maine.

Student Profile

2,167 students (35% male, 65% female); 25 states and territories; 2% minority, 1% international.

Faculty Profile

130 full-time faculty. 15:1 student/faculty ratio. Average class size is 19.

Residence Life

Moderately residential: 51% of students live on campus.

Athletics

NCAA Division III, North Atlantic Conference. 11 varsity sports (5 men's: baseball, basketball, cross-country, golf, soccer; 6 women's: basketball, cross-country, field hockey, softball, soccer, volleyball), 10 club sports, and 14 intramural activities.

Academic Programs

Art; arts administration; biology; business economics; community health education; computer science; creative writing; early childhood education; early childhood special education; elementary education; English; environmental planning & policy; environmental science; general studies; education studies; geography; geology; geology/chemistry; geology/geography; history; individualized studies; international studies; mathematics; music/arts; philosophy/religion; political science/social science; preprofessional (premed, predental, prepharmacy, preoptometry, and prelaw); psychology; rehabilitation administration; rehabilitation services; secondary education; sociology/anthropology; special education; theater/arts; women's & gender studies.

Costs and Aid

2007–2008: $14,040 in-state comprehensive ($6,688 tuition); $21,559 out-of-state comprehensive ($14,208 tuition). 80% of students receive some financial aid. Average award: $8,500.

Endowment

$10.7 million.

More Distinctions

• UMF has been named "One of America's Best Colleges" by U.S. News and World Report for ten consecutive years.

• UMF was selected as one of 20 institutions, out of 600, to participate in a national study to document effective practices to engage students in the learning process. It was selected based on students' scores on the National Survey of Student Engagement.

• UMF's campus dining service consistently ranks in the top 10 nationwide in consumer satisfaction among 400 ARAMARK college dining services.

Art Institute of Boston

MASSACHUSETTS

The Art Institute of Boston at Lesley University (AIB) offers students access to the broad resources of a large university as well as the attention of a small school. AIB's location in Boston connects students to a thriving arts community, a multitude of cultural options, a legendary music scene, and incomparable internship opportunities.

Admissions Contact:

Art Institute of Boston
700 Beacon Street
Boston, Massachusetts 02215
(800) 773-0494 x6710
Ph: (617) 585-6710
Email: admissions@aiboston.edu
www.aiboston.edu

The 4 Distinctions

Engaged Students

AIB offers students a professional environment to assist them in preparing for a career. Internships give students the opportunity to work as members of a professional team, to test and hone their technical and creative skills, and to connect with professionals in their chosen fields. AIB students have interned at leading corporations, design firms, advertising agencies, photography studios, galleries, museums, and more—including Allen & Gerritsen, Big Blue Dot, the Boston Globe, BrandEquity International, Design Continuum, Encompass Communications, Lego Systems, Mullen Advertising, Natural Health, Philographica, Reebok, and WGBH.

International study in all degree programs is encouraged, and AIB has study programs with colleges in Ireland, Italy, France, and the Netherlands. Students may choose to study in a number of fields, including studio art, humanities, and Italian language and culture at the Italian Language and Art Institute in Florence. Students with a fine arts major or a fine art/illustration major can study at the Burren College of Art in Ireland for a single semester or a full year. Students in AIB's department of design and department of illustration can attend the Willem de Kooning Academie in Rotterdam, the Netherlands for their junior or senior years.

Students also have the opportunity to spend a semester at one of thirty member colleges belonging to the Association of Independent Colleges of Art and Design (AICAD), of which AIB is a member. A yearlong program of study and studio art in New York City is among the most popular. Boston Architectural College and the Maine Photographic Workshops also have classes open to AIB students. AIB students also have the opportunity to interact with established artists from all over the world, who visit AIB to lecture, give workshops, and exhibit and critique.

AIB at Lesley University provides a nurturing, intensive environment for learning and growth. The students come to know, learn from, and inspire one another. The faculty and staff are incredibly accessible, and the small classes provide students with individual attention, effective learning environments, and opportunities for collaboration. AIB students have as deep a commitment to community service as they do to learning.

Great Teaching

Undergraduate programs specific to AIB include animation, graphic design, fine arts, illustration, photography, and art history. Graduate degree programs focus on visual arts.

AIB instructors provide an exceptionally high level of teaching and a solid commitment to advanced arts instruction. The faculty consists of full-time educators and adjunct members, a mix that allows students to draw from an incredible base of talent in all areas of the arts and academia. AIB students boast that their professors are not only "very knowledgeable and helpful aids in the learning process," but also "smart, unique, and respectable artists" who can shed valuable light on the prospects of earning a living in the visual arts.

Students and faculty are supported by facilities that are excellent for art education. From the state-of-the art darkrooms to the advanced computer labs, AIB's facilities provide the tools needed by aspiring artists to learn and explore. AIB offers expert instruction in the visual arts, with a focus on both the conceptual and the practical. To ensure a broad education, AIB emphasizes interdisciplinary study within the fine arts, as well as courses in the liberal arts. AIB's foundation courses give students an academic and artistic overview. All first-year students are required to participate in an intensive curriculum in drawing and visual perception, designed to introduce students to the skills and insights necessary for the advanced study of art. Photography students follow a unique first-year foundation in which they are immersed in the history, techniques, and concepts behind artistic photography.

Vibrant Community

Boston and Cambridge are architecturally beautiful cities filled with historic sites and a vast array of cultural and academic resources. Students regularly take advantage of the city, and appreciate Boston as a metropolitan area known for creativity and support for the arts. The Boston and Cambridge area is home to more than 230,000 students, and transportation is safe and easy to use.

While AIB's curriculum is rigorous, the hours in class are balanced by many opportunities for new experiences and fun—both on campus and in the city. AIB offers students a variety of activities, including visiting artist lectures, gallery and museum visits, student coffeehouses, clubs, athletics, and outings.

AIB is located in the Kenmore Square neighborhood, within downtown Boston. Most AIB facilities are located in two buildings within two urban blocks of each other. Both buildings include substantial computer labs, studio spaces, instructional rooms, and faculty offices. AIB has galleries at three locations. One gallery is used for traveling exhibitions, BFA and MFA graduate exhibitions, and the Faculty Biennial Exhibition. The Newbury Street gallery is used for student exhibitions, particularly in the department of fine arts. The third gallery hosts a variety of faculty, student, and visiting exhibitions. Admission to all galleries is free and open to the public.

There are plenty of activities on campus, such as clubs and organizations that vary in levels of commitment. The dodgeball club, Amnesty International, the Oxford Street Players, and Students for a Free Tibet are just a few examples. Students will also find a series of lectures on a variety of intriguing subjects, choir concerts, Sunday night movies, and Shakespearean theatre.

Athletics add significantly to the atmosphere at AIB. NCAA Division III teams compete in basketball, crew, soccer, softball, and volleyball. In addition, students can participate in intramural sports such as cross-country, tennis, and swimming. Those students who simply want to stay fit can choose from activities such as aerobics and yoga.

Successful Outcomes

The Career Resource Center provides career development and job-search services to Lesley University degree candidates and alumni. Students are taught job-search, career-assessment, and decision-making skills that they will use throughout their lifetime. Workshops include topics such as resume and interviewing skills, how to market your potential, and how to explore career directions. Students also have access to helpful job fairs featuring international and domestic opportunities.

On average, 98 percent of Lesley students who seek employment are placed in jobs immediately following graduation, while about one-third continue their education in graduate programs. Lesley's success rate is due to its solid curriculum, a productive internship program, and the hard work and determination of the students. Lesley's commitment to internships and field work provides all graduates with the confidence of experience.

It is this combination of expert faculty, stimulating classes, hands-on learning, career-focused internships, and wide variety of cocurricular activities that challenges, inspires, and prepares students to become catalysts and leaders. Whether they enter professional careers or pursue further study after graduation, students leave AIB with a strong commitment to social change, ready to make a difference in the world around them.

Fast Facts

Lesley University is comprised of two undergraduate schools, The Art Institute of Boston and Lesley College, as well as two Graduate schools and an adult learning division. It is a coeducational, private institution founded in 1909.

Web site

www.aiboston.edu

Location

Boston, Massachusetts

Student Profile

1,351 undergraduate students (33% male, 67% female); 42 states and territories, 15 countries; 21% minority, 3% international.

Faculty Profile

212 full and part-time faculty. 11:1 student/faculty ratio. Average class size is 15.

Residence Life

80% of freshmen live on campus and 50% of all undergraduates live on campus.

Athletics

NCAA Division III, North Atlantic Conference. 10 Varsity sports (4 men's: basketball, cross-country, soccer, volleyball; 6 women's: basketball, crew, cross-country, soccer, softball, volleyball).

Academic Programs

BFA degrees in animation; art history; fine arts; graphic design; illustration; photography; and a low-residency MFA degree in visual arts.

Costs and Aid

2007–2008: $35,550 comprehensive ($23,200 tuition). 73% of students receive some financial aid. Average award: $16,000

Endowment

$83 million.

More Distinctions

• In recognition of its work in community service, Lesley was selected in 2006 for inclusion on the exclusive President's Higher Education Community Service Honor Roll.

• *The Princeton Review* recognized Lesley College as one of the best regional colleges in the Northeast.

• *U.S. News & World Report* ranked Lesley among the best universities in the North.

• Great Colleges for the Real World chose Lesley to appear in its' annual listing.

• Lesley is featured in Princeton Review's Colleges with a Conscience.

• Lesley awards more master's degrees in education than any other institution in the U.S.

Assumption College

MASSACHUSETTS

Assumption College's student-centered community emphasizes the rich Catholic intellectual tradition and ecumenical outreach. The college seeks to educate students for critical thinking, thoughtful citizenship, and compassionate service.

Admissions Contact:

Assumption College
500 Salisbury St.
Worcester, MA 01609
Ph: (508) 767-7285
Email: admiss@assumption.edu
www.assumption.edu

The 4 Distinctions

Engaged Students

While augmenting their education and honing their professional skills by pursuing local, national, and international internships, Assumption's students work in diverse organizations across the globe, including the U.S. Departments of Commerce and State, Smith Barney, Fidelity Investments, Morgan Stanley, AT&T, and the Alliance Francaise in Paris. Members of the class of 2006 interned at more than 120 corporations, nonprofit organizations, and schools.

Students may also choose to spend a semester or year abroad. In recent years, Assumption students have studied in many countries, including China, France, England, Australia, the Netherlands, and the Czech Republic.

Students at Assumption also learn valuable lessons and practical skills through community service. During the 2006–2007 academic year, Assumption students provided ninety-three thousand hours of volunteer service to 130 different Worcester organizations.

Great Teaching

Father Emmanuel d'Alzon, founder of the Augustinians of the Assumption, envisioned a Catholic college that would embrace the "pursuit of truth" wherever it may be found. Today, the college maintains that mission through its liberal arts and preprofessional studies programs.

With an enviable student to faculty ratio of just 12 to 1, Assumption's academic atmosphere is closely knit and community oriented. Students first meet with faculty during orientation, when they are matched with an advisor who helps them choose courses. This is the beginning of an informed, personal conversation about their academic goals.

Regardless of their majors, all students take a general education curriculum that focuses on the liberal arts and sciences. These courses enable students and faculty to contemplate the books, ideas, and events that have shaped civilization, helping students prepare themselves to make their own future contributions to this ongoing process. In addition to the core curriculum, nearly 30 percent of

undergraduates major in business, while English, education and the natural sciences are other popular choices.

Students are also encouraged to enroll in honors classes or work with faculty on individual research projects. In honors courses, students pursue the broadest issues at the deepest levels, learning to ask questions, collect evidence, test answers, and arrive at conclusions. The Honors Program is a selective program designed to foster academic engagement inside and outside of the classroom.

In the classroom, faculty take a hands-on approach to learning through group projects, writing assignments, research, and tasks that encourage students to think, not just memorize. Classes are generally discussions, not lectures. Assumption undergraduates praise their professors for their ability to "engage the entire class in discussions and encourage thinking that goes beyond textbooks." They also like the way instructors "get to know you on a personal level" and are "available outside the classroom." Countless Assumption alumni report that they have been transformed by relationships with faculty who genuinely cared about them and actively guided them in reaching their potential.

Assumption prides itself on its "culture of inclusivity." "Encounters of the Assumption kind" is how the campus community describes the way in which faculty and students connect and influence each other. The campus itself is designed to ensure that teachers and students see each other regularly. Faculty reserve ten hours a week of office time; this time is often devoted to discussing a student's future goals.

Assumption is a member of the Colleges of Worcester Consortium, an association of the thirteen higher-learning institutions in Greater Worcester. Through the consortium, Assumption students can register for courses at the other twelve colleges, as well as participate in social and cultural events.

Vibrant Community

Home to more than 90 percent of the school's undergraduates, Assumption's campus is nestled on 180 parklike acres in a serene section of Worcester,

Massachusetts, the state's second-largest city. There, campus life is a rich mix of academics, athletics, service, and extracurricular activities, all designed to inspire students, help them learn to live lives of integrity, and prepare them for meaningful careers.

Assumption guarantees on-campus housing for all four years of a student's college experience. The school offers a wide variety of living options, ranging from traditional residence halls to townhouses and apartments. Four suite-style residence halls have been constructed in the last eight years.

Other new campus buildings include the Richard and Janet Testa Science Center, home to the department of natural sciences; the Information Technology Center, an eighteen-thousand-square-foot addition that features computer labs and technology-rich classrooms; and a multisport stadium with a synthetic turf field, lighting for night events, and grandstand seating for approximately 1,200 spectators. The Plourde Recreation Center includes a swimming pool, racquetball courts, an aerobic/dance studio, a jogging/walking track, and a fully-equipped fitness center.

Many social, recreational, and cultural activities are offered on campus providing students with a variety of opportunities to share interests and gain valuable leadership experience.

While Boston is less than an hour away, students also find that the city of Worcester offers many appealing restaurants, clubs, shops, and events, as well as chances to visit the city's other educational institutions.

Successful Outcomes

Assumption's office of career services works closely with students to identify potential career directions, creating and refining resumes and portfolios, and aligning students with potential employers. Career Services advisors assist students beginning in their freshman year.

CALLS (Career, Academic & Lifetime Learning Skills) is a unique program that addresses all facets of career and life planning. Through CALLS, students develop an "e-portfolio" of personal achievements including academic accomplishments, campus involvements, internships and special projects. This e-portfolio grows over four years, resulting in a comprehensive package that includes a resume and references that can be used in a job search.

After graduation, students stay connected to Assumption through the very active college Alumni Association which helps graduates stay connected through lifelong relationships. It also sponsors the college's reunion weekend, fall and winter homecoming, Reunion Leadership Day, regional club activities, and networking programs. The Assumption College Web site, alumni directory, and Assumption College Magazine also help alumni keep in touch with one another and the college.

Fast Facts

Assumption College is a Catholic liberal arts and preprofessional studies college founded in 1904.

Web site

http://www.assumption.edu

Location

Worcester, Massachusetts—about 45 miles from Boston.

Student Profile

2,125 students (40% male, 60% female); 24 states and territories; 8 countries.

Faculty Profile

12:1 student/faculty ratio. Average class size is 20.

Residence Life

Highly residential: 90% of students live on campus in guaranteed housing.

Athletics

Assumption College sponsors 23 intercollegiate teams, which include 11 varsity sports for men (basketball, baseball, cross-country, football, golf, ice hockey, lacrosse, soccer, tennis, and indoor and outdoor track) and 12 varsity sports for women (basketball, cross-country, field hockey, lacrosse, rowing, soccer, softball, swimming, tennis, indoor and outdoor track, and volleyball). Assumption College competes in NCAA Division II and is a charter member of the Northeast-10 Conference.

Academic Programs

Accounting; biology; biology with concentration in biotechnology & molecular biology; chemistry; classics; computer science; economics; economics with business concentration; economics with international concentration; education concentration (accompanying an appropriate major); English; English with concentration in writing and mass communications; environmental science; foreign languages; French; French with concentration in francophone culture & civilization; global studies; global studies with business concentration; history; human services and rehabilitation studies; international business; Italian studies; Latin American studies; management; marketing; mathematics; music; organizational communication; philosophy; political science; psychology; sociology; sociology with concentration in criminology or social policy; Spanish; Spanish with concentration in Hispanic culture & civilization; theology; visual arts.

Costs and Aid

2007–2008: $37,242 comprehensive ($27,320 tuition). 94% of students receive some financial aid. Average award: $15,972.

Endowment

$60 million.

More Distinctions

• *U.S. News and World Report* Best Universities, Master's Category.

• *Barron's* Best Buys in Education.

• Included in the *Princeton Review's* Best Northeastern Colleges, 2008 edition.

• Ranks eighth out of 105 New England schools for producing NCAA post-graduate scholars; eight Fulbright Scholars, one Woodrow Wilson Scholar, and one Marshall Scholar in the past five years.

Eastern Nazarene College

MASSACHUSETTS

Eastern Nazarene College (ENC) is the only evangelical Christian college in metropolitan Boston. Eastern Nazarene aims to offer a competitive academic education and a campus committed to a Christian lifestyle, based on the philosophy that there is no conflict between the best in education and Christian faith.

Admissions Contact:

Eastern Nazarene College
23 East Elm Avenue
Quincy, Massachusetts 02170
(800) 88-ENC-88
Ph: (617) 745-3711
Email: admissions@enc.edu
www.enc.edu

The 4 Distinctions

Engaged Students

Eastern Nazarene College is not only committed to offering students a well-rounded college experience on-campus, but sees off-campus study as an integral part of a student's education. Cooperative programs offer students the chance to engage in career-exploratory experiences. Students of all ages have the opportunity to get involved, from student government, to campus publications, to ministries.

As a member of the Council for Christian Colleges & Universities (CCCU) and one of eight regional Nazarene colleges and universities across the nation, ENC offers a multitude of opportunities for travel and study, both in the United States and abroad. Several students have attended Oxford University as part the "Scholar's Semester at Oxford." Students also participate in missions in Mozambique, choir tours in Fiji, Hawaii, and the United Kingdom, and environmental studies in New Zealand and Belize.

Campus Kinder Haus is an Early Childhood Education center that ENC operates for children ages 3 to 6. College students perform a vital role, connecting course work with experience in student teaching. For college students, Campus Kinder Haus presents a rich opportunity to experience the complexities and rewards of working with children.

Eastern Nazarene's mission lies in its dedication to building lives founded on a Christ-centered faith. Students are active in service in the community, ministering in nearly sixty different churches and organizations. "Open Hand, Open Heart," through which ENC students minister to the homeless of Boston, is an excellent example of students' desire to serve others.

Great Teaching

While ENC faculty actively publish and conduct research, and many are leaders in their fields, their primary emphasis is on teaching and mentoring students in a spiritually informed and academically supportive environment. The faculty at Eastern Nazarene represent five of the eight Ivy League schools, demonstrating the outstanding academic prowess of this Christian

college, and the fifteen to one student-to-faculty ratio means that dedicated faculty can give students the kind of individual attention that helps ensure growth and success. In ENC's small, personal environment, professors remain approachable. Students are also often invited to assist in professors' research, and faculty often bring students along on their travels, such as a trip to the Conference on Faith and History in Oklahoma City, or to present papers at Yale University.

Recently, an ENC professor received a grant from the Templeton Foundation to organize and run a conference in London on British abolitionism and moral progress, featuring sixteen of the world's leading historians. Another faculty member was recently invited to speak at a conference at the Vatican, and another ENC professor has served as a technical advisor in two U.S. military exercises, held at undisclosed locations, applying his research in artificial intelligence to the problem of combating improvised explosive devices. The Engineering program at Eastern Nazarene truly is a gem.

For many students, hands-on learning begins Freshman year. Students in the Education department begin student teaching during their first year at ENC. The Engineering department offers an annual robotics competition for engineering majors. A number of praxis, internship, and performance opportunities are available for all majors, from psychology, to biology, to music and theatre arts.

ENC provides students with an educational experience that combines high academic standards with a serious Christian perspective. All faculty are professing Christians and active members of a local congregation. ENC encourages rigorous intellectual investigation and broad exploration in the pursuit of truth, and students are expected to work equally hard on questions of faith and on academic pursuits.

Vibrant Community

Founded in 1900, the college moved to Quincy in 1919 from North Scituate, Rhode Island. Today, students at Eastern Nazarene are just minutes from all the city of Boston has to offer. Any day of the week students can walk to the Wollaston T station, one of the stops on the Red Line of Boston's public transit system. Twenty minutes later, they arrive at Park Street, in the heart of the city, to stroll through America's first public park after a ride on America's first subway. Another ten minutes and they can be at Harvard University in Cambridge. Students often visit the Theatre District and the Boston Symphony Orchestra, attend lectures at Harvard, shop along Newbury Street, or watch the Red Sox at Fenway Park.

On-campus, the Theatre arts program is in its thirtieth season. Presenting four to five productions each year, the department has produced over one hundred shows. The History department also hosts its own lecture series through the Historical Society at Boston University, featuring prominent historians from Tufts, Harvard, Johns Hopkins, and Oxford and Exeter University in England.

As members of a Christian community, students agree to a Lifestyle Covenant that promotes consistency and authenticity in Christian values at Eastern Nazarene College. Chapel attendance is a requirement and dormitories are separate for the sexes. ENC teaches students personal accountability, and the lifestyle guidelines are excellent standards for living out the practical aspects of life among a community of believers.

Successful Outcomes

Eastern Nazarene College has a history of graduating its students into top graduate programs, and alumni go on to do great things in the world. On average, 94 percent of ENC graduates who apply to medical schools and graduate programs for medical studies are accepted. In 2006, one ENC alumnus was granted a full scholarship and stipend for graduate work at Harvard University. More impressive, the prelaw program at ENC has maintained a 100 percent acceptance rate into law school for the past twenty-five years. These law schools include Yale, Harvard, the College of William & Mary, and Washington & Lee University. Graduates from the engineering program have attended schools like Rensselaer Polytechnic Institute for graduate work.

Notable ENC alumnus Neil J. Nicoll is president and CEO of the YMCA of the USA. David Bergers, the regional director for the Boston office of the Securities and Exchange Commission is an ENC alumnus who later went to Yale Law School. Eastern Nazarene's active alumni-relations office helps cultivate connections between ENC and its alumni, fostering mutual relationships in areas such as career networking and financial support.

Even after graduation, ENC's faculty and staff are deeply interested in the success of each student. ENC's Career Connection Program provides career information and personal insights on a variety of careers for current students and alumni. Created in 1996, the CCP has approximately 250 members who advise students in a variety of different careers, professions, and fields of study. It is not uncommon that college internships become full-time employment opportunities for ENC alumni.

Fast Facts

Eastern Nazarene College is a private, co-educational, four-year Christian college affiliated with the Church of the Nazarene. It is the only evangelical Christian college in metropolitan Boston.

Web site

http://www.enc.edu/

Location

Quincy, Massachusetts—0.5 miles from Wollaston Beach and 0.5 miles from the Wollaston MBTA station. Part of the Inner Core of Metropolitan Boston, Quincy is 6 miles south of the City of Boston, and ranked as the second-safest city in Massachusetts.

Student Profile

703 traditional undergraduate students (39% male, 61% female); 31 states, 21 countries; 24% ethnic minority. Students represent over 29 different church denominations. Students attend Chapel services 20-26 times per semester and abide by a common Christian Lifestyle Covenant.

Faculty Profile

46 full-time faculty. 15:1 student/faculty ratio. Average class size is 15. Faculty represent 5 of 8 Ivy League schools, among others.

Residence Life

Highly residential: 85% of students live on campus.

Athletics

NCAA Division III, Commonwealth Coast Conference. 11 varsity sports (5 men's: baseball, basketball, cross-country, soccer, tennis; 6 women's: basketball, cross-country, soccer, softball, tennis, volleyball).

Academics

Biology; business; chemistry; communication arts; computer science; criminal justice/sociology; education; engineering; English; environmental studies; forensic science; government; health science; history;, international studies; mathematics; movement arts; music; philosophy; physics; predentistry; prelaw; premed; prenursing; preoccupational therapy; prepharmacy; prephysical therapy; preveterinary science; psychology; religion; social work; sports management.

Costs and Aid

2007–2008: $27,969 comprehensive ($19,888 tuition). 100% of freshmen receive institutional aid. Average award for institutional aid is over $7,000. Federal Aid also available.

More Distinctions

• Graduates have a 94 percent acceptance rate into medical school/ graduate schools for medical fields.

• The prelaw program has had a 100 percent acceptance rate into law school for the past 25 years.

• The college has accredited Social Work and Teacher Education programs. The Education department faculty has over one hundred years of combined experience.

Elms College

MASSACHUSETTS

Founded in 1928, Elms College is a coeducational Catholic liberal arts college. Many students choose Elms for academic excellence, a focus on social justice, and an environment that is friendly, nurturing, and fun. Elms students receive a broad liberal arts education, explore a variety of social justice issues, and are empowered to make positive changes in the world.

Admissions Contact:

Elms College
291 Springfield Street
Chicopee, MA 01013-2839
(800) 255-ELMS
Ph: (413) 594-2761
Email: admissions@elms.edu
www.elms.edu

The 4 Distinctions

Engaged Students

Elms College students receive a broad liberal arts education. Through the exploration of a variety of subjects, they learn how to think, reason, and communicate intelligently and effectively.

There are 746 full-time undergraduate students at Elms, and the college's total enrollment has grown 69 percent in five years.

Elms College strives to develop character as well as intellect, and empowers students to use the knowledge they acquire to effect positive change in the world around them. Service learning, which includes a community service requirement, enables students to gain a better understanding of the needs of the community – and the world – in which they live, and their responsibility to help. Elms takes service so seriously that classes are canceled one day of the school year to allow the entire Elms College community to perform service projects throughout the region.

Students have traveled to Ecuador, Japan, Jamaica, and Honduras to reach out to others through service learning. Students of all majors can connect with the local youth; for example, accounting majors spent one morning in a local high school to encourage students to pursue college and the field of accounting. Education majors can take advantage of student teaching and tutoring opportunities to obtain experience in the classroom.

Social justice is interwoven into every aspect of student life at Elms. Each year, the social justice series conducts a yearlong examination of issues affecting the community and the world today. Past series have focused on diversity, capital punishment, and immigration, migration, and refugees.

Elms students also have a variety of internship options that put them into an environment where they can learn by doing, and be exposed to the world of work with all its challenges and benefits. Popular internships include the Basketball Hall of Fame and Massachusetts Mutual Financial Group.

Elms College works with the American Institute of Foreign Study to offer study-abroad opportunities, and our students have spent a summer, a semester, or a year in places such as Australia, France, Ireland, Japan, Italy, Spain, and Poland.

Great Teaching

At Elms College, students receive instruction, inspiration, and guidance from professors in an environment that fosters individuality, creativity, and scholarship. Our faculty has chosen to be a part of the Elms College community because teaching is their top priority. The faculty consists of 65 fulltime professors, and numerous adjunct professors, practicing professionals who bring experience from the working world into the classroom.

Faculty and advisors develop connections with students, and with a retention rate of 86 percent, Elms believes its students are well served.

The student-to-faculty ratio is eleven-to-one, and all teaching is done by professors – never by teaching assistants. In small classes, professors can more easily get to know each student's interests and aspirations, and can help them achieve their academic and personal goals.

Faculty members are usually willing to do an independent study with a student if a certain course does not exist. Students at Elms can also choose from courses at any of the eight Cooperating Colleges of Greater Springfield.

The school's core curriculum is built around the liberal arts and all students take a freshman writing course and an interdisciplinary first year seminar.

Elms College offers 33 majors within six divisions: Humanities and Fine Arts, Natural Sciences and Math, Business and Law, Education, Health Sciences, and Social Sciences.

The most popular majors at Elms fit into the school's tradition of graduates who serve the public: nursing, social work, education, and business management. Business students are prepared to enter the business world with a community consciousness.

Vibrant Community

Visitors to Elms College are often struck by the fact that everyone who passes on campus seems to know everyone else's name. Students, faculty, and staff get to know one another quickly, sharing experiences, scholarly perspectives, friendship, and support.

The campus is alive with events planned to appeal to student interests, expand perspectives, and reinforce a sense of community. Cultural offerings range from concerts, performances, and plays to movies, parties, and art exhibits.

On campus, renovations in many of the buildings have been done to accommodate the increase in enrollment. New state-of-the-art athletic fields have just been completed, and there are plans for improved science facilities and additional housing.

About 30 percent of students play a varsity sport for the Elms College Blazers. Men's basketball and women's softball are particularly successful in their Division III conferences and have reached the NCAA tournament numerous times. Intramural sports also draw a large number of participants.

Popular clubs and organizations include student government, social work, student nurses, international clubs, social justice theatre, and campus ministry.

Off campus, Springfield provides a vibrant nightlife. Many students visit Six Flags and the Basketball Hall of Fame for entertainment. Elms is less than two hours from Boston and less than four to New York, and many cultural activities take place just north of the college in the Northampton area. The area also features many outdoor activities, from skiing and snowboarding to hiking and biking along with parks, wildlife sanctuaries and a zoo. At the Chicopee Memorial State Park, students can swim, bike, fish, or picnic.

Successful Outcomes

Elms College's liberal-arts curriculum gives all students an advantage in the working world in critical areas such as thinking, writing, and communications. When our students graduate, they are well prepared for lives of personal accomplishment and professional success.

Elms College graduates have a 90 percent employment placement rate overall, with a 100 percent placement in the majors of nursing, education, and accounting. Nurses that come from Elms are considered some of the best in the state.

Most graduates of Elms College end up living and working in Massachusetts or Connecticut.

Fast Facts

Elms College is a coeducational, Catholic, liberal arts college founded in 1928.

Web site

http://www.elms.edu/

Location

Chicopee, Massachusetts—about two miles north of downtown Springfield, Massachusetts.

Student Profile

746 full-time undergraduate students (23% male, 77% female); 404 part-time students. The majority of students are from New England, New York, and New Jersey.

Faculty Profile

65 full-time faculty. 80% hold a terminal degree in their field. 11:1 student/faculty ratio. Average class size is 15.

Residence Life

Moderately residential: 46% of students live on campus.

Athletics

NCAA Division III, North Atlantic Conference (NAC). 15 varsity sports (7 men's: baseball, basketball, cross-country, golf, soccer, swimming, volleyball; 8 women's: basketball, cross-country, field hockey, lacrosse, soccer, softball, swimming, volleyball.)

Academic Programs

Accounting; biology; chemistry; communication sciences & disorders; computer information technology; education; English; fine art; health-care management; history; international studies & business; legal studies; liberal arts; management; marketing; mathematics; natural sciences; nursing; paralegal studies; professional studies; psychology; religious studies; social services/paralegal studies; social work; sociology; Spanish; speech language pathology assistant studies.

Costs and Aid

2007–2008: $34,250 comprehensive ($22,590 tuition). 92% of undergraduate students receive need-based financial aid. Average award: $14,959.

Endowment

$6.0 million.

Emmanuel College

MASSACHUSSETTS

A dynamic learning community in the heart of Boston, Emmanuel College is rooted in the liberal arts and sciences and shaped by a Catholic academic tradition. Highly regarded for the quality of its values-based academic programs, Emmanuel offers an environment that fosters academic excellence, intellectual integrity, and a strong social conscience.

Admissions Contact:

Emmanuel College
400 The Fenway
Boston, MA 02115
Ph: (617) 735-9715
Fax: (617) 735-9801
Email: enroll@emmanuel.edu
www.emmanuel.edu

The 4 Distinctions

Engaged Students

Student life is a vibrant part of the Emmanuel experience. Most students live on campus in the residence halls and participate in student organizations and/or on athletic teams. A wide variety of academic clubs, honor societies, media organizations, performance groups, leadership teams, and social and special interest organizations are available for student participation. Intercollegiate athletics include NCAA Division III sports for men and women.

Through Emmanuel's active office of campus ministry, students provide ongoing volunteer service at a number of agencies and institutions in the city of Boston and around the country. Sample service opportunities include elementary after-school programs, the Breast Cancer Walk, alternative spring break programs, Habitat for Humanity, and the peace and justice club.

Students can enrich their educational experiences and broaden their horizons by spending a semester or a year at a university in another country. Emmanuel's study-abroad coordinator helps students decide which country and program is right for them depending on academic and professional goals. Students can choose from over 500 programs and 70 countries. In recent years, Emmanuel students have studied around the world, including studying management in China, education in Australia, art in Italy, and political and economic development in Central America.

Emmanuel students become active members of the community and participate in internships with the city's most prestigious, leading-edge businesses and nonprofit organizations. A unique partnership with Merck & Co. Inc., which recently opened Merck Research Laboratories-Boston on the Emmanuel campus, provides unprecedented opportunities for students.

Great Teaching

With just 1,700 undergraduate students, Emmanuel provides a liberal arts and science education in a small-class atmosphere with personal attention from the faculty. Because professors provide individual attention, students feel important in the classroom. Emmanuel faculty members are both teachers and scholars. Regardless of their field, they all share a deep interest in teaching and in helping students reach their goals. Faculty know their students' names, and are always willing to meet with students to provide academic assistance, advice, or conversation. The college has seventy-seven full-time faculty members, 81 percent of whom have a doctorate or other terminal degree. The student to faculty ratio is fifteen to one.

Emmanuel College offers a variety of special academic opportunities, in addition to the traditional liberal arts and sciences curriculum. These include directed studies, an honors colloquium, honor societies, prelaw/prehealth professionals' advisory committees, leadership development programs, and a comprehensive career-development program though the internship and career development office.

Emmanuel and five neighboring colleges—Massachusetts College of Art, Massachusetts College of Pharmacy and Health Sciences, Simmons College, Wentworth Institute of Technology, and Wheelock College—collaborate as the Colleges of the Fenway. Students can cross-register for courses at no additional cost, attend social events, and use the academic facilities of all six institutions. This gives students from Emmanuel access to resources equal to those of a major university without losing any of the benefits of a small college environment.

Emmanuel offers major programs in seventeen disciplines, along with some twenty minors. The college recently added new majors in biostatistics and environmental science. Students with multiple interests or talents may design their own major programs, combining two or three subjects to create a major.

In support of student academics, the college's academic resource center offers peer tutoring, writing assistance, and language partners. Emmanuel also offers graduate and professional courses and programs at sites throughout eastern Massachusetts.

Vibrant Community

Emmanuel's students benefit both from being part of a community of educators and students that works together to enrich the world around them and from the easy access to the rich cultural, historical, and social life in and around Boston.

Students who desire a small, tight-knit academic community in the middle of a big, sprawling city need look no further than Emmanuel. Members of Emmanuel's small community all seem to know each other in one way or another. As one student said, "I always feel as if I could sit with anyone when I walk into the cafeteria and chat up everyone in the elevator going to class."

The Emmanuel campus is seventeen-acres of green in the heart of one of America's most exciting and cosmopolitan cities. The campus is alive with the energy of teaching and learning, of exploration and research.

The proximity to Boston gives Emmanuel students access to the ultimate extended classroom. Fenway Park, the Museum of Fine Arts, Symphony Hall, and renowned medical institutions are all just minutes away. For students looking for tranquility, Emmanuel's campus is right across the street from a section of Boston's Emerald Necklace—an area of parkland stretching in a six-mile loop.

Emmanuel's Jean Yawkey Center serves as a central gathering place for the entire Emmanuel College community and provides recreational, athletic, and dining facilities. The facility also houses the Jean Yawkey Center for Community Leadership, which focuses on developing service opportunities and leadership skills for Emmanuel students and building connections with the young people of the city of Boston through after-school and summer programs. The Carolyn A. Lynch Institute of Emmanuel College strengthens this connection by enabling the development and retention of teachers in urban school systems, focusing on training in math, science, and technology

Successful Outcomes

From students' first days at Emmanuel, they work with academic advisers to build academic plans that will take them where they want to go. Whether students arrive with a major in mind or want to use their college years to make a life plan, Emmanuel's academic advisers go out of their way to help students make the most of their college experience.

Academic support services are available for Emmanuel students, including academic advising, an academic resource center, and a busy office of internships and career development. Other services include job and internship postings; individual career advising; and career planning, programming, and networking events. At Emmanuel, these support services can help students learn to balance academics, work, and student life, and develop the skills necessary to begin a successful career.

A career advisory network has a group of over three hundred committed graduates who are available for networking, career advice, and mentorship for students interested in learning more about a certain field. Starting in their first year and continuing until graduation, students are exposed to career planning, assessment, and goal setting.

Fast Facts

Emmanuel College is a four-year, coeducational, liberal arts and sciences college affiliated with the Roman Catholic Church and founded in 1919.

Web site

http://www.emmanuel.edu/

Location

Boston, Massachusetts.

Student Profile

1,700 students (30% male, 70% female); 32 states and territories; 15% multicultural, 3% international.

Faculty Profile

77 full-time faculty. 15:1 student/faculty ratio. Average class size is 20.

Residence Life

Residential: 76% of students live on campus.

Athletics

NCAA Division III; GNAC, ECAC, NCAA, & NECVA Conferences. 14 varsity sports (6 men's: basketball, cross-country, indoor track, outdoor track, soccer, volleyball; 8 women's: basketball, cross-country, indoor track, outdoor track, soccer, softball, tennis, volleyball) and over 20 club and intramural sports.

Academic Programs

American Studies; art: art therapy; graphic design and technology, studio art; biochemistry; biology; Catholic studies; chemistry; communication; economics; education: elementary, secondary; English literature; environmental studies; global studies; history; individualized major, information technology; management; mathematics; neuroscience; performance arts; philosophy; political science; psychology: counseling and health, developmental, general/ experimental; Spanish; sociology; women's studies.

Costs and Aid

2007–2008: $37,835 comprehensive ($26,100 tuition, $11,200 room and board). 78% of students receive some financial aid. Average award: $15,624

Endowment

$71 million.

More Distinctions

• The National Association for Campus Activities honored Emmanuel with three awards during its regional conference from November 4–7 in Marlborough, Massachusetts. For the third straight year, Emmanuel College was named the most spirited institution in the Northeast.

• The National Academic Advising Association honored Emmanuel's Academic Advising Program (AAP) with an award in 2006. Emmanuel's AAP functions as integral part of the academic affairs of the college and has established strong links with offices throughout the institution.

Gordon College

MASSACHUSETTS

Gordon College is located in Wenham, Massachusetts—just 25 miles north of Boston and minutes to the coast of the Atlantic Ocean. A nondenominational Christian liberal arts college, Gordon offers a century-old commitment to character building and scholarship in a dynamic community that integrates Christian faith, learning and living.

Admissions Contact:

Gordon College
255 Grapevine Road
Wenham, MA 01984
Ph: (978) 927-2300
Email: admissions@gordon
www.gordon.edu

The 4 Distinctions

Engaged Students

Attending Gordon College means being part of a community that explores new ideas and cultivates excellence. Students take advantage of global opportunities for service and learning both in the United States and in international settings—included in the cost of tuition.

Gordon's proximity to Boston and other urban communities provides many opportunities for internships and hands-on work experience. Through the Gordon-in-Lynn program, students live and study in a city north of Boston where they gained real-world experience interacting through volunteer projects. Others have held internships in the city of Boston, including work in government, world-renowned hospitals, investment firms and other nonprofit organizations.

Service learning programs at Gordon help equip students with critical thinking and leadership skills as well as helping develop a vision for how Christian's can engage culture. Students also engage in ministry outreach and intercultural mission trips during school breaks throughout the year—serving in places like Belize, London, New York and South Africa.

Great Teaching

Professors, staff, and fellow students care about each other's development as scholars and as Christians. Gordon is the only nondenominational Christian college in New England.

Gordon is a Christian community where students are encouraged to wrestle with challenging questions and the faculty emphasize intellectual growth through rigorous academics. A charter member of the Council for Christian Colleges & Universities, the college enrolls 1600 students and offers 36 academic majors and 23 concentrations in the liberal arts and sciences. With an average faculty to student ratio of 13:1, students engage daily with a campus-wide culture that strives to connect intellect with Christian faith and vocation.

More than 90 percent of Gordon professors have earned a Ph.D. or the highest terminal degree in their field. Gordon faculty are creative teachers and faithful mentors. Teaching

at Gordon focuses on critical thinking, strong communication skills, writing, research, analysis and exploration of the student's creative and social gifts. What often sets Gordon professors apart is their ability to help students to think and morally lead with scholarly discourse and a Christian heart to serve—ensuring that graduates have a lot to offer the marketplace. Recently, a Gordon physics professor encouraged one of his students to present a poster on nuclear research at a national conference while another student conducted research through a project that introduced inner city high school students to the field of neuroscience (and who subsequently was recently accepted into a top medical school as a result of that research).

Gordon has a tremendous commitment to the study of science. In 2008 the college will open the new Ken Olsen Science Center—an 80,000 square-foot science and technology building. Gordon also offers an intensive month-long course on sustainable tropical agriculture with ECHO (Educational Concerns for Hunger Organization), where students travel—to Florida and either Haiti or Honduras—to study agricultural techniques used in developing worlds. As a result of Gordon's strong science curriculum, the college received national recognition when it was identified as a "Top College for Science" in the Peterson's Top Colleges for Science guidebook—one of only five Christian colleges in the United States to receive that recognition.

Along with a commitment to the sciences, Gordon is one of a handful of Christian colleges offering excellent programs in the arts—including painting, photography, music, and theatre. In addition to classes and Chapel services, the campus serves as hosts to a thriving creative community. Within the art department students are taught to consider the broader social function of art by faculty who endorse internships and class projects that use their artistic gifts in various cultural settings.

Vibrant Community

While almost all Christian colleges put a strong emphasis on behavioral expectations, regular chapel attendance and prayer before classes, Gordon goes beyond this by embracing a process of education that links the intellectual with the spiritual dimensions of a Christian life. Every professor integrates Christian thought and assumptions into classroom study.

In addition to the academic and spiritual ethos vibrant at Gordon, the college offers traditional residence halls and apartment-style living on its 400-acre campus. Residence halls are spread across the campus and provide students with opportunity for fellowship, prayer groups, and intramural floor competitions, while building friendships with their peers. Many residence halls are centered on themes like diversity, environmental issues, and community.

The college competes in NCAA Division III athletics and are always enthusiastically supported by dedicated Fighting Scots fans. Theatre is also an important part of life on campus and student clubs like Amnesty International, the Sweaty-Toothed Mad-men (improve group), Student Government, Advocates for Cultural Diversity, and the college newspaper contribute to this animated campus culture. Popular campus events include the highly prized Golden Globes and the theatrically competitive Golden Goose—where a recent "Super Mario" level-one video game reenactment even landed the number one spot on Google video. The city of Boston, the nearby beaches, and the ski resorts in the White Mountains offer recreational activities year round for students looking to explore and expand their New England college experience.

Successful Outcomes

Five years after graduating from Gordon, 63 percent of alumni have completed or are working on an advanced degree. Columbia, MIT, Princeton, Yale and Duke are just a few of the universities alumni are accepted into.

Gordon graduates are especially well represented in the career fields of business and finance, health care, and ministry. In a survey conducted on recent Gordon graduates, 100% of students said that Gordon helped them define their ethics, and 88% of graduates are frequently involved in their churches.

In addition to supporting students while attending Gordon, the college has an active and supportive alumni office. Gordon is committed to supporting both its students and alums throughout both their academic and professional tenures.

"One of my favorite things about being a student at Gordon College is the strong sense of Christian community offered and the relationships I have with my professors and mentors. The faculty at Gordon College care about your courses, your vocation and the lives of students."

-Brian Carlson is a Junior at Gordon College studying Business Administration

Fast Facts

Gordon College is a Christian, coeducational, four-year liberal arts and sciences institution. It is the only nondenominational Christian college in New England.

Web site

http://www.gordon.edu/

Location

Wenham, Massachusetts—two miles from the Atlantic Ocean and 25 miles from Boston.

Student Profile

1,600 undergraduates (40% male, 60% female); 7.2% international, 71% out of state.

Faculty Profile

97 full-time faculty. 90% of full-time faculty have earned doctorates or most advanced degree in their field. 13:1 student/faculty ratio. Average class size is 20.

Residence Life

Highly residential: 89% of students live on campus.

Athletics

NCAA Division III, Commonwealth Coast Conference. 20 varsity sports (9 men's: baseball, basketball, cross-country, indoor track & field (winter), outdoor track & field (spring), lacrosse, soccer, swimming, tennis; 11 women's: basketball, cross-country, field hockey, indoor track & field (winter), outdoor track & field (spring), lacrosse, soccer, softball, swimming, tennis, volleyball).

Academic Programs

Accounting; art; biblical & theological studies; biology; business administration; chemistry; communications arts; computer science; economics; education (early childhood, elementary education, secondary education, middle school education, music education); English language & literature; finance; foreign languages; French; German; history; international affairs; kinesiology; mathematics; music; music education; music performance; philosophy; physics; political studies; psychology; recreation & leisure studies; sociology; social work; Spanish; theatre arts; youth ministries.

Costs and Aid

2007-2008: $32,654 comprehensive ($24,652 tuition). 90% of undergraduate students receive financial aid. Average award: $13,500.

Endowment

$32,210,916.

More Distinctions

• The John Templeton Foundation includes Gordon in an exclusive list of 100 colleges nationwide that is known for its "strong commitment to character-building programs" and recognizes Gordon President R. Judson Carlberg as one of 50 presidents recognized for his exemplary leadership abilities.

Lesley College

MASSACHUSETTS

Founded in 1909, Lesley College's location—a few blocks from Harvard Square—connects students to a thriving arts community, a multitude of cultural opportunities, a legendary music scene, and incomparable internship choices. At Lesley, theory is illuminated by experience, and career is indistinguishable from social responsibility.

Admissions Contact:

Lesley College
Office of Admissions
29 Everett Street
Cambridge, MA 02138-2790
(800) 999-1959 ext. 8800
Ph: (617) 349-8800
Email: lcadmissions@lesley.edu
www.lesley.edu/lc

The 4 Distinctions

Engaged Students

Lesley places an equal emphasis on citizenship and scholarship. Lesley students have as deep a commitment to community service as they do to learning. Accordingly, the university provides plenty of opportunities for linking academic challenges and experiences in the classroom with those gained in the world at large.

At Lesley, there is a strong belief that learning should take place in many places, not just in classrooms. Students have the opportunity to participate in a number of Lesley-affiliated programs off campus in the U.S. and abroad. Lesley offers a number of summer travel-study courses that are generally ten days to three weeks in length. Planned study tours are led by distinguished members of the faculty and offer students the chance to discover the history, culture, and art of various regions. Through study tours, students also gain an in-depth understanding of significant world events, including tours of the Cuban experience in education and the arts, and tours focused on the British experience, learning from the Holocaust, the traditions and cultures of the Southwest, as well as the exploration of the Amazon and the rain forest in Peru and Ecuador.

For students who are passionate about the environment, the Audubon Expedition Institute (AEI) at Lesley offers students a dynamic educational experience. The earth and all its diverse terrain serves as the classroom, and lessons are taught in states like Hawaii and Alaska, as well as countries such as Mexico and Canada. AEI is unlike any other college experience; students spend a semester traveling in independent learning communities with two to four faculty and fifteen to twenty students.

Great Teaching

The teaching emphasis at Lesley is on exposing students to the real world through hands-on learning opportunities. Internships are the hallmark of a Lesley education and are carefully interwoven into every program. Combined with small seminars, students embark on field experiences beginning their very first year. Through classroom discussions, students will find themselves challenging prior assumptions and using their experiences from internships to examine theory.

Classroom learning at Lesley is a collaborative effort between students and faculty. The focus is on discussions instead of lectures, and discussions are often spirited and critical, encouraging no-holds-barred thinking. Classes are small, and students are completely immersed in the learning process. The faculty, who are dedicated and accomplished, are not only experts in their fields but are practitioners, as well. Furthermore, they are committed to providing the personalized attention required to satisfy inquisitive minds.

Art has long been used to depict, critique, and influence society. Those students who wish to expand their art horizons benefit from the classes available at the Art Institute of Boston (AIB). One of four colleges within Lesley University, AIB provides one of the finest professional art educations available, in a supportive and highly creative atmosphere where bold ideas are welcome.

Vibrant Community

While Cambridge is a cosmopolitan and dynamic city, the main campus at Lesley is located among quiet side streets. Residence halls and college-owned Victorian houses stand alongside stately trees within the campus courtyard.

Across Lesley University, there is an environment that empowers students to learn and grow, making connections with friends, peers, faculty, and staff. The office of student activities sponsors programs and events throughout the year. Clubs and organizations run the gamut from fun to serious. The dodgeball club, Amnesty International, the Oxford Street Players, and Students for a Free Tibet are just a few examples. Students will also find a series of lectures on a variety of intriguing subjects, choir concerts, Sunday night movies, and Shakespearean theatre.

Athletics add significantly to the atmosphere at Lesley. NCAA Division III teams compete in basketball, crew, soccer, softball, and volleyball. In addition, students can participate in intramural sports such as cross-country, tennis, and swimming. Those students who simply want to stay fit can choose from activities such as aerobics and yoga. All in all, there's something for everyone, whether students want to put on their sweats and participate, or just watch the action.

Few cities in America offer college students more to do than Boston. The Boston and Cambridge area is home to more than 230,000 students, so making all types of friends is a certainty. With everything from the Red Sox to the Museum of Fine Arts to dancing at one of the many clubs on Lansdowne Street, the city offers an abundance of sports, cultural, and entertainment options. Boston transportation is safe and easy to use, making it convenient for students to get where they need to go.

Successful Outcomes

On average, 98 percent of Lesley students who seek employment are placed in jobs immediately following graduation, while about one-third continue their education in graduate programs. This success rate is a tribute to Lesley's solid curriculum, a productive internship program, and the hard work and determination of the students. Lesley's commitment to internships and field work provides all graduates with the confidence of experience.

The Career Resource Center provides career development and job-search services to Lesley University degree candidates and alumni. Students are taught job-search, career-assessment, and decision-making skills that they will use throughout their lifetime. Workshops include topics such as resume and interviewing skills, how to market your potential, and how to explore career directions. Students also have access to helpful job fairs featuring international and domestic opportunities.

It is this combination of expert faculty, stimulating classes, hands-on learning, career-focused internships, and wide variety of cocurricular activities that challenges, inspires and prepares students to become catalysts and leaders. Whether they enter professional careers or pursue further study after graduation, students leave Lesley with a strong commitment to social change, ready to make a difference in the world around them.

Fast Facts

Lesley University is comprised of two undergraduate schools, The Art Institute of Boston and Lesley College, as well as two Graduate schools and an adult learning division. It is a coeducational, private institution founded in 1909.

Web site

http://www.lesley.edu/lc

Location

Boston, MA

Student Profile

1,351 undergraduate students (33% male, 67% female); 42 states and territories, 15 countries; 17% minority, 3% international.

Faculty Profile

212 full and part-time faculty. 11:1 student/faculty ratio. Average class size is 15.

Residence Life

80% of freshmen live on campus and 50% of all undergraduates live on campus.

Athletics

NCAA Division III, North Atlantic Conference. 10 varsity sports (4 men's: basketball, cross-country, soccer, volleyball; 6 women's: basketball, crew, cross-country, soccer, softball, volleyball).

Academic Programs

Art history; art therapy; child & family studies; communication technology; counseling; education; English; environmental science; environmental studies; global studies: politics, culture, & society; history; history & literature: American studies; history & literature: European & world studies; holistic psychology; human services; management; natural science: mathematics & science; self-designed.

Costs and Aid

2007–2008: $37,950 comprehensive ($25,600 tuition). 73% of students receive some financial aid. Average award: $16,000.

Endowment

$83 million.

More Distinctions

• In recognition of its work in community service, Lesley was selected in 2006 for inclusion on the exclusive President's Higher Education Community Service Honor Roll.

• The Princeton Review recognized Lesley College as one of the best regional colleges in the Northeast.

• U.S. News & World Report ranked Lesley among the best universities in the North.

• Great Colleges for the Real World chose Lesley to appear in its' annual listing.

• Lesley is featured in Princeton Review's Colleges with a Conscience.

• Lesley awards more master's degrees in education than any other institution in the U.S.

Massachusetts College of Liberal Arts

MASSACHUSETTS

Massachusetts College of Liberal Arts (MCLA) is a public, coeducational, liberal arts college, offering both undergraduate and graduate programs. Founded in 1894 as North Adams State College, MCLA today offers a challenging curriculum, including a rigorous collegewide honors program.

Admissions Contact:

Massachusetts College of Liberal Arts
375 Church Street
North Adams, MA 01247
(800) 969-MCLA
Ph: 413-662-5410
Email: admissions@mcla.edu
www.mcla.edu

The 4 Distinctions

Engaged Students

MCLA offers fifteen bachelor's degree programs with numerous concentrations. The most popular majors are English communications, incorporating broadcast media such as TV and radio; fine & performing arts; business; education; psychology; and sociology. Students are required to have a laptop and the general education program requires that students study a foreign language for at least one semester and present a senior capstone project, working closely with a faculty adviser to pull together what they've learned in their college academic experience.

Although internships are not required, many MCLA students take advantage of the wide range of choices available in the Berkshires, especially in the arts and art management through the Berkshire Hills Internship Program, which places students at the numerous local cultural attractions. MCLA is a member of the National Student Exchange, as well as forty-five other initiatives worldwide, providing students with easy access to study-abroad programs. Students also perform original research, including the work students can do using solar panels donated by the state. As one MCLA student put it, "learning is extended far beyond the classroom."

Great Teaching

With only 1,500 students, a low student to faculty ratio of thirteen to one, and a small average class size of eighteen, MCLA is a close-knit community. Hallmarks of its educational programs include flexibility, which allows students to shape their own courses of study, and the combination of traditional course work and experiential learning, including internships, study abroad, and other field experiences.

Recognized for its special focus on the liberal arts, MCLA is one of nine colleges within the Massachusetts Public Higher Education System.

MCLA professors are involved with their students, helping them develop the strong analytical and communication skills necessary for success in today's workforce. Just as the students are expected to be active participants in their education, MCLA faculty are committed to teaching and to using the opportunities for one-on-one interaction to help students acquire the knowledge and skills they need to adapt to change and to navigate through their lives with strong ethical compasses. Many students participate in the annual Undergraduate Research Conference, in addition to presenting papers with their faculty advisers at professional meetings.

Vibrant Community

MCLA is a residential college and three-fourths of its students live on campus. About two-thirds come from Massachusetts, although many students come from New York State, taking advantage of the reduced tuition offered to New York residents. On average, 90 percent of freshmen live together in coed dorms. Upper-level students live in town houses or apartments. There are forty organizations students can join, and four-fifths of MCLA students remain on campus during the weekends. The campus includes one fraternity and three sororities, though only a small percentage of MCLA students participate in Greek life.

A recent graduate noted that "MCLA is big enough that you will not meet everybody and do everything your first year, but small enough that you can do anything you want over the four years: sports, clubs, plays, music, newspaper, radio, travel, internships, politics . . ."

MCLA calls itself "a public college with a private atmosphere in the Berkshires." Noted for its comparatively low cost, MCLA's tuition and fees for Massachusetts residents are 80 percent less than the average private institution in New England. Tuition reductions are available for New York State residents and some residents of Maine, Rhode Island, and Vermont. Close to the Vermont and New York state borders, MCLA is two and a half hours by car to Boston, three hours to New York City, and one and a half hours to the closest airports in Albany, New York, or in Hartford, Connecticut.

The college's location in North Adams, a town of

about fifteen thousand in the Berkshire Hills, puts MCLA in the midst of an area renowned for its outdoor recreation opportunities and plentiful, quality cultural attractions, such as the Massachusetts Museum of Contemporary Art (MASS MoCA), the Clark Art Institute, the Norman Rockwell Museum, the Williamstown and Berkshire theater festivals, the Tanglewood Music Center, and the Jacob's Pillow dance festival. Williams College is located in nearby Williamstown, and MCLA students can cross-register at Williams to take classes there, use their libraries and museum, and attend events. The Berkshires offer natural beauty and a spectrum of recreational activities. The MASS MoCA arts center in North Adams has boosted the area's economy, attracting many artists to the area and offering unique cultural experiences for MCLA students.

Successful Outcomes

A majority of MCLA students participate in internship programs, taking advantage of the school's location in the Berkshires, preparing themselves with hands-on experience before entering the workforce after graduation.

Examples of recent internships include:

- MASS MoCA
- Berkshire Regional Planning Commission
- Massachusetts Office of Travel and Tourism
- Hasbro/Game Works
- WHDH-TV Boston
- Oprah Magazine
- The Washington Center
- Disney World
- Canyon Ranch
- The Berkshire Museum
- National Baseball Hall of Fame
- Berkshire Juvenile Court
- Mountain One Financial Partners

Fast Facts

Massachusetts College of Liberal Arts is a four-year, public, liberal arts college founded in 1894.

Web site

http://www.mcla.edu/

Location

North Adams, Massachusetts—a town of 14,700 located in the Berkshires in the northwest corner of the state, bordering both Vermont and New York.

Student Profile

1,454 undergraduate students (45% male, 55% female); 17 states; 9% minority, <1% international.

Faculty Profile

82 full-time faculty. 13:1 student/faculty ratio. Average class size is 18.

Residence Life

66% of students live on campus.

Athletics

NCAA Division III, Massachusetts State College Athletic Conference. 11 varsity sports (5 men's: baseball, basketball, cross-country, golf, soccer; 6 women's: basketball, cross-country, soccer, softball, tennis, volleyball.

Academic Programs

Anthropology; art; arts management; athletic training; biology; business administration; chemistry; computer science & information systems; education; English/communications; environmental studies; fine & performing arts; geography; history; interdisciplinary studies; mathematics; modern languages; philosophy; physical education; physics; political science; psychology; social work; sociology; women's studies.

Costs and Aid

2007–2008: $5,900 in-state, $14,900 out-of-state tuition. 85% of students receive some financial aid. Average award: $7,400.

Endowment

$7.2 million.

More Distinctions

- Ranked by U.S. News & World Report as one of " America's Best Colleges."

- Noted by Newsweek as a " Hot College" in the category "Most for Your Money."

- Member of the Council of Public Liberal Arts Colleges (COPLAC).

- Member of the National Student Exchange program.

Merrimack College

Admissions Contact:

Merrimack College
315 Turnpike Street
North Andover, MA 01845
Ph: (978) 837-5100
Fax: (978) 837-5133
Email: Admission@Merrimack.edu
www.merrimack.edu

MASSACHUSETTS

Merrimack College is a four-year, Catholic, Augustinian college offering liberal arts, business, science, and engineering programs within a residential campus. Located in a suburban setting twenty-five miles north of Boston, Massachusetts, Merrimack offers a strong cooperative education program for all majors, undergraduate research opportunities, and extensive service-learning experiences.

The 4 Distinctions

Engaged Students

What makes Merrimack College so distinctive is that active learning isn't just an educational philosophy, but a call to action. Students learn by doing at Merrimack—not only in the classroom and the laboratory, but also in the field and in the real world. With intensive, hands-on experiences such as internships, study abroad, or volunteer opportunities to complement class work, students make deeper connections to their studies, gain invaluable real-world experience, build their resumes, and boost their confidence.

Planning is underway for Merrimack's first major curriculum revision in twenty-five years, moving from a traditional five-course model to a four-course model, which, studies show, improves student learning by allowing subjects to be explored in greater depth. The curriculum changes will place the college squarely among a group of only thirty-five top-ranked liberal arts colleges in the country to adopt this innovative curriculum. It will be in place by fall 2008.

Merrimack offers thirty academic majors in the liberal arts, business, engineering, and the sciences, and has an outstanding faculty committed to helping students grow academically, morally, ethically, and socially. Merrimack's contemporary academic approach of fusing liberal arts with professional education means students become engaged and ready to make critical, moral, and informed decisions of thought, communication, and action in their own lives and in service to others. Merrimack graduates are able to demonstrate the knowledge, skills, competencies, and values needed to achieve their personal and professional goals.

Great Teaching

Merrimack's small class sizes and low student to faculty ratio of twelve to one, along with an energetic and inspiring faculty, provide the perfect recipe for active learning. Faculty members at Merrimack are engaged in wide-ranging studies, from chemistry to communications, and students often participate in this research to fulfill course credits, complete internships, or earn money as research assistants on government-funded studies.

Opportunities for undergraduate research are plentiful at Merrimack College. Merrimack's alumni go into the workforce at such places as the Dana-Farber Cancer Institute and the Harvard School of Public Health, and impress others with the caliber of the research experience they have achieved as undergraduates.

Students recognize the dedication of Merrimack professors. As one student said, "The best thing about the classes at Merrimack is the teachers. They're not only enthusiastic, they're accessible. You can see them any time because their office doors are always open, and they always encourage you to ask questions." Another student commented, "The faculty at Merrimack is amazing. They want you to do your best, so they grade really hard but are willing to meet with you any time to look over your work and help you make it better."

Vibrant Community

Students say Merrimack is a transforming place that helps students find their niches and make their own destinies. Filled with engaging and enthusiastic people, the Merrimack community is active and involved. Students transform themselves through a variety of active learning experiences in the classroom, on the athletic fields, and in countless extracurricular activities.

Merrimack's two thousand students are from twenty-eight states and seventeen countries. On average, 80 percent of students live on campus. Their closeness with one other and with faculty and staff spills over into the welcoming atmosphere of the college.

In addition to more traditional housing, several housing options are of interest to an increasing number of parents and students. Merrimack's wellness housing offers students the option of living on floors that are voluntarily free of any alcohol or drug use, an increasingly popular option. The college's Austin Scholars community offers students a living and learning program for students with intellectual curiosity and a commitment to continue the level of involvement they had in high school activities.

Merrimack College offers sixteen varsity sports (eight for men and eight for women). Fifteen of the sports compete at the NCAA Division II level in the Northeast-10 Conference, while men's hockey competes in the Hockey East Association.

Students have numerous opportunities to be involved in competitive sports, fitness activities, and recreation through Merrimack's intramural program, which includes sports like basketball, darts, dodgeball, hockey, swimming, indoor and outdoor soccer, softball, ultimate football, and volleyball.

Only five minutes from the commuter rail and a twenty-five minute drive to Boston, Merrimack offers fast connections to city activities, nightlife, shopping, culture, and events—not to mention the metro area's large college-age population. Whether students want to hone their career skills, see a Broadway show, or soak up some colonial history among the skyscrapers, Merrimack students think of Boston as their biggest classroom.

Successful Outcomes

Merrimack's office of career services offers one of the longest-running cooperative education programs in the Northeast, which includes a four-year and a five-year program for all majors.

Career development services at Merrimack connect students with hundreds of flexible cooperative education positions each year as well as with paid internships in every discipline. Career development staff host career fairs, information panels, recruitment days, seminars on job-interview techniques and resume writing, and career-exploration workshops. Employer recruitment on campus and alumni networking are also available through career development services. Further, Merrimack's career services extranet allows students to post their resumes for review by major companies and arrange interviews and meetings—all online.

On average, 92 percent of Merrimack students go on to full-time employment within six months of graduation, and 6.5 percent of Merrimack students enter a graduate school program immediately after graduation. Students have gone on to graduate study at some of the most prestigious institutions in the world, including MIT, Johns Hopkins, Cornell, Georgetown, the London School of Economics, and more.

"Students learn by doing at Merrimack—not only in the classroom and the laboratory, but also in the field and in the real world."

Fast Facts

Merrimack College is a selective, independent, four-year, coeducational institution that delivers a superior Catholic education in the Augustinian tradition and was founded in 1947.

Web site

http://www.merrimack.edu

Location

North Andover, Massachusetts—25 miles north of Boston and 25 miles from the seacoasts of New Hampshire and Maine.

Student Profile

2,000 undergraduate students (48 % male, 52 % female); 28 states; 4% minority, 1% international.

Faculty Profile

133 full-time faculty. 12:1 faculty/student ratio. Average class size is 15.

Residence Life

Moderately residential: 79% of students live on campus.

Athletics

NCAA Division II, Northeast-10 Conference, while men's hockey competes in NCAA Division I Hockey East Association. 16 varsity sport (8 men's: baseball, basketball, cross-country, football, hockey, lacrosse, soccer, tennis; 8 women's: basketball, cross-country, field hockey, lacrosse, soccer, softball, tennis, volleyball), and 6 intramurals.

Academic Programs

Accounting; biology; bio-chemistry; chemistry; civil engineering; communication studies; computer science; economics; education (elementary, middle, secondary, moderate disabilities); electrical & computer engineering; English; environmental science; finance; fine arts; French; health science; history; international business; management; marketing; mathematics; philosophy; physics; political science; predental; prelaw; premedical; psychology; religious studies; romance languages; sociology; Spanish; sports medicine (athletic training, prephysical therapy, strength & conditioning); urban studies; women's studies.

Costs and Aid

2007-2008: $41,100 comprehensive ($29,310 tuition; $11,790 room and board); 70% of students receive some financial aid.

Endowment

$33.6 million.

More Distinctions

• For the sixth consecutive year, U.S. News & World Report named Merrimack College a top ten regional school in its 2007 rankings of colleges nationwide.

• Ranked ninth in 2007 as a Best Comprehensive College – Bachelor's – in the north, Merrimack has been named a top tier regional school for nine consecutive years in its America's Best Colleges issue.

Pine Manor College

MASSACHUSETTS

Pine Manor College is a small, independent, liberal arts college for women. Based on the belief that just as much learning takes place outside the classroom as it does inside, Pine Manor aims to prepare women for inclusive leadership and social responsibility in their careers, their communities, and their families.

Admissions Contact:

Pine Manor College
400 Heath Street
Chestnut Hill, MA 02467
(800) 428-4484
Ph: (617) 731-7000
Fax: (617) 731-7199
Email: admissions@pmc.edu
www.pmc.edu

The 4 Distinctions

Engaged Students

With five hundred students, Pine Manor has a very diverse student body. At Pine Manor, students who have attended large, urban high schools; are first-generation college students; or who have different learning styles receive the same high-quality education as those who are fortunate enough to come from America's best high schools.

Pine Manor's Center for Inclusive Leadership and Social Responsibility seeks to enhance the leadership skills of young women from middle school through the college years. The center is an active hub of activity for women of all ages and backgrounds, reaching out to the community while providing learning opportunities for Pine Manor students. Through the center, Pine Manor provides leadership workshops to high schools and offers a college outreach program that helps high school-age girls to understand the college experience.

Pine Manor students wishing to study away from campus take part in programs affiliated with several study-abroad organizations, such as the Washington Seminar at American University, the American Institute for Foreign Study, and the University of Pittsburgh's Semester at Sea program.

All students are required to do an off-campus internship during their senior year, but students can also do internships during their junior and even sophomore years. Boasting one of the oldest internship programs in the country, the integration of practical, hands-on learning has been going on for a long time at Pine Manor. Often, these internships lead to postgraduation jobs at some of Boston's best corporations, hospitals, museums, and social-service agencies.

Some of the best learning occurs when students are engaged with one another in activities outside the classroom. At Pine Manor, there is an expectation to get involved; to participate in the inclusive leadership process; and to participate in community service, student organizations, athletics and physical recreation, and performing arts—all are considered a vital part of each student's development. Pine Manor's diversity and inclusive approach to learning creates wonderful and rare opportunities to engage with others. The international student adviser and the international student club seek to integrate Pine Manor's many international students fully into the life of the college.

Great Teaching

Pine Manor offers ten major fields—biology, management and organizational change, economic and financial systems, communications, English, history, liberal studies, psychology, social and political systems, and visual arts—but more than sixty options within these majors give students a wide array of academic choices. Students in English, for example, may choose to concentrate on English education or on creative writing. Within the social and political systems program, students may select national and international politics or criminal justice. One of the most popular programs at Pine Manor is biology.

Pine Manor's approach to education is focused on the process of both learning and teaching. Students are encouraged to engage in the process—to challenge one another in discussions and to remain open to new perspectives. The low student to faculty ratio of ten to one helps foster this environment. On average, 75 percent of full-time faculty hold the PhD or the highest equivalent degree in their field, and 68 percent of full-time faculty are women. With 72 percent of Pine Manor's classes having fewer than twenty students, the college ranks among the nation's top forty liberal arts colleges in class size.

Vibrant Community

Pine Manor is one of a very small number of nonhistorically black colleges in the nation to have more black students than white students. Other substantial numbers of students identify themselves as Hispanic, Asian-American, Native American, Haitian, Puerto Rican, and Cape Verdean.

Pine Manor's comprehensive, four-credit, first-year seminar, cotaught by faculty and staff, serves as an excellent orientation to the college experience. The seminar uses topics and issues selected by students to focus on academic issues such as reading, writing, and research, as well as such personal issues as moving away from home, living with a roommate, and being part of an intensely diverse community.

More than three-quarters of Pine Manor students live in residence halls on campus. Residence halls, each with thirty students, are grouped into three villages. Within each village, a first-year advisor, a resident assistant, and student-life staff members provide support.

Pine Manor has worked hard to create an inclusive environment. In line with this focus, the college does not have a typical student government. Rather, students have a strong voice in the life of the college through individual efforts and through clubs and organizations. It is an organic way of involving all members of the community in decision making.

Just three miles from downtown Boston and a short walk to the T—Boston's subway system—Pine Manor students enjoy all the amenities of one of the nation's great cities. Yet, located on seventy wooded acres, the campus has the feel of a college far from urban noise and congestion.

Successful Outcomes

Most Pine Manor alumni remain in New England. They are successful in many different career paths, notably in the sciences and in criminal justice. Pine Manor's office of experiential learning, internships, and career services helps students set career goals and offers more than one thousand internship opportunities, which often lead to students' first jobs upon graduation.

A few years ago, while the cost of college tuition was skyrocketing all across the country, one of Pine Manor's alumni gave a generous donation and Pine Manor took the extraordinary step to reduce their tuition by 30 percent. As a result, Pine Manor is one of the most affordable, private colleges in the country, offering a highly personalized, quality education.

Most Pine Manor alumni remain in New England. They are successful in many different career paths, notably in the sciences, business, education, and non-profit organizations. About 10% go directly to graduate school, and many others pursue graduate work within a few years of graduation. Pine Manor's office of Experiential learning, internships, and career services helps students set career goals and offers more than 1000 internship opportunities. Every student graduates with at least one internship experience, which often lead to students' first jobs upon graduation.

Fast Facts

Pine Manor College is a small, liberal arts college with a mission to prepare women for lives of inclusive leadership and social responsibility in their workplaces, families and communities. Pine Manor College offers women the chance to experience the benefits of a multi-cultural education in a collaborative, supportive learning environment. For nearly 100 years, students have enjoyed the benefits of a quality, personalized, affordable private education within sight of a world class city.

Web site
www.pmc.edu

Location
Chestnut Hill, Massachusetts—5 miles from downtown Boston.

Student Profile
500 undergraduate students (100 % female); 25 states and territories, 22 countries: 65 % minority, 9 % international.

Faculty Profile
75% of full-time faculty hold a terminal degree in their field. 10:1 student/faculty ratio. Average class size is 15.

Residence Life
Highly residential: 77 % of students live on campus.

Athletics
NCAA Division III, 7 varsity sports (basketball, cross-country, lacrosse, soccer, softball, tennis, volleyball).

Academic Programs
Biology; communication; English (literature & writing); economic & financial systems; history; liberal studies; management & organizational change; social & political systems; visual arts.

Costs and Aid
2006–2007: $26,628 comprehensive ($16,600 tuition). 89% of students receive some financial aid.

Endowment
$11 million.

More Distinctions
• The most diverse (#1) liberal arts college in the country, U.S. News and World Report.

• Top 60 liberal arts colleges in the country, Washington Monthly Magazine.

Regis College

MASSACHUSETTS

Founded in 1927 by the Sisters of St. Joseph of Boston, Regis College has been a four-year, private, liberal arts and sciences college for women for eighty years. That will change in fall 2007 when Regis began for the first time to admit men at the full-time undergraduate level.

Admissions Contact:

Regis College
235 Wellesley Street
Weston, MA 02493
(866) 438-7344
Email: admission@regiscollege.edu
www.regiscollege.edu

The 4 Distinctions

Engaged Students

Regis College offers a place for young men and women to become individuals, through an innovative personal approach in the classroom and a strong spirit of friendship throughout the campus community. Regis students are educated to succeed in their careers and in their lives. From the start, they are encouraged to take a leadership role in their education. Graduates of Regis College are prepared to make a difference in their career, in their community, and in the world.

Regis College offers several special academic opportunities that allow students to explore subjects they are interested in and to customize their learning experience. The college offers a number of areas in which students can extend their learning beyond the classroom, including seminars, off-campus study, study abroad, individualized study, preprofessional programs, special cooperative degree programs, special academic honors programs, and Regis service learning.

Students can study abroad for a summer, a semester, or a year. Regis is affiliated with Regent's College in London, England; University College Cork in Cork, Ireland; and Kyoto Notre Dame University in Kyoto, Japan. Regis also maintains a cooperative arrangement with Loyola University Chicago, offering students the opportunity to study at the John Felice Rome Center. In addition, students may receive credit for studying anywhere in the world through programs at other American universities.

Regis College students are encouraged to serve the community both on and off campus. Community service and outreach projects—sponsored by residence halls, class groups, and the college itself—are an integral part of campus life. Regis students participate in various fund-raising events; work at shelters for the homeless and women and children; assist at Greater Boston Food Bank; and make an annual spring break trip to Villa El Salvador, Peru, to experience service as well as culture and spirituality. Regis College is committed to exploring the needs and problems of the changing world.

Regis College believes that through participation in professional internships, students can begin to apply classroom learning to the world of work. The practical application of theory and principle serves to enhance the learning process. Internships thus become an integral part of each students' liberal arts and science education. Students have interned with companies such as the Charles River Museum of Industry, Citizens Bank, Faulkner Hospital, New England Cable News, the State Auditor's Office, and Theatre Espresso.

Great Teaching

Regis faculty members are exceptionally accomplished: nearly 85 percent hold the most advanced degrees in their fields. They are actively engaged in their disciplines, and conduct research, publish books and articles, and are recognized as leaders in their areas of expertise. Interaction between faculty and students is a hallmark of the Regis educational experience. Faculty members get to know each student individually. Faculty members are instrumental in helping students achieve their goals—assisting with everything from research and graduate school programs to internships and job opportunities.

Bachelor's degrees are offered in a wide variety of majors. Master's degrees are offered in nursing, teaching, management, communication, and health product regulation; Regis also offers a doctoral program in nursing practice. Among the most popular undergraduate majors are nursing and education. The core liberal arts curriculum inspires students to think both critically and creatively. Students learn how to write clearly, solve problems, and defend their point of view as they continue to reach new heights of intellectual capacity.

All first-year students take a two-semester first-year seminar, a writing seminar course, and a required math course. The small average class size of fourteen students cultivates an atmosphere in which students can voice their opinions in class, participate in learning, and initiate debate and discussion.

The honors program at Regis provides qualified students with an intellectually stimulating and challenging academic experience that extends beyond the classroom. Students in the honors program complete a total of six honors courses, including a required honors seminar and five other courses. With prior approval, upper-division honors students may also enroll in designated graduate courses. Honors program students provide tutoring for other Regis students, accompanied by a seminar in tutoring techniques and instruction methods. They also provide a substantial number of hours of voluntary service to the organization of their choice.

Vibrant Community

Regis College offers students a suburban setting with quick and easy access to the cultural and social activities of the Boston area. It is located in Weston, Massachusetts, a residential community twelve miles from metropolitan Boston. The college's shuttle service enables students to take advantage of programs at nearby colleges, as well as the business, government, entertainment, and cultural opportunities of Boston.

On average, 70 percent of the undergraduate student body lives on campus, and there are a number of different ways that students can get involved in campus activities. Over thirty active clubs and organizations on campus are open to the entire student body. Regis College is proud of its diverse student population and the different backgrounds and heritages they represent. The diversity of the students, clubs, and organizations is of utmost importance to the college. Among these organizations are the Student Government Association; AHANA, the African-American, Hispanic, Asian, Native American Association; AMISTADES, a Latino cultural organization; AAA, the Asian-American Association; Tower Activities Board (TAB) ; the Tower Society, a group of students who assist with recruitment; as well as clubs for social work, commuters, nursing students, theatre, and many more. Recent student initiatives include the formation of the dance company and the Cape Verdean Student Association, and the renovation of the student center, complete with a cybercafe and an arcade.

The office of student activities and various Regis clubs sponsor many events throughout the semester, including coffeehouses, musicians, comedians, cultural events, and parties, as well as a number of Regis College traditional events, including Welcome Week, Family Weekend, Oktoberfest Weekend, Spring Weekend, and the Christmas Banquet. Boston also offers students many exciting events and attractions such as Fenway Park, the Museum of Fine Arts, and Harvard Square.

Successful Outcomes

Regis College looks forward to graduating its first coeducational class in 2011. To date, Regis has educated more than ten thousand leaders in law, medicine, management, education, communication, social work, and other professional fields.

The office of career development provides a variety of career-development and job-search services for Regis College students and alumni. Career development staff assist students and graduates in planning careers, securing internships, developing resumes, implementing effective job-search strategies, identifying employers in various industries, and exploring graduate-school options.

Fast Facts

Regis College is a four-year co-ed liberal arts and sciences college, founded in 1927 by the Congregation of the Sisters of St. Joseph of Boston.

Website

http://www.regiscollege.edu/

Location

Weston, Massachusetts—1 2 miles west of Boston.

Student Profile

850 undergraduate students (100% female); 22 states and territories; 30% minority and international

*Regis announced their co-educational decision on August 31, 2006.

Faculty Profile

66 full-time faculty. 14:1 student/faculty ratio. Average class size is 12.

Residence Life

Moderately residential: 70% of full-time students live on campus.

Athletics

NCAA Division III, Commonwealth Coast Conference. 17 varsity sports (9 women's: basketball, volleyball, swimming & diving, track & field, field hockey, lacrosse, soccer, softball, tennis. 8 men's: 2007-08 basketball, swimming & diving; 2008-09 soccer, track & field; 2009-10 tennis, lacrosse, volleyball; 2010-11 golf).

Academic Programs

Biochemistry; biology; chemistry; communication; computer studies; English; graphic design; history; human computer interaction; information systems; international relations; law & government; liberal studies; management; mathematics education; museum studies; nursing; political science; psychology; public relations; social work; sociology; Spanish; theatre.

Teacher Licensure: early childhood education, elementary education, secondary education

Preprofessional programs: predental, prelaw, premedicine, preveterinary.

Costs and Aid

2007–2008: $37,590 comprehensive ($ 25,990 tuition); 87% of students receive some financial aid. Average award: $10,347.

Endowment

$22,512,941.

More Distinctions

• For the fourth consecutive year, Regis College is ranked in the top tier of Best Universities-Master's (North) according to the annual *U.S. News & World Report* survey for 2005. Regis placed 36th in the top group of 83 colleges and universities that offer master's as well as bachelor's degrees in the northern region.

• In 2001, the Carnegie Institute ranked Regis among the top thirty northern universities granting master's degrees.

• In 2000 and 2001, the National Survey of Student Engagement (NSSE) listed Regis among "benchmarking" colleges for its quality of educational experience.

Simmons College

MASSACHUSETTS

Located in the heart of Boston, Simmons College is a highly respected, small university with a cherished history of visionary thinking and social responsibility. Simmons offers an innovative liberal arts education for undergraduate women, integrated with professional work experience, as well as renowned graduate programs for women and men.

Admissions Contact:

Simmons College
300 The Fenway
Boston, MA 02115
(800) 345-8468
Ph: (617) 521-2000
Fax: (617) 521-3190
Email: ugadm@simmons.edu
www.simmons.edu

The 4 Distinctions

Engaged Students

Decades before women in America gained the right to vote, Boston businessman John Simmons had a revolutionary idea—that women should be able to earn independent livelihoods and lead meaningful lives. Simmons College was the result. Founded in 1899, Simmons has offered a pioneering liberal arts education for undergraduate women, integrated with career preparation for more than one hundred years. Today, Simmons encompasses the many benefits of a small university, including graduate programs for women and men in health studies, education, liberal arts, communications management, social work, and library and information science, as well as the nation's only MBA program designed for women.

Simmons's undergraduate women's college provides a strong liberal arts education integrated with interdisciplinary study, career preparation, and global perspectives. The college offers more than forty majors and programs. The most popular majors include nursing, psychology, biology, public relations and communications, sociology, education, art administration, physical therapy, prelaw, international relations, management, and economics. In addition, more than a dozen integrated degree and accelerated program options allow students to go directly from their undergraduate program to a graduate program at Simmons or one of its affiliated schools, often earning a bachelor's degree plus a master's or doctoral degree in less time than traditional programs. Nearly 30 percent of Simmons students choose to double-major.

Simmons's hands-on, interdisciplinary undergraduate curriculum ensures that each student explores a variety of subjects while gaining an in-depth theoretical and practical understanding of her major. First-year courses emphasize critical thinking and writing skills, while integrating two or more subjects—ranging from bioethics and Buddhist studies, to democracy, education, and economics.

Experiential learning is key, both in the classroom and beyond. Students fulfill an independent learning requirement through internship, fieldwork, and research projects. In doing so, they develop skills, impressive resumes, and a network of professional contacts. Simmons students typically spend one or more semesters interning for businesses, schools, government agencies, and nonprofit organizations, as well as in Boston's world-renowned research and teaching hospitals. Students also collaborate with faculty on professional research projects, and publish and present their findings at national conferences. Recent projects have included research on the causes of Alzheimer's disease, the molecular interactions involved in kidney-stone formation, and the development of organic light-emitting diodes (OLEDs).

Students also gain real-life experience through numerous service-learning and volunteer programs. Both undergraduate and graduate students participate in local and international service-learning courses each year, dedicating a total of approximately twelve thousand hours of community service to initiatives ranging from early childhood education in Boston public schools, to community health care in Nicaragua. Everyone at Simmons—from students, faculty, and alumni, to staff and senior administrators—gets involved in outreach such as the Promising Pals mentoring program, Special Olympics events, Global Community Service Day, and a silent auction that benefits the neighborhood food bank.

Acquiring a global outlook—including an understanding of languages, cultures, and world politics—is also part of the Simmons experience. From undergraduate programs such as Africana or East Asian studies, to graduate fieldwork with Boston's diverse immigrant communities, Simmons encourages students to move beyond familiar borders and connect with the world. To this end, Simmons encourages cross-cultural understanding and collaboration through on-campus colloquia and conferences; international scholarship; and outreach programs in Africa, Asia, the Middle East, Latin America, and Eastern Europe. Current initiatives include scholarships for Afghan women, community-health projects in Nicaragua, and library preservation in war-torn Iraq. Intensive study-abroad courses range from journalism in South Africa, to music in Austria, to history and culture in Japan. Students are also encouraged to spend an entire semester or year abroad, with scholarships and grants available for research and independent study.

Special academic opportunities include an honors program; Studio 5, a student-run, creative communications studio that produces projects for Boston-area nonprofits; and the Barbara Lee Family Foundation Intern Fellowship, which pairs undergraduate seniors with state legislators. In addition, several alumni mentoring programs allow students to gain professional experience and support. Through Success Connection, select undergraduate seniors shadow high-profile alumni in their places of work. Sistas Investing in Sistas connects Black undergraduate students and alumni for life-coaching relationships. The Mosaic Multicultural Program matches diverse alumni and undergraduate juniors for career mentoring opportunities.

Great Teaching

Simmons's distinguished faculty include noted researchers, authors, and experts in their respective fields. All are passionate educators, who take pride in personally teaching and mentoring their students. Students say that professors care about them, expect excellence, and go out of their way to offer guidance and support. A twelve to one student to faculty ratio ensures that every student receives individual attention.

Vibrant Community

The college's small but strong community attracts students and teachers who contribute to the school's life and meaning. The historic, tree-lined Simmons campus is located in Boston's eclectic Fenway neighborhood, which is alive with music, fine arts, research, education, activism, and the rowdy cheers of baseball fans at legendary Fenway Park. Numerous colleges, cafes, museums, parks, shops, and the Longwood Medical Area are all nearby.

Simmons has more than fifty student organizations, academic liaisons, and other activities, including student government, eight NCAA Division III athletic teams, cultural organizations, and volunteer projects. Campus traditions such as the Simmons Cup field day and "moonlight breakfasts" during finals week ensure a proud legacy of Simmons sisterhood. As members of the Colleges of the Fenway consortium, Simmons students attend social and cultural events with more than nine thousand undergraduates from five neighboring colleges.

Successful Outcomes

Simmons has a rich tradition of preparing women for high achievement. The challenging programs, exceptional internship opportunities, and collaborative community encourage dialogue, action, and respect, making the Simmons experience as thoughtful as it is thought provoking. Graduates say Simmons's intellectual focus, professional preparation, and supportive environment helped them develop the skills and confidence for successful careers.In communications and the arts, Bethany alumni and students continue to reach national prominence. Graduates include CBS News correspondent Bob Orr, Seattle Mariners play-by-play announcer Dave Sims, and former NBC anchor Faith Daniels. A Bethany student has been named a finalist in the National Broadcasting Society's student electronic media competition for seven consecutive years. So well-known is Bethany that the campus has attracted visits by U.S. Presidents Garfield, Kennedy, Nixon, Johnson, and Ford.

Fast Facts

Simmons College is a private college with more than thirty-five undergraduate majors and programs for women and numerous graduate programs for women and men. It was founded in 1899.

Web site

http://www.simmons.edu

Location

Boston, Massachusetts.

Student Profile

1,938 undergraduate female students; 44 states, 39 countries; 7% international, 16% multicultural.

Faculty Profile

109 full-time undergraduate faculty; more than 50% female. 78% hold doctorates or highest appropriate professional degrees. 12:1 student/faculty ratio. Average class size is 19.

Residence Life

Highly residential: 88% of students live on campus.

Athletics

NCAA Division III, Great Northeast Athletic Conference (GNAC), the Eastern Collegiate Athletic Conference (ECAC), and is affiliated with the Massachusetts Association of Intercollegiate Athletics for Women (MAIAW). 8 varsity sports: basketball, crew, field hockey, soccer, softball, swimming & diving, tennis, volleyball.

Academic Programs

Africana studies; art & music; arts administration; biology; biology/physician assistant; biochemistry; chemistry; chemistry/management; chemistry/pharmacy; communications; computer sciences; East Asian studies; economics/math; education; English as a second language; English; environmental studies; French; graphic design; history; international relations; information technology; management; managerial finance; management information systems; marketing; marketing communications/public relations; mathematics; modern languages & literature; nursing; nutrition; philosophy; physical therapy; physics; physics of materials; political science & international relations; premedicine; prelaw; predental; preveterinary; psychobiology; psychology; public policy; public relations; retail management; social science/education; society & health; sociology; Spanish; special education; women's studies.

Costs and Aid

2007–2008: $39,024 comprehensive ($27,468 tuition). More than 70% of Simmons students receive some financial aid. Average award: $14,638.

Endowment

$177 million.

More Distinctions

• Simmons was included in the 2007 Princeton Review "Best 361 Colleges" and was named one of the "best in New England" in the first-ever edition of Princeton Review's "Best Northeastern Colleges."

Stonehill College

MASSACHUSETTS

Stonehill College (SC), a private, Catholic, coeducational, liberal arts college, fosters campus life focused on community and service. Founded in 1948 by the Congregation of the Holy Cross, it aims to provide "a community of scholarship and faith, anchored by a belief in the inherent dignity of each person."

Admissions Contact:

Stonehill College
320 Washington Street
Easton, MA 02357-5610
Ph: (508) 565-1373
Fax: (508) 565-1545
Email: admissions@stonehill.edu
www.stonehill.edu

The 4 Distinctions

Engaged Students

With a full-time undergraduate enrollment of 2,248, Stonehill offers thirty-one academic majors, and thirty-seven minor areas of study in the liberal arts, natural sciences, and business. Its most popular programs are biology, biochemistry, English, political science, criminology, psychology, accounting, prelaw, and education. Stonehill's programs are unique because of the internship and research possibilities the college offers, reflecting its commitment to experiential learning.

SC students do real work in their internship experiences. By graduation, over 75 percent of students earn credits and gain valuable experience participating in a domestic or international internship, a study abroad program, or in a field-study experience. Close to 20 percent of students participate in both internship and study-abroad programs. Business students have interned at companies like Fidelity Investments and PricewaterhouseCoopers; English and writing students have had jobs in print media and public-relations firms; and science students have worked at hospitals in Boston and London.

Stonehill offers an innovative core curriculum called the Cornerstone Program, which includes team-taught freshman courses, the sophomore learning community, and a senior capstone course. The sophomore learning community is a cluster of classes that address an issue both in and out of the classroom. It includes two courses followed by a seminar frequently involving learning outside the classroom. A recent learning community on the conservation of the Everglades included courses in ethics and action, and ecology, as well as a one-week research trip to the Everglades, where students applied their learning to a real-world issue.

SC offers study-abroad opportunities at over 130 institutions in more than forty different countries throughout the world. Students can study abroad for a semester or for a full academic year. Other special academic programs include the Stonehill Undergraduate Research Experience (SURE) and an honors program.

Great Teaching

Stonehill aims to provide an "education of the highest caliber that fosters critical thinking, free inquiry, and the interchange of ideas." The low Stonehill student to faculty ratio of thirteen to one, and the average class size of twenty, allows faculty to know the students well, and they are committed teachers and mentors. They offer advice and help to students with courses and graduate-school applications. Like the majority of SC students, they are involved with cocurricular activities. Professors often invite guest speakers to come to the Stonehill campus, and sometimes as many as two thousand people attend these appearances.

The college's goal is to educate "the whole person so that each Stonehill graduate thinks, acts, and leads with courage toward the creation of a more just and compassionate world."

Vibrant Community

Stonehill is located in Easton, Massachusetts, a town of twenty three thousand, incorporated in 1725. The 375-acre campus is just twenty-two miles south of America's premiere college town, Boston. A free campus shuttle service provides students access to the Boston transit system.

Stonehill is a residential college, and 89 percent of SC students live on campus in mainly coed dorms. Nearly everyone, including the professors, participates in curricular and extracurricular activities. There are more than sixty-five student clubs and organizations, plus twenty competitive Division II varsity teams and numerous intramural, recreational, and intercollegiate club sport programs.

There are sixteen different community-service organizations such as Into the Streets, H.O.P.E., and the Center for Nonprofit Management, providing students with opportunities to serve in the local area and beyond. SC students travel to Boston and Providence to enjoy the many theaters, museums, and professional sport teams.

Successful Outcomes

Stonehill is committed to achieving successful outcomes. Faculty advisers help incoming students choose appropriate courses. The Office of Career Services assists in both career planning and placement by offering interest inventory testing, providing career information, and hosting activities such as mock interviews, job fairs, resume-writing workshops, and an active on-campus recruitment program. Within a year of graduation, 98 percent of last year's graduates were either employed, attending graduate or professional school, or participating in a service organization such as the Peace Corps. SC alumni can also take full advantage of the college's career resources. Alumni are also very involved on campus, offering internship and job shadowing opportunities, as well as externship experiences and full-time employment.

Each of the 556 graduates of the Class of 2006 has a special story to tell. The following are the profiles of four graduates:

E. Sletten received a two-year award from the Barry M. Goldwater Scholarship and Excellence in Education Foundation -- the third Stonehill student to receive a Goldwater and the first to do so in her sophomore year. A participant in the Stonehill Undergraduate Research Experience (S.U.R.E.), she collaborated with faculty, presented her research at conferences and was published in a professional journal. She will be pursuing her Ph.D. in Chemistry at the University of California, Berkeley.

While at Stonehill, M. Christian traveled to Honduras two years in a row to serve with the College's alternative spring break program (H.O.P.E.). Active in Campus Ministry, he also sang regularly with the Chapel Choir and started the first annual Celebration of Faith in the Arts. Upon graduation, this graduate will be returning for a year of service in Honduras.

In his junior year, competing against students from many leading colleges, D. Monaco landed a prestigious internship with Goldman Sachs where he spent one summer on Wall Street working on the New York Stock Exchange, gaining experience on an equities trading desk and learning about equity sales. A defensive lineman on the football team, Monaco was also engaged in many community outreach initiatives. Currently networking with Stonehill alumni in the finance industry, he is interviewing for a position in Boston.

Exploring international options, M. Mahmood developed her Arabic language skills as well as her knowledge of Islamic philosophy at the American University in Cairo. She also attended the University of Zaragoza in Spain where she perfected her Spanish. In addition, she interned at the Center for the Study of the Presidency and then at the Woodrow Wilson International Center for Scholars in Washington, D.C. After Commencement, she will return to Washington D.C. to work in the nonprofit sector before going on to pursue graduate studies.

Fast Facts

Stonehill College is a four-year college of arts and sciences and pre-professional studies affiliated with the Congregation of the Holy Cross of the Roman Catholic Church, founded in 1948.

Web site

http://www.stonehill.edu

Location

Easton, MA—22 miles south of Boston.

Student Profile

2,248 undergraduate students (41% male, 59% female); 28 states, 1 territory, and 10 foreign countries; 9% minority.

Faculty Profile

135 full-time faculty. 13:1 student/faculty ratio. Average class size 20.

Residence Life

Highly residential: 89% of students live on campus.

Athletics

NCAA Division II, Northeast 10 Conference. 18 varsity sports (8 men's: baseball, basketball, cross-country, football, ice hockey, soccer, tennis, track & field; 10 women's: basketball, cross-country, equestrian, field hockey, lacrosse, soccer, softball, tennis, track & field, volleyball), 8 club sports and 32 intramural sports programs.

Academic Programs

Accounting; American studies; biochemistry; biology; chemistry; communication; computer engineering*; computer science; criminology; economics; education; English; finance; fine arts; foreign language; French; gender studies; health care administration; history; international business; international studies; management; marketing; mathematics; multidisciplinary studies; neuroscience; philosophy; political science; psychology; public administration; religious studies; sociology; Spanish.

*The Computer Engineering Program is a 3 + 2 cooperative program with the University of Notre Dame, Indiana.

Costs and Aid

2007–2008: $39,870 comprehensive (28,440 tuition). 90% of students receive some type of financial assistance. Average freshman award: $16,946.

Endowment

$140 million.

More Distinctions

• In *U.S. News & World Report's* "America's Best Colleges 2008", Stonehill was ranked #106 of nearly 300 nationally-renowned baccalaureate institutions included in its new national "Liberal Arts Colleges" category.

• The *Kaplan/Newsweek College Catalog* deems Stonehill "a hidden treasure" and says it deserves more national recognition.

• *Princeton Review* praises Stonehill's student centered focus and its "academically challenging and mind-expanding curriculum."

Suffolk University

Admissions Contact:

Suffolk University
73 Tremont St, 6th Floor
Boston, MA 02108
1.800.6SUFFOL(k)
Ph: (617) 573-8460
Fax: (617) 557-1574
Email: admission@suffolk.edu
www.suffolk.edu

MASSACHUSETTS

Suffolk University (SU), founded in 1906, is a private university set on historic Beacon Hill in Boston, Massachusetts. The intellectual atmosphere in Boston helps students to thrive academically and culturally. At SU, there is a strong emphasis on preparing students for a diverse, global society.

The 4 Distinctions

Engaged Students

Suffolk and non-Suffolk students can travel to Suffolk's international campuses in Madrid, Spain, or Dakar, Senegal; participate in two-week intensive, faculty-led, credit-bearing courses conveniently offered during semester breaks; or enroll in one of thirty-eight international education semester programs around the world. One of the most unique study abroad programs at SU is the opportunity to begin your college career at Suffolk's Madrid campus – same curriculum, half of Boston's tuition.

SU is home to a substantial international student population. There are over 1000 international students from 104 countries. Additionally, forty-four states and Puerto Rico are represented in the student body.

SU is committed to encouraging students to explore the real-world applications of their education and to experience a global perspective. Many majors, particularly in business and in government, require students to complete internships and/or study abroad for at least one semester before they can graduate. For example, Global Business majors in the Sawyer Business School fulfill an overseas travel requirement by completing a minimum of one travel seminar or a semester study abroad while undergraduate Government majors in the College of Arts and Sciences following the International Affairs track are encouraged to complete a full- or part-time internship or study abroad semester.

Great Teaching

Suffolk University encompasses the Law School, founded in 1906; the College of Arts and Sciences, including the New England School or Art and Design(NESAD); and the Sawyer Business School. There are eighty undergraduate majors, as well as an array of exciting interdisciplinary majors, to choose from at SU. One of the most popular programs is the communications/journalism program, with areas of focus in media studies, film studies, and print journalism. Other popular majors are accounting, finance, and international business.

Of the many prestigious colleges and universities in the state, SU is home to the 2005 Massachusetts Professor of the Year. Walter Johnson, a professor of physics, was chosen in large part due to his enthusiasm for his subject and dedication to his students. Because classes are small, professors at Suffolk are free to express their passion for teaching, and their love for their fields of study. Many stay late after class or meet with students outside of office hours, and often take the time to answer urgent emails in the evening, or on the weekend before a test. They seek to inspire. They challenge ideas and explore differences. They serve gladly as mentors and advisers. It's no wonder that they know the names of all their students.

The student to teacher ratio is 13 to 1 and the average undergraduate class size is 21. The academic program stresses real-world teaching and learning. 94% of SU faculty hold a PhD or terminal degree.

Vibrant Community

When students arrive on the Beacon Hill campus, they are received with the phrase, "Welcome to Boston. Welcome to Suffolk. Welcome Home."

When students step out the door of any campus building they are on a city street in Boston. The State House, Boston Common, Quincy Market, and Financial District are all within walking distance. Public transportation is steps away. Because of this, Suffolk students can take advantage of Boston's rich entertainment, historical, and cultural resources; benefit from local commerce, government, and industry; and easily integrate their college experience into the local community. Boston is the quintessential college town, home to about 300,000 college students from all over the globe, which gives it a dynamic intellectual energy unmatched by other cities. Suffolk's satellite campuses in Barnstable, MA, and Franklin, MA, through partnerships with Cape Cod Community College and Dean College, add accessibility for the New England region.

Over seventy-five student organizations – including a TV production studio, performance opportunities, two student newspapers, diversity services, and "S.O.U.L.S." (Suffolk's Organization for Uplifting Lives through Service) – demonstrate SU's commitment to student involvement. The newly constructed Mildred F. Sawyer Library and newly renovated C. Walsh Theatre demonstrate SU's commitment to student academics and to student life.

Suffolk students don't hide behind campus gates and dorm room walls. Whether it's through internships, community service or working at local businesses, in learning and in action, they are empowered to interact with the city around them.

Successful Outcomes

The university's career counseling program helps prepare students for life after graduation. As one SU professor put it, "When it comes to launching a career, the key factor is experience, experience, experience." And when it comes to preparing for a career, the SU edge is "location, location, location." Boston, known as "the Hub," offers a wealth of co-operative education possibilities. Suffolk Madrid and Suffolk Dakar offer a global perspective and contact opportunities in Europe and West Africa as well.

The Office of Career Services and Cooperative Education guides students through an Undergraduate Career Timeline or "Road to Success." Freshman year, students can take a career-assessment test, visit the career library, and meet with career counselors to assess strengths, interests, and abilities. Sophomore year, students are encouraged to sharpen their focus, select a major, and conduct informational interviews with alumni in their chosen field. Junior year, students can revise their resumes, network with alumni, and interview with employers for internships. Senior year, the campus-recruiting program helps students find jobs with companies such as T-Mobile, Suffolk Superior Court, The Boston Globe, Ernst & Young, and Fidelity Investments.

Suffolk students benefit from the experience of both their professors and Suffolk alumni. In a recent survey, 90 percent of graduating seniors reported that Suffolk professors provided encouragement to further their education. Similarly, students can participate in a network of fifty five thousand active alumni around the globe.

Fast Facts

Suffolk University is a private, comprehensive, urban university.

Web site

http://www.suffolk.edu

Location

Boston, MA— located in historic Beacon Hill, three other Massachusetts locations and international campuses in Madrid, Spain, and Dakar, Senegal.

Student Profile

7,337 students including graduate students (42 % male, 58 % female); 44 states and territories, 99 countries

Faculty Profile

13:1 student/faculty ratio. Average undergraduate class size is 20.

Residence Life

Moderately residential: 16% of the student body lives on campus.

Athletics

NCAA Division III, Great Northeast Athletic Conference. 12 Varsity sports (7 men's: baseball, basketball, cross-country, golf, hockey, soccer, tennis; 6 women's: basketball, volleyball, soccer, softball, cross-country, tennis).

Academic Programs

Over 70 majors including: accounting; art & design; biology; chemistry & biochemistry; communication/journalism; computer science; economics; education & human services; electrical & computer engineering; English; entrepreneurship; environmental science; finance; government; global business; history; humanities; information systems; international economics; Latin American & Caribbean studies; legal studies; management; mathematics; marketing; medical science; modern languages; performing & visual arts; philosophy; physics; psychology; public administration; sociology; teacher preparation; theatre.

Costs and Aid

2006–07: $22,610 tuition, $12,756 room and board. 76% of freshman receive some financial aid. Average award: $21,835.

Endowment

$87,570,080.

More Distinctions

• The Princeton Review 2007 edition of The Best 361 Colleges.

• The Princeton Review 2005 edition of The Best 357 Colleges.

• The Princeton Review 2005 "Top 25 Most Connected Business Campuses."

• NAFSA: Association of International Educators – Internationalizing the Campus 2004: Profiles of Success at Colleges and Universities.

• The Princeton Review 2006 edition of The Best Northeastern Colleges.

Western New England College

MASSACHUSETTS

Blending the liberal arts and professional education, Western New England College values learning outside the classroom, a diverse campus community, innovation, and maintaining "an atmosphere of personal concern" for everyone. This powerful combination creates an outstanding environment for students seeking to succeed and lead in their professional and personal lives.

Admissions Contact:

Western New England College
1215 Wilbraham Road
Springfield, MA 01119
(800) 325-1122
Ph: (413) 782-1321
Fax: (413) 782-1777
Email: ugradmis@wnec.edu
www.wnec.edu

The 4 Distinctions

Engaged Students

For many students at Western New England College, study abroad is a passport to a world of remarkable opportunity. Beyond classes in international settings, students can also intern with the BBC in London; study art in Florence, Italy; or get a close-up look at business in Australia. Students have spent the semester or year in Australia, China, England, Finland, Ireland, Italy, and Spain.

The college also offers select courses abroad, including London through the Ages, and Introduction to the Mayan World, taught on-site in southern Mexico. Students have also had the opportunity to study French culture and history in Paris during spring break.

The college's Learning Beyond the Classroom program helps students discover learning opportunities all around them. Combining in-class study with out-of-the-classroom activities from community service to mentoring, the program gives students hundreds of ways to gain new and valuable life experience. Subsequent opportunities to reflect on the service activity help students draw important lessons from their involvement as it relates to their academic work.

The college has relationships with more than four hundred sponsoring organizations at which students perform fieldwork, research engineering design projects, student teach, or serve as interns.

Great Teaching

The college offers more than thirty undergraduate programs through its schools of arts and sciences, business, and engineering. Among the most popular majors are communication, criminal justice, management, psychology, and sport management. Another popular major, mechanical engineering, offers students lab time and a required senior design project that provides students with the chance to work one-on-one with department faculty. Western New England College professors inspire students to challenge ideas, think critically, and find creative solutions—to become active participants in their education.

Western New England College offers several joint degree programs. The school's 3+3 law program is a six-year course of study that leads to both an undergraduate and a law degree. Similarly, students can complete a five-year program leading to both an undergraduate degree and an MBA. The college offers the only program in the country that combines biomedical engineering with the law, a six-year curriculum that leads to both an undergraduate and a law degree.

The honors program at Western New England College gives students the opportunity to explore subjects in greater depth, interact with honors students across majors, and study topics that cross disciplines.

For over twenty-five years, Western New England College has set aside one day a year as Lecture Day, inviting students and the public to attend lectures and seminars exploring important topics facing society. To enhance the learning experience for students, many professors require students to attend and later participate in classroom discussions or write papers based on select lectures.

Vibrant Community

With over sixty student clubs and organizations, and a variety of athletic and creative outlets to choose from, many students find niches in appropriate cocurricular activities—from student government and athletics to the student newspaper (*The Westerner*), the cheerleading club, the Historical Society, the outing club, and many others. In their first year, students can join the Emerging Leaders program, where they explore personal strengths and test their capacities for leadership.

Opportunities for volunteering abound. Students can participate in the America Reads programs in which students read to young children in local schools; Helping Hands, a part of Campus Ministry; Make a Difference Day, when students volunteer in homeless shelters and soup kitchens; and alternative spring breaks, when students work with Habitat for Humanity or other organizations. Western New England College students also volunteer to teach computer skills and help to build computers for community agencies. Sports teams also get involved in projects such as distributing free books and helping with city beautification.

The college's setting in Springfield, Massachusetts, offers access to the Naismith Memorial Basketball Hall of Fame, Six Flags New England, The MassMutual Center, home to concerts and a minor-league hockey team, several museums, and a number of libraries. The campus is ninety minutes by car from Boston and sixty miles from skiing in Vermont. Western New England College is also part of a coalition of eight colleges in the Springfield area.

Three-quarters of Western New England College students live on campus, and many opt to live in themed housing, where they share housing with students with similar interests in academics, fine arts, sports, and wellness and health, as well as interests in other areas.

Successful Outcomes

Many Western New England College students are required to complete projects that serve as stepping-stones to real jobs. One student, for example, made a video for a local school for the deaf; she submitted the video to a local affiliate of ABC-TV and was offered and accepted an on-air reporter's job, while studying as a full-time student. Similarly, a mechanical engineering student who worked with United Technology on jet engines received an offer from NASA, after seeing her work, to pay for her PhD degree. Western New England College also boasts a former biomedical engineering student who developed an apparatus that surgeons were using a year later in open-heart surgeries.

Many students gain practical experience in internships. The college has a partnership with a public radio station in nearby Albany, New York— students serve as reporters of the station, producing news segments aired throughout the Northeast..

Through its career center, the college nurtures a network of alumni who serve as mentors for current students. Many alumni come back to campus to talk with students in classes. In engineering classes, for example, practicing engineers help students get a real-world perspective.

Western New England College's more than thirty-seven thousand alumni have a high rate of success. Graduates go on to prestigious graduate schools or to jobs in their chosen fields. Western New England College alumni are the CEOs, CFOs, and presidents of many of the region's banking and financial institutions; senior-level engineers at major corporations such as UTC and Pratt & Whitney; leaders in the law-enforcement community; managers of business strategies at corporations such as TJX Companies, Big Lots, Hasbro, and MassMutual Financial Group; and experts who make a difference every day in the sciences, health care, education, and social services sectors.

Fast Facts

Western New England College is a four-year private, independent, coeducational college founded in 1919.

Web site

www.wnec.edu

Location

Springfield, Massachusetts–90 miles from Boston.

Student Profile

2,405 undergraduate students (62% male 38% female); 28 states and territories, 60% students out of state; 8% minority.

Faculty Profile

177 full-time faculty. 15:1 student/faculty ratio. Average class size is 19.

Residence Life

Highly residential: 92% of freshmen live on campus.

Athletics

NCAA Division III, The Commonwealth Coast Conference (TCCC). 19 varsity sports (10 men's: baseball, basketball, cross-country; football; golf; ice hockey; lacrosse; soccer; tennis; wrestling; 9 women's: basketball, cross-country, field hockey, lacrosse, soccer, softball, swimming, tennis, volleyball). The College also offers two non-NCAA sports teams for men and women (bowling and martial arts).

Academics

Accounting; biology (general concentration, molecular concentration); biomedical engineering; business information systems; chemistry; communication (interpersonal communication concentration, mass media concentration); computer science; creative writing; criminal justice; economics; education (elementary, secondary); electrical engineering (computer concentration, electrical concentration); English; finance; five-year accounting Bachelor/MSA; forensic biology; forensic chemistry; general business; history; information technology; industrial engineering; international studies (European area concentration, developing societies concentration, economics & commerce concentration); 3+3 law program; law & society; mathematical sciences; management; marketing; marketing communication/advertising; mechanical engineering (manufacturing concentration, mechanical concentration); philosophy; political science; psychology; six-year biomedical engineering/law; social work; sociology; sport management.

Costs and Aid

2007–2008: $35,940 Arts & Sciences and Business comprehensive (25,942 tuition), $37,032 Engineering comprehensive (27,034 tuition).

More Distinctions

• Listed in top category among Master's Universities in the North in America's Best Colleges rankings by U.S. News and World Report.

• Western New England College is AACSB (The Association to Advance Collegiate Schools of Business) International accredited. Less than 10% of business programs worldwide are accredited by AACSB International.

Wheelock College

MASSACHUSETTS

Wheelock College (WC) is a small, private coed institution specializing in academic programs to prepare professionals to work with children and families. The campus is located on the Riverway in Boston, and attracts many applicants from New England, New York, and Pennsylvania.

Admissions Contact:

Wheelock College
200 the Riverway
Boston, Massachusetts 02215
(800) 734-5212
Ph: (617) 879-2206
Fax: (617) 879-2449
Email: undergrad@wheelock.edu
www.wheelock.edu

The 4 Distinctions

Engaged Students

During their time at WC, students have many opportunities to live the school's mission of improving the lives of children and families. The Center for Community Service is a student-run center that opened up on campus with a kickoff event to raise money for Rosie's Place, a sanctuary for homeless women. In addition to providing students chances to volunteer in the community, this Center sponsors and publicizes events to benefit groups such as the AIDS Action Committee, Toys for Tots, and MissionSafe.

WC students can study abroad in eighteen different countries or go on national or international service-learning projects lasting one week to ten days. Working with WC professors, students have traveled to Guatemala, Ghana, and Northern Ireland. Inside the United States, students traveled to New Orleans to help rebuild communities after Hurricane Katrina.

Being in Boston provides WC students with unlimited opportunities to enjoy time outside of the classroom. The campus is just a short walk from some incredible museums — such as the Museum of Fine Arts — and from Fenway Park, home of the Boston Red Sox. WC is located on the MBTA green line, which connects to all of Boston and the surrounding suburbs. There are plenty of opportunities to help the community through many volunteer opportunities. Students spend time volunteering in homeless shelters, cleaning the parks around campus, and fundraising and working with different non-profit organizations.

Great Teaching

With a student to faculty ratio of eleven to one, WC offers graduate and undergraduate programs through three schools: the School of Arts and Sciences, the School of Education and Child Life, and the School of Social Work and Family Studies. Popular programs of study include early childhood and elementary education, social work, and juvenile justice.

Small classes mean students enjoy thought-provoking dialogue with distinguished scholars and practitioners. It also allows the benefit of a close relationship between students and faculty who get to know each other as individuals. The Wheelock faculty includes renowned scholars, leaders, and advocates – nearly 90 percent of who hold the most advanced degrees offered in their fields of expertise. The WC faculty comprises members who are held in the highest regard for their seminal work in education, child life, social work, and most every profession that seeks to improve the lives of children and families.

Students also benefit from WC's participation in the Colleges of the Fenway Consortium (CoF), a network of six colleges. The consortium gives students access to a small college experience while providing the combined resources of a large university. Students can take classes at any of the consortium schools, use their libraries and dining facilities, and participate in intramural sports, cultural organizations, or student activities.

The course of study for WC programs is flexible depending on a student's interests, but every first-year student takes a foundation course about families, children, and community interactions. All WC students have the opportunity to gain valuable hands-on experience in real-world settings. The Field Experience Office works to connect students to internships and professional opportunities in the local community, many in area schools, hospitals, and community programs.

Vibrant Community

Convinced that early-childhood education was a solution for many of society's problems, Lucy Wheelock started Miss Wheelock's Kindergarten Training School for teachers in 1888. In 1939, the school became Wheelock College, and today has expanded its educational programs to include service to children's social and health needs.

WC is a private college with a public mission to improve the lives of children and families. This is achieved by infusing WC students' educations with achievement, integrity, mutual respect, multiculturalism, diversity, and social justice with a global perspective. Located in an urban environment, the college has a special commitment to urban, multicultural, and global education, a commitment exemplified by an annual lecture series on the education of black male youth.

Nearly seventy percent of students live on campus, though there are no requirements to do so. There are five residence halls, with options of coed or women's same-sex dorms, and first-year floors. Among the more than twenty clubs and organizations on campus are the sign choir, which brings deaf awareness to campus; the dance team; and Students Against Destructive Decisions (SADD). Wheelock athletes compete in the NCAA Division III conference in women's basketball, field hockey, soccer, softball, and swimming and diving; men's varsity teams in basketball and tennis will begin competition in the 2007 school year.

Successful Outcomes

Wheelock students and alumni are lifelong learners. The Alumni Relations Office sponsors events to help alumni maintain their connection to WC through events such as the annual Reunion Weekend, Alumni of Color Day, hot-topic continuing education seminars, and travel opportunities. WC alumni can be found in successful careers, helping children, families, and communities around the globe. The alumni community includes teachers, social workers, published authors and child-life specialists at hospitals. Margaret Hamilton, better known as the Wicked Witch of the West in The Wizard of Oz, was also an alumna of Wheelock.

WC alumni can participate in a travel tour with current students and faculty. In 2007, they traveled to the world-renowned municipal preschool system of Reggio Emilia, Italy. The trip was part of a two-week class and allowed participants to take part in a powerful educational and cultural exchange with innovative Italian educators.

"I want to serve my community and encourage others to become leaders themselves."

- Joel '10

Fast Facts

Wheelock College is an independent coeducational institution founded in 1888.

Web site

http://www.wheelock.edu

Location

Boston, Massachusetts.

Student Profile

675 students (6% male, 94% female); states and territories: New England, New York, New Jersey, Pennsylvania; 18% minority, 3% international.

Faculty Profile

65 full-time faculty. 11:1 student/faculty ratio. Average class size is 15.

Residence Life

Moderately residential: 73% of students live on campus.

Athletics

NCAA Division III, North Atlantic Conference (NAC). 7 varsity sports (2 men's: basketball, tennis; 5 women's: field hockey, soccer, basketball, swimming & diving, softball.)

Academic Programs

American studies; arts; certificate in human services; child care specialist; child life; early childhood care & education; elementary education; human development; humanities; juvenile justice & youth advocacy; math & science; social work; special education.

Costs and Aid

2006–2007: $34,800 comprehensive ($24,235 tuition). 85% of undergraduate students receive some financial aid. Average award: $14,176.

Endowment

$44.6 million.

More Distinctions

• Council on Social Work Reaffirmation for BSW and MSW programs.

• Partnered with Stonewall Communities Lifelong Learning Institutes for GLBT community.

Franklin Pierce University

NEW HAMPSHIRE

Named after the fourteenth president of the United States, Franklin Pierce was chartered in 1962 as a nonsectarian liberal arts college. Now a university, it offers small classes, award-winning professors who bring subjects to life, and rich opportunities to gain practical experience that meets each student's personal and professional goals.

Admissions Contact:

Franklin Pierce University
40 University Drive
Rindge, New Hampshire 03461
(800) 437-0048
Ph: (603) 899-4000
Fax: 603-899-4394
Email: shonkl@franklinpierce.edu
www.franklinpierce.edu

The 4 Distinctions

Engaged Students

Students are provided with numerous opportunities to gain leadership skills, enhance learning opportunities, and build connections to specific career paths. More than three-quarters of the students participate in academically oriented internships. One Franklin Pierce student completed an internship at the White House that resulted in a full-time position as assistant to the White House press secretary.

In a unique program known as the Walk, students spend a semester walking and camping through the European countryside. They become immersed in the culture, history, and language of other countries while developing leadership skills and engaging in personal reflection. Many students claim that the Walk is a life-transforming experience.

Public-opinion polls conducted through the Marlin Fitzwater Center for Communication are covered by the national and international press and provide students with experience in polling, statistics, and political analysis.

Business students compete in Students in Free Enterprise (SIFE), a global, nonprofit organization that arranges educational outreach programs. Franklin Pierce was the Northeast regional champion in 2005 and first runner-up the following year.

Franklin Pierce debuted in the American Parliamentary Debate Association circuit with two students placing fifth in the novice division after defeating a team from Harvard University. The team also defeated opponents from Boston University, Bowdoin College, Brown University, and Wellesley College on topics as diverse as major-league baseball, the death of Socrates, and casinos in Mississippi.

Great Teaching

Great teaching starts with a great curriculum. Franklin PieGreat teaching starts with a great curriculum. Franklin Pierce's innovative thirty-eight-credit general education curriculum, the Individual and Community Integrated Curriculum, has been recognized by the Templeton Foundation for its character-building emphasis. Most core curriculum courses are interdisciplinary, and some are team taught. All emphasize the active participation of students in the learning experience.

Franklin Pierce faculty members have received national recognition for their teaching excellence. In 2002 and 2003, the Carnegie Foundation named a member of the faculty as New Hampshire Professor of the Year. In 2005, another faculty member was selected to receive the Higher Education Faculty Member Award from the New Hampshire College and University Council.

Franklin Pierce faculty have been quick to embrace advances in technology to help deliver educational experiences that are more engaging and closer to the real-life challenges students face when they leave the classroom. For example, Franklin Pierce was the first college in the country to use dynamic newsroom management software that allows one group of students to act as assigning editors and a second group to serve as reporters.

Vibrant Community

Franklin Pierce's main campus is situated on more than one thousand wooded acres on the shore of Pearly Pond, near the base of Mount Monadnock. This environment is an essential part of campus life. With Franklin Pierce's seventy-two thousand-square-foot recreational facility and the university's location in a state that has always been a top choice for outdoor enthusiasts, students have endless opportunities for fitness, recreation, and competitive and noncompetitive sports.

The Monadnock Institute of Nature, Place and Culture, founded in 1996, fosters an appreciation of place for individuals and communities in the Monadnock region and beyond through research and interdisciplinary programs in education, community development, environmental stewardship, and regional heritage.

The Grand Monadnock Climb is a notable annual event when faculty, staff, and fellow students join the first-year students on a hike up Mount Monadnock. The climb gives first-year students an opportunity to interact with their advisors in an informal setting.

The Ecological Conscience Initiative is a program designed to minimize the impact of the school on the environment. This program seeks to protect scenery and wildlife habitat, decrease energy use and waste production, improve trails, and carry out other projects related to sustainability. The initiative also provides education about environmental issues through speakers, field trips, and other projects.

Community service is a campus tradition at Franklin Pierce. First-year students take part in an annual community-service fair, where they meet with representatives from local agencies. A popular program of choice for first-year students is mentoring middle-school children through the Pierce Pals and Boynton Buddies programs.

The New England Center for Civic Life (NECCL) at Franklin Pierce was founded in 1998 on the premise that an engaged, deliberative citizenry is vital to a healthy democracy. NECCL seeks to promote the practice and understanding of effective democratic citizenship. This nonpartisan center offers students, faculty, community leaders, and others opportunities to learn methods of dialogue and deliberation effective for building the capacity of citizens to make choices together and to act in the public interest.

The university community also enjoys Tuesday Briefings at the Marlin Fitzwater Center for Communication, a series of presentations by nationally known journalists and commentators. Recent speakers have included Victoria Clarke, former Pentagon spokeswoman; Gerald Boyd, former managing editor of the *New York Times*; Jim Miklaszewski, chief Pentagon correspondent for *NBC News*; and Marilyn Thompson, assistant managing editor for investigations at the *Washington Post*.

Successful Outcomes

Building on its use of academic portfolios to document and evaluate student progress and to assess its own programs, Franklin Pierce recently established an e-portfolio—a multimedia presentation of a student's academic accomplishments and related activities. Studies show that e-portfolios engage students more actively in learning and provide opportunities for reflection, advising, and academic planning. Portfolios also demonstrate outcomes that have immediate relevance to life after graduation.

Nearly three-quarters of graduating students in the last academic year had job offers within six months of graduation; 16 percent of students completing a bachelor's program went on to graduate school.

The alumni of Franklin Pierce College have made significant impacts on their communities and professions. Graduates work as federal prosecutors, teachers, freelance artisans, event planners, accountants, financial planners, marketing managers, college professors, entrepreneurs, and in numerous other fields.

Fast Facts

Franklin Pierce University is a four-year, private, independent, liberal arts college founded in 1962.

Web site

www.franklinpierce.edu

Location

Rindge, New Hampshire—65 miles from Boston.

Student Profile

1,704 full-time undergraduates (52% male, 48% female): representing 31 states and 15 international countries; 8% minority.

Faculty Profile

154 full-time and part-time faculty. 17:1 student/faculty ratio. Average class size is 16.

Residence Life

Highly residential: 90% of students live on campus. Four years guaranteed. Options include coed (by floor) dorms, townhouses, and apartment-style living.

Athletics

NCAA Division II, Northeast 10 Conference. 17 varsity sports (8 men's: baseball, basketball, crew, golf, ice hockey, lacrosse, soccer, tennis; 9 women's: basketball, crew, cross-country, field hockey, lacrosse, soccer, softball, tennis, volleyball).

Academic Programs

Accounting-finance; American studies; anthropology/archaeology; art education; arts management; biology; chemistry; criminal justice; computer information technology; creative writing; elementary education; English; environmental science; fine arts; graphic communications; history; management; marketing; mass communication; mathematics; music; political science; prehealth; prelaw; psychology; secondary education; social work & counseling; sociology; sports & recreation management; theatre & dance; women in leadership certification.

Costs and Aid

2007-08: $35,456 comprehensive ($25,516 tuition). 90% of freshman aid applicants received scholarship/grant assistance. Average freshman award: $16,500.

Endowment

$10 million.

Canisius College

NEW YORK

Admissions Contact:

Canisius College
2001 Main Street
Buffalo, NY 14208-1098
(800) 843-1517
Fax: (716) 888-2525
Ph: (716) 888-2200
Email: admissions@canisius.edu
www.canisius.edu

Founded in 1870, Canisius College (CC) is an independent, coeducational institution of higher education conducted in the Catholic, Jesuit tradition, exemplifying the Jesuit idea of cura personalis or "care for the individual." CC respects freedom of conscience and of worship, welcoming people of all faiths.

The 4 Distinctions

Engaged Students

CC classes are taught in state-of-the-art campus facilities and in out-of-the-classroom settings, providing students with real-world experiences to enrich their educations, to broaden their horizons, and to enable them to make positive contributions to the wider community. At CC, learning beyond the classroom takes many forms, such as internships, study-abroad programs, research, and service learning.

Internships connect students with employers in professional working environments, providing opportunities for practical application of classroom learning and for networking. Study-abroad programs allow CC students to study at their choice of a European, Asian, Australian, or Mexican college or university.

Service learning combines academics with community-service work and guided reflection in the Jesuit spirit of "men and women for others." Service-learning courses are offered in every academic area of the college, and include participating in after-school tutoring programs, teaching English to local refugees, and refurbishing computers for needy Buffalo youngsters. CC students can go on service-immersion trips, such as a winter service week in New York City working with the homeless.

Research projects both on and off campus also engage students at Canisius. CC students have traveled around the world performing research in the sciences, English, history, political science, and religion, including a recent trip to India, where students explored the evolution of different religions.

CC also offers an honors program for top students, featuring small, enriched classes and close faculty interaction; an Urban Leadership Program for inner-city students; and the Canisius Earning Excellence Program (CEEP) and Hughes Interdisciplinary Research Fellowships, which offer work-study opportunities closely related to a student's career or scholarly field.

Great Teaching

Canisius is a comparatively small college of 3,200 students that offers many of the amenities of a larger university, with more than seventy distinct academic programs. CC offers undergraduate programs built upon a liberal arts core curriculum in addition to master's programs in business, education, and other professional fields. About half of the students study in the School of Arts and Sciences, a quarter in the Richard J. Wehle School of Business, and the remaining quarter in the School of Education and Human Services. The most popular majors are psychology and general education.

The CC student to faculty ratio is twelve to one, and classes are typically under thirty. Professors teach all classes; there are no teaching assistants. Canisius emphasizes excellence in teaching, marked by intellectual vigor, close student-faculty relations, and active rather than passive learning. Canisius's tagline is "where leaders are made," and its mission is to prepare "leaders—intelligent, caring, faithful individuals—able to promote excellence in their professions, their communities, and their service to humanity."

The general education program reflects the rigor and tradition of Jesuit liberal arts education. In addition to a broad selection of courses across disciplines, each student must take two introductory English courses, an introductory philosophy course, and an introduction to religious studies that covers world religions.

Canisius also offers many unique minors that allow students to expand their experiences and their career options. The zoo biology minor provides students with access to five national zoos, and students get hands-on experience creating a working zoo on campus. A neuroscience minor gives students specialized course work for preparation to continue in PhD studies or medical school. The forensic psychology minor and computer forensics minor are both offered in collaboration with the criminal justice department. Prelaw and premedicine options are also available and can be combined with any major at the college.

Canisius offers capstone projects in most majors, and is building a new interdisciplinary science center. In addition, Canisius faculty members are recognized for their scholarly and creative work, including English professor Eric L. Gansworth, winner of the 2006 PEN Oakland-Josephine Miles Literary Award for his novel Mending Skins.

Vibrant Community

The majority of CC students are drawn from western New York, and most of the rest come from central New York State, Ohio, and Pennsylvania. The school's Division I athletics attract students from across the nation.

Residential housing consists of high-quality dorms and apartments; 72 percent of freshmen and 49 percent of all students live on campus. Freshmen and sophomores are required to live on campus unless living at home with family. Student housing includes a few single-sex floors, though most housing is coed by wing. Students also have the option of living in an international hall, honors housing, and a science-themed floor, the oldest living community at CC, reflecting the popularity of science studies.

CC students are involved on campus, where the active student government and one-hundred-plus clubs and organizations emphasize leadership training and help produce well-rounded graduates. In addition to the sixteen Division I athletics, there are eleven club sports; social, honor, cultural, and science clubs; and a college television station, radio station, and newspaper. It's no surprise that 85 percent of Canisius's students are found on campus on weekends.

The campus is in a residential area of Buffalo, close to Delaware Park and the zoo. Its Montante Cultural Center, an award-winning renovation incorporating much of the original stone and glass of a former church renowned for its architecture, serves as a general-purpose auditorium and performing-arts center for CC students, alumni, and the general public. The restored center is an example of how CC gives back to its wider community.

Buffalo, known as the Queen City for its rank as the second-largest city in the state after New York City, and as the City of Good Neighbors for its diverse population, lies at the confluence of Lake Erie and the Buffalo and Niagara rivers. Canisius takes advantage of the city's rich history, tradition of innovation, and varied economy.

Successful Outcomes

Many current Canisius students are the children of alumni, a sign that graduates are satisfied with their education. CC students take advantage of the hands-on internships available in every major and enjoy employment opportunities offered in Buffalo by leading companies in the health care, technology, nonprofit, and corporate professions, leading to successful postcollege placement. An example is CC's zoo biology program, which combines intensive class work with quality hands-on experience at the Buffalo Zoo, leading to an excellent track record in placing graduates.

A survey completed by CC alumni six months after graduation revealed that 92 percent were employed or in graduate school. Graduate school preparation is strong at Canisius: students score well on national tests and have strong resumes because of their experiential activities. CC graduates have a 95 percent acceptance rate into medical schools and more than a 90 percent acceptance rate into law schools.

Fast Facts

Canisius College is a private comprehensive university founded by German Jesuits in 1870.

Web site

http://www.canisius.edu

Location

Buffalo, New York

Student Profile

3,461 undergraduates (43% male, 57% female); 35 states, 21 countries.

Faculty Profile

215 full-time faculty. 12:1 student/faculty ratio. Average class size is 17.

Residence Life

Moderately residential: 49% of all students live on campus.

Athletics

NCAA Division I, Metro Atlantic Athletic Conference. 16 varsity sports (8 men's: baseball, basketball, cross-country, golf, ice hockey, lacrosse, soccer, swimming & diving; 8 women's: basketball, cross-country, lacrosse, soccer, softball, swimming & diving, synchronized swimming, volleyball).

Academic Programs

Accounting; accounting information systems; adolescence education (grades 7–12); anthropology; art history; athletic training/sports medicine; biochemistry; bioinformatics; biology; business economics; chemistry; childhood education (grades 1–6); clinical laboratory science; communication studies; computer science (BA & BS); criminal justice; digital media arts; early childhood education (birth–grade 2); economics; English; entrepreneurship; environmental science; European studies; finance; history; information systems; international business; international relations; management; marketing; mathematics/statistics; modern languages; music; philosophy; physical education/health education; physics; political science; psychology; religious studies & theology; sociology; special education/childhood education (grades 1–6); special education/early childhood education (birth–grade 2); urban studies.

Costs and Aid

2006–2007 $34,417 comprehensive ($23,930 tuition). 98% of students receive some financial aid. Average award: $17,238.

Endowment

$64.4 million.

More Distinctions

• Canisius College's regional accreditation was reaffirmed by the Middle States Association Commission on Higher Education in 2005.

• The School of Education and Human Services is accredited by the National Council for Accreditation of Teacher Education (NCATE) and the Richard J. Wehle School of Business by the AACSB International.

Daemen College

NEW YORK

Daemen College - a private college founded in 1947 offering liberal arts majors, professional degrees, and graduate programs – enhances its core curriculum through international education programs, collaborative research with faculty, clinical and field experiences, internships for credit, and service-learning opportunities.

Admissions Contact:

Daemen College
4380 Main Street
Amherst, NY 14226
(800) 462-7652
Ph: (716) 839-3600
Email: admissions@daemen.edu
www.daemen.edu

The 4 Distinctions

Engaged Students

In an academic atmosphere that leads to open inquiry and debate, Daemen develops skills that will benefit students personally and professionally throughout their lives, and fosters a strong commitment to civic responsibility and community well being. Integrated learning experiences, honors program, academic exchanges, and undergraduate research encourage students to think critically and creatively, work collaboratively, and thrive in environments that present challenges and demand innovation.

International study is one staple of the Daemen experience. Semester programs abroad, summer programs, and accelerated January term trips offer opportunities to learn about diverse cultures, political systems and histories, and to gain a global perspective. Most global experiences can be linked to a student's professional aspirations.

Students are expected to be active participants in their educations, and all seniors complete a culminating capstone/research experience - many of which are shared during a day-long Academic Festival which celebrates a wide variety of academic accomplishments.

Daemen believes in "learning through service," and virtually all undergraduate students engage in short- or long-term local, national or international service projects. For example, students may work with environmental organizations, refugee groups, residents of nursing homes, hospitals and clinics, or as a tutor/mentor to young students in city schools. The LADS program emphasizes lifelong learning and civic engagement.

Daemen prides itself on maintaining a student-centered atmosphere and a close professional and collaborative association among all members of the college community. Assisted by a supportive faculty, students are encouraged to pursue goals beyond their initial expectations, respond to academic challenges, and develop habits of mind that enrich their lives and their community.

Great Teaching

In an academically challenging atmosphere characterized by small classes taught by talented and committed professors,

Daemen students enjoy a personalized educational experience where they can develop a strong repertoire of knowledge and skills.

The core curriculum enables students to master seven essential skills and competencies that complement their majors: critical thinking and creative problem-solving, literacy in information and multi-media technology, communication skills, affective judgment, moral and ethical discernment, contextual competency and civic responsibility.

Some required courses are offered in a Learning Community format where small groups of students with different backgrounds, majors and extra-curricular interests learn how to apply critical thinking and problem-solving to study a common topic, issue, or subject.

Students with demonstrated excellence in learning can benefit from honors courses which examine complex issues from multiple perspectives, use primary sources rather than textbooks and present special opportunities for research and a variety of experience-based learning opportunities. Honors students oversee their own student organization and direct such campus events as film and speaker series, field trips and community service projects.

Daemen's student-faculty Interdisciplinary Research Think Tank offers students the opportunity to work with faculty members on significant research projects. Students may receive research scholarships and acknowledgement of their work through publications, presentations, or other forms of recognition.

A wide range of support services are in place to meet students' diverse needs. Each student has a full-time faculty professional advisor or mentor as well as access to academic coaches, supplemental instruction, peer led team learning, English as a second language, or disability services. Workshops help students build time management and study skills and offer assistance in the registration process, GPA improvement and other areas.

Vibrant Community

Located in Amherst, New York (rated by Money magazine as one of the safest cities in the United States), Daemen is near the city of Buffalo - and its exceptional theatre, music, art, restaurants, and major league sports. Daemen is also just 20 minutes from scenic Niagara Falls, and 1.5 hrs. from Toronto, ON.

Daemen offers excellent facilities and upscale residential living - for first-year students in the five-story suite style Canavan Hall and for upper division status students in Campus Village, a complex of seven two-story apartment style buildings.

Trained Residence Life staff members are available to assist students with their social, academic, and personal needs. Resident students work with staff to plan and conduct activities which enhance cooperation and develop a sense of community in the residence halls.

The college believes that there's more to being a student than studying and encourages students to use their Daemen experience to cultivate hidden talents, take new risks, and challenge themselves to grow. More than 50 organizations connect students who share similar passions and interests. Themed dinners, movie nights, musical theater, music performances, internationally famous speakers, and much more combine to create a dynamic campus atmosphere.

A member of the American Mideast Conference of the National Alliance of Intercollegiate Athletics, Daemen offers 8 varsity sports including men's basketball, cross country, soccer and golf, and women's basketball, cross country, volleyball and soccer. Student athletes can also participate in such club sports as cheerleading, indoor soccer, volleyball, lacrosse, rugby, and ice hockey. More casual athletes take part in intramural sports and keep fit in the exercise and weight rooms.

Successful Outcomes

Daemen graduates are poised for professional success. Prepared with sound communication and critical thinking skills and the ability to effectively access, evaluate, and apply relevant information using a variety of information resources, most move into the careers of their choice or graduate study within a year of graduation. They are also well-equipped for the eventuality of career changes.

Daemen's Office of Career Development and Cooperative Education provides a wide variety of career and professional services. For example, working with such organizations as the Washington Internship Institute and employers in business, sports, the arts, industry, government, non-profits, health, education, and cultural entities, the school connects students and graduates with internship and co-op positions which offer real world experience through local, national or international opportunities.

Graduates of Daemen College are also interesting people whose education has provided them with a large knowledge base and taught them how to make reasoned ethical choices and consider connections between values and behavior. With a lifelong hunger for learning, they are informed citizens, prepared to play productive roles in local and global communities both as effective participants and leaders.

Fast Facts

Daemen College, founded in 1947, is a private residential liberal arts institution for undergraduate and graduate study.

Location

Amherst, New York – just minutes from Buffalo and near Niagara Falls.

Student Profile

1705 undergraduate students (27% male, 74% female); 14% minority, 1% international; 838 graduate students.

Faculty Profile

102 full-time faculty members. 15:1 student/faculty ratio. Average class size is 20.

Residence Life

Moderately residential: 40% of students live on campus.

Athletics

NAIA, American Mideast Conference. 8 varsity sports (4 men's: basketball, cross country, soccer, golf; 4 women's: basketball, cross country, volleyball, soccer), Club sports: cheerleading, indoor soccer, volleyball, lacrosse, rugby, ice hockey. More casual athletes take part in intramural sports and keep fit in the exercise and weight rooms.

Academic Programs

Undergraduate degrees and programs in Arts & Sciences (Art, English, Foreign Language, Graphic Design, History & Government, Mathematics, Natural Sciences, Political Science, Psychology); Health & Human Services (Accounting, Business Administration, Education, Health Care Studies, Nursing, Physical Therapy, Physician Assistant, Social Work); Pre-professional Programs; Various Interdisciplinary Programs.

Graduate programs in Accounting; Education; Executive Leadership and Change; Global Business; Nursing; Physical Therapy; Physician Assistant.

Activity/Club/Organization Types

Academic honors, film/photography/visual arts, Greek life (national), health and fitness, hobbies, media (newspaper, radio, yearbook, etc.), minority/ethnic, outdoors/environmental, performance (theater/dance/mime), professional interest/academic subject, politics, religious/spiritual, service, support groups, student events/campus programming, student government, women's/gender studies.

Costs and Aid

2007-2008: Undergraduate full-time $18,750 comprehensive ($18,300 tuition plus $450 fees). Room and board (example Canavan Hall, 19-meal plan) $8610. 96% of students receive some financial aid. Average Award: $14,000.

Giving and Endowment Information

Alumni giving rate 12%. Endowment $5.2 million.

More Distinctions

• Awarded the Presidential Points of Light National Service Award for students' volunteer work and service-learning activities.

• Won seven American Mideast Conference North titles in the past four years.

• Internationally recognized Center for Special Education, Center for Wound Research and Education and Center for Sustainable Communities.

Fordham University

NEW YORK

Fordham University offers a distinctive, values-centered educational experience rooted in the Jesuit tradition of intellectual rigor and personal attention. Since 1841, Fordham's partner in this great enterprise has been New York City. Students enjoy the unparalleled educational, cultural, and recreational advantages of one of the world's most diverse and dynamic cities.

Admissions Contact:

Fordham University
441 East Fordham Rd.
Bronx, NY 10458
(800) FORDHAM
Email: enroll@fordham.edu
www.fordham.edu

The 4 Distinctions

Engaged Students

With its two distinctive residential campuses—green and gothic Rose Hill, on eighty-five acres adjacent to the New York Botanical Garden and the Bronx Zoo; and cosmopolitan Lincoln Center, in the heart of Manhattan, across from the Lincoln Center for the Performing Arts—Fordham offers students virtually unlimited possibilities for learning and personal growth. Students often say, "New York is my campus. Fordham is my school."

Fordham draws students from across the country and around the world, who want to live and learn in the global capital of commerce and culture. The University offers one of the most extensive internship programs in the country. Students choose from more than 2,600 internship options in business, communications, education, government, health care, biomedical research, law, the arts, and other fields. The Office of Career Services also offers workshops, career days, one-on-one career counseling, and on-campus interviews with major corporations. Students compete for and earn prestigious fellowships and scholarships—including Fulbright, Truman, and Mellon scholarships, and other competitive awards. And each year, more than 1,300 students engage in community service, both locally and in distant corners of the world, through the University's award-winning global outreach program.

Great Teaching

Fordham invites students to enjoy a wealth of resources and experiences, and dedicated professors who challenge students to excel within a supportive community.

With a proud history of approaching education in a distinctly Jesuit way, Fordham emphasizes *cura personalis*, a commitment to nurturing the whole person—mind, body, and spirit—and challenging students to surpass their perceived limitations. This kind of education unites both heart and mind, and at Fordham, this occurs within and beyond the classroom.

Fordham's world-class faculty are committed to teaching and research. In small classes (the average class size is twenty-two, and the University boasts a twelve to one student to faculty ratio), these scholars and mentors challenge students to develop to their full potential—and they give each student the individual attention he or she needs to excel.

Students choose from more than sixty-five majors and academic programs in the liberal and performing arts, sciences, and business. Every student also completes a rich core curriculum that spans literature, history, science, religion, philosophy, the social sciences, and the arts, and is designed to nurture curiosity and inspire a lifelong love of learning. Special academic offerings include honors programs; study abroad; dual-degree programs with Fordham's graduate schools; and preprofessional programs in law, medicine, and other health professions. Fordham's G.L.O.B.E. (international business) program combines liberal arts and business courses, and prepares students for multinational careers. Undergraduate students often collaborate with faculty on original research, and they also work with faculty and staff to prepare to compete for Rhodes and Fulbright scholarships and other prestigious fellowships and scholarships.

Vibrant Community

New York City provides unparalleled internship and career advantages, but it also offers students a never-ending list of things to see and do—from Broadway theater, museums, and concerts to major-league sports or a bike ride through Central Park.

Fordham's two residential campuses are easily accessible by public and private transportation. The University's Ram Van service also makes it easy for students to enjoy the academic and social life of the two campuses.

Strong orientation programs, special freshman seminars, and active faculty advising ensure a smooth transition to college life. Integrated Learning Communities in the residence halls on the Rose Hill campus give students the chance to collaborate with other students, staff, and faculty to design educational and service activities and events throughout the year. Students majoring in prehealth professions are mentored by resident upper-level students in the new Science Integrated Learning Community. The Lincoln Center campus features McMahon Hall, a twenty-story complex that provides apartment-style living and great views of Manhattan. Fordham's state-of-the-art facilities also include one of the most technologically advanced libraries in the country.

More than 130 student organizations offer a remarkable range of programming that capitalizes on the cultural resources of New York City. An extensive athletics program includes twenty-three varsity sports and a range of club and intramural sports. Each year, the community-service program gives hundreds of students an opportunity to work together on volunteer projects at dozens of sites in New York City, including soup kitchens, nursing homes, transitional shelters, hospitals, and community parks.

Successful Outcomes

A Fordham education blends a challenging curriculum with the resources, culture, and energy of New York City—a unique combination by any measure. Fordham students serve as interns at the United Nations and are mentored by CEOs of Fortune 500 companies. They win mtvU Student Filmmaker awards and capture prestigious Marshall and Fulbright scholarships. The opportunities Fordham provides students through close contact with influential professors and the school's urban setting translate into jobs and internships at graduation. More than 2,600 organizations in the New York metropolitan area offer students internships that provide hands-on experience and valuable networking opportunities in fields such as business, communications, medicine, law, and education. Students also earn admission to top graduate programs and win prestigious fellowships and scholarships for further study.

> "At Fordham, you will experience a Jesuit approach to education that begins with a deep respect for you as an individual and your potential, a principle called *cura personalis*. Because they respect you, our faculty will challenge you to strive for ever greater personal excellence in all aspects of life — intellectual, emotional, moral and physical."

Fast Facts

Fordham University is a four-year, private university affiliated with the Jesuit order of the Roman Catholic Church and founded in 1841.

Web site

http://www.fordham.edu/

Location

New York, New York.

Student Profile

8,477 undergraduate students (40% male, 60% female); 53 states and territories, 46 countries; 24.6% minority.

Faculty Profile

704 full-time faculty. 94% hold a terminal degree in their field. 12:1 student/faculty ratio. Average class size is 22.

Residence Life

Moderately residential: 60% of students live on campus. Undergraduate campuses at Rose Hill in the Bronx and Lincoln Center in Manhattan.

Athletics

NCAA Division I-A, Atlantic 10 Conference. 23 varsity sports (12 men's: baseball, basketball, cross-country, football [NCAA Division I-AA, Patriot League], golf, indoor track, outdoor track, soccer, squash, swimming & diving, tennis, water polo; 11 women's: basketball, cheerleading, crew, cross-country, indoor track, outdoor track, soccer, softball, swimming & diving, tennis, volleyball), 13 club sports, and 21 intramurals.

Academic Programs

Accounting information systems; African & African American studies; American Catholic studies; American studies; anthropology; applied accounting & finance; art history; biological sciences; business administration; business economics; chemistry; classical languages & civilization; communication & media management; communication & media studies; computer & information science; cooperative program in engineering (3-2); dance (Ailey/Fordham BFA Program); e-business; economics; engineering physics; English; entrepreneurship; finance; general science; history; human resource management; information systems; international business (G.L.O.B.E.); international/intercultural studies; international political economy; Latin American & Latino studies; literary studies; management of information & communications systems; management systems; marketing; mathematics; mathematics/economics; medieval studies; Middle East studies; modern languages & literatures; music; natural sciences; organizational leadership; peace & justice studies; philosophy; physics; political science; prearchitecture program; prelaw program; premedical & prehealth professions program; psychology; public accounting; religious studies; social science; social work (BASW); sociology; teacher certification program; theatre; theology; urban studies; visual arts; women's studies.

Costs and Aid

2007–2008: $44,100 comprehensive ($31,800 tuition, 12,300 room & board). 80% of students receive some financial aid. Average award: $15,386

Hamilton College

NEW YORK

Chartered as a college in 1812, Hamilton is an independent, residential, coeducational liberal arts college in Clinton, New York. Emphasizing individualized instruction and independent research, Hamilton's graduates make their voices heard through effective writing and persuasive speaking.

Admissions Contact:

Hamilton College
198 College Hill Road
Clinton, NY 13323
(800) 843-2655
Ph: (315) 859-4421
Email: admission@hamilton.edu
www.hamilton.edu

The 4 Distinctions

Engaged Students

About 40 percent of Hamilton students participate in international study, and Hamilton's own study-abroad programs are especially rigorous, with students pledging that they will speak only the native language during the entire time they are in their host country. These programs, which include a mix of Hamilton students and students from other colleges, have long and distinguished histories; the program in Beijing has been operating for ten years, the program in Madrid for thirty-four years, and the program to Paris for fifty years. Students also have access to study-abroad programs offered by other colleges and universities.

Hamilton also offers domestic study options. The nearly 40-year-old Washington, DC, program combines an academic seminar with internships as full-time staff members in a Congressional office and then in either an executive branch or non-governmental organization. Students can also spend the semester studying in New York City, taking an integrated course of study from a resident Hamilton professor that includes a seminar, a topics and issues course based on the expertise of the professor, an independent research project, and an internship in a globally focused firm or organization.

The Arthur Levitt Public Affairs Center connects Hamilton students with the world of public policy through its Community Outreach Office, service-learning projects, and faculty-student research.

Some classes have service components, including English and philosophy classes that participate in English as a Second Language programs in nearby Utica, New York. The student-run Hamilton Action Volunteer Outreach Coalition (HAVOC) is Hamilton's largest student organization and sponsors a variety of volunteer groups, including Big Brothers/Big Sisters, Habitat for Humanity, Food Salvage, Hope House, and English to Speakers of Other Languages (ESOL). Between three hundred and four hundred Hamilton students volunteer for one group or another every week.

Each summer, more than one hundred students in all academic disciplines remain on campus to conduct research, most of them receiving stipends for their research work. Nearly every year, Eugene Domack, professor of geosciences, travels with several Hamilton students to Antarctica for five weeks to conduct National Science Foundation-funded research.

Hamilton's graduates are among the most passionate and loyal of any U.S. college. One way the college's 17,000 alumni give back to their alma mater is by providing informational interviews, job-shadowing experiences and internships to current students. A new alumni-sponsored fund even makes summer stipends available to students who need the money but want to pursue unpaid internships with nonprofit organizations.

Great Teaching

Hamilton requires no core curriculum, and students tend to sample from many different academic disciplines. Hamilton's strong emphasis on writing differentiates it from most other colleges. Using outside reviewers, the college tracks the quality of students' writing over the course of their four years at Hamilton. The finest student writers are nominated to be peer tutors in the Writing Center, where 2,500 individual writing conferences are held each year.

During the past decade, two Hamilton professors were recognized as New York State Professors of the Year and one was named the nation's best liberal arts college professor. Interaction among students and professors is one of the hallmarks of the Hamilton experience. It is common for students to visit faculty members' homes, and faculty members even compete in intramural sports. The high level of faculty-student research also contributes to students' excellent relationships with their professors.

Vibrant Community

Hamilton has a four-year residency requirement. Some seniors apply to live off campus, but 98 percent of students live in college housing. Options include former fraternity houses that have been extensively renovated, townhouses, suites, apartment-style housing, and traditional dormitories. All housing is smoke-free, several residences are substance-free and nearly all college housing is coed. The college has made an effort to reduce the size of residences to encourage interaction and bonding among students.

The nearby Adirondack Mountains provide an excellent resource for students who love outdoor activities. Almost half of all first-year students participate in the Adirondack Adventure during preorientation, with activities including hiking, biking, climbing, and canoeing. Hamilton has just created an outdoor leadership center, and the college's active outing club, which has recently moved into a newly remodeled house, sponsors an annual challenge in the fall—not yet accomplished—of simultaneously placing a Hamilton student or other community member on each of the forty-six highest peaks in the Adirondacks.

Hamilton boasts a number of annual all-campus events, including the Citrus Bowl at the first men's ice hockey game of the season; the award-winning Acoustic Coffeehouse series; FebFest, a weeklong wintertime festival; ALHam Weekend, featuring the May Day Music Festival; and the HamTrek sprint triathlon.

Public speakers at Hamilton have included Colin Powell, Elie Wiesel, F. W. de Klerk, Margaret Thatcher, Bill Cosby, Jimmy Carter, Rudy Giuliani, Desmond Tutu, Bill Clinton, and Tom Brokaw.

Successful Outcomes

After graduation, most Hamilton alumni gravitate to Washington, DC, New York City, Boston, or San Francisco. About 21 percent of alumni end up in careers in finance, 16 percent in education, 10 percent in management, 9 percent in law, and 9 percent in media. About 25 percent of graduating seniors go straight from Hamilton to graduate school, and nearly all of the remainder are employed in their chosen areas within a few months of graduation. The Career Center helps students with resume writing, videotaped practice interviews, and introductions to recruiters who visit campus.

Alumni include Tom Vilsack, the first Democratic governor in Iowa in more than thirty years, and Mike Castle, former Republican governor of Delaware, who now represents his state in the U.S. House of Representatives.

"Hamilton requires no core curriculum, and students tend to sample from many different academic disciplines. Hamilton's strong emphasis on writing differentiates it from most other colleges."

Fast Facts

Hamilton College is a four-year, liberal arts college.

Web site

http:// www.hamilton.edu

Location

Clinton, New York.

Student Profile

1,798 undergraduates (50% male, 50% female); 43 states, 40 foreign countries; 5% international.

Faculty Profile

183 full-time faculty. 10:1 student/faculty ratio. Average class size: 16.

Residence Life

Highly Residential; 98 % of students live on campus.

Athletics

NCAA Div III, New England Small College Athletic Conference, the Liberty League, the Eastern College Athletic Conference and the New York State Women's Collegiate Athletic Association. 28 varsity sports (14 men's: basketball, ice hockey, squash, swimming, indoor track & field, baseball, crew, football, lacrosse, soccer, cross-country, golf, tennis, outdoor track & field; 14 women's: basketball, ice hockey, volleyball, squash, swimming, indoor track & field, crew, field hockey, lacrosse, soccer, softball, cross-country, tennis, outdoor track & field).

Academic Programs

Africana studies; American studies; anthropology (cultural anthropology & archaeology); art; art history; Asian studies; biochemistry/molecular biology; biology; chemical physics; chemistry; Chinese; classics (classical languages & classical studies); communication; comparative literature; computer science; dance; economics; English (literature & creative writing); environmental studies; foreign languages; French; geoarchaeology; geosciences; German; government; Hispanic studies; history; mathematics; music; neuroscience; philosophy; physics; psychology; public policy; religious studies; Russian studies; sociology; theatre; women's studies; world politics.

Costs and Aid

2007–08: $46,210 comprehensive ($36,500 tuition). More than half of all students receive some financial aid. Average award: $29,000.

Endowment

Over $700 million.

More Distinctions

• Hamilton is included in Princeton Review's Best 366 Colleges.

• Hamilton is included in Barron's Guide to the Most Competitive Colleges.

Hartwick College

NEW YORK

Hartwick College (HC) is a private, liberal arts college in the foothills of the Catskill Mountains. This nondenominational college is focused on providing an education that connects the classroom to the world. Students are encouraged to do research, internships, participate in the January term, and study abroad.

Admissions Contact:

Hartwick College
One Hartwick Drive
Oneonta, New York 13820
(888) HARTWICK
Ph: (607) 431-4150
Fax: (607) 431-4102
Email: admissions@hartwick.edu
www.hartwick.edu

The 4 Distinctions

Engaged Students

During their time at HC, 80 percent of students study off campus. In addition to faculty-led January-term programs, HC provides opportunities for semester- and yearlong study-abroad programs through an extensive network of other colleges and institutions.

Hartwick's January term offers students many opportunities for experiential learning. Three hundred students typically take part in off-campus programs during the January term. These programs provide study-abroad trips to over a dozen countries and several states, including Hawaii. Programs are faculty-led, and many are open to first-year students. Under this program, a Hartwick group has been studying a hill tribe in Thailand for more than ten years. A music professor annually leads a trip to Prague, with side trips to other cities in Europe. Other courses have explored Italian art and culture and the biogeography of the Bahamas. HC also offers funding for students to complete international internships or independent projects during the summer and January term.

HC students have recently interned with IBM, MTV, and Fidelity Investments; have partnered with such community organizations as the Da'Vida Fair Trade Center and the American Red Cross; and have conducted research on acid rain, memory, parenthood and politics, and local history. Nursing students receive multicultural training through fieldwork in Jamaica, and political science students have interviewed community members as part of HC's Thinking Citizen project, to assess citizens' political attitudes. Additionally, over spring break, many students participate in Habitat for Humanity projects in locations such as North and South Carolina, Kentucky, and West Virginia.

The MetroLink program at HC gives students a chance to go to Washington, DC; New York City; Philadelphia; or Boston for a week to shadow alumni on the job. The program is open to students of all career paths and helps students determine what they would like to do after graduation.

All students at Hartwick complete a senior research project or thesis. The college offers the Freedman Prize to students with particularly ambitious projects that require funding—recent examples have included paying a chemistry student's lab fees and helping to underwrite the recording of a music student's album.

Hartwick has a tradition of technological innovation in higher education. All students receive notebook computer systems for their personal use.

Great Teaching

HC students note the close relationships they establish with faculty and staff as a defining aspect of their college experience. Studies prove the trend: in the 2005 National Survey of Student Engagement, seniors rated Hartwick 15.8 percentage points above the national average for student-faculty interaction. With small average class sizes of eighteen and plenty of opportunities for student-faculty interaction, it's no surprise that students have such positive experiences.

Professors and students collaborate on groundbreaking research projects. Students from all majors may spend the summer conducting research with their professors. Recent projects focused on peer mediation programs in schools, leadership in top management firms, an analysis of brain structures and behavioral function, the archaeology of the Late Bronze Age in Russia's Samara Valley, community courts and restorative justice in South Africa, child composers, and sustainable nutrition in Thailand.

Service learning is an integral part of the student experience at Hartwick. Numerous courses are linked with community-based learning opportunities, combining classroom instruction and service in the community. For example, community-action teams in a sociology course titled Building Community—Children's Lives worked with the Violence Intervention Program, Catskill Rural AIDS Services, Head Start, and Saturday's Bread Soup Kitchen. Business students have worked with Opportunities for Otsego staff to update and create publications to improve public awareness of the agency's programs. Service learning does not stop at the U.S. border. January-term programs to Jamaica, Thailand, and Ireland have involved students in community issues in those areas, as well.

Hartwick academics are focused around an annual academic theme. Recent themes have included climate change, water works, food in our lives, health and the human experience, globalization, and sustainable living.

Hartwick offers an education program leading to teacher certification. In addition to student teaching, the program requires a service-learning component as well as some nonteaching work in local schools.

Vibrant Community

At HC, 75 percent of the student body are involved in campus clubs and organizations. From intramural soccer to basketball to student government, from ballroom dancing to Greek life, there are more than sixty-five activities to choose from.

Sports enthusiasts will love Hartwick. Division I men's soccer and women's water polo are traditions, and other opportunities to be active include competitive Division III athletic competition, club sports like cycling and skiing, and intramurals, including flag football and dodgeball. Oneonta is home to the National Soccer Hall of Fame and a Detroit Tigers A Minor League team, and nearby Cooperstown houses the National Baseball Hall of Fame.

The area around Hartwick—at the gateway to both the Catskill and Adirondack mountains—offers countless opportunities for hiking, boating, skiing, and other outdoor activities. The campus is located on 425 acres with a stunning view of the Susquehanna River Valley.

Students also have the option to live at the college's two thousand-acre Pine Lake Environmental Campus, eight miles from the main campus. Students who elect to live at Pine Lake focus on sustainable living, residing in cabins and eating food that they grow. These students take vans to travel to campus for class. Pine Lake is also the site of Hartwick's Challenge Education Program: over seven hundred students visit the campus annually to complete the ropes course.

Successful Outcomes

Among Hartwick's alumni are graduate students at institutions such as Yale University, the London School of Economics, and the University of Michigan; others alumni are professionals, working with organizations like the Boston Symphony Orchestra, Canon, Deutsche Bank, and the U.S. House of Representatives. Scott Adams, creator of the comic strip Dilbert, is a notable alumnus.

More than 95 percent of Hartwick students are employed or in graduate school within six months of graduation. The office of career services is dedicated to providing students with comprehensive career development and experiential learning opportunities. Career services staff help students find internships, get connected with MetroLink, and advise students on resumes. Hartwick is also one of the twenty-eight colleges in the Liberal Arts Career Network, which expands the network that students have to find jobs.

Fast Facts

Hartwick College is a private, nondenominational liberal arts college founded in 1797.

Web site

http://www.hartwick.edu

Location

Oneonta, NY—1 hour from Albany, NY; 3 hours from New York City.

Student Profile

1480 undergraduate students (44% male, 56% female); 38 states and territories, 19 countries; 11% minority, 3% international.

Faculty Profile

112 full-time faculty. 97% hold a terminal degree in their field. 12:1 student/faculty ratio. Average class size is 18.

Residence Life

Highly residential: 80% of students live on campus (including Pine Lake Environmental Campus). Students are required to live on campus through junior year.

Athletics

NCAA Division I and III; Empire 8 Conference, Atlantic Soccer Conference, Collegiate Water Polo Association, Intercollegiate Horse Show Association. 17 varsity sports (7 men's: basketball, cross-country, football, lacrosse, soccer [Division I], swimming & diving, tennis; 10 women's: basketball, cross-country, equestrian, field hockey, lacrosse, soccer, swimming & diving, tennis, volleyball, water polo [Division I]), 5 club sports, and 6 intramurals.

Academic Programs

Accounting; anthropology; art; art history; biochemistry; biology; business administration; chemistry; computer science; economics; education (certification), English; environmental chemistry; French; geology; German; history; individual student program (self-designed major); information science; mathematics; medical technology; music; music education; nursing; philosophy; physics; political science; psychology; religious studies; sociology; Spanish, theatre arts.

Costs and Aid

2007-2008: $39,350 comprehensive ($30,125 tuition). 95% of students receive some financial aid. Average award: $21,309.

Endowment

$59.4 million.

More Distinctions

• Ranked #8 on list of colleges with "highest percentage of students who study abroad" by U.S. News and World Report's "America's Best Colleges" (2007)

• Selected among "Best in the Northeast" by The Princeton Review (2007)

• Ranked #22 on list of 100 "hidden gems" by The Washington Post (2003)

Hobart and William Smith Colleges

NEW YORK

Hobart and William Smith Colleges (HWS) offers a flexible interdisciplinary curriculum. Students then layer and interweave guided exploration, study programs around the world, creative partnerships with faculty, and opportunities to serve and lead. The result is a distinctive, personalized education that prepares students to make an impact as citizens and professionals.

Admissions Contact:

Hobart and William Smith Colleges
629 S. Main St.
Geneva, NY 14456
(800) 852-2256
Ph: (315) 781-3622
Email: admissions@hws.edu
www.hws.edu

The 4 Distinctions

Engaged Students

Adhering to the liberal arts tradition, HWS provides a broad educational experience. This is realized through the requirement that students declare both a major and a minor, or two majors—one in a disciplinary and one in an interdisciplinary area of study.

Hobart and William Smith students' passions lead them in many directions. It is not uncommon for students to participate in a mosaic of activities, research topics, and majors. All students are free to explore and discover—in Geneva, the U.S., or abroad.

The world is increasingly complex, and HWS encourages students to take their places as responsible citizens within it. These experiences invariably change how students view themselves and others, as well as help them expand their views of who and what they can become. HWS offers one of the nation's broadest ranges of off-campus programs, with study abroad offered in twenty-seven countries. For example, students can choose to study in Australia, Ecuador, England, France, Germany, Hungary, India, Ireland, Italy, Japan, New Zealand, Russia, Senegal, South Africa, and Vietnam.

There's no substitute for experience, which is why Hobart and William Smith offers an array of internship opportunities. Local, national, and international programs give students a chance to put their knowledge to work. Recently, students have interned in Washington, DC; Boston; Chicago; New York; Geneva, New York; Geneva, Switzerland; London; and Hanoi with companies such as Yahoo! Inc., Ogilvy Public Relations, Comedy Central, Kenneth Cole Productions, Oppenheimer & Co., Sony Pictures, Yale Medical School's Hematology Department, and with Democratic New York Senator Hillary Clinton.

Central to the mission of Hobart and William Smith is a fundamental belief in service and service learning as critical components of a twenty-first-century liberal arts education. Students embrace service as an essential aspect of global citizenship and community enrichment. In a typical academic year, HWS students provide an estimated thirty-two thousand hours of volunteer community service, while more than 250 students take part in service-learning classes. Over the course of any given year, 75 percent of the HWS student body participates in community-service projects, performing service work for more than forty area organizations.

Great Teaching

Through the encouragement of HWS faculty, students know that nothing is intellectually off-limits. Students move easily across courses, programs, and departments to build a personally empowering education. Students can design their own majors or minors, allowing them to fully explore the areas and intersections that interest them. A student whose interests involve several disciplines may create an individual major by working with a faculty sponsor. The student plans the program, even down to the specific courses to be taken. Some recent individual majors include technology and society, social justice and economics, and performance theory and practice. In addition to creating their own majors, more than 60 percent of HWS students elect to invest their time and energy in an independent research project.

Students develop rewarding partnerships with faculty that enhance the traditional learning experience. Faculty are highly involved in students' education well beyond the classroom, providing exceptional mentoring and opportunities for students to partner with them in research. HWS has celebrated the great accomplishments of students who have recently been named a Rhodes Scholar, a Gates Cambridge Scholar, and Fulbright Scholars, as well as the many students who have been accepted at prestigious graduate schools.

HWS faculty members are accomplished scholars and leaders. The current HWS faculty includes nineteen Fulbright Scholars. HWS also boasts of an associate professor of English who has developed scripts for Hollywood films, including the Oscar-nominated "Election." The leading expert on the history of the New York City subway system teaches at Hobart and William Smith, and an associate professor of political science examines how the widespread belief in UFOs and aliens reflects disenchantment with political structure and rhetoric in this country.

Vibrant Community

Each year, dozens of speakers visit Hobart and William Smith to bring the world to Geneva. Most speakers visit classes and chat with students; all engage the community in conversation that is both interesting and thought provoking. Through the President's Forum Series, the college community is introduced to important politicians, intellectuals, and social activists. The Fisher Center Series explores issues of gender and sexuality in the arts, humanities, and social and natural sciences, in an effort to foster mutual understanding and social justice.

HWS is strongly committed to fostering a community in which the wide spectrum of individual differences is valued, celebrated, and integrated throughout its staff, students, faculty, and curriculum. The colleges cultivate an educational model that addresses the needs of a pluralistic and democratic society. The intercultural affairs office fosters interaction among people of many cultures and provides the opportunity for all students to celebrate their cultural heritage. The Center for Global Education provides enriching off-campus opportunities nationally and internationally for HWS students, while promoting an inclusive campus community by providing avenues for students to share what they've learned of other cultures through their experiences abroad.

With more than seventy organizations, students are free to try everything. HWS students can join the debate team, work for change through the myriad social-action groups, put out a weekly newspaper, broadcast with NPR-affiliate WEOS-FM, sing with an a cappella group, or develop their thespian talents with the Phoenix Players. Many HWS students enjoy intramural and club sports as an easy way to meet people and get involved.

Successful Outcomes

Pathways, a four-year, individualized career-development program, enables students to explore their interests and talents, develop career goals, gain experience, and launch a career or find the right graduate or professional program.

The Salisbury Center for Career Services offers one-on-one meetings with students and houses a career library, which contains books, directories, and periodicals focusing on career exploration; listings of part-time and full-time jobs; graduate-school information; company information; and information on job-search methods.

With more than forty-five different organizations recruiting on campus last year, it's no surprise that 70 percent of HWS's graduating class had full-time job offers and acceptances to graduate schools within six months of graduation. Recruiting organizations included companies, corporations, government agencies, and nonprofit organizations.

This year's graduating class has big plans. Among the graduates are a Fulbright Scholar going to Indonesia and students going to teach in Japan, as well as those off to become new employees of Yahoo! Inc. and Bank of America. They follow in the path of many successful alumni.

Fast Facts

Hobart and William Smith Colleges is a four-year, private liberal arts institution on the shores of Seneca Lake, one of New York's Finger Lakes. Hobart College for men was founded in 1822, and William Smith College for women was founded in 1908. Today, campus life is coeducational including classes, activities, and many residence halls. The Colleges still maintain separate athletics programs, deans offices and student governments.

Web site

http://www.hws.edu

Location

Geneva, New York—less than an hour to Ithaca, Syracuse, and Rochester.

Student Profile

1,970 students (47% male, 53% female); 41 states and territories; 13% minority, 2% international.

Faculty Profile

178 full-time faculty. 11:1 student/faculty ratio. Average class size 17.

Residence Life

Highly residential: approximately 87% of students live on campus.

Athletics

NCAA Division III, Liberty League. 22 varsity sports (11 Hobart: basketball, crew, cross-country, football, golf, ice hockey, lacrosse (Division I, ECAC), sailing, soccer, squash, tennis); 11 William Smith: basketball, crew, cross-country, field hockey, golf, lacrosse, sailing, soccer, squash, swimming & diving, tennis), 11 club sports and 11 intramurals.

Academic Programs

African/Africana Studies; American studies; anthropology; anthropology & sociology; architectural studies; art history; art (studio); arts & education; Asian languages & cultures; biology; chemistry; classics; comparative literature; computer science; critical social studies; dance; economics; English; environmental studies; European studies; French; geoscience; Greek; history; international relations; Latin; Latin American studies; lesbian, gay & bisexual studies; mathematics; media & society; modern languages; music; philosophy; physics; political science; psychology; public policy; religious studies; Russian area studies; sociology; Spanish; urban studies; women's studies; writing & rhetoric.

Special Programs:

4+3 architecture; 4 +1 business administration; education: childhood, childhood disabilities, adolescence, and MAT; 3+2 engineering; prelaw; premedicine; independent study; honors.

Costs and Aid

2006-2007: $43,516 comprehensive ($33,730 tuition). 77% of first-year students receive some financial aid. Average award: $30,098.

Endowment

$155,521,689.

Houghton College

NEW YORK

Houghton College is a four-year, Christian, liberal arts college, offering bachelor's degrees in forty-eight majors to its 1,200 students. Located in the rural Genesee Valley of southwestern New York State, Houghton has a secondary campus in a suburb of Buffalo and branches in Adirondack Park, Australia, Tanzania, and London.

Admissions Contact:

Houghton College
1 Willard Ave
PO Box 128
Houghton, NY 14744-0128
Ph: 1-800-777-2556
Fax: (585) 567-9522
Email: admission@houghton.edu
www.houghton.edu

The 4 Distinctions

Engaged Students

Forty-eight percent of Houghton students choose to enrich their education by participating in study-abroad or domestic off-campus programs. Houghton offers six of its own programs, and opportunities are available through programs run by numerous other colleges and organizations. Houghton's campus in Adirondack Park enables students to gain field experience in environmental science and apply classroom learning to the real world. Houghton Down Under provides students with a cross-cultural exploration of faith and life in Australia. Houghton in Tanzania plunges students into the language and history of East Africa while facilitating interaction with local people groups and missionaries. Students can also study abroad in the Houghton in London program or with Houghton Go ED in Uganda.

The first-year honors program combines an in-depth study of Western culture and civilization with either a spring semester in London or a May-term trip to Eastern Europe. Faculty members lead frequent trips during May-term and the summer to destinations such as Senegal, Honduras, Germany and Zambia. Houghton's intercollegiate sports teams integrate athletics with cross-cultural engagement, ministering in places like the Czech Republic, Ethiopia, Guatemala and the Bahamas.

Houghton students have conducted internships with such organizations as the Buffalo Bills and Merrill Lynch, and the new Chamberlain Scholars Program pairs students with faculty members for joint research projects.

Each spring, Houghton students participate in a campus-wide community-service day, assisting non-profit organizations at sites throughout western New York. In addition, Houghton students regularly travel to Buffalo to tutor refugees in English, assist at the King Center Charter School, and help run the Royal Family Kids' Camp for disadvantaged children and youth.

Great Teaching

Beginning with the first-year transition course, Houghton's academic program seeks to fulfill its mission by passing on an understanding of the Christian intellectual tradition. As educators in the liberal arts, Houghton faculty members excel at teaching disciplined ways of knowing and learning, developing character, and equipping students with the tools to succeed. The integrative studies curriculum forms the core of the Houghton educational experience and includes courses in history, literature, philosophy, mathematics, natural and social sciences, politics, fine arts and religion.

The well-regarded School of Education enrolls more than two hundred students in five majors: inclusive childhood education, adolescence education, TESOL (teaching English to speakers of other languages), music education, and physical education. Houghton's Greatbach School of Music offers a strong undergraduate program in general music, composition, conducting, and performance. Other academic areas of interest include biology, pre-med, intercultural studies, and equestrian studies.

Houghton's student-faculty ratio provides unique opportunities for collaboration between students and professors. In partnership with Houghton faculty, students have presented papers at literary conferences in Oxford, England, conducted photon light research at Cornell University, worked alongside researchers from MIT at the Los Alamos National Laboratory, and used computer science research to expand upon a discovery made by Nobel Prize-winning scientists.

Vibrant Community

An intentional and compassionate community is central to the learning process at Houghton. The majority of Houghton's faculty and staff live within walking distance of the campus, and this proximity allows for meaningful interaction between students and college personnel. The classroom, Bible study groups, a mentoring program and informal conversations combine to build relationships that enrich, challenge and encourage students to grow in academic and spiritual maturity.

In line with Houghton's Christian traditions, all students, faculty, and staff are required to sign a pledge of commitment to certain "standards of community life." Houghton faculty daily integrate faith with learning, and Houghton students, who represent all parts of the globe and over 30 different Christian denominations, learn to sharpen their skills, knowledge and faith together.

Houghton's 1300 acres of western New York woodland offers opportunities for exploring this beautiful region on foot, horseback (at out equestrian center) or cross-country skis. Over 80 percent of students live on campus, where the college has two all-male residence halls and two all-female halls as well as town-house accommodations for juniors and seniors.

Student groups active on campus include the Allegany County Outreach, Global Christian Fellowship, Student Government Association, Evangelicals for Social Action, Habitat for Humanity, Intercultural Student Association, Shakespeare Players, Equestrian Society and Youth for Christ. Over 75 percent of the students are active in Houghton's athletic program, whether playing an intercollegiate sport, joining an intramural team or participating in a fitness activity on campus.

Successful Outcomes

Houghton works to ensure students' success by requiring a first-year introduction course to ease the transition from high school to college; by pairing each student with an adviser; and by providing assistance with career planning, networking and resume writing.

Soon after graduation, 95 percent of education students are employed or enrolled in graduate school, and 98 percent pass the teaching certification exam. Houghton students' acceptance rate to medical school is about 90 percent, and Houghton graduates attend such law schools as Harvard, the University of Chicago, and the University of Virginia.

Houghton alumni are successful in a variety of fields, and many alumni take on the low-profile but rewarding task of discipleship or mission work in developing countries. Notable alumni include several professional soccer players, ABC News correspondent Barbara Pinto, Old Testament scholar Bruce Walke, British theologian and filmmaker Robert Beckford, and Fuller Theological Seminary president Richard J. Mouw.

As one Houghton College alum explains, "Houghton attracts people who study hard, who learn well and who want to serve—and that's exactly what Houghton graduates are doing all around the globe."

Fast Facts

Houghton College is a four-year, liberal arts college, affiliated with The Wesleyan Church, and founded in 1883.

Web site

http://www.houghton.edu/

Location

Houghton, New York.

Student Profile

1,335 students (35% male, 65% female); 35 states, 13 countries; 4% minority, 4% international.

Faculty Profile

87 full-time faculty. 13:1 student/faculty ratio. Average class size is 21.

Residence Life

Highly residential: 82% of students live on campus. Juniors and seniors have the option of living in apartments and townhouses.

Athletics

NAIA, 10 varsity sports (4 men's: basketball, cross-country, soccer, track & field; 6 women's: basketball, cross-country, field hockey, soccer, track & field, volleyball), 30 club and intramural sports.

Academic Programs

Accounting; applied physics - engineering; art; business; Bible; biology; chemistry; communication; computer science; earth science; economics; education; educational ministries; English; environmental studies; equestrian studies; family studies; foreign languages; forestry; French; general science; German; Greek; history; humanities; information technology management; intercultural studies; international relations; linguistics; mathematics; medical technology; ministry; missions; music; philosophy; physics; physical education; political science; prebioinformatics; predentistry; preengineering; prelaw; premed; preoptometry; prephysical therapy; prepharmacy; preseminary; preveterinary; psychology; recreation; religion; sociology; Spanish; TESOL; theater; theology; writing.

Costs and Aid

2007–2008: $28,480 comprehensive ($21,620 tuition). 88% of students receive some financial aid. Average award: $15,808.

Endowment

$35,542,335.

More Distinctions

• *U.S. News and World Report* – "America's Best College" has repeatedly named Houghton as one of the 161 national liberal arts colleges that are the 'most selective' and 'most solid' institutions in the country.

• *Fiske's Guide to Colleges* annually includes Houghton with 274 other colleges, as having solid academics, good social climate, and excellent quality of life.

Ithaca College

NEW YORK

Ithaca College (IC), a private, coeducational, nonsectarian college, offers the perfect blend of liberal arts education with professional preparation. From its founding in 1892 as a music conservatory, Ithaca's goal has been to provide a personalized, first-rate education and to develop in students the skills, values, and motivation to have a positive impact on the wider world.

Admissions Contact:

Ithaca College
100 Job Hall
Ithaca, NY 14850-7020
(800) 429-4274
Email: admission@ithaca.edu
www.ithaca.edu/admission

The 4 Distinctions

Engaged Students

Ithaca offers more than one hundred academic programs that emphasize real-world experience and provide students with an intellectual framework in their chosen fields of study. The college's Exploratory Program encourages students to take courses in any of Ithaca's schools and allows up to four semesters to declare a major. About 45 percent of new humanities and sciences students take advantage of the Exploratory Program.

Ithaca students gain hands-on experience in a variety of settings: in on-campus health and wellness clinics, in laboratories conducting original research with faculty, through partnerships with local businesses and nonprofit organizations, and via a nationwide internship network. Semester-long programs in Washington, DC, Los Angeles, and London, and study-abroad affiliations in some fifty countries provide more opportunities for personal and professional development.

The Center for Student Leadership and Involvement (CSLI) prepares IC students for "life in an ever-changing world." Its motto is "lead, serve, act," and it promotes experiences that encourage personal growth through connections with the greater Ithaca community. A campus clearinghouse for volunteer activities, CSLI monitors student-action organizations, offers training and personal-development workshops, and encourages the development of leadership and organizational skills. This emphasis on service begins the moment each student arrives on campus—freshmen are invited to join the Community Plunge, a program that links teams of students with local nonprofits for two days of volunteer work before classes begin.

IC students also benefit from the many distinguished guests who visit campus each semester to give lectures and performances, teach minicourses and master classes, and share their perspectives and professional expertise. Notable visitors include Olympic gold-medalist Scott Hamilton, award-winning journalist and Middle East correspondent Robert Fisk, Grammy Award-winning pianist Emanuel Ax, and filmmaker and media artist Naeem Mohaiemen.

Great Teaching

Ithaca's dedicated faculty are focused on teaching first. Faculty members—not TAs—teach all classes, and they serve as academic advisers, student clubs advisers, and mentors. Professors take pride in being on a first-name basis with their students and in challenging them to succeed.

The opportunity undergraduates have to collaborate on research and publish scholarly works with faculty—an experience typically reserved for graduate students elsewhere—is further evidence of this commitment to teaching. Recent student-faculty collaborations include a biomedical adhesives research project; studies of seismic signatures of the footfalls and calls of elephants; and research on the impact of foreign investments and toxic-waste issues in Ghana. These projects foster strong bonds among faculty, students, and their peers. Each year, IC celebrates these student-faculty partnerships at the James J. Whalen Academic Symposium, where students present their original work. Recent topics have ranged from studies of the portrayal of girlhood in children's and young-adult literature to original research on language acquisition in infants to experimental work on wind turbines. This event also includes art exhibits, performances, and readings.

When they're not working with students, Ithaca's accomplished faculty can be found creating award-winning films, videos, and art; conducting innovative research; presenting at national conferences; and writing journal articles and books that reflect and influence their fields. More than 90 percent of full-time faculty members have a PhD or a terminal degree in their field.

Vibrant Community

Located in Ithaca, New York, a lively and sophisticated residential community in the heart of New York State's Finger Lakes region, IC offers students many opportunities for community involvement, cultural enrichment, and outdoor recreation. The many parks, forests, gorges, and waterfalls in the area provide virtually endless opportunities for hiking, camping, water sports, and other activities.

The city of Ithaca is widely considered one of the nation's top college towns. It is further enriched by neighboring Cornell University and an international population from dozens of countries. This diversity is reflected in the local cable channel's international programming and in the variety of places of worship, grocery stores, and ethnic restaurants throughout the Ithaca area. Hundreds of concerts, lectures, theater performances, and events take place at the colleges and in the surrounding community each year. Notable performers such as cellist Yo-Yo Ma, the Strokes, and writer David Sedaris; events such as the Finger Lakes Environmental Film Festival; and a full season of theater performances at Ithaca College and local and regional community theaters provide year-round cultural offerings and entertainment.

Ithaca College is a vibrant, residential learning community. About 70 percent of students live on campus, where they can select from a variety of housing choices, including a Spanish-language immersion community, a sustainable-living community, and a freshmen-only option. Students earn one credit for choosing to live in Housing Offering a Multicultural Experience (HOME), which is popular among IC's international students.

After classes are over, IC students can be found participating in dozens of leadership, cocurricular, and extracurricular activities—the college has twenty-five highly competitive varsity teams and more than 150 campus clubs; it holds hundreds of concerts, recitals, and theater performances annually. Students manage the college's television station, two radio stations, two campus magazines, and a weekly campus newspaper—all of which consistently receive top awards from regional and national professional organizations.

Successful Outcomes

Ithaca alumni put into action the critical-thinking and hands-on learning skills they are taught. Within a year of graduation, 97 percent of IC graduates are employed or attending graduate school, and over the last five years, 100 percent of music-education graduates who sought a teaching position were placed.

Some prominent Ithaca alumni include Edward Glazer, executive vice president of the Tampa Bay Buccaneers; Michael Battle, director of the Executive Office for United States Attorneys; Judith Girard, president of HGTV; David Muir, anchor of NBC's World News Saturday and coanchor of Primetime; and Robert Iger, president and CEO of the Walt Disney Company. Dozens of alumni return to the campus each year to speak about their experiences, and students and graduates can take advantage of active alumni networks to develop internships and identify job openings.

Fast Facts

Ithaca College is a four-year, private, comprehensive college founded in 1892.

Web site

http://www.Ithaca.edu

Location

Ithaca, New York—in the heart of New York's Finger Lakes region.

Student Profile

6,000 undergraduate (56% female, 44% male). 47 states, 70 countries.

Faculty Profile

460 full-time, 210 part-time. 11:1 student-faculty ratio. Average class size is 15 students

Residence Life

Highly residential: over 70 percent of students live on campus

Athletics

NCAA Division III, Eastern College Athletic Conference (ECAC). 25 varsity sports (12 men's: basketball, swimming, wrestling, baseball, crew, football, lacrosse, soccer, cross-country, diving, tennis, track & field; 13 women's: basketball, volleyball, gymnastics, swimming, crew, field hockey, lacrosse, soccer, softball, cross-country, diving, tennis, track & field).

Academic Programs

Majors in the School of Business, School of Communications, School of Health Sciences & Human Performance, School of Humanities & Sciences, Division of Interdisciplinary & International Studies, and School of Music. Most popular majors: business administration/management; music/music & performing arts studies; communications.

Costs and Aid

2007–2008: $39,798 comprehensive ($28,670 tuition, $11,128 room, board, and fees). 85% of students receive some financial aid. Average award: $24,512.

Endowment

$205,700,000.

More Distinctions

• *U.S. News & World Report* has ranked Ithaca College among its top ten best master's universities in the North for ten years in a row.

• Ithaca College ranks in the top ten great schools at great prices in the same category.

• Ithaca was named one of the top 100 best campuses for LGBT students by the Advocate College Guide for LGBT Students.

Niagara University

NEW YORK

Niagara University (NU) is a Catholic, coeducational liberal arts institution. Founded in 1856 by the Vincentian community, NU is known for its beautiful campus, its quality academic programs, and its commitment to student engagement and community service.

Admissions Contact:

Niagara University
Bailo Hall
P.O. Box 2011
Niagara University, NY 14109
(800) 462-2111
Ph: (716) 286-8700
Fax: (716) 286-8710
Email: admissions@niagara.edu
www.niagara.edu

The 4 Distinctions

Engaged Students

Niagara strives to educate and enrich students through programs in the liberal arts and through career preparation informed by the Catholic and Vincentian traditions. The university develops a passion for learning in its students through teaching, research, and service, and its commitment to the Catholic faith allows students to experience the vision and reality of a service-oriented, value-centered education. St. Vincent de Paul's tradition of serving the poor is continued at NU, where all undergraduates participate in service learning. In addition, half do undergraduate research and many engage in study abroad, cooperative education, and internships. A Niagara education is designed to make a difference in the lives of students, leading them to make a difference in the community and the world.

Niagara offers seventy majors in its academic program. The most popular are: business/commerce; criminal justice; hotel & restaurant management; psychology; communication studies; biology and teacher education. Internships are frequently available to provide hands-on learning experience best fitted for the individual. Some NU students have even worked with David Letterman.

Learn and Serve Niagara is a program designed to promote the knowledge, values, and skills necessary for the lifelong engagement in the pursuit of social justice among all members of the university community. All major programs require completion of Learn and Serve components for graduation. Courses with service-learning components are offered in every college and in almost every academic department. Students are involved in projects ranging from working with the Niagara County District Attorney's Office in the domestic-violence program to doing historical research for nonprofit agencies to providing tax-preparation assistance to elderly community members. Education majors serve as teachers' aids, NU students provide tutoring for local children, and another group of students participates in Habitat for Humanity projects.

NU students can take advantage of other practical work experiences, too. College of Education students begin working in classrooms in their freshman year, and are given increasing amounts of responsibility with each succeeding year. The College of Business offers a five-year MBA with an undergraduate degree. The program emphasizes real-world experience with businesses from across the country as well as in the Buffalo area. As part of a cruise management course on Carnival Cruise Lines, students in the College of Hospitality and Tourism Management have the opportunity to work alongside management in a variety of jobs, including food service and guest relations. Students also have the opportunity to participate in a hotel management program in Italy, where students work alongside management at a hotel on Lake Como in Italy.

Great Teaching

NU has four academic divisions: the College of Arts and Sciences, the College of Education, the College of Business Administration, and the College of Hospitality and Tourism Management. The latter is no surprise, given Niagara's proximity to the famous falls of the same name, a must-visit destination for generations of travelers.

Niagara's low student to faculty ratio of seventeen to one means that classes are small, typically with fewer than thirty students and fewer than twenty students for labs and subsections. Faculty members serve as advisors to students, either in their major field of study or under the Academic Exploration Program for students who have not yet decided on a major.

Professors help students find internship placements through their contacts, and they also are involved in student clubs. Almost every major has a club, and faculty also offer special programs designed to stimulate and challenge the accomplished students who qualify for the honors program. Students contribute to research in a variety of fields, and their work is often presented at national conferences.

Addressing a student's whole life, NU offers continuing orientation throughout the college experience, including classes and seminars on drugs and alcohol, study habits, and other topics that count as credit for elective courses.

In addition to the internships and service-learning programs, students can earn credits for research projects, independent study, and cooperative-education programs. They may also participate in Army ROTC.

Vibrant Community

About 52 percent of NU's 2,900 undergraduate students live on campus in a variety of residential options. There are more than seventy registered student organizations, several of which serve the local community. Local elementary and secondary-school students are tutored by education majors, and the Learn and Serve program, for other majors, helps to involve NU students in the local community.

Niagara Falls is a dynamic town twenty miles from Buffalo and seventy miles from Toronto, Ontario. In addition to the cultural, entertainment, and sporting attractions these two great cities offer, Niagara Falls is rich in natural beauty beyond the well-known falls. The Niagara River (actually a strait between Lake Erie and Lake Ontario), Lake Ontario, and the Erie Canal all provide unique opportunities for NU students to study natural sciences and to take advantage of the area's many recreation possibilities.

Successful Outcomes

NU faculty and alumni are committed to helping students make connections. At NU's College of Hospitality and Tourism Management, alumni hold an all-day event each year to connect with current students and give them guidance. Alumni give presentations about their work experience and careers to help students choose their next step after graduation. NU's College of Business Administration also hosts both on and off campus events, including a "Meet the Accountants Night" where current students can network with alumni.

NU students can also take advantage of career counseling, help with resume writing, and training in business etiquette. Students from the Colleges of Arts and Sciences, Business, and Hospitality are eligible to participate in a co-op program in their junior or senior year, enabling them to gain both paid work experience and academic credit in their major. The Office of Career Development also facilitates on-campus interviews, which bring employers to campus throughout the year to interview students for full-time, part-time, and co-op employment opportunities.

"I came to visit Niagara and fell in love with the atmosphere. The campus is small enough that you can get to know many people and large enough that there's always someone new to meet.

- Emily Shuart, Communication Studies major from Hampton, VA

Fast Facts

Niagara University is a private, comprehensive, coeducational, liberal arts university in a Catholic and Vincentian tradition, and founded in 1856.

Web site

http://www.niagara.edu/

Location

Niagara University, New York—three miles from the world-famous Niagara Falls. Near American and Canadian cities of Buffalo and Toronto.

Student Profile

2,900 students (40% male , 60% female); 13% Out of State; 13% minority, 5% international.

Faculty Profile

137 full-time faculty. 17:1 student/faculty ratio. Average class size is 25.

Residence Life

Moderately residential: 52 % of students live on campus.

Athletics

NCAA Division I, Metro Atlantic Athletic Conference. 17 varsity sports (8 men's: baseball, cross-country, ice hockey, swimming & diving, basketball, tennis, soccer, golf; 9 women's: swimming & diving, ice hockey, lacrosse, tennis, soccer, volleyball, basketball, softball, cross-country).

Academic Programs

Hotel & restaurant management; tourism & recreation management; accounting; commerce; education (childhood (1-6), adolescence (7-12), early childhood & childhood (B-6), childhood & middle childhood (1-9), middle childhood & adolescence (5-12), special education & childhood (1-6), special education & adolescence (7-12), academic exploration program, prepharmacy, predental, premedical, prelaw, preveterinary, prepharmacology, ROTC-Army.

Costs and Aid

2006–2007: $30,090 comprehensive ($20,400 tuition). 75% of students receive some financial aid. Average award: $17,500.

Endowment

$66,000,000.

More Distinctions

• Niagara University offered the first bachelor's degree in tourism and is ranked in the top 20 programs of its kind in the country.

• Named three times to the U.S. News & World Report's top 20 "Great Schools at Great Prices."

• Named to the Princeton Review as one of the "Best Colleges in the Northeast."

Purchase College, SUNY

NEW YORK

Founded in 1967, Purchase College (PC) is a coeducational college offering liberal arts and sciences programs uniquely combined with conservatory training in the visual and performing arts, making it the cultural gem of the State University of New York's (SUNY) publicly funded network of sixty-four universities and colleges.

Admissions Contact:

Purchase College, SUNY
735 Anderson Hill Road
Purchase, NY 10577
Ph: (914) 251-6300
Fax: (914) 251-6314
Email: admissions@purchase.edu
www.purchase.edu

The 4 Distinctions

Engaged Students

Creativity is prized at Purchase College: its 3,901 students and 146 full-time faculty members are active culture generators. By choosing Purchase College, individuals make a conscious decision to pursue their studies and their careers in an intense cultural and intellectual center. About 65 percent of Purchase College's students are in the liberal arts and sciences programs, and the most popular majors are psychology and biology. The other 35 percent of students are in the visual and performing arts, where the most popular programs are dance, music, theater arts and film, and art and design. The general education program exposes fine arts students to the liberal arts and sciences, enabling interaction among different kinds of students. Many interdisciplinary studies are offered, as well.

Students prepare senior projects, directing their creative efforts toward completing a final piece of work, such as writing a play. The senior project gives students credible work experience, which is attractive to artists in many fields.

Great Teaching

Purchase College's goal is to ensure close contact between the two different styles of education, inspiring an appreciation for both intellectual and artistic talents in all students. Today, the college attracts students and faculty from around the world who seek a place to develop their talents, expand their minds, and prepare for a life of creative independence.

Purchase College's close proximity to New York City allows the college to attract and retain talented professors who appreciate the cultural opportunities available in the city. The low student to faculty ratio of fifteen to one makes it possible for students to know their professors well and to interact with them on a daily basis. Many faculty members choose to live on campus, creating a tight-knit community.

In a groundbreaking, new cross-campus initiative, Purchase College is embarking on a yearlong exploration of the rich cultural heritage of Africa and the African Diaspora. Public programs include events at The Performing Arts

Center featuring artists such as Urban Bush Women and Jant-B, Ronald K Brown/Evidence, Imani Winds, Jon Faddis Jazz Orchestra, Classical Theatre of Harlem, Peru Negro, Spirit of Uganda and much more. The Neuberger Museum of Art opens a dazzling re-installation of its acclaimed African collection. The School of the Arts presents concerts, dance and theater performances relating to the theme, and supports visiting guest artists: composer-conductor Tania Leon, Latin Jazz Master Ray Santos and choreographer Kevin Wynn. The School of Humanities and Natural and Social Sciences are offering public lectures and symposia in addition to courses that address cultural identity and expression, as well as complex socio-political issues. This initiative will stimulate and engage artists, scholars and the general public, making Purchase College a vibrant intellectual and artistic center for the community.

Vibrant Community

Purchase College's purpose is to bring together creative artists with intellectuals, which the residential campus supports by providing a common ground where both can work and learn. The student body is diverse for a SUNY campus: 20 percent of the students are from outside New York State. The dance and theater programs in particular attract students from across the nation.

Two-thirds of PC's students live on campus, and 70 percent are there on weekends, with about thirty active organizations students can choose to join. Students are so happy at Purchase College that when the college considered building a new dorm and asked the students to suggest a name, they chose Fort Awesome. There are no fraternities or sororities at Purchase. The campus features living-learning communities, and creative arts students in particular tend to live together throughout their four years at Purchase College.

The Purchase College campus is more than a learning facility; it's also a community venue and cultural center for the southeastern New York and southwestern Connecticut region. Its Neuberger Museum of Art is one of the largest campus museums in the country, and the Purchase Performing Arts Center, a multitheater complex, is the major professional, nonprofit arts presenter in the area. It seats up to 1,500 and draws two hundred thousand people to the more than six hundred performances, benefits, and events held there each year. The local community is fairly affluent, and they enthusiastically support Purchase College's arts through programs such as Adopt-A-Dancer, and by participating in a scholarship fundraising event held in conjunction with a performance of The Nutcracker ballet.

Purchase College's campus is located thirty-five miles northeast of New York City at the Connecticut state border. Originally a working farm, the campus was planned to be "a city within the country," with college buildings arranged in clusters to preserve open fields and meadows.

Successful Outcomes

Members of the Purchase College alumni community are Grammy, Emmy, and Oscar winners, and they share their experiences with current students. Purchase College alumni range from an award-winning molecular geneticist and other scientists to authors, filmmakers, dancers, dramatists, high-ranking international business executives, and newspaper reporters.

Notable alumni and former students of Purchase include Edie Falco, Hal Hartley, Josh Hartnett, Parker Posey, Michael Savage, Wesley Snipes, Stanley Tucci, Moby, Regina Spektor, and Ving Rhames.

Fast Facts

Purchase College is a four-year college offering Liberal Arts & Science programs as well as programs in the visual and performing arts. Purchase College is part of the State University of New York. Nelson Rockefeller founded Purchase College in 1967 as the SUNY campus dedicated to the arts, he also established on the site a school devoted to providing a liberal arts education.

Web site

http://www.purchase.edu/

Location

Purchase, New York— 35 miles northeast of New York City at the Connecticut state border. Near White Plains, New York.

Student Profile

3,901 total student body. 3,480 undergraduate students (46% male, 54% female); 45 states and territories, 21 countries; 23% minority.

Faculty Profile

146 of full-time faculty. 90% hold a terminal degree in their field. 15:1 student/faculty ratio. Average class size is 14.

Residence Life

Highly residential: 2,460 residence hall capacity.

Athletics

NCAA Division III, North Eastern Athletic Conference. 13 varsity sports (6 men's: soccer, basketball, cross-country, volleyball, baseball, tennis; 7 women's: soccer, basketball, cross-country, volleyball, softball, swim team, tennis.

Academic Programs

HUMANITIES: art history; cinema studies; creative writing; drama studies; history; Jewish studies; journalism; language & culture (Chinese, French, German, Hebrew, Italian, Spanish); literature; philosophy. NATURAL SCIENCES: biology; chemistry; environmental studies; mathematics/computer science; premed; psychology. SOCIAL SCIENCES: anthropology; economics; media, society & the arts; political science; sociology. INTERDISCIPLINARY STUDIES: Asian studies; global Black studies; Latin-American studies; lesbian & gay studies; liberal studies (arts, communications/media studies, legal studies); new media; women's studies. ART + DESIGN: graphic design; painting/drawing; photography; printmaking/art of the book; sculpture/3-D media; visual arts. CONSERVATORY OF MUSIC: performance- brass (trumpet, horn, trombone, tuba), classical guitar, harp, organ/harpsichord, percussion, piano, strings (violin, viola, cello, bass), voice, woodwinds (flute, oboe, clarinet, bassoon); composition; jazz studies; studio composition; studio production. CONSERVATORY OF DANCE: dance performance (modern and ballet); ballet; composition; dance production. CONSERVATORY OF THEATRE ARTS & FILM: scenic design; costume design; lighting design; costume technology; stage management; stage management/production management; technical direction/production management. GRADUATE PROGRAMS ARE OFFERED BY THE CONSERVATORIES AND THE SCHOOL OF ART + DESIGN.

Costs and Aid

2006–2007: $14,702 in-state comprehensive ($4,350 tuition); $20,962 out-of-state comprehensive (10,610 tuition). 78% of students receive some financial aid. Average award: $7,623.

Endowment

$37.298,000.

St. Bonaventure University

NEW YORK

St. Bonaventure University is a largely residential Catholic university in the Franciscan tradition offering undergraduate and graduate programs and an innovative liberal arts core. Founded in 1858, the school delivers challenging learning opportunities in a supportive environment which fosters the development of strong relationships among faculty, staff and other students.

Admissions Contact:

St. Bonaventure University
3261 West State Road
St. Bonaventure, NY 14778
(800) 462-5050
Email: admissions@sbu.edu
www.sbu.edu

The 4 Distinctions

Engaged Students

Learning extends beyond the walls of the classrooms at St. Bonaventure University, where students are encouraged to explore their options to serve, solve problems and make a difference to the lives of those in need – whether nearby or thousands of miles away. With service as the essence of rich out-of-class experiences, Bonaventure engages students through such opportunities as BonaResponds, a unique organization that recently worked with residents in hurricane-ravaged Mississippi as well as flood victims in Ohio. Students interact with neighbors in communities surrounding the SBU campus through such programs as the Warming House, the oldest student-operated soup kitchen in the United States, the Journey Project and Bona Buddies.

To ensure that first-year students get to know their instructors and fellow students quickly, the school's Learning Communities enable them to share two or three linked courses and gain common learning experiences.

Through Study Abroad opportunities at 38 colleges and universities in 27 foreign countries, St. Bonaventure helps students learn their role in the global community. Most programs require little or no language experience, and special tuition pricing ensures that there are enough prospects for everyone interested in participating in one of these programs.

Great Teaching

St. Bonaventure cultivates students' passion for learning and living through a curriculum which encourages critical thinking and focuses on connecting disciplines, people, places, events and ideas. Faculty members are at the school because they enjoy teaching, getting to know students, and serving not just as content experts but also as mentors. They remain active in their fields of study through research, publication, or professional activities, and they often invite students to join them in working on research projects or attend conferences. With just 15 students in the average class, faculty can interact with students individually during and after class.

All students are required to take 40 percent of their total credits in core liberal arts courses: literature, history, philosophy, classics, art and the fundamental sciences. Among the school's 31 undergraduate majors, the most popular are elementary education, journalism, psychology, accounting, marketing, finance, and management.

SBU's highly popular Dual Admissions Programs allow some students to have reserved seats in Dental, Medical, Physical Therapy, or Pharmacy school upon admission to the school.

High academic achievement students may participate in the honors program, which provides intellectual opportunities and challenges that complement and enrich their regular course work. Steered by faculty, the honors program courses enable motivated students to work collaboratively and tackle topics of current interest.

Vibrant Community

While it is located in a beautiful part of Western New York that is largely rural, the St. Bonaventure University campus is a vibrant and exciting community. From Division 1 and Intramural athletics, cultural exhibits, performances, and lectures to overnight events at Mt. Irenaeus Franciscan retreat or coffee house open mike nights, there is an endless supply of interesting things to do at SBU. During winter, many students ski at Holiday Valley, one of the best resorts in the East, just 20 miles away. And the Allegheny River Trail on campus offers a great place to relax, exercise, and enjoy nature's beauty during spring and fall months.

The Campus Activities Board is committed to bringing the most exciting, diverse and educational extracurricular programs to campus and gives students a voice in scheduling SBU activities throughout the year.

Students' experiences with the arts are expanded by exhibits at the world-class Regina A. Quick Center for the Arts and performances in the Center's Rigas Theatre.

Exciting NCAA Division I athletics teams turn even reluctant sports enthusiasts into Bonnies fans. Whether it's for a sold-out game at the Reilly Center Basketball Arena or a sunny afternoon in Fred Handler Sports Park, St. Bonaventure University athletics are the hottest ticket in town.

The friendly competition of Intramural programs also contributes to St. Bonaventure's tight-knit community. With 10 groups in action, the program attempts to offer something for every type of student, and more than 80 percent of SBU students participate in some intramural, recreational, or club sport activity.

Students can learn, grow individually and have fun socially by participating in SBU's more than 50 established campus clubs and organizations or – by working within the Student Government Association - start a new group to share their passions and interests.

Successful Outcomes

Armed with the skills, knowledge and experiences gained during their time at St. Bonaventure University, students graduate prepared to flourish in the real world. Within a year of graduation, 68 percent of survey respondents among 2006 graduates reported being employed full-time and 32 percent were attending graduate school.

Some of the most successful companies in the world either employ or are under the leadership of SBU graduates, including ESPN, Sirius Satellite Radio, The Pittsburgh Steelers, Procter and Gamble, Hartford Life, Inc., The New York Times, Lockheed Martin Global Telecommunications, and Wachovia, among many others.

SBU graduates remain a part of the university. In addition to 30 Alumni Chapters throughout the country, they can join their 500-plus fellow SBU alumni in the St. Bonaventure Alumni group online network which includes more than 11 million experienced professionals representing 150 industries from around the world.

St. Bonaventure University's strong emphasis on Franciscan values also stays with graduates, who retain a strong commitment to investigation and wonder, knowledge and love, reflection and wisdom, understanding and humility.

Fast Facts

St. Bonaventure University, founded in 1858, is an institution in the Catholic Franciscan tradition offering undergraduate and graduate degrees and a liberal arts core curriculum.

Web site

http://www.sbu.edu

Location

Southwest corner of New York state, between the towns of Olean and Allegany. 1.5 hours south of Niagara Falls and 1.5 hours east of Erie, Pennsylvania.

Student Profile

2,500 students (80 percent undergraduate, 20 percent graduate). 52 percent female, 48 percent male. 34 states and 12 foreign countries

Faculty Profile

Our distinguished faculty are committed to mentoring students in vitally engaging learning environments. With more than 150-full-time professors, many of whom have earned the highest degree in their fields; our students have access to scholars who are also excellent teachers.

Residence Life

Largely residential: 75 percent of students live on campus

Athletics

NCAA Division I - Atlantic 10 Conference. Men's varsity sports: baseball, basketball, cross country, golf, soccer, swimming and diving, tennis. Women's varsity sports: basketball, cross country, lacrosse, soccer, softball, swimming and diving, tennis. Club sports: women's field hockey, men's ice hockey, men's lacrosse, rugby (men and women), ski racing (men and women). Intramural basketball, dodge ball, flag football, floor hockey, golf, kickball, pool, soccer, softball, volleyball, wallyball.

Academic Programs

More than 50 undergraduate majors, including pre-health dual admissions programs and pre-law early admission, and 20 graduate programs from the schools of Arts & Sciences, Business, Education, Journalism/Mass Communication, and Franciscan Studies.

Costs and Aid

Undergraduates: $22,740 full-time tuition and fees; $680 per credit hour; room and meal plan (average) $8,485. Graduate students: $650 per credit hour. More than 90 percent of students receive financial aid; the average freshman package is $21,177. Of the $17 million in annual scholarships and grants students receive, $930,000 is from endowed/annual scholarships.

Endowment

$46.7 million.

More Distinctions:

-The University's soup kitchen, The Warming House, has operated for more than 30 years and is believed to be oldest student-run soup kitchen in the nation.

- St. Bonaventure University has five graduates who have earned journalism's highest honor, the Pulitzer Prize.

SUNY Cortland

Admissions Contact:

SUNY Cortland
SUNY Cortland Admissions
P.O. Box 2000
Cortland, NY 13045
Ph: (607) 753-4711
Email: admissions@cortland.edu
www.cortland.edu

NEW YORK

SUNY Cortland is a comprehensive college of arts and sciences offering undergraduate and graduate programs in the liberal arts and a variety of professional fields. Founded in 1868, it remains true to its roots as a teachers college and still graduates the most teachers in the state.

The 4 Distinctions

Engaged Students

Students have many opportunities to gain real-world experience outside the classroom while earning course credit. Education majors student teach at area schools, and science majors participate in fieldwork and research trips. Other opportunities include summer archaeological field school, a semester in Washington, and internships with the news media or social-service organizations.

SUNY Cortland students can study abroad in Australia, Belize, China, Costa Rica, Egypt, England, France, Germany, Ireland, Mexico, Spain, and Venezuela. Each year, students in marine biology spend part of their winter breaks observing marine life in the coral reef off the coast of Belize after a quick stop in the South American rain forest. Education students can travel to Australia for student teaching. Closer to home, geology students observe rock formations, and archaeology students dig for Native American artifacts right in central New York.

The school's annual Scholars Day offers students, faculty, staff, and alumni an opportunity to present research to an audience that includes the community and students from surrounding high schools.

Service learning typically takes place in Cortland at the YMCA, the YWCA, or Habitat for Humanity. Recreation and leisure studies majors often volunteer and develop programs in the local community. Recently, a SUNY Cortland student conducted research on disability participation in recreation.

Great Teaching

SUNY Cortland's mission statement affirms that quality teaching has been the highest priority since the school's founding in 1868, building on traditional strengths in teacher education and physical education and enhancing programs in the arts, humanities, and sciences.

Education remains the most popular major. Physical education, which also has a strong pedagogic orientation, is popular, too. Other distinctive majors include biological sciences (conservation biology and biomedical science) and sport management, in which students develop a business background in the world of sports.

SUNY Cortland's Faculty Development Center is designed to create an environment that facilitates the ability of each faculty member to develop his or her full potential as a teacher, scholar, researcher, and creative professional.

Cortland uses innovative technology for learning. The campus includes more than 850 computers in forty labs, and students in all majors engage in interactive learning exercises, using the latest software and consulting online resources. For example, the International Communications and Culture computer lab is the site of a multimedia materials course taught by Spanish professor Jean Leloup and French professor Robert Ponterio, in which students learn to master presentation software, streaming audio and video, and other high-tech tools. In the Geographic Information Systems laboratory, students create sophisticated computerized maps for a wide range of purposes, from urban planning to environmental conservation.

Vibrant Community

Located in central New York's City of Seven Valleys, SUNY Cortland also has a strong focus on sports and physical education. SUNY Cortland has had the most nationally successful men's and women's intercollegiate athletics program in New York over the past decade.

The school is committed to helping students maintain healthy lifestyles, offering on-campus health fairs and as many club sports as varsity sports. Last year, thirty SUNY Cortland athletes were all-Americans, and nine teams finished in the top ten nationally. In addition to the roughly seven hundred students who play on twenty-five varsity teams, more than half of all students participate in eleven club and forty-seven intramural sports, ranging from basketball and volleyball to biking and rock climbing. They have access to two state-of-the-art fitness facilities, two swimming pools, an ice arena, indoor and outdoor tracks, many basketball gyms and two outdoor courts, twenty-two tennis courts, ten squash and racquetball courts, and fifty acres of practice and game fields.

Campus activities include a Spring Fling festival and Winterfest. The entire campus community can also take part in weekly Sandwich Seminars, where faculty, staff, and guest speakers talk about their current research or topics ranging from college life and social issues to national and international politics.

About three thousand SUNY Cortland students live on campus. The residence halls are new or have been renovated in the last six to eight years.

Cortland students are involved with youth in the community through teaching, coaching, and participating in on-campus programs, such as the literacy department's effort to help children become better readers.

There are three ski resorts within fifteen minutes of campus, and numerous other outdoor sports activities at nearby lakes, rivers, and hiking and bike trails. Since 2001, the Outdoor Opportunities Program has helped coordinate a number of outdoor activities.

Successful Outcomes

Because of its strong focus on education, SUNY Cortland hosts a teacher recruitment program with a consortium of eleven different colleges. The program lasts three days and provides students with access to a number of teaching opportunities.

SUNY students can also take advantage of the Career Marketing Portal. This program helps students connect to campus careers, other students, alumni, and employers of all sizes and types, and serves as a one-stop shop for jobs, internships, vacation work, and careers.

Successful alumni include professional wrestler and best-selling author Mick Foley (aka Mankind), Hollywood director Ted Demme, top-ranked female U.S. army major General Ann Dunwoody, former New York governor Nathan L. Miller, and playwright Carol E. St. John.

"The student is key to education. So the learner comes first, not the subject matter, per se."

– Seth Asumah, chair African American Studies Department

Fast Facts

SUNY Cortland, founded in 1868, is a public comprehensive college of arts and sciences offering undergraduate and graduate programs in the liberal arts and a variety of professional fields.

Web site

http://www.cortland.edu/

Location

Cortland, New York—a short drive to Ithaca and Syracuse, New York.

Student Profile

5,960 undergraduates (42% male, 58% female); 9.5% minority, 1% international.

Faculty Profile

267 full-time faculty. 18:1 student/faculty ratio. Average class size is 22.

Residence Life

Moderately residential: 49% of students live on campus.

Athletics

NCAA Division III, SUNYAC Conference. 27 varsity sports (12 men's: baseball, basketball, cross-country, diving, football, gymnastics, ice hockey, lacrosse, soccer, swimming, track & field, wrestling; 15 women's: basketball, cheerleading, cross-country, diving, field hockey, golf, gymnastics, ice hockey, lacrosse, volleyball, swimming, soccer, softball, tennis, track & field), 17 club sports, and 3 intramurals.

Academic Programs

Adolescence education; African American studies; anthropology; art & art history; athletic training; biology; biomedical sciences; business economics; chemistry; chemistry/engineering; childhood education; communication studies; conservation biology; criminology; early childhood & childhood education; early childhood education; economics; English; English as a second language; environmental science & forestry; environmental studies; French; geographic information systems; geography; geology; health certification K-12; health science; human services; individualized degree program; international studies; kinesiology; kinesiology: fitness development; mathematics; musical theatre; new communication media; new media design; physical education certification K-12; physics; physics & engineering; political science; professional writing; psychology; recreation; social philosophy; sociology; Spanish; special education; speech & hearing science (non-certification); speech & language disabilities; sport management.

Costs and Aid

2007-2008: $14,200 in-state comprehensive ($4,350 tuition); $21,160 out-of-state comprehensive ($10,300 tuition). 70% of students receive some financial aid. Average award: $7,990.

Endowment

10 million.

More Distinctions

• Consumers Digest, in its May/June 2004 issue, ranked SUNY Cortland among its top 50 "best value" public colleges and universities in the nation.

• SUNY Cortland was ranked by Kiplinger's among its 100 Best Values in Public Colleges for 2007, a list that highlights national institutions "noteworthy for their combination of top-flight academics and affordable costs."

SUNY Oswego

NEW YORK

Admissions Contact:

SUNY Oswego
Office of Admissions
229 Sheldon Hall
State University of New York at Oswego
Oswego, NY 13126-3599
Ph: (315) 312-2500
Email: admiss@oswego.edu
www.oswego.edu

The State University of New York at Oswego (SUNY Oswego) is located on the beautiful shore of Lake Ontario. With 110 fields of study, SUNY Oswego is large enough to offer a comprehensive course of study, yet small enough to provide a personal education in a supportive environment.

The 4 Distinctions

Engaged Students

SUNY Oswego enrolls 6,620 full-time undergraduate students in an encouraging, challenging, and open-minded environment. Notable for its high level of student participation in international study, SUNY Oswego has been ranked in the top ten nationally among colleges of its size for overseas study programs. Overseas study options for Oswego students include programs in many locations around the globe, including Europe (the Czech Republic, England, France, Germany, Hungary, Ireland, and Spain), China, Japan, Australia, New Zealand, Mexico, Brazil, and Cuba. For SUNY Oswego students on study abroad, tuition remains the same as it is for on-campus students.

The Experienced Based Education office helps students connect to numerous internship opportunities. Recently, students have had internships with MTV, the Federal Aviation Administration, the Dolphin Research Center, General Electric, and Merrill Lynch, among many others.

The Center for Service Learning and Community Service focuses on providing opportunities for students to get involved in the local community in ways that enhance their academic interests. Some of the center's programs connect directly to the classroom, with political science students conducting exit polling during elections and psychology majors doing hands-on work at local mental health facilities.

Oswego provides students with a series of first-year programs that take place in the summer prior to fall enrollment. Orientation welcomes students with fun, family-friendly sessions that serve as a how-to manual for starting college. The First Choice program provides a menu of course offerings to help students transition to the responsibilities of college.

The First-Year Residential Experience presents an environment that shows Oswego's incoming freshmen how to make the most of their college years. The first-year advisement program offers sound advice on pursuing a degree. These innovative programs have won awards, have served as models for other institutions, and most important, they have helped thousands of Oswego students find the right start on their paths to success.

Great Teaching

More than half of SUNY Oswego's students major in the traditional liberal arts, while the nationally accredited schools of Education and Business offer programs tailored to more specific professional fields. SUNY Oswego offers a variety of programs for fostering interaction among students and faculty. Professors take part in the Take a Student to the Arts program, in which they attend performances and exhibits with students, and students widely take advantage of the Take a Faculty to Lunch program. Johnson Hall, a residence hall for first-year students, even includes a faculty advisor office to serve students from the convenience of their own residence hall.

A number of the programs within the School of Arts and Sciences offer unique teaching and learning opportunities. The Biology Department, for example, makes extensive use of its Rice Creek Field Station, located just a mile from campus, and students in the department's zoology program have the option of spending a semester or a year at Santa Fe Community College in Florida, which has a zoo adjacent to its campus. The Communication Studies Program offers a brand-new one million dollar media center with all digital TV and radio facilities. Psychology and public justice are other notable academic disciplines at SUNY Oswego. All three of Oswego's creative arts departments—art, music, and theatre—are now nationally accredited, and the college is one of only two SUNY schools, and one of a very limited number of schools across the northeast, to have received such recognition.

The School of Business, which enrolls roughly one in five undergraduates, offers seven diverse undergraduate majors, a graduate MBA, and is internationally accredited by the Association to Advance Collegiate Schools of Business (AACSB).

Accredited by the National Council for Accreditation of Teacher Education, SUNY Oswego's School of Education is strongly committed to learning by doing. The program offers student-teaching opportunities in a variety of settings, including schools in Syracuse, in underrepresented rural schools, and even overseas.

Vibrant Community

SUNY Oswego's nearly seven hundred-acre, tree-lined campus spread is along the southern shore of majestic Lake Ontario—an awesome sight and the backdrop for some of the world's most spectacular sunsets. On one side of the SUNY Oswego campus is over one mile of the scenic Lake Ontario shoreline, and on the other side is a town noted for its coffee shops and music venues. Students rave about their beautiful campus, which, they proudly point out, is also technologically advanced and mostly wireless. The SUNY Oswego campus is easily reached by car, rail, and air and is near Syracuse and Rochester, New York. The town of Oswego is known for its welcoming attitude toward SUNY students.

SUNY Oswego offers a variety of programs for incoming first-year students. The Hart Hall Global Living and Learning Center focuses on programs that emphasize community service, global-themed courses, and live-in faculty. Johnson Hall houses approximately 240 students who participate in the school's nationally recognized First Year Residential Experience program. This program focuses on the success of students their first year of college and throughout future years at SUNY Oswego. Participants in the Living and Learning Communities live in the same residence halls and take common classes with students who have similar interests, providing them with the opportunity to make connections with faculty, staff, and other students.

SUNY Oswego offers students more than 125 registered clubs and organizations to choose from, including academic, media and publication, religious, cultural, special interest, Greek life, arts, and community-service groups, as well as club sports. Participating in these student clubs and organizations offers students opportunities to build friendships and participate in active learning while promoting leadership and responsibility, experiences that often lead to higher levels of academic success.

Successful Outcomes

SUNY Oswego's learn-by-doing style of education helps prepare students for careers in nearly every profession. The alumni office offers the Alumni Sharing Knowledge (ASK) program, through which successful alumni visit the campus to present workshops and visit classrooms.

Although SUNY Oswego has received many awards and recognitions for its high standard of education and programs, the real testament to the quality of education are the nearly sixty thousand successful alumni who span the globe. An Oswego broadcasting degree launched the careers of NBC's Al Roker, ESPN's Linda Cohn and Steve Levy, and CNN's Kendis Gibson.

Oswego's career services office provides a broad range of services, such as career counseling, assessment, and advisement. Students can also connect with hundreds of major employers during annual job fairs and on-campus recruiting visits. Additional services include resume development and refinement, job search seminars and workshops, an information and upcoming events Listserve, use of the Discover career planning program, and graduate school research assistance.

Fast Facts

SUNY Oswego is a coeducational, comprehensive, public university and founded in 1861.

Web site

http:// www.oswego.edu

Location

Oswego, New York—35 miles northwest of Syracuse.

Student Profile

6,620 undergraduate students (46% male, 54% female); 28 states and territories, 19 countries; 10% minority, 1% international.

Faculty Profile

300 full-time faculty. 85% hold a terminal degree in their field. 18:1 student/faculty ratio. Average class size is 24.

Residence Life

Highly residential: 91 % of students live on campus.

Athletics

NCAA Division III, ECAC, NYSWCAA, and SUNYAC Conferences. 24 varsity sports (12 men's: baseball, basketball, cross-country, golf, ice hockey, lacrosse, soccer, swimming & diving, tennis, indoor & outdoor track & field, wrestling; 12 women's: basketball, cross-country, field hockey, ice hockey, lacrosse, soccer, softball, swimming & diving, tennis, indoor & outdoor track & field, volleyball), 8 club sports, and 11 intramurals.

Academic Programs

Accounting; adolescent education (grades7-12); American studies; anthropology; art; biochemistry; biology; broadcasting & mass communications; business administration; chemistry; childhood education (grades 1-6); cinema & screen studies; cognitive science; communication studies; computer science; creative writing; economics; English; finance; French; geochemistry; geology; German; global & international studies; graphic design; history; human development; human resource management; information science; journalism; language & international trade; linguistics; management accounting; operations management & information systems; marketing; mathematics; mathematics-applied; mathematical economics-applied; meteorology; music; philosophy; philosophy-psychology; physics; political science; psychology; public justice; public relations; sociology; Spanish; TESOL; technology education; technology management; theatre; vocational teacher preparation; wellness management; women's studies; zoology.

Costs and Aid

2006–2007: $14,904 in-state comprehensive ($4,350 tuition); $21,164 out-of-state comprehensive ($10,610 tuition). 70% of students receive some financial aid. Average award: $7,990.

Endowment

$8,600,000.

The King's College

NEW YORK

Committed to the truths of Christianity and a biblical worldview, and dedicated to preparing future leaders, The King's College aims to equip students with lifelong habits of mind, intellectual skills, and enduring motivations. The college boasts a rigorous curriculum that tightly integrates political theory, philosophy, economics, history, and theology.

Admissions Contact:

The King's College
350 Fifth Ave Suite 1500
New York, NY 10118
(888) 969-7200
Ph: (212) 659-3610
Fax: (212) 659-3611
Email: info@tkc.edu
www.tkc.edu

The 4 Distinctions

Engaged Students

Located in the Empire State Building in the heart of midtown Manhattan, The King's College attracts some of the brightest and best students in America, and is especially suited for students who seek to unlock their leadership potential.

New York City makes the perfect training ground for acquiring the skills and experiences necessary to become an influencer. Students participate in internships at organizations such as Fox News and Oppenheimer Funds.

King's students often show entrepreneurial initiative. Recently, a group of students designed a study trip to Albania that focused on politics, economics, and theology. While in the former Soviet bloc country, students studied how Albania struggles with democracy. They also debated at an Albanian university and appeared on Albanian radio. A similar trip is slated for this coming summer.

Great Teaching

The college's distinctive mission centers on preparing students for careers that will shape and eventually lead public and private institutions: to improve government, commerce, law, the media, civil society, education, the arts, and the church. The King's College does not offer students a traditional liberal arts experience, but instead offers an academic experience with a specialized curriculum focused on a philosophically and theologically informed examination of the nation's and the world's key institutions. The curriculum at King's College explores what spiritual, political, and economic freedom really involve. When asked what they are studying at college, a student at The King's College might answer, "God, money, power, and culture."

The King's College offers two degrees—the Bachelor of Arts in Politics, Philosophy, and Economics (PPE) and the Bachelor of Science in Business Management. The PPE program addresses the three subjects that examine the nature of human communities: politics, studying how we should govern ourselves; philosophy, studying what we can know through reason; and economics, studying how the community can prosper within the constraints of the material world. Students who major in PPE can choose from concentrations in media, literature, theology, and propaedeutics, a discipline that prepares students who seek to influence the field of education.

The teaching environment at King's is built around small classes, with a student to teacher ratio of fourteen to one. On average, 92 percent of full-time faculty hold terminal degrees. These faculty members bring together the rare combination of academic capability, professional experience, and a commitment to empower students. Dawn Fotopolus, one of the college's professors of business, is a great example. Professor Fotopolus, a former CitiCorp vice president and instructor at both NYU and Columbia University business schools, is known for giving rigorous finals, yet often invites students for meals at her Upper East Side apartment.

Because of its location in New York City, The King's College draws from a unique network of adjunct faculty, including Peter Kreeft, author of a textbook on Socratic logic; Gary Latainer, retired Morgan Stanley partner; Cabin Kim, CEO of Dermage; and Bret Schundler, mayor of Jersey City.

Students live and study by the college's mission, which seeks to provide a curriculum based on classical education that will provide students with understanding of politics, philosophy, economics, and commerce. With a focus on writing, speaking, and thinking critically, King's emphasizes not just regurgitating information but ensuring that students are able to make cogent, articulate arguments.

Every year, the entire campus takes part in Inter Regnum, a one-week break from classes during which the college community discusses an issue that pertains to current events.

Vibrant Community

The King's College holds classes in the Empire State Building. About 90 percent of students live in campus housing, which consists of apartments in two luxury buildings, one for men and one for women, located just steps from Macy's department store, the New York Public Library, and Madison Square Garden.

Following Harvard's model, the student body is divided into nine houses, each named after famous leaders. Students join a house as freshmen, and the house becomes their home within the college community throughout their time at King's. The house structure is the center of life and study at King's. Each house elects students to various positions and takes on responsibilities within residence life, academic performance, social life, and spiritual life. Within houses, students forge relationships that last a lifetime. Many campus events revolve around the house system, culminating in the annual House Cup, a competition based on GPA, sports contests, civic engagement, debate, and a drama presentation. The winning house is awarded a weekend away together as well as bragging rights.

King's students are committed to helping the local community, and often volunteer for blood drives, work in homeless shelters, and participate in other service opportunities. The school also hosts a campus retreat each year, outside New York City.

Successful Outcomes

An education at King's College prepares students for careers in which they will shape the future of government, commerce, law, the media, civil society, education, the arts, and the church.

The college works with students to place them in prestigious internships with organizations including Oppenheimer Funds, Goldman Sachs, ABC, ESPN, and Manhattan Mortgage. Recently, a King's student was given the opportunity to intern with the CEO of Alltel, including traveling with him in the corporate jet.

To help ensure success for each graduate, King's makes sure that each student works one-on-one with the director of career services. The career services office helps students identify their vocations, provides practical career preparation, and helps identify strategic placement opportunities, such as internships, study abroad, and jobs. Career services also assists students with everything from resume writing and interviewing to the art of the handshake. Students learn the ins and outs of professional networking, and benefit from the strong relationships the college has with employers.

"The school's vision is what first attracted me to King's, and I've been challenged each and every day by my professors and classmates to go beyond memorizing facts to applying theories and ideas to the world around me. This drive for excellence is tempered by an honest search for God's point of view on the subject at hand. I truly appreciate the concept of an education that can be applied to any future career or political endeavor."

Kristen Benz
North Manchester, IN
Class of 2010

Fast Facts

The King's College is a small 4 year Christian College. It was founded in 1938.

Web site

http:// www.tkc.edu

Location

New York, New York— located in the Empire State Building.

Student Profile

246 undergraduate students (35.8% male, 64.2% female); 35 states and territories, 19 countries; 11.8% minority, 8.1% international.

Faculty Profile

13 full-time faculty. 84.6 % hold a terminal degree in their field. 14:1 student/faculty ratio. Median class size is 15.

Residence Life

Highly residential: 90% of students live on campus.

Athletics

Club Sports (men: basketball, football, soccer, volleyball; women: basketball, soccer; coed: soccer, volleyball).

Academic Programs

Business management; politics, philosophy, & economics.

Costs and Aid

2007–2008: $29,190 comprehensive ($20,440 tuition). 98% of students receive some financial aid. Average award: $8163.

More Distinctions

• All American Colleges: Top Schools for Conservatives, Old-fashioned Liberals and People of Faith by ISI books 2006.

Utica College

NEW YORK

Utica College (UC) is a private, independent, coeducational, comprehensive, liberal-arts college. Founded by Syracuse University in 1946, UC began to grant master's degrees in 1999 and doctoral degrees in 2005.

Admissions Contact:

Utica College
1600 Burrstone Road
Utica, NY 13502
(800) 782-8884
Ph: (315) 792-3006
Fax: (315) 792-3003
Email: admiss@utica.edu
www.utica.edu

The 4 Distinctions

Engaged Students

UC offers thirty-two majors, twenty-six minors, and more than sixty areas of study. The most popular majors are business administration and management, criminal justice, and health services/allied health. Other unique programs include economic crime investigation, psychology-child life, and public relations. The college is also known for its highly competitive graduate programs in occupational and physical therapy.

Nearly 80 percent of UC students participate in work-study programs on and off campus. On-campus work-study opportunities are offered in a variety of offices, including admissions, athletics, financial aid, and maintenance. Off-campus work-study opportunities include tutoring at local middle and high schools.

Internship possibilities unique to the Utica area include working at Zogby International, Utica National Insurance, Rome Labs, Oneida Research, St. Elizabeth's Hospital, the Rome Police Department, and the New York State Attorney General's Office. UC students also study abroad, and can choose from programs in England, Ireland, Italy, Japan, Spain, Hong Kong, Poland, Finland, Hungary, Peru, Scotland, and Wales.

Great Teaching

UC uses a "foundation of values" to guide its decisions and actions. These include commitments to individual attention for students; lifelong learning; pragmatic approaches to teaching and learning; continual improvement in educational quality; diversity of perspective, background, and experience for education in an increasingly global society; and community and professional service. UC is dedicated to the highest ethical standards and integrity; freedom of expression and open sharing of ideas and creativity; open, honest, and collegial communication; and the well-being of others.

UC's low student to faculty ratio of seventeen to one, and small average class size of twenty-two enable students to develop strong relationships with faculty members. The college offers students a first-year seminar to help freshmen successfully transition to college. Students benefit from the faculty's strong commitment to quality teaching and to providing individual attention to their students. Nearly 89 percent of UC's faculty hold terminal degrees.

UC students often perform research, working closely with their professors. A sampling of recent research projects in biology includes a study of redback salamanders, an analysis of the growth of pond snails, and a report on squirrel tree frog communication.

UC's new science and technology facility, F. Eugene Romano Hall, provides classroom, laboratory, and clinical space, as well as modern technology for the health sciences. Utica College just broke ground on the Center for Identity Management and Information Protection (CMIP) building, and is an exciting new addition to the science and technology complex that will foster research on critical issues of the digital age. UC recently accepted its first students in the new cybersecurity and information assurance undergraduate major.

Vibrant Community

UC's 128-acre campus is within the city of Utica, the socioeconomic hub of the Mohawk Valley, just south of the state's Adirondack Park. Located on the Erie Canal, Utica is fifty-five miles east of Syracuse and ninety-five miles northwest of Albany.

UC has a diverse student body and offers a range of housing options. More than one third of the student body is from Utica other Mohawk Valley communities; the majority of the rest of UC students come from New York, New England, and the Middle Atlantic states. There are more than eighty on-campus clubs and organizations, including four fraternities and four sororities. UC has 21 Division III sports teams, and has recently nearly doubled the size of its Harold T. Clark Jr. Athletic Center's fitness center. A variety of cultural and entertainment activities occur on campus, including lectures, concerts, comedians, and drama productions.

The city of Utica and the surrounding Mohawk Valley provide many social, cultural, and recreational activities.

With a multicultural population of three hundred thousand, there are many restaurants, stores, and activities with easy access for UC students. There are also a variety of ways for students to become involved in the community, especially through programs UC has launched with local school districts and businesses to promote scholarship, such as the Young Scholars Liberty Partnerships Program, America Reads and America Counts challenges, and Project SHINE.

Successful Outcomes

UC alumni can be found in a variety of jobs, ranging from financial services to multinational corporations to nonprofits and government work. The career services office helps students and alumni with resume reviews, job leads, and mock interviews. UC students and alumni are encouraged to expand their learning beyond the classroom and the workplace in an effort to stay current in today's ever-changing global environment.

"Utica offers students a unique opportunity to become fully engaged in their education. Through a practical approach to mixing liberal arts with professional studies, Utica students emerge well prepared to handle the world in front of them."

-Colleges of Distinction

Fast Facts

Utica College is a comprehensive, independent, private institution founded in 1946 by Syracuse University.

Web site

www.utica.edu

Location

Largely residential section of west Utica, in the heart of central New York.

Student Profile

2,429 students; 26 states, 46 countries.

Faculty Profile

123 full-time faculty. 89% have earned their Ph.D. or the highest degree in their field. 17:1 student/faculty ratio. Average class size is 20.

Residence Life

Moderately residential: 41% of students live on campus. 7 residence halls.

Athletics

NCAA Division III, Empire 8 and Eastern College Athletic Conference (ECAC). 21 varsity sports (9 men's: baseball, basketball, cross-country, football, ice hockey, lacrosse, soccer, swimming & diving, tennis; 11 women's: basketball, cross-country, field hockey, ice hockey, lacrosse, soccer, softball, swimming & diving, tennis, volleyball, water polo; 1 coed: golf), 5 club sports, and 14 intramurals.

Academics

Accounting; accounting CPA; biology; business; business economics; chemistry; child life; communication; communication arts; computer science; criminal justice; criminal justice- economic crime investigation; cybersecurity & information assurance; economics; education; English; foreign language; government & politics; health studies (human behavior, management); history; international studies; journalism studies; liberal studies; management; mathematics; nursing; occupational therapy; philosophy; physical therapy; physics; psychology; preengineering; psychology-child life; public relations; sociology & anthropology; teacher education; therapeutic recreation.

Costs and Aid

2007–2008: $24,264 tuition. 90% of students receive financial aid.

More Distinctions

• UC has earned top-tier rankings in US News & World Report's America's Best Colleges.

Wagner College

NEW YORK

Admissions Contact:

Wagner College
One Campus Road
Staten Island, NY 10301
(800) 221-1010
Ph: (718) 390-3411
Email: admissions@wagner.edu
www.wagner.edu

Wagner College is situated on a hilltop overlooking the Manhattan skyline. Wagner's enduring bond with New York City allows for unmatched opportunities for experiential learning and interdisciplinary education. The heart of New York City is Wagner's laboratory.

The 4 Distinctions

Engaged Students

To prepare its graduates for a complex and interdependent world, Wagner links learning with practice, an educational approach clearly defined in the college's innovative Wagner Plan. Wagner provides students with the best of both worlds—an idyllic, small-town college campus, surrounded by a bustling city full of opportunity.

Internships, cooperative work, and service learning are a major focus of the curriculum at Wagner College. Beginning in their very first semester, students not only study issues and learn critical thinking, writing, and problem-solving skills, but they also have plenty of opportunities to put what they're learning into practice. Field experience is intrinsically linked to the subject matter of the freshman learning community. Recent projects have provided students with opportunities to work at the Museum for African Art, Ellis Island, the American Stock Exchange, and the Egger Nursing Home.

As one of only a handful of institutions recognized by Project Pericles as truly dedicated to service learning and engaged citizenry, Wagner College takes very seriously its role in developing the leaders of the new millennium. A centralized body on campus oversees the various leadership development and service-oriented initiatives, allowing for pervasive student involvement.

By partnering with the Institute for the International Education of Students, Wagner offers study-abroad programs in over twenty-two cities throughout the world. Often, students choose to combine an internship with their term abroad and make even greater connections between cultures. Wagner College also sponsors an exchange program with California Lutheran University.

Great Teaching

Since 1998, the Wagner Plan has redefined and reenergized the curriculum at Wagner. The freshman experience involves a three-class Learning Community (LC) with the same group of twenty-four students, as well as a thirty-hour field-study requirement. An additional LC takes place during the intermediate years, and a senior capstone LC cements the practical liberal arts program.

The Reflective Tutorial portion of the Wagner Plan illustrates the dedication Wagner faculty have to discussion-based, interactive learning. Each small tutorial group emphasizes writing skills and discussion. In these groups, students link their field experiences directly to the course readings in all three LC courses. With the direct link between field experience and course work, students practice applied learning and examine abstract ideas in light of real-world experience.

The faculty at Wagner are committed to the collaborative teaching aspect of the Wagner Plan. Each LC is taught in tandem, bringing together varied disciplines in innovative and enlightening ways. Topics such as *Sense and Nonsense in Science* bring together biology and psychology; *two lost worlds* connects anthropology and philosophy; and *Creativity and Conflict in Modern Times* links art and history.

Vibrant Community

Wagner's proximity to Manhattan enriches not only the educational potential of Wagner, but the social life, as well. With shuttles running to the ferry nearly 24 hours a day, students have easy access to all of the cultural opportunities the Big Apple has to offer. Students find that shopping, eating out in the Village, and visiting museums, the theater, and Central Park quickly become comfortable ways to spend their weekends.

With Wagner's state-of-the-art sports and recreation center it's easy for Wagner students to stay physically fit and participate in the twenty varsity teams and numerous intramural and club sports. The ninety-five-thousand-square-foot Spiro Center houses a fitness center, aerobics room, dance studio, and free weight training facility, as well as a basketball arena and a six-lane pool used both competitively and recreationally by the entire campus community.

On campus, students find a wealth of opportunities for excitement. Students can head down to Sutter Oval after dark and catch one of the popular outdoor movies on the big screen, or take part in educational and social events sponsored by the academic and cultural enrichment program, such as political discussions and environmental debates.

Successful Outcomes

Wagner College places great importance on life after Wagner, whether that takes the form of an entry-level position or admission to graduate school. On average, 28 percent of Wagner graduates choose to attend graduate school directly after college, at such prestigious universities as Yale, Princeton, NYU, and the University of Pennsylvania.

With an active Center for Career Development, Wagner students are privy to a host of information and valuable connections throughout the city and across the country. Wagner students can take advantage of a number of career development services, including an internship database of over six hundred employers, an online resume exchange, and mock interviews.

JPMorgan Chase, Goldman Sachs, Salomon Smith Barney, Credit Suisse, Bank of New York, Pfizer, Zenith Media, *The Late Show with David Letterman*, New Line Cinema, MSNBC, and AOL Time Warner are a few of the names participating in events at Wagner like career fairs, on-campus interviews, career workshops, and employer information sessions for interested students. Wagner's tight-knit association of alumni and friends of the college take an active interest in the success of future graduates.

Wagner College students have interned at the following organizations:

JPMorgan Chase, Roundabout Theatre Company, Universal Motown Records, New Line Cinema, Madison Square Garden, As the World Turns, CBS Network, Paul Taylor Dance Company, NYC Public Schools, NY Mercantile Exchange, US Secret Service, Department of Investigations, Division of Special Narcotics, and Johnson & Johnson.

Wagner graduates have located employment at the following organizations:

Bank of New York, Bellevue Hospital, Children's Aid Society, Columbia Presbytarian, Deloitte & Touche, LLP, L-Sea Transportation Inc., Marvel Entertainment, Hapag-Lloyd, Petry Media, Staten Island University Hospital, Shiseido Cosmetics, Sony Pictures/TV, Random House, US Department of Defense, Viacom International, The CollegeBound Network, The Grand Long Beach Event Center, and Walnut Street Theatre.

Internships that resulted in full-time jobs:

Nike Communications, Merrill Lynch, Citigroup, NJ Devils, Saatchi & Saatchi (now known as Zenith Media), Enterprise Rent-A-Car, Fastenal Company, Cosmopolitan Magazine, Morgan Stanley, and MTV Networks.

Fast Facts

Wagner College is a four-year, liberal arts college, affiliated with the Lutheran Church and founded in 1883.

Website

http://www.wagner.edu

Location

Staten Island, New York—one of the five boroughs of New York City.

Student Profile

1,929 undergraduate students (60% female, 40% male); 39 states, 13 countries; 14% minority, 1% international.

Faculty Profile

100 full-time faculty members and select adjunct faculty specialists. 13:1 student:faculty ratio. Average class size is 20.

Residence Life

Highly residential: 82.1% of students live on campus.

Athletics

NCAA Division I, Northeast Conference. 19 varsity sports (9 men's: baseball, basketball, cross-country, football (IAA), golf, lacrosse, tennis, track & field, wrestling; 10 women's: basketball, cross-country, golf, lacrosse, soccer, softball, swimming, tennis, track & field, volleyball, water polo), 1 club sport, and 5 intramurals.

Academic Programs

Accounting; anthropology; art; art history; arts administration; biology; biopsychology; business administration; chemistry; computer science; dance; drama/theater arts; economics; education; English; environmental studies; film and media; foreign languages; gender studies; German; government and politics; history; information systems; international affairs; journalism; mathematics; microbiology; music; nursing; philosophy; physician assistant; physics; prechiropractic; predentistry; preenginerring; prelaw; premedicine; preministry; preoptometry; prepharmacy; prepodiatry; preveterinary sciences; psychology; public policy & administration; religious studies.

Costs and Aid

2007–2008: $38,300 comprehensive ($29,400 tuition). 70% of students receive aid. Average freshman award is between $7,500 and $9,500.

Endowment

$21 million.

More Distinctions

• Wagner received the 2005 TIAA-CREF Theodore M. Hesburgh Award, which recognizes exceptional academic programs designed to enhance undergraduate teaching and learning.

• Wagner College is consistently ranked nationally in "Programs to Look For" by *U.S. News and World Report's America's Best Colleges* annual guide.

• *The Princeton Review* continues to cite Wagner College in their top 10 most beautiful campuses.

Bryant University

RHODE ISLAND

Bryant University is a private, coeducational university founded in 1863. Bryant prepares graduates for success in their personal and professional lives by offering challenging academic programs, a culturally enriching campus life, professional experiences, a curriculum including advanced technology, and a global perspective in course work and extracurricular activities.

Admissions Contact:

Bryant University
1150 Douglas Pike
Smithfield, RI 02917
(800) 622-7001
Ph: (401) 232-6100
Email: admission@bryant.edu
www.bryant.edu

The 4 Distinctions

Engaged Students

Bryant is committed to providing students with a balanced educational experience. Students with majors in the College of Business are required to choose a minor from the College of Arts and Sciences, and vice versa. This integration of business and liberal arts creates partnerships among disciplines and broadens students' career options after graduation.

Bryant students explore the world beyond the classroom by pursuing active internships and participating in study-abroad programs.

Internships at organizations such as Fidelity Investments (a financial services company located across the street from Bryant's campus), Walt Disney World, PricewaterhouseCoopers, the New England Patriots, Textron, media outlets, and a variety of nonprofit organizations give students practical, hands-on work experience. Entrepreneurial students can even develop their own businesses on campus. An example is the student-founded, on-campus, door-to-door laundry service.

Bryant also encourages all students to have a passport and to use it before they graduate. Study-abroad programs in forty-one foreign countries are available to qualified students, and can encompass a semester, a summer, or a full academic year. These programs give students a better understanding of world issues and make Bryant graduates more attractive as prospective employees in the marketplace.

Bryant has two unique international-study programs: the Sophomore International Experience and the Bryant-Lingan Summer Student Exchange. The Sophomore International Experience allows students to spend two weeks overseas, learning about other cultures and how businesses operate globally. Recent itineraries have taken Bryant students and faculty to Italy, Russia, China, Panama, and Ecuador.

The joint academic-exchange program between Bryant and Lingnan College of Sun Yat-sen University, China, is aimed at promoting cross-cultural cooperation and scholarly exchanges between students and faculty of the two universities. Overseen by the U.S.-China Institute at Bryant, the program's activities emphasize strength in language and academic training while promoting social and cultural understanding. Students participate in focused research projects and hands-on site visits, as well as in more traditional academic learning experiences.

Great Teaching

Bryant offers more than twenty major and twenty-four minor areas of study, encompassing the liberal arts, sciences, and business-related fields. The most popular areas of study are marketing, accounting, management, and finance. The academic programs focus on the intellectual and professional development of each student, preparing them for leadership positions in a wide range of careers. All students complete a core curriculum that integrates business and liberal arts, utilizing state-of-the-art technology.

The faculty is highly qualified: 98.5 percent of Bryant's full-time faculty hold PhD's or have earned the highest degree in their field of expertise. They continuously engage in research, publishing, consulting, community service, and practical experience. With a sixteen to one student to faculty ratio, each student can develop relationships with faculty members for guidance and support. Among the faculty members at Bryant are a practicing clinical psychologist, a nationally respected expert in advertising effectiveness and public policy, and the former poet laureate emeritus of Rhode Island.

Foundations for Learning is a required course for freshmen, designed to help them transition successfully from high school to college, preparing them for academic and social success. The classes are small and are taught by tenured and tenure-track faculty, as well as by administrators, including Bryant's president, Ronald K. Machtley.

Vibrant Community

Bryant is a student-centered university, and more than 83 percent of its three thousand-plus students live on campus, leading to important friendships and mentorships. Most students spend freshman year in the dorms, sophomore and junior years in suites, and senior year in on-campus townhouses. All Bryant housing facilities have been upgraded within the last four years, and new dorms and townhouses are being built. In addition to its modern facilities, Bryant's campus is 100 percent wireless, so students can send e-mails from their dorm rooms, the dining halls, the athletic fields, or while sitting in a tree.

Student life is stimulating, with seventy clubs and organizations on campus, and twenty-one NCAA Division II athletic teams. Intramural and club sports offer opportunities for all Bryant students to participate in athletics.

Bryant's 420-acre campus is about fifteen minutes from Providence, Rhode Island, forty-five minutes southwest of Boston, Massachusetts, and three hours from New York City. Providence, known as the Renaissance City, is the state capital, a transportation hub, and home to a robust cultural scene, as well as to the Roger Williams Park Zoo. Providence's 175,000 residents enjoy urban amenities typical of a city of this size, including a variety of restaurants, theaters, and shopping venues.

Successful Outcomes

Success means something different to everyone, but there are some things all Bryant students have in common. They are innovative thinkers and problem solvers, who come to Bryant with the drive to achieve their goals and graduate inspired and well prepared to do extraordinary things. Statistics support this assertion: within six months of graduation, 98.5 percent of Bryant's May 2006 graduates surveyed were employed or had entered graduate school.

Bryant University has experienced recent growth, building on its academic success, its student-centered approach to learning, its commitment to excellence within technology, its focus on the individual, and its diverse international community.

Whether in the classroom, on the playing field, or the business world, Bryant offers the tools for success. We graduate with confidence knowing that we are prepared to compete in any situation put before us.

- Shaun Leddy '07

Fast Facts

Bryant University is a four-year, private, business and liberal arts university founded in 1863.

Web site

http://www.bryant.edu/

Location

Smithfield, Rhode Island.

Student Profile

3,200 students (54% male, 46% female); 31 states and territories, 32 countries.

Faculty Profile

148 full-time faculty. 16:1 student/faculty ratio. Average class size is 25–30.

Residence Life

Highly residential: 83% of students live on campus.

Athletics

NCAA Division II, Northeast-10 Conference, Eastern College Athletic Conference. 20 varsity sports (10 men's; 10 women's), 12 club sports, and 10 intramural sports.

Academic programs

Actuarial mathematics; applied economics; applied psychology; business administration (concentrations in accounting, accounting information systems, computer information systems, finance, financial services, management, marketing communication); global studies; history; information technology; international business; literary & cultural studies; politics & law, sociology.

Costs and Aid

2007–2008: $40,954 comprehensive ($27,639 tuition). 68% of students receive some financial aid. Average award: $10,446.

Endowment

$167 million.

More Distinctions

• Listed as one of the top twenty universities in U.S. News & World Report's Master's in the North category.

• Listed in Barron's Best Buys in College Education.

• Listed in the Princeton Review's "Best 361 Colleges in America."

Providence College

RHODE ISLAND

Admissions Contact:

Providence College
549 River Avenue
Providence, Rhode Island 02918-0001
(800) 721-6444
Email: pcadmiss@providence.edu
www.providence.edu

Providence College (PC) is a Catholic liberal arts institution founded in 1917 by the Dominican order. Providence is the only institution in the United States administered by the Dominican Friars, who have a tradition of cultivating intellectual, spiritual, ethical, and aesthetic values in the context of a Judeo-Christian heritage.

The 4 Distinctions

Engaged Students

Providence students have a tradition of academic achievement: 45 percent of PC's incoming freshmen ranked in the top 10 percent of their class, and 83 percent were in the top 25 percent of their class; the middle 50 percent for SAT scores is 530–630 for critical reading, 550–650 for math, and 540–650 for writing; the middle 50 percent for ACT scores is 23–28.

Providence College provides both curricular and cocurricular service-learning outreach to the community. Through the Feinstein Institute for Public Service, Providence College students currently provide outreach to thirty-five different community organizations. Service learning has also been incorporated into academic disciplines, including education, military science, social work, and political science. In 1996, Providence College became the first institution to offer an undergraduate degree in public and community-service studies.

Over two thousand Providence College students engage in a vast array of voluntary community-service activities each year through campus ministry and numerous other campus groups, including service in local affiliates of Habitat for Humanity and Special Olympics, as well as visiting the elderly, cheering hospitalized children, and tutoring in Providence schools.

Students also teach literacy and English as a second language to adults, work in area soup kitchens and with Meals on Wheels, prepare Thanksgiving food baskets, support HIV/AIDS ministries, beautify the neighborhood, work to improve race relations, protest domestic violence, and work to protect the environment.

The study-abroad options are designed to augment the liberal arts perspective of Providence College. Programs include Africa, Asia, Australia and New Zealand, Central and Latin America, Europe and Russia.

The Washington, DC Semester Program combines academic study and experiential learning in a one-semester program spent at American University in Washington, DC.

In any one of a dozen areas of study, the program consists of a two-course seminar that features academic professors and professional policy makers; a one-course research project served by the excellent libraries of Washington, DC; and practical work experience in a one-course, two-day-per-week internship.

Great Teaching

Teaching is the primary focus of Providence College faculty—the school does not have any teaching assistants or graduate students teaching classes. Providence College students engage in original research and scholarship projects with the faculty in fields ranging from political science to bioinformatics. The results are often published in academic journals or presented at national conferences.

Providence College faculty members keep their office doors open, respond to e-mails late at night, and know details about their students' lives. From discussions in the cafeteria to invitations for dinner in their homes, to advice about graduate programs and careers, professors reach out to students, inside and outside of class.

The Development of the Western Civilization Program, or CIV, is the cornerstone of the Providence College core curriculum. Students take the required two-year interdisciplinary program during their freshman and sophomore years.

Western Civilization covers the areas of history, philosophy, literature, theology, and the fine arts from ancient Mesopotamia to modern times. It is team taught by four faculty members from each of these disciplines, who share their thoughts and perspective on the events, art, literature, philosophy, and religious ideals of the time. The program provides the foundation for undergraduate study and each student's pursuit of one of the college's forty-nine majors.

The Liberal Arts Honors Program offers students with exceptional academic achievement and initiative a more in-depth and rigorous version of the Providence College core curriculum. Students are required to take a minimum of six honors courses throughout their stay, with a capstone colloquium in the senior year.

Vibrant Community

Providence College's 105-acre campus is located within two miles of the heart of Rhode Island's capital city. The intimacy of the campus—with everything and everyone just a short walk away—enables students to enjoy a private, tranquil oasis for living and learning, with a vibrant city just minutes away.

Providence is home to an engaging blend of arts, culture, entertainment, and shopping—a city that has been nationally recognized for its urban renaissance. One of America's first cities, Providence is rich in history, culture, and tradition, and today enjoys a reputation as one of America's most desirable cities. Students can ride the RIPTA buses or trolleys for free to any location in Rhode Island.

In the last decade, the college has focused campus infrastructure improvements on enhancing its academic, residential, and spiritual facilities through the addition of buildings such as the Smith Center for the Arts, Suites Hall, St. Dominic Chapel, and the Concannon Fitness Center. On-campus living includes nine traditional halls, five apartment buildings, and a new suite-style residence completed in 2004.

The Office of Student Activities Involvement Leadership—known as the SAIL Office—works closely with the Board of Programers, the student organization that plans activities to meet the social, cultural, educational, and recreational interests of students. It also sponsors the college's leadership program, provides support to over sixty recognized student organizations, and coordinates the two-day summer orientation program for all new students. SAIL manages McPhail's entertainment facility, which is open seven days a week and hosts events throughout the academic year. In addition, the SAIL staff oversee operations in the Slavin Center, the College's student union.

Providence College also competes in nineteen Division I sports and supports student participation in intramural and club sports, including martial arts, sailing, rugby, snowboarding, basketball, and tennis.

Successful Outcomes

Typically, 95 percent of graduates are employed or pursuing graduate studies within six months of graduation.

The College's Office of Career Services office actively helps students throughout their time at Providence to prepare for joining the workforce. The staff maintains a database of about seven hundred internships, coordinates career shadowing and networking programs, and conducts numerous workshops to prepare students for employment or graduate school.

More than forty-five thousand Providence College alumni extend the reach of the college community to every corner of the nation and to many countries throughout the world. The ongoing support and involvement of alumni is strong, and the donor participation rate is among the highest in the country.

Fast Facts

Providence College, founded in 1917, is a four-year liberal arts college affiliated with the Dominican Order of the Roman Catholic Church.

Web site

http://www.providence.edu/

Location

Providence, RI

Student Profile

3,850 undergraduate students (43% male, 57% female); 42 states, 16 countries; 9% minority, 2% international.

Faculty Profile

295 full-time faculty. 12:1 student/faculty ratio. Average class size is 22

Residence Life

Highly residential: 92% of students live on campus.

Athletics

NCAA Division I, Big East Conference. 19 varsity sports (8 men's: basketball, cross-country, ice hockey, lacrosse, soccer, swimming/diving, track; 11 women's: basketball, cross-country, field hockey, ice hockey, soccer, softball, swimming/diving, tennis, track, volleyball), 9 club sports and 13 intramurals.

Academic Programs

Accountancy; American studies; anthropology; applied physics; art history; Asian studies; biochemistry; biology; Black studies; business studies certificate program; chemistry; classics; computer science; dance; development of western civilization; economics; elementary/special education; 3+2 engineering; English; film; finance; French; German; global studies; health policy & management; history; humanities; Italian; Latin American studies; prelaw; premedical science; liberal arts honors; linguistics; management; marketing; mathematics; military science/ROTC; music; natural science; 3+4 optometry; philosophy; political science; psychology; public administration certificate program; public & community service studies; secondary education; social science; social work; sociology; Spanish; systems science; studio art; theatre arts; theology; women's studies; writing.

Costs and Aid

2007–2008: $39,255 comprehensive ($28,920 tuition). 59% of students receive financial aid. Average award: $20,470.

Endowment

$115.3 million.

More Distinctions

• In the U.S. News America's Best Colleges - 2007 edition, PC consistently ranked in the top 2 masters level universities in the North every year since 1997

Roger Williams University

RHODE ISLAND

Founded in 1956, Roger Williams University is a four-year, independent, private, liberal arts university. Surrounded by the natural beauty of the historic Rhode Island coastline, Roger Williams offers a comprehensive and exciting education that merges academic ideals with practical career development.

Admissions Contact:

Roger Williams University
One Old Ferry Road
Bristol, RI 02809
(800) 458-7144 ext. 3500
Ph: (401) 254-3500
Email: admit@rwu.edu
www.rwu.edu

The 4 Distinctions

Engaged Students

Part of Roger Williams's mission is for students "to experience study and life abroad, to value cultural diversity, to develop ethical awareness, and to preserve intellectual curiosity throughout a lifetime." Students accomplish many of these goals through public service, experiential learning programs, and opportunities abroad.

Roger Williams's commitment to public service is one of its core values. The Feinstein Service Learning Program allows students to combine their classroom studies with meaningful public service, enriching their educational experience while helping the community in a tangible way. Students can earn their service-learning graduation requirement through a variety of local opportunities, including the semiannual University Day of Service and ongoing community-service projects.

Experiential learning programs allow students to integrate classroom theories with practical, hands-on work experiences. In the field, a student's formal education is reinforced as it is put into practice, and students return to the classroom with a more in-depth knowledge of the classroom material. Some majors at Roger Williams require students to undertake internships or co-ops, but all students are encouraged to participate, because these opportunities have become semester-long interviews and recruitment tools for employers.

Roger Williams offers students multiple study-abroad programs, including a flagship program in Florence, a theatre program in London, and programs in thirty-three other destinations around the world.

Additional special programs are offered through the various colleges in the school. For example, the Feinstein College of Arts and Sciences offers a Washington Semester; the School of Architecture, Art, and Historic Preservation offers a summer program for interested high school students; and the Gabelli School of Business offers an executive shadowing program.

Great Teaching

With over thirty-five majors, as well as five professional schools, and recently ranked in the top ten of comprehensive colleges in the north by U.S. News & World Report, Roger Williams offers students a strong liberal arts experience. Faculty at Roger Williams offer students plenty of personal attention by providing academic support in the classroom and opportunities to collaborate on research.

Roger Williams requires students to participate in the core curriculum, which is designed to help students build a solid foundation needed for lifelong adaptability, professional success, and personal fulfillment. Students gain a breadth of knowledge and experience, a deep understanding of an area they feel passionate about, and the ability to make connections and recognize the unity of knowledge. Over the course of four years, all students take five unique interdisciplinary courses, select a core concentration that they are passionate about, study on campus or in a foreign country, and finally choose a topical seminar that challenges students to synthesize all of their learning experiences.

The honors program is designed for outstanding students at the university, and provides challenging academic courses, research, and service opportunities designed to meet the aspirations of highly motivated students. Candidates who accept the invitation into the program receive either a dean's or a presidential scholarship. Students work closely with faculty to develop an in-depth course of study that will prepare students for a challenging senior research project.

Vibrant Community

There are many clubs and organizations to get involved with on campus. Students can promote diversity through the Multicultural Student Union; become politically involved through the Model United Nations; or get in shape by joining the cycling club. The Campus Entertainment Network is a student-run organization dedicated to bringing quality entertainment to the Roger William campus. In the past, the network has brought performers and speakers such as Third Eye Blind, Fuel, Tone-Loc, Busta Rhymes, Dr. Drew, the Sugarhill Gang, and Guster to campus. Students can participate in the eighteen varsity sports programs at Roger Williams, as well as club sports programs, including cheerleading, men's volleyball, crew, track and field, and rugby.

The town of Bristol is a quaint seaport community surrounded by the waters of the Mt. Hope and Narragansett bays. Outdoor activities are plentiful—students can sail, windsurf, take a jog, or a bike ride along the fourteen-mile East Bay Bike Path; relax on the beach; or just spend time shopping in the town's center. Bristol is located just twenty minutes from Providence or Newport, one hour from Boston, and four hours from New York City.

Successful Outcomes

Roger Williams students find that productive academic careers lead to fulfilling lives. Within six months of graduation, 94 percent of the recent graduating class had received full-time job offers. The Roger Williams University career center is committed to preparing students and alumni for life after college by helping individuals to understand their personal and professional values and interests and to acquire the skills necessary to obtain professional employment or admission into graduate school. Career center staff provide ongoing educational opportunities for students and alumni to learn to manage their careers. Career center professionals are dedicated to the pursuit of excellence in teaching, advising, and role modeling.

Recently, alumni Jason Pedicone, valedictorian of the class of 2004 and president of that class for two years, became the university's first Fulbright Scholar.

"Beginning on a beautiful coastline campus, Roger Williams' students build a bridge towards their future; armed with abundant tools, skills, and mentors to assist them."

-Colleges of Distinction

Fast Facts

Roger Williams University is a four-year, private, liberal arts, independent university founded in 1956.

Web site

http://www.rwu.edu/

Location

Bristol, RI

Student Profile

3,775 students (48% male, 52% female); 42 states, 41 countries; 5% minority, 3% international.

Faculty Profile

200 full-time faculty. 16:1 student/faculty ratio. Average class size is 21.

Residence Life

81% of students live on campus.

Athletics

NCAA Division III, Commonwealth Coast Conference. 19 varsity sports (9 men's: cross-country, sailing, soccer, basketball, swimming & diving, wrestling, baseball, lacrosse, tennis; 10 women's: cross-country, equestrian, tennis, volleyball, soccer, sailing, basketball, swimming & diving, lacrosse, softball), 5 club sports, 7 intramurals.

Academic Programs

Accounting; American studies; architecture; anthropology/sociology; art & architectural history; biology; business management; chemistry; communications; computer information services; computer science; construction management; creative writing; criminal justice; dance /performance studies; economics; elementary education; engineering; English literature; environmental science; financial services; foreign language (modern language); graphic design communication; history; historic preservation; international business; legal studies; marine biology; marketing; mathematics; philosophy; political science; psychology; secondary education; theatre; visual arts studies.

Costs and Aid

2007-2008: $23,040 tuition. 79% of enrolled students receive some financial aid. Average award is $18,000.

Endowment

$45,200,200.

More Distinctions

• *US News & World Report* has chosen Roger Williams as a top tier comprehensive, private, liberal arts college within their region for three consecutive years.

• Roger Williams is home to Rhode Island's only law school.

Salve Regina University

RHODE ISLAND

Admissions Contact:

Salve Regina University
100 Ochre Point Avenue
Newport, RI 02840
(888) GO-SALVE
Ph: (401) 341-2908
Email: sruadmis@salve.edu
www.explore.salve.edu

The liberal arts and professional programs at Salve Regina University teach students to think clearly and creatively, enhance their capacity for sound judgment, and prepare students for the challenge of learning throughout their lives.

The 4 Distinctions

Engaged Students

Salve Regina students are encouraged to become involved in the community and campus life and to pursue their future interests through internships and study abroad. Salve Regina encourages students to study abroad during their college experience to develop skills that can prepare them to work and live in an interdependent world. Possibilities include study in Italy, Greece, Australia, Mexico, London, Japan, Spain, France, or Ireland; a semester in Washington, DC; or a sea semester, during which students study at the Woods Hole Oceanographic Institution.

Community service at Salve Regina is more than just an activity; it is a way of life. Students may participate in a number of volunteer opportunities exist, such as the Feed-A-Friend food drive, Big Brothers of Rhode Island, the Positive Role Model Program, the Christian Appalachian Project, and the Special Olympics. Locally, Salve volunteers support the Dr. Martin Luther King, Jr. Center, the Potter League, the Salvation Army, area soup kitchens, literary projects, and Newport-area schools. As part of the Feinstein Enriching America Program, all students must complete ten hours of community service as a graduation requirement.

Salve Regina has developed a special program to help freshmen make new friends and get off to a great start both in and out of the classroom. Salve Regina freshmen live in one of two large, modern residence communities, where they meet many of their classmates. The residential life staff conduct a variety of programming activities in the first-year halls to help students adjust to college life.

Great Teaching

Salve Regina faculty have designed an exciting and innovative new core curriculum to provide a common academic foundation for students. Over four years, students take a sequence of courses designed to help them see and integrate connections among various subject areas. The theme of the Salve Regina core curriculum is developing lifelong learners and responsible citizens of the world.

First-year students at Salve Regina University are beginning a journey toward a lifetime of learning and responsible citizenship in a global context. The portal course, Seeking Wisdom: From Wonder to Justice, helps begin that journey, one which requires both liberal arts skills and a commitment to explore perennial moral and spiritual questions faced by humanity. This course is followed by Living Wisdom, a capstone core course for seniors that revisits the themes of the core curriculum.

Salve Regina's Pell Scholars Honors Program is unique given its connection with the Pell Center for International Relations and Public Policy. The Center was established at Salve Regina by the US Congress to honor Senator Pell. The Center offers programs and conferences to enhance international dialogue. Recent speakers have included Senators, journalists, Ambassadors and other notable figures such as General Romeo Dallaire and the Dalai Lama. Pell Scholars work on their honors thesis at the Pell Center and most lectures are open to all students at Salve Regina.

Vibrant Community

At Salve Regina, student activities are, for the most part, student-run activities. This makes it very easy for students to kick back, relax, and have fun meeting new people while getting involved in activities that interest them. Options include joining the multicultural organization, the dance company, the Model United Nations, or the surfing club. The campus activities board is open for any student to join and help to plan the campus social calendar. Committees include comedy, concerts, special events, outdoor adventure, and travel.

Newport is one of America's most popular tourist destinations. With mansions, the Tennis Hall of Fame, the Cliff Walk, the Jazz Festival, Ocean Drive, and a number of shops and restaurants on the harbor, the town's popularity is no surprise. Salve Regina students especially enjoy Newport in the fall and spring, when the city by the sea hosts a variety of festivals and events.

Many Salve students comment on the unity of the school—the feeling that the student body is "like a large family. Everyone is friendly and charitable." Students report that the majority of undergraduates are "very open to making friends" and "tend to live good Christian lives," which includes being "loving and caring and people you can trust." The small population makes for a situation where "you basically know everyone" and "there is no real sense of who is a senior and who is a freshman."

Students don't have to be a varsity athlete to get involved in Salve Regina athletics. They can enjoy intramurals, take a recreation or physical education class, or cheer on teams at a game. The Rodgers Recreation Center includes a five-thousand-square-foot weight room with free weights and the latest cardio and Nautilus machines. A full range of recreation classes are offered, ranging from Pilates and yoga to aerobics, kickboxing, and weight training.

Successful Outcomes

As a result of the university's core curriculum, Salve Regina graduates leave campus ready to be responsible world citizens. They understand and appreciate the diversity of the one human family that extends across the globe. They are concerned about major issues, whether local, regional, national, or global, and stay informed about them in order to debate them intelligently. They aspire to continue learning throughout their lives.

The Career Development Center has implemented a four-year guide to career success that students may use to help ensure career satisfaction and success. During their four years at Salve Regina University, students are encouraged to be proactive in career planning, and to utilize the services of the center. Career planning begins during the freshman year and continues throughout a student's academic life.

The university plays an active role in preparing students for the job market. Available services include career counseling; testing; work-study opportunities; complete résumé service; on- and off-campus job fairs; job shadowing opportunities; on-campus recruiting; four one-credit career and life planning courses; and assistance with internships, employment leads for full- and part-time work, Internet and company research information, transportation to job fairs, interviewing techniques, and graduate school searches.

Salve Regina University's latest alumni survey reports that 99% of respondents are either employed or attending graduate school. Graduate Schools include: Boston College, Boston University, Catholic Theological Union, Columbia University, Emerson College, Harvard University Kennedy School of Government, New England School of Law, Providence College, Roger Williams University School of Law, Sacred Heart University, Salve Regina University, Simmons College, University of Connecticut, University of Masachusetts, Boston, University of New Hampshire, University of Pennsylvania, and University of Texas Austin. Salve Regina's latest graduates are employed by well known firms that include: Beth Israel Deaconess Medical Center, Boston Red Sox, Ernst & Young, Genzyme Corporation, Golf Digest, Internal Revenue Service, KPMG, Massachusetts General Hospital, MEDITECH, New England Center for Children, Peace Corps, Progressive Insurance, Reebok International, Walt Disney Feature Film Productions, Women and Infants Hospital, Yale New Haven Hospital, and numerous public and parochial school systems throughout the country.

Fast Facts

Salve Regina University is a coeducational, private liberal arts college offering undergraduate and graduate degrees.

Web site

explore.salve.edu

Location

Newport, Rhode Island—30 minutes from Providence, 1 ½ hours from Boston.

Student Profile

2,100 undergraduate students (35% male, 65% female); 30 states, 12 countries; 7% minority, 1% international.

Faculty Profile

121 full-time faculty. 13:1 student/faculty ratio. Average class size is 19.

Residence Life

60% of the undergraduate student body lives on campus. Freshman and sophomores are required to live on campus.

Athletics

NCAA Division III, ECAC, CCC, and NEFC Conferences. 19 varsity sports (9 men's: baseball, basketball, cross-country, football, ice hockey, lacrosse, sailing, soccer, tennis; 10 women's: basketball, cross-country, field hockey, ice hockey, lacrosse, sailing, softball, tennis, track & field, volleyball), 12 club sports, and 7 intramurals.

Academic Programs:

Accounting; American/United States studies/civilization; art history; criticism & conservation; biology teacher education; biology/biological sciences; general; business administration/management; chemistry; clinical laboratory science/medical technology/technologist; communications & media studies; criminal justice/law enforcement administration; drama & dance teacher education; drama & dramatics/theatre arts; early childhood education & teaching; economics; elementary education & teaching; English language & literature; English/language arts teacher education; fine/studio arts; French language & literature; French language teacher education; historic preservation & conservation; history teacher education; history; information science/studies; international studies; liberal arts & sciences/liberal studies; mathematics teacher education; mathematics; music history, literature, & theory; music teacher education; nursing (registered nurse training: RN, ASN, BSN, MSN); philosophy, political science, & government; psychology; religion/religious studies; secondary education & teaching; social work; sociology; Spanish language & literature; Spanish language teacher education; special education.

Costs and Aid

2007–2008: $39,400 comprehensive ($26,750 tuition: includes a one time required laptop fee); 75% of students receive some financial aid. Average award: $18,616.

Endowment

$40 million.

More Distinctions

• Salve Regina University is one of 50 institutions in the country and the only in Rhode Island selected as a charter member of the Association of American Colleges and Universities' national campaign to advocate the value of quality liberal education.

Green Mountain College

VERMONT

Green Mountain College (GMC), founded in 1834, is a small, liberal arts school with a focus on environmental awareness and an emphasis on social consciousness. Members of the close-knit Green Mountain College community share a passion for making the world a better place in which to live, learn, and work.

Admissions Contact:

Green Mountain College
One College Circle
Poultney, Vermont 05764
(800) 776-6675
Fax: (802) 287-8099
Email: admiss@greenmtn.edu
admissions.greenmtn.edu

The 4 Distinctions

Engaged Students

The most popular majors at GMC are environmental studies, adventure recreation, business, psychology, and a three-year, hands-on program in resort and hospitality management. Students also have the option of completing an adventure recreation certification track, which is designed to allow students with a particular interest or focused career goal to seek appropriate levels of certification and obtain college credit with the American Canoe Association, the Association for Challenge Course Technology, the Professional Association of Diving Instructors, the American Mountain Guides Association, the Professional Ski Instructors of America, or the American Association of Snowboard Instructors. The college is also a credit-bearing institution for the National Outdoor Leadership School, which permits students to obtain credit for attendance while remaining enrolled at GMC. The college is an affiliate institution of the National Ski Patrol System and the Association for Experiential Education. Students may transfer credit for Outward Bound, National Outdoor Leadership School, and Wilderness Education Association courses completed for college credit from other institutions.

Exciting work-study and undergraduate research positions are available for GMC students. Students at GMC have many opportunities to study abroad at sister schools, through sponsored travel courses, or through other approved study-abroad programs. GMC has sister-school exchange programs with Hannam University in Daejeon, South Korea and the University of Wales in Aberystwyth, and both programs are popular with students. Shorter trips abroad for several weeks are also popular. GMC is a founding member of the Eco League, through which students may take a semester at any one of five environmentally focused colleges from Alaska to the Atlantic. Recent destinations through this program include New Zealand, Brazil, Italy, China, Wales, and Hawaii.

50 percent of GMC classes engage students in service learning. In one year, GMC students performed 5,829 hours of community service.

Great Teaching

Students find the professors at Green Mountain College to be accessible, as most live in the surrounding community and often eat in the campus dining hall. Among the teaching staff, Green Mountain has one Fulbright scholar, and 91 percent of faculty members have doctorates or terminal degrees. Classes are never larger than thirty-five students, and average about ninteen.

Among GMC's notable faculty members are Professor Jim Harding, who teaches natural resources management, was recently elected secretary of the Green Mountain division of the Society of American Foresters, an organization devoted to advancing the business of forestry in the state of Vermont. As a result, Harding serves on this organization's executive committee. Professor Jennifer Baker, who teaches arts and sciences, recently spent a week at the University of Oklahoma to participate in a workshop for facial reconstruction sculpture. Often referred to as forensic sculpture, this process employs facial reconstruction on a skull for forensic identification, but facial reconstruction also has museum, portrait sculpture, and law enforcement applications. Professor Steven Fesmire, who teaches philosophy and environmental studies, recently traveled to Unity, Maine to give the keynote address for Unity College's Inspired Speaker Series.

Green Mountain's faculty are as engaged in the curriculum as they are with the community, often starting new programs for students, such as the Asian studies and religious studies programs. One new special academic program is the campus farm, which is truly a part of the campus life in every sense. Students special order omelets in the dining hall made with eggs from Green Mountain's mobile chicken coop. Athletes walk past the farm road every day on their way to practice. Students collectively manage the farm, keep up with daily chores, and spend time there to relax and get away. The most important aspect of the farm is its level of integration with the central mission of the college, combining an unsurpassed environmental liberal arts education with practical experience.

Vibrant Community

Green Mountain College is located on a beautiful, traditional New England campus. The campus is aesthetically pleasing and easy to navigate. The 155-acre main campus features athletic fields, a farm with a garden and livestock, a ropes course, hiking trails, and a great swimming hole on the Poultney River. GMC is a close-knit community of 750 students; students come to GMC from thirty-three states and eleven countries.

There are six traditional residence halls on campus, and 90 percent of undergraduates live on campus. Within the dorms, some students have formed theme floors to welcome students with similar interests. Students who prefer a peaceful living environment can live on the quiet floor, and students who prefer an active social scene can room on the adventure recreation floor, which is always overflowing with kayaks and climbing gear. Other theme floors include creative arts, community, substance-free, and honors floors.

Green Mountain College is located in a small rural community with endless outdoor activities. A forty-minute drive will take visitors to world-class skiing at Killington, and beautiful hikes in the Green Mountains. Three urban hubs—New York, Boston, and Montreal—are also within a drive of a few hours. Most weekends, students have the opportunity to go on backpacking, kayaking, canoeing, rock-climbing, or ice-climbing trips led by the Green Mountain Adventure Programming Office. Located between the Adirondack, Green, and Taconic mountains, and just south of Lake Champlain, Green Mountain College is an ideal environment for adventurous activities.

Successful Outcomes

Green Mountain College graduates go on to a variety of jobs in different fields. Some of the college's former environmental studies majors have gone on to positions as environmental instructors and land-use and community planners. English majors have gone on to become staff writers, journalists, and arts editors. Green Mountain's psychology majors are now working in fields such as counseling, field archaeology, habilitation specialization, residential counseling, and teaching.

Many students choose to continue their education for a postgraduate degree, and have been accepted to colleges including American University; Boston University; Cambridge College; Columbia University; Cornell University; Fordham University; George Washington University; Harvard Graduate School of Education; Humboldt University; Naval Post Graduate Academy; New York Medical College; New York University; Princeton University; Rensselaer Polytechnic Institute; Skidmore College; Smith College; Stanford University; the University of North Carolina, Chapel Hill; the University of Vermont; and Virginia Commonwealth University. International graduate schools attended by Green Mountain alumni include Gothernburg University, School of Business and Commercial Law in Sweden; Heidelberg University in Germany; McGill University in Canada; the University of Aalborg in Denmark; and the University of Aberystwyth in Wales.

Fast Facts

Green Mountain College is a four-year, coeducational, private college, founded in 1834.

Web site

http://www.greenmtn.edu

Location

Poultney, Vermont.

Student Profile

750 undergraduate students (51% male, 49% female); 34 states, 11 countries; 14.5% minority, 1% international.

Faculty Profile

42 full-time faculty, 91% hold a terminal degree in their field. 14:1 student/faculty ratio. Average class size is 19.

Residence Life

Highly residential: 90% of students live on campus.

Athletics

NCAA Division III, Northern Atlantic Conference. 14 varsity sports (7 men's: basketball, lacrosse, soccer, skiing, golf, tennis, cross-country; 7 women's: basketball, cross-country, lacrosse, skiing, soccer, softball, volleyball), and club sports (ultimate frisbee, men's and women's rugby).

Academic Programs

Adventure recreation; business; economics; elementary education; elementary education with special education endorsement; economics; environmental management; environmental education; history; secondary education; natural resource management; psychology; sociology & anthropology; self-designed; resort & hospitality management; youth development & camp management.

Costs and Aid

2007–2008: $16,948 comprehensive ($11,886 tuition). 90% of students receive some financial aid. Average award: $12,600.

Endowment

$2.4 million.

More Distinctions

• The Green Mountain College Welsh Heritage Program seeks to maintain and cultivate the rich cultural legacy of the surrounding area and to foster an interest in Wales and Welsh culture among students and faculty. This unique program was founded to increase interest and commitment of young people in Welsh culture for the continued vitality of the Welsh-American community.

Saint Michael's College

VERMONT

A vibrant residential, Catholic, liberal arts college in Vermont, Saint Michael's College is devoted to education of the mind, body, and spirit. Some twenty-nine majors offer an abundance of ways to explore the liberal arts in pursuit of a career, under the guidance of faculty who are passionate about teaching.

Admissions Contact:

Saint Michael's College
One Winooski Park, Box 7
Colchester, VT 05439
(800) SMC-8000
Email: admission@smcvt.edu
www.smcvt.edu

The 4 Distinctions

Engaged Students

Known as a college that encourages students to make the world a better place, some 70 percent of students engage in community service, reflecting a unique passion for social-justice issues on campus. Saint Michael's encourages study abroad for a semester or a year. Students may study anywhere in the world, in one of several different types of international programs. Study-abroad language programs enable students to learn a language as they fulfill the college's language proficiency requirement. Field-study programs give students a hands-on academic semester, often in developing countries, focused on such themes as culture and development, ecology and conservation, and peace and conflict studies.

Saint Michael's prides itself on being a college that puts beliefs into practice. Its nationally recognized MOVE (Mobilization of Volunteer Efforts) program creates and implements projects that meet local needs effectively and directly, helping to build strong connections between the college and its surrounding community. Students can volunteer for a wide array of service organizations, from Big Brothers/Big Sisters and the Special Olympics to Habitat for Humanity.

The college's emphasis on community service manifests itself in its Fire and Rescue Squad, which deservedly has received a fair amount of media attention. An independent volunteer organization comprised of trained students, the squad serves the campus and much of the surrounding community. They respond to more than 2,000 calls annually—including respiratory and cardiac emergencies, motor vehicle accidents, and interhospital neonatal transports—and have provided continuous service twenty-four hours a day, 365 days a year, since 1969.

Great Teaching

Of Saint Michael's 150 faculty members, 94 percent have a PhD or the highest appropriate degree. With a student to faculty ratio of just twelve to one, students are ensured personal attention from professors both in class and out of class. Students and faculty interact in many settings—sharing meals on and off campus, collaborating on academic projects, and working together on community-service projects. For four of the last seven years, a Saint Michael's professor has been named Vermont Professor of the Year.

The Saint Michael's honors program gives exceptional students additional opportunities and challenges through small-group discussion, housing options, research, and extracurricular activities. Students can enroll in honors sections of classes in various disciplines. Saint Michael's also hosts a prestigious Phi Beta Kappa chapter on campus as well as many other departmental honors societies.

All first-year students enroll in a writing-intensive first-year seminar, which engages students through discussion and active learning on a particular topic. The interdisciplinary nature of the program focuses on analyzing primary texts and understanding cultural diversity. Past topics have included race relations in the United States, revolutionary ideas in the twentieth century, and science as a way of knowing.

The Edmundite Center for Peace and Justice seeks to integrate peace and justice concerns into the everyday life of the college community. Through lectures, symposia, and academic courses, the center seeks to promote human rights, global healing, and a respect for all humanity. Past lectures have explored the spiritual dimension of Dr. Martin Luther King's legacy, the ethics of global capitalism, and the ethical and policy considerations of stem cell research.

The college houses one of the oldest and most well-respected English language programs in the United States. Fifteen thousand alumni from more than forty countries have taken classes there. The school provides intensive language courses and teacher training courses in English as a second language, and partners with more than fifty high schools, universities, and businesses worldwide.

Engineering students have a choice of five-year cooperative programs with the University of Vermont or with Clarkson University.

Vibrant Community

Saint Michael's is located in Colchester, Vermont, just three miles away from Burlington, Vermont's largest city and a metropolitan college town of 100,000 residents. Home to the University of Vermont, Burlington provides many outstanding venues for live music and theater. The campus is only five minutes from Lake Champlain, where students can sail, swim, fish, and windsurf. In less than an hour-long drive, students can hit the ski slopes in beautiful Stowe, Vermont. All students in good academic standing receive an all-access season ski pass to Smugglers' Notch Resort, just forty-five minutes from campus. Students pay only a minimal processing fee for the pass, allowing them to enjoy the best of Vermont's winter recreation as part of their college experience and encouraging an active, healthy lifestyle.

Saint Michael's makes the most of Vermont's geography. Great places for kayaking, climbing, hiking, backpacking, and other outdoor adventures are just minutes from campus. The college's popular Wilderness Program offers environmentally conscious education, information, instruction, equipment, and recreational opportunities. The program coordinates an intensive five-day preorientation program for new students.

Saint Michael's is a true residential campus: nearly 100 percent of students live on campus, and the college guarantees on-campus housing for four years. International ambassador housing integrates international students and American students to promote intercultural awareness and global learning.

Saint Michael's was founded over 100 years ago by the Society of Saint Edmund, and it remains the only Edmundite college in the world. The Edmundites are known for their commitment to social justice and their role in leading desegregation efforts in Selma, Alabama with Dr. Martin Luther King, Jr. The Edmundite Campus Ministry program is an active part of Saint Michael's campus—open to all students, it is a resource for those wanting to explore their spirituality. The campus houses a beautiful chapel—one of the largest in the state—in which daily masses are held, serving both the campus and the community at large.

Successful Outcomes

Six months after graduating, 84 percent of Saint Michael's graduates are employed, 14 percent are in graduate school, and 5 percent choose to participate in a year or more of volunteer service—including some 125 alumni who have served in the Peace Corps.

Five years after graduation, 51 percent of Saint Michael's students have attended graduate or professional school. Ninety percent of graduates applying to medical school are accepted, as well as 71 percent of those applying to law school.

Many companies recruit on campus, including IBM, Readak Educational Services, Aetna/US Healthcare, New York Life Insurance Company, Fidelity Investments, Bear Stearns, General Electric, Deloitte Touche, Investors Bank & Trust, the U.S. Navy, and prestigious accounting firms such as KMPG.

Fast Facts

Saint Michael's College is a Catholic, residential, liberal arts college.

Web site

http://www.smcvt.edu/

Location

Colchester, Vermont—440-acre campus, situated between the shores of Lake Champlain and the majestic Green Mountains, overlooking Burlington, the state's largest city.

Student Profile

2,000 undergraduate students; 33 states, 13 countries; 79% from outside Vermont. 90% of entering students finish in the top half of their high school class. Middle 50% of students scored between 510-600 on the writing section of the SAT, between 500-600 on the critical reading section, and between 510-600 on the mathematics section.

Faculty Profile

150 faculty members. 12:1 student-faculty ratio.

Athletics

NCAA Division II, Northeast-10 Conference; East Collegiate Athletic Conference. 21 varsity sports (10 men's: baseball, basketball, cross-country, golf, hockey, lacrosse, skiing (alpine, Nordic), soccer, swimming & diving, tennis; 11 women's: basketball, cross-country, field hockey, lacrosse, skiing (alpine, Nordic), soccer, softball, swimming & diving, tennis, ice hockey, volleyball).

Academic Programs

Accounting; American studies; art; biochemistry; biology; business administration; chemistry; classics; computer science; East Asian studies; economics; education; engineering; English; environmental science/studies; finance; fine arts; French; history; gender/women's studies; geography; global studies; history; information systems; international business; Italian; journalism & mass communication; language; management; marketing; mathematics; medieval studies; modern languages; music; peace & justice; philosophy; physical science; physics; political science; psychology; religious studies; Russian; sociology/anthropology; Spanish; theatre.

Costs and Aid

$37,405 comprehensive ($29,695 tuition). Approximately 90% of admitted students receive financial aid.

Endowment

$58.6 million

More Distinctions

• Recently approved for chapter of Phi Beta Kappa, the nation's premier academic honor society. Only 10% of U.S. colleges and universities have PBK chapters.

• Included in *The Princeton Review's Best 366 Colleges* guidebook.

Colleges of Distinction
Mid-Atlantic Region Schools

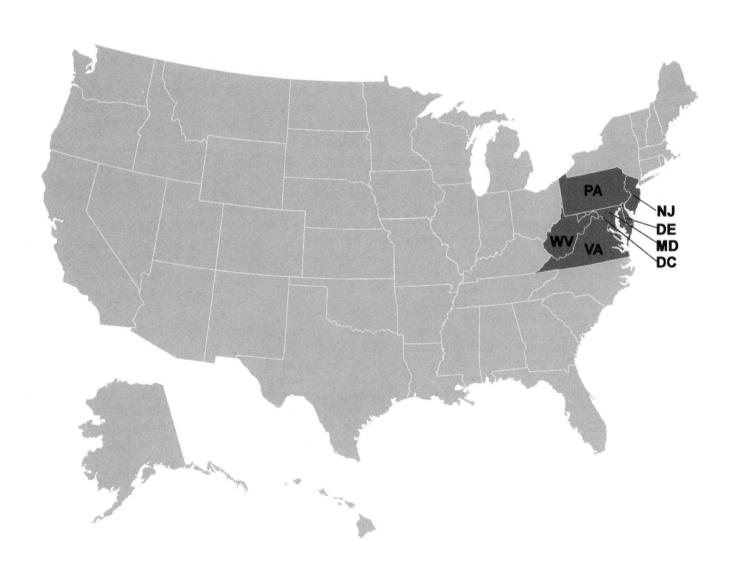

Photo: © iStockphoto.com/lisapics

Notes

_____

_____

_____

_____

_____

_____

_____

_____

_____

_____

_____

Loyola College in Maryland

MARYLAND

Loyola College in Maryland is a Catholic university committed to the educational and spiritual traditions of the Jesuits, to the ideals of liberal education, and to the development of the whole person. Loyola's mission is to prepare students to learn, lead, and serve in a diverse and changing world.

Admissions Contact:

Loyola College in Maryland
4501 N. Charles Street
Baltimore, MD. 21210
(800) 221-9107
Ph: (410) 617-5012
www.loyola.edu

The 4 Distinctions

Engaged Students

Loyola assists new students in integrating into campus life through a variety of first-year programs, including the first-year experience course. FE 100 is a one-credit elective course offering a combination of group social experiences, an excursion into the city of Baltimore, group discussions of important campus issues, and workshops led by support staff from the Loyola and Baltimore communities. The course is taught by an instructor team including the student's faculty core advisor, an administrator from student development or another division of the college, and a current upper-level student.

The Collegium program is a living-learning community of seventy-two first-year students who live on the same floor with classmates in two of their academic classes. Students in the Collegium program learn collaboratively, sharing questions about study methods and challenging one another's intellectual assumptions and abilities.

The Sellinger School of Business and Management is recognized as a premier business school in the region, responding to the needs and concerns in the business and management community. The only business school in Baltimore to be accredited by the Association to Advance Collegiate Schools of Business (AACSB), it is inspired by Jesuit values and guided by the principles of cura personalis ("care for the whole person"). Internships throughout the Baltimore-Washington, DC, metropolitan area are readily available, and experiential learning is required of all undergraduate business majors.

Various student research opportunities are provided at the Center for Social and Community Research, the Center for the Humanities, the Office of Institutional Research, the Office of First-Year Research, the International Technology Research Institute, the Office of Grant Services, and the Undergraduate Student Research and Scholarship Colloquium.

The college offers numerous programs, exchanges, and affiliations for studying abroad, including twenty Loyola programs. On average, 65 percent of students participate in some type of international experience in their time at Loyola (including summer sessions and short-term programs). Internship opportunities are available through specific departments, as well as through the career center.

The Center for Community Service and Justice offers students a chance to participate in service learning outside the campus. The center is made up of four distinct, yet interconnected components of community-based, justice-focused, experiential learning. Programs subscribe to the PARE model, which stands for Preparation, Action, Reflection, and Evaluation. The goal of the program is to make each service experience educative and to offer individuals the opportunity to learn about and grow in solidarity with people who are marginalized and, through this, to mature in their own faith or spirituality.

Great Teaching

All undergraduates complete a core curriculum that includes courses in English, philosophy, theology, ethics, history, fine arts, foreign language, mathematics, science, and social sciences. The purpose is to balance comprehensive education and specialized study in the major, and to challenge students to develop their interests, intellects, outlooks, beliefs, and values. The liberal arts core helps students to explore different fields while settling on their choice of majors. The core also encourages students to think and to solve problems in a variety of ways and to critically examine a cross section of ideas.

The student to faculty ratio is twelve to one, and the average class size is twenty-five. There is an 89 percent retention rate from freshman to sophomore year, and about 85 percent of the faculty hold doctoral or terminal degrees in their fields.

Vibrant Community

Founded in 1852, Loyola became a coeducational institution in 1971, following its merger with nearby Mount Saint Agnes College. Four out of five undergraduates come from out of state, from thirty-six states and twenty-seven countries. About 83 percent of undergraduates live on campus for all four years. A seventy-nine-acre traditional collegiate campus in northern Baltimore City primarily houses the college's undergraduate programs, with two satellite locations in the greater Baltimore metropolitan area for graduate programs.

On average, 60 percent of the student body engage in volunteer activity, either once during their stay or throughout all four years.

ALANA (African, Latino, Asian, and Native American) Student Services is committed to providing support, services, and programs for ALANA students at the college. The myriad of services offered fosters the academic, cultural, personal, spiritual, and leadership development of ALANA students. The office seeks to maintain an environment of respect and awareness, while advocating for ALANA students and responding to their needs.

The Best of Baltimore program for first-year students is designed to introduce them to the area's finest cultural and sporting events and to provide them with opportunities to socialize with other new students and with faculty and administrator hosts. The Best of Baltimore provides students with approximately one opportunity each month to do something out of the ordinary, including outings to the symphony, local theater events, and, of course, Orioles games. All transportation is provided, and each event includes a reception.

The Late Night program is designed to offer students social, cultural, and athletic programs on Thursday, Friday, and Saturday nights. There are several regularly scheduled Late Night programs offered through the office of student activities, including a midnight breakfast on Friday and Saturday nights, a coffeehouse on Thursday nights, monthly karaoke events, and a monthly concert series. In addition to these activities, students can participate in a number of social, cultural, and athletic events each weekend.

Loyola College's NCAA Division I intercollegiate athletic program maintains a reputation for athletic success and academic integrity that has become a model for institutions of similar size throughout the United States.

Successful Outcomes

Over 80 percent of Loyola College students graduate in four years. Within six to nine months of graduation, more than 75 percent of graduates are employed. About 30 percent of graduates go directly on to graduate or professional schools, and 10 percent do both.

The Sellinger Path to Graduation provides in-depth course information for each undergraduate concentration offered by the Sellinger School of Business and Management, detailing required business as well as liberal arts and science core courses. Each path is designed to assist students and faculty advisers in planning individualized programs of study.

The career center helps students and alumni discover their career passions by integrating the Jesuit core values and introducing a process of personal discovery and discernment. This process assists students with discovering their unique talents and gifts, as well as the relationship between their individual needs and their connections with others in a community. As an ongoing lifetime activity, this process helps students and alumni discern the appropriate direction for their lives.

Fast Facts

Loyola College in Maryland is a four-year Jesuit liberal arts college affiliated with the Catholic Church and founded in 1852.

Web site

http://www.loyola.edu/admission

Location

Baltimore, Maryland—the evergreen campus is situated on 79 acres of land.

Student Profile

3,500 undergraduates (42% male, 58% female); 36 states and territories; 14% minority, 1% international.

Faculty Profile

305 full-time faculty. 12:1 student/faculty ratio. Average class size is 25.

Residence Life

Highly residential: Over 85% of students live on campus.

Athletics

NCAA Division I, Metro Atlantic Athletic Conference (MAAC), Eastern College Athletic Conference (ECAC), Big East. 17 varsity sports (8 men's: basketball, crew, cross-country, golf, lacrosse, soccer, swimming & diving, tennis; 9 women's: basketball, crew, cross-country, lacrosse, soccer, swimming & diving, tennis, track& field, volleyball), 12 club sports, and over 25 intramurals.

Academic Programs

Accounting; biology; chemistry; classics; communication; computer science; economics; education; engineering science (computer, electrical, materials, mechanical); English; finance; fine arts (art history, music, photography, studio arts, theatre); international business; global studies; history; journalism; management; management information systems; marketing; mathematical sciences; modern languages and literatures (French/German/Spanish); philosophy; physics; political science; psychology; sociology; speech-language pathology/audiology; theology; writing.

Costs and Aid

2007–2008: $43,400 comprehensive ($33,150 tuition). 65% of students receive some financial aid.

Endowment

$175,490,880.

More Distinctions

• #2 Top Northern Master's Universities (*U.S. News & World Report*).

• #3 Dorms Like Palaces (*The Princeton Review*).

Salisbury University

MARYLAND

Salisbury University (SU) is nationally recognized for academic excellence. Its creative curriculum emphasizes undergraduate research, study abroad, professional internships and civic engagement. Located on Maryland's historic Eastern Shore, SU offers 42 undergraduate majors and 13 graduate programs.

Admissions Contact:

Salisbury University
1101 Camden Avenue
Salisbury, MD 21801
Ph: (410) 543-6000
Email:admissions@salisbury.edu
www.salisbury.edu

The 4 Distinctions

Engaged Students

SU's 7,500 students are active citizens locally, nationally and internationally. Through the Institute for Public Affairs and Civic Engagement (PACE), students promote the political process and assist local governments.

Many PACE students are involved in intensive, multi-faceted year-long civic experiences through the Presidential Citizen Scholar Program. Its Paul S. Sarbanes Lecture Series has attracted top political speakers including Senator Richard Lugar, Congressman and civil rights activist John Lewis, and Speaker of the House Nancy Pelosi.

A major part of the SU mission is to prepare global citizens. SU students are engaged internationally. Education students have taught elementary-aged children in New Zealand, and studied children's literature in Iceland, Poland and England. Nursing students have provided aid and education to villagers in Africa, while business students have studied economics in China and Germany. One philosophy professor has taken a group to India, where students embraced the culture, including local diet, to "live the philosophy."

Study abroad is possible for short periods during summer and winter sessions or for a semester or year. The results often last much longer. For example, through SU's Center for Conflict Resolution, students have researched and helped mediate disputes in contentious areas including Kosovo, Bosnia and Northern Ireland.

World leaders are campus visitors. Recent speakers in the center's "One Person Can Make a Difference" Lecture Series have included Nobel Peace Prize winners Lech Walesa, former president of Poland, and F.W. de Klerk, former president of South Africa. At SU, de Klerk received his first honorary degree from a U.S. institution.

Great Teaching

Enjoying both public and private support, all four of its academic schools are endowed, a rarity among public institutions. With its award-winning faculty, beautiful campus with arboretum status, exceptional academic and exemplary athletic programs, and a dynamic administration, Salisbury is earning recognition as a Maryland university of national distinction.

Lauded for its dedication to undergraduate research, SU offers students the chance not only to assist professors, but to perform their own independent study. Findings are presented on campus during the University's annual Student Research Conference, though many student scholars also have the opportunity to speak at national and international conferences. SU hosts the National Conference on Undergraduate Research in 2008.

Much of the learning at Salisbury takes place outside the classroom. A day in a lab at Henson Science Hall, for example, might mean helping research cures for tuberculosis or preparing a payload for a NASA rocket to test the effects of cancer metastasis in zero gravity.

Students in all majors have the opportunity to apply their studies through internships and field placements, which are strongly encouraged. In the Perdue School of Business, all majors must have an applied business learning experience. Other programs also provide unique benefits. The Bellavance Honors Center, for example, offers thriving seminars and small discussion-oriented classes. Students with minds for business may compete for the annual Bernstein Achievement Award for Excellence, a contest for young entrepreneurs that rewards the winner with $5,000 toward business startup costs.

The most popular majors at SU are business, education communications and nursing. The student to faculty ratio is 16:1, and the average class size is 27.

Vibrant Community

In creating a stimulating campus climate, SU not only involves its students, faculty and staff, but reaches out to the community at large. During Fun Day, held each September, area residents are invited to campus for a family festival celebrating the joy of learning—from exciting explosions in the chemistry lab to a chance for children and adults alike to try their hand at throwing their own clay pots.

Student organizations and volunteers are heavily involved in that celebration, as well as in the Sea Gull Century, SU's annual 100-mile or 100-kilometer bike ride, named a "Best Bicycling in America" event by The League of American Bicyclists.

The campus also give back to the area through activities such as The Big Event, a community cleanup initiative powered entirely by SU students—some 200 each year. SU's Relay For Life is consistently named one of the top collegiate Relays, raising more than $450,000 for cancer research since 2002. SU is also home to ShoreCorps/PALS, an AmeriCorps chapter allowing young adults to mentor students in local schools.

In addition, Salisbury's Division III athletics teams are engaged in the community. The field hockey team has volunteered for the American Cancer Society Leadership Conference and helped Habitat for Humanity with a house built entirely by women for a local mother and her daughter. Men's basketball players have assisted elementary students with reading, while some 30 football players run a Sunshine Club to mentor students at seven elementary schools. SU's student-athletes also excel on the field. The Sea Gulls have earned 11 NCAA Division III championships since 1994.

Culturally, SU offers a wide array of activities each semester through its University Galleries and Cultural Affairs programs. Past speakers have included environmentalist Jane Goodall, author and Nobel laureate Toni Morrison, Grammy winner Mary Youngblood, feminist pioneer Gloria Steinem, and journalist Robert MacNeil. Monks from the Deprung Loseling Monastery in Tibet have visited campus twice for week-long residencies.

SU is home to two National Public Radio affiliates, a student radio station and community access television. Students participate in a multitude of musical ensembles, including the Chorale and Chamber Choir—which have performed at Carnegie Hall—and the Salisbury Symphony Orchestra. Students also perform in six productions annually through the Bobbi Biron Theatre Program, recently highlighted on Playbill.com.

Off the main campus, students and visitors are always welcome at the Edward H. Nabb Research Center for Delmarva History and Culture—a treasure trove of regional history and information—and SU's Ward Museum of Wildfowl Art, named one of the "10 Great Places to See American Folk Art" by *USA Today*.

Successful Outcomes

Strong programs at SU have yielded a number of successful alumni. Among them: Baltimore Ravens owner Steve Bisciotti, Perdue Farms Inc. CEO Jim Perdue, Weather Channel meteorologist Mike Seidel, television writer Erica Messer (*Alias, The OC, Criminal Minds*) and Broadway actress Jennifer Hope Wills (*Phantom of the Opera, Beauty and the Beast, Wonderful Town*). SU graduates have also won Emmys for their involvement in the ESPN show *SportsCenter*.

With more than 35,000 alumni throughout the United States, SU has made its mark as a Maryland university of national distinction.

Fast Facts

Salisbury University is a public, four-year comprehensive university founded in 1925. SU is a member of the University System of Maryland.

Web site

http://www.salisbury.edu

Location

Salisbury, MD—on the Eastern Shore. 30 miles from the Atlantic beaches, 2.5 hours from Baltimore and Washington, D.C.

Student Profile

6,941 undergraduate students (43% men, 57% women); 32 states and territories, 59 countries.

Faculty Profile

495 faculty members; 16:1 student/faculty ratio.

Residence Life

Moderately residential: 10 undergraduate residence halls

Athletics

NCAA Division III, Capital Athletic Conference. 21 varsity sports (10 men's: baseball, basketball, lacrosse, soccer, swimming, tennis, football, indoor and outdoor track and field, cross country; 11 women's: basketball, field hockey, lacrosse, cross country, soccer, softball, swimming, tennis, indoor and outdoor track and field, volleyball), club teams and intramurals.

Academic Programs

Accounting; art; athletic training; biology; business administration; chemistry; clinical laboratory science/medical technology; communication arts; computer science; conflict analysis and dispute resolution; economics; early childhood education; elementary education; English; esl/k-12 certification; environmental health science; environmental issues; exercise science; finance; fine arts; French; geography; health education; history; information systems; interdisciplinary studies; international studies; management; marketing; mathematics; music; nursing; philosophy; physical education; physics; political science; psychology; respiratory therapy; social work; sociology; Spanish; theatre.

Costs and Aid

2007-2008: $6,412 in-state tuition, $14,500 out-of-state tuition. 68% of students receive financial aid.

Endowment

$35 million.

More Distinctions

• For the 11th consecutive year Salisbury University is ranked as a top 10 public comprehensive university—Master's category—in the North by *U.S. News & World Report*'s America's Best Colleges guide. SU ranks seventh in the 2008 edition.

Washington College

MARYLAND

Washington College (WC) is a private, coeducational, liberal arts college founded in 1782 under the patronage of George Washington. With an emphasis on appreciating America's heritage and strong support for hands-on learning opportunities, this friendly, residential college offers a supportive atmosphere for learning. WC's tagline is "Your revolution starts here."

Admissions Contact:

Washington College
300 Washington Ave.
Chestertown, MD 21620
Ph: (800) 422-1782
Email: adm.off@washcoll.edu
www.washcoll.edu

The 4 Distinctions

Engaged Students

Washington's dedication to connecting students to the world begins in the first year, when students take the required Community, Nation, and World seminars. In Community seminars, the focus is local: the political, social, artistic, economic, and environmental communities of the Chesapeake region. Next, students take Nation seminars, exploring a topic or issue of significance to the American community. Finally, students choose one spring-semester World seminar from a broad range of topics in the arts and sciences, looking at diverse traditions and cultures from around the world.

The most popular majors are biology (including premed), business management, psychology, and English. WC's vibrant creative writing program benefits the entire campus community by bringing writers such as Joyce Carol Oates and Robert Pinsky to campus for seminars, dinners, and time with students. As the head of the program notes: "Literature is an exercise in empathy—by reading thoughtfully, we learn more about what it is to be human."

Biology and environmental studies majors take advantage of WC's waterfront location and facilities, where students conduct fieldwork during the school year. During the summer, students can participate in fieldwork trips to Florida, the Virgin Islands, and elsewhere overseas.

Aspiring writers can enjoy the facilities of O'Neill House, a living/learning community for writers, or study for a summer at Kiplin Hall in England. One fortunate graduate will be selected to receive the Sophie Kerr Prize, the largest undergraduate prize in the nation. Recent winners have received over sixty thousand dollars to help them pursue the creative life after graduation.

WC's flagship academic enrichment program, the Douglass Cater Society of Junior Fellows, offers funding to students for a variety of self-directed projects. Requiring a grade point average of 3.6 or better, membership in the Cater Society is highly competitive and offered only to students who achieve distinction among the school's top scholars. Junior Fellows who have completed independent projects give short presentations to the entire campus community about their experiences. Recent funded internships have been with the Center for International Policy in Washington, DC; the British Museum; the dolphin research program at the Kewalo Basin Marine Mammal Laboratory in Hawaii; the Philadelphia Theater Company; and the International Human Rights Commission in Geneva, Switzerland.

Students may also take advantage of the opportunities offered by the C.V. Starr Center for American Study to explore the rich American heritage of the Chestertown region, including a public archaeology laboratory housed in the college's restored colonial-era Custom House on the Chester River. The Center for the Study of the Environment and Society also helps sponsor underwater archaeological explorations of the Chester River.

Great Teaching

"This school is as challenging as you want to make it," says one WC student. Students appreciate the college's emphasis on self-direction. It's not uncommon for professors to let students set class test dates and other deadlines. In return, they expect students to use their freedom wisely. The relaxed, egalitarian atmosphere promotes good discussion and collaborative learning—great practice for tomorrow's community and business leaders. When surveyed, 96 percent of students rank faculty accessibility as excellent, and WC alumni consistently cite "exceptional faculty" as the one factor that most enhanced their experience at the college.

As the tenth-oldest college in the nation, WC continues to follow the ideals of its presidential namesake: a better future achieved through education; respect for scholarship; and high standards for leadership, character, and service. As one professor puts it, "you won't be told what to think, but you'll learn how to think, to express, and to live life to the very fullest." While traditional in form, WC offers students a progressive atmosphere, where strong concern about environmental issues is matched by a keen awareness of the area's rich history and heritage.

Vibrant Community

The comfortable atmosphere of the small, historic community of Chestertown, Maryland, is shared by WC's intimate campus. Nearly 80 percent of WC's students live on campus, many in theme houses such as the Leadership and Service house, in which students agree to perform community and campus service. Service organizations range from well-known programs like Habitat for Humanity, Amnesty International, and the Special Olympics to local environmental programs like Furthering Outreach in the community and Environment (FORCE), and Hands Out, which coordinates local food drives, clothing drives, and special holiday projects. The fraternity and sorority community at WC is also active in service, sponsoring fundraising and other charitable events throughout the year.

WC offers over seventy clubs, a strong athletics program, and frequent concerts on campus. The college has a vibrant theater program, open to majors and nonmajors alike. The Riverside Players, for example, sponsor a number of programs, including the Royal Fakespeare Players, a parodic Shakespearean acting troupe. WC also offers a variety of intercollegiate and club sports, including rugby, ice hockey, and equestrian programs.

WC is located on the Chesapeake Bay's Eastern Shore, which is forty-five minutes from Annapolis, and ninety minutes from Washington, DC, Baltimore, and Philadelphia. Chestertown offers coffeehouses, art galleries, and a vibrant community theater in a peaceful small-town setting. Local residents attend college events, such as lectures given by top-notch speakers, including Senator John McCain, Ralph Nader, and Plácido Domingo. WC also hosts other community events and fund-raisers, and students are involved as members of local clubs and even the local volunteer fire department.

Successful Outcomes

Students praise WC's career services program for its strong influence. "They will find ways to help you do what you want to do," one student explained. About 25 percent of WC students attend graduate school at a top-ranked institution in the first year after graduation, 45 percent in the first five years. WC alumni are proud of their college and serious about preserving it; alumni regularly participate in fundraising and other school events.

Washington's alumni testify to the breadth of preparation available at the school, as well as to its commitment to public-minded service. Noted literary alumni range from the classic, James M. Cain, author of The Postman Always Rings Twice, to the contemporary, Christine Lincoln, author of Sap Rising. Other notable alumni include actress Linda Hamilton; Harris Whitbeck, head of CNN's Mexico City Bureau; Louis Goldstein, the longest-serving politician in the state of Maryland; and Jeff Alderson, a US Navy commander who served as media affairs officer for the Fifth Fleet during Operation Iraqi Freedom. Their varied paths mix community service, alumni loyalty, and creativity in a way that would surely please the school's most public-minded namesake.

Fast Facts

Washington College is a private, liberal arts college founded in 1782.

Web site

http://www.washcoll.edu

Location

Chestertown, Maryland—on the Chesapeake Bay's Eastern Shore, 75 miles from Baltimore, Philadelphia, and Washington, DC.

Student Profile

1,300 students (40% male, 60% female); less than half from Maryland and the balance from 40 other states and 30 foreign nations; 8% minority, 5% international. 5% of the WC student body is "non-traditional" (25 years old or older).

Faculty Profile

101 faculty; 92% hold Ph.D. or equivalent degree. 12:1 student/faculty ratio. Average class size is 17.

Residence Life

Highly residential: 80% of students live on campus. Students are required to live on campus during their first two years. 30 residence halls with a total capacity of 1000 students.

Athletics

NCAA Division III, Centennial Conference. 18 varsity sports (8 men's: baseball, basketball, lacrosse, rowing, soccer, swimming, tennis; 10 women's: basketball, field hockey, lacrosse, rowing, soccer, softball, swimming, tennis, volleyball; 1 coed: sailing). Club teams and intramurals are also offered, plus an Equestrian Team and a wakeboarding team.

Academic Programs

American studies; anthropology; art; behavioral neuroscience; biology; Black studies; business management; chemistry; computer science; creative writing; drama; economics; English; environmental & Chesapeake regional studies; French studies; German studies; Hispanic studies; history; human development; humanities; international literature & culture; international studies; mathematics; music; philosophy; physics; political science; psychology; sociology. The college also offers students the possibility to create self-directed majors.

Costs and Aid

2007–2008: $38,950 comprehensive ($31,570 tuition). 85% of students receive some financial aid. Average award is $17,500.

Endowment

$165 million.

More Distinctions

• Fred Rugg's top 100 "Just Good Schools" in Rugg's Guide to Colleges.

• US News & World Report Best Colleges 2005, Top 110 National Liberal Arts Colleges.

• Ranked in "100 Colleges That Are Better Than You Think" in Jay Mathews's Harvard Schmarvard.

• Rated Top 20 College Gems by Steven Antonoff in The College Finder.

• Recognized by the Princeton Review for inclusion in its Best 366 Colleges guide.

Rowan University

NEW JERSEY

Rowan University (RU) is a coeducational, comprehensive, public university, offering liberal education and professional preparation in a collaborative, learning-centered environment. The excellent and diverse faculty, staff, and students integrate teaching, research, scholarship, creative activity, and community service, enhancing the intellectual, social, and cultural lives of RU's campus and regional communities.

Admissions Contact:

Rowan University
201 Mullica Hill Road
Glassboro, New Jersey 08028
877-RU-Rowan
Ph: (856) 256-4200
Email: admissions@rowan.edu
www.rowan.edu

The 4 Distinctions

Engaged Students

RU encourages experiential learning outside the classroom, and its location in the greater Philadelphia metropolitan area provides many opportunities for internships. For example, the nationally ranked entrepreneurship program in the Business School sends its students to help local companies in a variety of ways, such as performing market research, and it even houses them together in a separate themed dorm on campus. Students from general business, engineering, and other majors are in demand for internships with a variety of area companies. Recent projects included developing PR action groups, creating an award-winning film about drug addiction, and working with People Magazine.

RU students who wish to study abroad can choose from among two hundred programs in more than fifty countries. Students in all majors are eligible, and all credits earned abroad count toward a RU degree.

All student groups on campus are involved in service learning. They volunteer for Habitat for Humanity, Relay for Life, and Big Brothers/Big Sisters, among other organizations. RU's fraternities and sororities also have a service requirement of their members, who form 11 percent of the student body.

Great Teaching

Students at RU have access to the resources of a large university without sacrificing the personal attention and small class size of a college. All classes are taught by professors, not teaching assistants. The average class size is twenty students, and the student to faculty ratio is twelve to one.

Because Rowan has a low student to faculty ratio, students have the opportunity to work with faculty on several research projects. For example, engineering students have traveled to Alaska to study oil spills, studied the Hope Creek Nuclear Facility to improve efficiency, and participated in research with NASA on the famous "Vomit Comet," an aircraft that simulates

zero gravity. Archeology students have been on archeological digs to Chile to excavate ancient burial grounds. Science and physics students work with faculty on research in new materials, environmental problems, and cancer cures. Last year forty-five grant projects were funded for a total of six million dollars from such agencies as the Department of Energy and the National Science Foundation.

RU offers forty-three undergraduate majors among seven academic colleges: Business, Communication, Education, Engineering, Fine and Performing Arts, Liberal Arts and Sciences, and the College of Professional and Continuing Education. Graduate students can choose from seven teacher certification programs, 38 master's degrees and specializations, 19 graduate certification programs, and a doctoral program in educational leadership. The most popular majors are business, communications, and elementary education and teaching. The entrepreneurship program in the Business School is ranked in the top twenty-five in the nation, and RU's student-run radio station was recently named the best in the country. The Engineering School is only ten years old, created in response to area need, and it already ranks twentieth nationwide. Education is RU's biggest school, reflecting its origins as a teachers college. It is nationally accredited, allowing its graduates to teach in every state.

Each college at RU offers a core curriculum tailored to its discipline, ensuring that RU students are generalists and well-rounded students, easily adapting to changing technologies and challenges. The core curriculum in every school includes a freshman seminar that focuses on critical thinking and writing, time management, career mapping and goal setting, and team building. Capstone experiences also vary by college. A fine arts major might create a show of his or her work, while a business student might lead a senior seminar.

RU is in the midst of an aggressive ten-year plan to develop a national reputation for excellence and innovation to make it the public university of choice in the region. The plan calls for a greater campuswide focus on academic and student support initiatives as well as campus construction and renovation projects. RU intends to create a West Campus on six hundred acres it recently purchased nearby. The anchor of the new tract will be the South Jersey Technology Park, which will play a significant role in the economic development of the region and will give faculty and students hands-on research opportunities that will allow them to participate in privately and publicly funded research projects.

Vibrant Community

RU's tree-lined campus is self-contained, and students walk from class to class. As the university grows and adds new buildings, its goal is to create a seamless intersection between the campus and the town. Glassboro, a city of about twenty thousand, is located in southern New Jersey, in the middle of the East Coast's "cultural corridor," an area that includes Boston, New York City, Philadelphia, Baltimore, and Washington, DC. This location gives students many options for off-campus learning and recreation on weekends. RU is thirty minutes south of Philadelphia, and an hour west of Atlantic City.

About one third of RU's 8,400 undergraduates live on campus, one third live in off-campus housing around the perimeter of the campus, and another third commute from a greater distance. Many students naturally come from New Jersey, since RU was founded as regional college for teachers in 1923. Its recent transformation into a national university now draws students from throughout the mid-Atlantic states and from thirty foreign countries.

RU offers a variety of housing choices, including all-freshman dorms, honors housing, and specific learning communities such as engineering, science, and entrepreneurship. Other housing options include townhouse and apartment complexes.

There are more than 150 student clubs and organizations, offering professional, cultural, and service activities. RU has one of the strongest NCAA Division III athletic programs in the country, earning eleven national championships in five different sports. About three thousand RU students are involved with intramural sports, and the Student Recreation Center is one of the most popular destinations on campus, providing fitness equipment and exercise classes as well as serving as the intramural sports hub.

Successful Outcomes

RU graduates are in demand. A total of 95 percent of the class of 2006 was employed or attending graduate school within one year of graduation. Between 30 and 40 percent of all RU graduates pursue advanced degrees. Engineering students have a 98 percent placement rate within a year, and premed graduates have a 100 percent placement rate.

Notable alumni include David Tarr, lead economist for World Bank; Jack Collins, former New Jersey Speaker of the House; Ric Edelman and Jean Edelman, president and owner of Edelman Financial Services; Susan Kroll, vice president of marketing for Warner Bros.; Betty Bowe Castor, former president of South Florida University; and Michael Stengel, general manager of the Marriott Marquis Times Square. Each year, more than thirty events are planned for alumni, and membership is free.

Fast Facts

Rowan University is a four-year comprehensive public university founded in 1923.

Web site

http://www.rowan.edu

Location

Southern New Jersey—18 miles southeast of Philadelphia and 50 miles west of Atlantic City.

Student Profile

8,430 undergraduate students (47% male, 53% female); 19 states and territories; 19% minority, 1% international.

Faculty Profile

451 full-time faculty. 12:1 student/faculty ratio. Average class size is 20.

Residence Life

Moderately residential: 35% of students live on campus.

Athletics

NCAA Division III, Conference: NJAC, varsity sports (7 men's: football, soccer, cross country, basketball, swimming & diving, baseball, track & field, 9 women's: lacrosse, soccer, cross country, basketball, swimming & diving, softball, track & field, field hockey, volleyball. 14 club sports, and 40 intramurals.

Academic Programs

Accounting; advertising; art education (general fine art); biochemistry; biological sciences; business (entrepreneurship, finance, human resources management, management, management information systems, marketing); chemical engineering; chemistry; civil engineering; communication studies; computer science; economics; electrical & computer engineering; early childhood education; elementary education; English; environmental studies; geography; health & exercise science (athletic training, teacher certification, health promotion & fitness management); history; journalism; law and justice studies; liberal studies (American studies, math/science); mathematics; mechanical engineering; music (composition, jazz studies, music education, performance); physical science; physics; political science; psychology; public relations; radio-TV-film; sociology; Spanish; studio art; theatre arts, writing arts.

Costs and Aid

2006–2007: $9,330 tuition and fees, $8,742 room and board. 83% of students receive some financial aid. Average award: $9,243.

Endowment

$169 million.

More Distinctions

• US News & World Report "Top Tier" of Northern Regional Universities

• Kiplinger's named Rowan one of the "100 Best Buys in Public Colleges and Universities"

• The Princeton Review included Rowan in the latest edition of "The Best Northeastern Colleges."

Seton Hall University

NEW JERSEY

The oldest diocesan university in the United States, Seton Hall University was founded in 1856 by Bishop James Roosevelt Bayley as a Catholic university offering students a close-knit and inclusive campus community. Only fourteen miles from Manhattan, the university is home to eight schools, over sixty majors, and about ten thousand students.

Admissions Contact:

Seton Hall University
400 South Orange Avenue
South Orange, NJ 07079
Ph: (800) THE-HALL
Email: thehall@shu.edu
www.shu.edu

The 4 Distinctions

Engaged Students

At Seton Hall, hands-on learning opportunities provide students with career-based, service-based, and leadership-based experiences. Every Seton Hall undergraduate student participates in at least one community service/volunteer project, and many students also participate in a career-based experiential education program prior to graduation. Career-based experiences include student teaching, clinicals, practicums, field placements, and internship experiences.

Offering a completely wireless campus, Seton Hall places a major emphasis on the use of state-of-the-art technology and facilities, such as the trading room at the Stillman School of Business and Sim Man, a portable and advanced patient simulator for College of Nursing students. In addition, Seton Hall's award-winning Mobile Computing Program provides all incoming, full-time freshman with a brand-new, fully loaded laptop. Incoming freshman receive their laptops the summer before they enter Seton Hall, giving them the opportunity to become part of the Seton Hall community as early as freshman orientation. The laptops also allow faculty to integrate technology and cutting-edge learning into the classroom.

But learning doesn't just take place on campus. Seton Hall is committed to providing students with a global education in today's increasingly interconnected world. The office of international programs offers study-abroad programs in Russia, London, China, Cypress, and even Bermuda, to name just a few. Seton Hall has also had a relationship with universities in China since 1951, giving students and faculty the opportunity to live and learn there. For students who would like a career with an international focus, the Whitehead School of Diplomacy and International Relations prepares diplomatic and business professionals to serve in public service, international business, law, technology, and the nonprofit sector. The Whitehead School boasts an impressive faculty, including five current and former U.N. ambassadors and officials.

Seton Hall's proximity to New York City and northern New Jersey offers students opportunities to intern with globally recognized companies and organizations, including Goldman Sachs, Merck, NBC News, Late Night with Conan O'Brien, Mercedes-Benz, and the New York Mets.

Great Teaching

Students are more than just a number at Seton Hall. Seton Hall offers all the resources of a large institution to about 5,300 undergraduates and approximately 3,100 graduate students, but with an average class size of twenty-five students or fewer, and more than 96 percent of courses taught by professors, students receive personal attention.

Undergraduate students can choose from majors within the College of Arts and Sciences, the College of Education and Human Services, the College of Nursing, the Whitehead School of Diplomacy and International Relations, the Stillman School of Business, and the Immaculate Conception Seminary School of Theology. Popular majors include the sciences, communications, political science, criminal justice, accounting, finance, and sports management.

Seton Hall's new core curriculum is a multifaceted program that will prepare students to become thinking, caring, communicative, and ethically responsible global leaders. Unique to Seton Hall, the new core consists of signature courses that provide an interactive and distinctive experience for students, and a focus on certain key proficiencies aimed to better equip students for life beyond college.

During their first two years, undergraduate students are exposed to a world of ideas from great scholars, opening their minds to the perspectives, history, and achievements of many cultures. This approach helps many students choose their majors and minors, while giving them plenty of time to focus on these areas in their third and fourth years.

The university's awarding-winning freshman studies program eases students into college life. Freshmen are paired up with a mentor who provides academic advisement and support, and a peer adviser to help students connect with and meet new people.

Students also benefit from opportunities to collaborate with dedicated, full-time faculty involved in notable and dynamic research. One such scientist, Sulie Chang, PhD, chair of the department of biology, has received more than $2.5 million in National Institutes of Health grants for her research.

Vibrant Community

Seton Hall's fifty-eight-acre campus in South Orange offers students an abundance of opportunities both on and off campus. On campus, there are seventeen varsity athletic teams that compete in the Big East Conference, over one hundred clubs and organizations, eighteen intramural sports, and Greek life to keep students with all interests involved and entertained. A short, ten-minute walk from campus brings students to the town center, which features bookstores, coffee shops, and restaurants. Once in town, students can hop on a train and arrive in the heart of New York City, the capital of fashion, finance, art, and entertainment, in under a half hour.

The Seton Hall campus community is guided by faith, with a beautiful historic chapel on campus and a campus ministry office. All Seton Hall students take classes in ethics and learn in a community informed by Catholic ideals and universal values. Students are engaged in learning about the importance of possessing integrity, compassion, and a commitment to helping others. This strong commitment to building character is extended to all students; Seton Hall welcomes students and faculty from all faiths.

Successful Outcomes

Seton Hall's location also gives students access to neighboring science- and technology-related companies, such as Johnson & Johnson, Merck, and ExxonMobile. The university's proximity to the "world's medicine cabinet" allows graduates to make connections within the pharmaceutical industry, which is expected to create approximately eighty thousand new science research jobs within the next decade.

Seton Hall's career center is one of few in the country that provide a dedicated career counselor to work with students throughout their college careers. Students begin this relationship in their freshman year, when they start exploring career interests and opportunities. These career counselors also work with students to organize internships with career insight. In addition, career workshops allow students to explore majors, choose their career fields, and begin to build professional relationships. Workshop topics include a focus on career options for different majors and tips on navigating the job market, writing resumes, and using the Internet as a career development tool.

The career center maintains an extensive job listings database and sponsors on-campus recruiting events. Hundreds of employers and alumni come to campus each year to mentor and recruit Seton Hall students for cooperative education programs and employment after graduation.

Notable alumni include Andrew Kohut, president of the Pew Research Center; George L. Miles Jr., CEO of WQED Multimedia and a director of AIG; Chris Modrzynski, COO of the New Jersey Devils; Frank Wilde, CEO of Tarantella, Inc.; Dick Vitale, ESPN sports anchor; Max Weinberg, drummer for Bruce Springsteen's E Street Band and bandleader on Late Night with Conan O'Brien; X. J. Kennedy, world-renowned poet; and Craig Biggio, Major League Baseball player.

Fast Facts

Seton Hall University is a private, four-year liberal arts Catholic university founded in 1856 as the first diocesan university in the United States.

Web site

http:// www.shu.edu

Location

South Orange, New Jersey—Seton Hall's 58-acre campus is located in the suburban village of South Orange, which is located only 14 miles from New York City.

Student Profile

5,300 undergraduate students (46% male, 54% female); 50 states and territories, 58 countries; 30% diversity rate.

Faculty Profile

860 full-time faculty. 92% hold a terminal degree in their field. 15:1 student/faculty ratio. Average class size is 25.

Residence Life

Moderately residential: 84% of freshmen live on campus.

Athletics

NCAA Division I, BIG EAST Conference. 17 varsity sports (8 men's: baseball, basketball, cross-country, golf, soccer, swimming & diving, indoor track, outdoor track; 9 women's: basketball, cross-country, soccer, softball, swimming & diving, tennis, indoor track, outdoor track, volleyball), 18 club sports, and intramurals.

Academic Programs

Accounting; Africana & Diaspora studies; anthropology; art education; art history; Asian studies; athletic training; biochemistry; biological sciences; biomedical engineering; broadcasting, visual & interactive media; business administration; Catholic studies; Catholic theology; chemistry; chemical engineering; civil engineering; classical studies; communication studies; computer engineering; computer science; criminal justice; diplomacy & international relations; economics (B.A. or B.S.); electrical engineering; English; environmental studies; finance; fine art; French; graphic, interactive & advertising art; history; honors program; industrial engineering; integrated elementary, early childhood, special education; Italian; journalism & public relations; leadership studies; liberal studies; management; management information systems; marketing; mathematics; mechanical engineering; modern languages; music education; music performance; nursing; nursing for R.N.; occupational therapy; philosophy; physical therapy; physician assistant; physics; political science; predental; prelaw; premajor arts; premajor sciences; premedical; preoptometry; pretheology; preveterinary; psychology; religious studies; Russian; secondary education; social & behavioral sciences; social work; sociology; Spanish; special education/speech-language pathology; sport management; theatre & performance.

*Note: Graduate programs available

Costs and Aid

2007–2008: $28,150 comprehensive (Flat rate for in-state or out-of-state students). Student room rates are just over $6,900 per year, with board costs ranging from $642 to just under $2,800 per year. 75% of students receive some financial aid. Average award: $15,920 per year.

Endowment

$230 million.

The Richard Stockton College

NEW JERSEY

The Richard Stockton College of New Jersey is a midsized, public, coeducational, liberal arts college located on a 1,600-acre campus in the pinelands of southeastern New Jersey. The college was founded in 1969 and emphasizes developing successful students who are leaders for the community, state, and nation.

Admissions Contact:

The Richard Stockton College
PO Box 195
Pomona, NJ 08240
Ph: (609) 652-4261
Email: admissions@stockton.edu
www.stockton.edu

The 4 Distinctions

Engaged Students

Stockton College offers unique study programs that encourage students to gain experience and knowledge about the world. Stockton's affiliation with the The Washington Center (TWC) has given students the opportunity to fulfill credit hours by interning and taking courses in Washington, DC. Through TWC, Stockton boasts the largest Washington internship program of any non-DC-area university. These internships are for all majors and can range from work in nonprofit organizations to media outlets to the White House.

A study tour is another unique option for many students at Stockton. These tours are led by Stockton faculty and are typically from one to four weeks in length. Students who go on a study tour take a course that goes along with the trip. Recent tours have taken students to Costa Rica, Poland, South Africa, Israel, and many other exciting locations. Students can also study abroad for a term or a year. All of these programs expose students to the world so they can develop academic competence, maturity, and an appreciation of culture. For a chance to travel and serve others, students from the Stockton Christian Fellowship take a trip during spring break to Exuma, a district of the Bahamas, to build and repair houses for the poor.

The Political Engagement Project (PEP) at Stockton College promotes the skills, understanding and motivation of students in their own political engagement, whether in the community, public policy or electoral politics. This is a non-partisan project aimed at encouraging political discourse among students, peers, faculty, and administration as well as civic action in all forms with the goal of increasing students' life-long political engagement. PEP addresses the serious problem of political disengagement in young people and advocates a dramatic increase in college and university efforts to strengthen student interest in politics. The project integrates political discussions, field trips, guest speakers, debates, literature, periodicals and other media into existing courses.

Great Teaching

The learning environment at Stockton is vibrant, fostered by professors who are passionate about what they teach. Freshman year, each student is paired up with a professor in his or her major to be a helpful guide through graduation. The average class size for a lecture is thirty; in a laboratory, twelve; and in a regular course, seventeen. Sciences are the strongest academic field at Stockton, preparing many students in premedical fields. The arts are vibrant, as well, with Pulitzer Prize–winning poet Stephen G. Dunn teaching in the creative writing department.

Some special facilities at Stockton include the new Carnegie Library and an astronomical observatory. Marine biology students can take advantage of the Marine Field Station to perform hands-on work in their area of study, while the Holocaust Resource Center is at the core of Holocaust and genocide studies at Stockton. The center includes a library and archives of video- and audio-taped histories of Holocaust survivors.

Two recently added, noteworthy programs at Stockton are the Computational Science (CPLS) Program and Homeland Security Track Master of Arts in Criminal Justice (MACJ). CPLS is an interdisciplinary five year B.S./M.S. dual-degree program in which students will acquire substantial knowledge in the sciences of his or her interest by taking courses offered in existing Division of Natural Sciences and Mathematics (NAMS) programs. This knowledge will be augmented by an introduction to sophisticated computational software and programming tools. The course work will be supplemented by special projects and internships at local industrial organizations to provide a capstone experience for students and a smooth transition into either an industrial career or graduate study in a computation-intensive field at a major university. The MACJ with a Homeland Security Track involves an all-hazards perspective, meaning that the program involves discussion about issues regarding the prevention of and reaction to natural and human-made disasters and terrorist attacks. The legal, moral and ethical issues pertaining to homeland security are an important component of the curriculum, as are studies of agency participation and cooperation in planning for and responding to crisis. The track examines issues from historical, cross-cultural, and interdisciplinary perspectives, drawing on experts in criminal justice, other social sciences, computer science, law, and natural sciences.

Vibrant Community

Stockton's campus is a twenty-minute drive from the Jersey shore, an hour from Philadelphia, and two hours from New York City. The Stockton community cares deeply for the environment: the campus has its own lake, keeps four hundred acres of land as an ecological reserve for natural science research, and uses an environmentally friendly, geothermal heating and cooling system, saving more than three hundred thousand in fuel costs each year.

The variety of clubs on campus brings students together to make an impact on people and the environment. One of the most popular clubs, Water Watch, organizes cleanups for surrounding bodies of water. Students, faculty, staff, and the community join together to clean the lakes and streams of southern New Jersey during the water cleanups. In addition to caring for the environment, students care for people, as well. The Stockton Christian Fellowship cares for the community by bringing meals to the Atlantic City Rescue Mission. Other organizations include Students Taking Action Now: Darfur, Stockton Hillel, and the Spanish Club.

On campus, an entertainment committee plans events and activities to keep the campus lively. Because there is no football team, soccer is the fan favorite at Stockton. The wooded campus provides many paths to run or walk on, and outdoor volleyball courts are situated near the dorms and apartments.

Successful Outcomes

The president of the college boasts that a Stockton student will obtain the educational benefits of a private college and the cultural benefits of a public university. Stockton alumni have found this to be the case, holding on to school pride once they have graduated.

About 35 percent of Stockton undergraduates go on to graduate school. The Washington Internship Program, which has sent over nine hundred students to Washington over the past twenty-five years, has provided many alumni with careers in DC. In Stockton's career services office, career counselors and peer career advisors assist students with identifying interests, exploring majors, setting career goals, writing resumes, preparing for interviews, searching for jobs or internships, and applying to graduate programs.

Fast Facts

Stockton College is a mid-sized, award-winning liberal arts college, founded in 1969.

Web site

http://www.stockton.edu

Location

Pomona, New Jersey—15 minutes from Atlantic City, one hour from Philadelphia, and two hours from New York City.

Student Profile

7,213 undergraduate students (42% male, 58% female); 17% minority; 30 countries represented.

Faculty Profile

461 faculty, 49% full-time. 94% hold terminal degrees. 17:1 student/faculty ratio. Average class size is 24.

Residence Life

Mildly residential: 31% of students live on campus in residence halls or garden-style apartments.

Athletics

NCAA Division III, New Jersey Athletic Conference. 15 varsity sports (6 men's: baseball, basketball, cross-country, lacrosse, soccer, indoor/outdoor track & field; 9 women's: soccer, volleyball, cross-country, tennis, field hockey, basketball, rowing, softball, cheerleading, indoor/outdoor track & field); intramurals.

Academics

Accelerated premed; audiology/audiologist & speech-language pathology/pathologist; biochemistry; biology/biological sciences; business administration & management; chemistry; communication studies/speech communication & rhetoric; computer & information sciences; computer science; criminology; economics; English language & literature; environmental studies; foreign languages & literatures; geology/earth science; history; information science/studies; interdisciplinary studies; liberal arts & sciences/liberal studies; marine biology & biological oceanography; mathematics; nursing—registered nurse training (RN, ASN, BSN, MSN); nursing science; pharmacy (dual-degree); philosophy; physics; political science & government; psychology; public health; social work; sociology; teacher education; visual & performing arts.

Costs and Aid

2006–2007: $17,600 comprehensive ($9,000 tuition). 65% of students receive some financial aid.

Endowment

$1,521,765.

More Distinctions

• Ranked sixth in the nation among public liberal arts colleges by U.S. News & World Report.

• Classified as a "highly selective college" by the Princeton Review.

• Listed as "A Best Northeastern College" by the Princeton Review.

Arcadia University

PENNSYLVANIA

Located on the outskirts of Philadelphia, Arcadia University is a private university, combining liberal arts and sciences with professional programs. Arcadia is noted for the strength of its international programs. Recognizing increasing internationalism in business and other fields, the university prepares its graduates to thrive in a culturally diverse world.

Admissions Contact:

Arcadia University
450 S. Easton Road
Glenside, PA 19038
877-ARCADIA - (877) 272-2342
Ph: (215) 572-2910
Email: admiss@arcadia.edu
www.arcadia.edu

The 4 Distinctions

Engaged Students

More than half of Arcadia's students study in another country before they graduate. In fact, international travel begins during the first year, with 87 percent of Arcadia freshmen using their passports. Many freshmen spend a semester of their first year in London, England; in Stirling, Scotland; or in Limerick, Ireland. During spring break, groups of freshmen travel to London, Scotland, and Spain for preview programs costing just $245. Transfer students have the opportunity to earn two credits while spending spring break in Italy for just $550.

The University's Center for Education Abroad, one of the largest campus-based international-study programs in the United States, offers more than ninety programs around the world. These include fairly traditional study-abroad destinations, as well as a number of unique programs, such as travel to the West African country of Equatorial Guinea, where students may work with elementary-school and adult education teachers, explore the nation's cultural and linguistic diversity, study the challenges of sustainable development, work in animal nurseries, and—on the island of Bioko—study tropical biodiversity as they participate in a census of primates and sea turtles. In Tanzania, Arcadia's graduate students in International Peace and Conflict Resolution focus on project-based student learning that supports such regional initiatives as establishing a conflict early-warning system.

Arcadia students frequently participate in internships in the United States and overseas. The university offers programs in Australia, England, Ireland, and Scotland that combine credit-earning course work with one to four days per week in a business setting or with politicians or governmental officials. These internships may last a summer or a semester.

Arcadia students are also involved in community service in the Philadelphia area and across the country. Last year, Arcadia freshmen contributed more than one thousand hours to valuable projects on that one day alone. Students also recently traveled to Louisiana during spring break to work on a home-building project.

Great Teaching

Many classes have an international component, often involving an overseas trip. On one recent class trip, students traveled to the Caribbean island of Dominica, where they worked with local tourism officials and with several commercial enterprises.

In the First Year Student Experience, freshmen are grouped by interest with faculty sponsors. Some of these seminars use the city of Philadelphia as a living laboratory. Each of Arcadia's academic areas has its own special characteristics. In psychology and biology, for instance, student-faculty research leading to professional publication is commonplace, and seniors present capstone projects in April of their final year. Recognized as a leader in special education, the education program is home to highly regarded professors in literacy and in math education, and seniors participate in an innovative integrative approach. Business students take advantage of internships in Philadelphia, and students in English and communications learn how to get their writing published.

Arcadia's General Education program provides an integrative and global experience for all Arcadia University undergraduate students throughout their academic careers. Students have significant flexibility in determining how and with what courses these General Education requirements are satisfied. This enables them to delve more deeply into their chosen major concurrent with a multidisciplinary look at how their work applies to the world.

All students participate in four types of required Curricular Experiences: a First-Year Experience, two University Seminars, a Global Connections Experience and Reflection, and a Senior Capstone Project. The seminar courses focus on integrative learning by providing vital and distinctive opportunities for students to make intellectual connections between normally discrete disciplinary ideas and the world beyond the classroom. Students also have a cross-cultural experience that places them in new cultural settings that may include study abroad or cross-cultural experiences in the United States.

Students take courses in four, theme-based Areas of Inquiry: Creative Expressions, Cultural Legacies, the Natural and Physical World, and Self and Society. Students enjoy project-based courses in the creative processes, explore cultural legacies and their relevance to contemporary societies, and experiment in natural and physical observations.

Students develop a series of Intellectual Practices through courses in various subjects. The five Intellectual Practices that Arcadia emphasizes are Global Connections, Modern Language, Quantitative Reasoning, Visual Literacy, and Writing. Students explore the interconnectedness of nations and societies and learn to express themselves through other languages, quantitative reasoning, and both visual and written literacy.

Vibrant Community

Arcadia offers numerous residential options, including residence halls, apartment-style living, and even quarters in the famous Grey Towers Castle, a national historic landmark. Residence life provides an opportunity for students to have fun and become leaders within their living groups.

Arcadia students participate in more than 45 clubs and organizations, including student government, academic, cultural and religious organizations, and community service groups, including the Latino Association, a popular club whose dance team has performed at a Philadelphia 76ers game.

Fast Facts

Arcadia University is a four-year, private, comprehensive university founded in 1853.

Location

Glenside, Montgomery County—just 25 minutes north of Center City Philadelphia.

Student Profile

3,700 students; (28% male, 72% female); 46 states, 26 countries; 17% minority.

Faculty Profile

332 full- and part-time faculty. 13:1 student/faculty ratio. Average class size is 16.

Residence Life

Highly residential: approximately 80% of students live on campus.

Athletics

NCCA Division III, Middle Atlantic States Collegiate Athletic Corporation (MASCAC). 14 varsity sports (6 men's: baseball, basketball, golf, soccer, swimming, tennis; 8 women's: basketball, golf, swimming, tennis, field hockey, lacrosse, softball, volleyball); club sports and intramurals available.

Academics

Accounting; acting; art; art education; biology; business administration; chemistry; chemistry & business; communications; computer science; computing technology; criminal justice; economics; education; engineering; English; environmental studies; finance; fine arts; global legal studies; global media; health administration; history; human resources administration; international business & culture; international peace & conflict resolution; international studies; liberal studies; management; management information systems; marketing; mathematics; modern languages; philosophy; political science; preart therapy; predentistry; prelaw; premedicine; prenursing; preoptometry; prephysical therapy; prephysician assistant studies; preveterinary; psychobiology; psychology; scientific illustration; sociology; Spanish cultural studies; special education; sport psychology; theatre arts & English.

Costs and Aid

2007–2008: $37,780 comprehensive ($27,440 tuition). 98% of students receive aid. Average award: $18,600.

Endowment

$42,424,000.

More Distinctions

• US News & World Report ranks Arcadia University 22nd among master's universities in the North.

• Included among Barron's Best Buys in College Education for the fifteenth year.

Cabrini College

PENNSYLVANIA

Admissions Contact:

Cabrini College (CC) is a Catholic, residential, coeducational college of liberal arts and professional studies, known for its commitment to community service. It was one of the first institutions of higher education in the nation to have a service-learning requirement for graduation.

Cabrini College
610 King of Prussia Rd.
Radnor, PA 19087-3698
Ph: (610) 902-8100
Email: admit@cabrini.edu
www.cabrini.edu

The 4 Distinctions

Engaged Students

CC offers thirty-five undergraduate majors as well as a series of preprofessional programs and concentrations. The most popular majors are education, English and communication, and business. Most education students are learning in actual school classrooms by their sophomore year, and 90 percent of CC's education majors go on to teach in elementary schools.

The results of the 2006 National Survey of Student Engagement (NSSE) show that CC's first-year and senior students are in the top half of students from 528 colleges and universities in all five benchmarks of effective educational practice: level of academic challenge, active and collaborative learning, student-faculty interaction, enriching educational experiences, and supportive campus environment.

Great Teaching

CC has a low student to faculty ratio of sixteen to one, allowing students to develop close relationships with professors. Jerry Zurek, PhD, was named Professor of the Year for 2005 in Pennsylvania, a prestigious award granted by the Council for the Advancement and Support of Education (CASE) honoring outstanding instructors who influence the lives and careers of their students. Dr. Zurek, a member of the CC faculty since 1977, has won numerous awards throughout his career. He has played an integral role in the development of the Hamilton Family Communications Center, which houses a state-of-the-art radio station, television studio, and newspaper and graphic-design laboratories, providing students with hands-on learning experiences.

The college's new Center for Science, Education, and Technology includes facilities for instructing future science teachers, and is the location for the Southeastern Pennsylvania Science Olympiad. The Crabby Creek Stream Monitoring Project, funded by an Environmental Protection Agency grant, will expand the environmental science curriculum to include science, psychology, and English students, and will provide environmental science education outreach for students from kindergarten through eighth grade.

CC students in all majors select from more than 1,300 co-op and internship opportunities in private industry, government agencies, media organizations and non-profit institutions.

Vibrant Community

Founded in 1957 by the Missionary Sisters of the Sacred Heart of Jesus, CC is named for St. Frances Xavier Cabrini. St. Cabrini, who was canonized in 1946, is the founder of the the Missionary Sisters of the Sacred Heart of Jesus and was the first American citizen to be elevated to sainthood. The college's mission, based on St. Cabrini's teachings, is to provide an "education of the heart," integrating intellectual competency with moral and social responsibility. The ideal is to "educate the whole person, [to] take action as a person, not just a professional." CC's educational philosophy prepares students for careers and enables them to live lives of dignity and purpose. Its new "brand promise," adopted in anticipation of its fiftieth anniversary in 2007 is "Do something extraordinary," an apt description of how members of the Cabrini College Community live, work, and grow.

As a participant in Campus Compact, CC is proud to be included "with distinction for general community service" in the President's Higher Education Community Service Honor Roll, awarded by Learn and Serve America.

CC is located on 112 acres in Radnor, a suburb thirty minutes or thirteen miles northwest of Philadelphia on the city's well-known Main Line. The area also is home to Villanova University, Eastern University, and Bryn Mawr College. Philadelphia, the City of Brotherly Love and the Birthplace of America, is the sixth most populous city in the U.S. It offers attractions, cultural events, and service opportunities typical of large, East Coast urban centers.

CC's campus is largely residential, with 1,100 of 1,650 undergraduates residing on campus. Thirteen residence halls offer living arrangements ranging from singles, doubles, triples/suites to apartments; and students may choose curricular-based living and learning communities: two for honors students and one for students still deciding on their majors.

On campus, CC offers competitive NCAA Division III intercollegiate athletics in eighteen men's and women's teams as well as a strong intramural sports program. CC students can take advantage of classes, facilities, and resources at eight local institutions, members of a consortium that includes Arcadia University, Rosemont College, Chestnut Hill College, and Immaculata University, among others. A free campus shuttle service connects with regional rail service to Philadelphia.

One important off-campus program is the Cabrini Classroom in Norristown, a mutually beneficial collaborative venture with Norristown community service providers such as Big Brothers/Big Sisters, the Police Athletic League, and Family Services. Benefiting from both the services of CC students and the expertise of CC's faculty and staff, the program provides at-risk youths with one-on-one mentoring, career development, science summer camps, cross-cultural events, and exposure to the college's exercise science and health promotion programs. CC students integrate service and community-based learning into academic course work in a real community setting, giving faces and names to social issues. The Cabrini Classroom in Norristown provides interactions that nurture in students an "Education of the heart," grounded in respect, community, justice, and a special concern for the most vulnerable in society.

Successful Outcomes

According to results of the most recent administration of the Collegiate Learning Assessment (CLA), CC students graduate with a larger-than-predicted growth in key communication and critical thinking skills, and only 20% of institutions in the study showed this "value-added" dimension. Nationally, 8,900 students from 123 colleges and universities participated in the CLA, a tool that measures student learning holistically and provides evidence of institutional effectiveness.

CC students and graduates maintain their focus on the wider world. Recently, a 9/11 quilt was displayed on campus, and both CC teachers and students participate in a partnership with Catholic Relief services, allowing them to be involved on a global level. CC students make presentations of their academic work at campus, local, regional, national, and international conferences/symposiums.

Ninety-five percent of Cabrini College graduates of the class of 2006 are employed or in graduate/professional school within ten months of graduation. 86% of employed graduates reported that their employment was related to their major, either directly or indirectly. Over half of students that participated in a co-op experience responded that they received a job offer from their co-op employer. Graduates go on to medical school, law school, graduate schools of education, graduate schools of business, and other graduate schools of arts and science.

Fast Facts

Cabrini College is a Catholic, residential, coeducational college of liberal arts and professional studies, known for its commitment to community service

Web site

http://www.cabrini.edu

Location

Radnor, Pennsylvania—13 miles northwest of Philadelphia on the city's Main Line.

Student Profile

1,814 undergraduate students (32% male, 68% female); 22 states and territories, 10 countries: 10% minority, 1% international.

Faculty Profile

63 full-time faculty. 77% hold a terminal degree in their field, 16:1 student/faculty ratio, Average undergraduate class size is 18.

Residence Life

Highly residential: 66% of full-time undergraduate students live on campus.

Athletics

National Collegiate Athletic Association (NCAA). 18 intercollegiate sports (8 men's; 10 women's).

Academic Programs

Accounting; American studies; biology; business administration; chemistry; computer information science; criminology; early childhood education; educational studies; elementary education; English; English/communication; exercise science & health promotion; finance; graphic design; history; human resources management; individualized major; information science; liberal arts; marketing; mathematics; organizational management; philosophy; political science; psychology; religious studies; Romance languages (French & Spanish); social work; sociology; special education.

Costs and Aid

2007–2008: $38,320 comprehensive ($27,200 tuition). 74% of students receive some financial aid. Average award: $10,387.

Endowment

$22,432,046.

More Distinctions

• Cabrini College has received over $923,000 in federal, state, and research grant funds for community engagement, institutional and environmental research, and its health and student-wellness programs.

• Cabrini has received a $2 million, five-year development grant through the United States Department of Education's Title III Strengthening Institutions Program.

Chatham University

PENNSYLVANIA

Admissions Contact:

Founded in 1869, Chatham University is a coed university with a residential women's undergraduate college as its historic heart. Chatham College for Women houses academic and co-curricular programs for undergraduate women at Chatham University and embodies the traditions and rituals of one of the nation's oldest colleges for women.

Chatham University
Woodland Road
Pittsburgh, PA 15232
(800) 837-1290
Ph: (412) 365-1290
Fax: (412) 365-1609
Email: admissions@chatham.edu
www.chatham.edu

The 4 Distinctions

Engaged Students

The University's mission is based on a desire to increase self-awareness, encourage social responsibility, enhance cultural awareness, develop leadership ability, establish a lifestyle of wellness and make connections with others as students endeavor to serve in the societies of today and lead in the world of tomorrow. For example, Chatham is one of several institutions that have joined together in Project Pericles, a national effort to prepare students for responsible and participatory citizenship. Through Project Pericles, student-faculty teams have attended the national gathering of Pericleans, and others have participated in the Pennsylvania Governor's Conference for Women.

The First-Year Student Sequence introduces students to the Pittsburgh region and its culture and provides opportunities to learn about the resources of the urban environment and to study issues of concern to women. These courses provide students with the analytical and communication skills essential for successful academic performance.

Each year, Chatham students complete thousands of hours of community service with organizations throughout the region. Students regularly volunteer for short-term projects, long-term service opportunities, and single events. Off-campus community service and volunteer opportunities are also available.

To help students gain an understanding of the world, Chatham Abroad involves a three-week travel experience with faculty members during Maymester of sophomore year; past Chatham Abroad trips featured Belize, Egypt, England, France, the Galapagos Islands, Ireland, Italy, Morocco, Russia, and Spain.

Great Teaching

Chatham's environment stresses the individual, both in and out of the classroom. The undergraduate student-teacher ratio of 8:1 ensures individual consideration and interaction between students and faculty members. Each student is assigned a faculty member who serves as her adviser through the completion of her degree program, including the Senior Tutorial capstone project. Ninety-four percent of all undergraduate faculty members hold terminal degrees.

Chatham's general education curriculum includes six required interdisciplinary courses, plus analytical reasoning, an international or intercultural experience, and wellness courses. Graduation requirements include the general education courses, a major, and the senior tutorial—an original research/capstone project. Students are mentored one-on-one by a faculty member throughout the tutorial process. The project provides an excellent bridge to graduate and professional schools and strong preparation for law and medical schools.

The University's 4-4-1 academic calendar consists of fall and spring terms, plus a three-week "Maymester" which features study abroad, concentrated study, experimental projects, travel and field experiences, internships, interdisciplinary study, and student exchanges with other institutions.

Chatham's Programs for Academic Advising, Career Development, and Educational Enrichment (PACE) offer students a comprehensive approach to academic and career planning as well as an academic-support network designed to maximize each student's academic success. Career services include counseling for undecided students, student internships, placement, workshops, recruitment, and mentor programs.

Vibrant Community

Chatham's 35-acre arboretum campus is located on historic Woodland Road in Pittsburgh's Shadyside neighborhood. The University's students can easily access Pittsburgh's dynamic career, cultural, and entertainment opportunities and can share in the educational and social offerings of the other nine area colleges and universities.

The undergraduate and graduate student body of almost 1,800 represents 34 states and 21 countries. Members of minority groups and international students compose 20 percent of the undergraduate student body. Resident and commuting students participate actively in the numerous professional, academic, social, and special-interest organizations at the University. Health services and personal and career counseling services are available on campus. There are several student publications, and Chatham sponsors frequent programs and speakers in the arts, environment, sciences, and public leadership arena.

Chatham's suburban campus is located minutes from downtown Pittsburgh. Steeped in history, the campus features towering trees, wandering paths, and century-old mansions which today serve as networked residence halls. Pittsburgh is one of the safest and most dynamic cities in the country and is headquarters to major businesses and industries in finance, health care, and technology. Students find eclectic neighborhoods that reflect Pittsburgh's historic qualities yet appeal to a wide audience. The city offers numerous arts and entertainment options in the Pittsburgh Symphony and world-renowned opera, ballet, and theater companies. Nearby parks and ski areas and the city's three rivers provide ample opportunities for such activities as hiking, biking, kayaking, skiing, whitewater rafting, and more. For sports enthusiasts, Pittsburgh's professional sports teams include the Penguins, Pirates and Steelers. Bus, rail, and air connections are available to and from most major cities.

Successful Outcomes

Chatham graduates are living their dreams as authors and activists, engineers and entrepreneurs, civic leaders and corporate CEOs, journalists and judges, educators and editors, doctors and designers, performers and pioneers. Chatham College for Women is proud of its history in preparing women for law school, medical school, or many other options including the College for Graduate Studies at Chatham University.

Notable alumnae include environmentalist Rachel Carson; Cynthia Montgomery, Timken Professor of Business Administration at Harvard University; Kathie Olsen, deputy director of the National Science Foundation; and Laurel Rice, first vice president of Morgan Stanley.

Fast Facts

Chatham University is a four-year, private, nonsectarian institution founded in 1869.

Web site
http://www.chatham.edu/

Location
Pittsburgh, Pennsylvania

Student Profile
610 undergraduates (all women); 34 states and 21 countries; 15% minority, 6% international.

Faculty Profile
78 full-time faculty. 94% of whom hold the terminal degree in their respective field 8:1 undergraduate student-faculty ratio (10:1 overall). Average class size is 14.

Athletics
NCAA Division III, Presidents' Athletic Conference (PAC) and Eastern College Athletic Conference (ECAC). Seven varsity sports (basketball, ice hockey, softball, soccer, swimming, tennis, volleyball), plus numerous intramurals and club sports, including basketball, bowling, crew, golf, soccer, softball, tennis, and volleyball.

Academic Programs
Chatham University offers the following majors leading to a Bachelor of Arts or Bachelor of Science degree: accounting, art (electronic media, photography, studio arts), art history, arts management, biochemistry, biology, business economics, chemistry, cultural studies, economics, education, English, environmental studies, exercise science, film and digital video-making, forensics, French, global policy studies, history, interior architecture, international business, management, marketing, mathematics, music, physics, political science, professional communication (broadcast journalism, print journalism, professional writing, public relations), psychology, public policy studies, social work, Spanish, theater, and women's studies.

Students may choose a traditional major, an interdisciplinary major, a double major, or a self-designed major. Pre-professional programs are offered in law, medicine and health professions, physical therapy, teaching certification, and veterinary medicine. A joint-degree engineering program is offered with Carnegie Mellon University. Chatham prepares undergraduate and graduate students for certification in four areas: early childhood, elementary (K-6), secondary (7-12), art (K-12), and environmental (K-12). In addition, certification in special education (K-12) and School Counseling is available at the graduate level through the Master of Arts in Teaching. Certification in music (K-12) is available through Carnegie Mellon University.

Costs and Aid
2007-2008 costs: $33,108 comprehensive ($25,216 tuition). More than 90% of students receive financial aid.

Endowment
$56.9 million.

Edinboro University

PENNSYLVANIA

Edinboro University of Pennsylvania is a comprehensive, residential, student-centered liberal arts university. Chartered in 1856 as the Edinboro Academy, it became a university in 1983, celebrating its 150th anniversary in 2006-07. Edinboro is a leading institution of higher education in its region and the state, standing for excellence in academics, technology and the arts.

Admissions Contact:

Edinboro University
200 East Normal Street
Edinboro, PA 16444
(888) 8GO-BORO
Ph: (814) 732-2000
Email:
www.edinboro.edu

The 4 Distinctions

Engaged Students

Edinboro University students – residential, distance, undergraduate and graduate – know that the University's motto – "Great Things Happen Here!" – is true. Edinboro offers more than one hundred degree programs and nearly 60 minor programs. The most popular majors are criminal justice, education, fine/studio arts, speech communication and general studies.

Edinboro students know their University is the place to pursue and realize their higher education aspirations leading to thousands of meaningful career opportunities from astrophysics to education, from journalism to high-tech animation, from health care to social work, from criminal forensics to music, from foreign languages to nuclear medicine, from anthropology to psychology, from industrial bio-chemistry to the environment and countless other diversified areas of career interest. Add to the mix a dozen nationally-accredited academic programs, internships and experiential learning in virtually every department, on-campus professional recruiting, and a networking alumni base of 50,000, and students easily understand why Edinboro University is synonymous with success.

Edinboro is not only distinguished, but nationally-famous for its animation programs, graphic design and sculpture. The University's largest major, the Art Department has 1,000 majors and more than 50 critically-recognized faculty members.

Criminal justice is another distinguished program at Edinboro with many alumni pursuing careers with the FBI, CIA and U.S. Secret Service. Some faculty are former FBI agents, while others are former leaders of state and national law enforcement agencies. Edinboro University is also home to the Pennsylvania State Police Computer Crime Laboratory.

Every department at Edinboro has its own internship program, and students in some fields are required to attain certification. Many students engage in research with faculty members. In addition, the Career Services Center links students with local employers and organizations offering internship opportunities within the students' areas of study. Edinboro's programs for students with disabilities is perennially ranked among the nation's top ten, providing total accessibility for physically challenged students.

Great Teaching

Teaching is another of the great things happening at Edinboro. With a low student-to-faculty ratio of eighteen-to-one and no teaching assistants, Edinboro's 408 tenured, tenure-track, full, part-time and adjunct faculty members mentor their students, working closely with them on research projects, classroom learning and hands-on laboratory assignments. They advise students through the internship process and give freely of their time to help ensure student success.

Edinboro University is well-known for its successful placement of students in many career tracks, particularly nursing, social work, forensics, accounting, business and education.

Edinboro professors strive to be not only responsive, but proactive in terms of preparing their students to thrive in the world around the university.

With the small class sizes, professors take a personal interest in their students in a learning environment that's caring and friendly. Because of Edinboro's highly qualified educational professionals, Edinboro students succeed in class – and in life.

Vibrant Community

Edinboro University is situated in Edinboro, a rural/suburban community located in the lush farmland and rolling hills of northwestern Pennsylvania, about 18 miles south of the cultural, sporting and shopping center of Erie. Edinboro's campus itself sits just off Interstate-79, a major north/south corridor putting Edinboro within an easy two-hour drive to Pittsburgh, Cleveland and Buffalo. Edinboro's main campus, home to about 7,800 undergraduate and graduate students, includes a five-acre lake, much open green space and wooded areas.

Known for its diverse student population, Edinboro University offers living and learning floors in its residence halls, including criminal justice, education, FLASH (Foreign Language, Anthropology, Social Work and History), Frederick Douglass African American Studies, art, science management technology, undeclared and Edinboro Success. Resident scholars often live in these residence halls with students. On the table are plans for a $105-million residence hall project that will provide some 1,700 beds in suite/apartment-style living. Edinboro's new $5 million music building will be ready for occupancy in late fall, while the $20 million expansion and renovation of the Student Center will be completed by late 2007 or early 2008.

The large, 585-acre campus – with branches in nearby Erie and Meadville – is dotted with hundreds of trees among the many red brick and more contemporary buildings. The oldest building, Academy Hall, constructed in 1857 in the Italian Renaissance style, was recently renovated and rededicated. Housing Undergraduate Admissions, Academy Hall is listed on the National Register of Historic Places and is believed to be the oldest former Normal School building in the nation still in use for educational purposes. All University buildings are accessible to the physically-challenged and well-maintained, and many are "green" or environmentally friendly.

When Edinboro students are not in class, they have the option of participating in any of more than 200 student organizations, a vibrant Student Government Association and an active Greek life. The busy social/cultural campus scene includes a concert/lecture series, ballet performances, a film series, plays, recitals, art exhibitions in the University's two galleries and even weekly "Bad Movie Nights."

Community projects and Student Philanthropy Days are also popular, encouraging students to perform good deeds in their daily lives, while taking a trusteeship and stewardship of their communities.

The University's classes and activities at its Edinboro, Erie and Meadville sites, as well as the shopping centers and attractions in Erie, are all connected via regular bus service which is free to all students.

Edinboro University students are engaged in an active men's and women's NCAA Division II sports program, including football and basketball, in the competitive Pennsylvania State Athletic Conference. Edinboro's Fighting Scots wrestling team competes at the Division I level, with frequent All-Americans and National Champions. Wheelchair basketball is also popular, with Edinboro competing and winning against national powerhouses.

Successful Outcomes

The proof that "Great Things Happen Here" can be found in Edinboro University's highly successful outcomes. Placement rates for undergrads and graduate students are consistently high, some at nearly 100%. Faculty members at prestigious law or medical schools say Edinboro's graduates are among the best-prepared to pursue advanced degrees in their disciplines.

The Edinboro University Alumni Association numbers more than 50,000, with nearly half of them remaining active in University affairs, providing a global networking system for recent alumni. A few famous alumni include award-winning actress and humanitarian Sharon Stone, Nortel CEO and President Mike Zafirovski, and NPR Morning Edition's Jack Speer.

Fast Facts

Edinboro University of Pennsylvania, established in 1857, is the largest comprehensive institution of higher education in northwestern Pennsylvania. It is one of 14 universities in the Pennsylvania State System of Higher Education.

Web site

http://www.edinboro.edu

Location

Edinboro, Pennsylvania—18 miles south of Erie, Pa., is within 100 miles of Pittsburgh, Cleveland and Buffalo.

Student Profile

6,800 undergraduate students (54% female, 46% male); 37 states and territories; 11% minority; 2% international.

Faculty Profile

408 full and part-time faculty, many with terminal degrees; 18:1 student/faculty ratio; average class size: 25.

Residence Life

Mildly residential: 27% of students live on campus. Construction of a major $105-million, 1,700-bed suite/apartment style residential complex is expected to begin in late 2007.

Athletics

NCAA Division I and II, Pennsylvania State Athletic Conference. 14 varsity sports (6 men's: football, basketball, cross-country, swimming, track, wrestling; 8 women's: basketball, cross-country, indoor track, soccer, softball, swimming, track, volleyball), club sports and intramurals.

Academic Programs

Accounting; animation; anthropology; art; art education; art history; biology; biology/premed; broadcast journalism; business administration; business/financial services; business/marketing; chemistry; communication studies; computer science; criminal justice; drama; earth sciences; economics; elementary education; elementary/early childhood education; elementary/special education; engineering; English; environmental studies/geology; foreign languages; forensic accounting; forensic sciences; geography; geology; health & physical education (teacher education, health promotion, recreation administration, sport administration); history; humanities; human services; industrial trades leadership; Latin American studies; mathematics; medical technology; music; natural science & mathematics; nursing; nutrition; philosophy; physics; physics/engineering; political science; preprofessional studies; preschool education; print journalism; psychology; secondary education (biology, chemistry, earth & space science, English, general science, German, mathematics, physics, social studies, Spanish); social science; social work; sociology; special education/elementary education; specialized studies; speech & hearing disorders; women's studies.

Costs and Aid

2007–2008: $12,510.78 in-state comprehensive ($5,177 tuition); $15,188.78 out-of-state comprehensive ($7,766 tuition). 85% of students receive some financial aid.

Elizabethtown College

PENNSYLVANIA

Founded in 1899, Elizabethtown College (EC) is a comprehensive, private, coeducational college affiliated with the Church of the Brethren, a group that has always stood for peace. EC's mission is to nurture sound intellectual judgment, keen moral sensitivity, and an appreciation for beauty in the world.

Admissions Contact:

Elizabethtown College
One Alpha Drive
Elizabethtown, PA 17022
Ph: (717) 361-1400
Email: murraydh@etown.edu
www.etown.edu

The 4 Distinctions

Engaged Students

Students can tailor an EC education to meet their needs by choosing from fifty-three majors and more than eighty minors and concentrations, more areas of study than other similar-sized colleges. The top majors are business and education. The business school, housed in a new building, offers a variety of specialties, including international business, information systems, economics, finance, accounting, entrepreneurship, and marketing. The international business major is particularly rigorous, requiring facility with a foreign language and study abroad. Many business students are involved in local businesses and international internships. The education department offers elementary and secondary education, placing a significant number of teachers in the local area. EC's five-year master's program in occupational therapy is well-known, and students gain practical experience within the first two years.

The Core Program, Elizabethtown's foundation curriculum, affords each student broad exposure to the arts, sciences, and humanities, complementing more intensive study in an academic major. The Core Program serves as the basis for development in critical thinking, writing, and communication skills. It is hands-on, providing students with opportunities for collaborative research projects such as producing a television show or organizing awareness programs. In addition to completing a first-year seminar and a colloquium, each student must take courses in "areas of understanding" ranging from foreign languages to physical health.

EC offers study abroad to twenty sites around the globe through affiliations with Brethren Colleges Abroad (BCA), the Queens University International Study Centre at Herstmonceux Castle in England, AustraLearn, and Nihon University in Japan. Elizabethtown's Center for Global Citizenship also focuses on international programs, as well as service learning and peacemaking. These programs take advantage of the opportunities created when these areas overlap, such as hosting international seminars, promoting experiential learning for students, providing justice-oriented service, embarking on nonviolent protest trips, and creating a center for training mediators and settling community disputes.

All students are encouraged to take advantage of internships and research opportunities, whether independent or collaborative. Both options are offered through most fields of study.

Great Teaching

EU is a learning community dedicated to educating students intellectually, socially, aesthetically, and ethically for lives of service and leadership as citizens of the world. The concept is embodied in the school's motto, "Educate for service." Elizabethtown College offers a supportive environment where students can stand out from the crowd and where faculty are eager to challenge them. Faculty, administrators, and staff work hand in hand with students in the classroom, during research projects, and while serving the community in order to prepare students for success after graduation.

Nearly 90 percent of the faculty hold a doctoral or terminal degree in their field, and 90 percent of the full-time faculty serve as student advisors. The low student to faculty ratio of thirteen to one allows for meaningful interactions with professors in small classes. EC's small size and attentive advisors help students meet and overcome the challenges of academic life.

Elizabethtown's honors program offers students the opportunity to work closely with faculty mentors, to participate in additional cocurricular activities, and to apply for academic grants that may be used for travel or research.

Short-term faculty-led study courses of one-to-three weeks permit students with limited time and means to experience the world, including travel to China, England, the Czech Republic, Costa Rica, Ecuador, Ireland, Japan, Canada, and Iceland.

Vibrant Community

The college is located in scenic Lancaster County in south central Pennsylvania, ten miles south of Hershey and twenty miles from Harrisburg, Lancaster, and York. Established in 1753, the rural community was named after the wife of its founder.

Nearly 85 percent of EC students live on campus, where they've discovered that there is always something to do or get involved in. The school's 1,900 students can choose from more than eighty clubs, as well as a variety of intramural teams and ten men's and ten women's intercollegiate athletic programs. About 80 percent of EC students remain on campus over weekends.

On-campus housing options include ten theme learning communities that provide educational opportunities for students. Students can choose to live in student-directed learning communities, houses that provide opportunities to design, present, and implement a self-motivated community-service project. One such project is Saturday's Special, dedicated to educational programs for area children in kindergarten through fifth grades.

S.W.E.E.T., a student-run organization that provides Elizabethtown students with a variety of entertainment both on and off campus, is responsible for the much-anticipated T.G.I.S. weekend that rings in the spring season, and also sponsors most of the entertainment on campus, from comedians to hypnotists to bands.

Both EC students and faculty actively engage in the surrounding communities to help those in need. The annual service program, Into the Streets, sends hundreds of students, alumni, faculty members, and administrators into the community to build playgrounds, rake leaves, and paint community buildings.

The town of Elizabethtown is a residential community of twelve thousand people, many of whom work in Hershey, Harrisburg, and Lancaster. As a result, the town is one of the fastest-growing municipalities in Pennsylvania. Three symphony orchestras, various professional athletic teams, many cultural centers, and a number shopping areas surround the community. The larger cities of Philadelphia, Baltimore, and Washington, DC are all within ninety minutes, and New York City and Pittsburgh are within four hours by car.

Successful Outcomes

Almost all Elizabethtown graduates find job placement within eight months of graduation. Business organizations and accounting firms recruit actively on campus. In addition, many faculty maintain active contact with Fortune 500 companies, national and regional accounting firms, and local businesses to identify career opportunities for graduating students and alumni. Career Services administers undergraduate and alumni networking and mentoring to facilitate job searches and career development. Each semester, EC students have access to graduate school fairs and job fairs to make contacts. Students seeking advanced degrees have been admitted to graduate programs at top universities across the country.

EC has an active alumni organization that maintains ties between graduates and the college. An online alumni portal offers news updates, message boards, career opportunities, and event registration.

Fast Facts

Elizabethtown College is a 4-year, private, comprehensive college that was founded by the Church of the Brethren in 1899.

Web site

http://www.etown.edu

Location

Elizabethtown, Pennsylvania—minutes from Hershey and Harrisburg; 90 minutes from Philadelphia, Baltimore, and Washington, DC.

Student Profile

1,900 undergraduate students; 30 states and 40 countries represented; 2% minority.

Faculty Profile

180 faculty, 90% of whom hold the terminal degree in their field. 13:1 student/faculty ratio. Average class size is 25.

Residence Life

Highly residential: 85% of full-time students live on campus.

Athletics

NCAA Division III, Middle Atlantic Conference. 20 varsity sports (10 men's: baseball, basketball, cross-country, golf, lacrosse, soccer, swimming, tennis, track & field, wrestling; 10 women's: basketball, cross-country, field hockey, lacrosse, soccer, softball, swimming, tennis, track & field, volleyball), 2 club sports, and 9 intramurals.

Academics

Accounting; actuarial science; biochemistry; biology; biotechnology; business administration; chemistry; citizenship education; communications; computer engineering; computer science; criminal justice; economics; elementary education; engineering; English; environmental science; fine art; forestry & environmental management; French; general science education; German; health & occupation; history; industrial engineering management; information systems; international business; Japanese; mathematics; music; music education; music therapy; occupational therapy (master's program); philosophy; physics; political philosophy & legal studies; political science; psychology; religious studies; secondary education; social work; sociology-anthropology; Spanish, theatre.

Costs and Aid

2007–2008: $36,600 comprehensive ($29,000 tuition). 90% of students receive some financial aid.

Endowment

$44.7 million.

More Distinctions

• Ranked as one the best regional comprehensive colleges by U.S. News & World Report's "Best Colleges" survey.

• Ranked as one of the country's "Best Values" by U.S. News & World Report.

• Listed in Barron's Guide to the Most Prestigious College, Peterson's Competitive Colleges, and Princeton Review's Best Mid-Atlantic Colleges.

King's College

Admissions Contact:

King's College
133 North River Street
Wilkes-Barre, PA 18711
(888) KINGS-PA
Ph: (570) 208-5858
Fax: (570) 208-5971
Email: admissions@kings.edu
www.kings.edu

PENNSYLVANIA

King's College (KC) is a private, coeducational, Catholic, liberal arts college sponsored by the Congregation of Holy Cross from the University of Notre Dame. Founded in 1946, KC is a small, student-centered community, known for its family atmosphere and for instilling in students the self-confidence that leads to personal success.

The 4 Distinctions

Engaged Students

KC offers thirty-five majors in business, humanities and social sciences, education, sciences, and allied health programs. The most popular are accounting, business administration, criminal justice, education, mass communications, and physician's assistant. KC's business department is accredited by the Association to Advance Collegiate Schools of Business, and in 2006, 100 percent of the physician's assistant graduates passed their boards.

KC faculty are committed to providing innovative learning opportunities. The biology department includes a Genomics Center with DNA sequencers similar to those cited on Crime Scene Investigation (CSI) television programs, which students use to study DNA and its importance in all living organisms, and the criminal justice department has attracted local media attention by staging a mock murder scene on campus in which teams of students investigate the case and present their findings.

Many KC students take advantage of local opportunities for internships that provide them with firsthand experiences and help students decide on career paths. Each year approximately 120 different organizations, from Walt Disney World to the White House to PricewaterhouseCoopers to DKNY, offer full- or part-time internships to students in most majors. These experiences add substance and experience to students' resumes and can help attract the attention of employers.

Great Teaching

KC's mission is to provide "students with a broad-based liberal arts education which offers the intellectual, moral, and spiritual preparation that enables them to lead meaningful and satisfying lives." KC's low student to faculty ratio of sixteen to one and small average class size of eighteen lead to close relationships between professors and their students. All teaching takes place in a classroom setting, not auditoriums, and all classes are taught by professors, not teaching assistants. Of KC faculty, 85 percent have a terminal degree in their field of study.

Vibrant Community

About half of KC's students live on the school's campus, which is characterized by beige brick buildings. Freshmen residence halls are single sex, while upper-level students can choose from among a variety of housing options.

Students can participate in fifty clubs and organizations based on majors and other interests, including the College Theater, an art gallery, TV and radio stations, nineteen varsity sports teams, and a variety of intramural sports. KC is also adding a new recreation and fitness center for fall 2007.

KC's thirty-three-acre campus is located in Wilkes-Barre, a commercial center of northeastern Pennsylvania with an area population of 175,000. Wilkes-Barre, known as the Diamond City because of its anthracite coal mines, is on the banks of the north branch of the Susquehanna River, one of the most ancient river systems on the planet. The Pocono Mountains, with their recreational offerings, are to the west, and major metropolitan areas are to the east. KC is two hours by car to Philadelphia; two and a half hours to New York City; three hours to Baltimore; three and a half hours to Hartford; and four hours to Washington, DC.

Wilkes-Barre has a suburban feel with many parks, and KC students are active participants in the local community. KC's campus is one and a half miles from the Wachovia arena, home to the Wilkes-Barre Scranton Penguins, an American Hockey League team and the Wilkes-Barre/Scranton Pioneers, a member of the Arena 2 Football League.

Successful Outcomes

KC alumni are successful: 100 percent are placed in a job or are pursuing higher education within six months of graduation. King's takes pride in their graduation rates; most students graduate in four years, getting them into the workplace ahead of their peers. King's hosts an annual employment fair featuring more than 120 employers, including national accounting firms, Fortune 100 and Fortune 500 companies, as well as numerous other organizations that provide excellent career opportunities for King's graduates.

KC alumni stay connected to the college; more than four thousand student/alumni contacts are made annually.

"The school's vision is what first attracted me to King's, and I've been challenged each and every day by my professors and classmates to go beyond memorizing facts to applying theories and ideas to the world around me. This drive for excellence is tempered by an honest search for God's point of view on the subject at hand. I truly appreciate the concept of an education that can be applied to any future career or political endeavor."

Kristen Benz
North Manchester, IN
Class of 2010

Fast Facts

King's College is a liberal arts, Catholic college located on a small, urban campus in Wilkes-Barre, Pennsylvania, founded in 1946 by the Congregation of Holy Cross from the University of Notre Dame.

Web site

http://www.kings.edu/

Location

Wilkes Barre, Pennsylvania—15 miles south of Scranton, Pennsylvania; 110 miles north of Philadelphia.

Student Profile

2,200 students (50% male, 50% female); 15% minority.

Faculty Profile

16:1 student/faculty ratio. Average class size is 18.

Residence Life

Highly residential: 59% of students live on campus or near campus.

Athletics

NCAA Division III, Middle Atlantic Conference (MAC). 19 varsity sports (10 men's: baseball, basketball, cross-country, football, golf, lacrosse, soccer, swimming, tennis, wrestling; 9 women's: basketball, cross-country, field hockey, lacrosse, soccer, softball, swimming, tennis, volleyball.

Academic Programs

Accounting; athletic training education; biology; business administration; chemistry; clinical lab. science/medical tech.; computers & information systems; computer science; criminal justice; early childhood education; economics; elementary education; English—literature; English—writing; environmental science; environmental studies; French; general science; history; human resource management; international business; marketing; mass communications; mathematics; neuroscience; philosophy; physician assistant (5-year master's); political science; prehealth; prelaw; psychology; secondary education certification; sociology; Spanish; special education; theatre; theology.

Costs and Aid

2006–2007: $31,130 comprehensive ($22,280 tuition). 95% of students receive some financial aid. Average award: $15,363.

Endowment

$60 million.

More Distinctions

• The American Association of Colleges and Universities Greater Expectations Initiative named King's as one of only sixteen Leadership Institutions nationwide as part of an organized effort to influence the future of liberal arts higher education. King's joins such institutions as Duke and Colgate universities as part of a national, organized effort to improve the future of undergraduate liberal arts education.

Lebanon Valley College

PENNSYLVANIA

Lebanon Valley College (LVC) is a private, coeducational, liberal arts-based college affiliated with the Methodist Church. Founded in 1866, the school's motto is "The truth will set you free." LVC students pursue life goals under the guidance of an involved and supportive faculty.

Admissions Contact:

Lebanon Valley College
101 N. College Avenue
Annville, PA 17003
(866) LVC-4ADM
Ph: (717) 867-6181
Email: admission@lvc.edu
www.lvc.edu

The 4 Distinctions

Engaged Students

Lebanon Valley offers thirty-five majors. The most popular majors are music, psychology, business, and education, particularly elementary and special education. Education students experience hands-on learning in local schools every semester, beginning in their freshman year. Unique music program offerings include courses in music recording technology and music business, and there are many opportunities for majors as well as non-majors to become involved in the college's strong music program.

LVC students are encouraged to study abroad regardless of their majors, and programs are available in Argentina, Australia, England, France, Germany, Greece, Italy, the Netherlands, New Zealand, Spain, and Sweden. Off-campus programs are available in Philadelphia and Washington, D.C. LVC students also take advantage of the wide variety of internship possibilities in the nearby Harrisburg area.

In the past two years, LVC athletic teams, music groups, and classes also have traveled to London, Mexico City, Paris, Vienna, Prague, Budapest, Salzburg, and elsewhere around the globe for College-sponsored activities.

Great Teaching

LVC rewards achievement by awarding scholarships based on high school academic work, not on SAT scores. If a student ranks in the top 30 percent of their high school class, they qualify for an academic scholarship that may cover up to half the cost of tuition.

The excellent faculty and low student to faculty ratio of fourteen to one is a key reason many students choose LVC. No two classes at LVC are quite the same, and whatever the subject, the classes are centered on real interaction.

The science curriculum is research-focused with a high level of student involvement in projects with faculty, including special summer programs. Currently, LVC faculty have three National Science Foundation grants directly involving students in research, presentation, and publication. Undergraduate students also have the opportunity to collaborate with teachers on research in quantum information science in the Mathematical Physics Research Group. LVC's actuarial science program, one of the few programs of its kind offered by a small liberal arts college, is also strong.

The college offers a six-year physical therapy program leading to a doctoral degree, as well as a digital communications program fusing art, business, English, and computer science.

Because of great teaching and advising, the majority of Lebanon Valley students earn their bachelor's degrees in four years. The College guarantees that full-time students can complete requirements for a baccalaureate degree in four years (basic requirements must be met), or the College will provide free tuition for additional courses.

Vibrant Community

Lebanon Valley College has excellent facilities, many of them new. About 72 percent of students live on campus in a variety of housing options, including traditional dorms, suites, and apartment-style facilities. About a third of the students participate in one of our 21 National Collegiate Athletic Association varsity athletic programs, and 80 percent participate in the popular intramural sports program. The school offers over 70 clubs and organizations, including a theater program, student newspaper, and numerous musical groups. About 10 percent of students are involved in fraternities or sororities.

Faculty and students enjoy daily interaction on campus and on school-organized trips to major cities like New York and Washington. LVC students also travel for public-service purposes, including a recent trip to Louisiana to rebuild houses. On-campus special events include a Thanksgiving Dinner put on by faculty for students, and Dutchmen Day, an impromptu holiday organized by students each spring, during which students and faculty take a break before final exams to relax and enjoy a day of fun, food, and games.

Lebanon County's tagline is "Not just country!" LVC's presence in Annville enlivens the small town, as local residents take advantage of the college's athletics, art gallery, annual themed colloquium lectures, panel discussions, forums, and other activities. The town itself has a movie theater and coffee shop that caters to LVC students.

Located on over three hundred acres in the broad valley between the Blue and South mountains, embracing the Schuylkill and Susquehanna rivers, LVC's campus in Annville is about eight miles from Hershey, the Sweetest Place on Earth, and twenty-five miles from Harrisburg, the state capital of Pennsylvania. Students can also make an easy, two hour trip to either Baltimore or Philadelphia.

Successful Outcomes

At LVC, students choose from a range of programs that provide them with professional skills in high demand. More important, students can also build the kind of skills that are always valuable: the ability to think critically and the power to communicate clearly and persuasively.

Within six months of graduation, 75 percent of LVC alumni have entered the job marketing a field related to their major. Between 13 and 15 percent of graduates continue their studies at the graduate or professional level. Science majors tend to choose research-focused employment or studies. Actuarial science graduates boast 100 percent job placement, and 100 percent of LVC's first class of physical therapy degree recipients passed their license exam.

LVC's Career Services Office supports students with a complete and highly effective career preparation program. In addition, the College's alumni can be an invaluable resource. Our graduates have gone from Annville, Pa., to success far beyond in just about every profession imaginable. By offering advice, connections, and internships, hundreds of LVC alumni actively work to assist current students and new graduates as they launch their careers.

This success is clearly shown by a spring 2007 LVC Alumni Survey in which 97 percent of our graduates said they would recommend LVC to a college-bound student. Further, a 2006 independent survey conducted by AICUP found that the class of LVC graduates studied were greatly satisfied with their educational experience at the Valley—97 percent of LVC respondents expressed satisfaction with the quality of instruction in their major and 100 percent professed overall satisfaction with their college experience.

Finally, LVC's success is regularly acknowledged by national education publications. We were rated NUMBER ONE for "Great Schools, Great Prices," in the North among Best Baccalaureate Colleges in U.S.News & World Report's 2008 America's Best Colleges and eighth overall.

Fast Facts

Lebanon Valley College is a private, residential, liberal arts college affiliated with the United Methodist church and founded in 1866.

Web site

http://www.lvc.edu

Location

Annville, PA—30 minutes from Harrisburg.

Student Profile

1,650 students (44% male, 56% female); 22 states, 8 foreign countries; 5% minority, less than one percent international.

Faculty Profile

100 full time faculty. 84% hold the terminal degree in their field. 14:1 student/faculty ratio. Average first-year class size is 20.

Residence Life

Highly residential: 72% of students live on campus.

Athletics

NCAA Division III, Middle Atlantic Corporation, Eastern College Athletic Conference. 21 varsity sports (11 men's: baseball, basketball, cross-country, football, golf, hockey, soccer, swimming, tennis, track & field (indoor & outdoor); 10 women's: basketball, cross-country, field hockey, soccer, softball, swimming, tennis, track & field (indoor and outdoor), volleyball), and 21 intramural activities.

Academic Programs

Accounting; actuarial science; American studies; art and art history; biochemistry and molecular biology; biology; business administration; chemistry; computer science; criminal justice; digital communications; economics; elementary education; English; French; German; heath care management; historical communications; history; individualized major; mathematics; medical technology; music; music business; music recording technology; philosophy; physical therapy; physics; political science; predentistry; prelaw; premedicine; preministry; preveterinary medicine; psychobiology; psychology; religion; sociology; Spanish; and teaching certification (English as a second language, elementary education, music education, secondary education, special education).

Costs and Aid

2007–2008: $35,230 comprehensive ($27,800 tuition). 97% of students receive some form of aid.

Endowment

$41 million.

More Distinctions

• *U.S.News & World Report* rated Lebanon Valley College among the top tier schools in its category for the 12th consecutive year.

• Named one of the "Best in the Mid-Atlantic" by *The Princeton Review.*

• Top three percent in the nation for its cohort in Average Graduation Rate according to *U.S.News & World Report.*

Lycoming College

PENNSYLVANIA

Founded in 1812, Lycoming College in Williamsport, Pennsylvania, is an independent, coeducational, liberal arts college affiliated with the Methodist Church. Lycoming's goals are to develop students' communication and critical thinking skills, to foster self-awareness, to increase receptivity to new concepts and perspectives, and to enhance social responsibility.

Admissions Contact:

Lycoming College
700 College Place
Williamsport, PA 17701
Ph: (570) 321-4000
Email: admissions@lycoming.edu
www.lycoming.edu

The 4 Distinctions

Engaged Students

Lycoming's 1,450 students hail from thirty-one states and twelve countries. Classes are small, averaging just eighteen students, and the faculty to student ratio is an excellent one to thirteen. Lycoming students take advantage of numerous opportunities for overseas study, often traveling aboard with faculty and staff. Art students travel to Europe and Asia with faculty members from their department, the Lycoming archaeology program takes students to the Mediterranean island of Cyprus for archaeological digs in the summertime, and business majors enjoy a four-week European Business Experience trip.

Biology students are frequently hired to do field analysis during the summer for Lycoming's Clean Water Institute, and chemistry students and their professors are funded to do cutting-edge research through the Merck Internship program.

The active Community Service Center offers scholarships to Lycoming students, and the Early Learning Center, coordinated by the psychology and education departments, runs an on-campus preschool.

The Scholars program is thriving at Lycoming. In the Spring of 2007, nearly 15% of the graduating class completed the rigorous four-year program. By invitation based on academic credentials, Lycoming's best and brightest students study side-by side with some of the College's finest teachers. All learn together as they explore a new theme each semester over a four-year period. This past year, through primary source readings, films, lectures and discussion, the scholars pursued the topic The Things You Know That Aren't So and The Arab World. As seniors, Scholars are also expected to complete and present a thesis paper or an honors project.

Great Teaching

Many Lycoming professors expand their courses outside the classroom. Ecology students, for example, go into the field with their professors to study hawk migration in central Pennsylvania, invertebrates in Virginia, and marine biology off the coast of Roatan, Honduras.

International relations students have the chance to study with Dr. Roskin, author of textbooks that are used by students at colleges and universities across the country. Political science students get hands-on research experience working with Lycoming's own Political Polling Institute.

Another star among the Lycoming faculty is Dr. Kolb, Assistant Professor of Business. Dr. Kolb's expertise is in Marketing for Cultural Organizations and Tourism Marketing. Her books are distributed widely in the United States, Europe, and the Pacific Rim. One of the students' favorite courses is Dr. Kolb's travel/study seminar, European Business Experience.

The most popular majors at Lycoming are business, biology, psychology, archaeology, and art. More then 90 percent of Lycoming professors hold a PhD or the highest degree in their field.

"Great teaching at Lycoming also means great advising. Hey, we're also here to help students find their way. We want to help these undergrads get through this maze of questions and uncertainties, and offer the right options, courses, and experiences to help them attain their goals." Dr. Gabriel, Associate Professor.

Vibrant Community

Lycoming students have an abundance of activities from which to choose. Popular traditions include the Campus Carnival, Homecoming bonfire and parade, the Halloween Hall Crawl, the all-college Thanksgiving Dinner, the Christmas Candlelight Concert, Mardi Gras, Concert Weekend, Greek Week, Ben Crever Day, and the All-college Formal.

More than 80 percent of Lycoming students live in residence halls or college-owned apartments and townhomes. Lycoming guarantees housing for all four years and offers coed and single-sex facilities, fraternity and sorority floors, special emphasis floors, and creative arts wings.

At Lycoming, leadership opportunities abound with student government, the campus activity board, student publications, and seventy-five chartered clubs and organizations. Lycoming students compete on eighteen varsity teams (Division III), and the college runs a popular intramural athletics program.

The college campus is adjacent to downtown Williamsport. The 'Port is a small, relaxed city of 35,000 situated in the Susquehanna River Valley of the Bald Eagle Mountains. While the Pennsylvania tourist guide refers to the area as the region of "woods, water and wildlife," Williamsport is a bustling center for business, manufacturing, government, finance, and entertainment. Lycoming students take advantage of the numerous coffee shops, restaurants, and jazz and blues clubs. One favorite student event is First Friday. This downtown celebration features the work of local artists as they display (and sell) watercolors, stone carvings, textile designs, drawings, jewelry, sculptures, and photography. Numerous art galleries, restaurants, and gift shops take part in the monthly event.

Successful Outcomes

"Lycoming prepared me for the real world by offering multiple opportunities, which became the foundation of my resume. I coordinated a community service project, sat as president of my fraternity, met hundreds of prospective students as a tour guide, and earned a White House internship with the Vice President of the United States." Tom Coale '03, attorney with McCarter and English in Baltimore, MD

Lycoming graduates include an Academy Award winner, a Pulitzer Prize winner, Hollywood screenwriters, a U.S. Congressman, and several presidents of Fortune 500 companies.

Six months after graduation, more than 95 percent of Lycoming students are typically employed or pursuing graduate degrees. Of Lycoming graduates, 30 percent go on to earn advanced degrees.

Alumni participate willingly in networking events with students, and the career development center provides students with workshops and individual counseling.

Fast Facts

Lycoming College is a four-year, coeducational, private liberal arts college affiliated with the Methodist church and founded in 1812.

Web site

http://www.lycoming.edu

Location

Williamsport, Pennsylvania--less than four hours from New York, Philadelphia, Rochester, Pittsburgh, and Baltimore.

Student Profile

1450 students (48% male, 52% female); 31 states, and 12 countries.

Faculty Profile

92 full-time faculty. 13:1 student/faculty ratio. Average class size is 18.

Residence Life

Highly residential: 83% of students live on campus.

Athletics

NCAA Division III, Middle Atlantic Conference, 18 varsity sports (9 men's: basketball, cross-country, football, golf, lacrosse, soccer, swimming, tennis, wrestling; 8 women's: basketball, cross-country, lacrosse, soccer, softball, swimming, tennis, volleyball) 4 club sports, and 8 intramural sports.

Academic Programs

Accounting; actuarial math, archaeology art & design, art history; astronomy; biology; business administration (finance, international business, management, marketing); chemistry, communication (corporate, digital media); criminal justice; economics; education (elementary, secondary, special); English (creative writing, literature); French; German; history, international studies, mathematics, music, philosophy; physics, political science; pre-dentistry; pre-ministry; pre-medicine; pre-law; pre-optometry; pre-veterinary; psychology; religion; sociology-anthropology; Spanish; theatre (acting, design, directing); women's studies; combined Degree opportunities: 3-2 Forestry- M.S. (Duke University). 3-2 Environmental Management - M.S. (Duke University).

Costs and Aid

2007-2008: $34,512 comprehensive ($26,624 tuition). 90% of students receive financial aid. Average award: $19,277.

Endowment

$140 Million.

More Distinctions

• Barron's lists Lycoming as one of 300 colleges offering above average education at below average cost.

• One of 400 colleges in Thompson Peterson's Guide to Competitive Colleges.

• One of "The Best Mid-Atlantic Colleges" by the Princeton Review.

Misericordia University

PENNSYLVANIA

Located on a suburban campus in northeastern Pennsylvania near the cities of Wilkes-Barre and Scranton, Misericordia University is a Catholic, coeducational, liberal arts college. Originally a women's college, 30 percent of today's student body are men. Overall, 97 percent of Misericordia's freshmen rate their experience as good or excellent.

Admissions Contact:

Misericordia University
301 Lake Street
Dallas, PA 18612
(866) 262-6363
Ph: (570) 675-4449
Email: admiss@misericordia.edu
admissions.misericordia.edu

The 4 Distinctions

Engaged Students

Providing a blend of academics and career preparation, Misericordia offers its 1,400 students a number of undergraduate research programs, internship opportunities, and service-learning programs in both Haiti and Guyana.

Misericordia's Insalaco Center for Career Development facilitates planning for semester-long, yearlong, and summertime study abroad to locations around the world. The project started small but is a growing emphasis for Misericordia. Many students arrange to do internships while on study-abroad trips, applying what they have learned in class to the international environment. Because of its founding by the Sisters of Mercy, Misericordia has a tradition of ties to Ireland, sending student teachers there each year for the last several years.

On average, 90 percent of Misericordia students participate in an internship during their college careers, often arranged by the college's Academic Internship Program. Nursing students undertake rigorous clinical placements. Other students help to run the college's Speech-Language and Hearing Center, and occupational therapy students work with local physicians. Students in business and other fields take on internships with companies and organizations in the nearby cities of Wilkes-Barre and Scranton. The university has long-standing, formal internship relationships with numerous hospitals and health-care facilities, including Johns Hopkins, as well as with organizations such as Walt Disney World, Prudential, Wachovia, the Philadelphia Phillies, the Baltimore Orioles, and NASCAR.

Students regularly participate in research in collaboration with their professors. History students and communications students have worked with faculty to collect oral histories of the communities that surround Misericordia. Other student-faculty projects have analyzed how well pill containers made of various materials preserve the potency of pharmaceuticals. Another project studied methods of teaching history in high schools and suggested innovative new teaching strategies.

Great Teaching

Misericordia offers thirty majors in three colleges: Arts and Sciences, Health Sciences, and Professional Studies and Social Sciences. About 44 percent of students earn their degrees in the health sciences (including nursing, physical therapy, and occupational therapy), 24 percent in business-related fields, 6 percent in psychology, 5 percent in social work, 5 percent in the humanities (English, history, communications), and 1 percent in education.

Misericordia boasts an excellent student to faculty ratio of eleven to one, and an average class size of just seventeen students. In the National Survey of Student Engagement, students consistently rank access to faculty and out-of-class guidance as a strong suit at Misericordia.

Misericordia is launching a Doctor of Physical Therapy degree and a Doctor of Occupational Therapy degree in the coming year, as well as a Master of Business Administration degree.

Vibrant Community

Misericordia has no fraternities or sororities. About 50 percent of students live in university housing, and the university assists other students in finding housing nearby in the community. Misericordia is building a new residence hall to accommodate the recent growth in resident students.

Misericordia students are active in volunteer activities, including such programs as Adopt a Grandparent, Habitat for Humanity, Salt and Light (a program that raises awareness of social justice issues), and sponsoring activities for preteens from a low-income housing project in Wilkes-Barre. Recent summer- and winter-break service trips have taken Misericordia students to Haiti and to Guyana.

There are twenty-five registered student organizations on campus, including campus ministry, Salad for the Soul (a multicultural organization), clubs for each academic program, a number of honors societies, a biweekly campus newsletter, and a literary magazine. The campus hosts comedians, concerts, student festivals, and a variety of all-campus recreational activities. Each fall, homecoming features classic events such as a parade organized by students and a tug-of-war over a mud pit.

The Student Outdoor and Recreation (SOAR) organization offers outdoor activities, including skiing (just fifteen minutes from campus) and rock climbing. The college has excellent athletic facilities, and its teams compete in NCAA Division III athletics.

Misericordia is located on a 120-acre campus in the suburb of Dallas, Pennsylvania. Frequent shuttle buses provide easy transportation to the nearby cities of Wilkes-Barre and Scranton, and there are regular trips to New York City and Philadelphia.

Successful Outcomes

Misericordia's distinctive Guaranteed Placement Program (GPP), through its Insalaco Center for Career Development, is a professional development program designed to supplement a student's formal education. GPP integrates classroom instruction, experiential education, service leadership on and off campus, and career-focused experiences. If any student fully participates in the program and does not receive a job offer or is not accepted into graduate or professional school within six months of graduation, the college guarantees that it will provide that student with a paid internship in his or her chosen field.

Misericordia's students have gone on to notable success in many fields. Graduates of the nursing program have become hospital chief executive officers; and medical imaging students have started their own companies, including Jonathan Brassington, founder of the computer company LiquidHub. The last several graduating classes have included students going on to medical school and veterinary school. In all, 97 percent of Misericordia graduates are working or attending graduate school within six months of graduation.

"The occupational therapy program at Misericordia really prepared me well to start my own business. The faculty were good at fostering confidence. The classes were small and professors taught to each individual student."

- Carolyn Catalano, MS, Occupational Therapy, Co-Owner of Kid Moves, Mahopac, NY

Fast Facts

Misericordia University is a coeducational liberal arts and sciences college founded by the Religious Sisters of Mercy in 1924.

Web site

http://www.misericordia.edu

Location

Dallas, Pennsylvania—just 8 miles from Wilkes-Barre, PA and 20 miles from Scranton, PA. Within a 2 hour drive of both Philadelphia and New York City.

Student Profile

2,343 full-time students (26% male, 74% female); 15 states and territories; 8 % minority, 1 % international.

Faculty Profile

92 full-time faculty. 11:1 student/faculty ratio. Average class size is 17.

Residence Life

Moderately residential: 55% of full-time students live on campus.

Athletics

NCAA Division III, Eastern College Athletic Conference. 20 varsity sports (9 men's: basketball, soccer, swimming, tennis, cross-country, baseball, golf, lacrosse, track & field; 11 women's: basketball, soccer, field hockey, volleyball, swimming, softball, cross-country, cheerleading, lacrosse, tennis, track & field), 1 club sport (men's tennis), and 11 intramurals.

Academic Programs

Accounting; biochemistry; biology/biological sciences; business administration and management; chemistry; clinical laboratory science/medical technology/technologist; communication studies; computer science; elementary education and teaching; English language and literature; history; information science/studies; interdisciplinary studies; kindergarten/preschool education and teaching; liberal arts and sciences/liberal studies; management information systems; marketing/marketing management; mathematics; medical imaging radiologic technology/science - radiation therapist; nursing; occupational therapy; philosophy; physical therapy; predentistry studies; prelaw studies; premedicine/premedical studies; preveterinary studies; psychology; secondary education and teaching; social work; speech language pathology; special education and teaching; sport and fitness administration/management.

Costs and Aid

2006–2007: $31,050 comprehensive ($20,830 tuition). 95% of students receive some financial aid. Average award: $11,031.

Endowment

$10,000,000.

More Distinctions

• Misericordia University places among the top 10-15 percent of colleges nationwide in an important national student survey related to high levels of success in learning and development in undergraduate education- NSSE.

• Misericordia University is ranked by the Princeton Review as a Best Northeastern College and by US News and World Report in the top tier, Master's North, in their America's Best Colleges Edition.

Mount Aloysius College

PENNSYLVANIA

Mount Aloysius College (MAC) is a comprehensive, liberal-arts-and-sciences-based institution that strives to provide a setting where students can synthesize faith with learning, develop competence with compassion, put talents and gifts at the service of others, and begin to assume leadership in the world community.

Admissions Contact:

Mount Aloysius College
7373 Admiral Peary Highway
Cresson, PA 16630-1999
(888) 823-2220
Ph: (814) 886-6383
Email: admissions@mtaloy.edu
www.mtaloy.edu

The 4 Distinctions

Engaged Students

The majority of MAC's students come from within the one hundred-mile radius of the campus, but there are approximately twenty states and fifteen countries represented in the student body.

The college provides a Center for Lifelong Learning that offers alternative academic programs and off-campus programs, and Mount Aloysius undergraduates have the opportunity to study abroad, volunteer, participate in rigorous undergraduate research, and complete service projects locally, nationally, and internationally.

Freshmen students also participate in service projects as part of a program called Cultural Literacy: A Seminar in Learning, Service, and the Mercy Tradition. Students receive three credits for this course, which helps develop writing skills and promote service. Service projects connected with the course include food drives, Gulf Coast projects, and fund-raisers for specific foundations and organizations. Speakers are also integrated into the course.

Great Teaching

The most popular majors at MAC are nursing, radiation sciences and health care programs, education, sign language, business administration/accounting, criminology, and biology. The nursing program partners with local and regional hospitals, including the Altoona Regional Health System and the Conemaugh Health System, both of which are approximately twenty minutes from campus. As a result of these partnerships, students have the opportunity to participate in hands-on clinical work starting in their first year.

Within the criminology major, students can concentrate in forensic science, which combines forensics, biology, and criminology. Another distinctive program is MAC's four-year American Sign Language program, which turns out successful graduates each year. Due to great programming and excellent teaching, Mount Aloysius College boasts a 99 percent job-placement rate within nursing and health care and a 97 percent placement rate overall with each graduating class.

Vibrant Community

Established in 1853, MAC is a comprehensive college specializing in both undergraduate and graduate education. MAC is affiliated with the Roman Catholic Church and sponsored by the Sisters of Mercy, but students of all faiths are encouraged to discover their own religious heritage and personal convictions. Approximately 60 percent of the 1,200 undergraduate students are Roman Catholic.

MAC's 165-acre campus is located in the Allegheny Mountains of west central Pennsylvania. Situated adjacent to the small town of Cresson, Pennsylvania, Altoona and Johnstown are a quick drive from the campus.

MAC's campus is an advancing residential campus, and with its small town location, is safe and secure. With the recent addition of the state-of-the-art Misciagna Residence Hall, students now have the option of choosing to live in apartment-style housing. The campus provides also a variety of high-tech facilities and is 100 percent wireless.

Mount Aloysius College athletics continue to advance! Their students are offered the opportunity to become involved in eleven varsity-level athletic programs, which compete in the National Collegiate Athletic Association (NCAA) Division III. Mount Aloysius College is also a member of the highly competitive Allegheny Mountain Collegiate Conference (AMCC). Students participating in athletics have access to a wide range of facilities. The Health and Fitness Center, home to the Mounties volleyball and basketball teams, houses: weight room, sauna, indoor walking track and training room. Student-athletes are also able to make use of the Walker Athletic fields, and the recreation rooms in the Cosgrave student center. If you are interested in continuing your athletic career at the next level, then Mount Aloysius College is the place for you!

Men's sports include Baseball, Basketball, Cross Country, Golf, and Soccer. Women's Sports include Basketball, Cross Country, Golf, Soccer, Softball, and Volleyball.

The college includes over one hundred clubs and organizations. MAC has numerous prelaw students, making for a successful mock-trial team. Students can also participate in the strong student government association, and MAC's premier theatre and choir groups have gained regional and national attention. Other organizations include the college newspaper, various academic and honor societies, a dance team, and a step team.

Successful Outcomes

Alumni stay involved with Mount Aloysius College and with one another, taking advantage of the college's strong, comprehensive alumni network. Twelve thousand Mount Aloysius alumni cover all fifty states and several international countries. Ranging from National Geographic Magazine to John Hopkins Hospital, Mount Aloysius College alumni work in a variety of fields and have continued their educations at graduate schools such as Notre Dame, Columbia, Boston College, Georgetown, and Princeton.

Fast Facts

Mount Aloysius College is a comprehensive, liberal arts and science-based institution, established in 1853.

Web site

http://www.mtaloy.edu/

Location

Cresson, Pennsylvania—Mount Aloysius College's 165-acre campus is located in the Allegheny Mountains. Adjacent to the College are two small cities, Altoona and Johnstown, Pennsylvania.

Student Profile

1,200 full-time undergraduates. Approximately 1,600 undergraduate and graduate students.

Faculty Profile

60 full-time faculty, 14:1 student/faculty ratio. Average class size is 18.

Residence Life

Advancing residential college with four residence halls, many providing private baths and apartment style living.

Athletics

NCAA Division III, Alleghany Mountain Collegiate Conference. 11 intercollegiate athletic programs (5 men's, baseball, basketball, cross-country, golf, soccer; 6 women's: basketball, cross-country, golf, soccer, softball, volleyball).

Academic Programs

More than 50 programs to choose from including:
Accounting (concentration in forensic accounting in criminal investigations); biology; biology (biological science specialization, environmental studies specialization, molecular biotechnology, pre-health); business administration (health care administration specialization, human resources management specialization, management, marketing and entrepreneurship); criminology (forensic accounting in criminal investigations, correctional administration, criminal justice addictions professional certificate, forensic investigation certificate); elementary education; early childhood education; English (theatre concentration); general science, history/political science, information technology (concentration in computer security); medical imaging (radiography 2+2, ultrasonography Concentration 3+1); nursing (2+2, telehealth certificate, RN-BSN, telehealth certificate); professional studies (behavioral and social science, humanities, math, science and technology, pre-law); psychology (counseling specialization, forensic criminal investigation specialization, general, human resources specialization); sign language/interpreter education, and undecided/exploratory.

Costs and Aid

2006–2007: $21,870.00 comprehensive ($14,800 tuition). 94% of students receive some financial aid. Noted as one of the most affordable, private Colleges in the USA.

Penn State Behrend

PENNSYLVANIA

Admissions Contact:

Penn State Behrend
4701 College Drive
Erie, PA 16563
(866) 374-3378
Ph: (814) 898-6100
Fax: (814) 898-6044
Email: behrend.admissions@psu.edu
www.behrend.psu.edu

Penn State Erie, The Behrend College, provides the opportunities and prestige of a major research university set in the atmosphere of a student-centered college. The college promotes innovative, integrated, and high-quality teaching, research, and outreach in support of the economic, intellectual, and social development of the college community and beyond.

The 4 Distinctions

Engaged Students

The faculty and staff at Penn State Behrend are committed to making research a major component of the undergraduate educational experience. Penn State Behrend's research and outreach programs are recognized as the leading resource for enhancing and enriching the region's economic, intellectual, and social quality of life.

Over the last several years, Penn State Behrend has worked toward this end by developing funding and recognition programs that enhance research opportunities at the undergraduate level. These opportunities include an undergraduate research grant program, an undergraduate student research award, an undergraduate research and creative accomplishment conference, and a summer research fellowship program. The college also supports undergraduate travel to attend professional meetings. Annually, the college provides nearly two hundred thousand dollars of support for undergraduate research.

Penn State Behrend grant programs include the Undergraduate Student Academic Year Research Grant Program and the Undergraduate Student Summer Research Fellowship. These programs are designed to provide incentive for student involvement in faculty research projects. Each student is eligible for grants of $500 to $1,200. The students are required to go through a formal proposal process, including selection of a faculty mentor, development of a research project, composition of a formatted proposal, and a review process at the school and college level.

At Penn State Behrend, an internship is a professional, career-related experience in an organizational or company setting. Students may have the opportunity to receive credit for the experience. Some students intern for the experience and networking opportunities rather than for course credit. Internships are often completed during the academic year in conjunction with classes or as a stand-alone experience in the summer. Interns often work ten to twelve hours a week during the academic year and ten to forty hours a week during the summer. Alternative schedules are possible and depend on the needs and expectations of the parties involved, including the student intern, a faculty adviser, and the intern supervisor for the company or organization. Many departments require a student to complete 120 career-related work hours to receive three credits.

Great Teaching

FTCAP, the First-Year Testing, Counseling, and Advising Program, is designed to introduce students to the academic programs and structure of Penn State. This includes a discussion of the majors and program requirements and an assessment of students' placement test results. Students meet individually with an academic adviser to discuss educational plans. Information gained through participation in this program benefits students significantly in working toward their educational goals.

Many student resources, both academic and extracurricular, are available to explore. Some of these include eLion, an interactive supplement to the student-adviser relationship; PSU advising, an information source for academic advice; Portals, the undergraduate information network; and the advising handbook, which provides information on university policies and procedures.

Vibrant Community

The 725-acre hilltop campus of Penn State Behrend is just a short drive from Lake Erie and Presque Isle State Park via the new Bayfront Highway. Original buildings donated by the Behrend family have been preserved, while more contemporary architecture complements state-of-the-art facilities. Each residence hall is named after a commander or ship involved in the War of 1812's Battle of Lake Erie.

Of the college's nearly four thousand students, roughly 1,700 students live on campus in four types of residential living arrangements, including traditional residence halls, eight-person suites, four-person suites, and apartments for juniors and seniors. Senat Hall is specifically for freshmen students enrolled in Freshman Interest Groups.

Penn State Behrend students participate in service to communities, governments, corporations, professional organizations, learned societies, and other external groups. Activities may include task forces, public hearings, professional performances, and other events that are based on the expertise of the faculty members involved.

A revitalized Lake Erie draws thousands of people to the area throughout the four seasons. Presque Isle, a 3,200-acre state park, offers more than a dozen miles of sandy beaches, boating, and a thirteen-mile trail for walking, jogging, in-line-skating, and cross-country skiing. The rejuvenated Bayfront District serves as home port to the U.S. Brig Niagara, a victor in the Battle of Lake Erie during the War of 1812.

The region boasts a thriving arts community, including a philharmonic and several theater companies, dance companies, and historical art museums. A seven-thousand-seat civic arena draws big-name performers to suit every musical taste. Erie is home to the SeaWolves, a Class Double-A baseball affiliate of the Detroit Tigers in the Eastern League; students also enjoy watching the Otters of the Ontario Hockey League.

The Office of Educational Equity and Diversity Programs supports and serves as an advocate for diverse populations within the college community. In addition to addressing the specific concerns of historically underrepresented racial and ethnic minorities, it also works in support of students with disabilities, international students, LGBT students, and women. The Multi-Cultural Council (MCC) is a student organization that serves as a liaison between the student government association and other registered student organizations made up of underrepresented groups.

Successful Outcomes

The Academic Advising and Career Development Center houses both the departments of academic advising as well as career development. The academic advising department is staffed by Division of Undergraduate Studies (DUS) advisers who act as resources for students in any Penn State major. DUS is an academic unit of enrollment for students who are exploring various majors and career opportunities. Once students enter a major, they receive academic advice from faculty in their selected major.

Career development staff assist students with the process of career and life planning through a full range of programs and services. Students may schedule appointments with a career counselor to discuss issues including interests, skills, values, and goal setting, as well as how to find career information, internships, full-time jobs, and graduate schools. Students are encouraged to utilize the services of the center every year, from first semester to graduation.

Today, Penn State Behrend boasts more than twenty-two thousand alumni. The Penn State Alumni Association—a powerful network of more than 159,063 members—is the largest dues-paying alumni association in the country. The association's mission is to connect alumni to the university and to one another, to provide valued services to members, and to support the university's mission of teaching, research, and service. Penn State Behrend encourages graduates to become active members of this growing community of Penn Staters and to take advantage of the many benefits of being a Penn State alumni.

Fast Facts

Penn State Behrend is a four-year and graduate coeducational institution. This research focused institution was founded in 1948 through a gift by Mary Behrend of her family's estate to Penn State University.

Web site

http://www.behrend.psu.edu/

Location

Erie, Pennsylvania—located within two hours of Buffalo, Cleveland, and Pittsburgh.

Student Profile

3,480 full-time students (67% male, 33% female); 29 states and territories, 19 countries; 9% minority, less than 1% international.

Faculty Profile

16:1 student/faculty ratio. Most frequent class size is 20-29.

Residence Life

Moderately residential: 47% of students live in campus.

Athletics

NCAA Division III, Allegheny Mountain Collegiate Conference (AMCC) and Eastern Collegiate Athletic Conference. 21 varsity sports (10 men's: baseball, basketball, cross-country, golf, indoor track, soccer, swimming, tennis, track & field, water polo; 11 women's: basketball, cross-country, golf, indoor track, soccer, softball, swimming, tennis, track & field, volleyball, water polo), and 20 intramural sports.

Academic Programs

Accounting; biology; business economics; business, liberal arts & science; chemistry; communication & media studies; computer engineering; computer science; creative writing; economics; electrical engineering; electrical & computer engineering technology; English; finance; general arts & sciences; history; international business; management; management information systems; marketing; mathematics; mechanical engineering; mechanical engineering technology; physics; plastics engineering technology; political science; psychology; secondary education in mathematics; science; software engineering.

Pre-professional programs: allied health, education certification, law, and medicine. Graduate degree programs: Masters of Business Administration, Masters of Project Management.

Costs and Aid

2006–2007: $18,948 in-state comprehensive ($12,098 tuition); $24,662 out-of-state comprehensive ($17,812 tuition).

Endowment

$34 million.

More Distinctions

• Named a National Best Value by the 2004 National Survey of High School Guidance Counselors.

• Ranks among the top four in student-to-faculty ratio, graduation rate, first-year student retention rate, and SAT scores among all public colleges and universities in Pennsylvania.

Rosemont College

PENNSYLVANIA

Admissions Contact:

Rosemont College
1400 Montgomery Avenue
Rosemont, Pennsylvania 19010
(888) 2ROSEMONT
Ph: (610) 527-0200 ext. 2966
Email: admissions@rosemont.edu
www.rosemont.edu

Rosemont College is a small, private, Catholic college eleven miles west of Philadelphia. Founded in 1921 by the Society of the Holy Child Jesus and situated on the Sinnott estate in Rosemont, Pennsylvania, Rosemont is dedicated to providing women of all faiths with opportunities for intellectual, spiritual, and emotional growth.

The 4 Distinctions

Engaged Students

Rosemont's core values are trust in and reverence for the dignity of each person, diversity in human culture and experience, and persistence and courage in promoting justice with compassion. Rosemont encourages students to meet diversity and change with confidence. Roughly 53 percent of the students at Rosemont are minority students, giving Rosemont the number two ranking for campus diversity among BA liberal arts colleges in U.S. News & World Report's America's Best Colleges 2007.

Rosemont offers undergraduate degrees to women through the Undergraduate Women's College and graduate and accelerated undergraduate degrees to women and men through the Schools of Graduate and Professional Studies.

Students can choose from twenty-one academic programs, four certification programs, and five preprofessional programs. There are two components to a Rosemont education: the curriculum and experiential learning. Students must complete the curriculum for their major as well as at least one related experiential component, such as service learning, an internship, or study abroad in order to graduate.

Rosemont students have the opportunity to study abroad for a summer, a semester, or a year. Recently, students have traveled to England, Italy, France, Ireland, Greece, Cuba, India, and Australia.

Great Teaching

The student body is comprised of four hundred undergraduate students, and the student to faculty ratio of eight to one and the average class size of twelve are hard to beat. The small class size allows for personal classroom attention. Approximately 90 percent of the faculty members hold a PhD or the highest degree in their field.

Rosemont offers distinctive programs to students. One course, entitled Analysis of Cuba, gave students the opportunity to travel to Cuba for ten days in order to enrich their classroom study and test research in their field. Students have also had the opportunity to go to Italy to work in studio art, study Italian Renaissance art history, study the history of Italian cities, learn the Italian language, and learn about Italian literature in a summer program abroad.

Vibrant Community

The resident staff provides programs, services, and support to student living in on-campus housing, and 70 percent of Rosemont students live on campus. There is usually at least one campus event per weekend that is open to the Rosemont community as well as to students.

Philadelphia is only a twenty-minute train ride away from campus, and the school's close proximity to the city provides students with plenty of cultural and social opportunities, such as the Philadelphia Museum of Art; the Philadelphia Orchestra; the Pennsylvania Ballet; and sporting events such as Phillies, Flyers, and Eagles games. There are also shops, movie theatres, restaurants, and bookstores located within walking distance of the campus.

Rosemont is a member of the NCAA Division III in six sports. Rosemont athletes and the entire college community enjoy the state-of-the-art McClosky Fitness Center, as well as a new lacrosse and field hockey field.

Successful Outcomes

Rosemont has been named to the John Templeton Foundation Honor Roll for Character-Building Colleges, a designation that recognizes colleges and universities that emphasize character building as an integral part of the college experience.

Faculty and staff impress upon Rosemont students that effective communication skills are a vital part of success in the careers they choose. As a result of the academic and personal growth that takes place at Rosemont, 92 percent of Rosemont's 2004 alumni are placed in professional positions within six months of graduation.

Rosemont Honors Programs

Counseling Programs

- BA in Psychology plus MA in Elementary or Secondary School Counseling with Certification (5 years)

- BA in Psychology plus MA in Professional Counseling (5 1/2 years)

Business Programs

- BS in Business plus Master of Business Administration (4 1/2 years)

Education Programs

- BA (any approved discipline) plus MA in Curriculum & Instruction with Elementary Certification (4 1/2 years)

English Literature, Publishing, and Writing Programs

- BA in English or Communication plus MA in English & Publishing (4 years)

- BA in English or Communication plus MA in English Literature (4 years)

- BA in English or Communication plus MFA in Creative Writing (4 years)

Health Science Programs

- BA in Biology/Health Sciences plus Graduate Certificate in Healthcare Administration (4 years)

Nursing

- BSN with Drexel University (2 years at Rosemont + 1 1/2 years at Drexel)

- BSN/MSN with Drexel University with tracks in Clinical Trials Research, Innovation & Entrepreneurship, or Leadership & Management (2 years at Rosemont + 1 1/2 years in Drexel's Nursing Program + 1 additional year at Drexel for MSN)

- BSN/MSN (Nurse Practitioner) with Drexel University (2 years at Rosemont + 1 1/2 years in Drexel's Nursing Program + 1 1/2 additional years at Drexel for MSN)

Accelerated bachelor's degree and dual-admissions opportunities. For admissions details on all honors programs, visit www.rosemont.edu.

Fast Facts

Rosemont College is a four-year, liberal arts, Catholic college, founded in 1921.

Web site

http://www.rosemont.edu

Location

Rosemont, PA—located just 11 miles west of Philadelphia on the suburban Main Line.

Student Profile

420 undergraduate women; 15 states and territories; 53% minority, 4% international.

Faculty Profile

30 full-time faculty and 64 part-time or adjunct faculty. 8:1 student/faculty ratio. Average class size is 12.

Residence Life

Highly residential: 70% of students live on campus.

Athletics

NCAA Division III, Pennsylvania Athletic Conference. Intercollegiate competition in basketball, field hockey, lacrosse, softball, tennis, and volleyball.

Academic Programs

Art history; studio art; biology; business; chemistry; communication; economics; education; English; French; history; humanities; Italian studies; philosophy; political science; psychology; religious studies; sociology; Spanish; and women's studies.

Costs and Aid

2007-2008 $31,735 comprehensive ($21,630 tuition), 90% of students receives some financial aid. Average award is $11,753.

Endowment

$6.9 Million.

More Distinctions

- Number Two for Campus Diversity Among BA Liberal Arts Colleges-*U.S. News and World Report*, 2007

- Best Northeastern College-*Princeton Review*, 2006

- Character-Building College-John Templeton Foundation's Honor Roll, 1997

Saint Francis University

PENNSYLVANIA

Founded in 1847, Saint Francis University is a four-year, coeducational, liberal arts university. Founded by Irish Franciscans, the university follows the traditions of the Franciscan Friars of the Third Order Regular, including a commitment to lifelong learning, environmental stewardship, and service to the poor and to one another.

Admissions Contact:

Saint Francis University
117 Evergreen Drive
Loretto, PA 15940
Ph: (814) 472-3000
Email: admissions@francis.edu
www.francis.edu

The 4 Distinctions

Engaged Students

Each year during the week of October 4, in conjunction with the feast of Saint Francis, the entire university community joins in a formal day of reflection in which students reflect upon Franciscan values and service to the community.

The university's global studies program links students with Franciscans around the world to offer study-abroad programs that typically integrate a substantial service-learning component. Saint Francis's students regularly participate in study-abroad programs in such locations as South Africa, England, and Italy. By agreement with Gamesa, a company that focuses on global renewable energy, students may also engage in internships in Spain, and the university recently purchased a historical monastery in France to serve as an additional study-abroad location. Students who participate in the university's France-based study abroad program participate in a variety of service projects all over Europe.

Other experiential programs include the Center for Renewable Energies, which concentrates on renewable energy sources such as wind-generated power; the Small Business Development Center, in which Saint Francis business students assist local businesses while learning to start and manage their own companies; the Global Music Program, which organizes an arts festival to spotlight global music; and the Dorothy Day Center, which focuses on community service.

Great Teaching

The university, which also offers graduate programs, prides itself on its concern with the personal development of each of its two thousand students and with helping to prepare students for career, family, and service. Saint Francis's faculty aim to provide students with broad intellectual development and specific career preparation, to develop students' abilities to communicate effectively, to integrate theory and practice in their teaching, and to instill in students a love of lifelong learning and service to others.

Saint Francis offers highly regarded, successful programs in premedicine, prelaw, education, and chemistry, and it offered the first comprehensive business program in central Pennsylvania.

"Although I have had countless positive experiences at SFU, one of the most life altering moments for me was my trip to South Africa at the end of my junior year. I spent 2.5 weeks working in a hospital/AIDS clinic, taking courses in philosophy and religion, and experiencing the fabulous South African culture. This trip changed my perception of the world, and helped me to grow mentally and spiritually. I can not thank the university enough for this wonderful opportunity."

- Miriam Sterner, Physician Assistant major, Saint Francis University, Class of 2007

Vibrant Community

Situated on a six hundred-acre campus in the Laurel Highlands of central Pennsylvania, Saint Francis is a ninety-minute drive east of Pittsburgh.

The university offers a variety of living-learning communities and is actively planning others. In the Honors Residence, students work in teams to support and promote ever higher academic standards. The Peer Ministers Residence is dedicated to enhancing values throughout the university community and ministering to other students. Soon to come are a Diversity House to support students from all cultures and backgrounds and a Business Community, where students interested in business will develop companies while living and learning together.

Fraternities and sororities have played a prominent role in the life of the university since its founding 160 years ago. Greek organizations work closely with the Dorothy Day Center on projects to make a positive difference in local social issues. On average, members of fraternities and sororities are quite academically successful.

"As a freshman, I felt welcomed and appreciated by the faculty and staff: they were easy to approach and seemed to really care about my education. I also found that the student body was unique and wonderful. I made strong friendships quickly and I found that with every month that passed I saw new and inviting faces that soon became my friends."

- Miriam Sterner, Physician Assistant major, Saint Francis University, Class of 2007

Successful Outcomes

Nearly 100 percent of Saint Francis graduates have begun graduate studies or are employed within six months of graduation.

The career services office provides career counseling and assists students in improving their interview and job-search strategies. The office also provides guidance on professional dress and etiquette and on preparing resumes and cover letters. Career service staff maintain cooperative relationships with a wide range of employers, students, faculty, and alumni to ensure effective outreach. By serving as a bridge linking job seekers with employers, the office supports community building, social responsibility, and economic development.

Notable alumni include industrialist Charles M. Schwab, NBA Hall of Famer Maurice Stokes, and MasterCard International senior vice president Joy Thoma.

Fast Facts

Saint Francis University is a four-year, coeducational, Roman Catholic, liberal arts institution college/university and founded in 1847.

Web site

http://www.francis.edu

Location

Loretto, PA—Located 90 miles east of Pittsburgh and six miles from the county seat of Ebensburg.

Student Profile

2,100 students total (41% male, 59% female); 25 states and territories; 15% minority, 3% international.

Faculty Profile

97 full-time faculty. 14:1 student/faculty ratio. Average class size is 19.

Residence Life

Highly residential: 90% of students live on campus.

Athletics

NCAA Division I, Northeast Conference. 21 varsity sports (9 men's: basketball, cross-country, football, golf, volleyball, soccer, tennis, indoor track, outdoor track & field; 12 women's: basketball, cross-country, field hockey, golf, volleyball, lacrosse, soccer, softball, swimming, tennis, indoor track, outdoor track & field) and 9 intramurals.

Academic Programs

Accounting; American studies; biology; computer science; criminal justice; economics and finance; elementary/special education; engineering (3-2); English, English/communications; environmental engineering; exploratory; forestry and environmental management (3-2); French; history; international business/ modern language in French or Spanish; interdisciplinary environmental studies; management; management information systems; marine and environmental; education specialties; marketing; mathematics; medical technology; nursing; occupational therapy; pharmacy (2-3) and (3-3 B.S./pharm. D.); philosophy; physical therapy; physician assistant; political science; psychology; public administration/ government service; religious studies; secondary education certification; self-designed major; social work; sociology; Spanish.

Costs and Aid

2006-2007: $31,478 comprehensive ($22,444 tuition). 90% of students receive some financial aid. Average award: $16,500.

Endowment

$22 Million.

More Distinctions

• Saint Francis University was voted one of the Top 100 Character-Building institutions by the Templeton Foundation.

• Saint Francis University is the only school in Central PA to be ranked among U.S.News & World Report's Top 15 "Best Value" Universities in the North Region.

Seton Hill University

PENNSYLVANIA

Seton Hill is a small, Catholic, liberal arts university located near Pittsburgh, Pennsylvania. Rooted in Judeo-Christian values, Seton Hill educates students to think and act critically, creatively, and ethically as productive members of society committed to transforming the world.

Admissions Contact:

Seton Hill University
One Seton Hill Drive
Greensburg, PA 15601
(800) 826-6234
Ph: (724) 834-2200
Fax: (724) 830-1294
Email: admit@setonhill.edu
www.setonhill.edu

The 4 Distinctions

Engaged Students

Founded in 1883 as a women's college by the Sisters of Charity, and named after their founder, Seton Hill became a coeducational university in 2002. The most popular majors currently are business, the sciences, and the arts programs. Business has been on the rise for the past few years, and the school has always been strong in art, with offerings in art, art history, art education, art therapy, and studio arts.

At Seton Hill, students will develop the life skills and leadership abilities to make positive decisions. Because of the variety of study options and activities, students are able to choose the best path to reach their individual goals. To help create the ideal educational experience, Seton Hill offers creative options such as independent study, study abroad, seminar work, and internships. The local Greensburg community includes a number of businesses and organizations that provide internships to Seton Hill students.

The January and May terms offer a time for students to venture away from campus for international study programs. Seton Hill students participate in programs such as languages and culture in Mexico; intensive French in Monaco; and art in London, Paris and Berlin.

Great Teaching

Seton Hill recognizes that all undergraduate students have a common major in the liberal arts, as well as a major in a particular discipline, resulting in a well-rounded person. Learning occurs from the perspective of the arts, mathematics, sciences, culture, history, and literature. Students are expected to learn through personal experiences and reflection as well as through critical reading, review of and participation in research, and understanding of theory and skills applications.

Seton Hill is known for its small class sizes, so students and faculty develop strong relationships. The student to teacher ratio of sixteen to one results in lively class discussions and thorough, individualized answers to questions. Professors get to know each student and provide guidance to help students get the most out of their education.

Seton Hill's curriculum reinforces entrepreneurial approaches to problem solving, resilience in overcoming obstacles, and skills in managing change in all facets of life. Faculty enhance the teaching and learning environment through the use of technology. Students benefit from the integration into their courses of the World Wide Web, multimedia presentations, chat rooms, threaded discussions, and academic support materials on CDs or online. Many classes have downlinked conferences as part of their curriculum, exposing students to national and international experts. Some classes interact with students on other campuses through videoconference study.

Vibrant Community

Situated on two hundred wooded acres in Greensburg, Pennsylvania, the Seton Hill campus is small enough to feel cozy, yet large enough to offer everything needed for college survival, including a library, theater, chapel, science labs, art studios, fitness center, gymnasium, athletic fields, and comfortable dorms. Beautiful, century-old buildings lend architectural distinction, while friendly students and faculty lend crucial support.

Students are never far from a cultural event or outdoor adventure. Greensburg is home to a wonderful art museum and a celebrated symphony orchestra. In the nearby Laurel Highlands, skiing, white-water rafting, and canoeing are available. A mere thirty-five miles away is Pittsburgh, with its cultural attractions and major-league sports teams. Each year, trips are offered to Pittsburgh, New York, and Washington, DC. In addition, with so many colleges nearby, students often join together for social and sporting events.

With a campus that puts everything within walking distance and a student body of 1,900, it's easy for students to make friends and get involved in activities. Seton Hill students can participate in anything from the campus newspaper to a wide array of sports. There are more than thirty different clubs and organizations for students. On-campus movies, performances, and art exhibitions are also popular diversions.

Students interested in intercollegiate, recreational, and fitness and wellness programs benefit from Seton Hill's new recreation complex, the McKenna Center. The center is the hub of student activity on campus and features incredible views of the Laurel Highlands. The centerpiece of the forty-four-thousand-square-foot facility is a gymnasium with seating for a thousand fans. The building also includes training rooms; offices; locker rooms; an indoor running track with stretching and warm-up areas; and fitness, dance, weight, and aerobic rooms.

After becoming coed in 2002, Seton Hill added men's athletic teams, including football. Seton Hill University recently moved to Division II of the National Collegiate Athletic Association (NCAA), and joined the West Virginia Intercollegiate Athletic Conference (WVIAC). The university will play its full conference regular season schedule with the WVIAC in 2007–2008.

Successful Outcomes

Seton Hill students are well prepared to enter the workforce of the twenty-first century. All Seton Hill students develop excellent communication skills, critical and creative thinking abilities, an understanding of historical and world perspectives, and the ability to reflect on their commitments to the world. What's more, students are asked to become risk takers and think outside the box, all skills necessary to be a leader in the next generation.

About one-third of Seton Hill's 2005 graduates went on to pursue graduate study at Seton Hill, as well as at schools such as the University of Pittsburgh, George Washington University, Ohio State University, and Georgetown, among many others.

Fast Facts

Seton Hill University is a private, Roman Catholic, liberal arts university founded in 1918.

Web site

http://www.setonhill.edu

Location

Greensburg, Pennsylvania—35 miles from Pittsburgh.

Student Profile

1900 students (35% male, 65% female); 35 states, 22 countries; 8 % minority, 2% international.

Faculty Profile

68 full-time faculty. 16:1 student/faculty ratio. Average class size is 15.

Residence Life

Moderately residential: 75% of students live on campus.

Athletics

Provisional member of NCAA Division II Athletics, West Virginia Intercollegiate Athletic Conference. 23 varsity sports (11 men's: baseball, basketball, cheerleading, cross-country, football, golf, lacrosse, soccer, tennis, track & field, wrestling; 12 women's: basketball, cheerleading, cross-country, equestrian, field hockey, golf, lacrosse, soccer, softball, tennis, track & field, volleyball).

Academic Programs

Accounting, art (art and technology, art education, art history, art therapy, graphic design, studio arts, visual arts management; biochemistry; biology; business (entrepreneurial studies, human resources, informational management, international organization, marketing); chemistry; communication; criminal justice; computer science; dietetics; education certification (art, biology, business, computer, and information technology); chemistry; dual elementary/ Special, early childhood; elementary, English, family and consumer sciences; French; mathematics; music; social studies; Spanish; special education; engineering (3 +2); English (creative writing, literature); family and consumer sciences (child care administration, family and consumer sciences education); forensic science; history; hospitality and tourism; international studies; journalism- new media; mathematics (actuary science); medical technology; music; music education, music therapy; performance; sacred music; nursing (2+2); political science; prelaw; preprofessional health sciences programs; psychology; religious studies/theology; social work; sociology; Spanish; theatre; technical theatre; theatre arts; theatre/business; theatre performance.

Costs and Aid

2007–2008: $32,746 comprehensive ($24,806 tuition). 91% of students receive some financial aid. Average award: $15,000.

Endowment

$9,852,132.

More Distinctions

• Named a 2005 Best College in the Mid-Atlantic Region by the Princeton Review.

Susquehanna University

PENNSYLVANIA

Susquehanna University (SU) is a national liberal arts college committed to excellence in providing student-centered experiences that prepare undergraduates for productive and reflective lives of achievement, leadership, and service. This collaborative and inclusive community, led by passionate faculty mentors with access to exceptional facilities, fosters a results-oriented education strong in experiential learning.

Admissions Contact:

Susquehanna University
514 University Avenue
Selinsgrove, PA 17870
Ph: 1(800) 326-9672
Email: suadmiss@susqu.edu
www.susqu.edu

The 4 Distinctions

Engaged Students

The university includes three schools: the School of Arts, Humanities and Communications; the School of Natural and Social Sciences; and the Sigmund Weis School of Business. Among the three schools, SU offers more than fifty majors and emphases, as well as forty-five minors, all of which allow SU students to tailor their educations to their interests and needs. In addition, students can design their own majors; recent examples of self-designed majors have included human resource communications, visual anthropology, and sports administration.

Susquehanna University offers numerous research opportunities for students, who work alongside their professors, travel to and present at conferences, and publish in scholarly journals. The Research Partners Program provides a stipend and campus housing assistance to some summer students working on projects with faculty

The Sigmund Weis School of Business offers a semester-long London Program for junior business majors that include field trips to various destinations in the European Union. The school encourages its students to pursue internships, and more than 80 percent of students complete at least one internship prior to graduation. The business foundation curriculum has a strong IT component required for all the school's majors.

By the time they are seniors, approximately one-third of SU students have traveled abroad. International studies and modern language majors already are required to study abroad. SU's innovative Focus Programs combine interdisciplinary course offerings with two or three weeks in the region studied, and allow even first-year students to study abroad. Recently, the university reached an agreement with the University of Macau in China to offer one-semester exchange programs between the two schools.

Students also have the chance to explore within the U.S. by spending time in Washington, DC, through the Washington Center for Internships, American University, or the Lutheran College Consortium. Other domestic programs that welcome SU students include the Drew University United Nations Semester and the Philadelphia Center program. The student-run radio station, WQSU-FM (The Pulse), is the third largest college radio station in Pennsylvania, broadcasting on 12,000 watts and serving about one-third of the state. The department also has TV production facilities, staffs the weekly school paper, and encourages internships with newspapers and other media. Award-winning members of SU's Students in Free Enterprise teams include communications and business majors, who use what they learn to develop and present community service projects.

Great Teaching

Dedicated to undergraduate education, Susquehanna University employs a faculty primarily focused on teaching, and committed to providing students with one-on-one mentoring and opportunities for student-faculty collaboration. Some 93 percent of full-time faculty have the highest degrees in their fields; many are published writers and award winners and have extensive work experience to draw upon in the classroom. SU's student-to-teacher ratio is fourteen-to-one, and the average class size is eighteen.

Frequently upgraded facilities enhance student-faculty collaboration and student research. Plans for a new science building and major renovations to the existing science facility promises to increase these opportunities in the years to come. Cross-disciplinary study is common at SU and has led to the development of majors and minors, including Asian studies, biochemistry, ecology, and international studies.

The department of music offers the Bachelor of Music degree in performance or music education, as well as a Bachelor of Arts in Music, which allows the student to pursue other areas of study. The Cunningham Center for Music and Art features a 320-seat concert hall, a number of music practice rooms, labs for digital keyboard and computer music, as well as an art wing with graphic design, photography, and other studios.

Vibrant Community

Susquehanna University is set on a scenic 220-acre campus in Selinsgrove, PA, near the banks of the Susquehanna River, about fifty miles north of Harrisburg, the state capital. Four-fifths of Susquehanna's nearly 2,000 students live on campus. The mostly Georgian architecture, including buildings on the National Register of Historic Places, feature state-of-the-art amenities including numerous smart classrooms, WiFi hotspots and Internet connection in every student's room. The sports complex, music and art center, business and communications building, town house-style residence halls, dining hall, and social space have all been recently built or renovated.

The nationally recognized Project House System offers fifteen to twenty-five student-initiated community service groups the opportunity to live in designated campus housing. Each year, the university holds a community service day, called SU G.I.V.E. (Get Into Volunteer Experiences) designed to introduce all first-year students to the numerous volunteer opportunities available in the community. Prior to the start of the first semester, a select group of first-year students are also chosen to participate in SU SPLASH (Students Promoting Leadership and Awareness in Serving the Homeless), an intensive week-long service project in Washington, D.C. Service-learning trips over winter and spring break include Su Casa trips to Nicaragua and Honduras, and Hurricane Relief Team efforts in the Gulf Coast.

The Arlin M. Adams Center for Law and Society, established in 2001, explores the intersections between law and the various other disciplines in contemporary thought. It provides a forum and research opportunities for the examination of issues impacting human rights and social responsibility, involving science and technology, and requiring constitutional interpretation.

There are more than one hundred student clubs and activities, including special-interest groups, honorary societies, literary magazines, music ensembles, leadership programs, volunteer service projects, religious organizations, intramural and club sports, and twenty-three Division III varsity sports teams.

Successful Outcomes

Susquehanna University offers a results-oriented education marked by an emphasis on experiential learning through such means as internships, student employment and research projects. Typically, about 96 percent of students are employed or enrolled in graduate school within six months of graduation. Since 2004, more than 80 percent of those students applying to law school have been accepted; 75 percent to medical, veterinary, and dental schools; and 100 percent to divinity schools.

Beginning with their first semester on campus, the Center for Career Services helps students navigate everything from resume writing and interview techniques to career fairs and internships. The center provides students with extensive online resources, on-campus recruitment opportunities and workshops on such skills as "power dining," business etiquette and networking. A credit-bearing career planning course focuses on the connections among career preparation, academic choices, and cocurricular activities.

SU students develop realistic goals and the strategies to meet them by working with academic advisers and taking advantage of internships, job contacts, and handson experiences. Many alumni recruit interns or potential employees, as well as visit the campus as guest speakers or panelists for career workshops.

Fast Facts

Susquehanna University is a four-year liberal arts college affiliated with the Evangelical Lutheran Church in America and founded in 1858.

Web site

http://www.susqu.edu/

Location

Selinsgrove, Pennsylvania—three hours from Philadelphia, Washington, D.C., and New York City, and four hours from Pittsburgh.

Student Profile

1,959 students (46% male, 54% female); 30 states; 8% students of color; 1% international.

Faculty Profile

185 full and part-time faculty. 14:1 student/faculty ratio. Average class size is 18.

Residence Life

Highly residential: 80% of students live on campus.

Athletics

NCAA Division III, Liberty League for football and Landmark Conference for all other sports, 23 varsity teams (11 men's: baseball, basketball, cross-country, football, golf, indoor track, lacrosse, soccer, swimming, tennis, track; 12 women's: basketball, cross-country, field hockey, golf, indoor track, lacrosse, soccer, softball, swimming, tennis, track, volleyball), club and intramural sports including intercollegiate crew, equestrian, and rugby.

Academic Programs

Accounting; art history; biochemistry; biology; business administration (with emphases in entrepreneurship, finance, global management, human resource management, information systems, marketing); chemistry; communications (with emphases in broadcasting, communications studies, corporate communications, journalism, mass communications, public relations, speech communication); computer science; creative writing; earth & environmental sciences; ecology; economics (with emphases in financial economics, general economics, global economy & financial markets); English; French; German; graphic design; history; information systems; international studies (with emphases in Asian studies, comparative cultural studies, developing world studies, diplomacy, European studies, international trade & development, sustainable development); liberal studies (with emphases in elementary/early childhood education, elementary K-6 education, secondary education certification available for many majors); mathematics; music (bachelor of arts, music education, music performance); philosophy; physics; political science; psychology; religion; sociology; Spanish; studio art; theatre (with emphases in performance, production, design).

Costs and Aid

2007–2008: $37,330 comprehensive ($29,330 tuition). More than 50% of students receive some form of financial assistance.

Endowment

$110.3 million.

University of Pittsburgh at Bradford

PENNSYLVANIA

The University of Pittsburgh at Bradford is a friendly, safe campus where students can earn a University of Pittsburgh degree in a personalized environment. Pitt-Bradford was founded in 1963 on the initiative of the local community to serve the higher-education needs of citizens in the northwestern/northcentral region of Pennsylvania.

Admissions Contact:

University of Pittsburgh at Bradford
300 Campus Drive
Bradford, PA 16701
Ph: (814) 362-7555
Email: admissions@upb.pitt.edu
IM: www.upb.pitt.edu/imadmissions.aspx
www.upb.pitt.edu

The 4 Distinctions

Engaged Students

The most popular majors at Pitt-Bradford are business management, nursing, education, criminal justice, sports medicine, athletic training, psychology, and biology. In addition to liberal arts and sciences such as English, history/political science, biology, and chemistry, the university offers professional programs in business management, entrepreneurship, nursing, accounting, broadcast communications, and hospitality management. Local industries frequently recruit Pitt-Bradford students into internships in field-placement positions.

Located near the oldest operating oil refinery in the country, Pitt-Bradford features an associate degree program in petroleum technology. Local oil and gas executives were instrumental in founding the school. A geologist, Raymond N. Zoerkler, launched an initiative in the early 1960s to set up a Pitt campus in Bradford. J. B. Fisher, president of Kendall Refining, was the first chairman of the advisory board.

Pitt-Bradford currently has a student population of 1,409 students. The school's goal is to have 1,500 full-time equivalent students. Of the total, 679 students live on campus, with the rest living off campus or in the surrounding area. About 48 percent of Pitt-Bradford students come from the six-county surrounding area, while 52 percent—a percentage that is rapidly increasing—come from outside the area.

Pitt-Bradford's active study-abroad program offers students opportunities for travel in such countries as Ireland, England, France, and Costa Rica, and a number of students participate in the Semester at Sea program.

Great Teaching

Pitt-Bradford offers forty majors and numerous resources to help its students "go beyond," as the tagline of the university proclaims. Unlike many public schools, Pitt-Bradford puts a strong emphasis on a core curriculum of liberal arts and sciences. Each major has a capstone—a one-year project with a strong focus on writing. A freshmen seminar seeks to engage students early in their academic lives at the university. Students come together to discuss topics and go over prospective areas of academic and career interest.

The University of Pittsburgh at Bradford is a regional college of the University of Pittsburgh. The University of Pittsburgh ranks nineteenth among public institutions in the U.S. and thirty-sixth among all research universities, so students receive the best of both worlds—they get a prestigious University of Pittsburgh degree while benefiting from a small, teaching-centered college.

Pitt-Bradford professors are dedicated to teaching. There are no graduate assistants teaching courses. The faculty to student ratio is fourteen to one, and the average class size is eighteen, allowing professors to work closely with their students and give them personal attention. Since professors know their students so well, they are able to help students secure valuable internships or research opportunities or to assist students in getting a great job after graduation.

Vibrant Community

Located 155 miles northeast of Pittsburgh on the Pennsylvania-New York border, Bradford is a welcoming and friendly city of eleven thousand in a county of fifty thousand residents. The university is seeking to address the workforce needs of the region, which is in strong need of an increased workforce in natural resource industries such as timber and oil. Pitt-Bradford's 317-acre campus, nestled in the foothills of the Allegheny Mountains, is located adjacent to the Allegheny National Forest, offering opportunities for skiing, snowboarding, white-water rafting, hiking, biking, fishing, and numerous other sporting activities.

Most of the buildings on campus are relatively new. Founded in 1963, Pitt-Bradford became a baccalaureate-level institution in 1979. There are no traditional dorm rooms on campus. A dozen apartment-style residence halls offer students a friendly space to call their own. The thriving residence life program offers movies, bands, cultural opportunities, and even field trips to nearby downtown skiing resorts and the Cedar Point Amusement

Park. Pitt-Bradford also offers one of the only fresh-food-only dining halls in the country, offering students fresh eggs, fresh vegetables, fresh everything.

There are approximately forty student clubs and organizations on campus, with new ones added all the time. Two of the most popular organizations are the student activities council, which brings entertainment to campus, and Students in Free Enterprise (SIFE).

The university president is attentive to the concerns and interests of students. When students expressed interest in programs such as accounting, entrepreneurship, hospitality management, and health and physical education, these programs were developed and implemented. The student government has regular meetings with the university president and open-discussion meetings with the president's cabinet. The university president and student government president even switch roles for a day.

Successful Outcomes

First-generation students make up a significant percentage of the student population. The Academic Success Center and the TRiO Student Support Services program have been put in place to support these students, and others, as well. The programs provide tutoring, career counseling, time-management workshops, test-taking and note-taking assistance, and other types of academic support. The career services staff offer individual and group counseling to help students identify their interests, abilities, and values, and to relate these to career opportunities.

Pitt-Bradford alumni have pursued careers in education, business, public service, and journalism, among other fields, both in the local area and beyond. Among Pitt-Bradford's successful alumni are Tom Gill, president of Saltt Custom Homes; Douglas E. Kuntz, president and CEO of the Pennsylvania General Energy Company; John Pavlock, district attorney for McKean County, Pennsylvania; Dr. Jill Owens, a physician who operates Bradford Family Medicine Inc.; Tom Lucas, the director for the 1:00 a.m. edition of ESPN's SportsCenter; Martin Causer, representative for Pennsylvania's sixty-seventh legislative district in the state House of Representatives; Dr. April Fisher, a psychologist with the Mifflin County School District in Lewistown, Pennsylvania; Ben Himan, violent crimes detective in the Durham City, North Carolina, police department; Jennifer Miller, an emergency veterinarian in Columbus, Ohio; Jeremy Callinan and Don Kemick, founders of a Web development company called protocol 80; and Jennifer Lewke, a reporter with WSYR-TV News Channel 9 in Syracuse, New York.

Many other alumni are attending graduate school, including John Skinner, who is attending the University of Pennsylvania; Jenaro J. Hernandez, who is a student at the University of Medicine and Dentistry of New Jersey's School of Osteopathic Medicine; Cecil Thomas, who is attending Lake Erie College of Osteopathic Medicine; and Lynette Fodor, who is a student at the University of Pittsburgh School of Health and Rehabilitative Sciences.

Fast Facts

The University of Pittsburgh at Bradford is a four-year college, located on 317 acres nestled along the Tunungwant Creek and was founded in 1963.

Web site

http://www.upb.pitt.edu/

Location

Bradford, PA—a welcoming and friendly town of about 11,000 people in northwestern Pennsylvania.

Student Profile

1,409 students (41% male; 59% female); 27 states and territories; 13% minority, 1% international.

Faculty Profile

77 full-time faculty. 14:1 student/faculty ratio. Average class size is 18.

Residence Life

Moderately residential: 45% of students live on campus.

Athletics

NCAA Division III, Allegheny Mountain Collegiate Conference. 15 varsity sports (7 men's: baseball, basketball, cross-country, golf, soccer, swimming, tennis; 8 women's: basketball, cross-country, golf, soccer, softball, swimming, tennis, volleyball).

Academic Programs

Accounting; applied mathematics; athletic training; biology; biology education 7-12; broadcast communications; business education k-12; business management; chemistry; chemistry education 7-12; criminal justice; economics; elementary education; English, English education 7-12; engineering science; entrepreneurship; environmental education 7-12; environmental studies; health & physical education; history/political science; hospitality management; human relations; information systems; interdisciplinary arts; liberal studies; mathematics education 7-12; nursing (AS); nursing (BSN); petroleum technology; physical sciences; psychology; public relations; radiological science; social sciences; social studies education 7-12; sociology; sport & recreation management; sports medicine; writing.

Costs and Aid

2007–2008: $10,590 in-state tuition, $20,170 out-of-state tuition. 95% of students receive some financial aid. Average award: $12,000.

Endowment

$16,234,191.

More Distinctions

• *U.S. News & World Report* ranked Pitt-Bradford one of the Best Baccalaureate Colleges in the North in its 2008 edition of America's Best Colleges.

• *The Princeton Review* listed Pitt-Bradford as one of the top 222 Colleges in the Northeast in 2007-2008.

Washington & Jefferson College

PENNSYLVANIA

The first college west of the Allegheny Mountains and the eleventh oldest college in the U.S., Washington & Jefferson College (W&J) is an independent, coeducational liberal arts college of about 1,500 students. W&J prides itself on being a community characterized by respect, collaboration, and inclusiveness.

Admissions Contact:

Washington & Jefferson College
60 South Lincoln Street
Washington, PA 15301
Ph: 888-W-AND-JAY
Ph: (724) 223-6025
Email: admission@washjeff.edu
www.washjeff.edu

The 4 Distinctions

Engaged Students

W&J built a reputation for undergraduate preparation for medical school and law school, but its excellent overall liberal arts curriculum serves as a highly successful foundation for many different fields, most notably chemistry, biology, history, and economics. W&J students participate in many internship opportunities, often working with alumni in the fields of financial analysis, health services, and law. A variety of W&J programs are engaged in the local communities. The entrepreneurial studies program, for example, works to help small businesses in the area, and the environmental studies program assesses the impact of local companies on the environment. Education students tutor local students, and health students work in the local hospital.

W&J's study-abroad program features programs in Asia, Africa, Europe, and South America, as well as in Mexico. Over 40 percent of W&J students study abroad at some time during their undergraduate years.

The college follows a 4-1-4 calendar, and during the monthlong January term, students participate in various programs that have been developed by professors, including a safari to Tanzania and theater trips to London. These programs are available to all students, including freshmen, and some students participate in as many as three January-term programs during their undergraduate years.

Great Teaching

W&J students, faculty, and staff often refer to "the hallmark of the college." By this, members of the W&J community mean a certain sense of closeness between students and faculty, which begins with the Freshman Forum. With about fifteen students, the forum is one of the largest classes offered at W&J. In the forum, professors act as advisors as students tackle some of the great questions of critical thinking.

Many of W&J's academic programs have earned national reputations for excellence. In recent years, for example, 100 percent of W&J graduates who have gone on to law school have passed the bar exam. The programs leading to medical study are characterized by their collaborative nature. W&J is especially successful in sending students on to medical school, and members of the W&J community will often note with pride that many of their successful doctors, lawyers, and scientists are first-generation college graduates, the children of local coal miners and blue-collar workers.

Engineering students at W&J are part of a dual-degree program. Students study for three years at W&J, and complete the remaining two years of study at an engineering school. Upon completion of the program, students receive a bachelor of arts degree from W&J and a bachelor of science degree in an engineering field from a partner school such as MIT.

Vibrant Community

Located in the small city of Washington, the school is about thirty minutes from downtown Pittsburgh. W&J offers regular shuttle buses to shopping, nearby attractions, and big-city events, such as ballet, opera, and live music performances.

In addition to its older residence halls, W&J has recently opened two suite-style residence halls that feature seminar rooms, as well as ten new Victorian houses, each designed for sixteen residents and built around themes such as music, business, or foreign language.

About half of W&J students are active in the college's six national fraternities and four national sororities. W&J competes in Division III athletics, and 35 percent of students are on a varsity sports team. The campus was recently voted one of the fittest by Men's Health magazine. The intramural program offers a wide selection of athletics. Participation is characterized by informality and enthusiasm as close, personal relationships color these events with friendly, traditional rivalries. Approximately 50 percent of the student body participates in intramurals.

Over the past decade, several W&J athletes and teams achieved outstanding success. The College's varsity teams have won more than 30 PAC championships, 35 students were selected as conference MVPs, 250 W&J athletes were awarded First Team All-Conference recognition, 27 received All-American honors, and 17 achieved Academic All-American status.

The football team has won 18 of the last 21 PAC Championships and advanced to the NCAA Division III playoffs 17 times, including two trips to the NCAA Division III National Championship Game (1992, 1994). In addition to the team's successes, W&J football players received a great deal of individual recognition, including 12 conference MVP awards and more than 120 First Team All-Conference selections. During that same time, six players were named to the Associated Press All-American Team and four players received an NCAA post-graduate scholarship.

Successful Outcomes

Founded in 1781, Washington & Jefferson has been producing successful alumni for over 220 years. Among them are Luke Ravenstahl, who became mayor of Pittsburgh at the age of twenty-six; current NFL commissioner Roger Goodell; Dr. Jesse Lazear, who discovered that yellow fever was transmitted by mosquitoes; Citicorp CEO John Reed; eighty-eight alumni who have gone on to become college presidents; and dozens of congresspeople, governors, and other prominent public servants.

"Washington & Jefferson College offers students an affordable education that puts liberal arts ideals into practice without abandoning pre-professional practicality. The end result is well over 200 years of impressive alumni achievement and distinction."

-Colleges of Distinction

Fast Facts

Washington & Jefferson College is a coeducational, four-year, private liberal arts college, founded in 1781.

Web site

http://www.washjeff.edu

Location

Washington, Pennsylvania—a city of 15,000, located 30 miles southwest of Pittsburgh.

Student Profile

1,500 students; 33 states, 7 countries, 23% out-of-state; 7% minority, 1% international.

Faculty Profile

89 full-time faculty and 19 adjuncts; 84% of full-time faculty have a Ph.D. or professional equivalent; 12:1 student/faculty ratio.

Residence Life

Highly residential: 90% or more of students live on campus.

Athletics

NCAA Division III level, President's Athletic Conference, and Eastern Collegiate Athletic Conference. 24 varsity sports (12 men's: baseball, basketball, cross-country, football, golf, lacrosse, soccer, swimming/diving, tennis, track, water polo, wrestling; 12 women's: basketball, cross-country, field hockey, golf, lacrosse, soccer, softball, swimming/diving, tennis, track, volleyball, water polo), 10 intramural sports, and three club sports (men's ice hockey and men's and women's rugby).

Academic Programs

Accounting; art; art education; biochemistry; biology; business administration; chemistry; child development and education; earth and space science; economics; education; engineering (3-2); English; entrepreneurial studies; environmental studies; French; German; history; human resource management; industrial chemistry and management; information technology leadership; international business; mathematics; mind, brain, and behavior; music; neuroscience; optometry(3-4); philosophy; physics; political science; predentistry; prehealth; prelaw; preoptometry; prephysical therapy; prepodiatry; preveterinary; psychology; sociology; Spanish; and theatre.

Costs and Aid

2006–07: $35,682 comprehensive ($27,680 tuition). 85% of students receive some financial aid. Average award: $19,000.

Endowment

$81.8 Million.

More Distinctions

• *U.S. News and World Report* ranked Washington & Jefferson College among the top liberal arts colleges.

• *Barron's Guide to Colleges* and *The Fiske Guide to Colleges* called W&J a "best buy."

Emory & Henry College

VIRGINIA

Founded in 1836, Emory & Henry College (E&H) is a residential, coeducational, liberal arts and sciences college. E&H is the oldest college in southwest Virginia, and is affiliated with the United Methodist Church. E&H is dedicated to uniting faith and learning, and to the ideals of freedom and civic virtue.

Admissions Contact:

Emory & Henry College
P.O. Box 10
Emory, VA 24327
(800) 848-5493
Email: ehadmiss@ehc.edu
www.ehc.edu

The 4 Distinctions

Engaged Students

E&H students are engaged in both academia and the world, with service-learning, research, and study-abroad opportunities.

The Appalachian Center for Community Service initiates many partnerships between the college and community that integrate education with service and citizenship. Service activities may be short- or long-term, and give students the opportunity to volunteer and create positive social change. Through the center, opportunities abound and exist both on and off campus. Some examples include the Afternoon Academy, an after-school program for local sixth-grade students; Big Brothers/Big Sisters of Washington County; Crossroads Medical Clinic, a mobile clinic providing primary medical services to those who have difficulty accessing the care they need; and the Meal Delivery Program, a volunteer delivery service for lunch and dinner to elderly and/or housebound individuals in the area.

Students can perform research in areas across the curriculum, and faculty encourage students and provide them with a variety of research opportunities. Recent topics have ranged from cell growth to attitudes toward men and women in nontraditional careers.

Study abroad is available to students in a variety of locations, including India, Costa Rica, Mexico, China, Bulgaria, Central Europe, Germany, and Italy. E&H helps students prepare for their study-abroad experiences with language study, a comprehensive international studies program, and an international studies and business program.

Great Teaching

The eleven to one student-to-faculty ratio at E&H allows students to benefit from small classes with plenty of personal attention. E&H requires students to complete a liberal arts core curriculum that emphasizes a global perspective on history, literature, and culture. In class, student participation is encouraged through writing assignments, discussion, and an active approach to thinking and reasoning. E&H professors are high caliber instructors, as well as mentors and

friends to students. Six E&H professors have been named State Professor of the Year by the Carnegie Foundation, an accomplishment unmatched by any other college or university in Virginia; one of these professors was even chosen as U.S. Professor of the Year.

Housed in the recently renovated King Athletic Center, the college's athletic training education program utilizes a newly constructed athletic training room, which serves as a treatment center to rehabilitate student athletes and as a clinical classroom for the athletic training education program. E&H is one of only a few schools to be fully accredited by the Commission on Accreditation of Allied Health Education Programs.

Within the international studies program, students can major in unique areas: East Asian studies, European community studies, Middle Eastern and Islamic studies, and international studies and business. The international studies and business major allows students to examine the impact of globalization in the business sector, combining studies of business education, economics, and advanced language training.

The Emory & Henry Theatre Department operates in association with the Barter Theater, , a professional LORT C Equity company located in Abingdon, Virginia. This partnership provides theatre majors with opportunities for professional internships, mentoring, workshops, and master classes. The Barter Theatre is ten minutes away from the E&H campus, and Barter staff members often serve as adjunct faculty members and guest artists in the Theatre Department.

Vibrant Community

Named after Bishop John Emory and Patrick Henry, E&H is located on a 331-acre campus in the Virginia Highlands, giving students a great view of the two highest peaks in Virginia: Mount Rogers and Whitetop Mountain. To explore the area surrounding campus, the outdoor club leads backpacking excursions, white-water rafting trips, and many other outdoor adventures. Students may earn certification through E&H's Outdoor Leadership Program by choosing a discipline in climbing, caving, canoeing/kayaking, mountaineering, or long-distance backpacking. Through a two-year process, students gain the experience and competence to lead their own adventures.

On campus, there are more than seventy student organizations. From Greek life to performing groups to academic and interest groups, there is a full range of activities to engage students. Religious and faith-based organizations give students an opportunity to express their faith. Among those groups is Kerygma, an organization that provides perspectives on church vocations, learning experiences, and service opportunities. The organization also sponsors a fellowship for those students considering a ministry-related vocation. Young Life Leadership study, Fellowship of Christian Athletes, and Campus Christian Fellowship are also faith-based organizations that involve many E&H students.

Athletics are popular at E&H, with 70 percent of students playing varsity or intramural sports. During homecoming weekend, the college's successful football team draws crowds of students, alumni, and community members. In addition to attending sporting events, participants enjoy seminars, performing arts productions, and social events.

The campus is close to the historic town of Abingdon, and is within easy driving distance of the metropolitan Tri-Cities region of Bristol, Johnson City, and Kingsport.

Successful Outcomes

Career services at E&H aids students in choosing a major, exploring careers, finding an internship, finding full-time and part-time employment, and planning for graduate school. Employers and alumni often post full-time, internship, and volunteer opportunities through career services. The E&H network offers experiential opportunities to E&H students through job shadowing and externships.

Emory & Henry graduates succeed in many fields and disciplines. Distinguished alumni include Dr. Tim Cloyd, president of Hendrix College; Morgan Griffith, majority leader of the Virginia House of Delegates; Harold Poling, former CEO of Ford Motor Company; and Toni Atkins, a San Diego city council member and a former interim mayor.

Emory & Henry graduates carry a commitment to service, leadership and character into a variety of fields, including medicine, law, engineering, education, the ministry, research, athletic training, psychology, business and mass communications. Employers and graduate school officials praise the institution for the preparation of its graduates and their conscientious devotion to their careers, their commitment to others, and their passion for lifelong learning and growth.

The following is a sampling of the pursuits of some recent graduates: vice-consul for the U.S. Foreign Service in Toronto, Canada; graduate student pursuing advanced in international public policy at the University of Michigan; doctoral candidate in the physical therapy program at Duke University; graduate student in biochemistry and molecular biology at Wake Forest University; accountant with PricewaterhouseCoopers; researcher with Dow Chemical Company; journalist with Forbes Magazine; and consultant with Salomon Smith Barney & Ketan.

Fast Facts

Emory & Henry College is a private liberal arts institution. Founded in 1836, Emory & Henry is the oldest college in Southwest Virginia. It is also one of the few colleges in the South to have operated more than 170 years under the same name and with the same affiliation: the United Methodist Church.

Web site

http://www.ehc.edu

Location

Emory, Virginia—in the Virginia Highlands, one-half mile off Interstate 81. Within easy driving distance is the metropolitan Tri-Cities region of Bristol, Johnson City, and Kingsport.

Student Profile

Just over 1,000 undergraduate students. (50% male and 50% female); 25 states, 7 foreign countries, and one territory are represented.

Faculty Profile

88 full-time faculty. 11:1 student/teacher ratio. Emory & Henry has been represented by the recipients of the Virginia Professor of the Year award six times in the last 17 years.

Residence Life

Highly residential: 70% of students live on campus.

Athletics

NCAA Division III, ODAC Conference. 14 varsity sports (7 men's: football, soccer, basketball, golf, baseball, cross-country, tennis, 7 women's, women's cross country, volleyball, basketball, softball, soccer, tennis, and swimming), and 12 intramurals.

Academic Programs

Art; athletic training program; biology; business administration; chemistry; computer information management; economics; education; English; environmental studies; international studies; geography; history; languages; mass communications; mathematics; music; philosophy; physical education; physics; political science; Preengineering; prelaw; premedical; psychology; public policy & community service; religion; sociology & anthropology; theatre.

Costs and Aid

2006–07: $28,220 comprehensive ($20,860 tuition). The average award for incoming first-year students including only grants and scholarships is $15,547.

Endowment

$84 million.

Hampden-Sydney College

VIRGINIA

Admissions Contact:

Hampden-Sydney College
P.O. Box 667
Hampden-Sydney, VA 23943
(800) 755-0733
Ph: (434) 223-6120
Email: admissions@hsc.edu
www.hsc.edu

Hampden-Sydney College is a liberal arts school for men located in Hampden-Sydney, Virginia. Founded in 1775, Hampden-Sydney is the tenth oldest college in the United States, and one of two remaining four-year, all-men's liberal arts colleges.

The 4 Distinctions

Engaged Students

Hampden-Sydney students are expected to be actively involved in community service and philanthropic activities, in addition to being fully engaged in their academic program. The College's faculty and administrators also expect students to demonstrate honesty and self-discipline in and out of the classroom. Hampden-Sydney men are bound by two commandments—one for Honor and one for Conduct—"The Hampden-Sydney Man will not lie, cheat, or steal, nor tolerate those who do," and "The Hampden-Sydney Man will behave as a gentleman at all times and in all places." So, our students are engaged academically, extracurricularly, and as good citizens.

Many academic organizations exist on campus in which our students are highly involved. Since many of our men go into the health professions, one of the largest of those is the Hampden-Sydney Pre-Health Society, which serves as a support group for students interested in all areas of the medical and health professions. The society offers preparatory classes for the Medical College Admission Test, maintains a media library in the Career Development Office, and organizes lectures on topics related to the interests of prehealth students.

One of the most popular majors at Hampden-Sydney is political science. Since many of our men wish to go into public service or the law, they feel that this major gives them a good background in those areas. Hampden-Sydney's principal vehicle for preparing undergraduates for this is the Public Service Certificate Program, which includes an internship and a major research paper. In past years, student internships have been arranged at many prestigious offices and organizations, including the White House, the American embassies in Brazil and Turkey, the United States Information Services office in the Czech Republic, the Virginia Port Authority in Belgium, and the European Parliament, as well as with state and local government agencies from Pennsylvania to Texas. Students from the program have been admitted to graduate and law programs at Columbia, Duke, Georgetown, Harvard, Johns Hopkins, Michigan, Texas, University of Southern California, Virginia, and Yale.

Because of the importance of a "world view" Hampden-Sydney's students are also engaged in study-abroad. More than one hundred programs in twenty-five countries are offered for students. These programs offer a variety of opportunities for study in Europe, Central and South America, South and East Asia, and the Middle East.

Great Teaching

Hampden-Sydney has 114 full-time faculty members, and a varying number of adjunct professors, all of whom are highly motivated and dedicated to teaching. About 92 percent of faculty members have obtained the highest degrees in their field. Many members of Hampden-Sydney's faculty have been employed by the college for more than twenty-five years. The college boasts a student to faculty ratio of eleven to one.

Hampden-Sydney faculty members also stay on the cutting edge of their fields, while providing opportunities for students to engage in research activities with them. Students can be mentored by faculty, while assisting in their research, often leading to published works co-presented at national conferences.

Hampden-Sydney conducts a five-week May term, which gives students an opportunity to take courses that are experimental in content, developed by members of the faculty in special topics within their disciplines. These courses are often those that require extensive time off campus. Past programs have included European Union studies in France; economics, political science, and culture studies in Eastern Europe; tropical biology in Mexico; theater in Scotland; language immersion in Spain; and area studies in Egypt. The College also offers the funding for ten to fifteen students to participate in their own summer research projects each year.

Students are also encouraged to take advantage of Hampden-Sydney's close connection to the Duke University Marine Laboratory (DUML) in Beaufort, North Carolina. DUML offers a variety of courses in marine science, policy, and economics. Students may enroll in the popular Beaufort-to-Bermuda program, during which students split time between DUML and the Bermuda Marine Biological Station.

Vibrant Community

Part of Hampden-Sydney's 1240-acre campus, set in Virginia's picturesque and historic Southside, has been designated a National Historic Preservation Zone. Major cities like Richmond, Lynchburg, and Charlottesville are less than an hour's drive; Washington, Norfolk, and Raleigh are also easily accessible. On a large scale, the campus is only a day's drive from most of the east coast.

About 96 percent of Hampden-Sydney students live on campus. Main campus buildings are centrally located, which allows for a short five-minute walk from one end of campus to another. Hampden-Sydney is known to be an outdoorsy campus, as many students hike, bike, and enjoy fishing and hunting in their free time. One-third of our students participate in the varsity athletic program; 85 percent participate in intramural sports. About 35 percent of the student body is affiliated with one of the school's eleven Greek organizations.

Hampden-Sydney offers more than forty clubs on campus. Each club is run by students—to aid in our focus on leadership—and the clubs come in a large variety. Students may choose from political clubs, sports clubs, religious clubs, a pep band, and multiple social fraternities, as well as volunteer groups such as the local Hampden-Sydney Volunteer Fire Department. Students can also participate in the college's various publications, as well as WWHS-FM, the student-run radio station. The Union-Philanthropic Literary Society is the oldest student organization at Hampden-Sydney College, and is the nation's second-oldest literary and debating society in existence today, having been founded in 1789.

The student-run College Activities Committee, as well as the College's Lectures and Programs Committee, bring academic, social, and performing arts groups to the campus throughout the year to add to the enrichment of the entire college community.

Successful Outcomes

Hampden-Sydney has an active Career Development Office, which regularly publishes a newsletter for students and organizes on-campus internship fairs. The college's alumni network plays an active role in fostering internship relationships among current students.

After graduation, most alumni enter the work force, but within five years approximately 50 percent of our men will go on to graduate school. One in ten of our alumni is president, CEO, or owner of a company.

Notable alumni of Hampden-Sydney include W. Randolph Chitwood Jr., MD, world-renowned heart surgeon; Paul S. Trible Jr., U.S. senator from Virginia and president of Christopher Newport University; Paul L. Reiber III, chief justice of the Vermont Supreme Court; John B. Adams Jr., CEO of the Martin Agency; Warren M. Thompson, head of Thompson Hospitality Corporation, the largest minority-owned food and facilities service company in the world; Hugh Stallard, former president and CEO of Bell Atlantic of Virginia; and Norwood Davis, former president and CEO of Trigon-Blue Cross Blue Shield.

Fast Facts

Hampden-Sydney College, a four-year, private, liberal arts college for men, has been in continuous operation since November 1775, eight months before Jefferson wrote the Declaration of Independence. The college is affiliated with the Presbyterian Church.

Web site

http://www.hsc.edu

Location

Hampden-Sydney, Virginia—located an hour from Richmond, Charlottesville, and Lynchburg, just 5 miles from the town of Farmville.

Student Profile

(100% male, 0% female); 32 states and 17 territories; 8.6% minority, 1.2% international.

Faculty Profile

114 full-time faculty. 92.2% hold a terminal degree in their field. 11:1 student/faculty ratio. Average class size is 14.7.

Residence Life

Highly residential: 96% of students live on campus.

Athletics

NCAA Division III, Old Dominion Athletic Conference. 8 varsity sports (baseball, basketball, cross-country, football, golf, lacrosse, soccer, tennis).

Academic Programs

Applied computational physics; applied mathematics; biochemistry; biology; chemistry; classical studies; computer science; economics; economics and commerce; English; fine arts (fine arts with a concentration in music, theatre, or visual Arts); French; German; Greek; Greek and Latin; history; humanities; Latin; mathematical economics; mathematics; philosophy; physics; political science; psychology; religion; religion and philosophy; Spanish.

Costs and Aid

2007–2008: $36,800 comprehensive ($28,100 tuition). 97% of students receive some financial aid. Average award: $20,700 (including scholarships, loans, and work-study appointments).

Endowment

$126 million.

More Distinctions

• The Princeton Review's "The Best 331 Colleges."

• The Princeton Review's "America's Best Value Colleges" [2006, 2007, 2008 Edition].

• U.S. News and World Report's "American's Best Colleges."

• Newsweek's "America's Hottest Colleges."

• The Templeton Foundation's Guide "Colleges that Encourage Character Development," and "The Templeton Honor Rolls for Education in a Free Society."

• Erlene B. Wilson's "The 100 Best Colleges for African-American Students"

• Loren Pope's "Looking Beyond the Ivy League"

Hollins University

VIRGINIA

Committed to active learning, personal growth, achievement, service to society, and fulfilling work, Hollins University (HU) challenges women, nurturing them in a community with a deep sense of purpose, a strong commitment to learning, and a track record of preparing graduates who take leadership roles throughout society.

Admissions Contact:

Hollins University
P.O. Box 9707
Roanoke, VA 24020
(800) 456-9595
Ph: (540) 362-6401
Fax: (540) 362-6218
Email: huadm@hollins.edu
www.hollins.edu

The 4 Distinctions

Engaged Students

HU's 4-1-4 calendar offers students a January term to spend participating in an internship, special course, or study abroad. During the January short term, students have travel and study opportunities in such countries as Italy, Spain, Germany, and Great Britain. Students can also opt to stay on campus, participating in an intensive seminar, or they may complete internships at places such as ABC World News; the New York Stock Exchange; the U.S. Naval Hospital in Naples, Italy; or Betsey Johnson Designs in New York City.

HU runs its own study-abroad programs in Paris and London, and students can also participate in one of HU's affiliate programs in Argentina, Ghana, Ireland, Greece, Italy, Japan, Mexico, and Spain. Science majors are able to study abroad during their junior or senior years through Hollins's affiliation with the School for Field Studies. In this program, students benefit from hands-on education while completing research in ecology, environmental issues, and sustainable development. They study with experienced scientist mentors in environmentally sensitive areas such as Costa Rica and Kenya.

Hollins students realize the importance of community, both on campus and off. Not only do HU women participate in community-service projects locally, Hollins annually sends students to Lucea, Jamaica, as part of a service-learning project.

There are over thirty-five clubs and organizations at HU, where being involved in the campus community is a part of life. Students can express themselves creatively through participation in one of the student publications, politically through the traditional college Democrats and college Republicans, or join a progressive organization such as OUTLoud, which promotes equal rights for everyone.

Great Teaching

HU students receive an education based on critical thinking, problem solving, verbal and written communication, investigation, management, and assessment. The university's unique Education through Skills and Perspectives (ESP) program enables students to customize their general education requirements to their interests and abilities.

The sixty-seven full-time faculty and thirty-four part-time faculty who are part of HU are active members of the campus community and the professional world. Teaching at Hollins is not just a job; professors are committed to being part of the community and encouraging students academically and personally. HU's distinguished programs in creative writing, art, and dance benefit not just those in the major, but enrich the cultural offerings on campus with art shows, readings, and dance performances.

Through the Batten Leadership Institute, students can earn a certificate in leadership studies. The certificate curriculum offers students executive-level training, helping them develop a range of skills that are essential for good leadership. Graduates of this program rave that the experience gave them the confidence to handle even the most unfamiliar situations with success.

Vibrant Community

Between faculty Christmas caroling, the Founder's Day celebration, and Tinker Day, students are entertained and experience the history of a strong Hollins community.

The latest addition to the Hollins campus is the new Richard Wetherill Visual Arts Center. This industrial-style building features many modern technological conveniences, including film editing suites, darkrooms, private studios for seniors, a ceramics studio, and a rooftop plein-air studio, and stands as proof of Hollins's commitment to the arts.

Inside the visual arts center is the Eleanor D. Wilson Museum, a partner of the Virginia Museum of Fine Arts. The museum offers world-class exhibits by such artists as Sally Mann (an alumnus of Hollins), Chakaia Booker, and Carrie Mae Weems, along with a senior art show each spring.

With 90 percent of students living on campus, options exist to meet a variety of needs. There are apartments, single- and double-occupancy residence hall rooms, and special housing for students interested in French, Spanish, the arts, community service, intercultural community, and the Hollins Outdoor Program (HOP).

HOP is a great way for students to take advantage of the array of activities made possible by the university's location. Combining "adventure, education, self-awareness, and leadership," students go caving in Starnes Cave, white-water rafting in the New River Gorge, or plan their own adventures through the fully equipped outing center.

Hollins's athletic teams are a source of pride within the university community. The campus riding team, for example, regularly places at or near the top in national meets.

Roanoke promotes an active arts culture, an emphasis on social equality, and a variety of community events. Students can enjoy shopping at the local farmers' market or take a day hike into the neighboring Blue Ridge Mountains.

Successful Outcomes

In addition to the career center, which provides students with on-campus interviews, a full career-planning library, one-on-one counseling, and an extensive alumnae network, Hollins also sends students to CHALLENGE, a nationally recognized career fair for graduating seniors from liberal arts colleges.

More than 80 percent of HU women participate in an internship, which provides them with experience and a competitive edge prior to entering the professional world. After graduation, 98 percent of HU alumnae report that they are prepared for "the real world."

When a student graduates from Hollins, she is not walking away from Hollins life. There are numerous alumnae activities that allow women to continue to participate in the Hollins community even after graduation. One of the most popular activities is participating in volunteer projects with other alumnae.

Hollins alumnae also boast numerous firsts. Ann Compton was the first woman to be named a White House correspondent, Charlotte Fox was the first American woman to climb three of the world's eight-thousand-meter peaks, Elizabeth Valk Long was the first woman publisher at Time Inc., and Kiran Desai was the youngest woman to win Britain's prestigious Man Booker Prize for Fiction.

Fast Facts

Hollins University is a small, private, women's, residential liberal arts university established as Valley Union Seminary in 1842.

Web site

http://www.hollins.edu

Location

Roanoke, Virginia—475-acre campus. Regional airport 10 minutes from campus; Blue Ridge Parkway and Appalachian Trail 20 minutes away; 35,000 undergraduates at 10 institutions within one-hour's drive.

Student Profile

799 undergraduate women; 43 states, 11 countries; 54% Virginians, 17% minority.

Faculty Profile

67 full-time faculty, 34 part-time. 97% hold a terminal degree in their field. 10:1 student/faculty ratio.

Residence Life

Highly residential: 90% of students live on campus.

Athletics

NCAA Division III, Old Dominion Athletic Conference. Intercollegiate competition in basketball, golf, lacrosse, riding, soccer, swimming, and tennis.

Academic Programs

Art history; biology; business; chemistry; classical studies; communication studies; dance; economics; education; English & creative writing; environmental studies; film & photography; French; history; interdisciplinary; international studies; mathematics & statistics; music; philosophy; physics; political science; prelaw; premed; prevet; psychology; religious studies; sociology; Spanish; studio art; theatre; and women's studies.

Costs and Aid

2007–2008: $34,785 comprehensive ($25,110 tuition). 98% of students receive some financial aid. Average award: $20,000.

Endowment

$123.5 million.

More Distinctions

• The Princeton Review's Best 357 Colleges (2005) gave Hollins four out of a possible four stars for academics.

• The 2005 Newsweek/Kaplan guide named Hollins the country's Hottest Riding School.

• The Fiske Guide to Getting into the Right College lists Hollins among the top 10 women's colleges in the country.

• Barron's Best Buys says Hollins has produced more published writers than any other college its size in the United States.

Mary Baldwin College

VIRGINIA

Founded in 1842, Mary Baldwin College (MBC) is a four-year, independent, liberal arts women's college. MBC is committed to empowering women and sustaining an inclusive community. The campus is located in the heart of the Shenandoah Valley on fifty-four acres of rolling hills in Staunton, Virginia.

Admissions Contact:

Mary Baldwin College
Administration Building
101 East Frederick Street
Staunton, VA 24401
(800) 468-2262
Ph: (540) 887-7019
Email: admit@mbc.edu
www.mbc.edu

The 4 Distinctions

Engaged Students

Students are able to get involved at MBC from the minute they set foot on campus. The First Year Experience introduces students to MBC and the local community by pairing small groups of students with an academic and student life advisor. The group connects through cultural outings (such as an afternoon at the only replica of Shakespeare's Blackfriars Playhouse located on the edge of campus), conversations with faculty members, and a bonfire on Cannon Hill.

International study and multicultural connections are valued at MBC because of the new perspectives and insights students gain through them. During May term, classes are offered all over the world, so it is a popular time to venture abroad. Students can also go abroad for spring break study trips, cultural exchanges, or for a full semester or a year.

Experiential learning is often achieved through internships. Political science majors may intern with an elected official or lobbyist, while business majors may find a nonprofit organization to intern for. Health-care administration requires a rigorous internship that may well lead to employment after graduation. Many majors require practical experience, and students work with a faculty supervisor to select the experience best tailored to their learning goals.

Great Teaching

Distinctive majors and a network of mentors are trademarks of the MBC academic experience. MBC also boasts small class sizes with plenty of personal attention. Guidance from a faculty advisor ensures an individual plan for each student that not only meets graduation requirements, but also builds important skills in preparation for life and careers. Faculty members in the residential college come to Mary Baldwin to teach; they believe in women's education. They mentor students as they progress in their majors and provide individual research opportunities, hands-on learning, and lively classroom

interaction. In the senior year, students complete the capstone project, a research project or creative work that is a culmination of all that students have learned. For studio art majors, this could mean displaying paintings in the Hunt Art Gallery on campus; for Asian studies majors, the capstone may be preparing a series of articles for publication.

The most popular majors are psychology, political science, sociology, business, and art. MBC offers the only fully endowed undergraduate health care administration program in the nation, and students in this major are highly sought after. In addition to distinctive majors, MBC offers unique minors such as African-American studies, public history, and peacemaking and conflict resolution. The most popular minor, education, leads to teacher licensure.

One unique program at MBC is the Virginia Women's Institute for Leadership (VWIL). Through rigorous academics, physical training, military leadership training, and broad-based leadership development, VWIL students become part of the Mary Baldwin College Corps of Cadets, the only all-female cadet corps in the world. The program requires dedication, because in addition to meeting all the requirements of the general education curriculum and a major field of study, VWIL students must take additional courses and participate in extra cocurricular activities. This makes for a demanding schedule and an intense undergraduate experience, and students must be in uniform three or four days a week. ROTC is required, but commissioning in the military is not. Women in the program earn a minor in leadership studies.

The Program for the Exceptionally Gifted (PEG) is another signature program offered at Mary Baldwin. Through PEG, students as young as thirteen become full-fledged undergraduate students on campus. There are about seventy-five PEG students on campus, all of whom live together for their first two years.

Vibrant Community

One in three students at MBC is a woman of color, and the college celebrates its diversity. The Ida B. Wells Society and the Quest Interfaith Village are two examples of how the MBC community values diversity in all its aspects. The Ida B. Wells Society is a learning community that explores and celebrates African-American heritage through activities, classes, lectures, and connections among students and faculty. The Quest Interfaith Village advances spiritual growth through community service, academic course work, discussion, and cocurricular activities. These are just two examples of the learning communities offered on MBC's campus.

About seven hundred of MBC's 850 students live on campus. The college is located in downtown Staunton, Virginia, a small community with a strong arts and music scene. Because of the campus' location in historic Staunton, students can walk to movie houses, shops, restaurants, theaters, and more. Mountains and rivers surround Staunton, so students can participate in outdoor recreation on hiking trails or white-water rivers. On campus and off, students stay active. The individualized wellness plan, which addresses making healthy life choices, is a key piece of the Mary Baldwin experience.

Successful Outcomes

The innovative offerings at MBC provide women with many paths to achievement and with preparation for the real world. MBC graduates women who function effectively as leaders in a variety of settings. Almost one fourth of graduates enter graduate or professional school within nine months of graduation; over the long term, 40 percent earn graduate degrees, two thirds engage in volunteer service, and half hold leadership positions. The majority of graduates report that they were better prepared for challenges after college than their colleagues who went to coeducational schools. MBC alumni have made their mark on practically every career field, from education to advertising, from laboratory research to international banking, from politics to art.

One alumnus avers, "I would never have been appointed by the president to work in the West Wing of the White House at the age of twenty-three if it had not been for Mary Baldwin. My political science professors were always challenging me to do better, while still praising me for the accomplishments I had achieved."

Fast Facts

Mary Baldwin College is a master's level university with the four-year, liberal arts Residential College for Women as its flagship program. Private, affiliated with the Presbyterian Church (U.S.A.); founded 1842.

Web site

http://www.mbc.edu

Location

Staunton, Virginia—2.5 hours from Washington, DC; 30 minutes from Shenandoah National Park and other natural areas.

Student Profile

Residential College for Women: 800 undergraduate students (100% female); 30 states: 33% minority, 2% international. Adult/graduate programs (main campus plus 5 regional centers): 1200 undergraduates, 200 graduate students (82% female, 18% male).

Faculty Profile

RCW: 76 full-time faculty:, 51% female, 97% with terminal degree. 11:1 student/faculty ratio. Average class size: 16.

Residence Life

Highly residential: 85% of students live on campus (special permission needed for off-campus residence).

Athletics

NCAA Division III, USA South Conference. 6 varsity women's sports: basketball, cross country, soccer, softball, tennis, volleyball. 4 club and individual sports: fencing, field hockey, lacrosse, and swimming.

Academic Programs

Art (history or studio); arts management; Asian studies; biochemistry; biology; business administration; chemistry; communication; computer science/mathematics; economics; education; English, French, healthcare administration; history; independent major; international relations; marketing communication; mathematics; music; philosophy; physics; political science; psychology; religion; sociology; sociology/social work; Spanish; theatre.

Costs and Aid

2007–2008: $29,200 comprehensive ($22,530 tuition). 93% of students receive some aid. Average award: $22,500.

Endowment

$38,029,857.

More Distinctions

• Virginia Women's Institute for Leadership – the only all-female corps of cadets.

• Program for the Exceptionally Gifted – high-ability girls skip high school, start college at 13 or 14.

• US News & World Report: top-tier master's university in the South (in top 25/top 20%).

Marymount University

VIRGINIA

Admissions Contact:

Marymount University
Undergraduate Admissions
2807 N. Glebe Rd.
Arlington, VA 22207
Phone: (703) 284-1500 and (800) 548-7638
Fax: (703) 522-0349
admissions@marymount.edu

Marymount is a comprehensive, coeducational Catholic university that combines a liberal arts foundation with career preparation and opportunities for personal and professional development. The University focuses on the education of the whole person and takes full advantage of the resources of Washington, DC. Scholarship, leadership, service, and ethics are hallmarks of a Marymount education.

The 4 Distinctions

Engaged Students

Marymount offers a wide range of majors through the Schools of Arts and Sciences, Business Administration, Education and Human Services, and Health Professions. The most popular are Business Administration, Nursing, Interior Design, Fashion Design, and Biology.

Students across the disciplines are encouraged to engage in research. At a recent student research conference, the wide-ranging subject areas included persistent viral infections, the effects of a mental disorder on the social perception of criminals, 19th century women in journalism, and a comparison of modern dance in the US with traditional African dance forms.

With students from more than 45 states and 70 countries, MU offers a student-centered learning community that values diversity and focuses on the education of the whole person.

Marymount students in every discipline gain hands-on experience through a required internship. The University's Career and Internship Center and academic internship mentors guide students in the search for a rewarding internship. Marymount alumni are also a resource.

Business students intern at international corporations like Morgan Stanley and Ernst & Young. Nursing students train in some of the most prestigious medical facilities in the nation, including Walter Reed Army Medical Center and Children's National Medical Center. Criminal Justice majors in the Forensic Science track intern with government agencies like the FBI and Homeland Security. Fashion Merchandising majors work with companies like Burberry and Saks Fifth Avenue. And, Politics majors work on Capitol Hill! Other popular internship sites include Gannett-USA Today, local television stations, the National Institutes of Health, The Smithsonian, The Export-Import Bank, and The White House.

Study abroad provides opportunities for growth and enrichment. Marymount has established study programs around the world, and internships can be combined with study in England.

A Marymount education emphasizes service to others. The entire Marymount community is involved in on-campus service events like HalloweenFest, which is for disadvantaged children, and holiday fund raisers. Through weekly volunteer service programs, MU students reach out to mentor young people and spend time with senior citizens. Alternative Spring Break participants serve in communities farther afield, such as rural South Carolina and the Dominican Republic.

At Marymount, students can't help but be engaged inside and outside the classroom. Opportunities abound to participate in student government, volunteer work, athletics (NCAA Division III sports, as well as intramurals like extreme Frisbee), and social and career-related clubs. Students can also choose to act in plays, write for the student newspaper or literary magazine, cheer on the Saints as a member of the Blue Crew, or sing with Blue Harmony.

Great Teaching

Marymount faculty are focused on teaching. They are experts in their fields, with 87-percent holding terminal degrees. They are also passionate about their subjects and convey that enthusiasm. One professor of English has just returned from India, where she spent a year teaching as a Fulbright scholar. She's now excited to share her experiences with her Marymount students. A Communications professor serves as the official timekeeper for US presidential and vice presidential debates. During the 2004 election, he arranged for several Marymount students to get a behind-the-scenes look at one of the debates.

Classes at Marymount are small (13/1 student/faculty ratio), and professors know each student by name and make themselves available for help and advising outside of class. With a liberal arts core curriculum, freshmen share many of the same courses, providing a foundation of common knowledge. The Freshman Seminar and Peer Mentor program help students make the transition to college work and campus life.

The MU learning community is enriched by the University's proximity to the nation's capital with its extraordinary cultural, business, and professional resources. Distinguished speakers of national and international stature are frequent visitors to campus. Recent Marymount guests have included Nobel Laureate Desmond Tutu; General Colin L. Powell (USA, Ret.); fashion designers Michael Kors and Carolina Herrera; and Vinton Cerf, vice president of Google.

The Marymount Honors program enables highly qualified students to dig deeper and get even more out of their college experience. Other benefits of the program include scholarship support and special educational and enrichment opportunities.

Marymount is a member of the Consortium of Universities of the Washington Metropolitan Area. Student can take courses at any of the Consortium institutions and have access to their libraries.

Vibrant Community

Located in a suburban Arlington neighborhood, Marymount's campus includes the Main House; academic buildings; residence halls; the Emerson G. Reinsch Library; and the Rose Benté Lee Center. The Main House, with its stately white columns, is the signature building on campus and many special events are hosted there. Academic facilities include classrooms and lecture halls; computer labs and wireless access areas; science and nursing labs; and studios for fine and graphic arts, fashion design, interior design, and video production; auditoriums; and the Barry Art Gallery. The Lee Center serves as the hub of campus life; it houses the Verizon Sports Arena, a recreational gym, swimming pool, exercise rooms, Bernie's café, and the bookstore.

Approximately 850 students live in on-campus and university-sponsored, off-campus housing. Students find that friendships developed on campus endure the test of time!

Part of the college experience takes place outside the classroom, At Marymount, there are lots of ways to get involved in campus life. From student government, theatre productions, and poetry readings to soccer, dance team, and career-related clubs – Marymount has something for everyone. The University fields 12 NCAA Division III collegiate teams, and intramural sports are also popular. Marymount is part of a larger community, and students reach out to help their neighbors through a variety of volunteer programs. They also take advantage of the cultural, professional, and social resources of the Washington area!

Successful Outcomes

For many students who earn their bachelor's degree at Marymount, the next step is graduate school. Many alumni choose to continue graduate study at Marymount. Others have received fellowships in doctoral programs at universities like Notre Dame, Penn State, the Maryland Institute College of Art, and Washington University. Law schools attended by Marymount graduates include The George Washington University, Wake Forest University, and The Catholic University of America.

Marymount alumni readily find employment upon graduation and are successful in their fields. With Marymount's location in the DC area, graduates also have excellent contacts with many government agencies. Prominent alumni include the CEO of DigitalNow, a vice president for Inova Health Systems, and the chief information officer of the U.S. Army. Many Marymount alumni stay actively involved with their alma mater, returning for professional development and social programs, and to assist current students.

Fast Facts

Marymount University is a comprehensive, coeducational Catholic university that emphasizes academic excellence at the undergraduate and graduate levels. Committed to the liberal arts tradition, the University combines a foundation in the arts and sciences with career preparation and opportunities for personal and professional development. Marymount is a student-centered learning community that values diversity and focuses on the education of the whole person, promoting the intellectual, spiritual, and moral growth of each individual. Scholarship, leadership, service, and ethics are hallmarks of a Marymount education.

Web site

http://www.marymount.edu

Location

Arlington, Virginia—in a tranquil neighborhood approximately 6 miles from Washington, DC.

Student Profile

2,295 undergraduate students (26% male, 74% female); 45 states, 76 countries; 14% African American, 8% Asian, 9% Hispanic, 6% international.

Faculty Profile

143 full-time faculty. Approximately 85 percent of full-time faculty hold the highest degree in their field. 13:1 student/faculty ratio. Average class size is 19.

Residence Life

Moderately residential: 33% of students live on campus.

Athletics

NCAA Division III, Capital Athletic Conference. 12 varsity sports (6 men's: basketball, cross-country, golf, lacrosse, soccer, swimming; 6 women's: basketball, cross-country, lacrosse, soccer, swimming, volleyball). The University also offers a variety of intramural programs, including extreme Frisbee.

Academic Programs

Art (art management, preart therapy); biology (ecology, general biology, molecular & cellular biology, premedicine); business administration (accounting, business law & paralegal studies, finance, general business, international business, management, marketing); communications; criminal justice; criminal justice/forensic science; economics in society; English; fashion design; fashion merchandising; graphic design; health sciences (health promotion, prephysical therapy); history; information technology (computer science, forensic computing, information systems); interior design; liberal studies; mathematics; nursing; philosophy; politics; psychology; sociology; social justice; teaching licensure (art, elementary education, ESL, learning disabilities, secondary education); theology; religious studies.

Costs and Aid

2007–2008: $29,105 comprehensive ($20,190 tuition, $8,705 room & board, plus fees). 77% of undergraduate degree-seeking students receive some financial aid. Average award (institutional grant): $8,847.

Endowment

$24,030,546 as of June 30, 2007.

More Distinctions

• *U.S. News & World Report* consistently includes Marymount in its listing of the top 100 master's degree-granting universities in the South. It also recognizes Marymount as one of the five most diverse universities in the southern region.

Randolph College

VIRGINIA

Admissions Contact:

Randolph College
2500 Rivermont Avenue
Lynchburg, VA 24503
(800) 745-7692
Ph: (434) 947-8100
Email: admissions@randolphcollege.edu
www.randolphcollege.edu

At Randolph, you'll explore issues that fascinate you in the best liberal arts tradition. You'll work with faculty whose passion for encouraging discovery is enriched by their own quest for knowledge. You'll thrive in small classes where discussions are engaging. You will benefit from an atmosphere of integrity and mutual trust fostered by the Honor System that has been in place since 1891.

The 4 Distinctions

Engaged Students

All Randolph students are encouraged to travel, to take on real problems, and pursue and achieve goals with personal meaning. Embedded within a student's education are opportunities for study abroad, national and international internships, career guidance, leadership development, and one-on-one faculty advising.

A member of the International 50 (a select group of fifty American colleges recognized for international programs and global awareness), Randolph College offers programs like the Gravely-Hampton Global Studies Fund to help support students traveling abroad. An especially popular program takes juniors to the University of Reading in England for a semester of study and culture. Then there's MIX: the Macon Intercultural eXchange, which takes students to a variety of educational and social settings to learn about cross-cultural communication and cultures around the world.

Recent student internships have included work with the American Embassy in Paris, the Lyric Opera of Chicago, GE Aircraft Engine services, and Virginia Baptist Hospital's neonatal intensive care unit. Randolph also offers a highly praised summer research program that allows students to collaborate with a mentor professor on a variety of professional-level projects. In recent years, research has included cloning genes, tracking the development of a sense of humor in early childhood, and designing a workbook for students of classical Greek.

Great Teaching

Whether it's helping students think through an assignment or clowning around in the much-beloved Faculty Show, professors treat students like family. "There is a real connection both in and out of the classroom," explains one graduate. A strong honor code and average class size of twelve students reinforces the comfortable, trusting atmosphere. Another graduate says, "the classes are basically run by students. Your thoughts are counted, you feel more confident, and you know what you learn in class is really practiced." In addition to the human touch, the campus features up-to-date technology in every classroom.

Randolph's global honors curriculum encourages students to consider questions and issues outside their usual sphere. The diverse student population and the emphasis on study abroad enables students "to see through the eyes of another culture." Randolph graduates understand the intellectual foundations of the arts, the sciences, and the humanities. The honor system is a vital part of life at Randolph, and all students are expected to behave ethically and honorably in all circumstances.

The American Culture Program examines American identity through a combination of in-class readings and travel experiences; in any given semester, students might explore blues on the Mississippi Delta; politics in Washington, DC; or other aspects of the country's heritage. There are also vibrant programs in the health sciences, English, and the classics. The Maier Museum of Art enriches strong programs in art and museum studies.

Whatever major is chosen, each adviser helps students craft a personalized Macon Plan, a road map to achieve college goals. The Learning Resources Center provides interactive workshops and seminars like PASS (Program to Achieve Success). There's also a separate writing lab and a math and science center for further assistance in those areas.

Vibrant Community

Randolph College's residence halls offer students spacious rooms with hardwood floors and high ceilings, generous lounge space, and extended quiet hours in all six residence halls. In fact, almost every building on campus has the grand look and feel of a fine old hotel.

The college's motto is "The life more abundant," and there are plenty of opportunities for students to live a full life on campus. Student athletes can choose from a number of Wild Cat sports, including basketball, cross-country, field hockey (club), soccer, softball, swimming, tennis, and volleyball for women and men's basketball, soccer, cross-country, and tennis. There's also a coed riding program, offering forty-three horses and one hundred acres in the foothills of the Blue Ridge Mountains. With the Blue Ridge Mountains so close by, there are plenty of opportunities for other outdoor activities like white-water rafting, rock climbing, and skiing.

The Sock and Buskin theater group and the a capella choir, Songshine, are a few of the other groups on campus. The Macon Activities Council arranges campus events and outings such as snow tubing, an all-day trip to Virginia Beach, comedians, laser tag, and more. Special events also bring a wide range of speakers and performers to campus. Black history celebrations have included authors, artists, politicians, gospel choirs, blues singers, and a Cajun zydeco band.

Students look for ways to make a real difference through their organizations and are creative about doing so. For example, the Muslim student group, UMMAH, sought and received funding from the Greater Lynchburg Community Trust to bring Islamic scholars and authors to campus for a daylong workshop and seminar event called Pathways to Understanding, which encouraged a better understanding of women's places within modern Islam.

Some twenty-five thousand college students live within a one-hour radius of Randolph College, and the one hundred and twenty thousand-person Lynchburg metro area offers restaurants, shopping, and most of the other amenities important to college students.

Successful Outcomes

Randolph ranks in the top 10 percent of BA institutions whose graduates go on to earn a PhD. Over the last ten years, Randolph's medical school acceptance rate has been nearly 29 percent higher than the national average, and 68 percent of students attend graduate school within five years of graduation.

By the time they graduate, more than 90 percent of Randolph's focused and motivated students will have held a campus leadership position.

A sense of the world is built into virtually every Randolph course.

Fast Facts

Randolph College is a coeducational, four-year, residential liberal arts college founded as Randolph Macon Woman's College in 1891.

Web site

http://www.randolphcollege.edu

Location

Lynchburg, Virginia—in the foothills of the Blue Ridge Mountains.

Student Profile

730 undergraduate students; 47 states, 44 foreign countries and territories; 16% minority, 10% international.

Faculty Profile

72 full-time faculty. 9:1 student/faculty ratio. Average class size is 12.

Residence Life

Highly residential: 88% of students live on campus.

Athletics

NCAA Division III, Old Dominion Athletic Conference. 14 varsity sports (6 men's: basketball, cross-country, lacrosse, riding, soccer, tennis; 8 women's: basketball, cross-country, lacrosse, riding, soccer, softball, tennis, volleyball).

Academic Programs

American culture; anthropology; art (art history, art history and museum studies; studio art); Asian studies; biology; business; chemistry; Chinese; Greek; Latin; classical civilization; communication studies; computer science; curricular studies; dance; economics; international economics; education/teacher licensure; English (literature and creative writing); environmental studies and science; engineering physics (dual degree); film studies; French; French civilization; French for commerce; German studies; global studies; health services (nursing/dual degree); health and physical education with teacher licensure; history; human services; Japanese; mathematics; music (history, performance, and theory); philosophy; physics; political science; psychology; religious studies; Renaissance studies; Russian studies; sociology; sport and exercise studies; Spanish; theatre; women's studies. Programs for specified careers in engineering; law; medical and health-related study; nursing; and teacher education.

Costs and Aid

2007–2008: $33,210 comprehensive ($23,900 tuition). 95% of students receive some financial aid. Average award: $22,117.

Endowment

$140.4 Million.

More Distinctions

• U.S. News & World Report recently ranked the College 7th in the nation for international diversity, 12th in the nation for alumni giving, and in the top 12 for number of classes given with under 20 students

• Barron's Best Buys in Education placed R-MWC in the top 10% of colleges and universities nationwide.

• The College was selected for inclusion in the 2007 guidebook Colleges with a Conscience.

• The College was recently chosen as one of 81 schools highlighted in Best Value Colleges.

• Princeton Review Guide to Best 361 Colleges ranked the College #18 for Class Interaction, 19 for Diverse Student Population, and #20 for Students Happy with Financial Aid.

Roanoke College

VIRGINIA

Roanoke College is a private, liberal arts college located in the scenic Roanoke Valley in Virginia. The college provides a learning approach that stresses intellectual, ethical, spiritual, and personal growth, preparing graduates for a diverse and changing world.

Admissions Contact:

Roanoke College
221 College Lane
Salem, Virginia 24153
(800) 388-2276
Ph: (540) 375-2270
Email: admissions@roanoke.edu
www.roanoke.edu

The 4 Distinctions

Engaged Students

Founded in 1842, Roanoke College is the second-oldest Lutheran-affiliated college in the country and is open to students of all faiths. The college's location in southwestern Virginia plays an important role in student choices. Because of Virginia's rich history, many Roanoke College students choose to major in history. The college also offers a semester in Washington, DC, for students interested in gaining experience and contacts in the national capital. Recent placements have included the White House, the U.S. Chamber of Commerce, the Department of Justice, and the U.S. Congress, as well as judicial offices, law offices, and various interest groups and service agencies.

Other popular majors include business administration, English, biology, psychology, athletic training, and political science. One of Roanoke's athletic training professors is the medical coordinator for NCAA championship tournaments held in Salem.

For business majors, the student managed fund course allows students to invest five hundred thousand dollars of the college's money in the stock market. Students make all the decisions. An intensive learning term in May allows students to focus on one nontraditional course, such as the history of Hawaii, tropical marine biology, or forensic economics. Many courses offer travel opportunities in the U.S. or abroad.

The Undergraduate Research Assistant Program (URAP) pairs incoming freshmen with professors doing research. Students are paid a stipend while being exposed to graduate-level research, and students have the opportunity to work on their assigned project for all four years of their college careers. The Summer Scholars program also allows students to conduct research with professors, and independent studies offering course credit can be completed in any major.

Roanoke offers students 145 study-abroad options in thirty-eight countries. Many May-term courses incorporate international travel. One special study-abroad program, inspired by the school's Lutheran affiliation, is the Roanoke College in Wittenberg spring semester in Germany. Martin Luther's Protestant Reformation originated in Wittenberg, where he posted the ninety-five theses to the door of the Castle Church. Roanoke professors provide instruction for courses in German language and literature, history, humanities, religion, and other topics.

About half of Roanoke's students come from Virginia. The other half of the student body represents forty states and twenty-six foreign countries.

A number of internship opportunities are available in the Roanoke Valley metropolitan area. Students can take advantage of the resources of the career services department to help them find internships in the Roanoke area or in other other cities.

Each year for the past twenty years, students have traveled to South Carolina to build Habitat for Humanity houses. Recently during orientation, incoming students constructed R House, a Habitat for Humanity house that was constructed on campus, then moved across town and presented to the recipient. Students have also participated in international trips to Nicaragua in recent years to help build libraries.

Great Teaching

Alumni report that their relationships with professors made the biggest impact on them during their college careers. Students rate faculty 4.6 out of five for openness to questions in class, and faculty take pride in their collaboration with students on out-of-class research projects.

One of Roanoke's suite-based residence halls has an apartment designed to house a faculty member, giving students further opportunities to interact with faculty. The apartment is currently occupied by a sociology professor.

About 95 percent of tenure-track faculty have terminal degrees. Roanoke professors Roland Minton and Greg Weiss have both been awarded the Virginia Outstanding Faculty Award, and Katherine Hoffman was named the Education Advocate of the Year. Weiss also won the Mauksch Sociology Award, and Minton authored a calculus textbook that is used by one hundred colleges on every continent except Antarctica.

Each student meets frequently with an adviser during the freshman year. In addition to offering guidance on academics, the adviser also offers guidance on cocurricular learning and service activities, with the goal of integrating the student into life outside the classroom.

Vibrant Community

Roanoke College is situated on an eighty-acre, tree-lined campus against the backdrop of the Blue Ridge Mountains in the heart of historic Salem, just outside Roanoke, Virginia. The Roanoke Valley serves as the area's cultural, economic, educational, and entertainment center, with about 283,000 citizens, and offers a number of the amenities found in a large city, but without the traffic congestion, urban sprawl, and pollution.

The campus is a mix of traditional buildings formed around two quads. The old library, Bittle Hall, now serves as the residence of the Virginia Synod bishop of the Evangelical Lutheran Church. The college has been embedded in the community throughout its history and was one of the few to continue teaching during the Civil War. The new president coming to the helm in July 2007, Michael Creed Maxey, is only the eleventh president in the school's history.

Campus housing options include housing based on themes such as the global village, health and fitness, honors housing, multicultural theme housing, Greek, and the natural sciences.

Greek organizations have a long history at Roanoke College. The Black Badge Society, established at Roanoke in 1859, was the second Southern Greek social organization. It didn't survive the Civil War, but remains a part of Roanoke's Greek history. Currently, chapters of eight Greek organizations, including four fraternities and four sororities, engage about 20 percent of the Roanoke student body.

Roanoke has over one hundred student organizations that provide many extracurricular opportunities other than Greek life. There are more than five hundred events on campus each year, ranging from plays to midnight dodgeball to lip-syncing contests to Fridays on the Quad. Roanoke competes in NCAA Division III athletics, and fields varsity teams in nine men's and ten women's sports.

Successful Outcomes

Some 95 percent of Roanoke students get jobs or go on to graduate school within six months of graduation.

Well-known alumni include John McAfee, founder of the antivirus software firm; and Henry Fowler, former U.S. secretary of the treasury.

Fast Facts

Roanoke College is a four-year, private liberal arts college affiliated with the Evangelical Lutheran Church in America founded in 1842.

Web site

http://www.roanoke.edu

Location

Salem, Virginia—in the Roanoke metropolitan area.

Student Profile

Approximately 1,900 students (56% female, 44% male); 40 states, 26 countries; 10% minority and international.

Faculty Profile

95% of tenure-track faculty members hold the highest degrees in their fields of expertise. 14:1 student/faculty ratio. Average class size is 18.

Residence Life

63% of students live on campus.

Athletics

NCAA Division III, Old Dominion Athletic Conference. 19 varsity sports (9 men's: baseball, basketball, cross-country, golf, lacrosse, soccer, indoor & outdoor track & field, tennis; 10 women's: basketball, cross-country, field hockey, lacrosse, soccer, softball, indoor & outdoor track & field, tennis, volleyball). Examples of club sports and intramurals include basketball, flag football, floor hockey, golf, ice hockey, indoor & outdoor soccer, lacrosse, powder-puff football, raquetball, softball, and volleyball.

Academic Programs

Art; art history; athletic training; biochemistry; biology (B.A.); biology (B.S.); business administration (B.B.A.); chemistry (B.A.); chemistry (B.S.); computer information systems; computer science; criminal justice; economics; English; environmental policy; environmental science; French; health & human performance; history; international relations; mathematics; medical technology; music; philosophy; physics (B.A.); physics (B.S.); political science; psychology (B.A.); psychology (B.S.); religion; sociology; Spanish; theatre; theology. Preprofessional programs: dentistry, engineering, law, medicine, ministry, veterinary medicine. Roanoke College also offers a Teacher Licensure Program.

Costs and Aid

$35,351 comprehensive ($25,550 tuition). 85% of students receive financial aid. Average award: $19,800.

Endowment

Approximately $120 million.

More Distinctions

• Named one of the "Best in the Southeast" by The Princeton Review.

• Listed by The Templeton Guide: Colleges That Encourage Character Development as an "exemplary program."

• Named the "19th Fittest College in America" by Men's Fitness magazine.

• Phi Beta Kappa honor society—one of only 276 out of more than 3,500 colleges and universities that have the academic credentials.

University of Mary Washington

VIRGINIA

The University of Mary Washington (UMW) is a coeducational public institution with a beautiful 176-acre campus large enough to support diversity but not so large as to be impersonal. Founded in 1908 as a school for women, the institution became coed in 1970, and adopted the university designation in 2004.

Admissions Contact:

University of Mary Washington
1301 College Avenue
Fredericksburg, VA 22401
Ph: (540) 654-2000
Email: admit@umw.edu
www.umw.edu

The 4 Distinctions

Engaged Students

The majority of UMW students are from Virginia, and 35 percent are from out-of-state. About 12 percent of the students come from traditionally underrepresented ethnic populations. UMW's liberal-arts education emphasizes excellence through freedom of inquiry, personal responsibility, and intellectual integrity. UMW's traditional and robust honor system allows some exams to be unproctored and taken at home. In addition to providing its students with a strong general education, UMW aims to provide students with a deep understanding of their responsibilities as citizens in the broader, diverse community, with the skills necessary for creative and productive lives.

UMW offers thirty different major programs, and students can work with a faculty advisor to design a special major. The most popular majors are business, education, and English. The university also offers a five-year master's degree program in education, which gives students the opportunity to teach in local schools. UMW articulates eight general education goals, plus five across-the-curriculum requirements, which include writing and speaking.

In addition to the self-designed major programs, UMW students take advantage of independent-study opportunities, internships, study-abroad programs, and double majors to ensure that they receive an enriching and well-rounded education. Other opportunities for involvement beyond the classroom include the more than 100 student organizations funded by a finance and budget committee, and the student-run entertainment agency that books on-campus events.

Great Teaching

With a total enrollment of nearly five thousand, UMW maintains its commitment to academic excellence, a strong undergraduate liberal arts program, and its commitment to lifelong learning and professional development.

Though faculty members are active and professionally engaged in their own research and scholarship, they teach all UMW classes; there are no teaching assistants. Most classes have fewer than thirty students, allowing faculty to focus on individual students and, when appropriate, to encourage the participation of undergraduates in research. In addition to being committed teachers, UMW faculty are also recognized for excellence in their own fields; a UMW creative writing professor was awarded a Pulitzer Prize for poetry in 2006. Students can accelerate their academic programs by participating in the university's summer session.

Vibrant Community

UMW students have a variety of options for interaction with the local community, including the Center for Historic Preservation, which takes advantage of the historic nature of Fredericksburg and the surrounding area. With more than one hundred student organizations and activities, students are involved on campus, and they typically stay there on the weekends. The university offers a full schedule of events and concerts, including its Fredericksburg Forum series, which has featured Tim Russert and James Earl Jones, among others. Campuswide events occur throughout the year, and faculty-hosted events, such as barbecues and socials are among the most popular.

About 70 percent of UMW students live on campus in a variety of different residence halls and apartment complexes. There are twenty-three varsity teams, and more than 180 UMW athletes have been granted All-American status. Club teams and an active intramural program provide choices for all levels of athletic interest and ability.

Fredericksburg, center of a dynamic and growing region of nearly three hundred thousand, is an hour south of Washington, D.C., and an hour north of Richmond, Virginia. This location allows UMW students to easily access federal and state internships and to take advantage of academic, cultural, and recreational opportunities found in these larger cities.

Successful Outcomes

Career Services provide UMW students with mock interviews, career days, and guest speakers, and each student is provided with a career advisor within his or her course of study. About 25 percent of UMW graduates attend graduate school, and of those remaining, 90 percent enter the job market in a field related to their major within six months of graduation.

UMW's graduates are successful and loyal. At 36 percent, UMW alumni have the highest giving rate in Virginia, a rate three times the national average for public colleges. Another distinctive quality of UMW alumni is the school's high number of Peace Corps volunteers, placing the university in the top 10 percent among colleges of similar size.

"In addition to providing its students with a strong general education, UMW aims to provide students with a deep understanding of their responsibilities as citizens in the broader, diverse community, with the skills necessary for creative and productive lives."

Fast Facts

University of Mary Washington is a four-year, coeducational, residential, public liberal arts college, founded in 1908.

Web site

http://www.umw.edu

Location

Historic Fredericksburg, Virginia—50 miles south of Washington, D.C., and 50 miles north of Richmond, Virginia.

Student Profile

4,173 undergraduate students (40% men, 60% women). 46 states and 24 countries represented; 35% from outside the state; 11% minority student body, 1% international.

Faculty Profile

321 faculty members. 63% full-time. 86% tenured/tenure-track. 15:1 student/faculty ratio. Average class size: 20-25.

Residence Life

Moderately residential: 70% of students live on campus. Residence options: coed and single sex residence halls and a new apartment complex.

Athletics

NCAA Division III, Capital Athletic Conference. 23 varsity sports (11 men's: basketball, swimming, indoor track, baseball, crew, lacrosse, soccer, cross-country, equestrian, tennis, track & field; 12 women's: basketball, volleyball, swimming, indoor track, crew, field hockey, lacrosse, soccer, softball, cross-country, equestrian, tennis, track & field), and 20 intramurals.

Academics

Accounting; anthropology; art; biology; business administration; business administration/management; chemistry; classics; computer science; economics; elementary education; English; environmental science; fine & studio arts; French; geography; geology; German; history; interdisciplinary studies; international relations; Latin (ancient and medieval); liberal arts & sciences/liberal studies; mathematics; modern languages; music; music teacher education; philosophy; physics; political science; predentistry; prelaw; premedicine; preveterinary studies; psychology; religious studies; secondary education; sociology; Spanish; theatre arts/drama.

Costs and Aid

2007–08: $13,100 comprehensive for Virginia residents (6,494 tuition and fees); $23,574 for non-Virginia residents ($16,968 tuition and fees). More than $15 million in financial aid awarded through a comprehensive program of grants, scholarships, loans, and student employment from federal, state, institutional, and private resources.

Endowment

$27.7 million

University of Virginia's College at Wise

VIRGINIA

Set in the mountains of southwest Virginia, The University of Virginia's College at Wise (UVa-Wise) is a public, four-year, liberal arts college. UVa-Wise has a history of pioneering education in its region, as there were no public colleges in Virginia west of Radford University before UVa-Wise was founded in 1954.

Admissions Contact:

University of Virginia's College at Wise
One College Avenue
Wise, Virginia 24293
Ph: (888) 282-9324
Email: admissions@uvawise.edu
www.wise.virginia.edu

The 4 Distinctions

Engaged Students

UVa-Wise remains the only branch college of the University of Virginia, and currently enrolls 1,911 students, many of whom are first-generation college students. Part of UVa-Wise's mission is to "continue to honor its commitment of service to southwest Virginia," and students have the opportunity to fulfill this mission through service learning. The first-year experience for freshmen provides a number of service opportunities. These can include participating in projects around the local community such as the Remote Area Medical Project, which includes a mobile medical unit that offers free medical care. Students shadow doctors, chart patient histories, and aid patients. Four national fraternities and sororities on campus are service based. They focus on beautification projects, constructing play units for the severely handicapped, and student cleanup days.

Students have an array of possibilities to study abroad because of UVa-Wise's relationship with sister schools in Turkey, Spain, Austria, and Mexico. UVa-Wise also sponsors weeklong trips to locales such as France, Greece, Italy, and Spain during fall and spring break weeks. Professors lead these trips, which are designed to spark students' interest in travel.

Great Teaching

Several members of the faculty have been honored with statewide awards for outstanding classroom teaching. UVa-Wise offers twenty-nine majors, twenty-seven minors, seven pre-professional programs, and twenty-four teaching licensures. The most popular majors are business, social science, history, and education. Recently, two new majors were added in music and biochemistry. Music majors can also complete the Pre-K–12 teacher's licensure in choral or instrumental music in conjunction with the Bachelor of Arts in Liberal Arts and Sciences.

UVa-Wise is the only school in Virginia with an undergraduate software engineering major. Companies such as Northrop Grumman, Sykes Enterprises, Inc., and CGI are closely affiliated with this program. Through partnerships with these companies, students have a wide variety of opportunities for internships, financial assistance, and future employment opportunities. Sykes Enterprises, Inc. has partnered with UVa-Wise and the Department of Business and Economics to offer UVa-Wise students a unique opportunity for student internships and job opportunities with the international technical-support company

Business students at UVa-Wise do well on the certified public accountant (CPA) exam and pass at a higher rate than any other school in Virginia. The department of business and economics is also planning to offer a new minor in international business.

Vibrant Community

The university is in a rural location, and has several building projects underway, including new residence halls, a dining facility, and renovations of historic buildings on campus.

UVa-Wise's campus of 367 acres is home to 75 percent of the freshmen class. All residence halls feature resident assistants who plan and coordinate activities and educational programs for their residents. In this scenic area, students can enjoy the outdoors by hiking, fishing, skiing, tandem skydiving, and a number of other opportunities through the Outdoor Recreation program. Intramural sports are also popular, and the majority of UVa-Wise's 1,900 students are involved. Varsity athletes compete at the Division II level, with notable football and women's basketball, softball, and tennis programs.

Successful Outcomes

The first classes of UVa-Wise graduates went on to become some of the region's most successful professionals, and the college continues to offer unique opportunities to its students. Many UVa-Wise students pursue graduate or professional schools, with approximately 65 percent of graduates going on to get advanced degrees. Graduates frequently pursue acceptance to medical schools and MBA programs, and graduates from all academic majors go on to a variety of professional or graduate programs at prestigious schools across the nation.

For students looking for an affordable college education, *U.S. News & World Report* noted that UVa-Wise students leave with the least amount of debt of any liberal arts school in the country. Notable alumni include Frank Taylor, actor; Ron Short, playwright; Jerry Kilgore, former attorney general of Virginia; Brent Kennedy, author; Judy Harding, President of Fortuna Energy in Canada; Valeri Colyer, Director of Human Resources at Norton Community Hospital; Aleta Childress, Training Manager at the Crutchfield Corporation; and Dr. Debbie L. Sydow, President of Onondaga Community College in New York.

"My overall experience at UVa-Wise really prepared me for the road that lay ahead. I was able to take advantage of several opportunities – such as study abroad, research, and attending and presenting at conferences – that enhanced my academic experience. In addition, the faculty and staff at the College were extremely helpful to me as I prepared to make the transition to graduate school."

Ella Smith '04
Double Major: Spanish and History
Profession: Spanish professor

Fast Facts

The University of Virginia's College at Wise is a public, four-year, residential college, founded in 1954 and the only branch college of the University of Virginia.

Web site

http://www.uvawise.edu/

Location

Wise, Virginia— located among scenic Appalachian Mountains in southwestern Virginia, 60 minutes from Tri-Cities, Tennessee and Virginia.

Student Profile

1,911 students (44% male, 56% female); 6% out-of-state, 1% international.

Faculty Profile

91 full-time faculty, 71 percent of full-time faculty hold the terminal degree in their area of instruction, 17:1 student/faculty ratio. Average class size is 17.

Residence Life

Mildly residential: 30% of students live on campus.

Athletics

NAIA Division II, Appalachian Athletic Conference and the Mid-South Conference (football only). 11 varsity sports (6 men's: basketball, baseball, football, cross-country, golf, tennis; 5 women's: basketball, volleyball, softball, cross-country, tennis).

Academic Programs

Accounting; administration of justice; art; biology; biochemistry; business administration; chemistry; college major (interdisciplinary studies); communication; computer science; economics; English literature; environmental science; foreign studies (concentration in French, German, or Spanish); French; government; health & physical education; history; liberal arts & sciences; management information systems; mathematics; medical technology/clinical laboratory science; music; nursing; psychology; sociology; software engineering; Spanish; Theatre.

Costs and Aid

2006–2007 $11,770 (Virginia residents)/ $22,806 (out-of-state residents) comprehensive ($5,692/$16,729 tuition). 80% of students receive some financial aid. Average award: $7,800.

Endowment

$36,104,384.

More Distinctions

• For three consecutive years, students at UVa-Wise have graduated with the lowest debt load of any liberal arts college in the nation, according to U.S. News & World Report.

• UVa-Wise now ranks among the top ten public liberal arts colleges in the nation, according to the U.S. News & World Report's annual college guide.

• UVa-Wise offers the only undergraduate degree in software engineering in the commonwealth of Virginia.

Virginia Military Institute

VIRGINIA

Virginia Military Institute (VMI) is a highly regarded liberal arts college with a strong engineering program. VMI takes pride in developing strong leaders for careers in the military, business, public service, academia, law, and medicine. The structured military environment provides challenges that nurture self-awareness, self-confidence, and pride.

Admissions Contact:

Virginia Military Institute
319 Letcher Avenue
Lexington, VA 24450
Ph: (800) 767-4207
Email: admissions@vmi.edu
www.vmi.edu

The 4 Distinctions

Engaged Students

About half of VMI's 1,300 students earn commissions as officers in all branches of the armed forces. About 20 percent of graduates make the active-duty military a career. For the others, the ethic of the citizen-soldier is so embedded that they seek careers of service in the reserve components of the military, in public service, in professions, or in service to their communities.

Service in the community is an important element of the VMI experience. Organized, led, and staffed by cadets, community-service projects are designed to develop leaders, as well as to provide services to the community. Projects range from rebuilding homes destroyed in natural disasters to mentoring elementary school children to cleaning and maintaining nature trails.

Active internship programs are available to nearly all cadets. From environmental internships in a national park in Canada, to internships with legislators, to internships with businesses, VMI cadets have the opportunity to learn on the job and to make critical early networking connections.

Great Teaching

As an entirely undergraduate college, every class section is taught by a faculty member, not by graduate assistants. VMI is a small college with a small faculty to student ratio. Professors know their students by name, and they work closely with them during class and after. Many departments have developed study areas clustered near faculty offices, allowing easy and direct communications between professors and students.

An active undergraduate research program pairs students with faculty mentors, and student research occurs throughout the academic year. VMI's Summer Undergraduate Research Institute provides an intense period during which research is the sole focus of students. VMI routinely has among the highest numbers of students presenting research findings to national conferences of the National Council on Undergraduate Research, as well as to regional conferences in a variety of disciplines. Student research is published in the institute's scholarly journal.

About 95 percent of the faculty members hold terminal degrees. The faculty includes professors who are respected leaders in their fields. Major scholarly journals are edited by members of the faculty, and many faculty members have published numerous scholarly articles and books.

Vibrant Community

VMI is rich in history and tradition, founded in 1839 and tested as no other college in America has been tested, when the entire student body was committed to combat at the Civil War's Battle of New Market. The campus, much of it designated as a National Historic Landmark, celebrates the traditions of VMI through a striking Gothic architecture.

Perhaps the most important building and the most important institution at VMI is the Barracks. Every cadet must live in the spartan barracks throughout his or her cadetship. This facility is a leadership laboratory, where values of sacrifice and service are learned, and where lifelong bonds of friendship are forged. Rooms are bare, with no televisions, refrigerators, or telephones. Every room has Internet access, however, and there are facilities nearby for recreation, such as television rooms, game rooms, and a canteen.

A cadet's day is highly regimented, with the daily schedule starting with a formation before breakfast and ending with taps, usually at 11:00 p.m. The 8:00 a.m. to 4:00 p.m. period is reserved for academics, with class schedules similar to those at other colleges. The remainder of the day, depending on the day of the week, is divided among military training, physical training, special training for cadets in their first year at the institute, club activities, student government activities, and dedicated evening study periods. It is a full day, but it does not preclude free time to visit local restaurants or to take in a movie in downtown Lexington, just a short walk away.

Successful Outcomes

VMI boasts many graduates who have gone on to successful careers. Perhaps the most revered of VMI's alumni is George C. Marshall, who led America's military in World War II as chief of staff of the Army, served as secretary of defense and secretary of state, and won the Nobel Peace Prize. Other graduates have served as generals, admirals, and CEOs of Fortune 500 companies. Others have had highly successful and fulfilling careers in other capacities and in all professions.

A key asset available to alumni is the VMI network. The challenges VMI cadets undergo during their first year, known as their Rat Year, creates enduring bonds among "Brother Rats." In addition, the ties forged between upper-level students who mentor cadets during their Rat Year last a lifetime. These bonds firmly tie graduates into the extended network of VMI alumni.

Alumni are extremely devoted to VMI. This, in large part, is demonstrated by the generous contributions alumni make to the VMI Foundation. This generosity has resulted in VMI having the largest per capita endowment of any public college in America when compared to the size of its student body.

"Graduates from VMI are trained in honor, loyalty, and strength of both character and body. The Institute combines academics with a unique military experience so cadets emerge well prepared to become leaders in any endeavor they choose."

-Colleges of Distinction

Fast Facts

Virginia Military Institute is a four-year, coeducational liberal arts college with a strong engineering program. It is an independent public college founded in 1839. It's highly regarded academic program is conducted within a military framework, providing a uniquely demanding and rewarding educational experience.

Web site

http://www.vmi.edu

Location

Lexington, Virginia—located in a small town in rural Virginia, VMI is 45 miles from Roanoke and less then a three hour drive from Washington, D.C.

Student Profile

1,300 undergraduate students (92% male, 8% female); 47 states and territories; 16.5% minority, 1.6% international.

Faculty Profile

114 full-time faculty. 97% hold a terminal degree in their field. 11:1 student/faculty ratio.

Residence Life

Highly residential: 100% of students live on campus.

Athletics

NCAA Division I, Big South Conference. 16 varsity sports (11 men's: basketball, baseball, cross-country, football, indoor & outdoor track, lacrosse, rifle, swimming, soccer, wrestling; 5 women's: cross-country, indoor & outdoor track, rifle, soccer), and 13 club sports.

Academic Programs

Biology; civil engineering; chemistry; computer science; economics & business; electrical & computer engineering; English & fine arts; history; international studies; mathematics; mechanical engineering; modern languages & cultures; physics & astronomy; philosophy; psychology.

Costs and Aid

2007–2008: $16,156 in-state comprehensive($5,062 tuition); $32,000 out-of-state comprehensive ($20,906 tuition). 42% of students receive some financial aid. Average award: $13,960.

Endowment

$288,086,372.

More Distinctions

• No. 1 public liberal arts college for seven years in a row by U.S. News and World Report.

Bethany College

WEST VIRGINIA

Bethany College is a private, coeducational, residential, liberal arts college in the beautiful panhandle region of West Virginia. Founded in 1840, Bethany is the oldest institution of higher learning in West Virginia.

Admissions Contact:

Bethany College
Bethany, WV 26032
(800) 922-7611
Ph: (304) 829-7000
Email: admission@bethanywv.edu
www.bethanywv.edu

The 4 Distinctions

Engaged Students

At Bethany, students do more than learn the liberal arts, they live them, exercising the mind so they become stronger and better prepared for a fast-changing and increasingly networked world. Bethany strengthens character and graduates students with sound tools for judgment, a reliable ethical compass, and the backbone required to make smart choices. Bethany teaches students how to think so that they can decide how to live. For more than 167 years, Bethany has been refining this approach to education by giving students "permission to dream," with the belief that every dream, and the life it inspires, grows from a bedrock of meaningful learning and support.

Here, students enjoy the benefits of a private, liberal arts college with a national reputation. Bethany's students choose from more than thirty majors, with many options for emphasis and several excellent pre-professional programs.

Bethany has affiliations with study-abroad programs in many countries around the globe and offers several scholarships for study-abroad programs. Bethany maintains programs at the Sorbonne in Paris, France; the Pädagogische Hochschule in Heidelberg, Germany; and the University of Navarra in Pamplona. There is no additional tuition cost to participate in these programs and student airfare costs are included.

Many student clubs and academic departments feature short-term travel. The Model United Nations club makes trips every semester to locations in Africa, the Caribbean, Central America, or South America. Several clubs in the department of political science offer two-week trips to such locations as Panama, China, Europe, and Africa. Some Bethany students have visited as many as a dozen different countries during their college years.

The career counseling office collaborates with academic departments to offer a number of internship opportunities in Wheeling, WV, or in Pittsburgh, PA. Along with professional, working internships, students take evening classes taught by real-world professionals.

Through Bethany's Washington Center Internship Program, students can spend a semester in Washington, DC, gaining experience in regulatory agencies, associations, and in other aspects of government, as well as with a number of companies. Students have had the opportunity to work with institutions such as the U.S. Department of State, the U.S. Congress, the White House, Amnesty International, CNN and FOX news, the Department of Energy, and the Middle East Institute. Over 70 percent of students who have participated in these internships have returned to DC for professional employment in their field of study.

Great Teaching

Great students emerge with the help of dynamic teachers and mentors. Bethany's faculty put teaching first and choose to be at a school where one-on-one engagement with students is top priority. Faculty regularly invite students to collaborate, giving them invaluable opportunities for research, discovery, publishing, and presentation.

In 2007, Bethany College professor of biology John Burns was named a Fulbright Scholar. His Fulbright application was built on years of faculty and student research conducted at Bethany in the areas of cycles and circadian rhythms. Joint faculty and student research is supported by Bethany College faculty development grants, and through other sources.

Many students have presented the results of their research at such meetings as the undergraduate research day in Charleston, West Virginia, and their results have been published in notable professional journals.

First-year seminar, designed to help first-year students make the transition from high school to college, offers such classes as tai chi, science and pseudoscience, and the Beatles and popular culture.

The senior project and senior comprehensive exams serve as practical capstones and give seniors the opportunity to demonstrate the breadth and depth of the knowledge they have acquired. The senior project is a required, faculty-directed research presentation. The comprehensive exams include a one-hour oral exam and an eight-hour written exam.

Vibrant Community

Located on 1,300 acres in the foothills of the Allegheny Mountains, Bethany provides a safe and stimulating learning environment. While the the town of Bethany has a population of only three hundred, Bethany is just a short drive from Wheeling, W V; and less than an hour from Pittsburgh, PA, recently voted America's most livable city-

Bethany's residence life program offers a variety of living and learning environments, including traditional residence halls, suites, and apartments. There are (number) coed residence halls, one male residence and one female residence. Morlan Hall houses students on its third and fourth floors, as well as several academic departments and a popular cafe.

The student activities council hosts a wide variety of performances, which have recently included Chinese poets, nationally known comedians, and various musical acts. Recent speakers on campus have included General Wesley Clark, former U.S. secretary of the treasury Paul O'Neill, and West Virginia Governor Joe Manchin III. Bethany's Project Red has sponsored speakers from the Congo.

About half of Bethany's students participate in Greek life, or in one of the 30 available varsity Division III sports teams.

For students with an interest in equestrian sports or studies, Bethany College offers one of the most well-equipped facilities of its kind anywhere. Peace Point Equestrian Center sits on 2,800 acres of hilltop land with miles of scenic trails. Amenities include 12' x 12' matted, deluxe Loddon stalls, each equipped with Nelson waterers and brass blanket, bridle, and saddle racks. Each barn has private hot-water wash stalls and an aisleway of cushioned interlocking brick. Turnout is available in large board fence paddocks, each with run-in shelters.

Successful Outcomes

Bethany College graduates have won a Pulitzer Prize; an Academy Award; have been named Gates, Madison, and Fullbright Scholars; and have been elected governor.

Alumni also include the sole American judge on the World Court in the Hague, and the director of the National Cancer Institute. Bethany has a strong reputation for preparing students for graduate and professional studies. Many Bethany graduates have launched rewarding careers in business, engineering, law, dentistry, and medicine from the foundation of Bethany's renowned pre-professional programs.

In communications and the arts, Bethany alumni and students continue to reach national prominence. Graduates include CBS News correspondent Bob Orr, Seattle Mariners play-by-play announcer Dave Sims, and former NBC anchor Faith Daniels. A Bethany student has been named a finalist in the National Broadcasting Society's student electronic media competition for seven consecutive years.

Fast Facts

Bethany College is a four-year, Liberal Arts College, affiliated with the Christian Church (Disciples of Christ) and founded in 1840.

Web site

http://www.bethanywv.edu

Location

Bethany, West Virginia—one hour from Pittsburgh; one-half hour from Wheeling, WV; one-half hour from Steubenville, OH.

Student Profile

902 students (51% male, 49% female); 22 states and territories; 6% minority, 3% international.

Faculty Profile

67 full-time faculty. 13:1 student/faculty ratio. Average class size is 20.

Residence Life

Highly residential: 88% of students live on campus.

Athletics

NCAA Division III, Eastern College Athletic Association, President's Athletic Conference (PAC). 20 varsity sports (10 men's: baseball, basketball, cross-country, football, golf, indoor track or outdoor track, soccer, swimming & diving, tennis; 10 women's: basketball, cross-country, golf, indoor track, outdoor track, soccer, softball, swimming &diving, tennis, volleyball), 7 club sports and intramurals.

Academic Programs

Accounting; biology; chemistry; communication; computer science; economics; education; English; environmental science; environmental studies; equine studies; fine arts; French; German; history; interdisciplinary studies; international relations; mathematics; music; philosophy; physical education & sports studies; physics; political communication; political science; psychology; psychology & education; religious studies; social work; Spanish; theatre arts; visual art.

Costs and Aid

2006–2007: $24,345 comprehensive ($15,750 tuition). 90% of students receive some financial aid. Average award: $7,500.

Endowment

$40 Million.

More Distinctions

• Bethany College is composed of 5 buildings on the National Register of Historic Places and two buildings are listed as National Historic Landmarks, out of 40 buildings that make-up the Bethany campus.

• The College was founded in 1840, making it the oldest college in West Virginia, and the longest continuous accredited college in the state.

West Virginia Wesleyan College

WEST VIRGINIA

West Virginia Wesleyan College (WVWC) is a private, residential, liberal arts college, affiliated with the United Methodist Church, with an enrollment of approximately 1,200 students. All of its forty majors offer the option of a five-year master of business administration degree.

Admissions Contact:

West Virginia Wesleyan College
59 College Avenue
Buckhannon, WV 26201
(800) 722-9933
Ph: (304) 473-8000
www.wvwc.edu

The 4 Distinctions

Engaged Students

Of WVWC's students, 25 percent identify themselves as United Methodist and 25 percent as Roman Catholic.

WVWC's four-hour freshman seminar program is designed to aid the transition from high school to college. The reading- and writing-intensive program, on average, covers a dozen different topics. Some recent examples have included ten things employers want, the economy, the sixties, baseball, and a study of Wal-Mart. The program has been so popular that it has been expanded to include all first-year students this fall.

Before graduating, every student participates in a community service experience, and 80 percent of students are actively involved in community service on an ongoing basis. As part of the Bonner Scholars Program, more than sixty students contribute more than ten hours of community service per week. Some students devote themselves to children's advocacy issues, while others work to support children at risk. During the alternative spring break, students have assisted economic start-ups in Belize, have participated in Hurricane Katrina relief efforts in New Orleans, and have repaired homes in Appalachia.

May term is a popular time for WVWC students to participate in international study. About seventy students travel abroad each May, earning three credits for this intensive period of study. The College has particularly close ties to study-abroad options in Northern Ireland and South Korea. Recent May-term courses have included trips to Australia, Greece, Ireland, Italy, Mexico, South America, Turkey, and the United Kingdom.

The College strongly encourages students to undertake internships as part of their college experience. The College's internship office facilitates such opportunities as internships with the Washington Center in Washington, DC; with a program in Pittsburgh; and with alumni, local businesses, and nonprofit agencies.

Research is another focus of academics at WVWC. At the annual regional undergraduate research conference hosted by WVWC, over sixty WVWC students participate in the research presentations each year. Five WVWC physics majors recently received four-thousand-dollar-NASA grants for special summer research projects. Student researchers work on a variety of projects, from social-policy mapping to working with local hospitals to conducting assessments of health care quality.

WVWC's Leadership Program is a four-year developmental program for emerging leaders. Enrolling about twenty-five freshmen each year, the program has a strong service component.

The campus is thoroughly connected to the Internet with 2,200 Internet ports and wireless access in common areas. All students are required to own a laptop computer.

Great Teaching

Though its curriculum is strongly based in the liberal arts, most major programs at WVWC have a deliberate vocational slant.

WVWC and the University of Virginia cooperate to offer a 3-2 engineering program and a 3-2 physics program, in which students earn a WVWC degree after three years and a master's degree from the University of Virginia after two additional years of study. WVWC and West Virginia University cooperate to offer a 3-2 engineering program that also offers students the option of earning two undergraduate degrees.

The business department, the most popular academic program at WVWC, offers a five-year MBA program available to majors from all areas who have a minor in business. The College offers five distinct business majors. WVWC also offers a five-year master's in education and in athletic training.

WVWC students benefit from the low student to faculty ratio of thirteen to one and an average class size of nineteen.

Vibrant Community

About 90 percent of students live on campus. WVWC has nine residence halls. Freshmen occupy three residence halls in an area called the Quad, and upper-level students can choose to live in singles or suite-style residence halls.

WVWC has a thriving Greek system, with four sororities and five fraternities. Members of Greek organizations are known for reflecting the values of the College.

The College's outdoor recreation program offers a wide variety of activities, including white-water rafting, paintball, cross-country and alpine skiing, caving, hiking, horseback riding, and rock climbing.

Wesley Chapel is the largest worship space in the state of West Virginia. Seating 1,600, it hosts performances by various campus musical ensembles, including a concert band, a percussion ensemble, Concentus Vocum, and the College's renowned concert chorale and jazz ensemble programs. International artists visit WVWC as part of the Arts Alive Program.

In the foothills of the Allegheny Mountains, Buckhannon is a town of about seven thousand inhabitants, an hour from Morgantown and seventy-five minutes from Charleston, the state capital.

The College's athletic teams, known as the Bobcats, compete in NCAA Division II and as part of the West Virginia Intercollegiate Athletic Conference. All of Wesleyan's eighteen teams successfully compete at the regional and national levels, and Wesleyan has won over 136 conference championships during the past fifteen years. On average, 30 percent of students take part in varsity athletics.

Successful Outcomes

The WVWC slogan is "Enduring values . . . transforming lives." WVWC graduates are committed to improving society.

Students who choose to continue their educations are successful: 90 percent of WVWC students who apply to graduate programs in law, medicine, and other disciplines are accepted.

Two recent graduates have been recognized with two of the highest international studies awards granted to college students. One graduate was selected to the prestigious U.S. Department of State Critical Language Scholarship program and studied in Tunisia for two months mastering the Arabic language. Of the more than 3,000 applicants for the Arabic Language Institute, only 150 students were selected.

Another graduate was awarded a Fulbright English Teaching Assistantship in Thailand and will be teaching conversational English to middle-high and high school students and will participate in all school activities. The Fulbright Scholarship Program is one of the most selective scholarship programs worldwide for college students.

Fast Facts

West Virginia Wesleyan College is a four-year, private, liberal arts college founded in 1890.

Web site

http://www.wvwc.edu

Location

Buckhannon, West Virginia—a quaint small-college town with an array of restaurants and fast-food eateries. The town is located within one hour of several beautiful state parks and within ninety minutes of West Virginia's nationally acclaimed ski resorts. The community includes department stores, movie theatres, antique emporiums, and a variety of independently-owned shops.

Student Profile

1,200 students (47% male, 53% female); 35 states, 26 countries; 8% minority, 3% international.

Faculty Profile

78 full-time faculty. 13:1 student/faculty ratio. Average class size is 19.

Residence Life

Highly residential: over 95% of students live on campus.

Athletics

NCAA Division II, West Virginia Intercollegiate Athletic Conference. 18 varsity sports (9 men's: baseball, basketball, cross-country, football, golf, soccer, swimming, tennis, track & field; 9 women's: basketball, cross-country, golf, soccer, swimming, tennis, softball, track & field, volleyball), women's lacrosse club team; intramural sports are offered each semester and the program includes flag football, volleyball, basketball, indoor soccer, ultimate Frisbee, and softball, among others.

Academic Programs

Accounting; art; art administration; athletic training; biology; business administration; chemistry; Christian education; combined elementary/secondary education; computer information science; computer science; criminal justice; economics; elementary education; engineering; English (education, literature, writing); environmental science; exercise science; graphic design: history; international business; international studies; management; mathematics; marketing; music; music education; nursing; painting and drawing; physical education; physics; philosophy; philosophy and religion; political science; predentistry; prelaw; premedicine; preoptometry; prepharmacy; prephysical therapy; preveterinary medicine; psychology; public relations; religion; secondary education; sociology; theatre.

Costs and Aid

2007–2008: $27,990 comprehensive ($20,850 tuition). 90% of Wesleyan's students receive some form of financial aid. Scholarships are available for academic, athletic, community service, leadership, and performing and visual arts achievement.

Endowment

$37 million.

Colleges of Distinction
South Region Schools

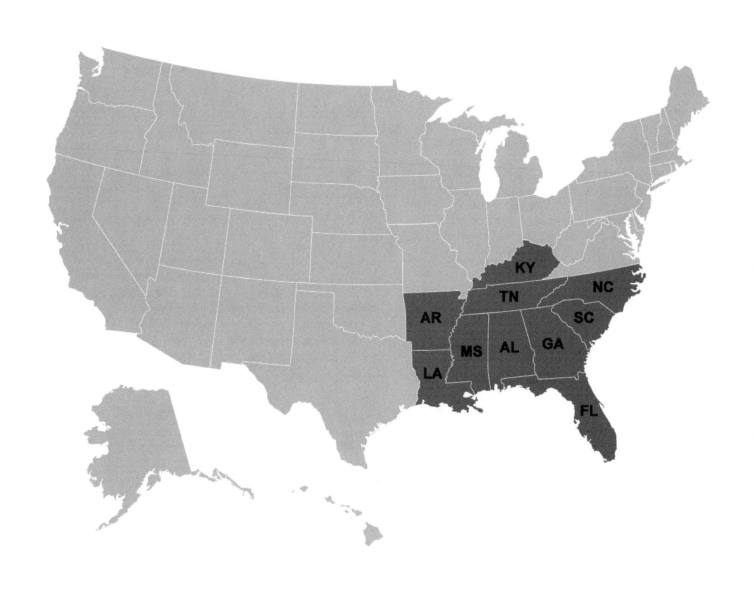

Photo: © iStockphoto.com/lisapics

Notes

_____

_____

_____

_____

_____

_____

_____

_____

Birmingham-Southern College

ALABAMA

Birmingham-Southern College (BSC) is a four-year, private, liberal arts institution affiliated with the United Methodist Church. Committed to providing a liberal arts education of distinctive quality, BSC challenges its students today to think independently, to examine the arts and sciences aesthetically and critically, and to communicate clearly.

Admissions Contact:

Birmingham-Southern College
900 Arkadelphia Road
Birmingham, AL 35254
(800) 523-5793
Ph: (205) 226-4696
Email: admitme@bsc.edu
www.bsc.edu

The 4 Distinctions

Engaged Students

Birmingham-Southern consistently ranks highest in Alabama for its academic programs, and it offers more than fifty majors. The most popular are business administration/management, health/medical preparation, and prelaw. BSC enjoys national recognition for the high percentage of its graduates accepted into medical, dental, and health career programs. Throughout its educational programs, BSC stresses critical-thinking skills, writing, and a collaborative, interdisciplinary approach, all essential for success in today's workplace.

BSC is noted for its strong service-learning program, in which 70 percent of its students participate; its study-abroad (including exchange programs with international colleges and universities) and leadership studies programs; and its January interim term, which provides flexible options for hands-on education. Other unique aspects of a BSC education are its requirement that all students attend forty cultural events during their college career, such as lectures, art exhibits, and musical and theatrical performances. Often, these events connect with students' course work. In addition, seniors give a public presentation of their research over four years, much like the oral requirement of doctoral programs.

During the school's January interim term, many students choose to study abroad or domestically. Scholarships and other funding are available, making these experiences accessible for many. BSC students who choose to remain on campus in January enjoy very small classes and often take advantage of internship opportunities in Birmingham, especially in the medical, legal, and fine arts fields. Birmingham's medical facilities are considered among the best in the nation.

Great Teaching

BSC fosters the advancement of scholarship, personal and resourceful learning, and comprehensive advising. BSC is distinguished by its dedicated faculty, undergraduate scholarship and research, leadership studies and service learning, cross-cultural opportunities, and on- and off-campus mentor relationships.

The low student to faculty ratio of twelve to one allows students to have personal interactions with faculty members often and in a variety of ways. Students are encouraged to explore the breadth of the college's academic programs through its general education foundations curriculum and its honors program.

Within the general education foundations program, freshmen take two first-year seminars their first year. These courses are interdisciplinary, often to include a service component, and provide an introduction to the liberal arts. One recent example includes BSC music students who worked with a local elementary school to create, compose, and produce an opera. First-year courses include language studies and courses with a deep engagement in the arts.

The honors program provides academic challenges to highly motivated, intellectually curious BSC students who are encouraged to take risks and explore new subject areas. About thirty-five students are admitted to the program each year.

In addition, students work side by side with faculty members on research projects. Many students even coauthor publications with faculty members, and together they present their findings at regional and national conferences.

Vibrant Community

Birmingham-Southern's 1,300 students come from about thirty-three states and sixteen foreign countries; about 70 percent are from Alabama. More than 85 percent of students live on the wooded 192-acre campus just three miles west of downtown Birmingham. The campus tone is friendly and courteous, typical of a Southern college. The campus police are highly respected and are seen as a great resource for students.

BSC housing includes residence halls, an apartment complex, and fraternity and sorority houses. Living and learning communities are available, and resident advisors are active and present in BSC students' daily lives. Students are involved in more than eighty student organizations, as well as NCAA Division III athletics, and 75 percent of students stay on campus on weekends. About 50 percent of BSC students are involved in Greek life, and fraternities and sororities provide many social activities and community-service opportunities.

Birmingham, Alabama, known as the Magic City, is located at the foothills of the Appalachian Mountains in the heart of the southeastern United States. It is a major urban center with more than one million people in the Birmingham metropolitan area. The city is a center for medical research, banking, music, technology, art, and engineering, as well as higher education. Birmingham itself is a leading urban center of the Sunbelt, and there are many opportunities for local community service, such as participating in Habitat for Humanity projects, tutoring elementary students, or working through the mayor's office on internships. BSC students also travel across the country and around the globe on service initiatives: in the past, students have traveled to Harlem and San Francisco domestically and to Zimbabwe and Mozambique internationally.

Successful Outcomes

BSC guarantees that students will graduate in four consecutive years if they follow guidelines set forth by the college, taking advantage of BSC's strong academic advising and careful planning of its course offerings. Students can also take advantage of career planning services such as interest inventories, career and job-search classes, resume assistance, interview training, on-campus job interviews, and an alumni network. Each year, almost 50 percent of graduates go on to graduate school. Nationally, the college ranks high in terms of graduates accepted to medical, dental, law, and professional schools. Within one year of graduation, 60 percent of BSC alumni enter the work force in a job related to their undergraduate fields of study. Many are hired by local Birmingham businesses and law firms, as well as by national corporations.

BSC alumni are studying and working in 38 foreign countries, from China and Australia, to Turkey, Ecuador, and Zimbabwe. In addition, the average BSC student graduates with far less debt than students at most other private colleges or major public schools.

Successful alumni include NASA employees, lawyers, doctors, a nationally acclaimed playwright, banking CEOs, college professors, and public-service professionals.

Fast Facts

Birmingham-Southern College is a four-year, private, liberal arts institution founded in 1856 and affiliated with the United Methodist Church.

Web site

http://www.bsc.edu

Location

Birmingham, Alabama—set on 192 wooded acres three miles west of downtown Birmingham.

Student Profile

1,315 students; 33 states, 16 countries; 16% minority, 2% international.

Faculty Profile

112 full-time faculty. 96% hold a terminal degree in their field. 12:1 student/faculty ratio.

Residence Life

Highly residential: 85% of students live on campus.

Athletics

NCAA Division III, Southern Collegiate Athletic Conference. 21 varsity sports (10 men's: baseball, basketball, cross-country, football, golf, lacrosse soccer, tennis, indoor track & field, outdoor track & field; 11 women's: basketball, cross-country, golf, lacrosse, rifle, soccer, softball, tennis, indoor track & field, outdoor track & field, volleyball).

Academic Programs

Accounting; art; Asian studies; biology; biology-psychology; business administration; chemistry; computer science; computer science-mathematics; dance; economics; education; engineering (3-2 program); English; English-theatre arts; environmental studies (3-2 program); French; German; history; history-political science; international studies; mathematics; music; musical theatre; nursing (3-2 program); philosophy; philosophy-politics-economics; physics; political science; psychology; religion; religion-education; religion-philosophy; sociology; sociology-political science; sociology-psychology; Spanish; theatre arts; urban environmental studies.

Costs and Aid

2006–2007: $30,440 comprehensive ($22,260 tuition, with the remainder being residence hall, books and supplies, meal plan, and fees). 99% of students receive some financial aid. Average award: $9,378.

Endowment

$122 million.

More Distinctions

• U.S. News & World Report has ranked Birmingham-Southern among America's best national liberal arts colleges for thirteen consecutive years. BSC also has been rated a Best Value college by U.S. News.

• The Fiske Guide to Colleges ranks Birmingham-Southern as one of twenty-six private colleges and universities nationwide as a Best Buy for the "quality of the academic offerings in relation to the cost of attendance."

• The Washington Times ranks Birmingham-Southern as one of the nation's top thirty colleges.

• Birmingham-Southern is included in Loren Pope's Colleges That Change Lives, recognizing colleges that are "outdoing the Ivies and the major universities in producing winners."

Henderson State University

ARKANSAS

As Arkansas's public liberal arts university, Henderson State offers its 3,500 students an education based on a comprehensive core of courses in the arts and sciences. Henderson State is located in Arkadelphia, a city of eleven thousand in a beautiful area of western Arkansas known for its rivers and lakes.

Admissions Contact:

Henderson State University
1100 Henderson Street
Arkadelphia, AR 71999-0001
(800) 228-7333
Ph: (870) 230-5000
Email: admissions@hsu.edu
www.getreddie.com

The 4 Distinctions

Engaged Students

Henderson encourages students in all disciplines to undertake research, and faculty members often invite students to collaborate with them on topics of interest. Some majors even require a research project for graduation. In recent years, as many as one-third of all participants in the annual statewide Arkansas Undergraduate Research Conference have been Henderson students.

Students in camping and outdoor education and in recreation and park management have easy access to abundant natural resources in Arkansas, providing opportunities to sharpen outdoor skills that will prove invaluable in their future careers as natural resource managers.

The Honors College provides opportunities for university service, as well as projects serving Arkadelphia and Clark County. Civic-minded students help families, put together programs for the public schools, and sponsor cultural events to bring the community and the university together.

Henderson has a Common Book Program which offers everyone on campus the opportunity to read and discuss the same book over the course of the semester. This creates a context for conversations about issues of importance in today's world, as well as within specific fields of study. It encourages students to create a community in and outside the classroom, while strengthening the students' reading, writing, and critical thinking skills.

Great Teaching

While the arts and sciences form the foundation for all academic programs at Henderson, the university has an excellent reputation in teacher education, business administration, and several other fields, too. The academic program at Henderson is divided into three colleges. The Matt Locke Ellis College of Arts and Sciences offers a comprehensive core of liberal arts courses, with majors in disciplines from fine arts and the social sciences to technology and the natural sciences. The School of Business offers the Bachelor of Business Administration degree, and it also runs

the aviation department which offers a bachelor's degree. Teachers College, Henderson, receives national recognition for the quality of its mentor-teacher program for first-year teachers; the Education Center, which opened in 2001, houses multimedia classrooms, a computer lab, the teacher resource center, a video-production laboratory, and an early childhood laboratory school.

Students in Henderson's well-regarded aviation program, the state's only four-year BS degree in aviation, are able to choose from three different Bachelor of Science tracks. The Caplinger Airway Science Academic Center offers high-tech classrooms, flight simulators, and on-site computerized FAA written-test facilities. Utilizing fifteen aircraft and more than fifteen flight instructors, the program provides students with the training and education necessary for careers in the professional aviation industry.

Henderson's nursing program, leading to the Bachelor of Science in Nursing (BSN) degree, is highly competitive, admitting only thirty-five new students each fall. Henderson also offers preprofessional programs in dentistry, engineering, law, medicine, physical therapy, optometry, and veterinary science.

The Donald W. Reynolds Science Center, which opened in 1999, houses state-of-the-art laboratories and classrooms, as well as the most advanced planetarium in Arkansas. Arkansas Hall, renovated and expanded in 2004, houses the departments of theatre, dance, and communications. The two-story building features a dance studio, a 162-seat studio theatre, and a 965-seat main auditorium.

Theatre students from Henderson frequently undertake internships and summer seminars with professional theaters in New York City, and the department regularly participates in the American College Theater Festival.

Vibrant Community

A pleasant town of about eleven thousand residents, Arkadelphia is just thirty minutes from Hot Springs and an hour from Little Rock. Amtrak stops in town, providing easy transportation throughout the region. Arkadelphia is considered an ideal college community, neither too big nor too small, making it a perfect place for students' first experiences living away from home.

Each residence hall has a hall council, charged with the task of integrating and exchanging members' ideas, promoting responsibility, and encouraging good citizenship and high academic standards.

Henderson students have a wide variety of extracurricular activities from which to choose, including six governing councils, twelve honorary societies, a number of service and departmental organizations, four different communications and media clubs, eight religious organizations, nine national fraternities, six national sororities, and an active intramural sports program that is open to all. Henderson State, an NCAA Division II school, competes in the Gulf South Conference. Student theatre productions, faculty concerts, and guest speakers enrich evenings and weekends. Each semester, first-run movies are shown on a large inflatable screen on the Quad and in the student union.

Henderson is committed to selecting and supporting a diverse domestic and international student population. The student body includes about one hundred students from over twenty countries around the world. The International Student Center provides housing for twenty-seven international students.

Henderson has an excellent program for incoming freshmen called the First-Year Experience (FYE). This program is designed to help new students gain essential skills in balancing issues of personal freedom and responsibility, including making important lifestyle decisions that can affect their personal success. It offers free tutoring and promotes involvement in clubs and organizations, community service opportunities, leadership programs, cultural events and campus activities.

FYE exposes new students to a wide range of majors and careers to help them discover and define their interests and abilities. Students also learn professional skills essential to any career, such as team building, presentation and writing skills, decision-making and group skills. The program gives students a chance to discuss issues of diversity in a small group setting.

Successful Outcomes

Henderson students have achieved national and international recognition, including Rhodes, Fulbright, and Rotary International scholarships.

The Center for Career Development at Henderson is committed to helping students develop career and life-planning skills, master job-search strategies, and seek rewarding employment. The center offers personal career counseling, mock interviews, resume preparation, on-campus interviewing, career fairs, graduate school search assistance, and a resource center.

Notable Henderson State alumni include Dr. Ann Chotard, founder of the Wildwood Park for the Performing Arts; Broadway actor Lawrence Hamilton; C. Vann Woodward, Pulitzer Prize-winning historian; Dwight Adams, vice president of player personnel for the Buffalo Bills; and Dr. Sam Barker, president of Squibb Corporation's U.S. pharmaceutical division.

Fast Facts

Henderson State University is a comprehensive, coeducational, four-year public institution, founded in 1890.

Web site

http://www.hsu.edu

Location

Arkadelphia, Arkansas—70 miles southwest of Little Rock, AR.

Student Profile

3,476 students (58% female, 42% male); 26 states and 24 countries; 22% minority, 2% international.

Faculty Profile

162 full-time faculty. 17:1 student/faculty ratio. Average class size is about 30.

Residence Life

Moderately residential: 29% of students live on campus.

Athletics

Henderson State is a NCAA Division II school. Students can participate in 12 varsity sports (5 men's: basketball; swimming; baseball; football; and golf; and 7 women's: basketball; volleyball; swimming; softball; golf; cross-country track; and tennis.

Academic Programs

Art; athletic training; aviation; biology; business administration; chemistry; child care; communication; computer science; dance; education {art, early childhood (P-4); elementary/secondary physical education; middle school (4-8); social science; vocational business education}; English; family and consumer sciences; general studies; history; human services; mass media; mathematics; medical technology; military science; music; nursing; physics; political science; predentistry; preengineering; prelaw; premedicine; preoptometry; prepharmacy; prephysical therapy; preveterinarian; psychology; public administration; recreation; sociology; Spanish; theatre arts; vocational business.

Costs and Aid

2007–2008: $2,900 in-state tuition, $5200 out-of-state tuition. 79% of students receive some financial aid. Average award: $2,800.

Endowment

$10 million.

More Distinctions

• The exclusive Arkansas member of the Council of Public Liberal Arts Universities (COPLAC).

Barry University

FLORIDA

Admissions Contact:

Barry University
11300 N.E. Second Avenue
Miami Shores, Florida 33161
800-695-2279
Ph: (305) 899-3100
Email: admissions@mail.barry.edu
www.barry.edu

Founded in 1940 by the Adrian Dominican Sisters, Barry University is a caring community where each student is valued and receives personal attention from distinguished faculty. Barry is well-known for its diverse student body and emphasis on community service.

The 4 Distinctions

Engaged Students

Barry offers more than fifty undergraduate majors, and the most popular are education, business, and biology. The progressive education program is constantly updating its curriculum to reflect the changing needs of society, and students are immersed in a wide range of courses designed to develop leaders in education who are technically savvy and who embrace integrity with a sense of service and stewardship.

Barry also encourages wholehearted engagement in community service. Since part of the University's mission is to encourage and develop learning opportunities in the community, most students are active off campus, helping solve local problems and performing service ranging from building Habitat for Humanity houses to aiding victims of Hurricane Katrina in the Gulf Coast. Recently, nursing students developed a program that alleviated pesticide rashes among the children of migrant farm workers.

Internships are available with a wide range of local businesses and corporations such as Bank of America, The Miami Dolphins, The Miami Heat, Carnival Cruise Lines, John Hancock Insurance and Financial Services, Target Brands, Dole Food Company, and Jackson Memorial Hospital. Public agencies also work with BU students in the fields of health care, mental health, criminal justice, and domestic violence, among others. On campus, students can work with most departments in work-study positions.

Each year Barry students make a difference by participating in a multitude of service projects locally, nationally, and overseas. Programs and foundations such as Sister to Sister, Habitat for Humanity, Alternative Spring Break, and Barry's own Campus Ministry raise money and send students to places where they can provide assistance, be it cleaning up flooded homes in New Orleans or teaching English in the Dominican Republic.

Great Teaching

Barry is committed to providing an affordable, high-quality education in a caring environment with a religious dimension, celebrating all faiths among its students. A hallmark of a Barry education is the personal and caring approach professors take toward their students. The small class sizes and low student to faculty ratio of fourteen to one allow instructors to interact closely with pupils. Faculty members often offer students help outside the classroom, making themselves accessible to provide personal attention. Barry's faculty are well-rounded and accomplished: more than 84 percent hold PhDs or the highest degree available in their fields.

Instructors such as economics Professor Robert McGee are recognized as leaders in their fields. Dr. McGee, a former consultant for the United States Agency for International Development, came to Barry after reforming national economies in Mozambique, and Bosnia-Herzegovina. The author of 49 books on economics, Dr. McGee brings a wealth of real-world experience to the classroom.

Biology Professor Allen Sanborn, considered to be among the leading experts in the study of cicadas, recently published findings where he identified two new species of the singing insect.

Barry's School of Podiatry's Dean Chet Evans and Professors John Nelson and James Losito were named among the most influential podiatrists in the nation by the journal Podiatry Management.

Barry University Professor of Physical Sciences, George Fisher edited and coauthored a textbook about D-amino acids. Dr. Fisher, among the few researchers to work in the pioneering field, has been studying D-amino acids at Barry since 1980 with the help of a grant from the National Institutes of Health.

Charles Rarick, professor of management in the Andreas School of Business, was named a Fulbright Distinguished Lecturer. One of the most prestigious of the Fulbright honors, the Distinguished Lecturer is awarded to only a few of the country's top scholars. The designation is Dr. Rarick's second Fulbright – he won a Fulbright Specialists Grant in 2005.

Vibrant Community

The University features an active, multicultural mix of students from the Caribbean, Central and South America, as well as Asia and Europe. There are more than eighty-nine clubs and student organizations—from cultural associations to honor societies—for students to join, offering something for everyone, including musical and dramatic performing groups, publications, ethnic and religious clubs, service and professional organizations, as well as three fraternities and two sororities.

Barry University is five miles from the ocean in sunny, suburban Miami Shores. The hospitable climate allows for swimming, sailing, waterskiing, scuba diving, golfing, and playing tennis, soccer, and other outdoor sports year-round. Nearby, the Florida Keys, the Everglades, and living coral reefs present both recreational and educational opportunities.

South Florida is an international business, tourism, and entertainment-industry hub with a cosmopolitan multicultural population, offering a wide range of internship and career options as well as a vibrant cultural scene. Highlights include Urban Beach Week; the Calle Ocho street festival; the Miami International Book Fair; and the prestigious art fair, Art Basel Miami Beach. The New World Symphony, the Miami International Film Festival, and the Miami City Ballet provide a full season of acclaimed performances. Miami also hosts the Miami Dolphins football team, the Miami Heat basketball team, the Florida Marlins baseball team, and the Florida Panthers hockey team.

Successful Outcomes

Barry graduates continue to be recognized in the professional arena, be it in business, education, medicine, or science.

The Independent Colleges and Universities of Florida (ICUF) ranked Barry among the two top private not-for-profit educational institutions whose graduates earn the highest wages upon graduation.

Barry's emphasis on low student-to-teacher ratios, community service, and academic excellence is not only effective, but is recognized by recruiters in the professional world.

Barry's Biology Pre-Dental class has had 100 percent acceptance to dental schools for the past thirty years. Ninety percent of Biology Pre-Medicine students were accepted to medical schools last year. Approximately ninety-eight percent of all of School of Natural and Health Sciences graduates are employed in their field of study. One hundred percent of anesthesiology and podiatric medicine graduates and ninety-eight percent of education majors who took certification exams last year passed. Ninety-four percent of nursing students who graduated May 2006 were successful on the NCLEX-RN exam. The School of Nursing also has a 100 percent placement rate.

Fast Facts

Barry University is a private, Catholic college founded in 1940 on a forty-acre tract of tropical vegetation located in residential Miami Shores.

Web site

http://www.barry.edu

Location

Miami Shores, Florida—7 miles from Miami and 14 miles from Fort Lauderdale.

Student Profile

2,800 undergraduate students.

Faculty Profile

340 full-time faculty. 14:1 student /teacher ratio.

Residence Life

Moderately residential: 60% of students live on campus.

Athletics

NCAA Division II, Sunshine State Conference. 12 varsity sports (5 men's: basketball, baseball, soccer, golf, tennis; 7 women's: basketball, volleyball, crew, soccer, softball, golf, tennis).

Academic Programs

Biological & biomedical sciences; business management & marketing; communications; computer & information sciences; education; English language & literature; foreign language & literature; health professions & clinical sciences; history; law & legal studies; liberal arts & sciences; mathematics; multi/interdisciplinary studies; natural resources & conservation; parks, recreation, & fitness; philosophy & religion; physical sciences; psychology; public administration & services; social sciences; theological studies & religious vocations; visual & performing arts.

Costs and Aid

2007–2008: $32,400 comprehensive ($24,500 tuition). 90% of students receive some financial aid. Average award: $15,599.

Endowment

$ 28,959,692.

More Distinctions

• 2007 *U.S. News & World Report* ranked Barry number one for student diversity among Southern schools of the same size and number one in the campus ethnic diversity category for universities in the South offering master's programs.

• Named "Best Private University or College" by South Florida *CEO magazine.*

• The Independent Colleges & Universities of Florida (ICUF) ranked Barry University graduates among the top two salary earners among the state's 28 private, not-for-profit educational institutions.

• *The Princeton Review* named Barry one of the 140 top colleges in the South for 2007.

New College of Florida

FLORIDA

New College of Florida (NCF) is a public, residential, coeducational college designated as the state of Florida's honors college for the liberal arts. Founded in 1960, NCF offers a quality undergraduate liberal arts education. As part of the school's unique approach, students craft their own individualized academic programs in consultation with faculty.

Admissions Contact:

New College of Florida
5800 Bay Shore Road
Sarasota, Florida 34243-2109
Ph: (941) 487-5000
Email: admissions@ncf.edu
www.ncf.edu

The 4 Distinctions

Engaged Students

NCF takes the life of the mind seriously, and its high standards demand rigorous student involvement and motivation. Its students develop a sense of personal responsibility and habits of mind that enable them to excel as lifelong learners in any vocation.

NCF offers more than forty standard academic programs, as well as the opportunity for students, working in close consultation with faculty, to craft their own individualized curricula. Top majors are literature in the humanities, psychology in the social sciences, and biology and environmental studies in the natural sciences. The latter is a natural, given the college's location on Sarasota Bay and its on-campus Pritzker Marine Biology Research Center. In any field, New College students are free to pursue their own interests and develop new ones in a directed, thoughtful, and disciplined way.

The majority of NCF students are from Florida, though NCF offers students numerous opportunities to explore the rest of the world through experiential learning programs. NCF students have studied in Kenya, India, Australia, the Netherlands, the UK, Germany, Finland, Mexico, Peru, and Brazil, among other places. Archaeological, ecological, and anthropological fieldwork is also popular, and the college's flexible curriculum makes extended fieldwork possible. Students have competed successfully for national grants, including securing funds to support research topics from the National Science Foundation. One student recently conducted microbiology research at the Oak Ridge National Laboratories for the U.S. Department of Energy.

NCF students also actively participate in the local community. NCF faculty and students helped found the Sarasota County Openly Plans for Excellence (SCOPE) program, through which area residents and members of the college explore issues of importance, ranging from race relations and aging to neighborhood development and environmental conservation. Likewise, the college's Student Outreach in the Sciences (SOS) program provides opportunities for students in the natural sciences to teach and tutor in area middle schools and high schools.

Great Teaching

With its low student to faculty ratio of ten to one and its unique series of seven academic contracts, plus independent study requirements, New College ensures that students and faculty work together toward each student's demonstrated competence and real mastery of specific subjects. Faculty get to know students well as they assist them in achieving their learning goals from course to course and project to project, and they often tailor class assignments to individual interests and abilities.

Instead of letter grades, faculty give narrative evaluations for each student. All NCF faculty are full-time, and 99 percent hold the PhD or terminal degree in their fields. Faculty value the one-on-one tutorials offered for upper-level students, more commonly found at the graduate school level. These tutorials define the personalized educational experience of NCF.

Modern facilities support many individual research options, including the R.V. Heiser Natural Sciences Complex, which features an on-site Raman spectroscopy lab; the Pritzker Marine Biological Research Center, which includes more than ninety saltwater and freshwater research aquariums; a two-thousand-volume library dedicated to Mesoamerican archaeology that includes an oral history archive; and the Caples Fine Arts Complex, which houses a performing arts center, practice rooms for musicians, sculpture and painting studios, and a welding shop and kiln for ceramics.

Each NCF student enters into seven semester-long contracts which ensure a broad exploration of the liberal arts. By the fifth semester, students are focused on their area of concentration. Three independent study projects—often using Florida as a resource—are completed during each of the first three January terms. The fourth January is reserved for work on the senior thesis, a final project each student defends orally before a faculty committee. A bound copy of each thesis is kept in the library, and topics have ranged from an analysis of the break shot in a game of pool to social and political factors contributing to the devastation of New Orleans by Hurricane Katrina to the development of a synthetic compound that may help reduce the risk of autism in young children.

Vibrant Community

Sarasota, located fifty-five miles south of Tampa on Florida's west coast, is known as the Circus City and offers a vibrant cultural life in addition to its world-renowned natural beauty and wildlife. Sarasota is home to the John and Mable Ringling Museum of Art, which sits adjacent to the New College campus. NCF's College Hall was the former home of circus magnates Charles and Edith Ringling. The Marie Selby Botanical Gardens and the famous Lido and Siesta Key beaches on the Gulf of Mexico are also nearby.

NCF students say that freedom and tolerance define the social tone of the college. Respect for sexual orientation, political affiliation, freedom of speech, ethnic heritage, and cultural associations are paramount. The idiosyncratic garb of individual students expresses these attitudes. New College is proud to note that 100 percent of its students receive some form of financial aid.

NCF students are actively involved in campus life and the local community. On average, 75 percent of all students live on campus in a variety of housing options, including five new residence halls that opened in fall 2007 and an historic residence hall complex designed by and named for renowned architect I. M. Pei. Residential life at NCF underscores the symbiotic relationship between academics and social life on campus, and it is typical on weekends for 95 percent of students to gather either formally or informally for student "walls," or parties, during which discussions of Hegel intertwine seamlessly with dancing and socializing. There are forty-five clubs and organizations on campus in which students can participate, and NCF's recreational facilities include an outdoor pool, a fitness center, scuba equipment, a boathouse for sailing, athletic fields, and a running trail.

Successful Outcomes

New College graduates are lifelong learners. Two-thirds of all NCF graduates go on for advanced degrees, with close to 80 percent of the natural science majors continuing on to graduate school. The NCF emphasis on its students' active involvement in designing their own academic program and on independent work experience means they are well equipped for challenging graduate work and they have close, long-term professional and collegial relationships with faculty members.

NCF graduates are successful in obtaining Fulbright Scholarships—twenty-five were awarded in the past six years—as well as a host of other prestigious postundergraduate research scholarships and grants. Recent graduates include a Gates Cambridge Scholarship recipient, a Jack Kent Cooke Scholarship recipient, and two National Science Foundation Research Fellows.

Although New College was founded as recently as 1960, its alumni include several notable people. Among them are Lincoln Diaz-Balart, U.S. congressman from Florida; Carol Flint, writer and producer of such shows as ER, L.A. Law, The West Wing, and others; Gregory Dubois-Felsmann, physicist and Rhodes Scholar; and William Thurston, winner of the Fields Medal, known as the Nobel Prize of mathematics.

Fast Facts

New College of Florida is the State of Florida's "Honors College for the Liberal Arts" located in Sarasota and founded in 1960.

Web site

http://www.ncf.edu/

Location

Sarasota, Florida—Located on 110 bay front acres on Florida's Gulf Coast in the resort city of Sarasota, noted for its beautiful public beaches, theater, art and music.

Student Profile

750 students (41% men, 59% women), all full-time; 80% Florida residents, 5% international.

Faculty Profile

73 full-time faculty. All teach and advise freshmen through seniors. 99% hold the Ph.D. or terminal professional degree. 10:1 student/faculty ratio.

Residence Life

Primarily residential: 75% of students live on campus.

Academic Programs

More than 40 academic programs offered, plus individualized curricula, including: anthropology; art; art history; biochemistry; biology; British & American literature; chemistry; Chinese language & culture; classics; computer science; economics; environmental studies; French language & literature; French studies; gender studies; German language & literature; German studies; Hispanic language & culture; history; humanities; international & area studies; literature; marine biology; mathematics; medieval & renaissance studies; music; natural sciences; neurobiology; philosophy; physics; political science; prelaw; premedicine; psychology; public policy; religion; Russian language & literature; social sciences; sociology; Spanish language & literature; theater; urban studies.

Costs and Aid

2007–2008:$10,884 in-state comprehensive ($3,850 tuition); $28,659 out-of-state comprehensive (21,625 tuition). 95% of all students receive some financial aid. Average award: $8,665. All freshmen who complete their admission application by February 15, and who are admitted, are guaranteed scholarship funding.

Endowment

$36,000,000.

More Distinctions

• The 2008 edition of The Princeton Review named New College the country's best value in public higher education, the second year in a row the college was so honored. In its 2007 edition, U.S. News & World Report also rated New College as the nation's top public liberal arts college and placed the school in the country's top tier of liberal arts colleges both public and private. New College is also one of only 40 colleges nationwide featured in Loren Pope's Colleges that Change Lives and regularly is included as a national best buy in publications ranging from the Fiske Guide to Colleges to Kiplinger's Top 100.

• Since 2001, New College has placed among the nation's leading colleges for per capita production of Fulbright Scholars, with students receiving 25 awards during the past 6 years.

Palm Beach Atlantic University

FLORIDA

Palm Beach Atlantic University (PBA) is a private, comprehensive, nondenominational Christian university with an emphasis on the liberal arts. Founded in 1968, PBA is dedicated to the development of moral character, the enrichment of spiritual lives, and the perpetuation of growth in Christian ideals.

Admissions Contact:

Palm Beach Atlantic University
901 S. Flagler Drive
West Palm Beach, FL 33401
(888) go-to-pba
Ph: (561) 803-2000
Email: admit@pba.edu
www.pba.edu

The 4 Distinctions

Engaged Students

PBA is unique among Christian colleges and universities for a variety of reasons: it is dedicated to conveying the value and significance of the American free-enterprise system, it requires that daytime undergraduates perform at least forty-five hours of service annually, it promotes and celebrates student diversity with more than thirty-seven nations represented in the student body in 2006, and its Office of Online Learning uses the eCollege Learning Management System to deliver Web-based courses. PBA offers students broad opportunities for spiritual growth through mission trips around the world, weekly worship services, and student-led prayer groups.

PBA is known for its signature community-service program called Workship, a combination of work and worship intended to instill in students the habit of giving back to their communities as well as to provide opportunities for students to gain experience. More than two million PBA student service hours have been recorded since the program's inception. One student volunteered at the local United Way by re-doing their accounting policies and procedures manual. His work was a great success, and it enabled him to land a job with one of the Big Six accounting firms. Other PBA students have been active in local churches.

Great Teaching

The school's motto captures PBA's goals: "Enlightening minds, enriching souls, extending hands." PBA offers about sixty different undergraduate academic programs. The most popular majors are management, biology, communications studies/speech communication, education, and psychology. All PBA programs emphasize learning inside and outside the classroom, taking advantage of the dynamic culture and thriving economy of the Palm Beach/Boca Raton area.

PBA's School of Business requires that students complete at least one semester of an internship and offers opportunities with local companies in a variety of industries, such as international business, computers, biotech, and finance, among others. The school also offers a placement office to coordinate students' internship and work-study arrangements.

PBA education graduates have a record-setting 100 percent state certification/licensing exam pass rate. They benefit from beginning their involvement in school classrooms in their freshman year and continue to use Workship opportunities to discover the age group with which they are most comfortable working.

The communications/media school is considered the heart of the school's culture, and its students have opportunities for a variety of hands-on experience, including script writing and other practical applications of media theories and techniques. The music and fine arts departments offer students a number of performance opportunities.

PBA is strong in the sciences. Its master's program in psychology meets state licensing requirements in three different areas. Its pharmaceutical school is one of four in Florida. Prepharmacy and nursing are popular fields of study, as is the marine and oceanography program, which benefits from the variety of marine environments in the West Palm Beach area.

The low student to faculty ratio of fifteen to one means that PBA students are well-known by their professors. PBA considers each faculty member a dean of students, each demonstrating a deep commitment to helping students learn and grow.

Vibrant Community

PBA's West Palm Beach campus is an enclave, including a number of multipurpose buildings with student residences located above lecture halls. The school features diverse living-learning communities and a variety of housing options, including traditional residence halls, suite-style rooms, and apartments. More than half of PBA's two thousand traditional undergraduate students live on campus, and a majority of those students spend their weekends there.

There are fifty-five registered organizations at PBA, including mutual-interest and honor clubs, as well a large intramural sports program, and other activities, such as the surf club, that take advantage of PBA's location.

PBA overlooks the Intracoastal Waterway in downtown West Palm Beach in the heart of Florida's Gold Coast, fifty miles north of Fort Lauderdale. West Palm Beach may be a small town, but it offers many big-city activities for students. The Kravis Center for the Performing Arts, the Norton Museum of Art, and the Flagler Museum are all nearby. Many professional sports teams play in town, and an annual highlight is Major League Baseball spring training. PBA also has satellite campuses in Wellington and Orlando.

Successful Outcomes

The career resource center offers PBA students an abundance of resources to help them make career decisions, and career counselors are available to help students choose a major. Counselors also help students assess what they will be able to do with their degree, offer resume help, and set up practice interviews. The on-campus Student Success Center helps students find part-time and full-time work.

The university has a strong reputation for producing graduates in business, education, and counseling. Half of PBA's graduates enter the job market in a field related to their major within six months of graduation. Students leave PBA with not only the ability to make a living, but with a better idea of how to live a life that honors God. PBA graduates are recognized as leaders in their communities and lay leaders in their churches.

Fast Facts

Palm Beach Atlantic University is a Christian university with a core emphasis in the liberal arts, founded in 1968.

Web site

http:// www.pba.edu

Location

West Palm Beach, Florida—60 miles north of Miami and 150 miles southeast of Orlando.

Student Profile

3,285 (36% male, 64% female); 51 states and territories; 33% minority, 3% international.

Faculty Profile

168 full-time faculty. 15:1 student/faculty ratio. Average class size is 18.

Residence Life

Moderately residential: 57% of students live on campus.

Athletics

NCAA Division II. 10 varsity sports (4 men's: soccer, basketball, baseball, tennis; 6 women's: soccer, volleyball, basketball, softball, tennis, cross-country).

Academic Programs

Bachelor of Arts

Acting for stage & screen; art (studio art); art/secondary ed. (K-12); biblical studies; Christian leadership; Christian social ministry; communication studies; cross-cultural & urban studies; dance; drama/secondary ed. (6-12); English; English/secondary ed. (6-12); film production; graphic arts; history; history/secondary ed. (6-12); music; musical theatre; news & information; organizational communication; philosophy; political science; political science/secondary ed. (6-12); popular music; prelaw; screenwriting; speech communication; television production; technical theatre production and design; theatre arts.

Bachelor of General Studies

General studies.

Bachelor of Music

Church music; instrument performance; keyboard performance; music composition; music/secondary ed. (K-12); voice performance.

Bachelor of Science

Applied finance & accounting; athletic training/concentration in exercise science; biology; elementary education (K-6); entrepreneurship and small business; international business; management; marketing; mathematics; mathematics/secondary ed. (6-12); physical education/non-teaching; physical education/secondary education (K-12); physical education/concentration; psychology.

Bachelor of Science in Nursing

Nursing; associate of arts; preengineering studies.

Costs and Aid

2007–2008: $28,296 comprehensive ($19,950 tuition). 95% of students receive some financial aid. Average award: $2,477.

Rollins College

FLORIDA

Founded in 1885 by New England Congregationalists seeking to bring their style of liberal arts education to the Florida frontier, Rollins College is the oldest recognized college in the state. Rollins is an independent four-year, nondenominational, coeducational institution with an international student body and a faculty dedicated to teaching.

Admissions Contact:

Rollins College
4701 College Drive
Winter Park, FL 32789
Ph: (407) 646-2000
Email: admission@rollins.edu
www.rollins.edu

The 4 Distinctions

Engaged Students

It is Rollins College's mission to educate students for global citizenship and responsible leadership, empowering graduates to pursue meaningful lives and productive careers. Rollins's programs in international relations, African studies, Asian studies, Latin studies, French, German, Russian, and Spanish demonstrate the college's long-standing commitment to providing students with a broad and deep international perspective.

More than 35 percent of Rollins College students study abroad, and two-thirds of the faculty are or have been actively engaged in international pursuits, including taking students abroad, conducting overseas research, and teaching international courses. Rollins offers its students a number of study-abroad options. Rollins's London Internship Program gives students the opportunity to live, work, and study for a full semester in one of the most historically significant cities in the world. Rollins's semester-abroad programs in Spain, Australia, and Germany immerse students in a foreign culture, language, and lifestyle. Rollins's affiliate programs expand international study options even further by providing international learning opportunities offered in conjunction with other schools.

Each year at Rollins, students have the opportunity to take part in field-study courses during the summer, winter, or spring break. Each of these sessions presents opportunities to examine visionary topics that have global implications. Field-study courses may include investigating alternative forms of economic development in Malaysia, conducting water purification relief in the Dominican Republic, or researching marine biology in Barbados.

Rollins's Living and Learning Center in Shanghai provides an educational facility in the Chinese city to serve U.S. college students and faculty, U.S. corporate employees, and the Chinese business and academic communities. The center provides opportunities for students to study and experience China; expands cultural and intellectual exchanges with Chinese scholars; facilitates collaborative programs with Chinese universities; advances research on China; and serves as a resource for students, faculty, and the community by sponsoring public lectures, cultural and networking events, and China-themed visitors. More than twenty-five faculty from Rollins—about 10 percent of the faculty—have traveled to China to study the Middle Kingdom on college-sponsored trips.

Internships also play an important role in a student's education at Rollins. The college's location near Orlando provides exceptional opportunities for internship positions with a wide variety of companies and organizations. In many cases, internships are salaried positions. Available internships include positions with the Winter Park Chamber of Commerce, Caribbean Travel & Life magazine, SeaWorld Florida, Merrill Lynch, World Trade Center Orlando, and the National Multiple Sclerosis Society.

Great Teaching

The college offers a wide range of majors and minors in a variety of areas, including expressive arts, humanities, interdisciplinary study, sciences and mathematics, social sciences, special programs, and preprofessional programs. The 3/2 accelerated management program allows students to graduate in five years with a bachelor's degree and an MBA from the college's prestigious Crummer Graduate School of Business. A variety of off-campus programs allow Rollins students the opportunity to extend their education beyond the campus, nationally and internationally.

On average, 92 percent of Rollins's faculty have a PhD or the highest degree in their field. Rollins offers thirty-three undergraduate majors and six graduate fields of study. Small class sizes and a student to faculty ratio of eleven to one provide Rollins students with an outstanding learning experience. Special programs include the honors degree program, the Rollins College Conference for first-year students, and a variety of international study opportunities.

Vibrant Community

The Rollins campus is a beautiful, seventy-acre lakefront setting, two blocks from downtown Winter Park and just minutes from Orlando and central Florida attractions. Students enjoy Rollins's tree-lined campus, stroll along the Walk of Fame, and take courses in magnificent Spanish Mediterranean-style buildings.

With the addition of men's and women's lacrosse in 2007–2008, Rollins will have twenty-three athletic teams, many nationally ranked. Other student activities include student government; publications; radio and television programming; Greek organizations; special-interest groups such as the Rollins Outdoor Club; and numerous artistic, musical, dramatic, and social opportunities.

Rollins's housing options include six traditional residence halls and eleven small houses for fraternities, sororities, and residential organizations. Pinehurst Cottage houses a special-interest group that promotes academic fulfillment outside the classroom, and Lyman Hall is home of the Rollins Outdoor Club, an active campus organization dedicated to broadening community awareness and enjoyment of outdoor activities.

Rollins College contributes to the cultural life of the central Florida community. It serves as home to one of the nation's oldest Bach festivals. The Annie Russell Theatre has a six-decade tradition of outstanding dramatic performances. The Cornell Fine Arts Museum is accredited by the American Association of Museums and boasts one of the finest collections of art of any college museum in the country.

Successful Outcomes

Rollins has produced Rhodes, Fulbright, Goldwater, and Truman scholars. In 1987, Donald Cram, class of 1941, received the Nobel Prize for chemistry. The most famous alumnus, the late Fred Rogers, class of 1951, found inspiration in the words, "Life is for service," he saw etched in stone on a wall on campus. Today he is known around the world for his landmark show Mister Rogers' Neighborhood.

The career services staff are available to assist current students and alumni with postgraduation plans and goals. Career counseling, career inventories, workshops, programs, the on-campus interview program, and a job-listing service are some of the many offerings of Rollins's career services office.

On average, 45 percent of Rollins's graduates continue their education at top-quality business and professional schools. Others graduates pursue career opportunities across the country.

Fast Facts

Rollins College is a four-year, coeducational, liberal arts college, founded in 1885.

Web site

http://www.rollins.edu

Location

Winter Park, Florida—50 miles from the Atlantic Ocean, 70 miles from the Gulf of Mexico.

Student Profile

3,100 students (44% male, 56% female); 44 states and 31 territories;16% minority, 3% international.

Faculty Profile

185 full-time faculty. 11:1 student/faculty ratio. Average class size is 17.

Residence Life

Highly residential: 78% of students live on campus. 20 residential facilities (coed residence halls, Greek houses, special residential organization houses, apartment complex).

Athletics

NCAA Division II, Sunshine State Conference. 23 varsity sports (11 men's: baseball, basketball, crew, cross-country, golf, lacrosse, sailing, soccer, swimming, tennis, waterskiing; 12 women's: basketball, crew, cross-country, golf, lacrosse, sailing, soccer, softball, swimming, tennis, volleyball, waterskiing).

Costs and Aid

2007–2008: $40,040 comprehensive ($30,420 tuition). 42% of students receive some financial aid. Average award: $25,398.

Endowment

$264,165,000.

More Distinctions

• For the 8th consecutive year, Rollins ranked second among regional universities in the south and first in Florida in the annual rankings of America's Best Colleges published by U.S. News & World Report.

• Selected annually for inclusion in Peterson's Competitive Colleges.

• Rated as "very competitive" by Barron's Profiles of American Colleges.

• Listed in The Princeton Review Student Access Guide to the Best 351 Colleges.

• Endowment of over $143 million places it in the top 10 percent of the more than 3,600 universities and colleges in America.

• Florida's oldest college.

Saint Leo University

Admissions Contact:

Saint Leo University
33701 State Road 52
PO Box 6665
Saint Leo, FL 33574-6665
(800) 334-5532
Email: admission@saintleo.edu
www.saintleo.edu

FLORIDA

Saint Leo University, Florida's first Catholic college, offers students of all faiths a distinctive education in a principled, character-enriching environment. Saint Leo remains anchored in the 1,500-year-old tradition of the Benedictine Order through its core values of excellence, community, respect, personal development, responsible stewardship, and integrity.

The 4 Distinctions

Engaged Students

Founded in 1889, Saint Leo aims to be a leading Catholic teaching university of international consequence for the twenty-first century. Offering undergraduate degrees in forty different majors and specializations, the university's flagship programs include business administration, criminal justice, education, international hospitality and tourism management, and sport business.

Students in virtually all programs of study have numerous opportunities to participate in practical internships, allowing them to put theory into practice in real-world settings. In addition to greater Tampa and Orlando, Saint Leo students have interned in Miami; Washington, DC; New York; London; Switzerland; and China. Significant personal interaction enables professors to facilitate internship options best suited to each student's specific interests, strengths, and career objectives.

The university's central Florida tourist-friendly location facilitates numerous internship opportunities for international hospitality and tourism students. Because of its great climate, Florida is also home to more major-league teams than any other state. Relationships with nearby teams offer outstanding internship options for sport business students.

Criminal justice students benefit from the university's unique relationships with local police academies in the form of high-level practical experience and officer certification options. Students can intern with high-profile organizations such as the U.S. Customs Service; the U.S. Marshals Service; the Drug Enforcement Administration; and the Bureau of Alcohol, Tobacco and Firearms.

The university offers unique study-abroad opportunities in a wide variety of locations including Australia, Ecuador, England, France, Ireland, Italy, Scotland, Spain, and Switzerland. Articulation agreements also afford study opportunities throughout Asia and the Pacific Rim.

Students are encouraged to give back to the community both now and in the future, and the campus includes a wide variety of service organizations. A popular alternative spring-break program allows students to volunteer in areas around the U.S. and the globe that are in particular need of assistance.

Great Teaching

Saint Leo University offers an environment where the needs of students always come first. With an average class size of eighteen, students receive personalized attention and develop close relationships with highly qualified professors. At Saint Leo, 84 percent of full-time instructional faculty hold terminal degrees in their fields.

Professors at Saint Leo challenge their students in the classroom and support them outside the classroom. They routinely meet with students to offer individual assistance, advice, and guidance. Students frequently acknowledge the value of their strong relationships with faculty members.

Saint Leo is committed to embracing the technology to support a twenty-first-century education. One of the first universities in America to widely integrate wireless access, Saint Leo remains on the cutting edge of educational technology, providing the tools for professors to teach and students to learn.

Saint Leo's LINK (Learning Interdisciplinary Knowledge) general education program is designed to ensure that students can communicate effectively, function at a high level both alone and as a part of a team, have a general knowledge base in many different areas, and can analyze and solve problems effectively. These skills – the foundation of a liberal arts education – are what today's employers demand.

All first-time college students are required to take SLU 100, foundation course designed to acquaint them with the university, equip them with vital skills vital for academic success, and instill in them the importance of community service.

Vibrant Community

Saint Leo University's lakeside campus is just thirty-five minutes from Tampa, known for its exciting nightlife, excellent ethnic restaurants, professional sports teams, and fine arts and concert venues. The beaches of Clearwater are just forty-five minutes away, while Orlando—the world's vacation destination with Walt Disney World, Universal Studios, and SeaWorld—is only ninety minutes from campus.

Saint Leo University is a community unto itself in a peaceful rural area with a beautiful climate all year. The combination of gracious Spanish architecture, lush vegetation and the brilliant Florida sunshine leave many first-time visitors commenting that Saint Leo looks more like a resort than a university campus.

Campus facilities include multiple housing options, ranging from traditional dorms to ultramodern apartments. The new state-of-the-art Student Community Center – opening in 2007 and featuring a dining hall, common areas, office and meeting space – will serve as the centerpiece of the university community.

Saint Leo University competes in 16 NCAA Division II intercollegiate sports and offers a variety of intramural activities. Students can utilize the campus fitness center and other year-round outdoor recreational activities, including the eighteen-hole Abbey golf course, Lake Jovita, and an Olympic-sized outdoor swimming pool on campus.

With more than fifty recognized campus clubs and organizations, there are a variety of ways for students to pursue their extracurricular interests. Through student government, Greek life, cultural and interest groups and service organizations, students forge bonds with each other and enrich not only the campus but also the surrounding community.

Successful Outcomes

Saint Leo continually graduates well-rounded, active learners who understand the importance of contributing to the communities in which they live and work. In a recent survey of graduates, 97 percent of respondents said they would recommend Saint Leo to a friend.

There are many successful alumni of Saint Leo. Among the students who have attended Saint Leo University or one of its antecedents are actors Desi Arnaz and Lee Marvin, singer Stephen Stills, major-league pitchers Red Barrett and Bob Tewksbury, Nicaraguan president Anastasio Somoza Debayle, and the current Chief Master Sergeant of the Air Force Rodney J. McKinley.

Alumnus Robert Diemer, a graduate of the school's criminal justice program, returned to Saint Leo to join the faculty after twenty-seven years in law enforcement. One Saint Leo student was selected as one of just 112 students from across the nation to participate in the highly competitive internship program with the Federal Bureau of Investigation.

Sport business department alumni are now working for top sports organizations, including the NFL's New Orleans Saints and Disney's Wide World of Sports. Saint Leo alumni from the education department have received numerous regional and national awards, including the Golden Apple teacher award and the prestigious Milken Family Foundation National Educator Award.

The common threads that seem to bind all Saint Leo alumni are commitments to lifelong, active learning; integrity; excellence; and a sense of personal responsibility to make a positive difference in the world around them. Saint Leo University is dedicated to providing students with highly personalized attention, flexible learning opportunities, and a solid foundation for personal fulfillment. It is an approach that has already proven successful for approximately fifty-three thousand Saint Leo alumni living in all fifty states and forty-nine countries.

Fast Facts

Saint Leo University is a Catholic, coeducational liberal arts university offering programs leading to the associate's and bachelor's degrees, the Master of Business Administration, Master of Education and master's degrees in counseling psychology and criminal justice. Chartered on June 4, 1889.

Web site

http://www.saintleo.edu

Location

Saint Leo, Florida—Located 35 minutes north of Tampa and 90 minutes west of Orlando.

Student Profile

1,514 students (46% male, 54% female); 38 states and territories and 45 foreign countries; 30% minority, 11% international. Average high school GPA is 3.18.

Faculty Profile

933 faculty members; 84% of full-time instructional faculty hold terminal degree in their field; 16:1 student/faculty ratio; average class size is 18.

Residence Life

Highly residential: 75% of students live on campus.

Athletics

NCAA Division II, Sunshine State Conference; 16 intercollegiate sports (8 men's: baseball, basketball, cross-country, golf, lacrosse, soccer, swimming, tennis; 8 women's: basketball, cross-country, golf, soccer, softball, swimming, tennis, volleyball)

Academic Programs

Accounting; applied science; biology; business administration (accounting, health services management, international business management); communication management; computer information systems; criminal justice (criminalistics, homeland security); elementary education (K-6); English (advanced literary study, creative writing, theatre); entrepreneurship & family business; environmental science; history; human resources administration; human services administration (administration, social services); international hospitality & tourism management; international studies; management; marketing; mathematics; medical technology; middle grades education (English, mathematics, science, social science); political science; psychology; religion; social work; sociology; sport business.

Preprofessional studies: dentistry, law, medicine, veterinary.

Costs and Aid

2007–2008: $24,522 comprehensive ($16,420 tuition and fees)

Endowment

$12,448,666.

University of West Florida

Admissions Contact:

University of West Florida
11000 University Pkwy
Pensacola, FL 32514
(800) 263-1074
Ph: (850) 474-2230
Fax: (850) 474-3360
Email: admissions@uwf.edu
www.uwf.edu

FLORIDA

The University of West Florida (UWF), with campuses in Pensacola and along the Emerald Coast of Northwest Florida, is one of the region's prized resources. UWF offers forty-nine bachelor's degrees, twenty-four master's degrees, two education specialist degrees, and one education doctorate to a student population numbering approximately 9,900.

The 4 Distinctions

Engaged Students

As one of eleven public universities in Florida, a personalized student experience is one of UWF's foremost attributes. Small classes afford students opportunities to interact with faculty and participate in hands-on academic projects in their chosen fields, including research, internships, and other multidimensional learning platforms. The average class size for freshmen lecture courses is thirty-two students.

The university encourages student civic engagement and community service. Through the Volunteer UWF! program, students spend more than fifty thousand hours each year assisting community partners, including elementary schools, nonprofits, and hospitals.

The UWF honors program has been recognized twice for excellence by Florida Leader Magazine. The program encourages students to take special interdisciplinary courses with top-notch faculty. Honors students engage in such community projects as cleaning up beaches and building homes for Habitat for Humanity. Members of UWF's honors program attend three conferences each year, including the National Collegiate Honors Council conference, the Southern Regional Honors Council conference, and the Florida Collegiate Honors Council conference. These trips provide students with an opportunity to make important contacts and gain new perspectives on improving the program. In addition to giving conference presentations, students have a chance to experience the local culture of cities like Salt Lake City, St. Louis, Philadelphia, and Washington, DC.

UWF's study-abroad program provides students with the opportunity to study at more than twenty institutions around the world. UWF's staff assists with application preparation and orientation for study abroad. Conversational foreign language courses are offered on a regular basis to provide basic skills for business, travel, or simply to learn more about different cultures. These short-term courses include Chinese, Japanese, Russian, Italian, and Spanish.

Great Teaching

With small classes and an emphasis on personal attention, UWF is often described as a private college atmosphere at an affordable, public college price. The emphasis on "interdisciplinary, integrative and interactive degree programs" also distinguishes UWF from larger schools.

The colleges of Arts and Sciences, Business, and Professional Studies are well equipped to provide a hands-on, active learning environment with state-of-the-art classrooms and labs.

UWF is known nationally for its landmark undergraduate and graduate programs in archaeology and public history. The rich cultural history of Pensacola and the Gulf Coast provide a perfect setting for these two unique programs.

Students pursuing the archaeology tracks for a degree in anthropology have literally unearthed history below the streets of the city and the waters of the Gulf of Mexico, producing evidence of Pensacola's international past. From the legendary galleons of the earliest Spanish explorers to the forts of Spanish and British settlements, UWF students have worked hand in hand with the university's renowned teaching archaeologists to contribute a wealth of knowledge about the city's past.

UWF's public history graduate students are engaged in documenting and preserving regional history. The twenty-two historic properties of Historic Pensacola Village and the T.T. Wentworth, Jr. Florida State Museum form the backdrop for one of the nation's most distinctive academic programs and classroom settings.

Other popular majors at UWF include marine biology, psychology, English, accounting, and nursing. The degree program in psychology currently attracts more than four hundred majors and provides students with a solid foundation for graduate study. UWF's department of English offers students a curriculum that is at the core of the modern liberal arts education. Courses in the English major contribute to the student's knowledge and understanding of human culture and to the relationship between literary texts and other bodies of human knowledge, such as philosophy, history, religion, psychology, the classics, and modern languages. The bachelor's degree in nursing prepares students to become clinical generalists who are leaders, managers, and lifelong learners who integrate research findings into their nursing practice.

UWF also offers a varied selection of distance-learning courses and several online degrees that provide extensive faculty-student interaction.

UWF's John C. Pace Library serves students at the main campus and branches along the Emerald Coast. Housing more than six hundred and twenty-eight thousand volumes, one million microforms, three thousand serial subscriptions, and nearly two thousand online journal subscriptions, the library is also designated as a regional depository for publications of the United States government and the state of Florida.

Vibrant Community

UWF's main campus is located in Florida's panhandle region, ten miles north of downtown Pensacola. Designated as a state nature preserve, the campus encompasses 1,600 acres of rolling hills and natural woodland along the Escambia River. The university's facilities complement the natural beauty of the campus landscape, which includes nature trails, streams, and bayous.

Nearly 1,500 students choose to live on campus at UWF. Within ten minutes, students can walk or catch a campus trolley to classrooms, the cafeteria, library, computer lab, gym, weight room, health center, post office, bookstore, theater, or tennis courts. The campus, close to stores, malls, and restaurants, is about twenty minutes from downtown Pensacola's historic areas and entertainment venues, and only thirty minutes from the Emerald Coast's famous white sand beaches.

Long celebrated for its caring, nurturing approach to helping students excel in and out of the classroom as they prepare to become contributing members of society, UWF has embraced Making Way for Excellence, a culture-changing campus renaissance program and quest to be recognized as one of the best places to work and best institutions of higher learning in the nation.

Successful Outcomes

UWF faculty are focused on ensuring that students maintain progress through the state of Florida's required curriculum. Critical thinking, communication, project management, values, ethics, and problem solving are also greatly emphasized. Academic learning compacts that serve as a model for Florida's public colleges describe the practical skills and knowledge students will attain upon graduation from a UWF program.

UWF students are valued partners and contributors in the university's community of learners. They help strengthen the school's shared values of caring, integrity, quality, innovation, teamwork, stewardship, and courage, and they fulfill the UWF mission—to empower each individual with knowledge and opportunity to contribute responsibly and creatively to a complex world.

Fast Facts

University of West Florida, a public four-year regional comprehensive university, opened for classes in 1967.

Web site

http://uwf.edu

Location

Pensacola, Florida—30 minutes from Pensacola Beach, 4 hours from New Orleans and about 6 hours from Atlanta. Branch campuses located along Northwest Florida's Emerald Coast.

Student Profile

9,882 students (39.6% male, 60.4% female); 50 states and territories; 22% minority, 1.4% international.

Faculty Profile

85.4% of full-time faculty hold a terminal degree in their field. 18:1 student/faculty ratio. Average undergraduate class size is 25.

Residence Life

Mildly residential: 14.7% of students live on campus.

Athletics

NCAA Division II. 15 varsity sports (7 men's: baseball, cross-country, basketball, golf, soccer, tennis, track; 8 women's: softball, basketball, cross-country, golf, soccer, tennis, track, volleyball), 16 club sports, and 30 intramurals.

Academic Programs

Accounting; anthropology; art; arts (fine); biology; career & technical studies; chemistry; clinical laboratory sciences; communication arts; community health education; computer engineering; computer science; criminal justice; economics; economics (business); electrical engineering; elementary education; engineering technology; English; environmental studies; exceptional student education; finance; health leisure & exercise science; health sciences; history; hospitality recreation & resort management; humanities; information technology; international studies; legal studies; management; management information systems; marine biology; maritime studies; marketing; mathematics; middle school education; music; nursing; oceanography; philosophy; physics; political science; pre-kindergarten/primary education; psychology; sciences; social sciences; social work; theatre.

Educational Specialist Degrees

Curriculum & instruction; educational leadership.

Costs and Aid

2007–2008: $13,319 in-state comprehensive ($2,860 tuition and fees); $24,152 out-of-state comprehensive ($13,702 tuition and fees). 68% of students receive some type of financial aid.

Endowment

$55,035,529.

Agnes Scott College

GEORGIA

Agnes Scott College is a private, four-year, liberal arts college for women. Located in metropolitan Atlanta, the school takes a holistic approach to education for women, acknowledging the primacy of intellectual development while integrating opportunities for physical, social, cultural, and spiritual development.

Admissions Contact:

Agnes Scott College
141 E. College Ave.
Decatur, GA 30030
(800) 868-8602
Ph: (404) 471-6000
Fax: (404) 471-6414
Email: admission@agnesscott.edu
www.agnesscott.edu

The 4 Distinctions

Engaged Students

Agnes Scott offers several different opportunities to study abroad. In addition to independent study-abroad options in more than thirty countries, students may opt to participate in the faculty-led Global Awareness Program. This program allows students to focus on one non-Western European country. The program includes two successive courses with a three-week international travel and study portion. Students examine the region through a variety of lenses, including history, language, culture, arts, geography, politics, and economics. About 40 percent of Agnes Scott students study internationally, compared to a national average of only 7 percent.

The Global Connections Program integrates an international study and travel component with a traditional academic course. Recent programs have included travel to Ireland, Gambia, Cuba, and the Czech Republic.

The Center for Writing and Speaking offers opportunities for students to enhance their writing and speaking skills. Individual peer tutors guide students by collaborating on ideas, offering course-specific assistance, and encouraging the intellectual progress of each individual.

The first-year seminars engage students through intensive small-group study on a particular topic. The small class size fosters group discussion and a sense of community.

Experiential learning opportunities include options for internships in an array of businesses, government agencies, and nonprofit organizations. Students may also participate in the Atlanta semester, which focuses on women, leadership, and social change. The Hubert Scholars Program enables students to intern for humanitarian services at home or abroad.

Great Teaching

All tenure-track faculty have a PhD or terminal degree in their field. Faculty members make themselves readily available to students. Collaborative learning, including opportunities for faculty-student research, is the norm. Students present their work at regional and national conferences and at Agnes Scott's Spring Annual Research Conference (SpARC).

With an average class size of only fifteen, students at Agnes Scott receive personal attention from instructors. The professors seek to understand each individual's strengths and weaknesses and foster an environment of cooperative learning.

A new state-of-the-art science facility offers the latest technology and includes laboratories for multiple disciplines, including biology, chemistry, physics, and psychology.

In addition to the thirty-three majors and twenty-six minors offered by the college, students may design their own courses of study through student-designed majors. Faculty members advise students on the creation and design of their individual course selections.

Vibrant Community

Founded in 1889 as the Decatur Female Seminary, Agnes Scott College adopted its present name in 1906 and remains affiliated with the Presbyterian Church. Agnes Scott College is located on a one-hundred-acre campus in Decatur, Georgia, that combines traditional Gothic architecture and modern renovations. The college recently completed a one hundred and twenty-million dollar renovation and expansion project that included the state-of the-art Bullock Science Center.

Decatur, a vibrant community of about twenty thousand, provides students with a comfortable home, while nearby Atlanta offers all the conveniences and advantages of a major metropolitan area.

The school's student-governed honor system dates back to 1906 and promotes a high level of integrity and ethics on campus.

One hundred clubs and organizations provide students with a diverse range of activities. In addition, the college hosts formals, band parties, concerts, and films, as well as lectures on classical and contemporary issues.

All traditional-aged students not commuting from their permanent residences are required to live in campus housing. In addition to traditional residence halls, upper-level women have the option to live in a more independent setting—the Avery Glen apartment complex. Additionally, three restored Victorian homes adjacent to the campus serve as theme houses, each of which focus on a particular language or discipline. Recent theme-housing options have included a Spanish language house, an environmental studies house, and an international house.

Agnes Scott College boasts several distinctive campus traditions. Every year, graduating seniors ring the bell in the Main Tower when they have secured a job or a placement in graduate school. For nearly one hundred years, October's Black Cat has marked the unofficial end of new student orientation. The celebration includes a weeklong spirit competition, a bonfire, and a formal dance.

Successful Outcomes

The career planning office works to fully understand the needs and goals of every student and to help students find employment opportunities. The career resource library and career observation days provide students with the necessary information to make informed decisions about their future. The career assessment and counseling program ensures that the women of Agnes Scott will be able to apply their college experiences in meaningful careers.

Graduates of Agnes Scott College succeed in finding employment or gaining entrance to graduate schools. Agnes Scott is ranked the top 6 percent of 1,325 baccalaureate-degree-granting institutions for the percentage of graduates who go on to earn a PhD.

Distinguished Agnes Scott alumnae include Jean Toal, chief justice of the South Carolina Supreme Court; Kay Krill, president and CEO of Ann Taylor Stores Corporation; and Amy Kim, with her team, winner of a 2007 Academy Award for best live action short film. The list goes on and on: Georgia's first female Rhodes Scholar, Fulbright, Goldwater, Truman, Rhodes, Pickering and Gates Millennium scholarship winners, the Chief Justice of the South Carolina Supreme Court, the first woman to be ordained a minister in the Presbyterian Church (U.S.A.) and the first woman to chair the Federal Commodity Futures Trading Commission and Agnes Scott's first United States Congresswoman.

Fast Facts

Agnes Scott College is a highly selective, independent national liberal arts college for women. Founded in 1889, the college is a diverse and growing residential community of scholars whose curriculum encourages women to become fluent across disciplines, across continents and across centuries. Agnes Scott has one of the largest endowments per student of any college or university in the United States.

Web site

http:// www.agnesscott.edu

Location

Decatur, Georgia—Agnes Scott College is located in a national historic district and residential community just six miles from Atlanta.

Student Profile

Approximately 900 undergraduate students (100% female) from 40 states and territories, 26 countries; 33% from under-represented ethnic backgrounds, 5% international.

Faculty Profile

82 full-time faculty. 100% of tenure track faculty hold a terminal degree in their field. 10:1 student/faculty ratio. Average class size is 15.

Residence Life

84% of students live on campus.

Athletics

NCAA Division III Conference. 7 varsity sports, 11 intramural clubs, and an assortment of fitness and recreational activities.

Academic Programs

Africana studies; art history; astrophysics; biochemistry & molecular biology; biology; chemistry; classical languages & literatures; classical civilizations; dance; economics; economics & organizational management; English literature; English – creative writing; French; German studies; history; international relations; mathematics; mathematics-economics; mathematics-physics; music; neuroscience; philosophy; physics; political science; psychology; religious studies; religious studies (religion & social justice); sociology-anthropology; Spanish; student designed major; studio art; theatre; women's studies.

Costs and Aid

2007–2008: $36,737 comprehensive ($26,600 tuition). In 2006-07, 50% of students received need-based financial aid, with an average need-based institutional award of $9,500. The average institutional award (merit and need-based) was $16,000.

Endowment

$294.7 million.

More Distinctions

Agnes Scott is among the top 10 liberal arts colleges in the South (*U.S. News & World Report* 2007).

ASC is # 28 as a "Great School, Great Prices" (*U.S. News & World Report* 2007).

Agnes Scott has one of the oldest and most respected student-governed honor systems in the country.

Berry College

GEORGIA

Since its founding in 1902, Berry College has focused on the development of the entire person through its integrated "education of the head, the heart, and the hands." Students learn, serve, work, and grow in an environment based on interdenominational Christian values and surrounded by breathtaking Georgia scenery.

Admissions Contact:

Berry College
2277 Martha Berry Hwy NW
Mount Berry, GA 30149
(800) BERRY-GA
Email: admissions@berry.edu
www.berry.edu

The 4 Distinctions

Engaged Students

A Berry College education begins with excellent academics, but it doesn't stop there. Berry students prepare for their futures by working on campus and providing community service during their college experience, giving them a head start on life after school.

At Berry, expanding students' multicultural and international experiences both on and off campus is a strategic focus. Approximately 30 percent of Berry students study abroad at some point during their undergraduate careers. Study-abroad programs are offered in Africa, Asia, Latin America and the Caribbean, Europe, and the Pacific Rim.

As active, integral, contributing members of the campus community, Berry students have countless opportunities to learn to lead by doing. Leadership training can start as early as the freshman year, when faculty and staff nominate first-year students to participate in a weekend Emerging Leaders seminar.

Great Teaching

Berry's classes are small, and students get personalized instruction from expert educators who have made a conscious decision to join a college where good teaching is valued and expected. The average undergraduate class size is twenty. Writing, language, and speech classes average just eighteen to twenty students, while general-education classes may have up to forty students. Laboratory classes are capped at just twenty students.

Berry professors are highly qualified and respected scholars. More than 96 percent of full-time faculty hold doctoral degrees, many from some of the best graduate schools in the country.

Berry offers a strong curriculum in the arts and sciences and exceptional professional programs in business, teacher preparation, and preprofessional opportunities. The educational program is characterized by high academic standards and an extraordinary level of collaboration among students and faculty in both research and study.

First-Year Seminar, a seven-week, fall-semester course, provides orientation for students new to the Berry experience. Taught by Berry faculty and staff, the course represents a number of disciplines. Each First-Year Seminar instructor is assisted by a first-year mentor—an upperclassman who provides a student's perspective on Berry College. A unique aspect of the seminar is a book discussion that allows freshmen to enjoy dinner and conversation with Berry faculty and staff, usually at their respective homes.

Vibrant Community

With more than one hundred clubs and interest groups, there is always something to do at Berry. Students contribute to student government; help publish the weekly newspaper, the literary magazine, or the yearbook; play a part in a musical or theatrical production; or participate in one of Berry's fourteen student-led religious organizations. The campus calendar is filled year-round with entertainment and cultural events, including concerts, films, dances, lectures, art exhibits, and student coffeehouse performances.

The student-led programming board sponsors at least seventy-five programs throughout the year, with two or three events each week. Dances, rafting trips, outdoor movies, cosmic bowling, comedians, and talent shows are just a few of the offerings.

As an interdenominational institution based on Christian values, Berry values ethics, religion, and service as important components of the Berry experience. Students contribute thousands of hours of community service in the religion-in-life, volunteer-services, and Bonner Scholars programs. Students begin and end their college careers with freshman and senior service days, perfect bookends for a Berry education.

Approximately 77 percent of students live on campus each year. Residence halls include all-women, all-men, and coed residence halls. Students can choose from singles, doubles, triples, and quads. Suite and apartment syle housing are also available for sophomores, juniors, and seniors.

Before arriving on campus, students get a reminder to bring their hiking boots. Berry's campus, the largest contiguous campus in the world, includes more than twenty-six thousand acres of forests, streams, mountains, and meadows situated in northern Georgia. Excursions for horseback riding, bicycling, hiking, and other outdoor activities are common, with student clubs dedicated to wilderness adventures.

Successful Outcomes

Berry alumni are prominent and successful; graduates include the chairman of the board of a Fortune 500 financial services conglomerate, the head of a NASA science directorate, a college president, and a federal judge. Every day, Berry graduates make significant contributions in cancer research, radiation physics, intelligence analysis, and on the operatic stage; they are also leaders in government, business, community service, science, the arts, church, medicine, and teaching.

With more than 90 percent of students working at some time during their college career, Berry College provides one of the strongest experiential learning programs in the country. More than 300 available job classifications offer plenty of opportunities for development and growth. As a result, many students build an extensive practical resume by the time they graduate.

The career development center offers tools to support a four-year approach to career planning. Starting with discovering values, skills, and interests during the freshman year and choosing a major, the program continues through the process of helping students find their first full-time jobs for after graduation. And after graduation, the career center is available to assist alumni at no charge.

Fast Facts

Berry College is a four-year, independent, interdenominational, Christian, comprehensive, liberal arts college founded in 1902.

Web site

http://www.berry.edu/

Location

Rome, Georgia—65 miles northwest of Atlanta and 65 miles south of Chattanooga, Tennessee.

Student Profile

1,737 undergraduate students (34% male, 66% female); 39 states and territories, 20 countries; 7.3% minority, 2.1% international.

Faculty Profile

135 full-time faculty. 12:1 student/faculty ratio. Average class size is 20.

Residence Life

Highly residential: 77% of students live on campus.

Athletics

Member of the National Association of Intercollegiate Athletics (NAIA) and Southern States Athletic Conference. Teams include basketball, cross-country, golf, indoor/outdoor running, soccer, and tennis for men and women; baseball for men; and volleyball and equestrian for women.

Academic Programs

Accounting; animal science; anthropology; art; biology; chemistry; communication; computer science; dual-degree engineering; dual-degree nursing; economics; education; English; environmental sciences; exercise science; finance; French; German; government & international studies; health & physical education; history; inter-disciplinary studies; management; marketing; mathematics; music; philosophy; physics; prelaw; premedicine; prepharmacy; preveterinary medicine; psychology; religion; sociology; Spanish; theatre.

Costs and Aid

2007–2008: $28,196 comprehensive ($20,570 tuition). 95% of students receive some financial aid. Average award: $16,000.

Endowment

$573 million.

More Distinctions

• After many years of being classified as a regional comprehensive college in *U.S. News & World Report*'s annual "America's Best Colleges" listings, Berry was included this year in the national liberal arts category due to a change in the basic classification system used by the Carnegie Commision on Higher Education. Of the 266 schools in this national category, Berry ranked 118 and was included on the list of 125 top-tier schools. Other publications in which Berry has appeared include the *Newsweek-Kaplan College Guide*, *Barron's Best Buys in Higher Education*, and the *Princeton Review's Best 290 Business Schools*.

Georgia College & State University

GEORGIA

Georgia College & State University (GCSU) is a public, coeducational, residential, comprehensive, liberal arts university committed to providing educational experiences typical of private liberal arts colleges at an affordable price. Founded in 1889 and part of the University System of Georgia since its formation in 1932, GCSU has been coeducational since 1967.

Admissions Contact:

Georgia College & State University
Campus Box 23
Milledgeville, GA 31061-3375
(800) 342-0471
Ph: (478) 445-1283
Email: info@gcsu.edu
www.gcsu.edu

The 4 Distinctions

Engaged Students

GCSU offers more than forty undergraduate degrees. The most popular majors are biology, psychology, nursing, English, health sciences, and professional education. Nursing students benefit from many hands-on experiences as undergraduates, as do professional education students. For the latter, an intensive cohort program begins in the junior year, and over 90 percent of education graduates remain in the field after nine years. GCSU also offers a five-year Masters of Arts in Teaching (MAT) program.

Residential learning communities (RLCs) bring friends, independence, discovery, and learning together as part of an enhanced on-campus housing program. There are three RLCs that span a single academic year, and three extended RLCs that run for two years and offer academic credit. Popular RLCs include Leadership, Entrepreneurship, Fine Arts, Honors and Scholars, Wellness, and Casa del Mundo, an international world house.

Work-study projects are available in almost every department, and they engage students in research, leading to close relationships with faculty members. The number of work-study projects is increasing steadily, as is the pay associated with them. Many students participate in research courses, though some perform independent research or take advantage of chemistry apprenticeships. The Corinthian is an on-campus student-written scholarly journal where students publish their research findings. Students also receive financial support to attend and present their research at professional conferences around the country.

GCSU students are also engaged in study abroad and internships. They can choose to study overseas through summer, semester, or yearlong programs. Mentorships are often offered in conjunction with the Georgia Chamber of Commerce. This program, funded by a grant, pairs students with chamber members, providing a semester-long experience leading to long-term relationships.

Great Teaching

GCSU graduates are "prepared for careers or advanced study and . . . instilled with exceptional qualities of mind and character, [including] an inquisitive, analytical mind; respect for human diversity and individuality; a sense of civic and global responsibility; sound ethical principles; effective writing, speaking, and quantitative skills; and a healthy lifestyle." The GCSU tagline sums it up this way: "We teach as if the world depended on it."

GCSU has a low student to faculty ratio of seventeen to one, and most classes have between fifteen and thirty-five students. Seminars, tutorials, and honors courses typically have twenty to twenty-five students with three faculty facilitators. GCSU faculty are "dedicated to challenging students and fostering excellence in the classroom and beyond . . . endow[ing] its graduates with a passion for achievement, a lifelong curiosity, and exuberance for learning."

To help students embark on a successful college career, GCSU offers a first-year seminar. Faculty from different departments teach small classes, aiding students in developing their own road map to graduation, and encouraging extracurricular experiential activities. These activities are tracked on a dedicated transcript maintained online that notes student internships, service, and leadership activities.

Vibrant Community

Visitors to GCSU fall in love with the campus on arrival. The classic campus features Corinthian columns, expansive lawns, and many historic buildings, including the old Georgia governor's mansion. Today, the college features state-of-the-art residence halls that house about 40 percent of students and a newly renovated library incorporating a museum, Starbucks, computer labs, and forty study rooms. In addition, GCSU is one of the top fifty wireless campuses in the nation.

GCSU's six thousand students are friendly and welcoming, offering assistance to new people. There are about 125 organizations and activities students can join. Relationships with the wider community are close, and many graduates stay in the area, remaining active in the town and its politics. The town's historic district is a block from campus, and many students are involved with local issues and events, including helping to organize the local Sweetwater Festival each year, an event featuring crafts, barbecue judging, and live music.

Service learning and community service help build relationships, encouraging students to apply what they learn in the classroom to the community and to lend a hand to those in need. GCSU IT students have worked to create Web sites and databases for local nonprofit organizations such as the Boys & Girls Clubs of America and the Red Cross; the mass communications department provides media services for needy organizations; and the health services department provides meals-on-wheels for the clients of local nonprofit organizations.

Other on-campus activities include a symposium on American democracy and performances by the GCSU jazz band. There is a strong Greek tradition at GCSU, including Panhellenic organizations and National Pan-hellenic Council organizations, as well as an off-campus community that caters to Greeks.

Minority students represent 13 percent of the student body. Hispanic students can take advantage of the Hispanic Foundation scholarship and a Hispanic virtual advisor for prospective students.

GCSU's forty-three-acre main campus is located in Milledgeville, the state's former capital in central Georgia. A city of twenty thousand today, Milledgeville's buildings were spared by General William Tecumseh Sherman's troops in their march to the sea in 1864, leaving columned buildings, green lawns, and tree-lined streets evocative of the southern charm of Georgia before the Civil War. Milledgeville offers proximity to a number of Georgia's larger cities. Atlanta is about ninety miles to the northwest, Savannah is about 160 miles to the southeast, and Macon is only forty minutes from campus.

Successful Outcomes

Science, chemistry, and premed graduates are particularly successful, and tend to have an above-average record of acceptance into medical schools. Famous alumni include the author, Flannery O'Connor, and corporate chief executives of Georgia Power and GEICO.

Fast Facts

Georgia College & State University was founded in 1889. Today, it is Georgia's public liberal arts university.

Web site

http://www.gcsu.edu/

Location

Milledgeville, GA—Located in the center of the state. It is about 30 miles northeast of Macon and 90 miles southeast of Atlanta.

Student Profile

6,040 students (39% male, 61% female); 25 states and territories; 13% minority, 3% international.

Faculty Profile

292 full-time faculty. 17:1 student/faculty ratio. Average class size is 20 students.

Residence Life

Residential: 40% of students live on campus.

Athletics

NCAA Division II, Peach Belt Conference. 10 varsity sports (5 men's: basketball, baseball, golf, cross-country, tennis; 5 women's: basketball, cross-country, soccer, softball, tennis), 5 club sports, and 16 intramurals.

Academic Programs

Accounting; art; athletic training; biology; chemistry; community health; computer science; criminal justice; early childhood; economics; English; environmental science; exercise science; French; general business; history; information systems; liberal studies; management; marketing; mass communication; mathematics; middle grades; music; music education; music therapy; nursing; outdoor education; physical education; political science; preprofessional programs (dentistry, engineering, forestry, health information management, law, medical technology, medicine, occupational therapy, optometry, pharmacy, physical therapy, veterinary medicine); psychology; rhetoric; sociology; Spanish; special education; theatre.

Costs and Aid

2006–2007: $12,272 in-state comprehensive ($3,574 tuition); $22,994 out-of-state comprehensive. Each year over 80% of the students receive some sort of financial aid.

Endowment

$18,280,363.

More Distinctions

• *Kiplinger Personal Finance* magazine recognized GCSU as one of the 100 Best Values in Public Colleges in the country.

• GCSU has been rated a top 20 public masters university in the South by *U.S. News & World Report.*

• GCSU was listed among the Top 50 Wireless College Campuses in the USA in a 2005 survey conducted by *Intel Corporation.*

• GCSU was named one of the 136 Best Colleges in the Southeast by *The Princeton Review.*

LaGrange College

GEORGIA

Founded in 1831, LaGrange College is a four-year liberal arts and sciences college affiliated with the United Methodist Church. The oldest private college in Georgia, LaGrange College strives to provide students with an ethical and caring community.

Admissions Contact:

LaGrange College
601 Broad Street
LaGrange, GA 30240
(800) 593-2885
Ph: (706) 880-8005
Email: admission@lagrange.edu
www.lagrange.edu

The 4 Distinctions

Engaged Students

LaGrange College students can choose from fifty academic and preprofessional programs offered on a calendar that includes two four-month semesters divided by a one-month January interim term. This term gives students the chance to explore a subject in-depth through traditional lecture formats, experiential learning, or study-abroad opportunities. For psychology students enrolled in the animal behavior course, the January interim term at LaGrange College is about expanding boundaries and geographical horizons as they venture to Costa Rica to study animal behavior.

For students interested in making a difference in the lives of others, LaGrange College supports a strong servant-leadership initiative. Students can get involved in service projects, Habitat for Humanity, after-school youth programs, or alternative spring breaks. Also available are Servant-Leadership Fellowships, which offer scholarships for students to pursue their own service projects.

Undergraduate research opportunities abound at LaGrange, as well. A number of faculty employ students as research assistants to help them with their work, and each year at Honors Day, dozens of LaGrange students are named research scholars for their efforts on individual and group research projects.

Great Teaching

All tenure-track faculty have a PhD or terminal degree in LaGrange's eleven to one student to faculty ratio allows professors to get to know their students well. Teaching in such an intimate setting, professors have the opportunity to learn their students' goals and to help them reach their objectives.

LaGrange professors, 87 percent of whom hold terminal degrees, strive to introduce their students to real-world situations as early and as often as possible. Whether they're composing musical scores in the MIDI recording lab, performing water tests at West Point Lake, or using the school's DNA fingerprinting lab in a biochemistry class,

LaGrange students know they will receive expert guidance from knowledgeable professors who seek to develop each student's research and problem-solving skills—skills that employers and graduate schools seek most.

The college is renowned for its offerings in drama, music, and art. The art department covers the academic side of art, with an art history major and the option of concentrating in museum studies. On the studio side, LaGrange offers an art and design major with four different concentrations, as well as the possibility of a double major and a major/minor. Students often present their work in the visual arts to the community through exhibitions, lectures, and workshops held at the Lamar Dodd Art Center. Recently, one LaGrange student won the Georgia Big Picture Conference Grand Prize for his film, which featured music by a LaGrange music student. The film was prepared for a January term visual music class.

Vibrant Community

LaGrange College maintains a 120-acre campus that features historic nineteenth-century buildings, as well as brand-new apartment-style residence halls.

With fifteen intercollegiate sports teams, more than forty-five clubs and organizations, and dozens of cultural enrichment events held on campus each year, there's always something to do at LaGrange. Students can take in or appear in a play at Price Theater, enjoy a concert in the newly renovated Callaway Auditorium, or view an art show at the Lamar Dodd Art Center, which houses a permanent collection of works by Picasso, Andy Warhol, and other famous artists. There are a number of religious groups on campus, including the Baptist Students Union, the Wesley Fellowship, and the Fellowship of Christian Athletes.

Within walking distance of campus, downtown LaGrange offers students further entertainment options. In addition to its unique shops and restaurants, the LaGrange downtown district also boasts a new ten-screen stadium-seat theater. Outside the city limits, West Point Lake and the world-famous Callaway Gardens are each within a short driving distance.

Students often get involved in the surrounding community through the office of community service, which provides volunteer service opportunities for all members of the LaGrange College community and encourages them to examine social and cultural issues by connecting them with their surrounding community and involving them in meaningful and responsible service. Students volunteer for organizations such as the American Red Cross, the Georgia Sheriff's Association Youth Homes, and the United Way.

Growing out of its history of service and its affiliation with The United Methodist Church, LaGrange College is committed to creating a caring and ethical community that challenges students' minds and inspires their souls. The College offers a number of opportunities for students, faculty and staff members to celebrate life and explore God's intention for human living, especially as it relates to living and working in the transitory environment of a college campus. Included in these opportunities are occasions for worship, fellowship and service.

Successful Outcomes

Over its more than 175-year history, LaGrange College has produced leaders in almost every field imaginable. Graduates have gone on to pursue successful careers in medicine, teaching, art, law, science, music, writing, entrepreneurship, and the ministry. Life's challenges aren't always predictable, so the broad curriculum at LaGrange prepares students for the inevitable surprises they will encounter along life's journey.

The LaGrange Career Center provides a wealth of information for students preparing to embark on their post graduate job search. They are host to career events and potential employers. Student need only visit the Career Center website to find all of the resources available to them.

Alumni often return to campus on homecoming weekend, which forms a sense of tradition and school spirit. Class reunions are often held that weekend, along with the other festivities.

Fast Facts

LaGrange College is a four-year, liberal arts and sciences institution affiliated with the Methodist church, offering undergraduate, pre-professional, and graduate degrees, founded in 1831.

Web site

http://www.lagrange.edu/

Location

LaGrange, Georgia—approximately 65 miles southwest of Atlanta.

Student Profile

1,100 students (36% male, 64% female); representing 19 states and 15 countries; 20% minority, 2% international.

Faculty Profile

63 full time faculty, 79% of whom hold the terminal degree in their field. 11:1 student-faculty ratio. Average class size is 11.

Residence Life

Moderately residential: 57% of students live on campus.

Athletics

NCAA Division III, Great South Athletic Conference (GSAC). 15 varsity sports (8 men's: baseball, basketball, cross country, football, golf, soccer, swimming, tennis; 7 women's: basketball, cross country, soccer, softball, swimming, tennis, volleyball), plus many intramural offerings.

Academic Programs

Accounting; art and design (art history, museum studies, art studio-ceramics, sculpture, photography, painting, drawing, graphic design, applied design, art education); biochemistry; biology; business management; chemistry; church leadership; coaching; computer science; English; French; history; human services; interdisciplinary studies; Latin American studies; mathematics; middle grades education; music (performance, creative technologies, church music), music education; nursing; philosophy; political science; psychology; religion (religion and philosophy, church leadership, philosophy); secondary education; sociology; Spanish, theatre arts; women's studies.

Costs and Aid

2007–2008: $18,760 comprehensive ($13,266 tuition). 69% of students receive some financial aid. Average award: $10,702.

Endowment

$57 Million.

More Distinctions

• LaGrange is ranked by *U.S. News & World Report* among the South's top comprehensive colleges and among that category's top 10 "best values."

• Founded in 1831, LaGrange is the oldest private college in Georgia.

• The college is widely recognized and renowned for its offerings in drama, music, and the arts.

Oglethorpe University

GEORGIA

Oglethorpe University, founded in 1835, is a private, coeducational, liberal arts university in the Southeast's leading metropolis, Atlanta. Located on one hundred acres, north of Buckhead, the campus is minutes from all Atlanta has to offer—internships, shopping, and cultural and sporting events. Oglethorpe's diverse student body encourages cultural exploration.

Admissions Contact:

Oglethorpe University
4484 Peachtree Road NE
Atlanta, GA 30319
(800) 428-4484
Email: admission@oglethorpe.edu
www.oglethorpe.edu

The 4 Distinctions

Engaged Students

Oglethorpe's new Center for Civic Engagement offers service-learning initiatives, including opportunities with four partner elementary schools and trips to New Orleans to aid in hurricane relief. The center's OUr Atlanta program gives students access to Atlanta's leading people and institutions, including the Federal Reserve Bank of Atlanta, the High Museum of Art, and the Atlanta Hawks, enriching students' classroom experiences.

Students engage on an international level through Oglethorpe University Students Abroad (OUSA), which offers four main areas of study through partner institutions in seven countries; independent study abroad at an institution of the student's choosing; short-term, for-credit trips in December, March, and May; and associate programs with Oxford University in England and the Umbra Institute in Italy.

Back on campus, popular majors include business administration, communication and rhetoric studies, accounting, and psychology. Oglethorpe offers twenty-eight majors and gives students an opportunity to design their own major, an opportunity many students take advantage of for interdisciplinary studies. Oglethorpe's thirteen to one student to faculty ratio guarantees personal attention for each student on his or her academic journey. Through course work or the honors program, many students publish papers or present research at academic conferences with faculty support. Oglethorpe's students have been actively engaged in the Atlanta community for years, through internships at some of the country's largest businesses or through the Rich Foundation Urban Leadership Program.

Great Teaching

At Oglethorpe, the promise of a great education is matched by a dedicated and passionate faculty. Recently ranked fifteenth in the nation by the Princeton Review, the Oglethorpe faculty are focused on fostering student learning. You won't find a lecture hall on campus, and Oglethorpe was ranked fourteenth in the Princeton Review's Class Discussions Encouraged list. Whether teaching courses in their discipline or a section of Oglethorpe's unique core curriculum, faculty members bring a wealth of knowledge to classroom discussions, while constantly pushing students to delve deeper into the subject at hand. Over 90 percent of faculty hold the terminal degree in their field. All undergraduate courses are taught by faculty members; there are no TAs. Included in the faculty are textbook authors, National Endowment for the Humanities fellows, a Guggenheim fellow, a French knight, a political columnist, scholars of Shakespeare and the Civil War, community activists, and academic organization leaders. Official office hours are posted by each professor, but students are also likely to stop professors on the academic quad for a short chat or see them at campus lectures, exhibitions, or performances.

Oglethorpe offers specialty programs as a result of the dedicated faculty. The Rich Foundation Urban Leadership Program, run by two politics professors, exposes students to civic life while researching the history and philosophy of citizen leadership through the ages. The urban ecology program, led by one of the first urban ecology PhDs in the nation, combines ecology, environmental science, economics, psychology, and public policy to produce scientists and urban planners focused on sustainable, equitable urban growth.

Students are guided by faculty through the freshman experience and the core curriculum, an integrated eight-course sequence that defines a liberal arts education. Courses are also offered to assist students with career options and the transition to life after college.

Vibrant Community

Oglethorpe is located on one hundred acres in Buckhead, a quiet oasis in a bustling metropolis. The residential campus houses over seven hundred students in nine residence halls and a six-house Greek row. Four residence halls, built since 2005, feature private bedrooms with shared bathrooms and common areas along card-access hallways.

Student activities are coordinated through the Oglethorpe Student Association, which hosts all-campus parties in the fall and spring, a homecoming dance, and a band competition. Oglethorpe's fourteen athletic teams provide plenty of opportunities for the campus community to show school spirit. Seven Greek organizations (three sororities and four fraternities) offer social events, fund-raisers, and community-service efforts on a regular basis. The residence life office also offers programming through its resident assistants. Campus traditions are growing, from first-year students signing the honor code at convocation to honor students being inducted during the Boar's Head holiday concert, and seniors ringing the carillon bells prior to graduation.

Off-campus events are plentiful, as well, with many trips and programs coordinated by the Center for Civic Engagement. Students explore Atlanta's cultural institutions through the OUr Atlanta program, often guided by the organization's leadership. Recently, students met with actors in a local theater before a debut performance, were shown a new exhibition at the High Museum of Art by the museum's director, and spoke with the director of the Federal Reserve Bank of Atlanta after an exclusive tour of the facility. Additionally, many public figures come to campus to speak. Recent guests have included Georgia governor Sonny Perdue, Congressman John Lewis, and playwright Eve Ensler. Oglethorpe students also benefit from the university's airline partnership. Students have taken day trips with classes to New York City, Chicago, and Washington, DC, to explore museums, theater, neighborhoods, businesses, politics, and culture.

Successful Outcomes

Oglethorpe students learn to make a life, make a living, and make a difference. As Oglethorpe president Lawrence Schall states, students are being educated for their third or fourth jobs, as well as for their first. Oglethorpe alumni graduate with the ability to think, contribute, and act as responsible and entrepreneurial citizens. Graduates go on to the most selective graduate programs in the country, including Brown, Columbia, Duke, New York University, Princeton, and Yale, to name a few. Over 80 percent (double the national average) of Oglethorpe students applying to medical school are admitted, thanks to their deep understanding of society and human nature.

Alumni are involved with campus life in a variety of ways. Whether helping students find a job, volunteering alongside them in universitywide days of service, serving on the board of trustees, or contributing to scholarship funds, alumni are deeply connected to Oglethorpe long after graduation. Notable alumni include poet Sidney Lanier, Hollywood director Vincent Sherman, National Baseball Hall of Famer Luke Appling, and Congressman Charles Longstreet Weltner.

Fast Facts

Oglethorpe University is a four-year, independent liberal arts college, founded in 1835.

Web site

http://www.oglethorpe.edu/

Location

Atlanta, Georgia—the lush, suburban campus is only 10 miles north of the heart of Atlanta. The historic district of the 100-acre campus has been designated in the National Register of Historic Places.

Student Profile

1,100 students (35% male, 65% female); 34 states and territories; 30% minority, 5% international.

Faculty Profile

57 full-time faculty. 13:1 student/faculty ratio. Average class size is 16.

Residence Life

Moderately residential: 56% of students live on campus.

Athletics

NCAA Division III; Southern Collegiate Athletic Conference. 14 varsity sports (7 men's: baseball, basketball, cross-country, golf, soccer, tennis, track & field; 7 women's: basketball, cross-country, golf, soccer, tennis, track & field, volleyball). An array of intramural and recreational sports options are available.

Academic Programs

Accounting; American studies; art history; behavioral science and human resources management; biology; biopsychology; business administration; chemistry; communication and rhetoric studies; economics; engineering; English; environmental studies; French; history; international studies; international studies with Asia concentration; mathematics; mathematics and physics; philosophy; politics; psychology; sociology; sociology with a social work concentration; Spanish; studio art and theatre.

Costs and Aid

2007–2008: $32,590 comprehensive ($24,242 tuition). 61% of students receive some financial aid. Average award: $18,497.

Endowment

$ 21,693,749.

More Distinctions

• Oglethorpe has consistently been listed favorably by multiple national publications including the Fiske Guide to Colleges, The Princeton Review Student Access Guide, Barron's 300 Best Buys in College Education, and US News and World Report Best Colleges.

• The National Review College Guide named Oglethorpe University one of "America's Top Liberal Arts Schools."

• Oglethorpe is a member of the Annapolis Group, an organization of the leading national independent liberal arts colleges.

Wesleyan College

GEORGIA

Wesleyan College (WC) is a small, private women's college. In 1836, WC was the first college in the world chartered to grant degrees to women. Today it is recognized as one of the nation's most diverse and affordable selective, four-year, liberal arts colleges.

Admissions Contact:

Wesleyan College
4760 Forsyth Road
Macon, Georgia 31210
(800) 447 6610
Email: admission@wesleyancollege.edu
www.wesleyancollege.edu

The 4 Distinctions

Engaged Students

The top majors at WC are biology, chemistry, psychology, business, communications, and early education. Research trips have taken students of all majors to various institutions such as art galleries and museums, and even to the Barrier Islands off the coast of Georgia. Most students take advantage of study-abroad opportunities, as well.

Pioneers for women in many fields, WC graduates include the first woman to receive a Doctor of Medicine and the first woman to argue a case before the Georgia Supreme Court. WC was ranked third for diversity in population by the Princeton Review in 2007.

WC's leadership institute program for rising seniors is a rigorous and competitive program that has taken students to a variety of cities across the US. Most recently, students have traveled to San Francisco to learn about urban development, political interaction, corporate development, public service, and community engagement. This program was started by three alumni, who also help fund it, and exemplifies the extraordinary alumni support offered to the college through endowed scholarships and special field-study opportunities.

Great Teaching

Students value the college's tradition of service and rigorous academic program renowned for its quality. An exceptional faculty teaches classes in seminar style. A student to faculty ratio of ten to one ensures that students are known by more than just a grade or a number. The acceptance rate of Wesleyan students into medical, law, business, and other graduate programs is exemplary.

Undergraduate degrees are offered in thirty-five majors and twenty-nine minors, including self-designed majors and interdisciplinary programs, plus eight preprofessional programs that include seminary, engineering, medicine, pharmacy, veterinary medicine, health sciences, dental, and law. A $12.5 million science center added to the college's offerings for 2007. Master of Arts degrees in education and an accelerated Executive Master of Business Administration program enroll both men and women.

Wesleyan's first-year integrative seminars are required for all students and are given over two semesters. The first seminar addresses problems and issues relating to women and the tools women need to be successful; the second seminar addresses problems and issues relating to women's goals and what women can give back in terms of careers and service in the larger community. The first-year seminar meets as a class once a week for lectures and seminars; on other days of the week, small groups meet with a designated faculty adviser. The seminar engages students in critical thinking about literature, introduces students to online discussion boards, and involves a rigorous writing component.

Vibrant Community

The four cornerstones of the college are academics, women, faith, and community.

Beyond the academic, Wesleyan offers students a thriving residence-life program, NCAA Division III athletics, a championship IHSA equestrian program, and meaningful opportunities for community involvement and leadership. The college's beautiful two-hundred-acre wooded campus, along with thirty historically significant buildings, is listed in the National Register of Historic Places as the Wesleyan College Historic District. Wesleyan is nestled in a northern suburb of Macon, the third largest city in the state, nicknamed the Heart of Georgia. Located seventy-five miles south of Atlanta, the city of Macon is home to about one hundred and twenty-five thousand people, 47 percent of whom are African-American.

Wesleyan's history of sisterhood and tradition fuels endless class competitions, but also keeps students passionate about academics, integrity, and a strong honor code. From hilarious costumes to moving candlelit ceremonies, tradition is alive and well at the world's oldest and boldest college for women. At the heart of Wesleyan sisterhood is a strong class-year system that dates back to the early years of the twentieth century. Each class is identified by color and mascot name, and has its own songs and cheers. Class mascot names include Pirates, Golden Hearts, Purple Knights, and Green Knights. Class traditions took the place of sororities, which were abolished in 1914 and determined to be too secretive and undemocratic. WC has a dry campus, stressing the value of responsible actions.

The college's Lane Center for Community Engagement and Service develops students as future community leaders and offers a wide variety of volunteer opportunities for students, including initiatives with local retirement homes and children's homes, and adult literacy programs to help empower women in the community. WOW! A Day for Macon is an integral part of Wesleyan's goal to promote service-based learning among its students. The college-organized event occurs twice each year and benefits dozens of nonprofit organizations, such as the Salvation Army's Safe House, the Georgia Children's Museum, Macon Outreach, and many more.

Successful Outcomes

On average, 50 percent of WC alumni go to graduate school, with a 95 percent admittance rate into law and medical school. The admittance rate to MBA programs is near perfect. In the last ten years, Wesleyan has had seven recipients of the Phi Kappa Phi Graduate Fellowship, which has financially assisted many students. Alumni include a Georgia Teacher of the Year, the first woman lieutenant governor of Florida, and even a former Miss America.

Today's Wesleyan women have big plans for the future. They enroll to study everything from engineering to early childhood education to environmental science. Once on campus, they refuse to limit themselves. Instead of choosing just one major, most choose double – or even triple – majors. Because they have combined major and minor programs in ways that separate them from other job-seeking candidates, Wesleyan graduates enter the workforce with unique qualifications. Some double major combinations of 2007 graduates include: political science with Spanish, biology with psychology, economics with international relations, economics with advertising & marketing communication, and economics with chemistry.

Overall, more 2007 Wesleyan graduates will pursue business-related professions than any other field. Distinctive seminar-styled instruction prepares students well. Wesleyan students taking the business ETS exit exam in 2006 ranked in the 95th percentile, nation-wide, in overall performance. This year Wesleyan advanced several students, majoring in economics and business, to the most competitive graduate programs in the nation and around the world.

According to the seventh annual report of the National Survey of Student Engagement (NSSE), Wesleyan College outperformed the Top 10% of colleges and universities nationally in all five categories studied: active and collaborative learning, enriching educational experiences, level of academic challenge, student-faculty interaction, and supportive campus environment.

Fast Facts

Wesleyan College is a four-year, private, liberal arts college for women affiliated with the Methodist Church. The college was founded in 1836 as the first college in the world chartered to grant degrees to women.

Web site

http://www.wesleyancollege.edu

Location

Macon, Georgia—85 miles south of Atlanta in the third largest city in the state. The beautiful 200-acre campus, located in suburban north Macon, has been designated the Wesleyan College Historic District and is listed in the National Register of Historic Places.

Student Profile

550 full-time undergraduate students; 23 countries, 23% out-of-state; 32% minority, 15% international.

100 graduate coeducational students in EMBA and MA programs.

Faculty Profile

52 full-time faculty. 94% with PhD. 10:1 student/faculty ratio. Average class size is under 20.

Residence Life

Highly residential: 80% of students live on campus.

Athletics

NCAA Division III, GSA Conference. 6 varsity sports (basketball, cross-country, soccer, softball, tennis, IHSA championship equestrian program), club sports, and intramurals.

Academic Programs

Advertising and marketing communication; African studies; African-American studies; art history; studio art; biology; business administration (accounting & management concentrations); chemistry; communication; computer information systems; computer science; dual-degree engineering; early childhood education; middle grades education; economics; English; environmental science; finance; French; history; interdisciplinary studies in humanities; international business; international relations; mathematics; music (emphasis in organ, piano, or voice); neuroscience; philosophy; photography; physics; political science; psychology; religious studies; self-designed interdisciplinary major; Spanish; technology in business administration; theatre; women's studies.

Costs and Aid

2006–2007: $14,500 tuition ($7,500 room & board). 85% of students receive some financial aid.

Endowment

$45 million.

More Distinctions

• Consistently ranked as one of the nation's best liberal arts colleges by The Princeton Review.

Berea College

KENTUCKY

Founded in 1855 by ardent abolitionists, Berea was the first interracial and coeducational college in the South. Berea is distinctly liberal arts in nature, and promotes understanding and kinship among all people, service to communities in Appalachia and beyond, and sustainable living practices.

Admissions Contact:

Berea College
Office of Admissions
CPO 2220
Berea, KY 40404
Ph: (800) 326-5948
Email: askadmissions@berea.edu
www.berea.edu

The 4 Distinctions

Engaged Students

Still firmly rooted in its origins and continuing its nondemonational Christian status, Berea's contemporary mission is to educate students "primarily from Appalachia, black and white, who have great promise and limited economic resources," expressing in action its motto that "God has made of one blood all peoples of the earth." Each Berea student receives a scholarship, a job in the private college's labor program, and a high-quality liberal arts education that allows students to experience and embrace the dignity of work, the impact of sustainability, and the value of service.

All students are employed by the college under its labor program, which uses competitive hiring standards and techniques, giving students invaluable work-related experience, as well as encouraging involvement on campus and with the college community. Every student works ten to fifteen hours per week while carrying a full academic load. Students' earnings cover a portion of their college expenses. Students develop an appreciation for the utility of labor, and gain valuable job experience for their future careers in over 130 student work areas.

Service permeates all facets of student life, and the Center for Excellence in Learning Through Service (CELTS) coordinates all service projects on and off campus, including activities such as tutoring at-risk students, reaching out to mentally and physically challenged persons, and assisting in local schools. Berea was the first institution to feature the Bonner Scholars program, still ongoing and active. The Entrepreneurship for the Public Good (EPG), a business program, provides hands-on experience for its fellows in projects including raising money for organizations such as Habitat for Humanity or working with local farmers to implement sustainable farming practices.

Over half of Berea's students participate in study-abroad programs, and 50 percent of the cost is covered by college grants. Study-abroad opportunities are available in locations in Europe, Asia, Australia, New Zealand, and Mexico, to name a few.

Berea students, faculty, and staff work together to address the needs of both their local Appalachian community and of the nation. By combining service and academic activities, students develop intellectual, physical, and spiritual characteristics that translate into committed action. The most popular majors are business, biology, technology and industrial arts, nursing, and child and family studies.

Great Teaching

Berea's teachers are committed to being engaged. The approach the college takes to developing the lives of its students attracts teachers with similar priorities. The intimate campus of 150 acres and small class sizes provide ample opportunities for students and faculty to interact on a daily basis. Enrolled students are provided with a laptop computer, which is kept by students upon graduation, allowing teachers to work with them using modern technology. Faculty members are also involved in the local community, where many hold positions on local councils.

Berea offers degrees in twenty-eight fields, including arts and sciences and select professional programs, as well as independent, student-designed majors. Students also have undergraduate research opportunities in multiple fields.

Vibrant Community

The town of Berea grew up around the college and is known as a progressive and enlightened rural community. The college previously owned many of the utilities, public works, and the hospital, and maintains working relationships with these organizations, affording students many work opportunities unusual for such a small school.

Campus life is active, with over fifty clubs and organizations providing students with a wide choice of activities. All students are expected to live in college residence halls and eat in college dining halls. Freshmen are housed together, and upper-level students are mixed throughout the campus. A number of student musical groups perform on campus and tour in the surrounding area. Some activities take students to cities in the region, such as Lexington and Louisville, Kentucky, and Nashville and Knoxville, Tennessee.

Berea offers varied opportunities for all interested students to create and perform, with four choral groups, seven instrumental ensembles, three dance performing groups, and five dance clubs on campus. The Jelkyl Drama Center mounts four annual student- and faculty-directed performances in the Musser black box theatre or in the McGraw convertible stage. The campus also includes gallery space for student and faculty art, as well as studio space for drawing, painting, design, fiber arts, printmaking, ceramics, and sculpture.

The college is committed to being a "green" campus, and newly renovated buildings are built with environmentally friendly, sustainable features in mind. The campus offers fourteen residential halls and nine specialty houses, as well as fifty family housing apartments, accommodating about 88 percent of students.

Successful Outcomes

Berea College only accepts students from families with limited incomes, and the high graduation rate of these low-income students is notable. Berea alumni enjoy a lighter debt burden than graduates of many other colleges, and they graduate with real work experience to assist them in a successful job search or in seeking higher education at top-ranked universities directly after their graduation.

There are over seventeen thousand living alumni in all fifty states, and in sixty nations outside the U.S. Distinguished Berea alumni include the 2002 Nobel Prize winner John Fenn; former U.S. secretary of commerce Juanita M. Kreps; Tony Award winner Tharon Musser; and automotive engineer and designer Jack Roush, owner of Roush Racing.

Fast Facts

Berea College is a four-year college founded in 1855.

Web site

http://www.berea.edu

Location

Berea, Kentucky—approxmately 40 miles from Lexington.

Student Profile

1,520 (40% male, 60% female); 39 states and territories; 69% minority, 7% international.

Faculty Profile

131 full-time faculty. 91% hold a terminal degree in their field. 10:1 student/faculty ratio. Average class size is 16.

Residence Life

88% of students live on campus.

Athletics

NAIA, Kentucky Intercollegiate Athletic Conference (KIAC). 16 varsity sports (8 men's: basketball, baseball, tennis, soccer, golf, swimming & diving, track & field, cross-country; 8 women's: basketball, volleyball, tennis, soccer, softball, swimming & diving, track & field, cross-country), 4 club sports, and intramurals.

Academic Programs

African & African American studies; agriculture & natural resources; applied science & mathematics; art; biology; business administration; chemistry; child & family studies; classical languages; economics; education studies; English; French; German; history; mathematics; music; nursing; philosophy; physical education; physics; political science; psychology; religion; sociology; Spanish; speech communication; technology & industrial arts; theatre; women's studies.

Costs and Aid

2007–2008: $6,282 comprehensive ($0 tuition). 100 % of students receive some financial aid. Average award: The equivalent of a four-year scholarship, up to $85,000.

Endowment

Over $1,000,000,000.

More Distinctions

• #1 Comprehensive College - Bachelor's in the South (*US News and World Report*).

• Best Colleges for African Americans (Daystar, Black Enterprise).

• Four-year tuition scholarship awarded to all enrolled students; only students with demonstrated financial need are eligible for admission; all students provided a paid, on-campus job; all students provided a laptop computer, which they keep upon graduation.

• Strong undergraduate/faculty research program; nationally recognized service-learning program CELTS (Center for Excellence in Learning Through Service).

Centre College

KENTUCKY

Founded by Presbyterian leaders in 1819, Centre College is a private, coeducational, liberal arts college in Danville, Kentucky. Centre's student body consists of approximately 1,175 students from throughout the United States and several foreign countries.

Admissions Contact:

Centre College
Centre College Admission Office
600 West Walnut Street
Danville, KY 40422
(800) 423-6236
Ph: (859) 238-5350
Email: admission@centre.edu
www.centre.edu

The 4 Distinctions

Engaged Students

Centre offers twenty-seven majors and twenty-seven minors. In addition to traditional majors, Centre encourages students to self-design majors to create a program that's right for them. Double majors are common, and Centre offers dual-degree engineering programs with four major universities.

As part of the Centre Commitment, all Centre students are guaranteed an internship, study abroad, and graduation within four years, or Centre will provide up to a year of additional study tuition free. Centre is ranked among the nation's top ten in study-abroad percentage (86 percent in 2006). Semester-long study is offered at campuses in England (London or Reading), France, and Mexico, with exchange programs in Japan, Northern Ireland, and England. A variety of three-week study opportunities are available at other locations around the world, including Italy, Vietnam, Barbados, Spain, and Turkey.

Centre students work closely with professors on collaborative research, allowing students to get to know their professors better and to learn firsthand from experts in their fields. Participating in joint research projects and publishing their research gives students valuable experience as well as resume credits.

Great Teaching

Unique to Centre is Professor Stephen Powell, the internationally known artist whose elaborately colored glass vessels are held in permanent collections throughout the world. Many of his students go on to success in their own glass careers. Powell puts in long hours of intense, small-group instruction to ensure that students master the technical aspects of hot glass. Powell also teaches the business aspects of art and gives his students hands-on opportunities to learn about kilns, ovens, and other equipment essential to ceramicists and glass artists. He has secured extensive donations that have made it possible for Centre students to build a thirty-foot anagama kiln that is hand fired two or three times each year for instructional purposes. Powell has also secured donations for and then supervised student

construction of one of the nation's finest, state-of-the-art hot glass studios in Centre's Jones Visual Arts Center, which opened in 1998.

Not only are Centre's teachers among America's best educated, they're also among America's most involved. To quote from Yale's 2006 Insider's Guide to the Colleges: "The 'accessible' and 'really amazing' professors at Centre" are "known for their personal attention that they give to students." Centre professors teach all classes—there are no teaching assistants. They also hold classes in their homes or in residence halls, and get to know students both in and out of class. Centre's average class size of eighteen allows students one-on-one time with their professors. Centre professors give students their home phone numbers, stop by and chat in the dining commons, and show up at students' recitals or soccer matches. Because professors know students personally, they help them stretch to achieve their very best.

A student's first year at Centre will include a small seminar—often with a fun, nonlecture format—during the three-week CentreTerm in January. This seminar gives students an opportunity to share a special interest with professors and classmates. Freshmen seminars often include field trips, dinner discussions, and other interesting learning activities.

Vibrant Community

Centre College is located in historic Danville, Kentucky, on a 150-acre campus with sixty-seven buildings, thirteen of which are included in the National Register of Historic Places. The College Centre, which features athletic, academic, and library facilities, opened in 2005. Nationally recognized for its high quality of life, Danville is progressive, safe, friendly, and perfectly placed as a gateway to the region and the world. It's called the City of Firsts for its many historical milestones, including the first courthouse in Kentucky and the first post office west of the Alleghenies. In 2000, the city helped Centre host the year's only vice presidential debate.

Centre students are bright and friendly. The majority of students live on Centre's campus, and all students will live on campus when Pearl Hall, the college's newest residence hall, opens in fall 2008. The new residence hall will be dedicated in 2009. Centre students are diverse both geographically (thirty-seven states and thirteen countries are represented in the student population) as well as socioeconomically (61 percent of students receive need-based aid). More than 60 percent of those ranked were in the top 10 percent of their high school graduation class. Centre students enjoy having fun, but are serious about their education. Centre students regularly win the nation's most prestigious fellowships and scholarships, including Rhodes, Rotary, Fulbright, Goldwater, and Truman. Centre offers students many ways to be actively involved in their educations, with nineteen varsity teams, about one hundred campus organizations, and more than two thousand events each year.

Successful Outcomes

Centre has been producing leaders for almost two centuries. From U.S. vice presidents and Supreme Court justices, to the founder of the Hard Rock Cafe and the inventor of plastic baggies, Centre's alumni have a tradition of extraordinary success. It starts with first-rate academics and opportunity. The college offers students many ways to develop their skills, including the Brown Scholars Leadership Program, the Bonner Leaders, athletics, Greek life, and a host of other student organizations. Volunteer, internship and externship opportunities encourage students to become directly involved in Danville and the surrounding communities.

Then the Career Services Office provides the services students need to help them succeed: one-to-one counseling, internships (guaranteed), employer interviews, eRecruiting (a powerful Internet job-search tool), and graduate school admission test preparation. After graduation, Centre continues to help its alumni with lifetime career counseling.

Thanks to an individual approach, Centre has the highest graduation rate in Kentucky. Recent graduates are employed by Fifth Third Bank, J.P. Morgan Chase, the Louisville Courier-Journal, U.S. Equestrian Federation, Office of Naval Intelligence, Columbus Museum of Art, AFLAC, Corporate Executive Board, and Boeing (among many others). And Centre graduates go on to prominent graduate schools, as well, just to name a few: Harvard, Yale, Duke, Wisconsin, and North Carolina.

Fast Facts

Centre College is a coeducational, residential college of the liberal arts and sciences.

Web site

http://www.centre.edu/

Location

Danville, Kentucky—35 miles from Lexington, 85 miles from Louisville, 120 miles from Cincinnati.

Student Profile

1,175 students (49% male, 51% female); 37 states, 13 countries; 5% minority, 1% international.

Faculty Profile

Approximately 100 full-time faculty. 98% hold a terminal degree in their field. 11:1 student/faculty ratio. Average class size is 18.

Residence Life

Highly residential: 94% of students live on campus

Athletics

NCAA Division III, Southern Collegiate Athletic Conference. 19 varsity sports and 15 intramurals.

Academic Programs

3-2 engineering program; anthropology; art; art history; biochemistry; biology; chemical physics; chemistry; classical studies; computer science; dramatic arts; economics; elementary education; English; financial economics; French; German studies; government; history; international relations; mathematics; molecular biology; music; philosophy; physics; political economy; prelaw; premedicine, psychobiology; psychology; religion; sociology; Spanish.

Costs and Aid

2007–2008: $35,000 comprehensive. Approximately 65% of students receive some financial aid. Average award: $19,900.

Endowment

$205 million.

More Distinctions

• Top Fifty National Liberal Arts Colleges (U.S. News & World Report, 2002).

• Most affordable of the U.S. News Top Fifty National Liberal Arts Colleges (2002).

• Number one in educational value among all U.S. private, liberal arts colleges (Consumers Digest, June 2007)"

• Number ten among baccalaureate institutions for study abroad (Black Issues in Higher Education, 2003).

• Included in the Unofficial, Unbiased Guide to the 328 Most Interesting Colleges (Kaplan, 2004 edition).

• One of the Best 345 Colleges (Princeton Review, 2003 edition).

Thomas More College

KENTUCKY

Thomas More College is a Catholic, liberal arts college of 1,500 students. Offering thirty-seven programs of study, Thomas More has appeared in several best-buy rankings. Just ten minutes across the Ohio River from downtown Cincinnati, the campus is situated on one hundred acres of beautiful rolling hills.

Admissions Contact:

Thomas More College
333 Thomas More Parkway
Crestview Hills, Ky 41017
(800) 825-4557
Ph: (859) 344-3332
Email: admissions@thomasmore.edu
www.thomasmore.edu

The 4 Distinctions

Engaged Students

As a member of the Cooperative Center for Study Abroad, Thomas More is able to offer its students study-abroad opportunities at locations on six continents around the globe. In addition, the college has five sister universities offering programs unique to Thomas More students: Gifu City Women's College in Gifu City, Japan; the Catholic University of Eichstatt, Germany; Mary Immaculate College in Limerick, Ireland; Sacred Heart University in San Juan, Puerto Rico; and Luhansk Taras Shevchenko National Pedagogical University in Ukraine. The college also has a special program with St. Andrew's College in Bearsden, Scotland.

The career center and academic departments work closely to provide internship opportunities for Thomas More students. Psychology students, for example, have the opportunity to do internships at local hospitals, businesses, and various research facilities.

The service-learning program coordinates community-service opportunities for Thomas More students. As conceived by the college, service learning consists of three components: the planning of a meaningful experience focused on an identified community need, the implementation of the experience itself within the context of a nonprofit organization, and a structured reflection in which students make connections between course objectives and the service learning experience. In addition to many projects in the local community, students have participated in Habitat for Humanity reconstruction projects in Louisiana, Florida, and various projects in Jamaica.

Great Teaching

The Thomas More core curriculum ensures that students receive a solid liberal arts education as well as a strong concentration in a major field. The core curriculum challenges students to examine the ultimate meaning of life, their place in the world, and their responsibility to others. Core requirements include the first-year seminar and courses in English, mathematics, social science, communications, world civilizations, foreign languages, natural science, theology, philosophy, and fine arts.

All freshmen at Thomas More enroll in the college's first-year seminar in the fall semester. Faculty from many different academic fields offer a variety of seminar topics. Incorporating issues and problems relevant to college freshmen into the seminars, professors introduce students to college-level learning and experiences. Research skills, study methods, time management, and college adjustment are part of every first-year seminar. Among the many first-year seminar courses offered have been Cincinnati culture, led by an art professor; an introduction to the principles of nonviolence, led by the campus minister; a course on claiming God during war, led by a history professor; abnormal psychology at the movies, led by a professor of psychology; and ethics and sports, led by a professor of philosophy.

The average class size at Thomas More is fourteen students, and the overall faculty to student ratio is one to thirteen. Among Thomas More professors, 60 percent have PhD degrees, and many work as consultants for various industries.

As a member of the Greater Cincinnati Consortium of Colleges and Universities, Thomas More students may enroll in classes at a dozen other local institutions, including the Art Academy of Cincinnati, the Athenaeum of Ohio, the University of Cincinnati, Hebrew Union College, Cincinnati State Technical and Community College, and Xavier University.

Many Thomas More students contract to perform an experiential learning project under faculty supervision, with the objective of enriching their education through experiences beyond the college's course offerings, acquainting themselves with the means for extending the learning process into their everyday lives, developing the habit of relating their educational activities to their career perspectives, and acquiring flexibility in their approach to learning. Students may earn up to sixteen credit hours in experiential learning projects.

Students also take advantage of the cooperative education program, in which students combine classroom instruction with related job experience. The paid, off-campus employment is integrated into the academic program, allowing co-op students to complete their degrees in the normal four years.

Thomas More is particularly well-known for its program in biology, with its field research center on the Ohio River. At this research station, students conduct research for the Environmental Protection Agency and hold workshops for elementary and secondary school students and teachers. The environmental studies program makes use of the field station in its collaborative research with the Museum Center of Cincinnati.

Physics and astronomy are strong programs at Thomas More; the college's observatory features four high-power telescopes and hosts monthly open houses for the public. Forensic science is a relatively new, but quite popular, program. Other well-regarded programs include nursing, business, education, and communications.

Vibrant Community

Student activities are as diverse as the student body itself. Commuters and on-campus residents count on a safe and fun learning environment on the Thomas More campus. The theatre department puts on three or four performances each year, and the choral ensemble is popular on campus and in the neighboring community. Thomas More competes in NCAA Division III sports, and half of all students take part in varsity athletics.

More than 40 percent of Thomas More students live on campus in four residence halls. Each resident is considered a "citizen" of his or her living community, achieving personal growth through a variety of activities and social interaction.

Cincinnati, just ten minutes away across the Ohio River, offers such urban amenities as the Cincinnati Bengals, the Cincinnati Reds, ballet, opera, a museum, the Cincinnati Zoo, a new aquarium, and a new shopping center called Newport on the Levee. The TANK bus line provides Thomas More students with easy access to the city.

Successful Outcomes

Thomas More's four-year graduation rate is an excellent 70 percent. On average, 90 percent of Thomas More graduates seeking work are hired within six months of graduation, 95 percent of applicants to law school are accepted, and in recent years, 100 percent of nursing graduates have received job offers in their field of choice. Some 75 percent of Thomas More graduates eventually enroll in graduate or professional schools.

Fast Facts

Thomas More College is a private, coeducational, liberal arts college affiliated with the Diocese of Covington, Kentucky and was founded in 1921.

Web site

http://www.thomasmore.edu

Location

Crestview Hills, KY—just 10 miles from downtown Cincinnati.

Student Profile

1,400 undergraduate and graduate students (53% male, 47% female); 13 states, 12 foreign countries; 22% minority.

Faculty Profile

68% hold a terminal degree in their field. 13:1 student/faculty ratio. Average class size is 14.

Residence Life

Mildly residential: 35% of students live on campus.

Athletics

NCAA Division III, Presidential Athletic Conference. 14 varsity sports (7 men's: basketball, baseball, cross-country, football, golf, soccer, tennis; 7 women's: basketball, cross-country, golf, soccer, softball, tennis, volleyball), 4 intramurals (softball, volleyball, 3-on-3 basketball, flag football).

Academic Programs

Accounting; art; art history; biology; business administration; chemistry; communications; computer information systems; criminal justice; drama; economics; education; English; exercise science; forensic science; history; international studies; mathematics; medical technology; nursing; philosophy; physics; political science; psychology; sociology; sports management & marketing; Spanish; theology.

Pre-Professional Programs in predental, preengineering, prelaw, premedical, preoccupational therapy, preveterinary, prepharmacy.

Costs and Aid

2006–2007: $19,500 full-time tuition. More than 90% of students receive merit-based or need-based financial aid.

More Distinctions

• Ranked among the best undergraduate programs in the South by U.S. News & World Report.

• Listed in Money's Guide to Best College Buys.

• Named a "Selective Liberal Arts College" by the Carnegie Foundation for the Advancement of Teaching.

• The Presidents' Athletic Conference (PAC) has announced the addition of Thomas More College as the seventh member of the conference beginning in the 2005-06 academic year.

• Thomas More College's safety statistics are tops in the nation. From parking safety to crime prevention, TMC prides itself on maintaining one of the safest campuses in the country.

Transylvania University

Admissions Contact:

Transylvania University
300 North Broadway
Lexington, KY 40508
(800) 872-6798
Ph: (859) 233-8242
Email: admissions@transy.edu
www.transy.edu

KENTUCKY

Transylvania University (Transy) is a private, liberal arts college affiliated with the Christian Church (Disciples of Christ). Founded in 1780, Transylvania offers its 1,153 students a liberal arts education combined with applied majors such as business and education.

The 4 Distinctions

Engaged Students

Transylvania's location just two blocks from the financial district of Lexington, a bustling city of 270,000 people, means that internships and part-time job opportunities are plentiful at banks, financial services companies, and accounting firms. As the legal and healthcare center for the eastern half of Kentucky, Lexington also offers internship opportunities for students interested in law and medicine. The rolling bluegrass countryside surrounding the city is home to some of the most beautiful and famous horse farms in the world, and the thoroughbred industry provides opportunities for students in many different fields. Recent internships have seen an accounting major at Pricewaterhouse-Coopers (where she became a full-time associate after graduation); a computer science major at Lexmark International, a major manufacturer of laser and inkjet printers; a sociology/anthropology major at Kentucky Refugee Ministries, a social services agency; and a history major at the Bluegrass Trust for Historic Preservation.

In addition, many students complete internships out of the state and abroad. Recent examples include internships with a member of the Scottish Parliament, at the Centers for Disease Control and Prevention in Atlanta, and at McGraw-Hill, a financial, publishing, and education services company in New York City. Transylvania's Canadian Parliamentary Internship program offers students the opportunity to work for five weeks in the office of a member of the Canadian House of Commons or Senate.

Transylvania graduates are known for their ability to think critically and to use inquiry to explore themselves and the world around them. More than half of Transy's students participate in study abroad programs, engaging in full-immersion experiences in which they learn culture and language, as well as the subject matter they are studying. May term classes, where students focus on one course for four weeks, frequently include domestic or international travel components. Recent courses have found Transy students studying at the School for International Training in Morocco, pursuing geology and tropical biodiversity in Ecuador, and studying international politics and economics in Mexico.

Great Teaching

Transy's faculty members have dominated the Kentucky Professor of the Year award (from the Carnegie Foundation for the Advancement of Teaching and the Council for Advancement and Support of Education), claiming the honor four times since 2001—more than any other Kentucky college or university. Faculty members also received the Acorn Award as Kentucky's outstanding professor from the Kentucky Advocates for Higher Education and the Council on Postsecondary Education in 2000 and 2006.

May term classes, many of which are interdisciplinary and team taught, foster an exceptional degree of interaction between students and faculty. A recent course on the chemistry of ceramics was co-taught by professors from the departments of art and chemistry, a course on contemporary Ireland was co-taught by professors in anthropology and political science, and one on advertising was co-taught by professors in communication and music technology.

Transy's Bingham Program for Excellence in Teaching was established to attract, inspire, and reward faculty members in their efforts to make the classroom an imaginative place of learning and discovery. The Bingham-Young Professorship allows outstanding Bingham professors to spearhead programs of curricular enrichment and teaching development for all the faculty, and the David and Betty Jones Fund for Faculty Development supports faculty research and scholarly activities, as well as faculty-directed student research projects.

Over 96 percent of faculty members hold the Ph.D. or the highest degree in their field, and Transy offers a student-faculty ratio of just thirteen to one. Professors engage students in small classes, encouraging them to go beyond the course assignments, seek out new knowledge, and see things in a different light.

Vibrant Community

Transy students are active in the local community and across the country through local urban outreach and alternative spring break programs. Many students arrive a week ahead of fall term to do community service in Lexington and other communities through the Jump Start and First-Year Urban programs. The Volunteer Income Tax Assistance Plan allows accounting students to provide free tax preparation help to less advantaged people, and Crimson Christmas is an annual campus holiday party for children of Big Brothers/Big Sisters of the Bluegrass.

With 80 percent of students living on campus, it's easy to meet friends and get involved in activities. There are over fifty student organizations, and students frequently create their own clubs. For example, a Transy student recently launched TERRA, an environmental activism group that has thrived, with new chapters at five different colleges and universities in Kentucky.

Transylvania hosts a wide variety of lectures, art exhibitions, music performances, film screenings, and on-campus entertainment. Recent speakers have included Nobel Peace Prize winner Elie Wiesel, authors Kurt Vonnegut and Joyce Carol Oates, historians Doris Kearns Goodwin and Shelby Foote, and U.S. trade ambassador Charlene Barshefsky. Two students recently organized an Iraq Teach-in for a non-partisan review of issues surrounding the war, and there are annual celebrations of Hispanic Heritage Month and African-American History Month.

Transy has a thriving Greek life, with four fraternities and four sororities, and approximately half of Transy's students join a fraternity or sorority.

Successful Outcomes

During its long history, Transylvania's notable alumni have included U.S. Supreme Court justice John Marshall Harlan; abolitionist Cassius Clay; Stephen F. Austin, founder of Texas; and Happy Chandler, Kentucky governor, United States senator, and commissioner of major league baseball. More recent alumni include a world-renowned marine zoologist at the Smithsonian Institution; the CEO, president, and founder of the National Rehabilitation Hospital in Washington, D. C.; a gallery director at the School of the Art Institute of Chicago; and a member of the surgical team that implanted the world's first self-contained artificial heart in a human being.

The Career Development Center sponsors seminars and conferences about graduate school, careers, and the working world, and convocation and various lecture series bring successful alumni to campus to meet with students.

Transylvania graduates are accepted at some of the most prestigious universities in the nation. Virtually all of the students that Transylvania recommends to law school and approximately 90 percent of the students recommended to medical school are accepted.

No matter what path a student chooses, Transylvania University works to develop in its graduates lifelong habits of learning, inquiry, and thoughtfulness, which lead to success in any career.

Fast Facts

Transylvania University is a private, four-year liberal arts institution affiliated with the Christian Church (Disciples of Christ) and founded in 1780.

Website

http://www.transy.edu

Location

Lexington, Kentucky— In the heart of Kentucky's Bluegrass region, Lexington is a vibrant city of 270,000. It is an hour's drive from Louisville and Cincinnati, and only three hours from Nashville, Indianapolis, and Columbus.

Student Profile

1,153 students (40% male, 60% female); 30 states; 6% minority, <1% international.

Faculty Profile

86 full-time faculty. Over 96% of tenured and tenure-track faculty hold the Ph.D. or highest degree in their field. 13:1 student/faculty ratio. Average class size is 18.

Residence Life

Highly residential: 80% of students live on campus.

Athletics

NCAA Division III, Heartland Collegiate Athletic Conference. 16 varsity sports (7 men's: baseball, basketball, cross-country, golf, soccer, swimming & diving, tennis; 9 women's: basketball, cross-country, field hockey, golf, soccer, softball, swimming & diving, tennis, volleyball).

Academic Programs

Accounting; anthropology; art (studio); art history; biology; business administration (concentrations in management, marketing, finance, and hospitality management); chemistry; classics; computer science; drama; economics; education; English; exercise science; French; history; mathematics; music (applied); music technology; philosophy; physics; political science; psychology; religion; sociology; Spanish.

Costs and Aid

2007–2008: $29,430 comprehensive ($21,400 tuition). Over 90% of students receive financial assistance. Average award: $17,629.

Endowment

$145 million.

More Distinctions

• Since 2001, four Transylvania professors have been named Kentucky Professor of the Year by the Carnegie Foundation and the Council for Advancement and Support of Education, in 2000 and in 2006, a Transylvania professor received the Acorn Award as Kentucky's outstanding professor from the Kentucky Advocates for Higher Education and the Council on Postsecondary Education.

Loyola University New Orleans

LOUISIANA

Founded by the Jesuits in 1912, Loyola University New Orleans combines the academic excellence of its faculty and programs, an ideal size that fosters individual student success in a positive learning experience, and a commitment to educating the whole person.

Admissions Contact:

Loyola University New Orleans
6363 St. Charles Avenue
New Orleans, LA 70118
(800) 4-LOYOLA
Ph: (504) 865-3240
Email: admit@loyno.edu
www.loyno.edu

The 4 Distinctions

Engaged Students

Loyola offers students many exciting educational and cultural opportunities to travel and study abroad. Recent options have included summer programs in Belgium, England, France, China, India, Ireland, Spain, and Mexico, among others. Loyola's Center for International Education also coordinates semester programs in a variety of destinations throughout the world. Students receive academic credit for their participation and gain many significant experiences they can apply to their education at Loyola, graduate work, or employment.

Loyola offers students various internship opportunities with both local and national companies and organizations. By participating in an internship, students are able to gain relevant career-related experiences that reinforce what they have learned in the classroom and make them more marketable after graduation.

At Loyola, there are opportunities for students in many academic disciplines to become involved in research conducted by faculty. Students are also able to conduct their own research with faculty supervision and present their findings at national conferences. Often, students are able to continue their research as they progress to graduate school.

In its recent partnership with the Thelonious Monk Institute of Jazz Performance, Loyola students will participate with students from the Monk Institute in rebuilding the New Orleans jazz scene. This partnership will include efforts to strengthen the school system and community jazz education programs; to offer employment opportunities for New Orleans musicians; to attract displaced musicians; and to unite the jazz, arts, and cultural communities of New Orleans.

Loyola University Community Action Program (LUCAP) directs volunteers in service-oriented activities within the community and the university, while promoting involvement in the area of social justice. Students involved in LUCAP volunteer with organizations focused on environmental action, hunger relief, the death penalty moratorium movement, assisting local elderly citizens, and have taken an active role in rebuilding the New Orleans community. The program aids in promoting social and spiritual growth through involvement in service activities.

The Office of Service Learning at Loyola coordinates opportunities for students to combine community service with classroom instruction. The projects focus on critical, reflective thinking, as well as civic and personal responsibility. Students volunteer in many capacities and at many sites, including shelters for battered women, schools, homeless shelters, hospitals, elderly care facilities, literacy centers, programs that serve the needs of the physically and/ or mentally challenged, and programs that address the special needs of inner-city youth. Faculty and students collaborate to select a specific site and activities that correlate to the course content. The faculty member grants the students academic credit based on the learning achieved through service, not for completing the hours. Service learning not only benefits the student, but also the greater New Orleans community.

Great Teaching

Loyola prides itself on the positive learning environment its ideal size affords students. Loyola's beneficial student to faculty ratio of eleven to one allows for meaningful faculty communication and mentoring with students. Loyola's diverse and experienced faculty are available to give students the personal attention they need to achieve success.

Faculty advisers are selected for students according to their academic interests and are available for consultation throughout the academic year, especially during orientation and registration periods.

Students benefit from the diverse services of the Career Development Center, Disability Services the Mathematics Center, the Monroe Library, the Ross Foreign Language Center, and the Writing Across the Curriculum program. Students can receive additional instruction and tutoring in multiple disciplines, enhance their writing and critical thinking skills, and explore potential career opportunities.

The common curriculum offers a broad range of courses for students to explore multiple disciplines and all students are required to take common curriculum courses, regardless of their declared major. The common curriculum consists of introductory courses such as composition, literature, history, philosophy, mathematics, science, and religious studies. The advanced common curriculum courses are designed to ensure a rewarding and well-rounded education.

Vibrant Community

Loyola's scenic uptown campus is set in the heart of one of the most prestigious neighborhoods in New Orleans. Students enjoy the numerous venues of New Orleans jazz as well as cuisine from the finest restaurants. The university is located directly across from the Audubon Zoo and Park, the city's premier recreation center. With its unique cuisine, numerous museums and historical sites, and flourishing arts community, New Orleans provides a cultural experience few cities can match.

There is also plenty to do on campus. Loyola students participate in more than 120 student organizations and activities. Organizations include the environmental action club, the economics club, College Democrats and Republicans, the outdoor recreation club, and many more. Besides social interaction and relaxation, students gain many useful skills, such as time management, leadership, problem solving, and critical thinking abilities through extracurricular activities. In addition, the student-run University Programming Board (UPB) sponsors films, concerts, TGIFs, and many ethnic and cultural experiences on campus throughout the academic year.

Loyola is also home to an active Greek system, including five national fraternities, six national sororities, and three governing boards.

Loyola houses students in four residence halls. Approximately 65 percent of Loyola freshmen come from outside of Louisiana, and all freshmen from outside the metropolitan New Orleans area are required to live on campus. Honors students have the opportunity to live on a designated floor in the residence halls.

Successful Outcomes

The Career Development Center assists students in assessing career opportunities, exploring career resources, and developing skills for the job search. Publications housed in the center include information on a wide range of career choices, graduate school directories, scholarship and financial aid directories, and field-specific directories of employment. In addition, the center hosts recruiters and on-campus job fairs.

Loyola graduates have gone on to law schools such as Georgetown School of Law, the University of Notre Dame, and William and Mary School of Law; medical schools such as Columbia University, Duke University, and Stanford University; and a variety of graduate programs at universities such as Rice University and the University of Edinburgh.

Fast Facts

Loyola University New Orleans is a four- year, private, coeducational, Jesuit, Catholic institution founded in 1912 for graduate and undergraduate study.

Web site
http://www.loyno.edu

Location
Uptown section of New Orleans, Louisiana—15 minutes from downtown and the French Quarter.

Student Profile
2,685 undergraduate students (41% male, 59% female); 50 states, the District of Columbia, Puerto Rico and 48 foreign countries; 36% minority.

Faculty Profile
259 full-time faculty. 85% have terminal degrees in their field. 11:1 student/faculty ratio. Average class size is 22.

Residence Life
Four residence halls; single sex and coeducational. All freshmen from outside metropolitan New Orleans are required to live on campus.

Athletics
NAIA Division I, Gulf Coast Athletic Conference. 8 varsity sports (4 men's: baseball, basketball, cross-country, track; 4 women's: basketball, cross-country, track, volleyball.

Academic Programs
Advertising; accounting; biology; biology/premed; chemistry; chemistry/forensic science; chemistry/premed; classical studies; criminal justice; economics; English literature; English writing; finance; French; history; journalism; international business; management; marketing; mathematics; music (composition, jazz studies, instrumental performance, music industry studies—performance track, music industry studies—non-performance track, music education, music therapy, music with elective studies, vocal performance); philosophy; physics; political science; psychology; psychology/premed; public relations; religious studies; religious studies/Christianity; religious studies/world religions; sociology; Spanish; theatre arts; theatre arts communications, theatre arts with a minor in business administration; visual arts, graphic arts.

Costs and Aid
2007–2008: $35,746 comprehensive ($25,632 tuition). 84% of students receive some financial aid.

More Distinctions
• Ranked as one of the top regional colleges and universities in the South and one of the top 60 in the United States by U.S.News & World Report.

• Named one of "America's 300 Best Buys" in Barron's Best Buys in College Education, and ranks in the top seven percent of the 1,500 colleges and universities ranked by Barron's.

• Students have been awarded Rhodes, British Marshall, Mitchell, and Fulbright scholarships.

Millsaps College

MISSISSIPPI

Admissions Contact:

Millsaps College
1701 North State Street
Jackson, MS 39210-0001
(800) 352-1050
Ph: (601) 974-1000
Fax: (601) 974-1229
Email:
www.millsaps.edu

Millsaps College is an independent institution of higher learning affiliated with the United Methodist Church and founded in 1890 with a gift from civic leader Reuben Webster Millsaps. With small class sizes and distinctive programs, today Millsaps offers a full spectrum of education in liberal arts and sciences.

The 4 Distinctions

Engaged Students

Millsaps has a long tradition of offering one of the best and strongest premed programs in the state. Graduates of the college claim a significant number of the one hundred open slots at University of Mississippi Medical School every year. About 15 percent of each year's graduates major in biology or chemistry. Millsaps also offers a strong prelaw program with its political science and history majors.

Millsaps's business program is fully accredited by AACSB, and accounts for 15 to 20 percent of total graduate and undergraduate enrollment every year. Millsaps is one of the handful of very strong liberal arts business schools. Accounting, economics, and business administration are the main focuses in the business division.

The school also boasts an exceptionally strong anthropology department, as strong as any liberal arts program. Fieldwork is done at the college's 4,500-acre biocultural reserve in the Yucatán province of Kiuic. Millsaps was the first school to begin excavation of this site, which was inhabited around 600 BCE. Geology, too, offers many experiential trips to Alaska, Yucatán, and Yellowstone National Park. Altogether, eight to nine courses in math, art, sociology, business, and other disciplines are offered in the college's Yucatán programs. Through its solar-powered, neo-Mayan architecture on the reserve and a newly renovated house and classroom facility in a nearby city, Millsaps creates a living and learning environment for students.

There are many other opportunities to venture off campus and abroad, including lab research and NCUR conferences for chemistry and biology students; language immersion programs of four to eight weeks in Nice, Costa Rica, and other venues; summer business programs in London, Munich, and the Netherlands; and a sociology program in China.

The college's location just one mile from downtown Jackson, the state's capital and financial center, affords students the opportunity to intern with high-level executives who agree to spend a substantial amount of time with students talking about the industry and various aspects of their professions. Mentorship programs are in place for medicine, business, law, and all other areas of study.

The Millsaps College Faith & Work Initiative, funded by the Lilly Endowment, provides an array of seminars, courses, and internships that allow students to explore their personal and professional futures as they relate to issues of ethics, values, faith, and the common good.

Great Teaching

Millsaps's faculty are dedicated to teaching, first and foremost. Research is secondary, and frequently involves work with undergraduate assistants. The college boasts one teacher for every eleven students and an average class size of fifteen. Millsaps employs ninety full-time faculty members, and virtually all of Millsaps' tenure-track faculty hold a PhD or the terminal degree in their field.

Millsaps professors have won various teaching awards, including the McGraw-Hill Undergraduate Anthropology Teaching Award, the CASE Carnegie U.S. Professor of the Year Award, and three professor of the year awards for Mississippi in the last five years, including a recent award to a geneticist in the biology department.

Millsaps's Heritage program is a wide-ranging study of the history of ideas, cultures, religions, creative works, and pivotal problems that have shaped humanity for thousands of years. Beginning with fossils and ending with speculations about the future, this program brings together history, literature, philosophy, religion, and the arts in an integrated approach to the study of a global cultural history. The program is the equivalent of two yearlong courses.

Unlike many colleges, Millsaps has developed a writing program that is independent of the English Department. The program teaches students how to develop the art of communication, an essential skill that can be used in any major or career. Millsaps embraces the philosophy that writing cannot be taught in one semester of freshman composition. Instead, it is taught continuously, and within the context of the discipline, from English to biology, and even accounting. The college's required writing portfolio allows students to gather and reflect on a variety of their academic writings.

Millsaps is working to expand experiential education, internships, and study abroad, seeking to internationalize students through semester-long programs.

Vibrant Community

The school has one thousand-plus undergraduates, with 80 percent of the students living on campus. There is currently one specifically designated residential service-learning community of twenty-five students, and steps are being taken to create further communities, including those based on themes of environment and leadership. Fully half of the student body is Greek, helping to support a vibrant community on campus.

First-year students at Millsaps take an introduction to liberal studies seminar, a rigorous reasoning- and writing-intensive course. Topics of the seminars vary, though all seminars cover the same objectives.

Millsaps's Student Foundations program is designed to help students adjust to the transition of college. Students meet once a week to learn about personal responsibilities such as dealing with alcohol, drugs, and other issues that may arise while living away from home.

There are many opportunities for service at Millsaps; students are active in tutoring programs, Habitat for Humanity, and local soup kitchens, among other organizations. The college's One Campus, One Community program focuses on community-service projects in local North Midtown (an area near Millsaps) and Jackson's K-12 schools.

The city of Jackson features a number of cultural opportunities, including a symphony, ballet, art museum, and many jazz clubs. Farish Street, a historic district in town, is going through a revamping that will provide students with a number of other off-campus options.

Successful Outcomes

Along with eight Methodist bishops, distinguished Millsaps alumni include Joanne Edgar, cofounder of Ms. magazine, and Ellen Gilchrist, a distinguished novelist and winner of the American Book Award for fiction.

Other alumni include Ken Blackwell, one of the founders of Bristol Technology, a software company recently acquired by Hewlett-Packard; Mississippi Supreme Court justice James Graves; and the late General Louis Wilson, who enlisted in the Marine Corps in 1941 as a senior and went on to become commandant of the Marine Corps.

Fast Facts

Millsaps College is a four-year independent liberal arts college, founded in 1890 and affiliated with the United Methodist Church.

Web site

http://www.millsaps.edu/

Location

Jackson, Mississippi—200 miles south of Memphis.

Student Profile

1,003 undergraduate students (49% male, 51% female); 31 states and territories; 18% minority, 2% international.

Faculty Profile

90 full-time faculty. 11:1 student/faculty ratio. Average class size is 15.

Residence Life

Highly residential: 80% live on campus.

Athletics

NCAA Division III, SCAC Conference. 14 varsity sports (7 men's: baseball, basketball, cross-country, football, golf, soccer, tennis; 7 women's: basketball, cross-country, golf, soccer, softball, tennis, volleyball), 4 clubs, and 26 intramurals.

Academic Programs

Accounting; American studies; anthropology; art; biochemistry; biology; business; chemistry; Christian education; classical studies; computer science; economics; education; English; environmental studies; European studies; faith & work initiative; film studies; French; geology; German; history; human services; international studies; mathematics; music; philosophy; physics; political science; psychology; public management; religious studies; sociology; Spanish; teacher licensure; theatre; women's/gender studies; writing program.

Preprofessional programs in predental, preengineering, prelaw, premedical, and preministerial.

Costs and Aid

2006–2007: $22,032 comprehensive ($20,660 tuition). 96% of students receive some financial aid. Average award: $18,892 for students with financial need.

Endowment

$95,592,000.

More Distinctions

• Ranked in the top 100 liberal arts colleges by U.S. News's America's Best Colleges.

• Named as one of only 40 Colleges That Change Lives.

• Cited by Fiske Guide to Colleges as one of the "Small Colleges and Universities Strong in Business" and for "its focus on scholarly inquiry, spiritual growth, and community service."

Lees McRae College

NORTH CAROLINA

Located high in the Appalachian Mountains, Lees McRae College is a private, four-year, coeducational college affiliated with the Presbyterian Church (U.S.A.). Since 1900, the college has sought to educate the whole person: mind, body, and spirit.

Admissions Contact:

Lees McRae College
Banner Elk, NC 28604
Ph: (828) 898-5241
Fax: (828) 898-8814
Email: admissions@lmc.edu
www.lmc.edu

The 4 Distinctions

Engaged Students

With performance, technical theater, and management opportunities extended to students during their first year, the Lees-McRae College performing arts program has been one of the college's most successful programs. In addition, Lees-McRae offers extensive hands-on opportunities in unique fields such as wildlife biology, wildlife rehabilitation, athletic training, sport management, and communication arts. Whether working with student athletes in the trainer's clinic or rehabilitating a wounded great horned owl at the Blue Ridge Wildlife Institute, Lees-McRae students can expect to work in real-world situations early in their college careers.

Lees-McRae students have a number of opportunities to serve others. The school's intermediate Spanish class volunteered over 1,200 hours using their Spanish skills to teach English as a second language to migrant workers from Avery County. The college offers a variety of community-service opportunities, social-awareness weeks, and alternative spring-break trips. Service-learning courses are also available to students, incorporating community service into academics.

Internships, study abroad, and honors courses give students opportunities to gain skills and build a strong personal character. Community theaters, law-enforcement agencies, and hospitals are some of the many settings where Lees-McRae students can intern. The college encourages practical experience, and assists students in coordinating their ideal internship placement. Lees-McRae also provides students with the option of studying abroad, and in recent years, students have studied in England, Ireland, Scotland, France, Italy, Australia, Africa, Germany, and Nicaragua. Students enrolled in the honors program have a unique opportunity to live in the honors residence halls and take challenging courses together.

Great Teaching

A student to faculty ratio of twelve to one enables Lees-McRae to keep classroom sizes small. In addition, roughly 80 percent of the college's faculty and staff have a PhD or a terminal degree in their field, and prospective students can feel comfortable knowing that they will be educated by qualified professors who are highly motivated and dedicated to seeing each student succeed. It is not unusual to find professors' offices open beyond their scheduled office hours in order to further class discussions or to give a little extra help to those who may struggle with a difficult topic.

The education program at Lees-McRae promotes a holistic development of teachers. Lees-McRae consistently ranks number one in the percentage of student teachers licensed, overall GPA, and Praxis I test scores for all North Carolina education programs.

The Blue Ridge Wildlife Institute on campus annually cares for more than six hundred injured or orphaned wild animals from western North Carolina, providing wildlife rehabilitation/preveterinary science students with hands-on learning.

Vibrant Community

Located in the heart of the High Country in North Carolina, Lees-McRae's mountain campus offers limitless activities to outdoor enthusiasts of all levels. For those who are just looking for a nice place to relax and open a book, Lees-McRae's four-hundred-acre campus offers everything from rivers to open green spaces. On campus, there are many cultural and entertainment activities. Movies, comedians, various musical groups, and scholarly speakers make up just some of the activities that are sponsored by the college.

Lees-McRae fields eighteen intercollegiate sports teams, including a three-time Division II National Champion mountain-biking team. In the past several years, Lees-McRae athletic teams have won thirty-one Carolinas-Virginia Athletic Conference Championships. Intramural sports teams are also an option, and students can join in on the intramural fun through softball, soccer, flag football, billiards, tennis, and much more.

The region provides plenty of outdoor activities for students. Skiing, mountain biking, white-water rafting, and fly-fishing are readily available, and the famed Appalachian Trail passes a few miles from campus. Nearby attractions for students to enjoy include Linville Caverns, Linville Falls, and Wiseman's View. Lees-McRae's outdoor programs group provides students and the community with a series of outdoor educational experiences that exercise the mind, body, and soul of the student, while developing essential leadership and developmental skills vital to success in life.

It is not unusual to find members of the college community out serving the local community during their free time. Over the last year, members of the college volunteered a combined sixteen thousand hours of service in the local community.

Successful Outcomes

Some alumni see their career at Lees-McRae College as successful because of their success in law school. Others may consider their Lees-McRae experience successful because they have the skills to enter the job of their choice in the field of performing arts. Still more feel they are well prepared for careers in an ever-changing business world. Regardless of discipline, all Lees-McRae graduates will agree that their lives, not just their minds, were enriched. Dr. David Bushman, president of Lees-McRae College, summed up the mission of the college when he said, "Education is meant to change lives. . . . We'll prepare you for a life of engagement, and you'll develop the tools to live a life that matters, a life in which you can make a difference for others."

Fast Facts

Lees McRae College is a four-year, liberal arts college affiliated with the Presbyterian Church and founded in 1900.

Web site

http://www.lmc.edu

Location

Banner Elk, North Carolina—2.5 hours from Charlotte, North Carolina and Knoxville, Tennessee.

Student Profile

900 students (49% male, 51% female); 30 states and territories; 11% minority.

Faculty Profile

80% of faculty are full-time. 14:1 student/faculty ratio. Average class size is 15.

Residence Life

Highly residential: 78% of students live on campus.

Athletics

NCAA Division II, CVAC Conference. 18 varsity sports (9 men's: basketball, cross-country, cycling, golf, lacrosse, soccer, tennis, track & field, volleyball; 9 women's: basketball, cross-country, cycling, lacrosse, soccer, softball, tennis, track & field, volleyball), 0 club sports, and varying number of intramurals.

Academic Programs

Athletic training; biology (prehealth sciences, prevet, wildlife biology, wildlife rehabilitation); business administration (accounting, information systems, management, small business development); communication arts; criminal justice; elementary education; history; humanities; interdisciplinary studies; international studies; literature; mathematics; performing arts studies; physical education; psychology; religious studies; sociology; sport management; theater arts education.

Costs and Aid

2007–2008: $26,000 comprehensive ($19,500 tuition). 90% of students receive some financial aid.

Endowment

$20,062,954.

Meredith College

NORTH CAROLINA

Admissions Contact:

Meredith College
3800 Hillsborough Street
Raleigh, NC 27607-5298
800-MEREDITH
Ph: (919) 760-8600
Fax: (919) 760-2874
Email: admissions@meredith.edu
www.meredith.edu

Meredith College is one of the largest private women's colleges in the country. With a strong liberal arts tradition dating back to 1891, Meredith offers a rich program of undergraduate and graduate study in the vibrant environment of Raleigh, North Carolina, with its wealth of educational and research institutions.

The 4 Distinctions

Engaged Students

At the undergraduate level, Meredith offers more than fifty programs of study. Each major is grounded in a new general education curriculum that emphasizes interdisciplinary study, experiential learning, and global awareness.

One of every five Meredith College students takes part in the study-abroad program, an increase of more than 50 percent since 2001. Study-abroad coordinators work to customize the program to students' needs. Meredith offers exciting study-abroad opportunities, including humanities programs in Italy, Switzerland, and England; business, child development, interior design, women's studies, criminology, and biology programs in Denmark; science field research in Costa Rica; humanities programs in Austria; language and cultural studies programs in Spain; digital imaging programs in Italy; and fashion studies programs in France.

The most popular majors are biology, business, psychology, and interior design. The biology departments are housed in the eighty-thousand-square-foot Science and Mathematics Building, which includes a scanning electron microscope.

The college's interior design program is accredited by the Council for Interior Design Accreditation. Meredith's design program has many partnerships with the local design community and facilitates mentoring relationships, which provide students with exposure to the professional world.

The School of Business is working towards AACSB accreditation, the highest level of accreditation for business programs. The school offers a Masters of Business Administration degree, in addition to undergraduate majors in accounting, business administration, and economics.

Each of Meredith's academic departments includes an internship coordinator, and the career center also helps place students in internships. Meredith's close ties to the Environmental Protection Agency, TV and radio stations in the area, as well as many pharmaceutical and biotech companies often lead to student internship opportunities.

The undergraduate research program supports collaborative work with faculty across the curriculum. Students can also travel to conferences, receive stipends, and earn course credit for research. Meredith offers summer stipends for students who apply to work with faculty on a particular research endeavor. Meredith's annual Celebrating Student Achievement Day showcases student work. Recent projects have included research on rhetoric during the English Renaissance, theoretical molecules in chemistry, global inequality and political violence, and emerging leadership in girls and women.

Great Teaching

There are no teaching assistants at Meredith College. A student to faculty ratio of eleven to one allows students to get to know professors and work one-on-one on undergraduate research.

In 2001, Meredith College launched a laptop program that provides full-time students with a laptop computer at the beginning of their freshman year and then replaces it in their junior year.

The Meredith Autism Program (MAP) is a behaviorally based, early intervention program for preschool children with autism and pervasive developmental disorder (PDD). Offering both a clinical/research model and a workshop model, the program allows Meredith students to gain experience working with children with autism and PDD. Meredith students help children reach their potential through developing language, social, self-help, and motor skills.

The Carolinas Psychology Conference (CPC), which began in 1976, is sponsored by the department of psychology at Meredith College and by the department of psychology at North Carolina State University. The conference gives undergraduate students an opportunity to present the research they have been working on to other students and faculty members with similar interests in a comfortable but professional setting. Many future psychologists make their first research presentations at the CPC.

Meredith students benefit from the accomplishments of their professors. Recently, a Meredith College biology professor won a Fulbright fellowship to Kenya to study HIV and AIDS. This created the opportunity for a Meredith sophomore to work in the clinics, as well.

Vibrant Community

Meredith's 225-acre campus is located on the western edge of Raleigh, North Carolina, the state capital, near the Research Triangle, one of the country's leading research hubs. The college has 2,100 undergraduate students, 54.4 percent of whom live on campus. Raleigh itself is home to one hundred thousand college students from other institutions.

A lecture series in the 1,200-seat outdoor amphitheater next to the lake is open to the surrounding community. The venue also hosts concerts, guest speakers, and other special events in the fall and spring.

Meredith Votes is an all-campus, nonpartisan, voter education, voter registration, and voter turnout campaign. Led by students in Meredith's political science 941 course, Meredith Votes takes place each election year and often includes a series of voting education articles in the campus newspaper, a debate of presidential campaign issues between College Democrats and College Republicans, and a meet the candidates forum.

Meredith students also participate in LeaderShape, a nationally recognized leadership development program through which participants practice decision-making skills for ethical dilemmas, learn how to work in high-performance teams, discuss how to understand and respect one another's values, and clarify personal values and standards. Meredith is the first women's college and the first college in North Carolina to hold its own session of the LeaderShape Institute.

Many courses with service-learning elements are built into the curriculum, and most student organizations also make service projects a focus. For example, the student government has funded an emissions-free service project and other environmental awareness programs as part of its Campaign for a Greener Meredith. In the Meredith Reads program, students, faculty, alumni, and even the college president go into local schools each week for a semester-long service project.

Meredith students participating in alternative spring break service trips have traveled as far as Sri Lanka for tsunami relief and to Louisiana for Hurricane Katrina rebuilding programs.

Successful Outcomes

Some 96 percent of graduates find employment within six months of graduation. Nearly one quarter of graduates go on to graduate school. Meredith's career center offers programs for students starting in their freshman year, focusing on a holistic approach. The center offers mock interviews, resume workshops, networking events, career panels, and career fairs.

Meredith's sixteen thousand alumni tend to stay very close and connected. They often serve as mentors to students and provide them with internship opportunities.

Distinguished alumni include Silda Wall Spitzer, the current first lady of New York; Broadway performer and Tony award winner Beth Leavel; and longtime CNN anchor Judy Woodruff, who recently returned to PBS's The NewsHour with Jim Lehrer.

Fast Facts

Meredith College is a four-year private, independent, women's college founded in 1891.

Web site

http://www.meredith.edu

Location

Raleigh, North Carolina—the state's capital city, which with Durham and Chapel Hill makes up North Carolina's Research Triangle area.

Student Profile

2,015 undergraduate students (153 graduate students); 30 states, 16 countries, 13% out of state; 19% undergraduate multi-cultural population.

Faculty Profile

132 full-time faculty. 10:1 student/ faculty ratio. Average class size is 17.

Residence Life

Moderately residential: 54.4% of students live on campus.

Athletics

NCAA Division III, USA South athletic conference. 6 varsity sports (basketball, cross-country, soccer, softball, tennis, volleyball).

Academic Programs

Accounting; American/United States studies/civilization; art history criticism and conservation; art teacher education; biology/biological sciences; business administration/management; chemistry; child development; communications studies/speech communication & rhetoric; computer & Information sciences; computer science; dance; drama & dance teacher education; drama & dramatics/ theatre arts; economics; English language & literature; environmental science; environmental studies; family & consumer sciences/human sciences; fashion merchandising; fashion/apparel design; finance; fine/studio arts; French language & literature; graphic design; history; human resources; management/personnel administration; interior design; international business; international relations and affairs; kinesiology & exercise science; management science; marketing/marketing management; mass communications/ media studies; mathematics; molecular biology; music performance; music teacher education; physical education teaching & coaching; piano & organ; political science & government; predentistry studies; prelaw studies; premedicine/premedical studies; prepharmacy studies; preveterinary studies; psychology; religion/religious studies; social work; sociology; Spanish language & literature; sports & fitness administration/management; voice and opera.

Costs and Aid

2007–2008: $28,650 comprehensive ($22,350 tuition). In 2006-07 1,901 students received some form of financial assistance, totaling $28.2 million.

Endowment:

$78.5 million.

Salem College

Salem College is the oldest women's college in the country. Established in 1772 by the Moravian settlers who founded Salem, North Carolina, today the liberal arts college features state-of-the-art facilities, preserving many of the Moravian traditions while continuing to foster independence in women.

Admissions Contact:

Salem College
601 S. Church Street
Winston-Salem, North Carolina, 27101
(800) 32-SALEM
Ph: (336) 721-2600
Email: admissions@salem.edu
www.salem.edu

The 4 Distinctions

Engaged Students

The Salem Signature, an innovative, four-year series of courses, truly distinguishes Salem from other colleges. The Salem Signature leads students along a path of self-knowledge, community service, and career preparation, ensuring that graduates are fully equipped to excel in the world.

The first year of the Signature series is designed to facilitate self-discovery. By examining cross-cultural, gender, and societal issues, the student gains an understanding of the diversity of human experience. The sophomore year provides students with an appreciation of the community beyond the campus—its needs, resources, functions, and the roles of those involved in its well-being. This year includes a minimum of thirty hours of social service. The junior year is a journey into the world of work and career through credit-bearing internships and work opportunities. The senior year focuses on values, leadership, identity, and ethics.

The most popular majors at Salem are psychology, English, and sociology. The most distinctive is the not-for-profit major. All majors require an internship, facilitated by faculty through internship lists and by contact with alumni. Winston-Salem businesses include companies such as Sara Lee, Wachovia, and Krispy Kreme, and many Salem students intern at these companies. Premed students intern in local hospitals and emergency rooms. Communications students intern at various television and radio stations.

Salem's January term provides students with an opportunity to concentrate on one subject area of particular interest. During this month, students may enroll in travel programs, independent studies, internships, or courses on campus. Students also have the option of enrolling in courses or programs at other 4-1-4 institutions. Classes offered during the January term are more distinctive than those offered during the rest of the year, and some are team taught by two professors from different fields.

Recent on-campus courses have included classes on Cuba through the eyes of film and literature; unlocking the Da Vinci Code; the aftermath of disaster, which included a trip to the Gulf Coast region affected by Hurricane Katrina; Rastafarianism and social resistance in the Caribbean; and science fiction and photography. Recent travel courses have included study in Ireland, Italy, Mexico, China, and England.

Great Teaching

The faculty to student ratio at Salem College is thirteen to one, and the average class size is thirteen. Understanding that the best teachers are also committed to their own intellectual development, members of the faculty engage in continued professional development as educators and scholars. Salem College faculty pursue research in their fields of study and in the pedagogy of their disciplines. They lead creative and productive lives as they model for students the value of professional accomplishment, service, and leadership within and beyond the Salem community.

The college offers in-depth programming in three areas of distinction. The Center for Women Writers at Salem College provides an opportunity for writers to express their creativity in conversation; in workshops; in community and college courses; and through readings, lectures, and other special programs. The School of Music offers the Bachelor of Music degree in performance (with a concentration in flute, organ, piano, or voice), the Bachelor of Arts degree with a major in music, and a Bachelor of Arts degree with a double major consisting of the degree requirements in music together with those of another major. Women in Science and Mathematics (WISM) offers career counseling, group discussions, and trips to conferences, as well as a yearlong series of lectures open to the community.

Vibrant Community

Salem College's sixty-four-acre campus is located in the heart of downtown Winston-Salem in the Old Salem historic district. The eighteenth-century Moravian village of Salem is now an internationally recognized living history museum complex. The campus includes five buildings that date from the original town of Salem, and shares Salem Square with Old Salem and with Home Moravian Church (built in 1800).

The city of Winston-Salem offers a wide variety of cultural activities that Salem students enjoy. The city's performing-arts groups include the Winston-Salem Symphony and the Piedmont Opera Theatre. A short walk from Salem's campus, Winston-Salem's downtown has a vibrant arts and music scene featuring the Roger L.Stevens Center, a nationally recognized facility for the performing arts, as well as many restaurants, clubs, and galleries.

Within a few hours of campus are mountains for skiing, camping, or hiking; rivers for white-water rafting; and the beautiful beaches of North Carolina.

Salem College enrolls six hundred undergraduates. Students are required to live on campus all four years. There are two freshmen dorms, while upper-level students live in suite-style or apartment-style dorms.

There are more than fifty clubs on campus, including many multicultural, political, and religious groups. Salem also boasts six varsity sports in Division III athletics and three club sports.

The school has many special traditions, some of them dating back to the original Moravian community. Among them are a Christmas candlelight service; Fall Fest, when classes compete against one another to show school spirit; a Founder's Day celebration; Convocation Day; a Leadership Banquet; and the Fall Lawn, an annual party held on campus.

Salem also features a Big Sister/Little Sister program in which juniors adopt a freshman, offering an honorary introduction to the college and helping to facilitate the transition into college life. The program features a number of organized social activities, including a spring banquet for big and little sisters.

Successful Outcomes

Salem graduates have successful careers with companies such as BB&T Bank, Nike, JP Morgan-Chase, and other local organizations. Half of Salem alumnae go on to graduate school within five years.

The Salem College Alumnae Association, under the leadership of its own board and with the support of the alumnae office, fosters a spirit of continuing service, fellowship, and support of Salem College. It promotes active interest in the progress and welfare of Salem and enables the college to maintain educational and cultural relationships with alumnae.

Over nine thousand Salem College alumnae live in forty-nine states, two U.S. territories, and thirty-three foreign countries. They are successful in business, the media, international affairs, politics, education, medicine, science, the arts, and many other areas. Salem College alumnae have long been recognized for service to their communities.

Although Salem alumnae have chosen many paths, they share many common ties—the integrity of adhering to a cherished honor code, an excellent education received from caring and talented faculty, memories of being a part of Moravian traditions, and of course, that special bond of sisterhood with generations of Salem women.

Fast Facts

Salem College is a four-year college of liberal arts founded in 1772.

Web site

http://www.salem.edu

Location

Winston-Salem, North Carolina—20 minutes from Piedmont Triad International Airport in Greensboro.

Student Profile

600 traditional students; 28 states and territories; 25% minority, 18% international.

Faculty Profile

75 full-time faculty. 13:1 student/faculty ratio. Average class size is 13.

Residence Life

Highly residential: 80% of students live on campus.

Athletics

NCAA Division III, Association of Independents. 7 varsity sports (soccer, basketball, cross-country, softball, swimming, tennis, volleyball), 2 club sports (equestrian and field hockey).

Academic Programs

Accounting; American studies; art, art history; arts management; biology; business administration; chemistry; communication; creative writing; economics; English; French; German; history; interior design; international business; international relations; mathematics; medical technology; music; music education;

not-for-profit management; philosophy; psychology; religion; sociology; Spanish.

Special Programs: education licensure, honors program, preengineering, prelaw, premedicine, Salem signature, women in science & mathematics.

Costs and Aid

2007-2008: $28,900 comprehensive ($18,850 tuition). 75% of students receive some financial aid. Will meet 100% of demonstrated financial need.

Endowment

$47,450,334.

More Distinctions

• *Money magazine* has named Salem one of the top 10 "Best Buys" among women's colleges seven years in a row. (Salem was also ranked in the top 150 "Best Buys" for all colleges and universities in the U.S and one of the top 25 "Best Buys" among liberal arts colleges in the Southeast).

• Salem is one of the top "Character-building Colleges" in the nation by the John Templeton Foundation, in large part because of the unique Salem Signature program.

St. Andrews Presbyterian College

NORTH CAROLINA

St. Andrews Presbyterian College is a four-year, liberal arts and sciences college in the Sandhills Region of North Carolina. Known for its innovation and academic excellence, the college's unparalleled interdisciplinary curriculum is primarily discussion based, with small-group activities and projects rather than lecture-style classes.

Admissions Contact:

St. Andrews Presbyterian College
1700 Dogwood Mile
Laurinburg, NC 28372
(800) 763-0198
Email: admissions@sapc.edu
www.sapc.edu

The 4 Distinctions

Engaged Students

St. Andrews offers semester-abroad study programs in China, Ecuador, and Italy, as well as shorter trips to Greece, India, Cuba, Australia, and Vietnam, among other destinations. The college has formal exchange agreements with Kansai Gaidai University in Japan and with Hannam University in Korea. In addition, arrangements can be made for students to spend a semester at the University of St. Andrews in Scotland.

St. Andrews offers an excellent equestrian program that includes high-caliber instructional and competitive components. Students have the option of pursuing majors in therapeutic riding, therapeutic horsemanship, prevet, and equine business management, in addition to a minor in equine science. The academic program is known for its strong experiential component. Five of the six equine studies courses include extensive fieldwork. Students have the opportunity to participate in equine internships with some of the industry's top professionals, often leading to career opportunities after graduation.

St. Andrews offers a creative writing degree and encourages aspiring writers through the Chapbook publication, a writing contest open to juniors and seniors. The winner of the contest has his or her book published by the St. Andrews Press and receives fifty copies of the three hundred copies printed. Students can also publish original writing and photography in Gravity Hill or the Cairn, annual literary magazines that publish work by students and emerging writers outside the St. Andrews community.

Symposia provide a forum for the presentation and discussion of philosophical issues outside of the classroom through paper presentations by students, faculty, and visiting philosophers, and open discussion of those papers. Science and Religion Roundtable events quarterly examine the moral and ethical dilemmas of the future with guests, faculty, and students.

Great Teaching

At St. Andrews, the liberal arts provide undergraduates with the widest and most in-depth preparation for becoming global citizens. St. Andrews faculty have a passion for learning and a love for their disciplines. They are skilled interdisciplinary teachers who can move across intellectual divides. Students learn new ideas, different ways of thinking, and sharpen their means for intellectual engagement, all with the support of St. Andrews faculty.

Faculty work to ensure that students claim ownership of their learning. Faculty and students create an intellectual community for the exchange of ideas and the development of critical thinking, and employ many different writing, research, and problem-solving techniques. Through academic advising, faculty support students as they develop interest in a major and find their fit in the St. Andrews community.

St. Andrews offers an honors program with its own series of special courses for exceptional students. Students invited to participate in this program join a rowdy group of scholarly peers tackling controversial topics as they learn to find their own voices, both verbally and in writing. The honors program curriculum includes an integrative capstone seminar, which calls for students to prepare and defend a thesis related to their major.

Student mentors help first-year students navigate academic expectations and requirements. They also work under the direction of the Quest 1 faculty advisers to support first-year students.

The St. Andrews campus is home to an impressive Scottish Heritage Center, which houses a collection of old and rare books of Scottish and Scottish-American history, genealogy, and culture, as well as current scholarly titles and periodicals. The center also houses exhibitions of the Scottish settlement of southeastern North Carolina and sponsors a number of concerts, lectures, and other events, including the annual Charles Bascombe Shaw Memorial Scottish Heritage Symposium. The archive for the Thistle and Shamrock, a popular National Public Radio program heard nationwide, is stored at the center. It is the largest collection of Celtic music of its type in the United States. St. Andrews proudly sponsors its own competitive pipe band, bringing pipers and drummers from all over the world to pursue their education.

Vibrant Community

Education at St. Andrews goes beyond the curriculum. Students have the opportunity to participate in all kinds of campus activities. Opportunities include serving as a first-year mentor; volunteering on a Habitat for Humanity project; participating in Christian Student Fellowship; completing faculty-guided research projects; singing on tour with the college choir; acting in a theater production; editing publications for the St. Andrews Press, the yearbook, or the student newspaper; competing as part of an NCAA Division II athletic team; tutoring local school children; or working as residence assistant.

On-campus clubs and organizations focus on everything from academic interests to pure fun. They include the psychology and physical therapy clubs, music and art groups, cycling and volleyball, and even rugby and paintball, as well as the Writers' Forum.

St. Andrews is residency required, with about eight hundred students on campus, hailing from forty-six of the fifty states and fourteen foreign countries, creating a wonderfully diverse and exciting student body. The college has an award-winning pipe band, a seven-time national champion equestrian team, twenty-one NCAA Division II athletic teams, a state-of-the-art Electronic Fine Arts Center, multimedia art facilities, and a multidisciplinary science lab the size of a soccer arena.

St. Andrews is located on a 640-acre campus in Laurinburg, North Carolina, just two hours from spectacular mountains, magnificent beaches, and major metropolitan cities. The campus includes a seventy-acre lake in the middle of campus and a three-hundred-acre equestrian facility.

Successful Outcomes

Each year the college conducts an outcomes survey of recent graduates. Over the last decade, the placement rate for graduates has exceeded 96 percent. This is an impressive rate and an indicator that the educational program at St. Andrews prepares graduates for the rigor of graduate school and professions. Within six months, 98 percent of graduates are employed or in graduate school. St. Andrews has an alumni network all over the world, and graduates are successful in entering professional programs in medicine and health, law, veterinary medicine, and engineering.

Fast Facts

St. Andrews Presbyterian College is located in southeastern North Carolina, in Laurinburg, a community of 18,000 people.

Web site

http://www.sapc.edu/

Student Profile

808 students (38% male, 62% female); 28 states and territories, 14 countries; 17.9% minority.

Faculty Profile

42 full-time faculty, 41 part-time. 13:1 student/faculty ratio. Average class size of 15-20.

Residence Life

Highly residential: 92% of students live on campus. 8 residence halls with rooms arranged in suites that accommodate 12 to 16 students. One hall under renovation, opening Fall 08.

Athletics

NCAA Division II, CVAC Conference. 21 varsity sports (11 men's: baseball, basketball, cross-country, golf, lacrosse, soccer, swimming, tennis, track & field, volleyball, wrestling; 10 women's: basketball, cross-country, golf, lacrosse, soccer, softball, swimming, tennis, track & field, volleyball).

Academic Programs

Accounting; applied ministries; art; art therapy; biochemistry; biology; business administration; business management; chemistry; computer science; communication; creative writing; economics; elementary education k-6; engineering; English; finance; history; international business management; management and information technology; marketing; mathematics; philosophy; physical education; politics; psychology; religious studies; sport and recreation management; sports management, theatre arts; therapeutic horsemanship & therapeutic horsemanship business management.

Costs and Aid

2007–2008: $26,184 comprehensive ($18,192 tuition). 90% of students receive some form of financial aid.

Endowment

$12.8 million. Alumni giving: 21%.

More Distinctions

• St. Andrews Presbyterian College is one of only twenty colleges in the mid-Atlantic region identified by Washington Post education reporter Jay Matthews as "hidden gems." St. Andrews is also featured in Matthews' new book Harvard Schmarvard: Getting Beyond the Ivy League to the College that is Best for You.

Warren Wilson College

NORTH CAROLINA

Warren Wilson College is a small liberal arts college in the Blue Ridge Mountains of western North Carolina. A "work college," it bases its curriculum around the Triad Education Program, which encourages a student focus on academics, work, and service.

Admissions Contact:

Warren Wilson College
P.O. Box 9000
Asheville, NC 28815
(800) 934-3536
Ph: (828) 771-2073
Email: admit@warren-wilson.edu
www.warren-wilson.edu

The 4 Distinctions

Engaged Students

One unique feature of the college is that all students work fifteen hours a week on any of more than one hundred campus work crews. This student work helps defray the cost of room and board. One of the largest work crews runs Warren Wilson's farm, which was recently named Outstanding Conservation Farm Family for the mountain region of North Carolina. Other students work in office jobs or on other outdoor crews such as forestry.

About 70 percent of Warren Wilson's students take part in the Warren Wilson Worldwide program, which provides a cross-cultural field experience. Recent destinations have included Japan, Korea, Ireland, Mexico, Vietnam, Thailand, and New Zealand.

All students are expected to complete at least one hundred hours of community service before graduating. Service projects in the local community have included helping to clean up a local center for domestic violence, performing stream renovation, working in a food bank, and volunteering at a Presbyterian home for children. Students have also worked at soup kitchens in Washington, D.C., and in New York City, and some have traveled several times to the Gulf Coast to help rebuild homes destroyed by Hurricane Katrina.

Internships are offered through the college's Environmental Leadership Center and the career services office. The most popular internships focus on conservation work with a variety of governmental agencies and nonprofit organizations.

Students in the sciences conduct their own research under the direction of a mentoring professor. They regularly present the results of their research at the annual conference of the North Carolina Academy of Science, where Warren Wilson students have won more awards than students from any other school in the state.

Warren Wilson is closely affiliated with the North Carolina chapter of Outward Bound, located on the western edge of campus, so many students experience an Outward Bound course during their undergraduate years. In addition, the Warren Wilson Worldwide Program offers an Outward Bound course as one of their study-abroad options.

Great Teaching

Warren Wilson's average class size is fourteen students. First-year and transfer students take part in a first-year seminar featuring small groups of students. The goal of these seminars is to help students develop their learning, research, and problem-solving skills. Recent first-year seminar topics have included courses on great trials throughout history and on Caribbean literature.

The most popular majors at Warren Wilson are environmental studies, art, and biology. The school has developed a specialized double major that pairs Spanish with studies in psychology, outdoor leadership, or art. Through a partnership with one of the largest private universities in Mexico, students receive bilingual training in these fields.

Warren Wilson students engage in deep, significant learning. An abiding commitment to the liberal arts provides a curriculum that challenges students while expanding their minds and creating a foundation for lifelong study. Professors come from the nation's top graduate schools, including Duke, Harvard, Northwestern, Stanford, UC-Berkeley, and Yale. The liberal arts focus encourages students to explore various fields of study before choosing from 41 majors and concentration areas, and 26 minors. Choices can be broadened further with several dual degree programs, including Forestry and Environmental Management with Duke University, and a special concentration in Pre-Peace Corps, International and Non-Government service.

Programs of distinction flourish throughout the curriculum:

• Discovery Through Wilderness, International Field Study, and Peace Studies.

• The Environmental Studies curriculum, one of the longest-standing programs in the country, recently featured in the National Wildlife Federation's Campus Yearbook.

• The Outdoor Leadership Program, focusing on education, facilitation, and experiential learning, which partners closely with the North Carolina Outward Bound School and the Nantahala Outdoor Center, the nation's leading whitewater rafting organization.

Vibrant Community

The 1,100-acre campus includes six hundred acres of forest and three hundred acres of farmland. Roughly 90 percent of Warren Wilson's students live in college-owned housing. Living-and-learning residences include a wellness dorm, which focuses on promoting healthy decisions, and physical and mental well-being; and the EcoDorm, a live-in educational facility that models energy-efficient designs and renewable-energy sources. Warren Wilson students were heavily involved in the conception and planning of the 36-bed residence hall.

A sense of community is one of the main reasons students give for choosing Warren Wilson College. The college's academics, work, and service philosophy, seamlessly integrated into its environmental commitment, creates a natural connection between students, faculty, and staff. Each student has an important voice, and helps to shape campus life and college policies. Forums abound for finding a voice, through the Student Caucus, Community Meetings, and other venues. Many faculty and staff live on campus, as educators deeply committed to overseeing internships, helping with individual study, assisting research, and taking students to conferences.

Life at Warren Wilson is rich and diverse, with a range of clubs and organizations, student and faculty readings, and guest speakers. The college has an abundance of visiting writers and musicians due to the Master of Fine Arts Program for Writers and The Swannanoa Gathering. The college's theater offers half a dozen productions annually, and many musical events enliven campus life. Notable environmental speakers are frequent visitors to campus.

Warren Wilson has been featured in Outside Magazine for its ready access to outdoor activities. The outdoor programs office offers trips and technical skills workshops. Activities available include backpacking, day hiking, cycling, running, rock climbing, bouldering, caving, surfing, snowboarding, skiing, canoeing, kayaking, and rafting. Most of these activities are organized and facilitated by student trip leaders who are trained and certified as wilderness first responders, as well as having backgrounds in leading and teaching groups in an outdoor setting.

Successful Outcomes

Warren Wilson produces a high number of professionals, particularly in environmental education, service professions, social work, and teaching. The college's alumni work in almost every field, from urban planning to veterinary medicine. Warren Wilson alumni include Tony Earley, author of "Jim the Boy," musician David Wilcox, perinatal physician Dr. Anne Graham Masters, and songwriter Billy Edd Wheeler, who has written many chart hits including "Jackson" by Johnny Cash and June Carter. Alumni satisfaction with Warren Wilson is demonstrated by the high rate of alumni giving.

An average of 17 percent of Warren Wilson graduates begin advanced study each year at respected institutions around the world. Through research practices provided by the Warren Wilson experience, students have the tools crucial for entering these programs.

Fast Facts

Warren Wilson College, founded in 1894, is a four-year, liberal arts college affiliated with the Presbyterian Church.

Web site

http://www.warren-wilson.edu

Location

Asheville, North Carolina—about 2 hours west of Charlotte, North Carolina.

Student Profile

838 students (38% male, 62% female); 44 states and territories; 5% minority, 4% international.

Faculty Profile

62 full-time faculty. 12:1 student/faculty ratio. Average class size is 16.

Residence Life

Highly residential: 90% of students live on campus.

Athletics

United States Collegiate Athletic Association. 12 varsity sports (6 men's: basketball, soccer, cross-country, mountain biking, canoe & kayak, swimming; 6 women's: basketball, soccer, cross-country, mountain biking, canoe & kayak, swimming), 3 club sports, and other intramurals.

Academic Programs

Art; biology; business administration & economics; chemistry; creative writing; education; English; environmental studies; global studies; history & political science; humanities; integrative studies; mathematics; outdoor leadership; philosophy; psychology; religious studies; social work; sociology/anthropology; Spanish; women's studies.

Costs and Aid

2007–2008: $25,384 comprehensive ($21,384 tuition). 90% of students receive some financial aid. Average award: $12,374.

Endowment

$35 million.

More Distinctions

• Chosen to receive the 2006 Campus Sustainability Achievement Award by the Association for the Advancement of Sustainability in Higher Education.

• Named a Best Buy in the 2008 Fiske Guide to Colleges.

• Cited as a leading school, and the only school in North Carolina, in more than one category in the National Wildlife Federation report, State of the Campus Environment: A National Report Card on Environmental Performance and Sustainability in Higher Education.

• One of six four-year work colleges in the United States, and one of only two that require each residential student to work at least fifteen hours per week.

• Ranked as one of the Best 366 Colleges by the Princeton Review's college guidebook

Western Carolina University

NORTH CAROLINA

Western Carolina University (WCU), a campus of the University of North Carolina system, is a public, coeducational, four-year university focused on scholarship, teaching, and learning, with an emphasis on engagement. Founded in 1889, Western now serves almost nine thousand students from North Carolina, forty-six other states, and thirty-nine countries.

Admissions Contact:

Western Carolina University
Office of Admissions
102 Camp Building
Cullowhee. NC 28723
(877) WCU-4-YOU
Ph: (828) 227-7317
Fax: (828) 227-7319
Email: admiss@wcu.edu
www.wcu.edu

The 4 Distinctions

Engaged Students

Most of WCU's academic programs include a strong element of experiential learning, including internships, co-ops, and other activities that allow students to apply what they learn in class to experiences that build both competence and confidence.

For example, engineering students have worked with a local surgeon to develop knee replacement devices. Marketing students develop direct sales plans for local businesses. Education majors are required to serve in partnering schools, first as observers, and later as interns for a year as they prepare for licensure. Nursing students are required to practice their skills under supervision in various clinical settings. Radio- and television- production majors have access to network-quality equipment used by some of the nation's most advanced broadcasters, equipment they use to operate the campus TV station and an FM radio station, serving both the campus and the surrounding community. Forensic anthropology students will soon have the opportunity to work at Western's new decomposition research station, only the second in the nation.

Western also encourages students, faculty, and staff to become involved in service to the community by volunteering on projects such as Habitat for Humanity, Relay for Life, the annual river cleanup, holiday toy collection, domestic- and child-abuse prevention efforts, and more. Western's new service-learning department helps to coordinate volunteer activities with area nonprofit agencies, and recognizes outstanding achievement with annual service awards.

Great Teaching

Students are attracted not only by the university's vibrant Honors College and WCU's wide range of academic programs but also by Western's small class sizes, close interaction with faculty, and beautiful mountain campus.

Western offers more than 120 areas of undergraduate study in the arts and performing arts, sciences, business, education, health and human services, technology, and humanities. Among the most popular and fastest-growing majors are construction management, forensic anthropology, engineering, security and protective services, motion picture and television production, athletic training, and entrepreneurship. The university also maintains a strong tradition of excellence in business administration, teacher education, and nurse preparation.

Western's faculty includes nationally and internationally recognized experts in business, education, environmental science, television production, motion-picture production, and electronic-music production, as well as winners of Emmy, O. Henry, and National Endowment for the Arts awards.

Generous endowments have allowed Western to attract distinguished professors in more than a dozen areas, including engineering, commercial and electronic music, elementary and middle grades education, special education, business innovation, gerontological social work, construction management, regional economic development, advanced optics manufacturing, Appalachian culture, musical theatre, educational technologies, Cherokee studies, communication disorders, environmental science, physical therapy, and nurse anesthesia.

The university's tightly knit and rapidly growing Honors College offers a focused living and learning environment for more than one thousand high-achieving students seeking advanced academic challenges, more choices for independent study, and extra help in preparing for prestigious national awards and for professional schools of medicine, dentistry, physical therapy, optometry, and veterinary medicine.

For the past few years, Western has ranked in the top twenty in the number of papers accepted at the National Conference on Undergraduate Research. In 2006, Western arrived with the second highest number of participants from any school in the country. The thirty-one students invited from Western to this year's conference presented their findings on such topics as the genetics of river cane; microorganisms in elk; Cherokee dyes; the death penalty; the works of Emerson, Plato, Gunter Grass, and Milton; the politics of U.S. House races, and more. Western ranked eighth among the nation's colleges in the number of student abstracts accepted to the prestigious conference.

Vibrant Community

Located in a beautiful valley between the Great Smoky and Blue Ridge mountains, Western is uniquely positioned to offer the advantages of a safe and friendly community with a thriving focus on outdoor recreational activities such as hiking, biking, rafting, and climbing, along with research possibilities on air and water quality, environmental sciences and geosciences, the habitat and well-being of wildlife populations, the heritage of the Southern Appalachians, the culture of the Cherokee, and much more.

The university itself recently doubled in size to about six hundred acres with the addition of the Milliennial Campus, which will serve as a multiuse neighborhood with a mix of academic buildings, research facilities, business, industry, and housing. The area will become a "knowledge enterprise zone" where university, private industry, and government partners conduct research and development into scientific and technological innovations that have commercial applications. Students are expected to be involved in some aspect of every venture.

WCU's campus is residential: most of the first-year undergraduates live in university housing, as do half of the rest of the student body. Housing options include coed and single-sex residence halls; apartments for married students; and Greek, honors, special-interest, and international housing. There are dozens of on-campus organizations and clubs focused on students' interests, including the arts, zoology, fraternities and sororities, leadership and student government, artistic and musical performances, faith communities, health and wellness, intramural and club sports, and service learning.

With the opening of its Fine and Performing Arts Center, Western has become a cultural destination for the region. The center features a one-thousand-seat performance hall designed for world-class music, theater, dance, and literary performances by talented faculty, students, and guest artists, and has enjoyed mostly sold-out shows since it opened. A separate wing of the center houses state-of-the art classrooms, labs, and studios, as well as a fine art museum with nearly ten thousand square feet of exhibit space for its permanent and guest collections.

Successful Outcomes

Western is well-known for the caliber of its graduates, who typically score well above average on state and national exams for professions such as teaching, nursing, public accounting, construction management, and project management. WCU students also qualify for entry into graduate and professional schools of all kinds.

Famous alumni include Brad Hoover, a member of the NFL's Carolina Panthers football team; Frances Owl-Smith, the first female member of the Eastern Band of Cherokee to earn a medical degree; Michelle Hicks, principal chief of the Eastern Band of Cherokee; and Tony White, whose company accelerated the race to decode the human genome.

WCU is accredited by the Commission on Colleges of the Southern Association of Colleges and Schools, holds twenty-one separate program accreditations, and is a member of more than thirty state and national associations and organizations.

Fast Facts

Western Carolina University, a University of North Carolina campus, is a four-year, residential, coeducational university, founded in 1889.

Web site

http://www.wcu.edu/

Location

Cullowhee, North Carolina—52 miles west of Asheville, North Carolina.

Student Profile

8,665 (46% male, 54% female); 46 states, 39 foreign countries.

Faculty Profile

433 full-time faculty. 14:1 student/faculty ratio. Average freshman class size is 23.

Residence Life

42% of students live on campus.

Athletics

NCAA Division I, Southern Conference. 14 varsity sports (6 men's: baseball, basketball, cross-country, football, golf, track & field; 8 women's: basketball, cross-country, golf, track & field, soccer, softball, tennis, volleyball).

Academic Programs

Anthropology; art/fine arts; art education; athletic training; biology; business administration and law; chemistry; clinical laboratory sciences; communication; communication sciences & disorders; computer information systems; computer science; construction management; criminal justice; electrical and computer engineering technology; electrical engineering; emergency management; emergency medical care; engineering technology; English; English education; entrepreneurship; environmental health; environmental sciences; finance; forensic science; geology; health information administration; history; hospitality & tourism management; humanities; interior design; international business; management; marketing; mathematics; mathematics education; motion picture & television production; music; music education; natural resources management; nursing; nutrition & dietetics; parks & recreation management; philosophy; physical education; political science; psychology; science education; social sciences; social sciences education; social work; sociology; Spanish; Spanish education; special education; speech & theatre arts; sport management; teacher education (B-K, elementary & middle grades); theatre; recreational therapy.

Costs and Aid

2007–2008: $12,305 in-state comprehensive ($2,028 tuition); $22,488 out-of-state comprehensive ($11,611 tuition). 74% of students receive some financial aid. Average award: $7,525.

Endowment

Approximately $30,030,000.

Anderson University

SOUTH CAROLINA

Affiliated with the South Carolina Baptist Convention, Anderson University (AU) is a comprehensive, private, coeducational, liberal arts university offering a high-quality education in a Christian environment. Founded in 1911, it is located in the upstate region of South Carolina, near the foothills of the Appalachian Mountains.

Admissions Contact:

Anderson University
316 Boulevard
Anderson, South Carolina, 29621
(800) 542-3594
Pam Bryant, Director of Admissions
Ph: (864) 231-2032
Email: pbryant@andersonuniversity.edu
www.andersonuniversity.edu

The 4 Distinctions

Engaged Students

Anderson University offers more than fifty majors and other academic programs. The most popular majors are elementary and early childhood education, graphic/interior design, business, biology, and Christian ministries. AU's education majors make up one-third of the student body, and the education program is consistently ranked in the top two among South Carolina's public and private universities.

Most majors at Anderson require participation in internship programs. Beginning in their freshman year, education students benefit from field experience in local public classrooms. Business school internships take advantage of the university's close proximity to the national headquarters for Michelin and BMW, and human resource management students participate in programs at Bosch, a large local manufacturer.

Great Teaching

AU's core values espouse personal attention and genuine Christian committment, while focusing consistently on teaching, building a caring community, and upholding rigorous academic standards. In addition to topical classes that introduce them to college academics, students take two religion courses as part of their general education.

Anderson University professors have a student-focused approach, encouraging an open forum to create an individualized learning experience. They are committed to helping students develop and grow intellectually, physically, socially, morally, and spiritually. While the faculty's principal emphasis is on teaching, most also are also engaged in research in their fields.

When they arrive at Anderson, freshmen are paired with mentoring professors. This highly successful advising and mentoring program allows for the formation of close relationships, many of which develop into local research and other joint projects.

In addition, Anderson University's campus is designed to encourage faculty-student interaction. The Cohesive Coffeehouse features regular musical performances by student and local groups in a comfortable setting, where students, faculty, and staff enjoy coffee and dessert.

Vibrant Community

In 1911, the town of Anderson wanted a Christian college to operate in the community. Almost one hundred years later, the university exceeds early expectations. In addition to hosting many civic events that bring students and the local community together, more than 50 percent of Anderson students participate in community-service projects.

Many of these are fostered by the campus ministries department. Its numerous clubs and activities focus on public service, continuously demonstrating and reinforcing the school's strong community bond. Anderson also regularly takes groups of athletes into local public schools, while other students participate in Habitat for Humanity area initiatives. In addition, the campus worship center features different speakers each week, often Anderson alumni working as missionaries.

Anderson offers an intimate, welcoming environment in which students can explore the possibilities and mature in their own unique way while having fun. A Christ-centered education provides additional opportunities for personal growth through emphasis on service to others. Regardless of personal religious affiliation, community service provides double value to each student as an individual: first and foremost is the value it provides to the community, to individuals in need and to society as a whole. But beyond that, personal growth is dependent on experiences that expose students to people from different walks of life and from other cultures. Anderson University students have a great opportunity to make a difference in the community, and many who go on to successful careers in service-oriented professions found their future through volunteer activities during their college years.

The Student Development department at Anderson University is concerned with programs for students outside the classroom. Anderson University's faculty and staff are committed to assisting students as they strive to develop intellectually, physically, socially, morally, and spiritually. The University provides a comprehensive program of student development. All activities and programs are designed to help students to have positive and rewarding personal growth experience while at Anderson University.

Successful Outcomes

Anderson graduates frequently find employment in the surrounding area. Based on their practice teaching and other experiences in the local schools, education majors enjoy a natural fit in the community. Anderson places 100 percent of its education graduates in both public and private school positions.

Biology and art students, too, find a local niche in the area's thriving research and artistic communities. Of the students that apply to graduate schools, 90 percent are accepted to the institution of their choice.

After graduation, Anderson alumni continue to be strongly involved in the school. The university's new slogan, "Knowledge for the journey," reflects students' and graduates' shared commitment to a life mission, whether in ministry or the professions.

"Anderson University seeks to be a premier place of learning that combines the best of the liberal arts and professional education in a distinctly Christian community. You see it in the success that is achieved there."

-Colleges of Distinction

Fast Facts

Anderson University is a comprehensive university located in Anderson, South Carolina, established in 1911.

Web site

http://www.andersonuniversity.edu

Location

Anderson, South Carolina—35 miles south of Greenville, 132 miles from Columbia.

Student Profile

1,750 undergraduate students (40% male, 60% female); 16% out-of-state; 3% international.

Faculty Profile

80 full-time faculty. 65% hold a terminal degree in their field. 13:1 student/faculty ratio.

Residence Life

Moderately residential: 65% of students live on campus.

Athletics

NCAA Division II, Carolinas Conference. 16 varsity sports (8 men's: baseball, basketball, cross-country, golf, soccer, tennis, track & field, wrestling ; 8 women's: basketball, cross-country, golf, soccer, softball, tennis, track & field, volleyball).

Academic Programs

Accounting; art/art studies; art teacher education; business administration/management; ceramic arts & ceramics; Christian studies; communications & media studies; creative writing; criminal justice/law enforcement administration; drama & dramatics/theatre arts; drawing; elementary education & teaching; English language & literature; English/language arts teacher education; finance; fine/studio arts; graphic design; health & physical education; health/health care administration/management; history; history teacher education; human resources management/personnel administration; interior design; management information systems; marketing/marketing management; mass communications/media studies; mathematics; mathematics teacher education; music/music & performing arts studies; music performance; music teacher education; painting; physical education teaching & coaching; psychology; public relations/image management; religion/religious studies; religious/sacred music; social studies teacher education; Spanish language & literature; special education.

Costs and Aid

2007–2008: $24,600 comprehensive ($16,600 tuition). 91% of students receive some financial aid. Average award: $ 7,280.

Endowment

$17 million.

More Distinctions

• America's Best Christian Colleges.

College of Charleston

SOUTH CAROLINA

The College of Charleston is a public liberal arts and sciences university located in the heart of historic Charleston, South Carolina. Founded in 1770, its mission remains to provide a superior quality undergraduate education at an affordable price for its ten thousand students.

Admissions Contact:

College of Charleston
66 George Street
Charleston, SC 29424
(800) 960-5940
Ph: (843) 805-5507
Fax: (843) 953-6322
Email: admissions@cofc.edu
www.cofc.edu

The 4 Distinctions

Engaged Students

At the College of Charleston, learning is not confined to the classroom. Students are encouraged to study abroad, participate in independent research projects, and engage in experiential learning opportunities that typically would be available only at the graduate level. Opportunities provided by the city of Charleston and its environs are essential components of a College of Charleston education. Students can take advantage of a beautifully preserved historic city, a vibrant arts community, a diverse natural environment, an innovative business climate, and a consortium of area schools.

Service-learning courses allow students to learn through meaningful work with the community. Students' hands-on experiences help others and make classroom theory real and applicable to daily life. Service-learning opportunities change each year, but some examples of service-learning courses offered at the College include Exploration in Community Involvement and Global Awareness, Clinical Education Experience in Athletic Training, and Social Gerontology. A variety of volunteer opportunities also are available to College of Charleston students.

The College offers several study-abroad options, including semester and summer programs, bilateral exchanges, and independent-study programs. Each year, the College's Center for International Education (CIE) offers six semester-long, faculty-led study-abroad programs in places ranging from Santiago, Chile, to La Rochelle, France, to Havana, Cuba. The College also offers a consortium program at Annot, France.

Great Teaching

The College of Charleston is first and foremost a teaching institution. Its low student to faculty ratio of thirteen to one allows students to work closely with nationally recognized faculty and to be valued as an integral part of the College's close-knit community of scholars. As a member of the Council of Public Liberal Arts Colleges (COPLAC), the College of Charleston is committed to its focus on teaching. In fact, the college has capped enrollment at ten thousand undergraduate students, ensuring that classes remain small.

The College of Charleston offers more than forty majors; the school's most popular majors are business and economics, education, and arts. The College also boasts a strong program in biochemistry and a well-regarded Honors College that draws 6.5 percent of College of Charleston's students. Building on it founding principles, the College has rigorous general education requirements, supporting its liberal arts context. All students must take at least two years of a foreign language. The school offers thirteen different languages and numerous cultural studies programs, reflecting the College of Charleston's global focus and international orientation. In addition to modern languages, the College offers two majors in Classics: an AB degree for students whose primary interest is the study of Greek and Latin, and a BA degree, which focuses on Greek and Roman culture and civilization.

Undergraduate research and creative projects are encouraged at the College. Faculty members serve as mentors to students, and funding is available through competitive grants. Science, theater, sociology, and Spanish majors alike take advantage of these grants. Many projects utilize Charleston—a modern, urban, and historically significant city—as a living and learning laboratory.

Vibrant Community

The College of Charleston is the oldest institution of higher education in South Carolina and the thirteenth-oldest in the country. Founded in 1770—three of its founders were signers of the Declaration of Independence—it became a state college in 1970. Its fifty-two-acre campus, outlined by herringbone-patterned brick sidewalks, is located in historic Charleston, also known as the Holy City. In addition to its historic significance and beauty, Charleston is an important seaport and has a population of about one hundred thousand. Spoleto Festival USA, the world-renowned cultural festival, is held in Charleston every spring, highlighting a wide range of the performing arts. The College hosts dozens of performances each year, as well.

About 15 percent of the College's ten thousand students are from an area within one hundred miles of Charleston, and while no more than 38 percent are from outside South Carolina, they represent fifty-two states and territories and seventy-five foreign countries. There are approximately 150 student groups and clubs on campus, as well as fraternities and sororities. The College's athletes compete at the Division I level, and the sailing, crew, basketball, soccer, golf, and equestrian teams are especially strong.

College of Charleston students can choose from a variety of residential options, including a living and learning community for honors students in an historic house with a seminar room and study area. In keeping with the College's strong sense of tradition, many buildings on campus are listed on the National Register of Historic Places. Another traditional touch is the graduation dress code: men wear summer tuxedos and women wear white dresses and carry bouquets of red roses.

College of Charleston students explore the world beyond Charleston, participating in alternative spring-break service projects such as helping the homeless in Chicago, doing environmental work in Seattle, and working with schools in the Dominican Republic. Closer to home, CofC students and faculty work together in the Charleston community on service projects such as the annual MLK Challenge.

Successful Outcomes

Many College of Charleston alumni are willing to offer career assistance and advice to students through the College's Career Center. The Career Mentor Network allows students to connect with alumni to gather information about a particular position or field, including required skills and information on the employment market in a variety of geographical areas. Students can supplement their academic transcript with a cocurricular record of campus involvement and activities to showcase their skills and expertise when applying for jobs and graduate programs.

The Higdon Student Leadership Center provides programs that create opportunities for student involvement and learning through individual and group leadership activities. One such program, Leadership College of Charleston, gives thirty junior and senior student leaders, selected through a competitive application and interview process, the opportunity to meet monthly with one another and to meet local and state leaders to discuss issues facing them as future leaders of society, communities, and corporations. The opportunity to network with off-campus leaders creates opportunities to explore internship and employment possibilities.

Fast Facts

College of Charleston is a four-year public liberal arts and sciences university founded in 1770.

Web site

www.cofc.edu

Location

Charleston, South Carolina—on the coast, 116 miles from Columbia, South Carolina; 322 miles from Atlanta, Georgia; 238 miles from Jacksonville, Florida

Student Profile

9,820 undergraduate students (36% male, 64% female); 52 states and territories, 75 countries, 10% minority, 2% international.

Faculty Profile

522 full-time faculty, 13:1 student/faculty ratio. Average class size is 20.

Residence Life

Moderately residential: 30% of students live on campus.

Athletics

NCAA Division I, Southern Conference, 19 varsity sports, 8 men's and 11 women's teams, 20 club sports, and 23 intramurals.

Academic Programs

Accounting; anthropology; art history; arts management; athletic training; biochemistry; biology; BS with dentistry emphasis; BS with medicine emphasis; business administration; chemistry; classical studies; communication; computer information systems; computer science; discovery informatics; early childhood education; economics; elementary education; English; French; geology; German, historic preservation & community planning; history; hospitality & tourism management; international business; Latin American & Caribbean studies; marine biology; mathematics; middle level education; music; philosophy; physical education; physics; political science; psychology; religious studies; sociology; Spanish; special education; studio art; theatre; urban studies.

Costs and Aid

2006–2007: $16,728 in-state comprehensive (7,234 tuition). 26,728 out-of-state comprehensive; ($16,800 tuition). 59% of full-time undergraduates who applied for need-based aid were awarded it. Average full-time undergraduate need-based award: $2,866.

Endowment

$54,430,000.

More Distinctions

• The Fiske Guide to Colleges includes CofC as one of the nation's best and most interesting colleges.

• Newsweek named the college as one of the country's most interesting schools.

Converse College

SOUTH CAROLINA

Converse College is a four-year, private, liberal arts college for women, founded in 1889. Converse's mission is to shape young women of today into leaders of tomorrow by fostering exploration, discovery, commitment, and vision. Converse aims to prepare students for lifelong learning, leadership, and service.

Admissions Contact:

Converse College
580 East Main Street
Spartanburg, SC 29302
(800)766-1125
Ph: (864) 596-9000
Email: info@converse.edu
www.converse.edu

The 4 Distinctions

Engaged Students

Study abroad experiences are an important aspect of Converse students' experiences. Study abroad is used to complement learning, and many courses include study-travel opportunities. These trips, led by Converse faculty, vary every year and include international and national destinations. The college also features formal study-abroad programs with seven colleges in five different countries.

Converse students also have an abundance of exciting internship opportunities with national and international organizations. Converse students have interned at O magazine, NASA, Entertainment Tonight, Merrill Lynch, the National Endowment for the Arts, and Oak Ridge National Laboratory. Research is also an option, with Converse students regularly earning research grants to tackle a wide range of topics in the sciences. Both independent and collaborative research projects with faculty are common.

Great Teaching

Converse College offers its 750 undergraduate students forty-four undergraduate majors and twenty-one minors. There are 86 full-time faculty at Converse. Of the tenure-track faculty at the college, 89 percent have PhDs or terminal degrees in their fields, and 57 percent of the faculty are women. At Converse, the faculty conduct 100 percent of the teaching. From the beginning of classes as a freshman to the completion of senior year, students will have abundant opportunities to work side by side with their professors, stake their place in a team research project, or investigate on their own in a directed independent study project.

Converse students develop their unique voices through a challenging liberal arts curriculum, a century-old honor tradition, and the Daniels Center for Leadership and Service. Across the board—from art and design to science, business, music, and education—professors actively mentor and challenge students through spirited discussions inside and outside of the classroom. The Nisbet Honors Program, Petrie School of Music, independent and collaborative research opportunities, leading national debate teams, study-

abroad and internship programs, and a nine to one student to faculty ratio differentiate the Converse learning community.

Converse's Petrie School of Music is the nation's only comprehensive professional music school within a liberal arts college for women. With a goal to link the classroom with the world beyond, the Daniels Center for Leadership and Service is a partnership between academic affairs and student affairs that provides students with opportunities to learn, serve, and lead on campus and in the community. The center oversees service-learning programs, service projects in the Spartanburg community, and leadership programs that develop each student's leadership potential.

In freshman honors seminars, students and professors explore great literature, groundbreaking ideas, enduring works of art, and new perspectives. The Nisbet Honors Program challenges academically gifted students to investigate topics through interdisciplinary honors seminars, courses that are team taught by professors from different fields.

Converse is recognized as a national powerhouse in the Model League of Arab States program, a competitive simulation in which students write, debate, and pass resolutions on issues of concern in the Arab world. In its first year of competition at the Model NATO conference in 2005, Converse earned best delegation honors.

Vibrant Community

Located in the heart of Spartanburg, South Carolina—home to six colleges and twelve thousand college students—Converse helps women develop the skills necessary to balance a full life. While academic quality receives top priority, campus-life and residential-life programs are designed to build community and involvement. A big sister/little sister mentoring program begins in the freshman year and often creates lifelong friendships, as do the college's sixty student organizations. Traditions such as the Peppermint Ball, 1889 Week, Sophomore Celebration, and May Day are hallmarks of the Converse experience. The student activities committee is student-led and provides a diverse calendar of social and educational events. SAC sponsors coffeehouses, movies, comedians, DJs, karaoke, and bands, in addition to programs honoring Women's History Month and Black History Month.

The proximity to neighboring colleges provides Converse students with opportunities to socialize with other college students. For example, Converse women have traditionally had a strong relationship with the coeducational Wofford student body, just a couple of miles away. Converse women experience the best of both worlds: the benefits of a single-gender education within a college town of students from a variety of other institutions.

Each of Converse's seven residence halls are within a five-minute walk to all classes and labs. Students are also within walking distance of downtown Spartanburg, where a number of social activities are hosted by College Town—a partnership among all six colleges in Spartanburg County. Spartanburg has a wealth of indoor and outdoor recreational opportunities.

The Blue Ridge Parkway and the Great Smoky Mountains are just thirty minutes away, and Asheville, Atlanta, Charleston, Charlotte, and Myrtle Beach are all within a short drive. Greenville-Spartanburg International Airport, located twenty minutes west of the city, is served by six major airlines.

Successful Outcomes

More than one hundred international firms—including German automaker BMW—make Spartanburg an international and cultural center. The city offers a multitude of internship and job-placement opportunities, and local and regional companies visit the campus each year to recruit Converse graduates.

Each year, Converse graduates are accepted to notable graduate-school programs across the country, including Emory University, the Harvard Divinity School, Vanderbilt University, the New England Conservatory, the Peabody Conservatory, New York University, and the University of California. Employers visit campus each term to interview students for full-time positions and internships. Converse also participates in the South Carolina Independent Colleges and Universities (SCICU) Senior Interview Day each January term in Columbia. Graduating seniors submit resumes to participating employers and are preselected for interviews.

Converse alumnae distinguish themselves in both career and community leadership. Just a few examples of successful alumnae are a deputy assistant director in the Office of U.S. Presidential Personnel, a Texas Supreme Court justice, a member of a renowned heart research group, a Pulitzer Prize-winning novelist, a global sales manager for Wachovia Bank, a Broadway performance artist, and an interventional radiologist.

Fast Facts

Converse College, founded in 1899, is a four-year, independent, women's liberal arts college with coed graduate programs in education, music and the liberal arts

Web site

http://www.converse.edu

Location

Spartanburg, South Carolina.

Student Profile

700 undergraduate students (women only) and 1,100 graduate students (men and women); 28% out-of-state; 25% minority, 2% international.

Faculty Profile

86 full-time faculty. 9:1 student/faculty ratio, 7:1 in Petrie School of Music.

Residence Life

Highly residential: 85% of students live on campus.

Athletics

NCAA Division II, Conference Carolinas. 5 varsity sports (basketball, volleyball, soccer, tennis, and cross country); intramurals are also available.

Academic Programs

Accounting; art (art education, art history, art therapy, interior design, studio art); biology; business administration (concentrations in economics, finance, human resource management, international business, marketing); chemistry (biochemistry); computer science; economics; education (early childhood, elementary, secondary minor); English (creative & professional writing); engineering; foreign languages & literatures (French, German, Spanish, Modern Languages); history; individualized major; mathematics; music (composition, music business, music education, theory, music therapy, performance, piano pedagogy); politics; psychology; religion; special education (comprehensive, deaf & hard of hearing, educable mental disabilities, emotional disabilities, learning disabilities); theatre.

Costs and Aid

2007–2008: $30,534 comprehensive ($23,344 tuition). 93% of students receive some financial aid. Average award: $ 19,900. Scholarships are awarded for academics, leadership, music, theater, art, and involvement with Girls Scouts and Girls' State.

More Distinctions

• U.S. News & World Report ranks Converse a top college and third best value in the South.

• Converse competes at the highest NCAA level of any women's college and is a member of the Conference Carolinas.

• Converse is the only women's college in the world named to the prestigious roster of All-Steinway schools.

• The Chapman study-abroad endowment provides financial assistance to enable students to experience studying abroad.

Presbyterian College

SOUND CAROLINA

Admissions Contact:

Presbyterian College
503 South Broad Street
Clinton, South Carolina 29325
(864) 833-2820
Ph: (123) 456-7890
Email: need_email@presby.edu
www.presby.edu

SOUTH CAROLINA

Presbyterian College (PC) is a coeducational, Carnegie I liberal arts college that provides a rigorous academic program and encourages students to uphold the school's motto— While we live, we serve. PC's broad curriculum is designed to aid students in an educational quest, and encourages student service in the community.

The 4 Distinctions

Engaged Students

PC's commitment to service in the community begins with students' arrival on campus. As part of the orientation process, new students take part in a community-service project. PC also requires all students to participate in an intercultural experience, an internship, or a study-abroad experience. Students have had local internships in banks, hotels, hospitals, and law offices, and the college collaborates with Millekin, a large textile company, to provide students with an integrated internship and leadership training experience. Some students have ventured to Washington, DC, to intern for the National Geographic Society and to Atlanta to intern for CNN and Delta Air Lines.

Study abroad is available during the semester or during PC's "May-mester." Professors develop the May term programs of study, and past "May-mester" learning programs have traveled to Vietnam, Europe, South America, and Kiawah Island. There are currently fifteen different learning trips, and the program keeps expanding to offer more in the future. A partnership with Ghuizhou University in China offers students opportunities to study Chinese language and history on campus and then travel to China with faculty for immersion in Chinese culture. The Cuba study program is one of only fifteen in the country. Traveling to and studying about Cuba has allowed PC to provide students with a very unique experience while attending a small liberal arts institution.

Exposing students to other cultures comes to life in a living learning environment residence hall named Carol International House. Students are chosen to live in CIH and are offered numerous programming opportunities to understand world cultures at a deep level.

The most emphasized type of experiential learning at PC is performing service. Whether in a children's home, at the Special Olympics, or at a local school, mentoring students, 60 percent of PC students participate in service projects. Recently, students have rolled up their sleeves to work with a Habitat for Humanity house on McMillian Street in Clinton. About 45 percent of the student body has gone

Greek, and as one would imagine, these organizations have strong connections to numerous service organizations.

Great Teaching

Some popular majors at PC include business administration, premed, history, and music. Many history majors are prelaw and are able to intern in the local area with circuit court judges.

Professors have noted that they chose to teach at PC because of the high amount of contact with their students. In the first year, students participate in a seminar with twelve other freshman students led by a faculty member who is their advisor. Of the professors at PC, 95 percent hold terminal degrees in their field, and PC has had six professors receive the CASE Professor of the Year award—more than any other school in South Carolina.

Students have many opportunities to perform research on their own or with a professor, a process that begins with open dialogue with professors who act as mentors and help students develop a field of interest. There is also a Summer Fellows Research program which provides stipends for students to work very closely with faculty in a concentrated manner on various research projects. Many of our students present their research at national professional conferences.

The faculty-student relationships at PC are expressly unique. There are many evenings that students are invited to dine at faculty homes in a very informal manner. Students feel comfortable stopping by a professor's office because they know that professor cares about them as an individual. Lifelong friendships with faculty are developed while students are at PC.

Vibrant Community

Incoming students take a pledge that begins, "On my honor, I will abstain from all deceit . . . ," and professors testify that this oath of honor weighs heavily on students' choices. The honor code affects the campus atmosphere by giving students the freedom to trust one another. Because of this honor code, professors will often allow students to take tests back to their rooms to complete, and a PC student doesn't think twice about the safety of his or her laptop if it is left in the library during mealtime.

There are five traditional residence halls on campus: two freshman halls, one men's hall, and four apartment-style halls for upperclassmen. Students can also choose to live in the Carol International House, a living-and-learning residence hall with a goal of promoting cultural awareness.

PC strives to truly be a part of the community. To foster this relationship, PC has moved its bookstore downtown, and allows all events on campus to be open to the surrounding community, including the renowned Russell Program, a lecture series on different aspects of the media.

Successful Outcomes

PC graduates have proven that the program at PC has opened many doors and avenues to endless possibilities. Presbyterian College alumni were valedictorian for the past two years at the Medical University of South Carolina. A recent graduate received a full fellowship to study in the doctoral program of economics at Duke University. Penn State welcomes a 2007 graduate into its acoustical engineering program as the Annenberg School of Jounalism at the University of Southern California welcomes another 2007 graduate into its magazine journalism school. In 2006, all three seniors applying for entrance into the highly selective School of Veterinary Medicine at the University of Georgia were accepted. Mercer Law School offered their full Woodruff Fellowship to a 2007 PC graduate.

PC students are equipped to be productive citizens in this global society, and graduates are very successful in many careers. But above all that, service is a big part of the PC experience. *Washington Monthly* has recognized PC as the top liberal arts college in the nation for what its students and alumni contribute through service to their communities and to the country.

During the summer of 2007, a current PC junior served in an internship at the Kennedy Center for the Performing Arts in Washington, DC. A PC Senior participated in an internship at National Geographic in the summer of 2006, and a current senior is conducting an internship at Vera Wang's in New York.

Fast Facts

Presbyterian College is a private, residential, college affiliated with the Presbyterian Church (U.S.A.) and founded in 1880.

Web site

http://www.presby.edu/

Location

Clinton, South Carolina—a small city of 10,000 located between Greenville, South Carolina, and Columbia, South Carolina.

Student Profile

1,185 students (50% male, 50% female); 29 states and territories, 9 countries; 10% minority.

Facuity Profile

84 full-time faculty. 95% hold a doctorate or terminal degree. 13:1 student/faculty ratio. Average class size is 14.

Residence Life

Highly residential: 95% of students live on campus.

Athletics

NCAA Division I (FCS). 16 varsity sports (8 men's: baseball, basketball, cross-country, football, golf, soccer, tennis, lacrosse; 8 women's: basketball, cross-country, golf, soccer, softball, tennis, volleyball, lacrosse) and 2 club sports.

Academic Programs

Art; biology; business/accounting; business/management; chemistry; computer science; early childhood education; economics; English; fine arts (concentrations in art, drama/speech, & music); French; German; history; mathematics; medical physics; middle school education; modern foreign languages; music; music education; philosophy; physics; political science; psychology; religion; religion—Christian education; sacred music; social science; sociology; Spanish; special education; theater arts.

Costs and Aid

2007–2008: $33,930 comprehensive ($24,030 tuition). 90% of students receive some financial aid. Average award: $21,500.

Endowment

$101 million.

More Distinctions

• "*Washington Monthly* ranks PC as the top liberal arts college in the nation for contributions to communities and the country by their alumni."

• The Princeton Review has named PC one of "America's Best Value Colleges" for 2008."

• The John Templeton Foundation named Presbyterian College a "Character Building College."

• PC has six South Carolina CASE professors of the year; twice more than any other college or university in the state.

Belmont University

Admissions Contact:

Belmont University
1900 Belmont Boulevard
Nashville, TN 37212
Ph: (615) 460-6785
www.belmont.edu

TENNESSEE

Belmont University, the largest Christian university in Tennessee, is a private, coeducational, comprehensive university offering undergraduate degrees in more than seventy major areas of study. Founded in 1891, Belmont continues to offer its students an atmosphere of warmth, acceptance, and possibility within a student-centered, Christian community.

The 4 Distinctions

Engaged Students

Belmont is home to 4,700 undergraduate and graduate students, and is an especially great choice for students interested in the music business. The Belmont Experience: Learning for Life Core curriculum (BELL Core) is part of the general education curriculum, evidence of Belmont's belief in the importance of experiential learning. Through this curriculum, students complete general education requirements and must fulfill participation requirements through activities such as undergraduate research, study abroad, service learning, internships, clinicals/practica, or recitals.

Belmont offers long-term as well as short-term study-abroad programs. In the early 1990s, Belmont was one of the first universities to develop ties with universities in Eastern Europe and Russia. Belmont has long-standing relationships with these schools today. A member of the Cooperative Center for Study Abroad, students can participate Belmont-faculty-led summer programs in Britain, Barbados, Belize, Ghana, Ireland, Kenya, Scotland, and Singapore.

The junior cornerstone, a problem-based course required in the general education core, gives students the opportunity to perform undergraduate research. For fifteen years, undergraduates have been able to present research findings to a community of peers at the Belmont Undergraduate Research Symposium. In addition, the disciplines of science, sociology, and psychology each host their own research symposia.

Belmont's Engaged Scholars Program recognizes and promotes undergraduate students' participation in forms of active learning that extend beyond the traditional classroom. After applying to the Engaged Scholars Program, selected students must complete experiences in at least 5 of the categories of Engaged Learning: Independent Research, Creative Projects, Service Learning, Internships, Study Abroad, Off-Campus Experiences, Peer Tutoring, Co-Curricular Activities, and Student Leadership. Students then write a reflection of each experience to put together in a portfolio in order to graduate with the distinction of being an Engaged Scholar.

Belmont's Students in Free Enterprise (SIFE) team won the Rookie of the Year award at the 2006 SIFE USA National Exposition and first runner up in the Entrepreneurship competition.

Belmont wants students to have a common or shared experience that promotes the development of a well-rounded individual by encouraging learning outside the classroom and life-long learning. The Convocation Program, a graduation requirement for all undergraduates, requires students to attend a number of on campus events from five categories: Academic Lectures, Culture and Arts, Community Service, Faith Development, and Personal and Professional Growth.

Great Teaching

Belmont features seven undergraduate colleges and schools: Arts and Sciences, Business Administration, Entertainment and Music Business, Health Sciences and Nursing, Religion, University College, and Visual and Performing Arts. The student to teacher ratio at Belmont is thirteen to one, and 50 percent of Belmont classes enroll twenty students or fewer. Belmont boasts the only College of Entertainment and Music Business in the world, a program specifically designed for those students who intend to pursue a career in the entertainment and/or music business. Belmont's location in Nashville is especially beneficial for students hoping to gain experience in the field. The internship program in the College of Entertainment and Music Business sends hundreds of students each year to work in every facet of the music industry, from industry record labels, to publicists, to law firms.

Belmont's BELL Core requires that a student's first semester consists of a common book, a common movie, a seminar, and a writing course. Two religion courses are required, one freshman year, and one junior year. Also required are four global-studies courses, two experiential learning courses, and a senior capstone.

Vibrant Community

Students at Belmont meet needs in the community through a variety of service-learning activities. English and education majors gain valuable teaching experience by tutoring students at local schools. Spanish students team up with community role models in the Belmont-YMCA Hispanic Achievers program, a program designed to empower Hispanic youth through activities and mentoring specific to their career goals. Accounting students help neighborhood residents of all ages improve their computer skills. These projects help Belmont students connect to and serve the community.

The Curb Event Center, Belmont's five-thousand-seat multipurpose arena is home to basketball games, concerts, and much more. Belmont participates in Division I athletics and has a strong basketball program. The school's rivalry with Lipscomb University draws many spirited students out to root on the Belmont Bruins basketball team. Many students also get involved athletically by participating in Belmont's extensive intramural sports program.

There are more than eighty clubs and organizations active on campus. Students can join one the many different campus ministry groups, such as Belmont's Christian Music Society, an organization designed to educate and expose students to issues involving Christian ethics within the entertainment industry.

Successful Outcomes

Many Belmont alumni have been successful at breaking into the country-music industry. Country singers Josh Turner, Brad Paisley, and Trisha Yearwood all attended Belmont. Kimberly Locke and Melinda Doolittle, both Belmont grads, found success on American Idol.

Belmont's career services department provides students with the Career Exploration Series, a program designed to help students explore how their chosen majors can give them opportunities in broad and growing fields. As part of this series, students participate in career fairs as well as workshops on resume and interviewing skills, global opportunities, and career choices. The university's Belmont and Beyond program helps students transition into postcollege life, including sessions with Belmont alumni and advice on networking.

After an internship with "The Oprah Winfrey Show", and a stint at Oprah's Leadership Academy for Girls in South America, Journalism major Rachel Smith was crowned Miss USA.

With a 97% first time pass rate on the NCLEX, Belmont's Nursing graduates are helping address the nationwide shortage of nurses.

Fast Facts

Belmont University is a four-year, coeducational Christian university whose roots began in 1891.

Web site

http://www.belmont.edu

Location

Nashville, Tennessee—at the heart of Music Row.

Student Profile

4,700 students; 47 states, 25 countries; 10% minority, 1% international.

Faculty Profile

200 full-time faculty. 13:1 student/faculty ratio. Average class size is 19.

Residence Life

Moderately residential: 60% of students live on campus.

Athletics

NCAA Division I, Atlantic Sun Conference. 15 varsity sports (7 men's: baseball, basketball, cross-country, golf, soccer, tennis, track; 8 women's: basketball, cross-country, golf, softball, soccer, tennis, track, volleyball), and many intramural sports.

Academic Programs

Accounting; applied discrete mathematics; art education; audio & video production; audio engineering technology; biblical languages; biblical studies; biochemistry & molecular biology; biology; business administration; chemistry; Christian ethics; Christian leadership; church music; classics; commercial music; communication studies; computer science; design communications; early childhood education; economics; engineering physics; English; entertainment industry studies; entrepreneurship; environmental studies; European studies; exercise science & health promotion; finance; French; German; health; history; information systems management; international business; international economics; journalism; management; marketing; mass communication; mathematics; medical imaging technology; medical physics; medical technology; middle school education; music business; music composition; music education; music performance; music theory; musical theatre; music with an outside minor; neuroscience; nursing; pharmaceutical studies; philosophy; physical education; physics; piano pedagogy; political economy; political science; psychology; public relations; religion & the arts; religious studies; science & engineering management; secondary education; social work; sociology; songwriting; Spanish; studio art; theatre & drama; web programming & development.

Costs and Aid

2006-2007: $26,300 comprehensive ($17,470 tuition). 75% of students receive some financial aid.

Endowment

$52 million.

Christian Brothers University

TENNESSEE

Christian Brothers University (CBU) is renowned and respected for its distinctive, vibrant, and vigorous educational program. This small, friendly, and remarkably diverse campus in central Memphis helps students develop ethical values even as it prepares them to "step up, stand out, and lead" in professional careers.

Admissions Contact:

Christian Brothers University
650 East Parkway South
Memphis, Tennessee 38104
(800) 288-7576
(901) 321-3205
Email: admissions@cbu.edu
www.cbu.edu

The 4 Distinctions

Engaged Students

Regularly rated one of the best universities in the South, CBU traces its roots to a seventeenth-century educational innovator, Saint John Baptist de La Salle. While strongly rooted in the twenty-first century, education at CBU honors those Lasallian traditions, especially in the University's focus on faith, service, and community.

CBU capitalizes on its small size and passionate faculty to deliver a unique curriculum. Courses of study are divided into four distinct schools: arts, business, engineering, and sciences. Within those core areas, CBU offers a wide variety of majors that are popular with students. Many students are drawn to CBU's psychology program, often as a gateway toward work in counseling or teaching. The University recently inaugurated a biomedical science major to enhance the skills and experience of students headed to medical, dental, and nursing schools. CBU's popular law-enforcement curriculum is enhanced by university ties with law-enforcement practitioners across the greater Memphis community.

CBU knows that study abroad engages learners in a rich cross-cultural educational experience, leading to insights about different people and cultures; providing on-site observation of historical, scientific, and cultural phenomena; and offering the chance to study foreign languages in a cultural context. CBU students recently studied in Rome, Assisi, Paris, London, Florence, Bath, Madrid, Costa del Sol, and in the countries of Brazil and Uganda.

CBU's Career Center and academic departments help students find internships with businesses and nonprofit agencies in and around the Memphis area. CBU structures its internships as a complement to classroom learning, and of course, as a chance for students to gain professional experience through a supervised field placement in an appropriate company or agency. Student interns apply their developing professional knowledge and skills, learn on-site processes, clarify career options, and gain experience that almost invariably provides an advantage when it comes time to find a job after graduation. Industries across the mid-South region welcome CBU engineering interns, and many accounting majors find positions with local businesses. A number of recent science majors have interned at the local zoo.

Whether they are students, professors, or staff, members of the CBU community regularly volunteer time and services for the greater good. There's a strong tradition, for example, of tutoring children of various ages in the local community.

Great Teaching

The Lasallian tradition emphasizes that all people, especially the young, have an inherent dignity, which comes from their being created in the image of God. For Lasallian educators, education is a means of developing this dignity for the well-being of each student as well as for the well-being of society. Following those traditions at CBU today, Christian Brothers and their lay faculty colleagues continue the work of Saint John Baptist De La Salle.

In the context of CBU's close-knit campus community, faculty and staff mentor students as well as teach; many times they know a student so well that they can offer personal attention tailored to that student's particular situation.

During spring break and the summer, faculty lead off-campus study trips, often to international destinations. Many of these trips give students the chance to collaborate on original research, and many also incorporate an aspect of community service, in keeping with CBU's mission.

CBU's honors program nurtures and challenges students with proven academic abilities who seek a more intensive educational experience. Honors students take at least one special-topics course, all of which are led by instructors carefully chosen for their teaching expertise.

Vibrant Community

CBU is a proudly Catholic university, operated under Catholic and Lasallian educational traditions. But it celebrates diversity, too—more than 24 different faiths are represented in the CBU student body, and just over 25 percent of the student body is Catholic. Baptists, Muslims, Presbyterians, Hindus, Jews, and Buddhists are all well represented and more than welcome. Religious observances are not required, but all students are encouraged to practice their faith openly and actively.

There's further diversity in the student body—40 percent of CBU students are from traditionally minority populations. Once open only to men, CBU in 2007 was 56 percent female, 44 percent male.

CBU is home to more than forty student clubs and organizations, including groups involved in theater, art, music, academic areas, and publications. The Student Government Programming Council helps develop and host cultural, educational, and entertainment programs.

Many campus clubs are service oriented, providing channels for students to get involved locally for a common cause. One event, Up 'til Dawn, has students finding sponsors to keep them awake all night, completing activities and challenges—all to raise money for St. Jude Children's Research Hospital.

The eighteenth-largest city in the United States, Memphis offers up a world of opportunity and fun for CBU students. The city has an NBA team, the Memphis Grizzlies, and hosts great concerts and festivals. Students can hear the blues most every night on the city's famed Beale Street. Memphis boasts great restaurants and abundant parks, and its downtown entertainment district has seen a major resurgence in the last decade.

Successful Outcomes

CBU is known for producing graduates who are fully ready to launch successful careers. In any given year, as many as two hundred companies, corporations, government agencies, and nonprofit organizations come to CBU to recruit for employees. Alumni can be found working for corporations and organizations across the nation and the world, including American Express, AT&T, Boeing, FedEx, Hewlett-Packard, IBM, NASA, Pricewaterhouse Coopers, and Xerox, as well as many highly regarded local and regional firms.

Typically, some 85 percent of CBU graduates receive full-time job offers within six months of commencement. Students who elect to go on for an advanced degree regularly find that the CBU degree opens the door to admittance at top-tier graduate programs. From 2002 to 2006, CBU graduates from the school of science had a 91 percent acceptance rate into medical school, exceeding the nationwide rate of 46 percent, and an 87 percent acceptance rate into pharmacy school, again exceeding the nationwide rate of 30 percent.

CBU alumni play an active and enthusiastic role in helping students before, during, and after their time on campus, including the postgraduation job search. Many alumni are active in the local Memphis community and help CBU students network there.

The CBU career center provides testing, analysis, and professional tips for students, all as part of a full complement of services designed to help students find the right professional path—and the right employer.

Fast Facts

Christian Brothers University is a four-year, private university affiliated with the Roman Catholic Church. The University was founded in 1871 by the De La Salle Christian Brothers, a Catholic teaching order.

Web site

http://www.cbu.edu

Location

Memphis, Tennessee—about four miles east of downtown; near Interstates 40, 240, and 55; and close to major medical centers.

Student Profile

1,800 students (44% male, 56% female); 31 states, 14 countries; 43% minority; 2% international.

Faculty Profile

92 full-time faculty. 13:1 student/faculty ratio. Average class size is 16

Residence Life

Moderately residential: 40% of students live on campus.

Athletics

NCAA Division II, Gulf South Conference. 13 varsity sports (6 men's: basketball, baseball, soccer, cross-country, tennis, golf; 7 women's: basketball, soccer, tennis, golf, cross-country, softball, volleyball), club sports, and intramurals.

Academic Programs

Applied psychology; cultural studies (licensure 4-8); English; English for corporate communications; history; liberal studies (licensure K-6); prelaw; psychology; religion & philosophy; accounting; finance; information technology management; management; marketing; chemical engineering; civil engineering; electrical & computer engineering; mechanical engineering; biology; biomedical science; chemistry; computer sciences; engineering physics; mathematics; natural sciences; physics; preprofessional health programs; studio arts.

Costs and Aid

2007–2008: $27,040 comprehensive ($21,360 tuition and fees). 91% of students receive some financial aid. Average award: $15,808.

Endowment

$27.1 million.

More Distinctions

- Ranked 17th among the best Southern universities in *U.S. News & World Report's America's Best Colleges* (2008 edition).

- Listed in Peterson's Competitive Colleges.

- Ranked among the best Southeastern colleges by the Princeton Review.

- Listed in Michael Viollt's Great Colleges for the Real World.

Maryville College

TENNESSEE

Admissions Contact:

Maryville College
502 E. Lamar Alexander Parkway
Maryville, TN 37804
(800) 597-2687
Ph: (865) 981-8010
Email: info@maryvillecollege.edu
www.maryvillecollege.edu

Maryville College (MC) is a private, coeducational, liberal arts college affiliated with the Presbyterian Church (U.S.A.). Founded in 1819, it is the twelfth oldest institution of higher learning in the South. Maryville provides students with the skills and opportunities to be successful and to make a difference in the world.

The 4 Distinctions

Engaged Students

MC offers fifty major fields of study. The most popular are biology, business, education, and psychology. MC draws students from across the nation for its major in sign language interpreting. In all its academic programs, the college focuses on taking students beyond their expectations. Course work includes hands-on applications of the material, giving students a well-rounded education through service-learning, research, and study-abroad opportunities. Students are encouraged to work collaboratively to prepare for effective interactions in the workplace.

The Maryville College Covenant was created by students in 1990. It promotes basic shared values and ideals in order to strengthen and affirm the college community. The covenant sets high standards for expected behavior regarding scholarship, respect, and integrity, and is enforced by MC students themselves.

All MC students participate in its nationally recognized first-year program, which addresses the transitions students need to make to achieve academic and social acculturation to college life. It is designed to help students establish effective study habits, learn fundamental skills, and acquire an understanding of what it means to be an educated person.

Every student also takes part in Mountain Challenge, an outdoor experiential program. Mountain Challenge is based on the MC campus and utilizes the nearby natural resources to present students with unfamiliar and challenging tasks, leading to a new, expanded sense of achievement.

Great Teaching

All MC students fulfill requirements thru the distinctive Maryville curriculum, which has been collaboratively structured by the faculty to enable MC graduates to think critically, creatively, and ethically; communicate effectively; discover connections and synthesize solutions; develop broad knowledge and global perspectives; and cultivate a love of learning for a lifetime

The low student to faculty ratio of fourteen to one, and Maryville's strong sense of community encourage close

relationships between students and their professors. Faculty are often viewed as mentors and friends as well as advisors and instructors.

Every degree candidate at MC completes a senior study project, a capstone experience to their education at the college in which students work one-on-one with a professor in their major field. Students propose the subject and shape of the project, which can take a variety of forms, including literary, scientific, and historical investigation; work in a laboratory, studio, or in the field; and interpretive or creative activity. Students plan their projects, perform research, and complete the work, gaining the confidence and pride that comes from accomplishment. In 2006, subjects of senior studies ranged from "A Day of Grace: Evangelical Theology in Uncle Tom's Cabin," to "A Survey of Arthropod Biodiversity in the Canopies of Southern Red Oak Trees in the Maryville College Woods."

Vibrant Community

Maryville has about 1,200 students and 75 percent come from Tennessee, most from within a three hour drive of the campus. Most are graduates of public high schools from the top of their classes, and approximately one-third are first-generation college students.

MC's residential community is cohesive, with over 70 percent of students housed on campus. All freshman students live in one of three first-year residence halls; upperclassmen select from a variety of residence-hall options, including apartment-style suites and a wellness hall. Students have never felt that Greek life would be a good fit with the MC community, so there are no fraternities or sororities on campus.

There are about fifty clubs and organizations for students to choose to join. Popular groups include Ultimate Frisbee, the student programming board, the student government association, Global Citizenship Organization, the Black Student Association, Peace & World Concerns, and Habitat for Humanity. Students' leadership and service contributions were acknowledged in November

2006 when MC was named to the first President's Higher Education Community Service Honor Roll in recognition of the extraordinary volunteer efforts by the college and its students to serve area neighborhoods and Gulf Coast communities devastated by Hurricane Katrina.

The college's Nonprofit Leadership Certificate program connects Maryville students with a national alliance of colleges, universities, and nonprofit organizations to prepare and certify college students for professional careers in youth and human-service agencies. Recent activities of the program include attending the national convention in Washington, DC, and participating in a mission trip to Biloxi, Mississippi.

The college's 320-acre campus is in Maryville, Tennessee, a town of about twenty-six thousand with a historic downtown and nine-mile greenway winding through the city and county. It is located about fifteen miles north of the Great Smoky Mountains National Park and fifteen miles south of Knoxville, the state's third largest city.

Successful Outcomes

Students who graduate from Maryville are prepared for lives of citizenship and leadership. Between 40 and 50 percent of MC's alumni go on to employment in education, public service, ministry, and other nonprofit fields, and 25 percent go on to immediate postgraduate work.

The college's Center for Calling & Career fosters moral, spiritual, and personal reflection on issues of vocation and vocational discernment. It helps students to discover who they are and determine what they want to become, leading to a satisfying vocation with a profound sense of purpose. Integrated with the academic affairs department, the center assists with major selection, resume and cover-letter writing, interviewing, networking, conducting job and internship searches, applying to graduate school, and other issues of professional and vocational development.

Fast Facts

Maryville College is a four-year, liberal arts, private, coeducational college founded in 1819.

Web site

http://www.maryvillecollege.edu

Location

Maryville, Tennessee— Ideally situated between the Great Smoky Mountains National Park and Knoxville, TN. By car, the college is accessible by Interstate 40 from the east and west, and by Interstate 75 from the north and south.

Student Profile

1,155 students (54% female, 46% male); 33 states and territories, 23 countries; 21% out-of-state.

Faculty Profile

76 full-time faculty. 14:1 student/faculty ratio. Average class size is 20.

Residence Life

Residential: 70% of students live on campus.

Athletics

NCAA's Division III. 14 varsity sports (7 men's: baseball, basketball, cheerleading, cross-country, football, soccer, tennis; 7 women's: basketball, cheerleading, cross-country, soccer, softball, tennis, volleyball. Club sports include an equestrian team, ultimate Frisbee and dance. Intramural sports are also offered.

Academic Programs

American Sign Language and deaf studies; art; art history; biochemistry; biology; business & organization management; chemical physics; chemistry; child development and learning; computer science/business; computer science/mathematics; economics; engineering; English; English as a second language; environmental studies; health care (nursing); history; individualized major; international business; international studies; mathematics; music; music theory/composition; music performance; outdoor recreation; philosophy; physical education; political science; psychology; religion; sign language interpreting; sociology; Spanish; teaching; theatre studies; writing/communication.

Costs and Aid

2007–2008 $33,150 comprehensive ($24,675 tuition, $3,900 room and board); More than 90% of students receive both financial aid and scholarships. Average Award: $15,000.

Endowment

$42 million.

More Distinctions

• The College consistently ranks among *U.S. News & World Report's* best colleges in the South.

Rhodes College

TENNESSEE

Rhodes College is a four-year, private liberal arts school located in Memphis, Tennessee. Founded in 1848, Rhodes seeks to educate students with a lifelong passion for learning, a compassion for others and the ability to translate academic study and personal concern into effective leadership and action in their communities and the world.

Admissions Contact:

Rhodes College
114 Palmer Hall
2000 N. Parkway
Memphis, TN 38112-1690
(800) 844-5969
Ph: (901)843-3700
Email: adminfo@rhodes.edu
www.rhodes.edu

The 4 Distinctions

Engaged Students

Rhodes students have access to more than 150 academic internships each semester, and about 60 percent take advantage of these opportunities. Memphis is home to more than 100 medical, government, business, cultural, and artistic facilities and through these, students have the chance to shape their skills for the future. Local options are as diverse as St. Jude Children's Research Hospital, FedEx, the FBI, the National Civil Rights Museum, the Blues Foundation, and the United States Attorney's Office.

At Rhodes, more than 80 percent of the student body participates in community service. The Rhodes curriculum includes courses that include service components and related internships for academic credit. Additionally, Rhodes students independently operate several service outlets, including a downtown soup kitchen and the country's first campus-based chapter of Habitat for Humanity. A large portion of the student body also volunteer as tutors and mentors in local schools and urban youth programs.

Rhodes offers a wide range of study abroad options, such as its European Studies program, which gives students the opportunity to spend two weeks at the University of York in England; six weeks with British tutors at Lincoln College, Oxford; and five weeks of travel to major cultural centers on the continent. Other Rhodes-sponsored programs include special study in Argentina and Chile. Summer Programs include British Studies at Oxford, intensive language programs in France, Spain, Mexico, or Russia, Coral Reef Ecology (Honduras) and service leaning programs at several international locations.

There are a number of social fraternities and sororities at Rhodes. Approximately 50% of the students are members of Greek organizations. The fraternity and sorority lodges are not, however, residential, and most Greek-sponsored parties and activities are open to the entire campus.

Great Teaching

The Rhodes faculty is composed of gifted scholars who challenge, engage, and connect students in life-changing ways. With a faculty-student ratio of just 11:1, faculty members interact with students both inside and outside the classroom. The Rhodes faculty works with students to offer unique research experiences. These are the kinds of opportunities usually afforded only to graduate students at large research universities. Whatever the program – astrophysics, English, history, mathematics, pre-med, or any one of 31 major programs — students have the opportunity for hands-on research and study.

In addition, flexible independent and off-campus study is encouraged at Rhodes. Choices include pre-designed or self-designed interdisciplinary majors, individualized study options such as the honors program, directed inquiry projects, the tutorial plan, and study abroad. State-of-the-art technology is everywhere on the wireless campus at Rhodes. "Smart" classrooms, located throughout the campus, offer Internet access and computer and video displays, while the college's science facilities have recently been updated, offering students top-of-the-line technology and instruments.

Vibrant Community

The campus consists of 100 acres in midtown Memphis, across from Overton Park which contains the Memphis Zoo, the Brooks Museum and the Memphis College of Art. The campus design includes stone Gothic architecture buildings, 13 of which are currently listed on the National Register of Historic Places. A 140-foot bell tower was named in honor of explorer Richard Halliburton.

The Honor Code, a century-old tradition, makes a huge difference in the Rhodes community. Upon enrolling at Rhodes, students pledge not to lie, cheat, or steal. Faculty members feel free to leave the classroom when they give a test; students trust each other; and individuals live in harmony with the community. The Honor Code makes Rhodes an easy place to live, and a great place to learn.

Rhodes offers outstanding opportunities in music, theatre, and other fine arts. Rhodes' McCoy Theatre gives students the opportunity to perform alongside veteran community actors in a variety of stage settings by hosting at least four productions annually with student cast and crew. For musicians, Hassell Hall offers practice rooms, teaching studios, a recital hall, and more than 8,000 recordings in the Adams Music Library. Students ensembles tour in the U.S., Europe and beyond with the Rhodes Singers who have performed twice in Carnegie Hall in recent years. Others join the chamber orchestra or chamber groups.

Rhodes was recently named high on the Princeton Review's list of colleges with "dorm rooms like palaces." Each room offers wireless Internet access and cable television. Living options include halls with limited or 24-hour visitation, theme housing, large double or triple rooms, and the "East Village" apartments, which offer four-person suites with a shared living area and either individual or double bedrooms.

Rhodes' $22.5 million Bryan Campus Life Center offers state-of-the-art recreational and intercollegiate athletics facilities including a performance gymnasium, a multi-use gymnasium, racquetball courts, international squash courts, free weights and state-of-the-art cardiovascular equipment. Adjacent to the center are a stadium for football and track, 10 tennis courts, a swimming pool, intercollegiate baseball and soccer fields, football practice fields, and additional playing fields for intramural and club sports.

There's more than Graceland and Elvis Presley in Memphis. From blues on Beale Street to stadium sports, Memphis offers a rich mix of entertainment options. Memphis, the 18th largest city in the United States, is an exciting river city renowned for its great food and outstanding museums, as well as its rich Southern heritage.

The $42 million Barret Library, the social and intellectual hub of the campus, is a technology center with a theater, complete media production facilities and a teaching and learning center that gives professors the capacity to hold virtual global classes with colleagues around the world. The collection includes books and traditional resources as well as databases and online journals. Barret also has dozens of collaborative study spaces where students can work with professors and each other and actually talk out loud.

Successful Outcomes

Virtually all Rhodes graduates either secure jobs or are accepted into graduate or professional school. Recent graduates have received a wide variety of prestigious scholarships including Carnegie Fellowships, Rhodes Scholarships, Fulbright grants, Luce Scholarships and Watson Fellowships.

The Rhodes Career Services Office offers a strong career-counseling program. About one-third of Rhodes students continue their education after graduation. The acceptance rates to law and business schools are around 95 percent for Rhodes graduates. The broad-based foundation offered by Rhodes includes teaching students to think for themselves and to solve real problems. Rhodes helps students grow into the people they want to be, and to find not just a job, but a career that will bring a lifetime of rewards and satisfaction.

About one-third of Rhodes students continue their educations after graduation. The acceptance rates to law and business schools are around 95 percent for Rhodes graduates. The broad-based foundation teaches students to think for themselves and to solve real problems.

Fast Facts

Rhodes College is a four-year liberal arts and sciences college affiliated with the Presbyterian Church, and founded in 1848.

Web site

http://www.rhodes.edu

Location

Memphis, Tennessee—home of great music and a vibrant business and medical center that provides exciting internship opportunities.

Student Profile

1,699 students (43% male, 57% female); 43 states and territories: 15% minority, 1% international.

Faculty Profile

129 full-time faculty. 11:1 student/faculty ratio. Average class size is 13.

Residence Life

Highly residential: 74% of students live on campus.

Athletics

NCAA Division III, Southern Collegiate Athletic Conference. 19 varsity sports (9 men's: baseball, basketball, cross-country, football, golf, soccer, tennis, swimming & diving, track & field; 10 women's: basketball, cross-country, field hockey, golf, soccer, soft-ball, tennis, swimming & diving, track & field, volleyball), 10 club sports, and 8 intramurals.

Academic Programs

American studies; anthropology; art; Asian studies; biology; chemistry; economics & business administration; earth system science; economics and international studies; education; English; film studies; French and international studies; geology; German and international studies; Greek & Roman studies; history; international studies; international studies and history; international studies and political science; Latin American studies; mathematics & computer science; modern languages (Chinese, French, German, Italian, Russian, Spanish); music; philosophy; physics; political science; psychology; religious studies; sociology; theatre, and urban studies.

Costs and Aid

2007-2008: $41,010 comprehensive ($30,342 tuition). 77% of students receive some financial aid. Average award: $20,413.

Endowment

$278 million.

More Distinctions

• Named "Mostly Likely to Succeed" because of its extremely high rate of graduates accepted to law school, medical school and other graduate programs by Newsweek / Kaplan Guide to Colleges

• Ranks consistently in the Top Tier of America's Best National Liberal Arts Colleges in U.S. News & World Report

• Ranked amongst the top 10 most active campuses in the country by Mother Jones magazine (2003).

• Rated 35th in the "Top 100 Best Values in Private Colleges and Universities" by Kiplinger's Personal Finance Magazine and Consumer Digest.

Union University

TENNESEE

Union University is a private, four-year, coeducational, liberal arts-based university. Union is a Christ-centered university with a focus on academic excellence and intellectual curiosity. Students are encouraged to develop an attitude of service, a passion for truth, and a desire for a greater understanding of God and the world.

Admissions Contact:

Union University
1050 Union University Drive
Jackson, TN 38305
(800) 33-UNION
Ph: (731) 661-5422
Email: info@uu.edu
www.uu.edu

The 4 Distinctions

Engaged Students

Union integrates its commitment to academic excellence with a Christian worldview. This approach allows students in all one hundred programs of study to explore how the Christian faith impacts all aspects of learning and life. Popular majors include nursing, business, education, and Christian studies.

The university started the first nursing program in West Tennessee, and has ties with fourteen hospitals, including the largest hospital in the state. Business and education majors benefit from extensive internship programs that help students apply their new learning to practical situations; internships are required of all business students. The Christian studies program encourages students to connect with the great Christian intellectual tradition.

During spring, summer, and winter breaks, Union University students are sent on short-term mission projects, called Global Outreach Trips, throughout the world. Recent destinations have included multiple locations in the United States, Europe, Asia, and Central America.

Union students are encouraged to think deeply about the issues of the day, including life, justice, and racial reconciliation, and to act accordingly in their service opportunities. Union encourages community service by setting aside an entire day during the school year to serve the local community. The day commemorates the community response to the campus when a tornado hit in 2002. Students, faculty, and staff choose from more than sixty different volunteer projects on this Day of Remembrance.

Great Teaching

As a freshman, every student is enrolled in College Life at Union (CLU), an eight-week course covering time management and the discovery of individual gifts. The course helps students choose a major that fits their interests and their God-given talents.

All majors require research, and many require a capstone project or thesis. Juniors and seniors have a chance to present their research on campus and on a national level through the annual Scholarship Symposium. Creative writing majors present original works that often culminate in professional portfolios. Most research and writing projects are completed under the close mentorship of a professor.

Faculty and students connect outside of the classroom. Faculty lead or participate in Rounders, an extracurricular book study group open to all Union students. There are usually six to eight meetings per semester. Rounders participants meet within small groups to discuss the most important literary works in light of a Christian worldview. Books by Aleksandr Solzhenitsyn, Dorothy Sayers, Martin Luther King Jr., and C. S. Lewis have been examined during recent Rounders discussions.

Vibrant Community

All students have their own private bedrooms and share a common living space with roommates. About 1,200 students live on campus, and because of this, the on-campus community thrives. In addition to sixty student organizations, there are intramural sports, world-renowned guest speakers, a wide range of mission trips, student seminars on a variety of relevant topics, student-led Bible studies, plays, and musical performances. There are six Greek organizations on campus, and about 20 percent of students are involved in these organizations. Greek life at Union is service oriented, and each of the three sororities supports a local charity. Greek life also provides a strong social outlet.

Though not required, about 95 percent of Union freshman join LIFE Groups. These student-led groups for new students provide encouragement, assistance, and support through a network of relationships. LIFE Groups give new students a chance to meet other students within a relaxed and comfortable small-group setting.

Union's campus is located in Jackson, Tennessee, a city between Nashville and Memphis. Jackson is surrounded by fourteen rural counties, which makes it the hub city in the area. There is a professional symphony, a professional theater group, and a Double-A baseball team in the area.

Union encourages students to serve in the community as well as in local churches. Most students have cars, but those without a car function well because of the generosity of other Union students.

Successful Outcomes

Union graduates have strong job-placement rates. Local hospitals traditionally hire many Union nursing graduates. Around 30 percent of Union students go on to graduate school immediately after graduation, and Union graduates have recently been accepted to graduate study at Yale, UVA, Emory, NYU, Boston University, Northwestern, and Vanderbilt. In the last ten years, 97 percent of all students who applied to medical school with recommendations from a faculty committee were accepted.

Beginning in their freshman year, students are encouraged to visit the career services offices and take advantage of their workshops, seminars, and resume help. There are twenty alumni chapters around the world, and Union's Young Alums program organizes activities and milestone events. Famous alumni include former U.S. Supreme Court justice Howell E. Jackson, former NBC News correspondent John Dancy, Jimmy Neutron creator Kirby Atkins, and contemporary Christian singer and songwriter Chris Rice.

For decades, Union University graduates have assumed leadership roles in their fields of study. A few brief examples:

David Melvin ('64) pioneered the heart transplant program at Cincinnati's University Hospital, leading a team of doctors through more than 100 surgeries. At the height of his career, Melvin traded his surgical mask for freshman engineering texts, eventually earning a doctorate in that field. He's developing innovations such as a patented exterior harness for powering diseased hearts.

Autumn Ridenour ('02) earned a graduate degree from Yale University and became program coordinator for that institution's Bioethics Center. She has explored a wide range of difficult ethical issues, including a focus on aging and disability. Ridenour is pursuing a Ph.D. in theological ethics at Boston College.

Brody McMurtry ('03) completed a law degree at the University of Virginia and is finishing a graduate program in international affairs at Georgetown University. McMurtry has served with the International Justice Mission as a volunteer in Uganda, where civil war has had a devastating effect on children and families.

Brian Taylor ('05) finished his studies at Union and received a full fellowship and annual stipends for five years to do research at M.D. Anderson Cancer Center at the University of Texas, one of the leading facilities of its kind in the nation.

Fast Facts

Union University is a private, four-year, coeducational liberal arts-based university offering bachelors, masters and doctoral degrees. Founded in 1823, Union is affiliated with the Tennessee Baptist Convention.

Web site

http:// www.uu.edu

Location

Jackson, Tennessee (area population: 100,000), 80 miles east of Memphis and 120 miles west of Nashville.

Student Profile

Student count: 3,157 (41% male, 59% female); 40 states and 35 countries: 13% minority. 2% international.

Faculty Profile

Faculty count: 331. 11:1 student/faculty ratio.

Residence Life

Moderately residential: 54% of students live on campus.

Athletics

NAIA Division I. TranSouth Conference. 11 varsity sports: (5 men's: basketball, baseball, cross-country, golf, soccer; 6 women's: basketball, cheerleading, cross-country, soccer, softball, volleyball), and an extensive intramural program. Union provides fitness opportunities for all students.

Academic Programs

Art*; biology*; business administration*; chemistry; Christian studies; communication arts; computer science; education*; engineering; English*; history & political science, history*, political science*; honors; intercultural studies; language; mathematics*; music; nursing; physical education, wellness & sport; physics*; preprofessional programs; psychology; social work*; sociology & family studies.

*Teacher Licensure Available

Costs and Aid

2007-2008: $24,850 comprehensive ($17,990 tuition). 89% of students receive financial aid. Average award: $15,387 including all aid types—federal, state, university.

Endowment

$25 million.

More Distinctions

• "U.S.News & World Report ranks Union University in the top 20 of Universities-Master's in the South category."

• Named one of America's 100 Best College Buys by an independent research firm.

• America's Best Christian Colleges for nine consecutive years.

• Included in the Time 500 best.

Colleges of Distinction
Midwest Region Schools

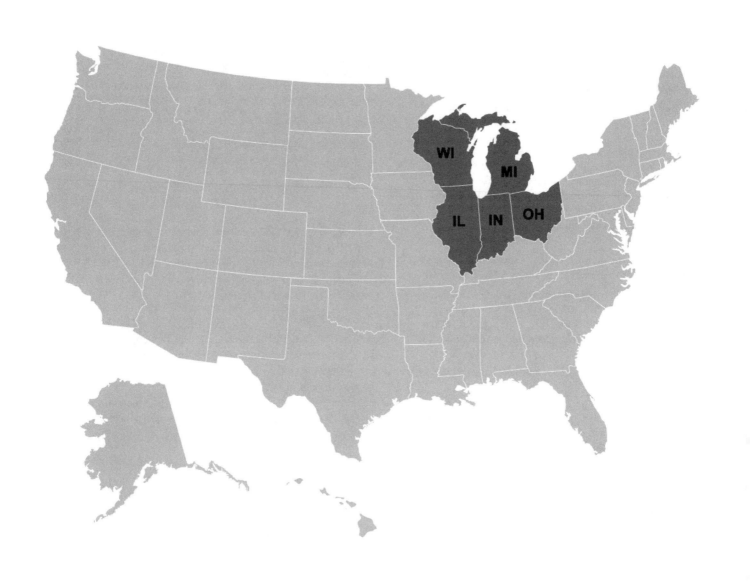

Photo: © iStockphoto.com/lisapics

Notes

_____

_____

_____

_____

_____

_____

_____

_____

_____

_____

Augustana College

ILLINOIS

Admissions Contact:

Augustana College
639 38th Street
Rock Island, IL 61201
Toll Free: (800) 798-8100
Ph: (309) 794-7341
Fax: (309) 794-8797
Email: admissions@augustana.edu
www.augustana.edu

Founded in 1860, Augustana College is private, selective, liberal arts college affiliated with the Evangelical Lutheran Church in America. The college enrolls 2,500 students of diverse social and cultural backgrounds. Located in Rock Island, Illinois, Augustana is the only liberal arts college in the metropolitan area known as the Quad Cities.

The 4 Distinctions

Engaged Students

At Augustana College, students find an array of learning opportunities to challenge and prepare them for meaningful work in a complex world. Much of the rich variety of the academic program is grounded in Augustana's many options for experiential learning: intensive global learning experiences, domestic and international internships, service learning, and programs that focus on one's purpose or path in life.

Augustana's international study programs are known for both cultural immersion—such as summer or year-long language programs in Ecuador, France, Germany, or Sweden—as well as for variety and range. Besides the popular international terms in Asia, Europe, and Latin America, the college offers focused terms in such places as Ghana, India, Ireland, or Vienna, each providing in-depth experience in a more focused region.

Not all learning abroad is for credit, however: international internships provide opportunities to gain language, cultural, and professional skills through working in another culture. An exciting program is the eight-week internship program in Sydney, Australia, where Augustana business and speech communication students intern in settings directly related to their fields.

Augustana students also take responsibility as world citizens through helping with relief efforts. Recently, groups of students spent their spring breaks in Mississippi and Louisiana, working to rebuild homes destroyed by Hurricane Katrina. Other groups organize an annual trip to Meru, Kenya, working together with the Mutuuma community to renovate primary school classrooms. Still others focus their efforts locally, volunteering with a neighborhood elementary school or taking part in raising funds to relieve the effects of natural disasters or social disparity.

Such opportunities for social action and service learning are popular in part through the work of campus ministries as well as the Augustana College Center for Vocational Reflection—a resource for students and others to apply their skills, gifts, and talents through meaningful work and a purposeful life.

Great Teaching

Augustana students become engaged in their communities and in the world partly because they are inspired by great teachers. Close connections with faculty mentors and a dynamic culture of exploration and inquiry foster collaboration in research, the arts, and social service.

The close, productive relationships among students and professors begin the first year, with the Augustana General Education Studies (AGES) program. Working with an advisor, students select their courses in the series, an interdisciplinary sequence that provides deeper relevance to their individual study in a major field. AGES faculty work together to provide meaningful learning experiences that encourage students to think critically and creatively, communicate well, view issues from multiple perspectives, and make connections among disciplines. This supportive, collaborative learning environment is carried through in subsequent years as faculty promote the skills, gifts, and talents of individual students.

The academic program culminates in Senior Inquiry, in which each senior student investigates, creates, and carries out a capstone project in collaboration with a faculty mentor in his or her field. Projects vary as widely as the individual students and professors who bring them to life, and include such examples as cancer research, the history of a landmark building, an analysis of political rhetoric, or the organization of a mile-by-mile cleanup of a river. Through their work with an award-winning chemist, historian, or poet on campus, students hone their skills, expand their knowledge, and build the academic confidence that comes through working closely with a respected mentor. They also complete a meaningful capstone project that both demonstrates and further develops their abilities in their field.

Vibrant Community

Augustana's beautiful 115-acre campus extends into the culturally diverse Quad Cities—a midsized metropolitan community on the banks of the Mississippi River. The diversity of the Quad Cities offers something for every Augustana student's talents and interests, from internships in global corporations or local businesses and not-for-profit organizations, to an astounding array of social opportunities and cultural experiences—including the arts, athletics, ethnic festivals, and social outreach. Augustana College offers students more than one hundred extracurricular clubs and organizations in part because these experiences find practical outlets and a welcoming environment in the Quad Cities.

Augustana also benefits from close ties to the community as a college that offers a successful balance of liberal arts education and preprofessional study. Along with the arts and humanities, programs such as accounting, business administration, communication sciences and disorders, education, and pre-health thrive in an environment that offers many different settings for experiential learning.

On campus, Augustana's residential life program and award-winning office of student activities offer many leadership and social opportunities to engage students throughout the year.

Successful Outcomes

Within six months of graduation, 99 percent of graduates report having jobs or being enrolled in graduate or professional degree programs. Augustana ranks among the top 10 percent of all colleges and universities based on the number of graduates who go on to earn a PhD.

Augustana alumni are members of Congress, college presidents, CEOs of Fortune 500 companies, humanitarians, parents, mentors, teachers, coaches, community leaders, and so much more. They're working at places like the Quad Cities' own Deere & Company and around the globe in international embassies, for the U.S. Senate, and for organizations like the United States Olympic Committee and the United States Agency for International Development, to name a few. Alumni have won awards including Fulbright scholarships, the Nobel Prize, and the Illinois Professor of the Year Award. Through AlumNet, a powerful networking tool sponsored by Augustana's career center, alumni share a wealth of information, advice, and countless success stories with students searching for their own paths in life.

Fast Facts

Augustana College is a private, residential, four-year college of the liberal arts and sciences founded in 1860, related to the Evangelical Lutheran Church in America.

Web site

http://www.augustana.edu

Location

Rock Island, Illinois— within the Quad Cities, a metropolitan area of 375,000 located 2 1/2 hours from Chicago.

Student Profile

2,500 undergraduate students (42% male, 58% female); 40 states and territories; 9% minority, 1% international.

Faculty Profile

165 full-time faculty. 90% hold a terminal degree in their field. 13:1 student/faculty ratio. Average class size is 20.

Residence Life

Highly residential: 80% of students live on campus (most seniors live off campus).

Athletics

NCAA Division III, College Conference of Illinois and Wisconsin (CCIW). 19 varsity sports (10 men's: baseball, basketball, cross-country, football, golf, soccer, swimming, tennis, indoor & outdoor track, wrestling; 9 women's: basketball, cross-country, golf, soccer, softball, swimming, tennis, indoor & outdoor track, volleyball) and club sports.

Academic Programs

Accounting; art; art education; art history; biology; business administration (finance, international business, management, management information systems, marketing); chemistry; classics; communication sciences & disorders; computer science/mathematics; earth science teaching; economics; elementary & secondary education; English; French; geography; geology; German; history; mathematics; medicine; music; music education; music performance; philosophy; physics; political science; predentistry; prelaw; preoptometry; prephysical therapy; preveterinary medicine; psychology; public administration; religion; Scandinavian; sociology; Spanish; speech communication; theatre.

Augustana offers coordinated degree programs in the following: Engineering, Environmental Management, Forestry, Landscape Architecture, and Occupational Therapy.

Costs and Aid

2007–2008: $33,717 comprehensive ($26,484 tuition). 90% of students receive some financial aid.

Endowment

$101 million.

Benedictine University

ILLINOIS

Benedictine University, founded in 1887, is a private, Catholic, coeducational, comprehensive liberal arts university dedicated to the education of undergraduate and graduate students from diverse ethnic, racial, and religious backgrounds. A Catholic university in the Benedictine tradition, Benedictine provides a values-centered liberal arts education enriched by excellence in science.

Admissions Contact:

Benedictine University
5700 College Road
Lisle, IL 60532
(888) 829-6363
Ph: (630) 829-6300
Email: admissions@ben.edu
www.ben.edu

The 4 Distinctions

Engaged Students

Benedictine offers forty-five undergraduate majors through the College of Science, the College of Liberal Arts, the College of Business, the College of Education and Health Services, and the Margaret and Harold Moser College of Adult and Professional Studies. The most popular majors are management, biology, psychology, elementary education, and health sciences.

Benedictine has a reputation for providing a solid education in science. Students have the opportunity to participate in research projects using the latest technology, such as the Modulus Single Tube Fluorometer, a multifunctional instrument that helps chemistry students quantitate the amount of various chemical compounds and biological macromolecules in samples, and a DNA sequencer, which enables students to investigate the structural information encoded in the human genome.

There are three options for study-abroad. Students can enroll in partner institutions through Partnership Exchange Programs, or they can participate in programs offered by third parties or in programs developed by Benedictine faculty. For example, during school breaks, business students travel to Tijuana, Mexico, to see the consequences of business decisions made in the U.S. They study poverty, urban development, human rights, manufacturing, industrial facilities, working conditions, and the impact of NAFTA. Students have also visited China, Japan, France, Spain, Korea, Ireland, and Denmark.

Alternative Spring Breaks are popular, and students have traveled to Louisiana to rebuild homes destroyed by Hurricane Katrina and to Bolivia to help in orphanages, hospitals, and day-care centers.

Great Teaching

As an academic community committed to liberal arts and professional education—distinguished and guided by its Roman Catholic tradition and Benedictine heritage—the university prepares its students for a lifetime as active, informed, and responsible citizens and leaders in the world community. Benedictine is grounded in the spirit of the founders, who based their lives and work on St. Benedict's *Rule for Monks*, written in the early sixth century. The university builds its educational life on the values of the Benedictines, including the central celebration of community as a gathering of people who share a commitment to a common mission. A Benedictine education is designed to be flexible so that it can meet current social needs, developing in its graduates the capacity to adapt as they enter the working world, and the ability to manage change and difficulties in a confident and positive manner.

Benedictine fulfills its commitment to its mission through excellence in teaching and interaction between students and faculty. A liberal arts core prepares all undergraduate students to participate fully in a diverse and dynamic society, balancing their rights and duties as individuals with the demands of the common good. Benedictine's core curriculum unites all students with a shared base of broad knowledge. Each student must take courses covering basic skills, enroll in a freshman seminar, and choose from a series of courses about cultural heritage.

Benedictine teachers are committed and accomplished. Faculty are frequently honored with local, regional, national, and international grants, fellowships, and awards.

Benedictine's students take their studies seriously, and the low student to faculty ratio of thirteen to one, combined with an average class size of twenty-five, allows students to enjoy a close familiarity with professors.

Vibrant Community

Benedictine considers residential life an important element of the college experience and offers a variety of housing options: all-male, all-female, or coeducational residences in a mix of residence hall rooms, suites, and apartments. Freshmen may have cars on campus.

In addition to intercollegiate athletics, students can choose from more than forty different organizations for extracurricular activities—each with a faculty advisor and often formed around mutual interests such as the *Candor* (the student newspaper), the Political Sciences Student Organization (an active group that recently brought a senatorial candidate to campus) and the Tri-Beta Biology Club.

Benedictine was named to the President's Higher Education Community Service Honor Roll for its participation in a range of volunteer-service activities during the 2005–2006 school year, including Hurricane Katrina relief efforts and the American Cancer Society Relay for Life. Students also help their neighboring community through participating in food and clothing drives, offering tax preparation services for low-income citizens, cleaning the campus lake, taking part in Big Brothers/Big Sisters programs, and partnering with local businesses to distribute holiday dinners to the needy.

The local area has many restaurants, a park, and golf courses. Members of the wider community attend Benedictine's Great Issues-Great Ideas Lecture Series, featuring world leaders, members of the media, and astronauts, among other notables. The Village of Lisle-Benedictine University Sports Complex, featuring a lighted multipurpose football/soccer stadium with a nine-lane track and lighted baseball and softball fields, hosts numerous events year-round.

Benedictine is one of only five colleges and universities across the United States selected to host twenty-two students from the Middle East and North Africa as part of the U.S. Department of State's Middle East Partnership Initiative Study of the United States - Summer Institutes for Student Leaders for a six-week summer program.

Benedictine's modern academic and sports facilities are situated on a rolling, tree-covered 108-acre campus 25 miles southwest of Chicago in Lisle, recently named one of the top twenty places to live in the U.S. by *Money magazine*. Benedictine also offers programs in Springfield, Illinois and in China.

Successful Outcomes

Benedictine's broad-based liberal arts program creates well-rounded students because the university believes that even if students pursue a career in science, they should be able to read, write, and speak well. Benedictine graduates contribute to and are functional members of society, making a difference in the world.

Career counselors meet with students to discuss opportunities, prepare resumes, and establish goals for what students need and want to learn. A career service library houses all career-related information for easy access by Benedictine students.

Benedictine's alumni program is active. Students can bounce ideas off graduates and can expect their resumes to be referred to friends and business associates of alumni. Benedictine graduates also bring their companies to campus for recruiting and for informational purposes.

Successful Benedictine alumni include many physicians due to the university's strength in science. Other notable alumni include Bill Callahan, former head coach of the Oakland Raiders, and David Reynolds, a Disney writer best known for The Emperor's New Groove.

Fast Facts

Benedictine University is a comprehensive, Catholic, coeducational liberal arts institution founded in 1887.

Web site

http://www.ben.edu

Location

Lisle, Illinois—25 miles west of Chicago.

Student Profile

2,657 undergraduate students (43% male, 57% female); 41 states and territories, 14 countries; 29.1% minority, 1.1% international.

Faculty Profile

94 full-time faculty. 80% hold a terminal degree in their field. 13:1 student/faculty ratio. Average class size is 25.

Residence Life

Mildly residential: 25% of students live on campus.

Athletics

NCAA Division III, Northern Athletics Conference (NAC) and Illini-Badger Football Conference (IBFC). 19 varsity sports (9 men's: baseball, basketball, cross-country, football, golf, soccer, swimming, track & field (indoor & outdoor); 10 women's: basketball, cross-country, golf, soccer, softball, swimming, tennis, track & field (indoor & outdoor), volleyball).

Academic Programs

Accounting; bilingual journalism; biochemistry/molecular biology; biology; business & economics; chemistry; clinical laboratory science; communication arts; computer information systems; computer science; diagnostic medical sonography; economics; elementary education; engineering science; English language & literature; environmental science; film studies; finance; fine arts; gender studies; global studies; health science; history; international business & economics; international studies; Latin American studies; life span services; management & organizational behavior; marketing; mathematics; music; nuclear medicine technology; nutrition; philosophy; physics; political science; prepharmacy; preprofessional programs (chiropractic, dentistry, medicine, occupational therapy, optometry, physical therapy, podiatry, veterinary medicine); psychology; radiation therapy; religious studies; secondary education; social science; social work; sociology; Spanish; special education; sports management; sports marketing; studio art; writing & publishing.

Costs and Aid

2007–2008: $28,263 comprehensive ($20,800 tuition). 92% of students receive some financial aid. Average award: $14,682.

Endowment

$20 million

More Distinctions

• *U.S. News & World Report's 2008* rankings listed Benedictine sixth in Illinois for campus diversity and as a top school in the Midwest.

Bradley University

ILLINOIS

Bradley University is a private, independent, coeducational, comprehensive university founded in 1897. With six thousand students, Bradley offers extensive resources not available at most small colleges and the personal attention not typically found at large universities.

Admissions Contact:

Bradley University
1501 West Bradley Avenue
Peoria, IL 61625
(800) 447-6460
Email: admissions@bradley.edu
www.bradley.edu

The 4 Distinctions

Engaged Students

Bradley emphasizes experiential learning and hands-on career preparation in addition to traditional classroom work; 75 percent of students have benefited from one or more of these experiences during their four years at Bradley. Additionally, nearly 15 percent of Bradley's students spend a semester or a two-week term abroad in programs ranging from studying ruins of ancient pyramids in Egypt to studying art history and language in France. Bradley students have also studied abroad in London, Madrid, Dublin, Copenhagen, Beijing, Helsinki, and in Peoria's sister city of Friedrichshafen, Germany.

Each spring, Bradley features an Undergraduate Research Expo to showcase students' research efforts. Some undergraduates go on to publish the projects presented there in scholarly journals or present the work at national conferences.

Service learning is also emphasized throughout the university, with opportunities such as a minor in leadership studies, a cross-curriculum theme in the college of Education and Health Sciences, and the Bradley Fellows program. Each year, fifteen new students enter as fellows and focus on service through volunteering. Students who participate in this program receive a stipend in return for their time commitment.

Internships are available to Bradley students in most programs. Examples include education majors who teach in one of the largest school districts in the state; health and medical students who work in one of the various facilities throughout the Downstate Medical Center of Illinois; and engineering students who often intern at Caterpillar, a leading manufacturer of construction and mining equipment and related services, whose corporate headquarters are located in Peoria.

Great Teaching

Bradley was the first coeducational, nondenominational institution in the country to be founded by a woman: Lydia Moss Bradley. The school's mission is to nurture "the multifaceted development of students to enable them to become leaders, innovators, and productive members of society." Bradley graduates are prepared "for life and professions in a changing world, and they are able to cross academic, geographic, and cultural boundaries." Bradley provides an environment of opportunities, choices, and technologies found at large universities, combined with the quality, personal attention, and challenges of a small, private college. Because of its size, Bradley has strengths in many areas. The university is especially successful at providing a balance between strong academic preparation and experiential and career-related skill development.

Bradley's unique academic structure allows the school to offer more than one hundred undergraduate and thirty graduate programs of study in five different colleges. Among the most popular majors are nursing, communications, education, accounting, and mechanical engineering. With a low student to faculty ratio of fifteen to one, professors can provide personalized attention in learning and academic advising. They serve as mentors and professional guides for their students, who benefit from working directly with professors; there are no teaching assistants.

In addition to excellent teaching, Bradley's faculty members are known for their research, scholarship, and creative abilities. More than a dozen are Fulbright scholars, who bring their experiences from around the world back to Bradley's campus. Faculty also serve as advisors for clubs and organizations such as the Model United Nations and dozens of preprofessional student organizations.

Bradley's five colleges are Education and Health Sciences, with a direct-entry doctorate program in physical therapy; Communications and Fine Arts, which features a multimillion-dollar communications center; Engineering and Technology, one of the top-ranked programs in the nation; Liberal Arts, with a broad diversity of courses; and Business Administration, with a 3/2 accounting program, a professional selling program, and a major in entrepreneurship.

The Academic Exploration Program (AEP) at Bradley offers focused undergraduate guidance to undecided majors. Nearly 20 percent of Bradley students begin their college careers with the Academic Exploration Program. Undecided students take AEP 100, an introduction to ideas that may be unfamiliar to freshmen. The course is designed to help students choose majors and gather information about careers and internship options.

Vibrant Community

Bradley is located one mile from downtown Peoria in a metropolitan area of more than 360,000 people. One of the oldest communities in the state, Peoria is located along the banks of the Illinois River in central Illinois, about three hours by car from Chicago, Indianapolis and St. Louis. The Greater Peoria Regional Airport offers direct flights to Atlanta, Chicago, Dallas, Denver, Detroit, Las Vegas, Minneapolis, St. Louis, and Tampa. Bradley's eighty-five-acre campus is self-contained: no major streets or city buildings run through the campus. The amenities of a large city are close by, including a variety of shops and restaurants.

All freshmen and sophomores live on campus in residence halls offering many different housing options. Most junior and senior students live within three blocks of campus in apartments owned by Bradley or in privately owned apartments and houses.

About 30 percent of Bradley students choose to join one of the sixteen fraternities or twelve sororities on campus, making Greek organizations a popular part of campus life. Each Greek organization provides leadership opportunities for service and friendship, and is integrally involved in student life.

Bradley offers more than two hundred clubs and organizations for students to join, so most students spend their weekends on campus. There is a spectrum of diverse student organizations such as the Bradley Ultimate Frisbee Fanatics (BUFF), the Deep-Thinkers Club, Fish Philosophy Facilitators (a group that teaches people to enjoy what they do), Habitat for Humanity, and Worship at Full Volume, a nondenominational Christian music service. With fourteen different religious organizations on campus, students have many opportunities to explore their beliefs and celebrate diversity, reflecting Bradley's wide acceptance of all religions.

Successful Outcomes

Bradley's Smith Career Center has a large staff and a variety of resources available to Bradley students. The career center offers a broad spectrum of activities to help graduates embark on successful careers. The center's resources are available to Bradley alumni throughout their lifetime.

On average, 94 percent of Bradley graduates seeking a job or admission to graduate school are placed within six months of graduation. Recent graduates have attended schools as diverse as Escuela Libre de Derecho in Mexico, the Savannah College of Art and Design, and the Vancouver Film School, as well as Boston, Duke, Georgetown, and Northwestern University.

Notable Bradley graduates include Gerald Shaheen, group president of Caterpillar Inc. and chairman of the U.S. Chamber of Commerce; Tammy Lane, Academy Award winner for best makeup in Chronicles of Narnia; Major Robert Lawrence, the nation's first black astronaut; Keith Bane, founder of Nextel phones; Neil Flynn, cast member of NBC's sitcom, Scrubs; and Dr. Nora Zorich, director of new drug development at Proctor & Gamble Pharmaceuticals.

Fast Facts

Bradley University is a comprehensive, independent, private university founded in 1897 offering bachelors and masters degrees as well as a doctorate in Physical Therapy.

Web site

http://admissions.bradley.edu

Location

Peoria, Illinois

Student Profile

5,300 undergraduate students (45% male, 55% female); 42 states and territories, 39 countries.

Faculty Profile

330 full-time faculty. 14:1 student/faculty ratio. Average class size is 23.

Residence Life

Highly residential: 90% of students live on campus. All new freshman students must live on campus or commute from home.

Athletics

NCAA Division I, Missouri Valley Conference. 14 varsity sports (6 men's: baseball, basketball, cross-country, golf, soccer, and tennis; 8 women's: basketball, cross-country, golf, indoor track, outdoor track, softball, tennis, and volleyball), 15 club sports, and 18 intramurals.

Academic Programs

Accounting; actuarial science; advertising; art; art education; art history; biochemistry; biology; business economics; cell & molecular biology; chemistry; civil engineering; communication; computer information systems; computer science; construction; criminal justice; dietetics; early childhood education; economics; electrical engineering; electronic media; elementary education; engineering physics; English; entrepreneurship; environmental science; family & consumer sciences; family & consumer sciences education; finance; foods & nutrition; French; German; graphic design; health science (leads to Bradley's Doctorate of physical therapy); history; industrial engineering; international business; international studies; journalism; learning behavior specialist; management & administration; management information systems; manufacturing engineering; manufacturing engineering technology; marketing; mathematics; mechanical engineering; medical technology; multimedia; music; music business; music composition; music education; music performance; nursing; organizational communication; philosophy; physics; political science; psychology; public relations; religious studies; retail merchandising; secondary education; social work; sociology; Spanish; teacher education; theatre arts; theatre performance; and theatre production.

Costs and Aid

2007–2008: $28,428 comprehensive ($21,200 tuition). 90% of students receive some financial aid. Average award: $14,200.

Endowment (as of June 2006)

$ 205,800,000.

Dominican University

ILLINOIS

Dominican University (DU) is a Catholic, coeducational, comprehensive, teaching university, founded in 1901. As DU enters its second century, its mission continues to be to prepare students "to pursue truth, to give compassionate service and to participate in the creation of a more just and humane world."

Admissions Contact:

Dominican University
7900 West Division Street
River Forest, IL 60305
(800) 828-8475
Ph: (708) 524-6800
Email: domadmis@dom.edu
www.ican.dom.edu

The 4 Distinctions

Engaged Students

DU's study abroad and experiential learning opportunities are particularly noteworthy. One of the first schools to provide off-campus study opportunities for its students, DU now offers programs around the world in places such as England, France, Italy, Spain, El Salvador, South Africa, and China.

Service-learning programs at Dominican take advantage of the school's Chicago-area location. These programs combine community service with academic instruction focused on critical, reflective thinking and civic responsibility. Students are involved in organized community service addressing local needs and directly linked to the curriculum. Dominican offers over thirty service-learning courses that allow students to earn credit while helping others. In 2006, Dominican's service-learning program was recognized with the prestigious Jimmy and Rosalyn Carter Partnership Award for Campus-Community Collaboration.

DU's internship program, staffed by a full-time director, helps students make the most of the school's location in the Chicago area. DU students have worked with fashion buyers, designed brochures for a park district, researched investment options for a venture capitalist firm, helped a state senator run for reelection, and worked on historic preservation projects at the Frank Lloyd Wright Preservation Trust. Students have interned at two hundred different sites, including a variety of businesses, the Chicago Cubs baseball team, and local cultural organizations.

Great Teaching

A key advantage to the Dominican education is the relationship between faculty and students. The twelve to one student to faculty ratio allows professors to become involved in students' individual academic pursuits. Small classes are typical at DU; 73% have fewer than 20 students. In addition, faculty members often sponsor student organizations and clubs related to academic subjects, encouraging faculty/student interactions beyond the classroom.

The three most popular majors, in order, are business and its related subjects, sociology, and psychology. Business-related major subjects appeal to many students because of their practical applications, entrepreneurial outlook, the international focus of the curriculum, and opportunities to study abroad. Edward Brennan, the retired CEO of Sears, Roebuck and Co., and his wife Lois (class of 1955) think so highly of the value of a Dominican education that they have made a generous gift to ensure that DU's Brennan School of Business has the resources to prepare the next generation of ethical business leaders. Sociology majors have a strong desire to understand society and effect positive change. A psychology major offers students challenging internships and service opportunities in the Chicago area and superb laboratory resources, as well as the most active academic club on campus.

Parmer Hall, a new, state-of-the-art academic building, was designed to promote student-faculty interaction. The facility includes dedicated space for student-faculty research projects as well as numerous areas for group and individual study. The sciences are the fastest growing majors at Dominican. Many students prepare for future careers in the health sciences and participate in a unique internship program with Rush Oak Park Hospital.

Students benefit from DU's respect for the individual, an attitude that encourages authentic self-expression for students from all backgrounds, nationalities, and religious traditions. Faculty members work one-on-one with students to help them succeed in achieving their goals and preparing for the next stage of their lives.

In DU's Rosary College of Arts and Sciences, each undergraduate student has a dedicated faculty advisor—initially the student's freshman seminar professor and, later, a professor from the student's chosen major field. Small class sizes allow faculty members to get to know and to encourage each of their students, regardless of their major field of study. Most DU alumni say they value their relationships with faculty above all other experiences at DU.

Vibrant Community

Dominican University welcomes students from all faith backgrounds and values diversity among its students, faculty, and staff. DU students are culturally aware and active in the world beyond the campus. DU's convenient location—a twenty-minute ride via public transportation or an easy drive from downtown Chicago—allows the student body to take advantage of the Windy City's unique and multifaceted cultural life, including museums, professional sports, and theater, as well as many diverse communities.

As the cultural and financial hub of the Midwest, Chicago offers a wide range of excellent museums, restaurants, sporting events, and cultural activities. Chicago Transit Authority and Metra Rail stations are conveniently located just a few minutes away from campus. Chicago's diverse communities and thriving business environment provide a broad spectrum of opportunities for DU students seeking jobs or internships.

DU's atmosphere is energetic and diverse. Its small campus size encourages intimacy among different groups of students, and opportunities for all students to intermingle with the faculty. In a recent survey, students said they loved DU's size, small learning groups, teamwork, and student diversity. Most students take part in at least one of the many ethnic and cultural, academic, departmental, or special interest clubs and organizations on campus. Involvement transcripts record students' participation in service or activities outside the classroom. The Campus Activities Board sponsors many campuswide activities, ranging from music and comedy nights, trips to Cubs and White Sox games, casino nights, and dances.

Many students choose Dominican for the opportunity to participate in intercollegiate athletics. Dominican is a member of the NCAA Division III and the Northern Athletic Conference. Men's teams include baseball, basketball, cross-country, soccer, and tennis. Women compete in basketball, cross-country, soccer, softball, tennis, and volleyball. The men's soccer team has advanced to the NCAA Division III tournament for the last several seasons, and the men's club volleyball team also competes successfully at the national level.

Dominican University offers students many opportunities to participate in the arts. The performing arts series brings a wide variety of musical acts to campus. Students can participate as stage crew and ushers or take advantage of discounted student tickets. The theater arts program mounts at least three major productions a year, including a popular musical. Students build sets, make costumes, and perform.

Successful Outcomes

DU graduates have an advantage in a competitive job market and the graduate school application process because of their service and internship experiences. A survey of recent DU graduates showed that 25 percent are full-time graduate students, 14 percent are part-time graduate students, 72 percent are employed, and 80 percent of those who are employed are working in a field related to their major.

Alumni say that the theme of providing service and giving back to the community is common across all DU programs. Regardless of occupation, DU alumni feel compelled to live out the school's mission—"to pursue truth, to give compassionate service and to participate in the creation of a more just and humane world" —in everything they do.

Fast Facts

Dominican University is a Catholic, comprehensive, teaching university founded in 1901.

Web site

www.ican.dom.edu

Location

River Forest, Illinois—10 miles from downtown Chicago.

Student Profile

1,462 undergraduate students, 3,292 total; 24 states, 18 countries; 30% minority, 2% international.

Faculty Profile

97 full-time faculty. 92% hold a terminal degree in their field. 12:1 student/faculty ratio. Average class size is 15.

Residence Life

60% of freshmen and 42% of all eligible undergraduates live on campus.

Athletics

NCAA Division III, Northern Athletics Conference (NAC). 11 varsity sports (5 men's: baseball, basketball, cross-country, soccer, tennis; 6 women's: basketball, cross-country, softball, soccer, tennis, volleyball), 3 club sports, and 7 intramurals.

Academic Programs

Accounting; addiction counseling; African/African American studies; American studies; apparel design; apparel merchandising; art; art history; biology; biology-chemistry; business administration; chemistry; communication arts & sciences; computer information systems; computer science; corporate communication; criminology; economics; education (early childhood, elementary, secondary); English; environmental science; food industry management; food science & nutrition; French; graphic design; history; information technology; international business; international relations & diplomacy; Italian; mathematics; mathematics & computer science; natural sciences; nursing; nutrition & dietetics; pastoral ministry; pharmacy; philosophy; photography; political science; preprofessional programs (predental, prelaw, premedical, prepharmacy); psychology; social science; sociology; Spanish; theatre arts, theology.

Costs and Aid

2007–2008: $29,450 comprehensive ($22,350 tuition). In 2006, 75% of first-year students received need-based financial aid.

Endowment

$18 million.

More Distinctions

• *U.S. News & World Report* consistently rates Dominican a best value in recognition of excellent academic programs provided at a moderate price. The publication has consistently ranked the school in the top tier of Midwest regional universities.

• Dominican is a member of Peterson's Competitive Colleges.

Elmhurst College

ILLINOIS

A private, four-year college in the liberal arts tradition, Elmhurst College consistently ranks among the top colleges in the Midwest. In small classes, Elmhurst students work with faculty whose top priority is teaching and mentoring. The college is located in a quiet suburb sixteen miles west of downtown Chicago.

Admissions Contact:

Elmhurst College
190 Prospect Avenue
Elmhurst, Illinois 60126-3296
(800) 697-1871
Ph: (630) 617-3400
Email: admit@elmhurst.edu
www.elmhurst.edu

The 4 Distinctions

Engaged Students

Academic programs at Elmhurst are characterized by their real-world connections and responsiveness to student needs. Students conduct research and defend their results. They analyze data, think critically, solve problems collaboratively, study and write across the disciplines, and learn to formulate new ideas and to convey them effectively. Each year, students of all majors share their original research at the college's Undergraduate Research and Performance Showcase.

Off campus, students can participate in a wealth of internship and job-shadowing experiences, both in the Chicago area and beyond. One student recently shadowed a renowned neurosurgeon in San Francisco; another worked on staff at the Mayo Clinic in Rochester, Minnesota; a third traveled to New York to participate in a high-level discussion of medical ethics.

Elmhurst offers international education experiences in many countries, including Spain, the Netherlands, Poland, Bulgaria, and England. Students can go abroad for a semester, a year, or for a month during the college's distinctive January Term.

"My two Elmhurst internships were incredible experiences. I learned first-hand about fundraising, disaster response, coordinating volunteers and a lot more. I also got a chance to study abroad. Best of all, I've met friends who are willing to meet me head-on and talk about the big issues. It's tested me as a person and enabled me to grow."

- Ashley Greuel

Great Teaching

About 85 percent of Elmhurst's full-time faculty members hold the highest degree in their academic field, usually a PhD. Elmhurst professors, who have studied at some of the nation's best colleges and universities, are scholars, researchers, and practitioners whose professional expertise enriches classroom discussions.

Faculty members' top priority is teaching. Every class at Elmhurst is taught by a faculty member, never a teaching assistant. The faculty to student ratio is only thirteen to one, and the average class has nineteen students. These small classes help to promote lively discussions. In addition to knowing students by name, Elmhurst professors often know their students' interests, strengths, and concerns. Professors at Elmhurst are known for their availability, meeting students during office hours, giving out their cell phone numbers, and performing research with undergraduates.

The most popular majors at Elmhurst are business, education, and nursing. The large school district and nearby hospitals provide many opportunities for education and nursing majors. The Center for the Health Professions assists nursing majors as well as all other majors in health professions. The center brings together students from across the health-care spectrum for an innovative mix of academic and cocurricular programs, and offers advisors to help students identify career goals and select the courses to help them achieve those goals.

At Elmhurst's Niebuhr Center, students can live out the mission of service to society. The center's Callings for the Common Good is an academic program for students who are motivated by faith—whatever their religious background or spiritual beliefs. The program guides and supports students in any major who are considering a calling to a service profession or ministry. Through courses, paid internships in the ministry, and opportunities to preach or participate in a local ministry, students explore their calling to better the world.

Vibrant Community

Elmhurst College is located in the quiet suburb of Elmhurst, a community of 43,000 that has been called "the quintessential Chicago suburb." Downtown Elmhurst is just two blocks north of the campus and is filled with family-owned stores and restaurants. Within walking distance from campus are two art museums, a library, an eight-screen movie house, a number of restaurants, and more. About 50 percent of Elmhurst students live on campus.

Life at Elmhurst is active and creative. Students get involved in more than one hundred activities, from theater to intramurals to the mock trial team. The student newspaper has been honored with awards, and Elmhurst College's radio station has been on the air since 1947. The campus regularly hosts performances, art exhibits, and an array of excellent guest speakers.

Student athletes at Elmhurst compete on eighteen teams in NCAA Division III. About one fourth of the freshman class comes in as athletes. In the past decade, Bluejay teams have won conference championships in five sports. They compete in first-rate facilities such as Langhorst Field, which sits in the center of campus and attracts crowds of students to watch the games, and which is home to the football, soccer, and track and field programs.

The college is just a short train ride from downtown Chicago, where students enjoy unlimited access to world-class cultural and professional opportunities from internships to sporting events to concerts of all kinds.

Successful Outcomes

An Elmhurst education is practical. Students at Elmhurst don't have to choose between a great liberal education and strong professional preparation. In today's world, students need both—and at Elmhurst, they get both. Each major offers both cutting-edge theory and abundant opportunities to examine and practice how the theory actually works. The result is a rigorously intellectual preparation for life. For example, a business class might craft a marketing plan for an area nonprofit organization. An assignment for a speech pathology class might include asking students to evaluate patients at the college's own Speech-Language-Hearing Clinic.

Outside the classroom, Elmhurst offers hundreds of internships with some of the Chicago area's leading employers. Each internship is designed to help students explore their career options and sharpen their professional skills.

Within six months of commencement, nearly every member of each year's graduating class has launched his or her career in a job, in graduate school, or both. Elmhurst graduates build successful careers in corporations, nonprofit organizations, educational institutions, law firms, medical centers, research laboratories, and countless other venues. They thrive in demanding careers because they've learned to embrace new ideas, master advanced technologies, and create original solutions to problems old and new.

Fast Facts

Elmhurst College is a four-year liberal arts college founded in 1871 and affiliated with the United Church of Christ.

Web site

http://www.elmhurst.edu

Location

Elmhurst, Illinois—16 miles west of Chicago.

Student Profile

2,400 undergraduate students (40% male, 60% female); 17 states and territories, 12 countries; 19% minority, 2% international.

Faculty Profile

85% of full-time faculty hold a terminal degree in their field. 13:1 student/faculty ratio. Average class size is 19.

Residence Life

Moderately residential: 50% of students live on campus.

Athletics

NCAA Division III, Conference of Illinois and Wisconsin. 18 varsity sports (9 men's: baseball, basketball, cross-country, football, golf, soccer, tennis, track & field, wrestling; 9 women's: basketball, bowling, cross-country, golf, soccer, softball, tennis, track & field, volleyball) and 7 intramurals.

Academic Programs

Accounting; American studies; art; art business; art education; biology business administration; chemistry; communication studies; computer game & entertainment technology; computer science; early childhood education; economics; elementary education; English; environmental geosciences; exercise science; finance; French; geography; German; history; information systems; interdepartmental; interdisciplinary communication studies; international business; jazz studies; logistics & supply chain management; management; marketing; mathematics; music; musical theatre; music business; music education; nursing; organizational communication; philosophy; physical education; physics; political science; psychology; religion & service; secondary education; sociology; Spanish; special education; speech-language pathology; theatre; theatre arts education; theological studies & Christian ministry; theology & religion; urban studies.

Costs and Aid

2007-2008: $31,884 comprehensive ($24,600 tuition). 86% of students received some financial aid. Average award: $18,200.

Endowment

$81 million.

More Distinctions

• Elmhurst College has an extensive program of scholarships based on academic credentials.

• Elmhurst is ranked in the top tier of Midwestern 'best universities-master's colleges' by *U.S. News & World Report*.

Illinois College

ILLINOIS

Illinois College (IC) is a private liberal arts college with a rich history, committed to the highest standards of scholarship and integrity. The oldest Phi Beta Kappa college in the state, IC was founded in 1829 by students from Yale University during their travels west to establish institutes of higher learning.

Admissions Contact:

Illinois College
1101 West College Avenue
Jacksonville, IL 62650
(866) 464-5265
Ph: (217) 245-3030
Fax: (217) 245-3034
Email: admissions@ic.edu
www.ic.edu

The 4 Distinctions

Engaged Students

From the moment they arrive on campus, IC students are engaged – academically, athletically, socially and in outreach to the community.

Illinois College's most popular majors are education and business-related programs, while premed and prelaw are growing in popularity. Education majors participate in a service-learning practicum, and students regularly offer their services to alternative schools. Recently, more than twenty-five education majors provided a personal boost for at-risk elementary and high school students when they took part in an innovative program that sought to enrich the academic experience for students who desperately need additional teaching resources.

Students have the opportunity to participate in collaborative research within several academic programs throughout the college's curriculum. For example, a significant number of science majors have worked under the supervision of staff at the Southern Illinois University School of Medicine in Springfield in order to complete scholarly research on a number of conditions commonly found among the population of the nearby Jacksonville Mental Health and Developmental Center. Their efforts have been an important addition to the ongoing study of ways to effectively treat these conditions.

Other popular educational opportunities at IC include internships and study-abroad opportunities. Each year, more than 87 students intern at both local and national companies, gaining invaluable experience in their chosen field of study. In addition to encouraging students to participate in study-abroad programs, IC's "BreakAway" program offers participants the chance to travel with professors on short trips, instead of spending entire semesters abroad. This year students are headed to Greece, Morocco, and Spain.

The ongoing development of Illinois College's Intercultural Exchange Program with Kyoto's Ritsumeikan University offers IC students an opportunity to explore the culture of Japan either through studying at Ritsumeikan or by welcoming a Ritsumeikan student to the IC campus. Since the program began in 1987, several IC graduates have gone into international education and served as English-language instructors at schools across Japan.

Great Teaching

Great teachers abound at Illinois College. The college's innovative IC Connections Program instantly establishes the student professor relationship as the cornerstone of a successful academic experience. Even before the official start of classes, professors and students meet in small groups to discuss the importance of making a successful transition to college, creating a partnership that remains in place throughout a students' undergraduate career. IC places great emphasis on mentoring, and personal access to faculty is instrumental in the journey.

Great teachers bring a wealth of resources with them to IC and students are encouraged to take advantage of their professors' wide spectrum of academic interests and scholarly pursuits outside the classroom. A growing number of professors are engaged in collaborative research with students, and their efforts have led to an increasing number of student publications and scholarship presentations.

Vibrant Community

With two colleges and a number of other educational institutions located within its borders, the Jacksonville community is vibrant and alive offering students many cultural and artistic opportunities. Students can be found participating in programs through the Strawn Art Gallery and the Jacksonville Theatre Guild as well as hanging out at The Three Legged Dog coffee house in downtown plaza or at IC's Common Grounds coffee house. The Bruner Fitness and Recreation Center on campus offers a variety of classes and programs from yoga to spinning or students can relax and catch a movie at one of the three theatres in town or take in any number of high school and/or college sporting events throughout the seasons.

Located just 35 miles west of the state capital of Springfield and ninety miles north of St. Louis, IC boasts a New England-style academic quadrangle along with new facilities from one end of the campus to the other, including the state-of-the-art Parker Science Center and Bruner Fitness and Recreation Center.

IC students can choose to reside in single-gender, coed, suite-style, and apartment-living residence halls, along with two foreign-language houses. The introduction of language houses on campus has provided students with added opportunities to practice their conversational skills in German and Spanish while our newest residence hall – a coed hall was built as a totally "Green" building, helping students reside in an environmentally conscious setting.

The college offers unlimited opportunities to get involved with over seventy-five clubs, organizations, and leadership opportunities on campus, including academic honor societies, student publications, music groups, and religious organizations.

IC students also understand the importance of civic engagement as they prepare for lives of service and leadership. IC students regularly volunteer at such organizations as the American Cancer Society, Big Brothers/Big Sisters, Habitat for Humanity, and the Special Olympics to name a few.

While a small campus, IC has had a long history of inviting prominent speakers and visitors to campus to engage the student body. Among the prominent visitors to campus during the college's early years were such well-known individuals as Abraham Lincoln, Ralph Waldo Emerson, Mark Twain, and Daniel Webster. Recent guests on campus have included Paul Rusesabagina, human rights activist and subject of Hotel Rwanda; the late Coretta Scott King, civil rights leader; and Peter Arnett, Pulitzer Prize-winning journalist.

Successful Outcomes

IC students receive extraordinary recognition and honors both during their time at the college and after graduation. Earlier this spring, IC senior Cindy Arnold was honored at the International Convention of the Sigma Tau Delta English Honor Society. Seniors Jessica Rubino, a biology and chemistry major, and Erin Kennelly a Spanish major, presented abstracts at the National Conferences on Undergraduate Research.

Illinois College has an outstanding career center that assists students with resume preparation, cover letter writing, and interview skills. The college also offers workshops, access to numerous career fairs, off-campus interviews, and the latest in computerized job searches. Employers are eager to hire IC graduates because IC students have garnered valuable practical experience through local, national, and international internships. Employers of recent IC graduates include the Boeing Company, Caterpillar Inc., the Chicago Board of Trade, the Department of Homeland Security, Ernst & Young, the Federal Deposit Insurance Corporation, General Electric, the Illinois House of Representatives, Motorola, Pepsi, Roche Pharmaceuticals, and Wells Fargo Financial.

IC graduates are also increasingly choosing to continue their educational pursuits; each year Illinois College students are admitted to the nation's top medical, law, and graduate schools. Recent graduates are currently studying at Boston University, Clemson University, Harvard University, the John Marshall Law School, Saint Louis University, the University of Chicago, the University of Pennsylvania, and Washington University.

Fast Facts

Illinois College is an independent, residential, four-year, liberal arts institution affiliated with the Presbyterian Church (U.S.A.) and the United Church of Christ. Founded in 1829, Illinois College is considered the cradle of higher education in Illinois. College-level instruction in the Prairie State began at Illinois College in 1830, and the College awarded the state's first bachelor's degree in 1835.

Web site

http:// www.ic.edu

Location

Jacksonville, Illinois—the 65-acre campus is situated in a community of 20,000 in west-central Illinois, located 35 miles west of the state capital in Springfield, 90 miles north of St. Louis and 235 miles southwest of Chicago.

Student Profile

1,023 undergraduate students (48% male, 52% female); 21 states and territories, 14 countries; 7.3 % minority, 2.2% international.

Faculty Profile

72 full-time faculty. 82% hold a terminal degree in their field. 13:1 student/faculty ratio. Median class size is 16.

Residence Life

Highly residential: 70% of students live on campus. Freshman, sophomore and junior students are required to live on campus.

Athletics

NCAA Division III, Midwest Conference. 20 varsity sports (10 men's: baseball, basketball, cross-country, football, golf, indoor track, outdoor track, soccer, swimming, tennis; 10 women's: basketball, cross-country, golf, indoor track, outdoor track, soccer, softball, swimming, tennis, volleyball), 3 club sports and 10 intramurals.

Academic Programs

Accounting; American studies; art; biology (occupational therapy, exercise science); biochemistry; chemistry; communication & rhetorical studies; computer science; economics (finance); education (early childhood, elementary, physical education, secondary education); English (literature, expository writing, creative writing); environmental biology; environmental biology/chemistry; fine arts; French; German; history; interdisciplinary studies; international studies; management & organizational leadership (management, sport management); management information systems; mathematics; music; philosophy; physics (engineering); political science; psychology; religion; sociology; Spanish; theatre.

Combined degree programs: cytotechnology, engineering, medical technology, occupational therapy.

Costs and Aid

2007–2008: $25,770 comprehensive ($18,600 tuition). 97% of students receive some financial aid.

Endowment

$124 million.

Illinois Wesleyan University

ILLINOIS

Founded in 1850 and affiliated with the Methodist Church, Illinois Wesleyan University (IWU) is a liberal arts university located in Bloomington-Normal. Dedicated to undergraduate study and offering a diverse curriculum in liberal arts, fine arts, and professional programs, IWU fosters the development of multitalented students through commitment to diversity, social justice, and environmental sustainability.

Admissions Contact:

Illinois Wesleyan University
1312 Park Street
Bloomington, IL 61701
Ph: (309) 556-3031
Email: iwuadmit@iwu.edu
www.iwu.edu

The 4 Distinctions

Engaged Students

IWU offers a balanced liberal arts education that fosters the success of its multitalented student population and provides its students with the diverse experiences needed to prepare them for a global society.

As a solely undergraduate community, IWU dedicates all of its resources and unique opportunities to its 2,100 undergraduate students. Many students choose to conduct research in their fields, and this work is supported by the annual John Wesley Powell Research Conference held on campus. In 2007, nearly 140 students participated in the conference. Presentations traditionally deal in a wide range of subjects, from the natural and social sciences to areas such as music composition, international studies, history, and more.

IWU students often complement their education with a study-abroad experience. Students can take advantage of nearly two hundred semester- and yearlong programs in over sixty countries, or participate in monthlong study-abroad courses offered during the distinctive May term portion of the 4-4-1 academic calendar. IWU is also one of twelve schools nationwide to have an exchange program with Oxford University.

The community surrounding Illinois Wesleyan offers distinctive opportunities as students look to supplement their classroom experiences with off-campus learning experiences. The best example of this is the Action Research Center, which coordinates research projects undertaken by Illinois Wesleyan University students, faculty, and staff in partnership with groups in the larger central Illinois community. Current projects include work on McLean County's ten-year plan to end homelessness, a tutoring and mentoring program, and work with the Ecology Action Center to reduce pesticide use.

Great Teaching

All of Illinois Wesleyan's courses are taught by professors, and 92 percent of the faculty members hold terminal degrees in their fields. Through the faculty advising program, every student has a faculty advisor during their entire four-year college career. With a student to faculty ratio of eleven to one and an average class size of eighteen, faculty members are drawn to IWU by the one-on-one interaction that students themselves are seeking.

Relationships with professors are developed early with the help of the distinctive Gateway Colloquium course—a small, discussion-oriented course designed to develop first-year students' proficiency in writing academic and public discourse. This course is capped at fifteen students.

Every professor holds at least five office hours each week, but this is just one example of the accessibility of faculty. Faculty members actively seek out students for participation in independent studies and research projects. While the traditional semesters afford opportunities for these types of endeavors, the May term is often utilized for these experiences, as well.

Most classes at IWU are small, personal, and discussion-based. In fact, only six students need to register for a course in order for the course to be taught. There are exceptions to this rule, and courses with as few as two students have taken place.

Dr. Narendra Jaggi, professor of physics, was recently named Illinois Professor of the Year by the Carnegie Foundation for the Advancement of Teaching. IWU faculty members consistently receive grants to help them continue and expand upon their work and research. Recently, grants have been awarded in areas such as music composition, green chemistry, and nursing.

Vibrant Community

IWU has an eighty-acre campus located in suburban Bloomington-Normal, Illinois, about two hours south of Chicago and within three hours of St. Louis and Indianapolis. Bloomington-Normal is one of the fastest-growing communities in Illinois, with a population of 125,000 permanent residents. With Illinois State University located eight blocks north of IWU's campus, there are roughly twenty-two thousand college students in town nine months of the year. With two universities so closely situated, Bloomington-Normal thrives as a college town, replete with numerous restaurants, coffee shops, an indoor and outdoor mall, movie theaters, and a diversity of entertainment. The local media pay close attention to IWU sports and campus events, and the university is a centerpiece of this central Illinois community.

On campus, the school's ten Greek fraternities and sororities account for 30 percent of the campus population, providing a balance between Greek life and independent life. With a diverse student body, professional schools of music and theatre, eighteen successful NCAA Division III sports teams, an active and engaged student senate, and a residential campus with over 80 percent of the students living on campus, students are never lacking for things to do beyond academics.

In recent years, entertainers and guest lecturers have included Maya Angelou, Ben Folds, Kurt Vonnegut, Cornell West, Gavin DeGraw, Angela Davis, Dr. James Watson, John Updike, Magic Johnson, Mat Kearney, Dmitri Martin, and many others.

Successful Outcomes

In a typical year, about 30 percent of IWU graduates will pursue an advanced degree, whether at graduate school, medical school, law school, or other type of institution. Recently, IWU graduates have attended institutions such as: Harvard, Yale, Princeton, Columbia, Brown, Georgetown, Duke, Oxford, Stanford, and Emory.

IWU graduates benefit from the school's diverse, flexible liberal arts curricula, and about 20 percent of each year's graduates complete a double major. Students also benefit from a diverse student body—IWU's diversity enrollment has increased by 50 percent over the last ten years.

IWU boasts a medical school acceptance rate nearly twice the national average—the acceptance rate typically hovers around 90 percent. Challenging, fast-paced courses; research and internship/externship opportunities; and small classes and labs all play a role in preparing students for the MCAT and medical school.

Overall, IWU has a 92 percent employment placement rate. IWU's School of Nursing has a 100 percent employment placement rate, and the Music Education program has placed all of its graduates into the teaching profession over the last eight years. Also, in 2006, IWU accounting students had the highest CPA pass rate in the state of Illinois.

Famous Illinois Wesleyan alumni include Mike Mason, executive assistant director of the FBI ; Adlai Stevenson, former U.S. vice president ; Dawn Upshaw, three-time Grammy winner; Jack Sikma, seven-time NBA All-Star ; B. Charles Ames, former CEO of BFGoodrich, Kinko's, and Lexmark; Ed Rust, State Farm CEO; and Frankie Faison, actor.

Fast Facts

Illinois Wesleyan University is a private, four-year, liberal arts college affiliated with the Methodist Church, and was founded in 1850.

Web site

http:// www.iwu.edu

Location

Bloomington, Illinois.

Student Profile

2,137 undergraduate Students (43% male, 57% female); 85% in-state students, 15% out-of state students.

Faculty Profile

170 full-time faculty. 12:1 student/faculty ratio. Average class size is 18.

Residence Life

Highly residential: 80% of all undergraduates live in college housing.

Athletics

NCAA Division III. 18 varsity sports (9 men's: baseball, basketball, cross-country, football, golf, soccer, swimming, tennis, track & field; 9 women's: basketball, cross-country, golf, soccer, softball, swimming, tennis, track & field, volleyball), club sports, and intramurals (badminton, cheerleading, diving, equestrian, football non-tackle, ice hockey, lacrosse, track & field, water polo.)

Academic Programs

Area, ethnic, cultural, & gender studies; arts (visual & performing); biological & biomedical sciences; business, management, & marketing; computer & information sciences; education; English language & literature; foreign language & literature; health professions & clinical sciences; history; mathematics; natural resources & conservation; philosophy & religion; physical sciences; psychology; social sciences.

Costs and Aid

2007-2008: $38,010 comprehensive ($30,580 tuition). Average percent of need met: 91%. Average financial aid package: $21,636.

Endowment

$171,000,000.

More Distinctions

- The Princeton Review Top 361 Colleges.

- Fiske Guide to Colleges "Best Buy."

- The Unofficial, Unbiased Insider's Guide to the 320 Most Interesting Colleges.

- Visiting Scholars program to Oxford University.

Lake Forest College

ILLINOIS

Lake Forest College (LFC) is an independent, national, liberal arts college founded in 1857. The college's 1,400 students come from forty-seven states and fifty-four countries, providing many cross-cultural learning opportunities. LFC students learn to read critically, reason analytically, communicate persuasively, and think for themselves.

Admissions Contact:

Lake Forest College
555 N. Sheridan Rd.
Lake Forest, Illinois 60045
(888) 828-4751
Ph: (847) 234-3100
www.lakeforest.edu

The 4 Distinctions

Engaged Students

Every year, almost 50 percent of LFC students graduate with internship credit, and all students take advantage of an experiential-learning opportunity outside the classroom during their time at LFC. The Center for Chicago Programs connects the college community to the cultural, historic, and educational riches of Chicago. This program facilitates academic experiences and internships at Chicago institutions. It also brings experts and artists to campus for classroom discussions, as well as public lectures and performances.

LFC offers five study-abroad programs of its own and ten other opportunities through its affiliation with the Associated Colleges of the Midwest (ACM). The college's own programs include international internship programs in France and Chile, an interdisciplinary humanities program in Greece and Turkey, a new Asian-studies program in Beijing, and a special course on tropical ecology with a spring-break trip to a tropical biology research center.

The school's special program for outstanding first-year students, the Richter Apprentice Scholar Program, provides students with an additional opportunity to enrich the learning experience. During the second semester of their first year, Richter Scholars take a special interdisciplinary seminar that explores the range of disciplines encompassed within a liberal arts education. Over the summer, Richter scholars are employed for ten weeks as research assistants, working one-on-one with a member of the faculty. Recent research topics include the neurobiology of memory capacity, the psychological process of people involved in genocide, the role of federal housing policy on residential segregation, and a variety of other topics. Richter Scholars are frequently cited as coauthors on academic papers.

Great Teaching

The distinguished scholars on the faculty take pride in their commitment to teaching, and they know students by name. There are no teaching assistants at Lake Forest; all classes are taught by faculty members. LFC faculty members, 98 percent of whom hold PhDs, have won national teaching awards and have spoken and consulted throughout the United States and abroad. More than 30 percent have published books in their disciplines.

Members of the faculty frequently build on what students are learning in the classroom with trips to Chicago. For example, a political science professor takes students to public housing developments to learn about housing issues by talking with tenants, housing authority employees, and community leaders. Students also regularly travel to the Chicago Shakespeare Theater, the Chicago Board of Trade, and the Chicago Mercantile Exchange.

The general-education curriculum begins with a course in the First-Year Studies Program, special first-year seminars that every student is required to take. Many of these courses take advantage of Chicago as a "geographically extended classroom." Students are also required to meet the terms of a writing requirement in addition to taking two credits in the humanities, social sciences, and natural and mathematical sciences. The general-education curriculum also includes a cultural diversity requirement.

Students with a strong academic record during their first two years can apply at the end of their sophomore year to participate in the Independent Scholar Program. The program allows students to work with a faculty advisor to design their own major.

Vibrant Community

The campus' 107 acres combine open vistas and wooded ravines, where modern buildings are complemented by renovated late nineteenth- and early twentieth-century architecture. About 85 percent of students live on campus, and students play an active role in governing the LFC community. The board of trustees, the college council, and most all governance committees have at least two student representatives. More than 30 percent of the student body participates in varsity athletics and another 35 percent participate in nonvarsity athletics. In addition to its seventeen varsity teams, LFC offers over thirty club and intramural sports, ranging from aikido and rock climbing to sailing, lacrosse, and rugby. Lake Forest has two national fraternities and five national sororities. Approximately 15 percent of the student body is involved in Greek life.

LFC's ten residence halls encompass a number of different living environments, including all women's, coed, upperclassmen's, predominately first year, or twenty-four-hour quiet. All residence halls are smoke free.

The vibrant resources of downtown Chicago, located thirty miles from campus, enrich the LFC experience, as does the proximity to Lake Michigan. Chicago's North Shore suburbs provide many entertainment opportunities. Downtown Lake Forest, within walking distance from campus, has many shops and restaurants, and the Lake Forest beach is just a short stroll away. The college provides a daily shuttle to many surrounding towns, and the train to Chicago and the North Shore suburbs is located in downtown Lake Forest. The Lake Forest area also provides opportunities for outdoor pursuits such as hiking and biking on trails and natural prairies. Whether it's participating in college-sponsored trips, attending live concerts or performances, or just hanging out with friends in the new Mohr Student Center playing pool or watching a sporting event on the large-screen TVs, there are plenty of activities for LFC students to take advantage of.

Successful Outcomes

Providing interactive workshops and individual career counseling, the career advancement center helps students to establish skills, assess interests and values, learn about career opportunities, and make connections with alumni in their fields of interest. It also helps students plan for internship and study-abroad experiences.

The college and its alumni association host events around the country. 12,250 alumni in sixty countries and all fifty states are actively engaged in the college. Many are involved with student-mentor programs, assist with internships, and support the college through participation and financial donations.

LFC graduates go on to do interesting things in a variety of fields. Alumni include a producer with Fox Sports Chicago, a portfolio manager with Goldman Sachs, a gospel recording artist, and a space tactics officer with the Air Force. Other notable alumni are Forbes magazine's 2001 Entrepreneur of the Year, James Foster; designer Nate Berkus; Pulitzer Prize administrator Sig Gissler; and singer/songwriter Steve Goodman.

Fast Facts

Lake Forest College is a coeducational undergraduate institution offering students the opportunities and challenges of a liberal arts education. The institution was founded in 1857.

Web site

http://www.lakeforest.edu/

Location

Lake Forest, Illinois—30 miles north of downtown Chicago on the western shore of Lake Michigan.

Student Profile

1,400 students (42% male, 58% female);47 states and 54 countries; 14% minority, 13% international.

Faculty Profile

117 faculty. 12:1 student/faculty ratio. Average class size is 19.

Residence Life

Highly residential: 85% of students live on campus.

Athletics

NCAA Division III, Midwest Conference and Northern Collegiate Hockey Association. 17 varsity sports (8 men's: basketball, cross-country, football, handball, hockey, soccer, swimming & diving, wrestling; 9 women's: basketball, cross-country, handball, ice hockey, soccer, swimming & diving, tennis, volleyball, softball) and more than 30 club and intramural sports.

Academic Programs

African-American studies; American studies; area studies; art (studio & art history); Asian studies; biology; business; chemistry; classical studies; communications; computer science; economics; education; English (literature & writing); environmental studies; history; independent scholar program; international relations; Latin American studies; mathematics; metropolitan studies; modern languages & literatures (Arabic, Chinese, French, German, Italian, Japanese, Portuguese, Russian, & Spanish); music; philosophy; physics; politics; preprofessional programs (law, medicine, dentistry, veterinary medicine); psychology; religion; sociology & anthropology; theater; women's & gender studies.

Costs and Aid

2006–2007: $36,124 comprehensive ($28,700 tuition).

Endowment

$64.3 million.

More Distinctions

- Lake Forest is one of forty liberal arts colleges selected by U.S. News & World Report as a Best Value in the 2007 list of "Great Schools at Great Prices."

- Lake Forest is ranked number two for Students Happy with Financial Aid in the Princeton Review's 2005 The Best 357 Colleges.

- Lake Forest College maintains an active chapter of Sigma Xi, the Scientific Research Society. The college is one of only five hundred institutions worldwide to have a Sigma Xi chapter.

Loyola University Chicago

ILLINOIS

One of the largest U.S. Jesuit Catholic universities, Loyola University Chicago prepares students to lead extraordinary lives by building upon its Jesuit tradition with an innovative Core Curriculum, which equips students with skills for lifelong success, and a strong commitment to develop the whole person—intellectually, socially, physically, and spiritually.

Admissions Contact:

Loyola University Chicago
6525 N. Sheridan Rd
Chicago, IL 60626
(800) 262-2373
Ph: (312) 915-6500
Email: admission@luc.edu
www.luc.edu

The 4 Distinctions

Engaged Students

Loyola enrolls more than fifteen thousand students from fifty states and eighty-two countries, and offers sixty-nine undergraduate majors. Through its John Felice Rome Center in Italy, The Beijing Center for Chinese Studies, and sixty study-abroad programs in twenty-nine countries, Loyola provides excellent venues for student-faculty research and opportunities for international education.

The Loyola Undergraduate Research Opportunities Program (LUROP) offers students excellent opportunities to participate in collaborative research with faculty, often under grants from such sources as the National Institutes of Health and the U.S. Department of Defense. The Quinlan Life Sciences Education and Research Center, a forty-two million dollar facility, offers high-tech classrooms, fiber-optic workstations, and a stream lab.

Loyola's Information Commons, scheduled to open in spring 2008, is a four-story lakeside research facility that will be open around the clock. The facility will provide an individual and group study space for students, state-of-the-art technology with more than 250 computers, wireless Internet connections, and a lakefront cafe.

Each fall, spring, and summer break, University Ministry's Alternative Break Immersion sends more than one hundred students to ten domestic and three international community organizations for intense experiences of action for social justice.

Great Teaching

With a thirteen to one student to faculty ratio, students easily interact with Loyola's superior faculty. Of Loyola's faculty, 97 percent have earned the highest degree in their fields, and they use their knowledge to foster student learning. Loyola professors are committed to teaching and being accessible to students, encouraging them to e-mail or to stop by during office hours for additional assistance.

Loyola's interdisciplinary honors program serves the most intellectually talented and highly motivated students at the university. In an atmosphere charged with challenging teaching and enthusiastic student participation, professors and students work together, exploring critical issues in each discipline. The most motivated students capitalize on this through involvement with faculty research and by attending colloquia with resident and visiting scholars.

Loyola's Eliciting Vocations through Knowledge and Engagement (EVOKE) project strives to encourage, support, and challenge the people of Loyola to be true to their personal callings. EVOKE enhances the university's commitment to service and activism through participation in targeted programs, courses, and personal development.

Loyola's Center for Urban Research and Learning (CURL) promotes an innovative model of teaching and learning that develops partnerships between the university and Chicago's communities. CURL places strong emphasis on research that addresses community needs and involves the community at all levels of research.

Vibrant Community

Students lead and participate in more than 150 clubs and organizations, including social, cultural, ethnic, professional, academic, and special-interest groups. Whatever the interest or passion, Loyola has something for every student.

Loyola combines the best of campus and city life with diverse living and learning opportunities in Chicago. Loyola's picturesque Lake Shore Campus is situated on the shores of Lake Michigan and provides a campus oasis just eight miles north of downtown Chicago. Loyola provides five traditional residence halls and ten apartment-style residences. Living on campus offers students the opportunity to make lifelong friendships, meet new people, and experience college life. Classrooms, labs, libraries, sport facilities, a chapel, and the lake are all within walking distance of residence halls. The residence hall staff are committed to providing a living environment that is conducive to academic, personal, and spiritual development. Access to parks with running trails and bike paths is a big advantage, as is Loyola's location in Rogers Park, one of the most diverse neighborhoods in Chicago.

Loyola's Water Tower Campus, on Chicago's Magnificent Mile in the heart of the city, connects students to myriad internship, job, and service opportunities. The Water Tower Campus is also home to Baumhart Hall, a twenty-five-story residence hall that features a student center, fitness center, study lounge, food court, outdoor terrace, cafe, wireless access, and more.

Loyola students have immediate access to concerts, museums, plays, vibrant nightlife, and other cultural and recreational activities. Getting around town is easy: both campuses have stops on the local CTA transit line, and the student U-Pass provides unlimited rides throughout Chicago's public transportation system. Recent campus developments include two new residence halls, the state-of-the art Quinlan Life Sciences Education and Research Center, and the Loyola University Museum of Art (LUMA).

Successful Outcomes

Loyola has nearly one hundred and twenty thousand alumni—eighty thousand in Chicago alone—who live and work in all fifty states and nearly 120 foreign countries.

Among Loyola's leading alumni are L. Scott Caldwell, BA '94, actress, Tony Award winner, and recurring performer on the ABC hit TV show *Lost*; Stephen Dynako, BA '89, vice president of new product approval process and change management for Harris Financial Corporation; Lisa Madigan, JD '94, Illinois attorney general; Bob Newhart, BBA '52, actor and comedian; Bob Parkinson, BBA '73, CEO of Baxter Labs and former COO of Abbott Labs; and Bill Rancic, BA '94, entrepreneur and winner of the first season of Donald Trump's *The Apprentice*.

Loyola's Career Development Center (CDC) provides all of the resources students need to start their careers after graduation. The CDC annually lists more than thirty thousand available jobs, including information on more than two thousand part-time jobs, one thousand internships, and six hundred seasonal positions.

Opportunities for internships, clinical experiences, and service opportunities abound throughout Chicago and beyond, from such well-known companies and organizations as Abbott Laboratories, the American Medical Association, the Chicago Bears, Chicago Public Schools, Children's Memorial Hospital, the City of Chicago, the Ford Motor Company, Kraft Foods, Leo Burnett, McGraw Hill, Motorola, NBC, the Target Corporation, the Tribune Company, Verizon Wireless, Walgreens and many more.

The city's vast cultural, business, and civic resources enrich Loyola's curriculum with numerous service-learning, immersion, and volunteer programs.

Fast Facts

Loyola University Chicago is a four-year, private, liberal arts university founded in 1870 by the Roman Catholic Order of the Society of Jesus (Jesuits).

Web site

http://www.luc.edu/

Location

Chicago, Illinois.

Student Profile

9,725 undergraduate students (35% male, 65% female); 50 states and territories, 82 countries; 30% minority, 1% international.

Faculty Profile

668 full-time faculty. 13:1 student/faculty ratio. Average class size is 29.

Residence Life

82% of freshman live on campus. Freshmen and sophomores are required to live on campus, unless they live at home with a parent or guardian.

Athletics

NCAA Division I, Horizon Collegiate Conference. 13 varsity sports (6 men's: basketball, cross-country, golf, soccer, track& field, volleyball); 7 women's: basketball, cross-country, golf, soccer, softball, track& field, volleyball), 12 club sports, and 14 intramurals.

Academic Programs

Accounting; advertising & public relations; anthropology; bilingual/bicultural education; biochemistry; bioinformatics; biology; Black world studies; chemistry; classical civilization; communication; communications networks & security; computer science; criminal justice; ecology; economics; elementary education; English; entrepreneurship; environmental studies; environmental sciences (chemistry); finance; fine arts; forensic science; French; Greek (ancient); health systems management; history; human resource management; human services; information systems; information technology; interdisciplinary honors program; international business; international film & media studies; international studies; Italian; journalism; Latin; marketing; mathematics; mathematics & computer science; molecular biology; music; nursing; philosophy; philosophy: social justice; physics; physics & computer science; physics & engineering; political science; psychology; operations management; religious studies; science education; secondary education (dual-degree program); social work (also available in a combined bachelor's and master's degree in social work); sociology; sociology & anthropology; software development; Spanish; special education; sport management; statistical science; theatre; theology; theoretical physics & applied mathematics; women's studies (as a second major only).

Costs and Aid

2007–2008: $37,130 comprehensive ($27,200 tuition). 94% of students receive some financial aid. Average freshman award: $17,793.

Endowment

$305,664,0221.

More Distinctions

• Loyola is consistently ranked a top national university and best value by *U.S. News & World Report*.

• Loyola is one of the largest of the 28 Jesuit Catholic universities in the United States.

McKendree University

ILLINOIS

Founded in 1828, McKendree made the transition from Illinois's oldest college to Illinois's newest university in July 2007. McKendree cherishes its rich history and valued traditions. The men and women of McKendree find tremendous diversity on a small campus filled with personal, family-like relationships with professors.

Admissions Contact:

McKendree University
701 College Road
Lebanon, IL 62254
(800) 232-7228
Ph: (618) 537-6831
Email: inquiry@mckendree.edu
www.mckendree.edu

The 4 Distinctions

Engaged Students

As a campus of 1,400 students, McKendree is well-known for being extremely student focused. The university provides students with opportunities to excel in a number of areas. McKendree is located only twenty-five minutes from downtown Saint Louis. This location gives students endless career opportunities, including a range of internships. Through the office of career services, students can find internship programs that will provide them with valuable work experience as well as class credit. Student interns work with close supervision of faculty members, on-site supervisors, and the director of career services.

The office of career services provides a variety of resources to acquaint students with career options. Individual career counseling, interest and personality assessments, and career exploration workshops offer students the opportunity to examine possible majors and careers. The career services resource center provides access to computer-based information, as well as books, magazines, and brochures dealing with career planning, job searches, and interview skills. Information on and applications for graduate school admission examinations are available, as well. Workshops and individual counseling provide assistance with resume preparation, job search correspondence, and interview skills. The office also hosts career information days and job fairs to introduce students to available fields of work and to prospective employers.

Other student-focused resources include the university's academic success center, which offers assistance to all students in organizing written work, improving reading skills and study methods, and reviewing mathematics. Free tutoring in all subjects is also available through the center. The academic success center also provides assistance for those students with special needs. McKendree's writing resource center offers assistance with all aspects of the writing process and research documentation. Through the help of experienced peer and faculty tutors, this center offers a range of services to all students, staff, and faculty on an appointment or walk-in basis. Health services are available through the university's full-time, on-campus nurse and counseling services. All of these services are free and open to all students.

In addition to internships, there are a number of opportunities for students to learn outside the classroom. Many students earn credit through independent study. A large majority of McKendree professors are published and are well-known and respected for their writing and research. Faculty often receive assistance from their students in exchange for college credit, a valuable opportunity that allows students to help a professor conduct research for a book or work on an experiment that will one day be published.

McKendree's study-abroad program is coordinated through the Institute for Study Abroad at Butler University. This program gives McKendree students the option of studying at ninety-three different universities across thirteen countries and five continents. In addition, any institutional aid awarded to students that is not linked to participation will go with students to assist with their tuition at the international university of their choice.

Great Teaching

The most unique thing about the McKendree experience is the relationship between faculty and students. This relationship is best described as a mentor-mentee relationship. Students frequently address professors by their first name. It is very common for faculty members to include their home and cell phone numbers on the class syllabus or to have classes over to their homes for dinner. Many professors can be found helping students in their offices hours after their last class ended.

The atmosphere on campus is family oriented, and this family feeling begins with the students and faculty. McKendree boasts a unique faculty-in-residence program, in which a faculty member is selected to live on campus. Dr. Betsy Gordon, associate professor of speech communication and chair of McKendree's division of language, literature, and communication, has been selected as McKendree's newest faculty-in-residence. Dr. Gordon finds the prospect of "developing learning activities that are designed to engage students outside the classroom" an exciting one.

Faculty also influence students as faculty advisers. Each student is assigned a faculty adviser to provide guidance in developing a course plan that meets curriculum requirements and nurtures the student's own interests and goals. For first-year students, this adviser may or may not be from the field of a student's declared interest, but as a major focus develops, a student may choose a new adviser from faculty in the appropriate division.

Vibrant Community

In addition to the unique relationship between the students and faculty at McKendree, another unique distinction of campus is the location. McKendree's location is a blend of small town and suburban. The 120-acre main campus is within twenty-five minutes of downtown Saint Louis to the west, and is equally close to the popular Carlyle Lake outdoor recreation area to the east. McKendree students truly get the best of both worlds: the serenity and security of a small town and the advantages of a large metropolitan area, including career opportunities, cultural events and institutions, shopping, professional sports, and entertainment.

Although McKendree is located in a small town, there is always something happening on campus. Students are directly involved in planning and implementing campus events. The Campus Activities Board (CAB) offers students the chance to gain leadership skills while providing entertaining and enriching programs for their fellow students.

McKendree has a long and rich tradition of Greek life extending back to 1837. Throughout their history, Greek organizations have encouraged their members to cultivate skills in leadership, scholarship, character development, and service to the community. A variety of Greek organizations are available for students to join, including fraternities, sororities, and coed organizations.

Successful Outcomes

McKendree graduates experience an impressive amount of success postgraduation. Within one year of receiving their bachelor's degrees, 31 percent of McKendree graduates enter graduate or professional programs, including students attending law school, medical school, MBA programs, and other graduate or professional programs. The acceptance rate for McKendree graduates into these programs is extremely impressive, with over a 99 percent acceptance rate to law schools, medical schools, and MBA programs. Also impressive is McKendree's 100 percent acceptance rate into Washington University's occupational therapy masters and doctoral programs. With the exception of Washington's own graduates, McKendree is the largest feeder school for this Washington University program.

For those students who choose not to continue their education after receiving their bachelor's degree, 98 percent accept a job in their field or a related field within six months of graduation. The success of McKendree graduates is due to the distinguished education they receive at McKendree University, the hard work of the career services office, alumni networking opportunities, and the university's location near an area with a number of career development opportunities.

Fast Facts

McKendree University is a four-year liberal arts college. It was established in 1828 by pioneer Methodists.

Web site

http://www.mckendree.edu

Location

Lebanon, Illinois—25 minutes from downtown St. Louis and minutes from Lake Carlyle.

Student Profile

1,500 undergraduate students (47% male, 53% female); 48 states and territories; 19% minority, 3% international.

Faculty Profile

204 full-time faculty. 14:1 faculty to student ratio. Average class size is 12.

Residence Life

Moderately residential: 55% of students live on campus.

Athletics

NAIA Division I, American Midwest Conference, Mid-States Football Conference, and American Collegiate Hockey Association. 20 varsity sports (11 men's: baseball, basketball, bowling, cross-country, football, golf, hockey, soccer, tennis, track & field, wrestling; 9 women's: basketball, bowling, cross-country, golf, soccer, softball, tennis, track & field, volleyball), and a significant intramural sports program.

Academic Programs

Accounting; art; athletic training; biology; business administration; chemistry; computer information systems; computer science; economics/finance; education studies; elementary education; English; health education; history; international relations; management; marketing; mathematics; medical technology; music, music education; occupational therapy; organizational communication; philosophy; physical education; political science; psychology; religious studies; secondary education certification; social science; sociology; speech communication.

Costs and Aid

2007-2008: $29,120 comprehensive ($20,570 tuition). 95% of undergraduates receive financial aid.

Endowment

$23,000,000

More Distinction

• McKendree is ranked 6th among 108 colleges in the Midwest for offering classes with fewer than 20 students by the U.S. News & World Report.

• McKendree is ranked number one for class size by U.S. News & World Report by having no classes with more than 50 students.

• McKendree placed in the top five percent of five categories used in the rankings – ACT scores, number of freshmen in the top 10 percent of their high school class, number of classes with less than 20 students, number of classes not exceeding 50, and acceptance rate for new students.

Millikin University

ILLINOIS

Millikin University (MU) is a small, comprehensive university located in Decatur, Illinois, a metro area with a population of about one hundred thousand. The university is dedicated to challenging the minds and lives of its students through a classic and literary liberal arts education that accompanies a practical study of professions.

Admissions Contact:

Millikin University
1184 West Main Street
Decatur, Illinois 62522
(800) 373-7733
Email: admis@millikin.edu
www.millikin.edu

The 4 Distinctions

Engaged Students

Founded in 1901 by local businessman James Millikin, MU's mission is to deliver on the promise of education and to prepare students for professional success, democratic citizenship in a global environment, and personal lives of meaning and value.

Millikin offers more than sixty academic programs, including preprofessional programs, master's degrees, and adult learning majors. Hands-on learning is the backbone of a student's academic experience at MU. All majors offer opportunities for students to gain practical experience in their fields of interest right on campus. For example, business students team up with art majors to run the Blue Connection art gallery in Decatur, which showcases MU student, faculty, and alumni artwork. First Step Records, First Step Publishing, and Bronze Man Books, are also university-owned, student-run companies, which allow students to do everything from recording their own CDs in Millikin's state-of-the-art recording studio to publishing their own original sheet music and literary compositions.

Millikin also offers students opportunities for hands-on learning off campus—in Decatur, throughout the nation, and across the world. Business majors have the unique opportunity to consult for companies outside the United States as part of an international business class. The university encourages students to gain a global perspective by taking advantage of at least one of the many study-abroad opportunities available for a whole semester or for a two-week winter or summer immersion session. Education majors have traveled to China and Taiwan to teach English in schools, art majors have traveled to Italy to study glassblowing, and political science majors intern in Washington, DC. Nearly every program of study at Millikin offers opportunities to gain practical, interactive career experience outside the classroom. Nursing majors work in local hospitals. Education majors begin observing and shadowing teachers in local classrooms as early as the sophomore year. And many MU students participate in internships with local Fortune 500 and Fortune 100 companies such as Archer Daniels Midland Company (ADM), Caterpillar, and Tate & Lyle.

Service learning is required for all freshmen. MU offers a scholarship program for students who prove to have a strong interest in and commitment to service to their communities.

MU's honors program provides the university's best and brightest students with opportunities throughout their four years to create unique research projects on the subjects in which they are most interested. Students have written their own music, produced broadcast television audition tapes, illustrated children's books, and researched human genes. Honors students travel to conferences to present their work at national events, and MU hosts a banquet each year to allow these students to showcase their work for the entire university.

Great Teaching

Millikin offers four colleges and schools: the College of Arts & Sciences, the College of Fine Arts, the College of Professional Studies, and the Tabor School of Business.

In a recent survey, MU students were asked what makes the university so unique. The most popular answer was, "The professors." Unlike at other institutions where faculty are primarily expected to conduct research, Millikin's primary expectation of its faculty is to teach, and teach well. Faculty members at MU give generously of their time and resources to their students. Many live close by in Decatur and are easily accessible outside of class. They dedicate their time and resources to the art of teaching and to providing students with opportunities to learn inside and outside of the classroom. Professors lent a hand to students in starting Blue Connection, First Step Records, and Bronze Man Books. Faculty also lead immersion trips and alternative spring-break trips to locations such as New Orleans to do community service.

The faculty in the Tabor School of Business at MU have provided students with opportunities to accompany them to national conferences and present research and work. They have also used connections within the Dominican Republic and Korea to allow students to conduct market research for international corporations.

Vibrant Community

There are over ninety student organizations on campus, including honorary societies, fine art and business clubs, and community-outreach programs. Six fraternities and four sororities offer Greek life to those who want to join. On average, 50 percent of students are involved in athletics at some point during their four years at Millikin. Twenty NCAA Division III varsity teams, junior varsity sports, intramurals, cheerleading, and the dance team keep a large portion of the student body physically active.

Approximately 65 percent of MU students live on campus in university residence halls, Greek chapter houses, or the Woods—MU's apartment complex for upper-level students. Some residence halls allow groups such as honors or fine arts students to live together in a learning community.

The Decatur community is located 180 miles from Chicago and 120 miles from Saint Louis. Members of the Decatur community enjoy performances at the Kirkland Fine Arts Center by MU students as well as traveling professional acts who perform in the 1,900-seat auditorium. Students can work out at the Decatur Indoor Sports Center, located on MU's campus. The center features a rock-climbing wall and an indoor track and fitness center.

Successful Outcomes

Millikin's hands-on learning philosophy, which students are introduced to freshman year has proved to educate students and prepare them for the professional world. Of 2006 graduates, 100 percent entered graduate or professional school or found jobs after graduation. Many students are offered employment in Decatur after completing internships with those local companies. Graduates also go on to work in Chicago, New York City, Los Angeles, and throughout the world. Graduates of MU's theatre program can be found on Broadway, in nationally touring theatre groups, and on network television programs.

Alumni are passionate about Millikin. Many alumni reside in Decatur, and alumni chapters are active in Chicago, Saint Louis, Indianapolis, Atlanta, and throughout the United States. Alumni learn the latest Millikin news and happenings via the Millikin Quarterly magazine and the Big Blue e-newsletter. The Big Blue Club also allows MU alumni sports fans to support their alma mater years after they leave MU. Homecoming brings many alumni back to campus, and some even lead career-oriented discussion groups during that week. MU alumni are a loyal and connected group that often offer MU students a strong network when job searching.

Famous Millikin alumni include Jodi Benson, the voice of Ariel in The Little Mermaid; Matthew West, a Christian musician; and George Musso, former player for the Chicago Bears and member of the NFL Hall of Fame.

Fast Facts

Millikin University is a coeducational, independent, four-year university, which focuses in studies in the arts & sciences, business, fine arts and professional studies (Education, Nursing, and Exercise Science). It was founded in 1901 and is affiliated with the Presbyterian Church.

Web site

http://www.millikin.edu/

Location

Decatur, Illinois—120 miles north of St. Louis, 180 miles south of Chicago, 150 miles west of Indianapolis.

Student Profile

2,400 undergraduate students (44% male, 56% female); 31 states and territories, 7 countries.

Faculty Profile

145 full-time faculty. 12:1 student/faculty ratio. The average class size is 23 students.

Residence Life

Moderately residential: 65% of students live on campus.

Athletics

NCAA Division III, College Conference. 20 varsity sports (10 men's: baseball, basketball, cross-country, football, golf, soccer, swimming, track & field (indoor & outdoor), wrestling; 10 women's: basketball, cross-country, golf, soccer, softball, swimming, tennis, track & field (indoor & outdoor), volleyball), 8 intramurals.

Academic Programs

Accounting; applied mathematics; art (studio); art education; art management; art therapy; athletic training; biology; biology education; chemistry; chemistry education; commercial art/computer design; commercial music; communication; computer science; early childhood education; elementary education; English education; English literature; English writing; entrepreneurship; finance; fitness & sport (sports management emphasis); history; human services; interdisciplinary; international business; international & global studies; management; management information systems; marketing; mathematics education; music; music business; music education (instrumental emphasis, vocal emphasis); music performance (instrumental emphasis, piano emphasis, vocal emphasis); musical theatre; nursing; philosophy; physical education; physics; political science; psychology; social sciences education; sociology; Spanish; theatre (acting emphasis, stage management emphasis, technical/design emphasis, theatre administration emphasis).

Costs and Aid

2007–2008: $31,155 comprehensive ($23,250 tuition). 99% of students received some financial aid in 2006-2007.

Endowment

$80,251,527.

North Central College

Admissions Contact:

North Central College
30 North Brainard Street
Naperville, IL 60540
(800) 411-1861
Ph: (630) 637-5800
Email: admissions@noctrl.edu
www.northcentralcollege.edu

ILLINOIS

North Central College is a private, four-year, comprehensive, liberal arts college, primarily undergraduate and residential. Founded in 1861, it is affiliated with the United Methodist Church. North Central is committed to teaching leadership, ethics, and values both inside and outside the classroom.

The 4 Distinctions

Engaged Students

North Central offers fifty-eight undergraduate majors. The most popular are education, business management, and psychology. Education majors take advantage of the college's proximity to both rural and urban areas, offering students a variety of choices for their student teaching experiences. The college also offers elementary through high school students the opportunity to come to campus for tutoring and exposure to college life under the Junior/Senior Scholars program.

North Central students take advantage of off-campus and study-abroad opportunities, too. There are thirty-four programs on five continents available for students to choose from. The college's December interim term, a significant break between Thanksgiving and the beginning of the new calendar year, allows North Central students to participate in unique trips. Some, like the Verandah Experience, involve faculty-led trips to cultural events and explorations of ethnic neighborhoods in the Chicago area. Others are study-abroad programs that often involve internships.

Alternative Spring Break is another opportunity for North Central students to learn outside of the classroom. In recent years, the football team has traveled to Texas to build houses for Habitat for Humanity. Examples of learning outside the classroom also include the Students in Free Enterprise (SIFE) group, which competes nationally in business, entrepreneurial, and leadership activities. Recently, participants who were working to promote free-trade coffee from Guatemala traveled there to meet with coffee producers.

Great Teaching

North Central's mission is to foster a community of learners dedicated to preparing informed, involved, principled, and productive citizens and leaders over a lifetime. The college fulfills its mission by recognizing the individual needs of students at different stages of life and from different ethnic, economic, and religious backgrounds, while ensuring that all students experience quality teaching in small classes and are held to common standards. Educational programs are augmented by work experiences, providing practical skills necessary to prepare North Central graduates for successful careers.

North Central's low student to faculty ratio of fourteen to one, and small average class size of nineteen allow students to work closely with their professors. About 87 percent of North Central's faculty have doctorates or terminal degrees, and teaching assistants do not teach undergraduate students at North Central, affirming the college's commitment to quality teaching.

Students also interact with faculty outside of the classroom, including under the Chicago Term program. Chicago Term courses are taught in the city, taking advantage of North Central's convenient location. Students commute into Chicago with their professors and experience the museums, landmarks, and other urban offerings.

North Central provides a quality experience on campus, as well. A new thirty million dollar arts facility is under construction to be ready in 2008. It will serve as a concert hall, theater, art gallery, rehearsal space, and more.

Vibrant Community

Many of North Central's undergraduate students live on campus in traditional residence halls and townhouses. Students are required to live on campus their first two years, and cars are permitted. Some themed townhouses are available, such as a career-oriented house.

Clubs and activities are strong at North Central. About a third of North Central's students are involved in athletics, and there are fifty-five other clubs and activities to join. Many are tied to academic programs. A high number of North Central students participate in fine-arts programs, though they may not be majors. The college's radio station is nationally known, and students run it 24/7. While the station benefits broadcast and communications majors, providing them with real-world experience, anyone can participate—and they do.

North Central students, known as Cardinals after the college's mascot, actively participate in community service. A service-oriented program called Cardinals in Action provides help to needy residents of Naperville. Students also participate in local call-to-action activities such as the March to Naperville, raising awareness of social issues.

Naperville, ranked by Money magazine as the number two place to live in the country, has a national reputation. It is a top-rated suburban community of about one hundred and forty thousand with a lively and historic downtown. It is located thirty miles west of Chicago on the DuPage River, forty-five minutes by car. The affluent suburb offers internship and networking opportunities for North Central students, as well as a certain measure of safety. Great dining is available within two blocks of North Central, and a beautiful park on the DuPage River borders the campus.

Chicago is accessible by commuter train, and the trip takes only thirty minutes. North Central students can live on campus and take advantage of the proximity to Chicago for access to internships, fine arts and museums, and music, especially jazz. North Central students feel they are attending a first-rate college in the middle of somewhere as opposed to the middle of nowhere.

Successful Outcomes

North Central students are well-prepared for the real world because of their hands-on experiences. They learn and exercise their minds both in and out of the classroom. Nearly 97 percent of North Central's graduates are in jobs or in graduate programs within six months of graduation, and many stay in the dynamic Naperville and Chicago area.

North Central's career center brings alumni back to campus to connect with current students in small seminars. Alumni also return for the annual Athletic Hall of Fame induction ceremony, highlighted by recent graduates' moving stories of the importance of their North Central experiences.

In addition, there are a dozen alumni clubs across the nation, providing networking opportunities for alumni and graduating students. Alumni also meet with potential students, assisting in the admissions process. Famous alumni include F. L. Maytag, founder of the Maytag Corporation, and a former speaker of the House of Representatives.

Fast Facts

North Central College is a private, selective, four-year, comprehensive, liberal arts college affiliated with the United Methodist Church and founded in 1861.

Web site

http://www.noctrl.edu/

Location

Naperville, Illinois—29 miles west of Chicago.

Student Profile

2,000 undergraduate students (42% male, 58% female); 30 states and territories; 13% minority, 2% international.

Faculty Profile

125 full-time faculty. 87% hold the highest degree in their field. 14:1 student/faculty ratio. Average class size is 19.

Residence Life

Moderately residential: 55% of students live on campus.

Athletics

NCAA Division III, College Conference of Illinois & Wisconsin. 19 varsity sports (10 men's: cross-country, football, soccer, golf, swimming, basketball, tennis, wrestling, baseball, track & field; 9 women's: cross-country, volleyball, soccer, golf, tennis, swimming, basketball, softball, track & field) and a variety of intramural sports for men and women.

Academic Programs

Accounting; actuarial science; anthropology; applied mathematics; art; athletic training; biochemistry; biology; broadcast communication; business administration; business management; chemistry; Chinese; classical civilizations; community conflict resolution; computer science; dance; East Asian studies; economics; education; engineering; English; entrepreneurship & small business management; exercise science; finance; French; gender & women's studies; German; global studies; history; history of ideas; humanities; human resources management; individualized major; information systems; interactive media studies; international business; Japanese; jazz studies; journalism; management information systems; marketing; mathematics; music; music education; nuclear medicine technology; nursing; organizational communication; organizational leadership; philosophy; physical education; physics; political science; professional conflict resolution; psychology; radiation therapy; religious studies; science; social change & public advocacy; social science/history; sociology; sociology & anthropology; Spanish; speech communication; sport management; theatre; urban & suburban studies.

Costs and Aid

2007–2008: $32,241 comprehensive ($24,159 tuition). 90% of freshman students receive some financial aid.

Endowment

$70 million.

Rockford College

ILLINOIS

Rockford College is a private, coeducational, comprehensive liberal arts college. Founded in 1847, its mission is "to prepare students for fulfilling lives, careers, and participation in a modern and changing global society through the total academic and co-curricular experience."

Admissions Contact:

Rockford College
5050 E. State Street
Rockford, IL 61108
(800) 892-2984
Ph: (815) 226-4000
Fax: (815) 226-2822
Email: rcadmissions@rockford.edu
www.rockford.edu

The 4 Distinctions

Engaged Students

Rockford College is committed to teaching students to be thoughtful, active citizens who can make a very real difference in the world. It starts with the Plunge, the all-college, fall event during which students, faculty and staff immerse themselves in volunteer projects throughout the community. For as much as the students are able to help make improvements, they also reap the personal reward of knowing that they, like many before them, are able to make a difference.

Rockford College offers more than seventy programs, and the most popular are education, nursing, business and psychology. Many courses have a community-based learning component, and Rockford College students are encouraged to become involved in the community beyond the classroom and the campus. The college's Jane Addams Center for Civic Engagement serves as the clearinghouse for information about community-service projects in the surrounding area and abroad.

The college's Humanitarian Action Response Team (HART) was formed in January 2005 in response to the devastating Asian tsunami. Members of HART include students, faculty and staff. As "global citizens responding to community needs," its mission is to stimulate learning and develop leadership in the performance of needed service. HART's first project was to build a shelter in Thailand for the victims of the tsunami. Rockford College students also participate in Habitat for Humanity projects, such as the Alan Hutchcroft Alternative Spring Break, named in honor of the late Dr. Alan Hutchcroft, a professor at Rockford College and supporter of the event. In the spring of 2007, thirty-nine students, faculty, staff and alumni traveled to Starkville, Mississippi for the annual trip.

Rockford College students can also perform community service through study-abroad programs at Regent's College in London and in Argentina. The service component for study abroad is similar to on-campus requirements at Rockford, providing a continuity of experience for Rockford College students.

Great Teaching

Rockford College's faculty members are dedicated to their students. Their commitment to making connections with students both in the classroom and beyond is supported by the college, which also encourages continuing education for faculty members. More than 70 percent of faculty members have the highest degrees in their fields. The low student to faculty ratio of eleven to one, and small class size of fewer than twenty students allow professors to have significant one-on-one contact with their students.

Many faculty members are accomplished authors, researchers, and authorities in their fields. Members of the art and performing arts departments have strong regional and national reputations and provide a great resource for Rockford College students. Science professors have strong outreach programs in the scientific community, as do members of the economics, business and accounting department in the business world.

Hands-on programs are common in every discipline. The Student Academic Showcase, held at the end of the spring semester, celebrates students' academic interests and achievements. The Student-Faculty Research program is available to students who wish to do a summer research or creative project under the guidance of a faculty member.

Rockford College's general education requirements extend the meaning of a liberal arts education beyond its usual definition. The first-year advising program pairs each student entering with fewer than thirty credit hours with a first-year adviser, a specially trained faculty or academic staff member. Each adviser helps students formulate educational goals prior to starting classes at Rockford College and supports them in attaining those goals throughout that first year. All students take rhetoric classes to prepare for their upper-level course work. Health and wellness courses are also required.

Vibrant Community

While the majority of Rockford College's students are from Illinois, the college does have a strong out-of-state representation. A high number of Rockford College's students are first-generation college students.

Rockford's campus includes nine residence halls. Some are small houses, and one large complex includes independent houses within it. Resident assistants in the halls help foster a sense of community, and residents are active participants in the development of the rules for their halls. All halls are coed, and each hall has a variety of rooms, including suites, doubles and supersingles with private baths.

The college has twenty-five clubs and organizations representing students' interests in culture, academics, the environment, health and recreation. Students may propose and start new clubs if they see a need. Drawn from every major, about a quarter of Rockford College's students are involved in athletics.

Rockford College's 130-acre campus is located in the city of Rockford, a metropolitan area along the Rock River, about ninety miles northwest of Chicago. With a population of one hundred and fifty thousand, Rockford is the third largest city in the state behind Chicago and Aurora, a suburb of Chicago. Rockford has a lively arts, music and cultural scene with residential dance and theater companies, several choral organizations and the Rockford Symphony Orchestra. There are also ten museums, including the Burpee Museum of Natural History, home to Jane the dinosaur, the most complete, best-preserved juvenile T. rex skeleton ever found. On the Waterfront, Illinois' largest music festival, is held in downtown Rockford over the Labor Day weekend. Rockford also has a number of professional sports teams, including the Rockford IceHogs hockey team and the Rockford RiverHawks baseball team. The college's Rockford Regents baseball team played its 2007 season home games at the Riverhawks' brand-new, state-of-the-art stadium. Rockford College students enjoy their park-like campus, located in the heart of a bustling city.

Successful Outcomes

Rockford College's most famous alumna is Jane Addams, founder of Chicago's Hull House and winner of the 1931 Nobel Peace Prize. The College today maintains a commitment to civic engagement, adhering to the words from Addams' valedictory address: "We stand today united in a belief in beauty, genius and courage, and that these can transform the world."

Rockford College Alumni hold true to Addams' words in their careers. Many have joined or started social service organizations in their communities or continued on as teachers, molding the future leaders of tomorrow. The College can count among its distinguished Alumni accomplished artists, authors, business and community leaders and entrepreneurs.

Rockford College Alumni find jobs in all fields, but most common are education and the health professions. In a recent survey, 17 percent of Rockford's 4,750 alumni have reported completing a higher degree in arts and sciences, business, education, health or law science since graduating.

Fast Facts

Rockford College is a four-year, private, liberal arts college founded in 1847.

Web site

http:// www.rockford.edu

Location

Rockford, Illinois—90 miles northwest of Chicago.

Student Profile

880 undergraduate students (35% male, 65% female); 20 states and territories, 8 countries; 14% minority, 1% international.

Faculty Profile

62 full-time faculty. 74% hold a terminal degree in their field. 11:1 student/faculty ratio. Average class size is 12.

Residence Life

Mildly residential: 31% of students live on campus.

Athletics

NCAA Division III, Northern Athletics Conference. 15 varsity sports(men's: baseball, basketball, cross-country, football, golf, soccer, tennis, track & field; women's: basketball, cross-country, golf, soccer, softball, tennis, track & field, volleyball), and intramurals/recreational sports (dodgeball, basketball).

Academic Programs

Accounting; anthropology & sociology, art (BA or BFA); art history; biochemistry; biology; business administration; chemistry; classics; computer science; economics; elementary education (Illinois certification K-9, middle school endorsement); English; French; history; humanities; international studies; Latin; mathematics; music; musical theatre performance; nursing; philosophy; physical education; political science; psychology; romance languages; science & mathematics; social sciences; Spanish; special education; theatre arts. Preprofessional programs: prelaw, presocial work, predentistry, premedicine, prepharmacy, preveterinary medicine. Graduate programs in business administration and teaching.

Costs and Aid

2007–2008: $22,950 tuition. 98% of students receive some financial aid. Average award: $16,387.

More Distinctions

• One of 11 Illinois schools with a Phi Beta Kappa chapter.

• Recognized by Princeton Review as one of the 81 Colleges with a Conscience.

• Recognized by Princeton Review as one of the Best in Midwest, 2005, 2006, 2007.

• Recognized by Carnegie Foundation for the Advancement of Teaching with Community Engagement Classification with an emphasis on outreach and partnership.

• Rockford College was selected for the premiere Guide to Service-Learning Colleges and Universities, which spotlights excellent institutions that integrate community service with academic study to enrich learning, teach civic responsibility, and strengthen communities.

Roosevelt University

ILLINOIS

Founded in 1945, Roosevelt University provides students with a rigorous education, balanced with a commitment to social equality and justice. Named for Franklin and Eleanor Roosevelt, Roosevelt University was one of the first educational institutions in the nation to admit all qualified students regardless of race, age, gender, or ethnicity.

Admissions Contact:

Roosevelt University
430 S. Michigan Ave.
Chicago, IL 60605
Ph: (877) 277-5978
Email: ApplyRU@roosevelt.edu
www.roosevelt.edu

The 4 Distinctions

Engaged Students

Befitting the mission of the university, students have many opportunities to learn from real-life experiences while serving in the community. Recent service-learning projects have included animal rescue efforts, Big Brothers/Big Sisters events, blood drives, support for Habitat for Humanity and Gear Up events, and numerous food drives. Roosevelt was one of the first universities in Chicago to partner with the nationwide early childhood education program, Jumpstart. Roosevelt students work with Jumpstart to provide one-on-one mentoring and organized activities that encourage literacy, language, and social interaction.

In addition to serving, students have an opportunity to intern in the Chicago area with respected companies. Recent internship sites have included Wachovia Securities, Morgan Stanley, Whole Foods, Tribune Interactive, and Citicorp Investment Services.

Roosevelt University offers exchange and nonexchange study-abroad options all over the world. Recent locations include Finland, Germany, Scotland, England, and various sites in Asia and Latin America. In all, students have exciting opportunities to immerse themselves in global cultures.

Great Teaching

Roosevelt offers more than eighty undergraduate majors and preprofessional programs, while keeping a low student to faculty ratio of sixteen to one. Social justice is at the heart of Roosevelt's educational mission, and students can experience this commitment as they interact with the diverse student body and faculty, take part in service-learning courses, and participate in programs that reach out to Chicago area communities. Though Roosevelt's academic programs are offered through five distinct colleges (Arts and Sciences, Business, University College, Education, and Performing Arts), they are all linked by Roosevelt's commitment to excellent teaching, personal guidance, and the foundation of social justice.

There are two hundred dedicated faculty members at Roosevelt, and in one recent year they have written or otherwise contributed to the publication of several books; conducted 115 major university lectures and workshops; edited and reviewed thirty-three publications; published 113 essays, papers, and articles; and attended and presented at numerous national conferences. Students benefit from opportunities to learn from and conduct research alongside this distinguished faculty.

While insisting that its students meet standards of academic excellence, Roosevelt has kept its doors open to the economically disadvantaged, to students who work full-time to support themselves, and to students who are the first members of their families to attend college. Roosevelt has kept education affordable for its students, and is known as one of the most affordable private universities in the Midwest, due to generous scholarship and financial aid programs. Nearly 75 percent of Roosevelt students receive financial aid in the form of scholarships, grants, loans, and work-study opportunities.

Vibrant Community

Roosevelt University has two main campuses, one in downtown Chicago and one in the northwest suburb of Schaumburg. These two campuses, along with several off-campus sites and a large online program, reflect the mission of a metropolitan university.

There are plenty of things to do on campus. Every year, Roosevelt's Center for Student Involvement plans dozens of events, hosts visiting speakers on a wide variety of subjects, and schedules musical performances and topical student programs. On the Chicago campus, students can enjoy a variety of programs staged in the university's world-famous Auditorium Theatre, known for its perfect acoustics and classic Chicago architecture.

On both campuses, students have access to fitness facilities with state-of-the-art workout equipment. Roosevelt's new University Center overlooks Lake Michigan and Chicago's popular State Street. The building offers semisuite quad and semisuite double units for freshman and sophomores, and it offers studios and two- or four-bedroom apartments for juniors, seniors, and graduate students.

Roosevelt's Chicago campus is located on South Michigan Avenue, in the heart of Chicago's Loop. The area is often referred to as the South Loop Education Corridor, because Roosevelt and half a dozen other colleges and universities, enrolling thirty-five thousand students, are located within a mile of one another. Chicago is home to more than one hundred corporate headquarters, thirty Fortune 500 companies, three hundred U.S. banks, more than forty museums, more than 150 theaters, more than six thousand restaurants, five major professional sports teams, and the world's largest public library. Roosevelt's location leaves students with no shortage of excitement and activities.

Successful Outcomes

Roosevelt's office of career services is staffed with professional counselors who provide students with the resources necessary for effective career and postgraduate education planning. More than 90 percent of Roosevelt graduates are employed in their chosen field or are accepted to graduate school within six months of graduation.

The Chicago area offers students opportunities to work with some of the top companies, firms, and organizations. The Art Institute of Chicago, General Mills, Pepsi, the Ford Motor Company, Hilton Hotels, United Airlines, and AT&T are just a few examples of companies that seek Roosevelt graduates.

Roosevelt alumni include Andrew Barrett, former commissioner of the Federal Communications Commission; Ira Berkow, sportswriter for the New York Times; Sylvia Flanagan, senior editor for Jet Magazine; Patricia Harris, assistant vice president of diversity for McDonald's; Ramsey Lewis, jazz musician; Harold Washington, the first African-American mayor of Chicago; Bob Wattel, executive vice president for Lettuce Entertain You Enterprises; and David Woolridge, former corporate vice president of Motorola.

Roosevelt University was one of the first educational institutions in the nation to admit all qualified students regardless of race, age, gender, or ethnicity.

- Colleges of Distinction

Fast Facts

Roosevelt University is a private, independent, and coeducational institution founded in 1945. Roosevelt University, named for Franklin and Eleanor Roosevelt, balances a rigorous education with an unwavering commitment to social equality and justice.

Web site

http://www.roosevelt.edu

Location

Chicago, Illinois— Roosevelt's location on Michigan Avenue is in the heart of Chicago's Loop.

Student Profile

3,975 undergraduate students; 86% from Illinois; 35% minority, 6% international.

Faculty Profile

210 full-time faculty. 13:1 student/faculty ratio.

Residence Life

On-campus residence required through sophomore year.

Academic Programs

Accounting; actuarial science; African-American/Black studies; art; art history, criticism & conservation; biology/biological sciences; biotechnology; business administration & management; business/commerce; business/managerial economics; chemistry; clinical laboratory science/medical technology; clinical/medical laboratory science & allied professions; communication/speech communication & rhetoric; community organization & advocacy; comparative literature; computer science; computer systems networking & telecommunications; dramatic/theater arts; economics; education (elementary, kindergarten/preschool, music, secondary, special education); electrical, electronic & communications engineering technology; English; finance; foreign languages & literatures; geography; gerontology; health/health care administration; health science; health/medical laboratory technologies; health/medical preparatory programs; history; hospitality administration; human resources management; human services; insurance; international business/trade/commerce; international relations & affairs; jazz/jazz studies; journalism; labor & industrial relations; law & legal studies; legal assistant/paralegal; liberal arts & sciences/liberal studies; literature; management science; marketing/marketing management; mathematics; medical radiologic technology; music; music history, literature, & theory; music pedagogy; music performance; music theory & composition; nuclear medical technology; philosophy; piano & organ; political science & government; predentistry studies; prelaw studies; premedical studies; prepharmacy studies; psychology; public administration; public administration & social service professions; public relations/image management; radio & television; social sciences; sociology; Spanish; statistics; telecommunications; urban studies/affairs; violin, viola, guitar & other stringed instruments; voice & opera; wind & percussion instruments; women's studies.

Costs and Aid

2007–2008: $27,550 comprehensive ($16,680 tuition). Full-time tuition and fees vary according to course load and program. Part-time tuition: $600 per semester hour. Nearly 75% of Roosevelt students receive some financial aid. Average award: $13,173.

Southern Illinois University Edwardsville

ILLINOIS

Emphasizing teaching, research, and public service programs, Southern Illinois University Edwardsville (SIUE) is a premier metropolitan university with nearly 13,500 students. Founded in 1957, SIUE is a fully accredited public institution, beautifully situated on 2,660 acres just twenty-five minutes from Saint Louis.

Admissions Contact:

Southern Illinois University Edwardsville
Campus Box 1600
Edwardsville, IL 62026
Ph: (618) 650-3705
Email: admissions@siue.edu
www.siue.edu

The 4 Distinctions

Engaged Students

The College of Arts and Sciences (CAS) offers forty-four degree programs in the arts, humanities, and social and natural sciences. The College is committed to ensuring that its graduates acquire the skills and knowledge necessary to function as educated individuals, lifelong learners, and responsible citizens. To these ends, the college fosters the development of the following characteristics and capabilities: communication, critical thinking, problem framing and solving, knowledge, integration and application of knowledge, self-development, citizenship, and lifelong learning. All undergraduates begin their academic career in CAS, which administers the university's general education classes.

The School of Dental Medicine is second in the nation in final scoring on national board dental exams. As the only dental school in Illinois outside Cook County, and the only dental school within 250 miles of the Saint Louis metropolitan area, the school serves as a vital oral health care provider for Southern Illinois.

SIUE's School of Business has been accredited by the Association to Advance Collegiate Schools of Business (AACSB) since 1975. Fewer than 15 percent of business schools worldwide have earned this prestigious seal of approval. The School of Business provides students with many opportunities to experience international business. The skills they develop from that exposure provides them with a competitive edge when they graduate. Each year, a number of faculty and students participate in the school's international exchange programs in France, Germany, Mexico, and China.

The School of Education offers degree options in psychology, speech pathology/audiology, exercise/wellness, and a variety of teacher preparation areas. Students blend their classroom experiences with field experience in rural, urban, and metropolitan settings, all within thirty-five miles of campus.

School of Engineering graduates are recruited by industry-leading firms all over the world. With a state-of-the-art facility, highly qualified faculty, and active partnerships with area industries and agencies, students prepare for challenging careers in engineering, computer science, and construction management.

The School of Nursing is fully accredited by the Commission on Collegiate Nursing Education, the gold standard for baccalaureate and graduate degree nursing programs. In 2005, students placed among the top 10 percent nationally on the national licensing exam.

The only pharmacy school in downstate Illinois, the School of Pharmacy offers a highly competitive program in which only one of five applicants is accepted. The school collaborates with rural and urban health-care institutions to meet the health-care needs of Central and Southern Illinois and the Saint Louis metropolitan area.

Great Teaching

SIUE faculty are committed to making sure that students have all the resources needed to complete their education. They share their knowledge, but just as important, they engage students in the learning process by encouraging students to share their own thoughts and ideas, cultivating interesting classroom discussions.

SIUE is one of only a few universities across the country to offer a capstone undergraduate project that allows students to apply what they have learned prior to graduation. In addition, through the SIUE Undergraduate Research Academy, students participate in research typically available only to graduate students. Offering tremendous learning opportunities, both programs give students valuable preparation for graduate school or a career. SIUE has captured national attention for innovative learning opportunities. In fact, *U.S. News & World Report* ranked SIUE among the best universities in the country for the capstone senior project program.

SIUE faculty members have prestigious and widely varied backgrounds. Faculty members come from Yale, Rutgers, Brown, Vanderbilt, the University of California, the University of Texas, the University of Wisconsin, the University of Minnesota, and from around the world, including the Republic of China, New Zealand, Canada, Columbia, India, Africa, and Europe.

Vibrant Community

More than 65 percent of new freshmen live on campus. SIUE University Housing was awarded the 2006 Commitment to Excellence Award by Educational Benchmarking, Inc. for demonstrated dedication to continuous quality improvement.

Focused Interest Communities (FICs) are clusters of students pursuing the same major or with similar interests who live in the same general area in Bluff Hall. These communities are designed to provide residents with the support of other students studying the same subjects. By sharing their experiences in a community setting, students participating in FICs will expand their understanding of special-interest areas and develop an appreciation for the contribution of perspectives different from their own.

SIUE athletics finished fourth nationally in the United States Sports Academy Directors' Cup among NCAA Division II schools, and the school has won seventeen national championships. Men's basketball, volleyball, men's soccer, women's soccer, softball, baseball, men's golf, women's golf, men's indoor and outdoor track and field, and women's indoor and outdoor track and field have all made appearances in NCAA Division II tournaments, and the women's softball team recently was crowned national champions. SIUE has obtained approval from its board of trustees to move to Division I in the near future.

Students interested in developing their leadership potential may wish to become active in one or more of the 170 recognized student organizations. In addition to honorary organizations that encourage and recognize academic achievement, student organizations address educational, religious, social, recreational, and political interests. All enrolled students may take part in student organizations and their activities. Student government, the student leadership development program, student organizations, fraternities and sororities, university committees, honorary organizations, and departmental activities offer such opportunities.

The Kimmel Leadership Center provides students with numerous services, programs, and activities to help them develop their potential. The Kimmel Leadership Center is the focal point for student government and its functions, the Student Leadership Development Program, the Campus Activities Board, student organizational activities, and several related student-sponsored activities.

The Vadalabene Center offers fitness options such as a natatorium (an indoor pool), a rock-climbing gym, four racquetball courts, a walleyball court, a group activities room, a dance studio, table tennis, lockers, shower rooms, and a sauna.

Successful Outcomes

SIUE prepares students to become leaders in their communities and professionals in their fields of study. With more than 75,000 alumni, SIUE prepares graduates for the challenges of today's competitive workforce and graduate programs. SIUE alumni are proud of their educational foundation and continue to support the university. Alumni stay in touch with their peers through the alumni association and via *e-Connection*, the school's alumni magazine.

Fast Facts

Southern Illinois University Edwardsville (SIUE) is a premier metropolitan university, offering a broad choice of degrees and programs ranging from career-oriented fields of study to the essential, more traditional, liberal arts located in Edwardsville, Illinois.

Website

http://www.siue.edu

Location

Edwardsville, Illinois—suburban 2660-acre campus about 20 miles from St. Louis, Mo.

Student Profile

10,960 undergraduate students (45% male, 55% female); 43 states, 46 nations; 15.1% ethnic minorities.

Faculty Profile

815 faculty. 71% full-time. 17:1 student/faculty ratio

Residence Life

Mildly residential: 27% of students live on campus. In the fall of 2007, SIUE opened Evergreen Hall. It is the newest Residence Hall to join the University Housing family at SIU Edwardsville. Evergreen Hall accommodates 511 residents, which brings the total on-campus student population to approximately 3,500.

Athletics

NCAA, All Division II. 16 varsity sports (8 men's: baseball, basketball, cross-country running, golf, soccer, tennis, track & field, wrestling; 8 women's: basketball, cross-country running, golf, soccer, softball, tennis, track & field, volleyball) and intramurals.

Academic Programs

Accounting; advanced education in general dentistry; anthropology; art; art and design; art therapy counseling; biology/biological sciences; biotechnology management; business administration; business economics and finance; chemistry; civil engineering; computer engineering; computer management and information systems; computer science; construction management; criminal justice studies; dentistry; early childhood education; earth and space science education; economics; economics and finance; educational administration; electrical engineering; elementary education; English; environmental science management; environmental sciences; foreign language and literature; geographical studies; geography; health education; history; museum studies; industrial engineering; instructional design and learning technologies; kinesiology; learning, culture and society; liberal studies; literacy education; manufacturing engineering; marketing research; mass communication; media literacy; mathematical studies; mathematics; mechanical engineering; music; nursing; pharmacy; philosophy; physics; political science; psychology; public administration; school psychology; secondary education; social work; sociology; special education; speech communication; speech language pathology and audiology; teaching; theater & dance.

Costs and Aid

2007–2008: $13,812.50 in-state comprehensive ($5,227.50 tuition); $21,654.50 out-of-state comprehensive ($13,069.50 tuition). 63% of students receive some financial aid.

Anderson University

INDIANA

Anderson University has grown since its founding in 1917 to include an undergraduate liberal arts program (organized into three colleges), a graduate School of Theology, and a center for adult education. The university's mission is to educate strudents for a life of faith and service in the church and society.

Admissions Contact:

Anderson University
1100 East Fifth Street
Anderson, IN 46012
(800)428-6414
Ph: (765) 641-4080
Email: info@anderson.edu
www.anderson.edu

The 4 Distinctions

Engaged Students

Opportunities abound at AU for students to get involved and discover which activities are most meaningful for them. For some, this means assisting professors in research projects and other professional endeavors. Students can also pick from a range of extracurricular activities that includes student government, Model U.N., intramural sports, Multicultural Student Association, theatre productions, and the AU student newspaper- just to name a few. Whether it's traveling with the Chorale to sing at the Cathedral of St. John the Divine in New York City, crafting business strategies with local entrepreneurs, or working behind a camera with an award-winning production company in Tanzania, there's always something to discover at Anderson University.

Anderson University is a member of the Council for Christian Colleges and Universities (CCCU). Through this organization, AU students are eligible to apply for a semester at one of the seven off-campus programs in overseas locations such as Costa Rica, Egypt, Russia, England, and China, as well as programs in Washington, DC, and Los Angeles. Affiliation with the CCCU allows for easy transfer for credits and externally funded financial aid.

The honors program provides a series of small, discussion-based, interdisciplinary courses that satisfy particular liberal arts program requirements. These courses, as well as close interaction with faculty and peers, offer intellectually challenging experiences that will stimulate and refine the skills of clear expression, acute analysis, critical thinking, and imaginative problem solving.

Tri-S (study, serve, and share) was designed along the lines of the Peace Corps program in the 1960s. Today, more than one-fourth of the AU student body travels to Africa, Europe, Asia, Latin America, the Caribbean, and the Middle East each year. The program is so affordable that some students take a number of trips before they graduate. Depending on the project, students can volunteer their skills in construction and painting or share their abilities in counseling, singing, nursing, or teaching. Living and working daily with their international hosts, students are exposed to the arts, culture, and language of the host country.

Great Teaching

For students who call this campus home, Anderson University is a place of academic and Christian discovery. Because of the university's commitment to providing mentoring relationships, students work closely with renowned faculty in a variety of fields. Such mentors include a biology professor known for his focused attention toward environmental stewardship, a glass sculptor who once taught in one of England's most respected glass programs and has exhibited around the world, and an English professor who travels the country portraying nineteenth-century American author Henry David Thoreau.

AU professors are not on campus to become nationally known for their research. They are there, rather, because they share AU's vision of a premier teaching-learning community and because they specialize in teaching undergraduates. In fact, it's not unusual for the faculty, 81 percent of whom hold doctorates or terminal degrees, to involve students in their research.

Anderson thinks the education of today's young people is too important to leave in the hands of anyone but experienced and professionally qualified faculty. At AU, the student to faculty ratio is fourteen to one. These numbers become more meaningful when faculty members join students in service projects, offer a listening ear during midterms, or provide an important job connection.

Anderson provides quality liberal arts preparation in more than sixty majors and programs. An educational ministry of the Church of God, the university welcomes students from all denominations into a campus community dedicated to a Christian lifestyle.

Vibrant Community

Anderson University is defined more by what its students do than what they don't do. A vital spiritual life program includes campus Bible studies, a ministry at a nearby reformatory, retreats to urban ministry projects, and an arts festival for expressions of faith. Anderson believes that a student body can become a believing body, and asks that students attend chapel twice a week.

Students can take their pick of extracurricular activities that include student government, Model UN, intramural sports, the multicultural student association, the international student association, theater productions, and the AU student newspaper or yearbook, to just name a few. To assist students along the way, AU staffs a very active campus activities office and provides helpful resident directors and resident assistants to help students become accustomed to and involved with the life of the campus community. The mission of the Anderson University student life staff is to develop a community with Christian principles, a community focused on relationship development, serious learning, and lots of fun.

Just forty miles northeast of Indianapolis and the Indianapolis International Airport, the tree-lined campus in Anderson, Indiana (population 60,400), features the $5.5 million Reardon Auditorium and the $17.4 million, 132,000 square-foot Kardatzke Wellness Center.

Successful Outcomes

Historically, AU students have been drawn to ministry, education, and social services. That is still true, although recent generations of graduates have realized the opportunity and the need for ministry in a number of professional fields. For that reason, you'll find Anderson alumni pursuing careers in business management, marketing, medicine, law, mass communication, the music industry, music performance, and computer science, as well as teaching, social work, and areas of professional ministry.

Recent graduates have won fully funded placements in graduate programs at the University of Chicago, Vanderbilt University, and Harvard University. Others have attended the Indiana University School of Medicine, the Princeton Theological Seminary, and Washington University.

The career development office offers a variety of resources, such as a seminar that assesses students' marketable skills, helping them identify careers that would be a good fit. Through this office, Anderson graduates can learn effective job-search skills not only for entry-level positions but also for the eight or nine vocational changes they will likely undertake during their working lives.

Fast Facts

Anderson University is a private, four-year institution established in 1917 and supported by the Church of God.

Web site

http://www.anderson.edu/

Location

Anderson, Indiana—a city of 60,000, 35 miles northeast of Indianapolis.

Student Profile

1,965 students (40% male, 60% female); 45 states, 40 foreign countries; 5% minority, 1% international

Faculty Profile

135 full-time faculty. 81% hold a terminal degree in their field. 14:1 student/faculty. Average class size is 24.

Residence Life

70% of students live on campus

Athletics

NCAA Division III, Heartland Collegiate Athletic Conference. 16 varsity sports (8 men's: baseball, basketball, cross-country, football, golf, soccer, tennis, track & field; 8 women's: basketball, cross-country, golf, soccer, softball, tennis, track & field, volleyball).

Academic Programs

Accounting; athletic training; Bible; Bible & religion; biochemistry; biology; chemistry; Christian ministries; church music; computer science; criminal justice; economics; education; English; exercise science; family science; finance; fine arts; French; general studies; history; information systems; instrumental performance; management; marketing; mass communication; mathematics; music; music business; music education; nursing; philosophy; physics; political science; psychology; social work; sociology; Spanish; theatre studies; visual communication design; voice performance.

Costs and Aid

2007–2008: $29,520 comprehensive ($21,920 tuition). 90% of students receive some financial aid. Average award: $11,216.

Endowment

$17,056,000.

More Distinctions

• AU has been selected as one of the top liberal arts colleges in the Midwest by U.S. News & World Report's America's Best Colleges.

• AU was also selected for the John Templeton Foundation Honor Roll for Character Development.

Goshen College

INDIANA

A four-year, Christian, liberal arts college established in 1894, Goshen College has an impressive history and offers student access to a unique international education program. Goshen is committed to graduating students prepared to make positive contributions to their communities, their churches, and to the world.

Admissions Contact:

Goshen College
1700 South Main Street
Goshen, Indiana 46526
(800) 348-7422
Ph: (574) 535-7000
Fax: (574) 535-7609
Email: admission@goshen.edu
www.goshen.edu

The 4 Distinctions

Engaged Students

Goshen College provides a top-tier, Christ-centered academic experience that emphasizes passionate learning, global citizenship, compassionate peacemaking and servant leadership. Goshen prepares students for successful careers and vocations that allow them to transform lives and change the world.

Goshen College was one of the first colleges in the United States to make international education a part of its core curriculum. More than 80 percent of the most recent graduating class studied abroad. Students can choose from a range of host countries, including Ethiopia, Nicaragua, Senegal, Cambodia, Germany, Peru, China, and Jamaica. Study-Service Term, the college's unique three-month study-abroad program, offers students the opportunity to participate in life-changing experiences. Since 1968, more than 6,900 students and 230 faculty leaders have lived, studied and provided service throughout the world. A recent Goshen survey of randomly selected alumni found that 91.5 percent consider SST one of their most important life experiences.

In 2007, the college's American Sign Language (ASL) Program sent students to Jamaica with ASL as their primary language. Students learned about Jamaican culture and also Jamaican Deaf culture.

Students are accepted into Goshen on the basis of GPAs and standardized test scores, as well as by references and a personal essay.

Great Teaching

With a faculty to student ratio of thirteen to one and 83 percent of classes containing less that twenty-five students, Goshen offers plenty of personal attention from faculty and an assurance that students won't get lost in the crowd. Faculty members are dedicated and talented. More than two-thirds of the faculty have earned their doctorate or the equivalent degree in their field, and over half have lived, worked, or studied abroad.

Goshen's vast array of academic programs offer hundreds of challenging and practical interdisciplinary options.

Students interested in a marketing career, for example, might combine multimedia communication, entrepreneurship, and art. The possibilities are nearly endless.

Learning at Goshen is hands-on. Students in education, social work, multimedia, psychology, communication, nursing, accounting, and many other fields are placed in positions that help them establish their careers.

The peace, justice and conflict studies program, with a major and two minors, covers a wide range of peace-related issues, while being deeply rooted in Christian faith.

Goshen College also offers a premier center for ecological studies, the Merry Lea Environmental Learning Center, which is among Indiana's best-assembled land preserves. This Merry Lea preserve is known for its diversity of ecosystems and its quality educational programs. More than 7,000 school children visit each year. It has a "green" biological field station, designed to earn a Platinum LEED rating from the U.S. Green Building Council – the only LEED building in Indiana registered at this level.

Vibrant Community

As a Christ-centered college, service is a key component to the Goshen experience. Goshen students volunteer with local agencies such as the Child Abuse Prevention Center, Goshen General Hospital, and the Teenage Parent Program.

Community is not just a buzzword at Goshen College. While students come to Goshen from around the world and from a range of different backgrounds, they share a sense of common purpose. Students regularly report that friendships made at Goshen are central to the entire college experience.

This private, coeducational northern Indiana college is owned by Mennonite Church USA. Like members of other historic peace churches (Church of the Brethren and Quaker), Mennonites have a strong orientation toward peace-and-justice issues. They also are committed to welcome other religions traditions. While about 55 percent of Goshen's enrollment is Mennonite, more than thirty different Christian denominations and several world religions also are represented on campus. International students are 8 percent of total enrollment and come from thirty-seven countries. Another 10 percent of students are minorities from within the United States.

Goshen is a solidly residential campus—more than 80 percent of students live on campus. The college's nineteen major buildings include the well-equipped Roman Gingerich Recreation-Fitness Center and a sixty-eight thousand square-foot music center, including a one thousand-seat performance hall known for its fine acoustics.

The college's Westlawn cafeteria offers a wide variety of hot food, vegetarian selections, sandwiches, salads, all-day breakfast items, ice cream, desserts, and international dishes, as well as flexible hours and frequent mealtime entertainment like open mic night and pumpkin-carving contests.

With dozens of clubs and organizations on campus, cocurricular and extracurricular opportunities abound, including student government, ministry, community volunteerism, theater, music, multicultural issues organizations, newspaper, radio, television, and Bible studies, as well as fourteen athletic teams and nine intramurals. Goshen offers a variety of options for a rich student life.

Successful Outcomes

Goshen graduates are everywhere. More than twenty thousand Goshen alumni can be found throughout the United States and in nearly eighty countries.

The journey for Goshen students doesn't end with graduation. Goshen College graduates experience success on many levels. Goshen alumni regularly matriculate at some of the most prestigious graduate programs in the country, including Harvard, Columbia, Princeton, Notre Dame, and Northwestern University.

Goshen College alumni have assisted with the creation of the United Nations, chaired international science gatherings (including one that reclassified Pluto), discovered J. S. Bach's original tuning method for pipe organs, worked for peace around the world, received film awards (including the Sundance Film Festival), published poems in national magazines and reviews, served as leaders in agricultural research (including being credited with creating the seedless watermelon), started countless small and large businesses, and conducted internationally-leading molecular biology research.

Goshen students are accepted into medical school at twice the national average; English majors score in the top one percent on the Education Testing Service Exam; nursing, social work, and elementary education graduates regularly score higher than average on state exams; and accounting majors successfully complete the CPA exam at a rate three times greater than the national average. Goshen ranks in the top 17 percent of liberal arts colleges for producing graduates who earn doctoral degrees, according to a study by Franklin and Marshall College.

Fast Facts

Goshen College, established in 1894, is a residential Christian liberal arts college rooted in the Anabaptist-Mennonite tradition.

Web site

http://www.goshen.edu

Location

Goshen, Indiana—2 ½ hours from Chicago, 3 hours from Indianapolis.

Student Profile

951 undergraduate students (40% male, 60% female); 32 states and territories, 27 countries; 10% minority, 8% international.

Faculty Profile

67 full-time faculty. More than 66% hold a terminal degree in their field. 13:1 student/faculty ratio. 85% of classes have fewer than 25 students.

Residence Life

Highly residential: 76% of students live on campus. Students under the age of 22 and not living with immediate family members are required to live on-campus.

Athletics

NAIA, Mid-Central College Conference. 14 varsity sports (7 men's: baseball, basketball, cross-country, golf, soccer, tennis, track & field; 7 women's: basketball, cross-country, soccer, softball, tennis, track & field, volleyball) and 9 intramurals.

Academic Programs

Accounting; American Sign Language interpreting; art; Bible & religion; biology; business; business information systems; chemistry; communication; computer science; computer science and applied math; education (elementary); English; environmental science; history; history and investigative skills; mathematics; molecular biology/biochemistry; music; nursing; organizational leadership; peace, justice and conflict studies; physical education; physics; psychology; social work; sociology/anthropology; Spanish; special education (K-6); TESOL (Teaching English to Speakers of Other Languages); theater.

Graduate programs are available.

Costs and Aid

2007–2008: $28,300 comprehensive ($21,300 tuition). 99% of students receive some financial aid. Average award: $17,555.

Endowment

$105.8 million.

More Distinctions

• U.S.News & World Report's "America's Best Colleges."

• Barron's Best Buys in Education.

• Making a Difference College Guide."

Manchester College

INDIANA

Manchester College (MC) is a private, coeducational, liberal arts and sciences college, one of six across the nation affiliated with the Church of the Brethren. The tree-shaded, 125-acre campus is an attractive setting for MC's diverse atmosphere, where dialogue about difficult issues and differing opinions is encouraged.

Admissions Contact:

Manchester College
604 E. College Ave.
North Manchester, IN 46962
Ph: (800) 852-3648
Email: admitinfo@manchester.edu
www.manchester.edu

The 4 Distinctions

Engaged Students

Founded in 1889, MC's mission remains to respect "the infinite worth of every individual and graduate persons of ability and conviction who draw upon their education and faith to lead principled, productive, and compassionate lives that improve the human condition." MC offers more than forty-five areas of study. The most popular majors are teacher education, accounting, biology, and chemistry. MC was the first college in the nation to offer peace studies, an area of study focused on conflict resolution for personal or international contexts, and taught by professors from a variety of disciplines.

Many of MC's academic programs are highly regarded. The accounting program was recently ranked third in the nation based on MC graduates' successful performance on the CPA qualifying exams. In addition to classroom work, students take advantage of opportunities to gain hands-on experience. The biology and chemistry programs take advantage of a field station on a pond near campus to perform research, and internships are available in a wide variety of majors.

MC's 1,050 students participate in service-learning and study-abroad programs to augment their classroom experiences. MC's Spanish students teach English to local immigrants, helping them fill out forms and prepare resumes so they can find employment. Other students tutor children in schools within thirty miles of MC under the Indiana Reading Corps (IRC) program.

About a 40 percent of MC's students study abroad, often during the January session, although some students prefer to take classes on campus in January. Students also can study abroad for a semester or an academic year in one of eleven countries. Students also participate in summer research projects, applying for funds and working closely with a faculty member.

Great Teaching

MC's low student to faculty ratio of fourteen to one and small class size, averaging twenty-one students, allow students to work side by side with their professors. The highly qualified faculty—93 percent have earned their PhD or the highest degree offered in their field—teach full-time. MC's faculty prepare their students to articulate their ideas, support them with research, and make a case to defend them successfully.

As part of this preparation, all first-year MC students take a colloquium focused on teaching students to handle differences in an articulate and civilized manner. Students read and discuss texts in small groups and attend a lecture series and convocations based on difficult dialogues. Junior and senior students take critical connections courses, which approach different issues from an interdisciplinary perspective.

Vibrant Community

The campus is located in North Manchester, a classic, small Hoosier town of about six thousand, located thirty-five miles west of Fort Wayne and one hundred miles north of Indianapolis, providing students with access to nearby internship opportunities.

About three-quarters of MC's students live on campus, and some choose to live in learning communities, where groups of students attend classes together, encouraging collaborative learning and allowing students to form close bonds. Choices in housing include a women-only building, two traditional residence halls that are coed by floor, and two suite-style halls with mixed-gender floors.

There are more than fifty different clubs MC students can join. The Intercultural Center houses Hispanos Unidos, the Black Student Union, and an international student club.

Other student organizations are service oriented, such as Habitat for Humanity, or are organized around academic and other interests.

MC's diverse student body enjoys intramural sports such as basketball and sharbade (a combination of hockey, lacrosse, and soccer, played on scooters). Major weekend and campus events include Camp Mack Day, when students and faculty play softball, May Day weekend, when students compete in a serious mud-volleyball tournament, and Little Sib's Weekend, when students' little brothers and sisters invade campus.

Successful Outcomes

MC students graduate with ability, skills, values, and conviction. Nearly 97 percent of MC's alumni are employed or pursuing higher education within six months of graduation. Roughly 85 percent of MC's prelaw and premed students are accepted at professional schools.

MC is so confident of their graduates' success that they offer an employment guarantee: students who meet certain requirements with the career center can return to the college for another year of schooling, tuition free, if they aren't employed within six months of graduation.

Fast Facts

Manchester College is an independent, coeducational college in the liberal arts tradition, affiliated with the Church of the Brethren, founded in 1889.

Web site

http://www.manchester.edu

Location

North Manchester, Indiana—35 miles from Fort Wayne and 100 miles from Indianapolis.

Student Profile

1,050 students (45% male, 55% female); 23 states and 30 countries; 8% minority. 5% international.

Faculty Profile

68 full-time faculty, 92% of whom hold the terminal degree in their field. 14:1 student/faculty ratio. Average class size is 21.

Residence Life

Moderately residential: 74% of students live on campus.

Athletics

NCAA Division III, Heartland Collegiate Athletic Conference. 17 varsity sports (9 men's, 8 women's) and an extensive intramural program.

Academic Programs

Accounting; art; athletic training; biochemistry; biology; biotechnology; business; chemistry; coaching (minor only); communication studies; computer science; criminal justice (minor only); economics; elementary education; engineering science; English; environmental studies; exercise science; finance; fitness & sport management; French; gender studies (minor only); German; gerontology (minor only); history; information systems (minor only); interdisciplinary major; journalism (minor only); management; marketing; mathematics; media studies (concentration); medical technology; music; peace studies; philosophy; physical education; physics; political science; prelaw; premedicine; preoccupational therapy; prephysical therapy; psychology; public relations (concentration); religion; secondary education; social work; sociology; Spanish; sport management (fitness & sport management), TESOL (Teaching English to Speakers of Other Languages), theatre arts (concentration).

Costs and Aid

2006–2007: $28,210 comprehensive ($20,440 tuition). 98% of students receive some financial aid.

Endowment

$34 million.

More Distinctions

• The A Cappella Choir of Manchester College has performed at some impressive venues, including Carnegie Hall in 2001 and the Vatican in 2004.

• Manchester received acclaim for its exceptional academic program and its affordability in U.S. News & World Report's 2005 America's Best Colleges guide. The magazine ranks the college seventh as a "Great School/Great Price" and as a "Best College" among midwestern liberal arts colleges.

• The Princeton Review's 2004 and 2005 editions of The Best Midwestern Colleges both include Manchester.

Saint Joseph's College

INDIANA

Founded in 1889, Saint Joseph's College (SJC) is a private, Catholic, liberal arts college founded and sponsored by the Missionaries of the Precious Blood (C.PP.S.). Located in northwest Indiana, SJC strives to prepare men and women to lead successful professional and personal lives consistent with Gospel values.

Admissions Contact:

Saint Joseph's College
US Highway 231
Rensselaer, IN 47978
Ph: (800) 447-8781
Email: admissions@saintjoe.edu
www.saintjoe.edu

The 4 Distinctions

Engaged Students

Saint Joseph's College has developed a unique series of classes called the Core Program. Students receive a well-rounded academic foundation through this team-taught, interdisciplinary approach to general education. The program focuses on linking different disciplines, demonstrating how subjects influence one another, and applying the information to students' majors.

SJC's Core Program allows students to integrate required courses throughout all four years so that students can begin the study of their majors right away. The most popular majors are education, business, biology-chemistry, psychology, and criminal justice. In their first semester, education majors have the opportunity to observe in elementary and secondary schools; by their sophomore years, they are able to directly participate in classroom learning. Criminal justice professors take students to crime scenes to see real evidence, while business students conduct market analyses of nearby cities.

Saint Joseph's liberal transfer policy allows students to spend up to a full semester in another country. With the standard programs, all credits earned abroad count toward graduation. As early as sophomore year, SJC students can study abroad in places such as the Netherlands, Mexico, Spain, England, Austria, France, Wales, China, and Australia. Research can also lead students abroad, as it did for one biology student who attended a conference in Africa with a professor.

Great Teaching

Professors at SJC are there to teach. There are no teaching assistants, so students learn directly from experts in their fields and gain valuable hands-on instruction. Saint Joseph's College boasts over seventy majors, minors, and preprofessional programs.

SJC professors have an open-door policy and always find time to connect with individual students. Faculty members accommodate students' needs and even serve as advisers for student-run clubs. This role adds another dimension to the student-faculty relationship and allows faculty to get to know students outside the classroom setting. Professors also show their support by attending events that feature students' creative endeavors, such as poetry readings sponsored by *Measure*, the college's literary magazine; art gallery displays; band and choral concerts; theatrical productions; and sporting events.

Vibrant Community

Open to all faith denominations, campus ministry serves as an integral part of SJC's Catholic identity. The operating philosophy behind the organization is based on the needs of the students, and programming is geared to provide students with opportunities to further their relationships with God and others. Programming—from Sunday liturgies to retreats—is student organized and led. Students explore and enhance their spiritual, moral, and ethical principles through activities and programs such as Kairos Retreats and work for social justice in the Volunteer Corps.

Over 70 percent of students reside on the college's 180-acre, parklike campus, and 86 percent of full-time students are involved in campus clubs and organizations. By joining clubs, students are able to develop strong leadership skills, a highly valued quality in the workplace. One of the college's most popular clubs, the Diversity Coalition, hosts an annual Martin Luther King Jr. parade and program that incorporates members of the Rensselaer community. Rensselaer, known as the county seat for Jasper County, is a bustling community that continues to expand. The city offers such amenities as a movie theater, art gallery, roller rink, bowling alley, and a downtown area with unique dining and shopping options, all within the confines of a safe and friendly atmosphere.

Successful Outcomes

SJC graduates are no strangers to success. Within twelve months of graduation, 95 percent of graduates are building careers in their preferred fields or furthering their education in graduate or professional schools. In addition, several SJC graduates continue their education at some of the country's most prominent graduate and professional schools.

Alumni are essential to SJC students, constantly willing to take Pumas under their wings for mentoring and to provide community-driven networking opportunities. A number of alumni seek out current Pumas for job placement, including Michael Evans of the class of '67, owner and CEO of American Institute of Toxicology (AIT Laboratories). Evans offers semester-long internships and postcollege careers to SJC students each year.

The college's Career Development Center (CDC) provides assistance with everything from skills assessments to resume workshops to career fairs. The CDC also works closely with the Center for Indiana Partnerships to provide students with a variety of exciting internship opportunities and field experiences while enrolled at SJC. Whether preparing a resume for the first time, securing an internship, or connecting with SJC's vast Alumni Career Network, these centers serve as powerful resources for the career success of SJC students.

The most rewarding aspects of teaching at Saint Joseph's College are 1) gaining new expertise as I conduct original research jointly with my students, 2) smiling and waiting patiently as students command new skill sets they were positive they would never master, and 3) getting e-mails from alumni going back to '93 who say the skill sets they learned in my class have been the foundation for their careers."

- Dr. David Dixon, Assistant Professor of Political Science and International Studies

"The Core Program builds upon itself, increasing your academic abilities and strengthening your morals and character. Core 1 helped me improve my writing skills and evaluate my beliefs and values."

- Philip W. Jobst, sophomore

"Being bored is not an option here at SJC; there is always something to do as long as you keep your eyes and ears open!"

- Avriel Mullett, senior

Fast Facts

Saint Joseph's College is a private, liberal arts college affiliated with the Catholic church, but welcoming to students of all faiths. The College was founded in 1889 by the Missionaries of the Precious Blood (C.PP.S).

Web site

http:// www.saintjoe.edu

Location

Rensselaer, IN—90 miles from Chicago & Indianapolis.

Student Profile

1,031 undergraduate students (41% male, 59% female); 20 states and territories; 15% multicultural enrollment, 1% international.

Faculty Profile

58 full-time faculty. 15:1 student/faculty ratio. Average class size is 14.

Residence Life

Moderately residential: 73% of full-time students live on campus.

Athletics

NCAA Division II, Great Lakes Valley Conference. 18 varsity sports (9 men's: baseball, basketball, cross-country, football, golf, soccer, tennis, track & field (indoor & outdoor); 9 women's: basketball, cross-country, golf, soccer, softball, tennis, track & field (indoor & outdoor), volleyball).

Academic Programs

Accounting; art; biology; business administration; chemistry; computer science, criminal justice; economics; education; English; history; international studies; lay ecclesial ministry; mass communication; mathematics; music; nursing; philosophy; physical education; political science; psychology; religion; social work; sociology; theatre arts.

Costs and Aid

2007–2008: $28,820 comprehensive ($21,710 tuition). 97% of students receive some form of financial assistance.

More Distinctions

• Princeton Review - "Best Midwestern College."

• Templeton Foundation - "Character-Building College."

• US News & World Report - one of the Top 40 "Best Midwest Comprehensive Colleges."

• National Council for Accreditation of Teacher Education (NCATE) awarded an "unconditional" accreditation, the highest rating an institution can achieve.

• Barron's Best Buys in College Education.

Saint Mary-of-the-Woods College

INDIANA

Founded in 1840 by Saint Mother Theodore Guerin, Saint Mary-of-the-Woods College (SMWC) is a Catholic, liberal arts college for women. The college is committed to helping students develop their abilities to think critically, communicate responsibly, engage in lifelong learning and leadership, and to effect positive change in a global society.

Admissions Contact:

Saint Mary-of-the-Woods College
Saint Mary-of-the-Woods, IN 47876-0067
(800) 926-7692
Ph: (812) 535-5106
Email: smwcadms@smwc.edu
www.smwc.edu

The 4 Distinctions

Engaged Students

In keeping with the school's theme, "Life in progress," students at SMWC are active and involved, and have many opportunities to gain real-life experience through service learning, internships, research, and student performances.

At SMWC, service is integrated throughout the curriculum. Students may choose from several courses that incorporate service learning in a variety of disciplines, such as English, education, accounting, or theology. Students enrolled in service-learning courses develop knowledge and skills as they provide hands-on service to the local community.

The internship program at SMWC enables students to put their academic training to work in a professional environment, to refine their career objectives, and to gain valuable insight and experience. Examples of recent internships include a history and political science major interning for a U.S. senator, an elementary education major interning at the Children's Museum of Indianapolis, and a journalism and digital media communications major serving as a reporting intern at LEO Weekly. Internships and externships are arranged through the career services office, whose staff carefully guides students through the experience.

Students have the opportunity to participate in authentic research projects and to carry out their own scholarly work. On Student Academic Achievement Day, students showcase their projects, research, artwork, musical performances, video productions, and other creative endeavors. Each year, several students have opportunities to present or copresent their scholarly work to professional audiences.

Students have a number of opportunities to showcase their work at the SMWC Art Gallery and, in the Conservatory of Music, students hold junior and senior recitals. Students with interest in theater have opportunities to direct, perform, and design sets, costumes, and lighting for productions in Cecilian Auditorium and the Guerin Little Theatre.

Great Teaching

With a twelve to one student to faculty ratio and an average class size of ten, SMWC offers a personal setting for students to develop knowledge and skills. Professors at SMWC are experienced in their respective disciplines, and they represent diverse views and faith choices.

SMWC faculty members participate in professional development workshops to continuously strengthen and update their use of active learning strategies and instructional methods. At SMWC, students can take classes in various formats, including traditional face-to-face instruction, online courses, independent study, and study abroad.

SMWC has a growing international student population, as well as an exchange student program. Students can participate in the college's affiliated programs for study abroad in London, Ireland, Mexico, and Taiwan.

Vibrant Community

SMWC is located in Saint Mary-of-the-Woods, Indiana, in a quiet, peaceful, and secluded environment. The spacious wooded campus allows students to go for calm walks through the rich oak trees, engage in study sessions in the fresh air, and play volleyball or take a bike ride after class. At the same time, several metropolitan areas are only a car ride away. In addition, there are plenty of opportunities to meet and interact with students from Indiana State University, Ivy Tech Community College, and the Rose-Hulman Institute of Technology through Fusion, a social consortium offering concerts, lectures, community projects, and social events.

There are dozens of clubs and organizations for students to join, including the Education for Peace and Justice Committee; the Student Activities Committee; the Woods, the college's newspaper; and campus ministry. SMWC's clubs, organizations, sports, music ensembles, theater, and student government association provide students with ample opportunities to develop leadership skills.

SMWC celebrates several long-standing traditions, including Junior Ring Day, the Faculty-Senior Reception, and the Senior Dinner. Students actively participate in campus activities; they attend athletic events, join in late-night movies, and participate in campuswide events such as Race for the Cure, Diversity Week, and Family Weekend.

Terre Haute is a mere five miles southeast of campus, and provides a variety of places to shop, eat, and hang out. Indianapolis is just an hour and a half east of SMWC.

Successful Outcomes

SMWC students are closely connected with the Career Development Center throughout their college years, participating in job shadowing, internships, career workshops, and interview coaching opportunities. The Career Development Center's Web site connects students with a database where they can apply for jobs and post resumes; learn more about internships, externships, and supplemental learning experiences; and register for workshops and job fairs. The Career Development Center sponsors a networking day with the National Alumnae Board for students to network with alumnae and for alumnae to identify talented students as prospective employees for their companies.

After graduation, SMWC students pursue successful careers and advanced learning. Graduates go on to work for companies such as Eli Lilly, Pfizer, Coca-Cola, Barnes and Noble, Beazer Homes, and Riley Hospital for Children. Notable alumnae include Mari Hulman George, chair of the Indianapolis Motor Speedway; and Caroline Myss, mystic and medical intuitive.

"SMWC and especially the Career Development Center were invaluable in helping me prepare for the 'real world'," Wagner said, "As a result of the help of the Career Development Center and attending all of the Career Workshops, I found myself ahead of schedule with respect to both job and graduate school searches. The faculty members were very willing to help me consider my options post SMWC and offer advice about what career would suit me the best. I spent many afternoons in professors' offices discussing the future and gaining a better understanding of what I needed to do in order to reach my goals after [graduating from] SMWC."

Mary Wagner
Majors: Psychology and Music

Fast Facts

Saint Mary-of-the-Woods College is the oldest Catholic liberal arts college for women in the United States. SMWC was founded by Saint Mother Theodore Guerin in 1840. SMWC is a four-year college, sponsored by the Sisters of Providence.

Web site

http://www.smwc.edu

Location

Saint Mary-of-the-Woods, Indiana—5 miles northwest of Terre Haute, IN.

Student Profile

1,700 students. 300 campus-based undergraduate students.

Faculty Profile

65 full-time faculty. 12:1 student/faculty ratio. Average class size is 10.

Residence Life

Highly residential: 66% of students live on campus.

Athletics

USCAA Division III. 3 varsity sports (basketball, soccer, softball). IHSA Equine Teams (western, hunt seat).

Academic Programs

Accounting; advertising; art; biology; business administration; criminal justice; digital media; education majors; English; equine majors; graphic design; history/political science(prelaw); human resource management; human services; humanities; individualized major; journalism; marketing; mathematics; medical technology; music; music therapy; paralegal studies; preprofessional studies; professional writing; psychology; social science (history); theology; women & theatre.

Costs and Aid

2007–2008: $27,560 comprehensive ($19,530 Tuition). 90% of students receive some financial aid. Average award: $8,000.

Endowment

$13 million.

More Distinctions

• *U.S.News and World Report*: 2008 Top 20 Midwest Comprehensive Colleges.
• *Princeton Review* "Best of the Midwest" Distinction.

Saint Mary's College

INDIANA

Saint Mary's College is a Catholic, women's, liberal arts college. Founded in 1844 by the Sisters of the Holy Cross, it is one of the nation's oldest women's colleges. Located near the University of Notre Dame, Saint Mary's enjoys a national reputation for academic excellence and vitality of campus life.

Admissions Contact:

Saint Mary's College
Notre Dame, IN, 46556
Ph: (574) 284-4587
Fax: (574) 284-4841
Email: admission@saintmarys.edu
www.saintmarys.edu

The 4 Distinctions

Engaged Students

All Saint Mary's students complete a senior comprehensive project commonly referred to as the senior comp. Projects vary by discipline, but all are modeled on graduate-level thesis projects or examinations. Some students complete extensive research projects, some write novels, and others prepare advertising campaigns for local companies.

Titles of some recent senior comps included "Creation of Constructive Discontent in Advertising," "To Live Amongst the Gods: The Choice of Medieval Life," "Short-Term and Long-Term Effects of Methylphenidate on Response to Anesthesia and Blood Pressure in Male Spraque-Dawley Rats," and "Incidence of Breast Cancer in Indiana: A Comparison Among Caucasian and African American Women." Another recent project consisted of writing a full-length play.

Nearly 55 percent of Saint Mary's students complete study-abroad programs offered in more than twenty different locations. The college has maintained a campus in the historic center of Rome since 1970.

The Hispanic Outlook in Higher Education magazine has listed Saint Mary's as a top pick for Hispanic students.

Great Teaching

On average, 92 percent of Saint Mary's full-time faculty hold a PhD or the highest degree in their field. Because there are no graduate teaching assistants, Saint Mary's faculty are accessible to all students, and an eleven to one student-faculty ratio ensures that teachers and students discuss, discover, and learn together.

The Templeton Guide: Colleges that Encourage Character Development has recognized Saint Mary's as one of only forty-five institutions across the nation that offer opportunities in the classroom for students to examine, reflect on, and articulate a set of moral ideals and commitments.

The Center for Academic Innovation (CFAI) was founded in 1993 to create and foster programs in faculty and curriculum development, student research, teacher-student collaborations, and innovation in teaching and learning. The CFAI sponsors fellows each academic year to implement specific programs. Recent CFAI fellows have included Susan Vance of the department of business administration and economics with a program called Why Ask Why? Exploring a Faculty Response to Campus Alcohol Issues; Mana Derakhshani and Julie Storme of the department of modern languages, with a program titled Fostering Cross-Cultural Awareness in the Saint Mary's College Community; and Sr. Miriam Cooney of the department of mathematics with Collaborative Learning: Developing Alternative Teaching Styles.

Vibrant Community

Saint Mary's 75-acre campus, set alongside the St. Joseph River, features great natural beauty. Located just across the street from the University of Notre Dame and adjacent to Holy Cross College, the three schools form an educational community consisting of nearly ten thousand students. These campuses are located just minutes from the city of South Bend, with a population of one hundred and fifty thousand.

Campus activities include over seventy clubs and organizations, including eight varsity athletic teams and an active intramural program; the daily newspaper, the Observer, published jointly by Saint Mary's and Notre Dame; the combined Notre Dame and Saint Mary's radio station, WVBL; numerous drama and musical ensembles; religious clubs; and service and social organizations. Over 70 percent of students are engaged in social and civic organizations.

Saint Mary's Center for Women's Intercultural Leadership (CWIL) was founded in 2000 with a twelve-million-dollar grant from the Lilly Endowment. The role of CWIL is to foster the intercultural knowledge and competence critical to educating the next generation of women leaders. CWIL promotes intercultural engagement across Saint Mary's campus, connecting with communities at the local, state, national, and global levels.

In 2006, more than two hundred Saint Mary's and Notre Dame students combined to raise in excess of twenty-one thousand dollars during an all-night dance marathon to benefit Riley Hospital for Children in Indianapolis. The first SMC Dance Marathon, based on a proposal by two members of Saint Mary's Board of Governance, has now become an annual spring event.

Through the Office of Civic and Social Engagement, nearly thirty different volunteer and civic opportunities await student input. Last year, Saint Mary's students gave over five thousand volunteer hours to benefit the Marquette School Partnership.

Successful Outcomes

Saint Mary's vibrant network of alumna includes three members of the current 110th Congress, the most from any women's college in the country.

Saint Mary's graduates move up quickly in their chosen professions. Last year, 100 percent of students who applied to graduate programs in the health professions were accepted, and 100 percent of accounting graduates also found placement in their field. Over the past ten years, 95 percent of all health profession graduates were admitted to graduate programs.

Approximately 95 percent of Saint Mary's College graduates will earn their degree in four years. Of those who graduate, 93 percent report being well satisfied with the overall Saint Mary's experience; and 65 percent report seeing a relationship between their major and their first job. Some 45 percent have careers in industry, business, and government; 10 percent in nursing; and 18 percent in teaching; while 25 percent attended graduate or professional school immediately after graduation. Four-fifths of those in graduate school reported satisfaction with their preparation for graduate study.

"My family definitely needed financial assistance for me to attend college since my older sister is also in school. I found that I was getting similar grants and scholarship offers from most of the colleges/universities that offered me admission but the atmosphere and warmth of the community brought me to Saint Mary's. Professors took time to not only get to know me but they demonstrated a genuine interest in my goals and interests. It helped that my sister also attends Saint Mary's and has loved her experiences here; when I visited campus, it just felt like a place I could call home."

Kristle Hodges '10
English major
South Holland, Illinois

Fast Facts

Saint Mary's is a Catholic, residential, liberal arts, women's college founded in 1844 by five Sisters of the Holy Cross who came to the U.S. from France to teach.

Web site

http://www.saintmarys.edu

Location

Notre Dame, Indiana—75 acres of landscaped campus along the St. Joseph River; just a few miles north of South Bend. Saint Mary's is approximately 1 ½ - 2 hours east of Chicago, IL.

Student Profile

Approximately 1550 undergraduate students (100% female); 44 states and territories, 7 countries; 10% minority, 1% international.

Faculty Profile

125 full-time faculty. 92% hold a terminal degree in their field. 11:1 student/faculty ratio. Average class size is 16.

Residence Life

Highly residential: 84% of students live on campus. Six semester on-campus residency policy which includes approved, campus-sponsored, study abroad housing.

Athletics

NCAA Division III, Michigan Intercollegiate Athletic Association. 8 varsity sports (basketball, cross-country, golf, soccer, softball, swimming & diving, tennis, volleyball), and intramurals (dodgeball, basketball, soccer). Cheerleading, dance, lacrosse, and triathlon teams are Saint Mary's sponsored clubs. Other co-sponsored clubs with the University of Notre Dame include equestrian, figure skating, gymnastics, water polo, and field hockey.

Academic Programs

Accounting; art; biology; business administration; chemistry; communication studies; computational mathematics/computer science; economics; elementary education; English literature; English writing; French; history; humanistic studies; Italian; management information systems; mathematics; music; music education; music performance; nursing; philosophy; political science; psychology; religious studies; social work; sociology; Spanish; statistics & actuarial mathematics; student-designed major; studio art; theatre. Secondary education certification in art, biology, business administration, chemistry, English literature, English writing, French, history, mathematics, music, political science, psychology, sociology, and Spanish.

Costs and Aid

2007-2008: $ 35,550 comprehensive ($26,285 tuition). 90% of students receive some financial aid. Average award: $17,400.

Endowment

$120 million.

More Distinctions

• In its 2008 annual survey of America's Best Colleges, *U.S. News & World Report* ranked Saint Mary's among the Top 10 National Liberal Arts Colleges; having previously ranked Saint Mary's the #1 Comprehensive Midwest College 12 of the last 13 years.

Taylor University

INDIANA

Taylor University is a private, interdenominational Christian university with campuses in Upland and Fort Wayne, Indiana. Founded in 1846, it is one of the oldest evangelical Christian colleges in the country.

Admissions Contact:

Taylor University
(800) 882-3456
Fax: (765) 998-4925
Email: admissions@taylor.edu
www.taylor.edu

The 4 Distinctions

Engaged Students

Intellect and spirituality coexist harmoniously at Taylor University, where students find a high-quality learning experience based on Christian ideals of truth and life. Taylor students enjoy the university's many strong points, such as its nationally recognized study-abroad program and its cutting-edge scientific research opportunities. Students may choose from more than one hundred undergraduate majors; the most popular programs include education, business, biblical studies, communication, and psychology. In 2003, Taylor began offering graduate-level programs, and current degrees offered include a Master of Environmental Science, a Master of Business Administration, a Master of Arts in Higher Education, and a Master of Arts in World Religions.

Taylor faculty regularly win contracts to conduct research for major companies, government agencies, and other organizations. Physics professors and students recently received grants for research from NASA, the air force, Lockheed Martin, the EPA, and the National Science Foundation. In addition to possessing the only lightning receiver in the Midwest, Taylor's research capabilities are enhanced by a partnership with Stanford University through which Stanford PhD candidates use Taylor's resources to study lighting effects in space.

The Council for Christian Colleges & Universities has recognized Taylor University for having the largest number of students participating in study-abroad programs. Taylor supports its own Irish studies program, which offers a program for freshman to spend their first semester of college in Ireland. Students can also travel through Taylor World Outreach on weeklong or monthlong mission trips. Real-world experience is required of all graduates. Taylor students have the opportunity to develop their leadership abilities through the Leadership Initiative of Taylor. The four-year program combines special classes with seminars, community service, and hands-on leadership experience.

Taylor's liberal arts curriculum builds on the foundational belief that all truth has its source in God. The academic program includes a core set of general education requirements, and seniors must complete an integrative, interdisciplinary, general education seminar. According to the 2005 National Survey of Student Engagement, students rated their Taylor experience significantly higher than their peers at other institutions in overall satisfaction with their entire educational experience, the quality of their relationships with other student and faculty members, and enriching educational experiences. The survey also asked students to what extent their experience at Taylor contributed to their knowledge, skills, and personal development in specific areas. Taylor students rated their experience significantly higher than their peers at other institutions in acquiring a broad general education, writing clearly and effectively, understanding of self, and developing a personal code of values and ethics. Taylor's faculty members are highly accessible to students, with about 80 percent living in the greater Upland region.

Great Teaching

Students are admitted to Taylor based on their potential to contribute to the learning experience as well as their potential to learn from it. Faculty and students work collaboratively, both in class and out, to achieve learning outcomes appropriate to each student's vocational calling.

Members of the Taylor faculty are noted for their ability to reconcile intellectual pursuits and faith. Taylor's honors program emphasizes the integration of faith and learning, ideas and values, and discussion and student initiative.

In addition to programs of study leading to academic degrees, Taylor offers many programs throughout the year that are designed to challenge students in all disciplines to be good stewards and citizens. Taylor offers a summer honors program called CRAM, during which high school students participate in course work that requires deep thinking, while challenging them to consider their studies in light of the culture at large. CRAM participants also experience a taste of college life while receiving college credit.

Vibrant Community

Students at Taylor are active in campus organizations, community leadership, outreach ministries, study-abroad programs, and in many other ways. Student life at Taylor provides the chance to learn outside the classroom. The biblical concept of the Body of Christ is evident as students live, serve, and learn together. Whether competing with their residence floor in the intramural flag football championship, working with Project Mercy alongside a team of fellow students in Ethiopia, or creating an award-winning DVD for the Indiana Department of Homeland Security, Taylor students are engaged in a variety of events that contribute to their growth and to the campus community. Chapel services, during which the entire student body gathers in worship, are held three times a week, from 10:00–10:45 a.m. on Monday, Wednesday, and Friday. Attendance is not taken at chapel, yet the seats are consistently full because the students choose to be there.

Taylor's student activities council sponsors more than fifty-five events per year, with a total attendance of eighteen thousand. Last year, Taylor students volunteered 54,294 hours in community service and ministry. More than 1,100 students are involved with voluntary discipleship groups, while 90 percent play intramural sports. Taylor also hosts club lacrosse and equestrian teams. Nearly three hundred Taylor students are involved in the university's fifteen intercollegiate sports. Other activities include a variety of clubs and organizations, including twelve music ensembles and an award-winning student media. A variety of activities take place in Taylor's residence halls, where personnel assistants help coordinate a wide variety of activities ranging from hog roasts to pick-a-date night, when roommates pick each other's companion for a group date.

A foundational document for the Taylor community is the Life Together Covenant. All community members sign this document, affirming that they will live under the basic assumption that joining this intentional community is a privilege coupled with responsibilities that help shape rather than control.

Successful Outcomes

Taylor's commitment to service and faith leaves a lasting impression on its graduates. Of Taylor alumni, 68 percent report that they are still living out the Taylor mission statement within their communities. Over half of alumni—52 percent—report that they are involved in charity, social welfare, relief agencies, and school or youth organizations.

Taylor's alumni giving rate of 46 percent is ranked as the second highest among midwestern comprehensive colleges, according to U.S. News & World Report. More than 90 percent of Taylor grads are either working in a field related to their major or attending graduate school within ten months of graduation, while 90 percent report being satisfied or extremely satisfied with their undergraduate experience.

"Taylor is recognized by U.S. News and World Report rankings as the #1 Midwest Baccalaureate College. Taylor is also named A Best Midwestern College by The Princeton Review."

Fast Facts

Taylor University is a four-year, private, coeducational, interdenominational Christian university and was founded in 1846.

Web site

http://www.taylor.edu

Location

Upland, Indiana—1 hour from Indianapolis.

Student Profile

1,853 students (46% male, 54% female). 44 states, 23 countries; 69% from outside of the state; 7% American ethnic and international students.

Faculty Profile

192 faculty members (137 full-time). Student/faculty ratio13:1. Average class size is 21.

Residence Life

Highly residential: 80% of students live on-campus.

Athletics

NAIA Division II, Mid-Central Conference, Mid-States Football. 15 varsity sports (8 men's: baseball, basketball, cross-country, football, golf, soccer, tennis, track; 7 women's: basketball, cross-country, soccer, softball, tennis, track, volleyball), 2 intercollegiate club programs, and an active intramural program with over 90% student participation.

Academic Programs

Accounting; accounting/systems; art; art education; Art/Systems; biblical literature; biblical literature/systems; biology; biology science education; biology/systems; chemistry; chemistry (environmental science); chemistry science education; chemistry/systems; Christian educational ministries; Christian educational ministries/systems; communication studies; communication studies/systems; computer engineering; computer science; computer science (new media); computer science (new media/systems); computer science/systems; early childhood education; economics; economics/systems; elementary education; engineering physics; engineering physics/systems; English; English education; English/systems; environmental engineering; environmental science; exercise science; finance; French; French education; geography; health & physical education; history; history/systems; individual goal oriented; interdisciplinary mathematics; international business; international business/systems; international studies; liberal arts; management; management information systems; management/systems; marketing; marketing/systems; mathematics education; mathematics (environmental science); mathematics/systems; music; music education; media communication; media communication/systems; natural science; philosophy; philosophy/systems; physical science education; physics; physics science education; physics/ mathematics education; physics/systems; political science; political science/systems; premajor; psychology; psychology/systems; social studies education; social work; sociology; sociology/systems; Spanish; Spanish Education; sport management; theatre arts; theatre arts/systems; visual arts (new media); visual arts(new media/systems).

Costs and Aid

2007–2008: $29,360 comprehensive fee ($23,030 tuition). 89% of students receive financial aid from Taylor University. Average award: $15,131.

Tri-State University

INDIANA

Admissions Contact:

Tri-State University
1 University Ave.
Angola, IN 46703
800.347.4TSU
Ph: 260.665.4100
Email: admit@tristate.edu
http://www.tristate.edu

Located in Angola, Indiana, Tri-State University (TSU) is an independent university devoted almost entirely to undergraduate education. Tri-State enrolls 1,100 students, and with small classes and a low student to faculty ratio of thirteen to one, students find it easy to build solid relationships with their professors.

The 4 Distinctions

Engaged Students

Tri-State's students regularly take advantage of internship opportunities. Criminal justice students, for example, have had internships with the Internal Revenue Service and local sheriff's offices. Other companies and agencies that have offered internships to Tri-State students include Abbott Laboratories, Bank of America, BASF, the Eastman Chemical Company, the Federal Bureau of Investigation, the Indiana House of Representatives, Motorola, Northwestern Mutual Life, and Pfizer Global Research & Development.

In addition to unpaid internships, Tri-State's cooperative education program has relationships with many different companies. Under this program, students take up to half a year off from their regular studies to work for a company. They receive a monetary stipend for their work, as well as gaining valuable learning experience. Companies taking part in the program include BorgWarner, Caterpillar, DuPont, Kodak, General Electric, Merck & Co, Inc., and Westinghouse Electric Company.

Through TSU's direct affiliation with International Studies Abroad (ISA), students can participate in affordable summer semester and yearlong programs in Spain, Italy, France, England, Mexico, Costa Rica, the Dominican Republic, Chile, Peru, Argentina, and Australia.

Great Teaching

Tri-State's faculty are dedicated to undergraduate teaching, and there are no teaching assistants in any of the academic programs. The largest classroom on campus seats forty-five students. The university's small classes provide a stimulating learning environment, and teachers at Tri-State are known for having an open-door policy.

Tri-State's program in engineering has built an especially solid reputation over the years. All professors in the engineering program bring not only academic backgrounds, but also professional experience in their fields of expertise. Tri-State has introduced Master of Engineering degrees in mechanical and civil engineering, which allow qualified students who commit to the program as freshmen to earn a Bachelor of Science and Master of Engineering simultaneously. The Master of Engineering degree can be completed in five years, including one summer design project.

The university also offers bachelor's degrees in education, criminal justice, and most of the sciences. Students who like to hit the links are drawn to the golf management program, which is complimented by an eighteen-hole golf course on campus. Tri-State also offers a major in entrepreneurship. Drawing from the areas of marketing, management, accounting, and finance, this program provides the foundation for students hoping to launch their own enterprises or assume the operation of family-owned businesses.

Vibrant Community

Under its Vision for the Future capital campaign, TSU has embarked on a ninety million dollar campus improvement plan, which includes the unveiling of its new University Center and Center for Online Technology in fall 2007. The $1.5 million project will include a 250-seat theater, a library, cafe dining for students and the community, cutting-edge technology, a global workplace, a sports and wellness center, and even a rock-climbing wall. The renovaton of the historic Sniff Building into the C.W. Sponsel Administration Center will provide generous space for university departments. New student apartments will continue the university's update of student housing, and freshman honor villas will give students even more incentive to strive for academic excellence. The connection of Hershey Hall in the fall will make the TSU environment totally wireless, as part of a two million dollar campuswide technology upgrade.

All freshmen and sophomores live in one of the university's six residence halls, or they apply to reside in the university's new freshman honor villas. All students under the age of twenty-one live in university housing, which includes on-campus apartments for juniors and seniors.

On campus, there are plenty of ways to get involved, including sixty student organizations and thirteen fraternities and sororities. About 25 percent of students join national fraternities and sororities. Students can also participate in Bingo for Books, Library Putt-Putt, the Home Sweet Dorm contest, or a pickup game of sand volleyball.

Tri-State is a member of the Michigan Intercollegiate Athletic Association, a Division III NCAA affiliate and the association's oldest. The university's full NCAA status in fall 2007 brings a total of twenty-one varsity men's and women's sports, including lacrosse, to the field or arena to entertain fans and challenge student-athletes. Intramural sports include basketball, billiards, dodgeball, the spring golf scramble, flag football, ping-pong, racquetball, Wiffle ball, and volleyball.

Tri-State students regularly take advantage of the natural features of the area, which afford opportunities for fishing, waterskiing, sailing, camping, and cross-country skiing. Theatrical performances, speaker series, and other cultural events are also popular activities for students. Students have volunteered for Habitat for Humanity, the Special Olympics, and at blood drives. One of the most popular groups on campus is the Christian Campus House.

Successful Outcomes

Professors play a major role in advising students about their career plans, writing letters of recommendation, and suggesting graduate schools. The career services office starts working with students during the freshman year, offering job fairs, resume building, workshops, and even etiquette dinners. About 90 percent of graduates have full-time jobs in their fields within six months of graduating. TSU has been listed for three consecutive years in U.S. News & World Report among colleges with graduates carrying the least amount of debt.

Among Tri-State University's notable alumni are NASA project manager Timothy Adams; Florence Cramer Bratton, the nation's first woman engineering graduate; Westinghouse, Korea president Tim Collier; Dr. John McKetta, science advisor to three U.S. presidents; and inventor Robert Molitor.

"The focus level of students at Tri-State University is astonishing. Every single person has a future goal in mind, and their drive to succeed in the real world is apparent."

-Colleges of Distinction

Fast Facts

Tri-State University is an internationally recognized, comprehensive, private, independent, co-educational institution. It was founded in 1884.

Web site

http://www.tristate.edu/

Location

Angola, Indiana—located on U.S. 20, accessible just off I-69 or I-80/90. It is less than a three-hour drive from Chicago, Cleveland, Detroit, and Indianapolis.

Student Profile

1,100 undergraduate students (72 % male, 28 % female); 24 states and territories, 8 countries; 5 % minority, 2 % international.

Faculty Profile

69 full-time faculty. 13:1 student/faculty ratio.

Residence Life

Moderately residential: 65% of students live on campus. All students under age 21 live in university housing, unless they commute from nearby homes.

Athletics

NCAA Division III, Michigan Intercollegiate Athletic Association (MIAA). 21 varsity sports (11 men's: baseball, basketball, cross-country, football, golf, lacrosse, soccer, tennis, wrestling, indoor track, outdoor track; 10 women's: basketball, cross-country, golf, lacrosse, soccer, softball, tennis, indoor track, outdoor track, volleyball), 0 club sports, and 8 intramurals.

Academic Programs

Accounting; biology; chemical engineering; chemistry; civil engineering; communication; computer engineering; criminal justice; design engineering technology; electrical engineering; elementary education; engineering administration; English; English education; environmental science; finance; forensic science; golf management; health education; health promotion & recreational programming; management; management information systems; marketing; mathematics; mathematics education; mechanical engineering; physical education; physical science; premedical; psychology; science education; social sciences; social studies education. Graduate programs in mechanical and civil engineering and engineering technology are available.

Costs and Aid

2007–2008: $28,750 comprehensive ($22,250 tuition). 95% of students receive some financial aid. Average award: $18,300 including all sources.

Endowment

$21 million.

The University of Evansville

INDIANA

The University of Evansville (UE) is a student-centered, liberal arts institution dedicated to active learning and scholarship. Founded in 1854, Evansville endeavors to prepare women and men for lives of professional service and leadership.

Admissions Contact:

The University of Evansville
1800 Lincoln Avenue
Evansville, IN 47722
(800) 423-8633 ext. 2468
Ph: (812) 488-2468
Fax: (812) 488-4076
Email: admission@evansville.edu
www.evansville.edu

The 4 Distinctions

Engaged Students

Evansville students are encouraged to explore their interests, conduct research, study abroad, and gain real work experience. With more than eighty areas of study, students can easily find the program they want, and they are encouraged to take classes from outside their major, providing them with a well-rounded educational experience.

More than two-thirds of University of Evansville graduates have studied abroad, making it one of the top five comprehensive universities in the United States for student travel. Students have studied in France, England, Russia, Japan, Italy, Kenya, the Netherlands, and many more locations. Since UE strongly encourages its students to study abroad, students are allowed to use federal, state, and university aid for these approved programs, making a study-abroad experience available and affordable. Harlaxton College, owned and operated by UE and located in Grantham, England, provides a home to approximately 150 students each semester. Students living at Harlaxton Manor spend a four-day week in classes and then have time to take field trips to Ireland, Italy, Greece, France, and other European countries.

UE students live on campus and are encouraged to get involved. With over 170 clubs, organizations, and activities, it's easy for students to find something that interests them. Social, professional, and musical organizations—Evansville students can explore them all. The Center for Student Engagement maintains a list of all students' involvement with organizations and volunteer activities and provides them with records of these activities, which can be used to enhance students' resumes and graduate school applications.

Great Teaching

Evansville professors are accessible and care about their students. They challenge students, expose them to new ideas, encourage them, and offer support. With UE's small class sizes, students receive one-on-one attention and build personal relationships with their professors. When students apply to graduate school or for jobs, professors are able and willing to write recommendations because they know their students.

This individualized attention begins during the students' freshman year, with the world cultures sequence, the cornerstone of an Evansville education. Students are placed into small-group world cultures sections during welcome week and continue with the same class throughout their freshman year. The world cultures two-semester curriculum is carefully planned to give students an appreciation of the complex cultures and ideas that have influenced the evolution of civilization from ancient times to today. Students are challenged to see how their actions and choices will inevitably impact diverse peoples, cultures, and environments now and in the future, developing students' confidence to face challenges.

For those students who are interested and meet academic criteria, the University of Evansville offers an honors program that incorporates unique courses with distinct learning environments providing enhanced educational learning experiences. Students openly discuss different viewpoints in small, seminar-style classes offered in various academic disciplines. Intellectually curious students who desire academic challenges will enjoy the collaborative learning atmosphere of the honors program, as well as the opportunity to engage in advanced independent study, a senior project, and special social programs. Honors program students may register on the first day of registration, giving them priority course selection. Honors students may also live in Powell Residence Hall, the honors program hall.

The university also sponsors UE Explore, an undergraduate research program designed to provide students and faculty the opportunity to work together on research projects. Research project ideas may be generated by students or faculty, and projects can occur over the summer or during the academic year. Many of these projects have culminated in students publishing and presenting their research in national venues. Recent examples have included students studying the effect of the Internet on interpersonal relationships and the use of drugs or eating disorders on athletes. Additionally, students have designed chemical techniques to improve the environment and have developed new understandings of ancient religious texts.

Vibrant Community

Evansville provides numerous opportunities for students to get involved both on and off campus. With students from thirty-nine states and fifty countries, students are exposed to different ideas and cultures, all while experiencing a quality education.

The University of Evansville is nestled in a residential neighborhood where students walk, jog, and shop. The campus has eight residence halls, and all buildings are conveniently located near other campus buildings, making any destination no more than a ten-minute walk across campus. Evansville, Indiana, is the economic and cultural center of southwest Indiana. With over four hundred global corporations located in the community, students have opportunities for a variety of co-ops and internships. Every year the Broadway series and concert tours visit Evansville, adding to the many entertainment opportunities that occur within the city.

Moore Residence Hall provides students with an opportunity to participate in a global living and learning community. International House, open to all university students, enhances the experience of all students attending UE by helping them to understand cultures from around the globe. Weekly meetings, located in Moore Residence Hall, provide information about various cultures and countries, and are the basis for this learning experience.

With more than 170 student organizations, students are able to become involved and meet others with similar interests. Whether volunteering to teach individuals in the community how to read or speak English, leading student government, raising funds for community agencies with a fraternity or sorority, or participating in intramurals, UE students are challenged to share their time and talents.

Successful Outcomes

From the moment they arrive on campus, Evansville students are being prepared for not only their first job, but their best job. Internships, cooperative education experiences, clinicals, undergraduate research, and course work give students the knowledge and skills they need to succeed.

The university's office of career services and cooperative education works with students to help them achieve their goals. Students participate in internships and cooperative experiences throughout the United States and abroad, providing them with real-world experience. For students who are undecided about their areas of study, UE offers the Do What You Are career survey, helping students determine their strengths and appropriate potential career paths.

Over the past ten years, more than 97 percent of University of Evansville graduates were employed within one year of graduation, four out of five graduates were working in their field of study, and over half had attended graduate school.

Fast Facts

The University of Evansville is a private, liberal arts and sciences university affiliated with the United Methodist Church and founded in 1854.

Web site

http://www.evansville.edu

Location

Evansville, Indiana.

Student Profile

2,471 students (40% male, 60% female); 39 states, 50 countries; 6.3% minority, 5.8% international.

Faculty Profile

179 full-time faculty. 90% hold a terminal degree in their field. 13:1 student/faculty ratio. Average class size is 18.

Residence Life

Highly residential: 90% of students live on or within walking distance to campus.

Athletics

NCAA Division I, Missouri Valley Conference. 14 varsity sports (6 men's: cross-country, golf, basketball, swimming & diving, soccer, baseball; 8 women's: tennis, cross-country, golf, basketball, swimming & diving, soccer, softball, volleyball), and intramural sports.

Academic Programs

Accounting; archaeology; art; art education; art history; athletic training; Biblical studies; biochemistry; biology; business administration; chemistry; civil engineering; classical studies; clinical laboratory science; cognitive science; communication; computer engineering; computer science; creative writing; economics; electrical engineering; elementary education; environmental administration; environmental science; exercise science; finance; French; German; global business; graphic design; health services administration; history; international studies; legal studies; literature; management; marketing; mathematics; mechanical engineering; music; music education; music management; music performance; music therapy; neuroscience; nursing; philosophy; physical education; physical therapist assistant; physical therapy; physics; preart therapy; political science; predentistry; prelaw; premedicine; preoptometry; preveterinary medicine; psychology; secondary education; sociology; Spanish; special education; sport communication; sport management; theatre design & technology; theatre education; theatre management; theatre performance; theatre studies; theological studies; visual communication; writing. Graduate programs are available.

Costs and Aid

2007–2008: $32,990 comprehensive ($ 23,710 tuition). 92% of students receive some financial aid. Average award: $ 19,036.

Endowment

$74,912,074.

The University of Southern Indiana

INDIANA

The University of Southern Indiana (USI) is a public, coeducational, comprehensive university with a liberal arts and sciences curriculum as the foundation for all of its undergraduate programs. Founded in 1965, USI is regionally responsive and needs- driven: a university "by the people, for the people."

Admissions Contact:

The University of Southern Indiana
8600 University Boulevard
Evansville, Indiana 47712-3596
(800) 467-1965
Ph: (812) 464-8600
www.usi.edu

The 4 Distinctions

Engaged Students

As an institution, USI embraces change and emphasizes teaching students about morals, values, traditions, ethics, and respect for others. USI offers undergraduate programs through five colleges: the College of Business, the College of Education and Human Service, the College of Liberal Arts, the College of Nursing and Health Professions, and the College of Science and Engineering. The university's most popular majors are business administration and management, elementary education and teaching, and psychology. USI is a public university offering a "private education," unmatched for value in the state of Indiana. Students value the core curriculum, which gives them backgrounds in multiple fields and helps ensure that USI graduates are multidimensional.

USI students excel at accounting. They are the best in the state, having won the last three Indiana Case Study competitions. Other competitive programs include nursing and health professions, and premed. The Baccalaureate/ Doctor of Medicine (BM/D) program has six slots available each year, guaranteeing its students seats at Indiana University Medical School. USI's brand-new engineering program is growing faster than expected, responding to the needs of employers.

Increasing numbers of USI students take advantage of study-abroad programs. A collaborative effort with the University of Evansville's Harlaxton campus sends students to England with faculty members to study in a castle. Internships are also possible: over 250 seniors participated in internships in 2005–2006. The school also features an active cooperative education program that matches students with employers.

Great Teaching

USI's environment puts its greatest emphasis on teaching and learning, and the energy and dedication of its faculty and staff serve as models for other universities. The faculty's commitment to continual improvement in teaching has led to a high quality of instruction and enhanced graduate preparedness, making USI a "creator of opportunity" for thousands of students, many of whom are the first in their families to attend college.

The relatively low student to faculty ratio of twenty to one allows professors to get to know their students as individuals, providing support and focused instruction, and responding to students' needs. There are no teaching assistants or graduate assistants at USI, allowing students to develop close relationships with their professors, who take pride in advising and guiding their students toward successful careers. USI's commitment to cutting-edge technology in the classroom enhances teaching and learning.

Vibrant Community

The beautiful, contemporary USI campus is five miles or six minutes by car west of downtown Evansville, in a wooded area of rolling hills with two nearby lakes. The University enrolls about ten thousand students, who come from both public and private schools. Most students come from Indiana, though thirty-five other states and forty-two countries are represented, as well.

USI was established in an underserved area of the state, and by serving the people's needs, the area as a whole now is thriving. Evansville is the third largest city in Indiana, with a population of about 125,000. Known as River City for its location on a horseshoe bend of the Ohio River, Evansville serves as a regional hub for Indiana, Illinois, and Kentucky. It provides great shopping as well as many internship and co-op opportunities for USI students.

Originally, the student population was commuter oriented. Today, 30 percent of USI's students reside on campus, and that number is increasing every year. All USI housing is on campus, and many residence halls feature new suite-style units, including "super-singles" and apartments, representing advanced and modern residential options for students.

USI offers nine living-learning communities programmed by faculty, such as an international floor and an engineering floor. Students in these communities take courses together, and strong bonds are created between their experiences in the residence hall and their course work. There are four living-learning experience residence halls with two hundred students each, living in suites with their own bathrooms. Residence-life staff develop additional programming for these living-learning communities.

USI students are active, and the student government is well run, supported by a large budget. There are over ninety organizations students can join, as well as opportunities to create new clubs of interest. Intramural sports are enormously popular, with ninety-two intramural football teams. On-campus activities include lectures, a film series, and musical performances. Students can also participate in Greek life by joining one of six fraternities or four sororities.

The campus's thirty-one million dollar library includes a Starbucks, and the University Center is undergoing a thirteen million dollar renovation. In student housing, a community center is being renovated and will include laundry machines connected to the Internet to alert users when their wash is done.

USI students are involved with service in the community, and there is an active religious life on campus. USI students participate in Habitat for Humanity projects, and some USI students recently traveled to New Orleans to help Katrina victims as part of an alternate spring break program.

Successful Outcomes

Two-thirds of USI's alumni live in the region and continue their involvement with the university by counseling students, supporting athletics, and mentoring current students in community-service roles in the Volunteer USI program.

USI listens to employers, learning what they need and are looking for in prospective employees. The university invests in the latest technical equipment so that students will be familiar with the tools they will use in the workplace. Career counselors are assigned to each undergraduate college, and they bring large companies to USI, including Dell Computers, a company known for being selective in its recruiting efforts. Dell recruiters visit only a few institutions across the country, and the company was so pleased with the students it found at USI that it plans to increase its recruiting efforts at USI.

"I like studying math at USI because I always have my professor, not a teaching assistant, working with me. Professors are willing to help me one-on-one after class or during office hours. They know how hard students work, and they want us to succeed."

- Jillian Myrick, mathematics major

Fast Facts

The University of Southern Indiana is a four-year public university founded in 1965. USI is a state supported institution with enrollment of more than 10,000 students.

Web site

http://www.usi.edu

Location

Evansville, Indiana— situated in a beautiful 300+ acre site at the southwestern edge of the city of Evansville.

Student Profile

9,298 undergraduate students (40.0% male, 60.0% female); 36 states and territories, 42 countries; 6.1% minority, 1.1% international.

Faculty Profile

307 full-time faculty. 20:1 student/faculty ratio. Average class size is 25.

Residence Life

Moderately residential: 27.6% of students live on campus.

Athletics

NCAA Division II, Great Lake Valley Conference. 15 varsity sports (7 men's: baseball, basketball, cross-country, golf, soccer, tennis, track & field; 8 women's: basketball, cross-country, golf, soccer, softball, tennis, track & field, volleyball), 5 club sports, and 60 intramural activities offered.

Academic Programs

Accounting & professional services; applied studies; art; biology; biophysics; business administration; business education; chemistry; communication studies; computer information systems; computer science; dental hygiene; early childhood (teacher education); economics; economics (teacher education); education (secondary); electronic business; elementary education; engineering; English; English (teacher education); exercise science; finance; food & nutrition; French; French (teacher education); geology; German; German (teacher education); health services; history; history (teacher education); individual studies; industrial supervision; international studies; journalism; management; marketing; mathematics; mathematics (teacher education); nursing; occupational therapy; philosophy; physical education; physical education (teacher education, grades K-12); physical education (teacher education, grades 5-12); political science; political science/government (teacher education); psychology; psychology (teacher education); public relations & advertising; radiologic & imaging sciences; radio & television; science (teacher education); social science (teacher education in history, government, economics, psychology, or sociology); social work; sociology; sociology (teacher education); Spanish; Spanish (teacher education); special education (teacher education); theatre arts; visual arts (teacher education, K-12); visual arts (teacher education). Graduate programs are available.

Costs and Aid

2006–07: $4,460 in-state; $10,631 out-of-state. 67% of students receive some financial aid. Average award: $6,786.

Alma College

MICHIGAN

Alma College is a private, coeducational, liberal arts and sciences undergraduate college that highlights personalized education, social responsibility, and extraordinary achievements. Founded in 1886 by Michigan Presbyterians, Alma maintains a close relationship with the Presbyterian Church (U.S.A.) while welcoming students of all religious backgrounds.

Admissions Contact:

Alma College
614 W. Superior St.
Alma, Michigan 48801
800-321-ALMA
Ph: (989) 463-7111
Email: admissions@alma.edu
www.alma.edu

The 4 Distinctions

Engaged Students

Alma's general-education requirements include a spring term class, typically in the month of May, where class participants cross boundaries and explore experiences beyond the classroom, often including travel abroad. Recent spring term classes include a Chaucer class that traveled to Canterbury in England, an ornithology class that studied birds in Peru, and a history class that explored relevant historical sites in China. One class, studying Holocaust literature in Poland, restored a Jewish cemetery, and students said it was one of the most important experiences of their lives.

About 80 percent of Alma's students take a service-learning class. Many of these class projects are ongoing over several years. For example, a Pine River environmental sciences project located five miles down the river from the college tests the water and studies the effects of various environmental events. This project has been ongoing for more than ten years.

The Center for Responsible Leadership, an emerging hallmark program at Alma, prepares students to be ethical leaders with the ability to initiate and manage change, and encourages students to focus on long-term decision making as opposed to short-term gain. Leadership qualities are encouraged in all Alma students, following its mission, and the entire curriculum is designed with this in mind. On-campus training and off-campus retreats are offered to help students define their individual mission statements. Junior-year internships continue this work, and senior-year leadership projects are intended to provide students with opportunities to help Michigan companies and communities.

Alma also encourages its students to look beyond Michigan's boundaries. Its Posey Global Program supports international study through nonprofit internships; independent research projects; and participation in colloquia, seminars, conferences, and training opportunities. This competitive program awards stipends to cover the costs of overseas travel, program fees, living expenses, and other relevant costs.

The Model United Nations (UN) program provides students with an opportunity to explore pressing international issues as they prepare to compete at regional and national conferences. Alma's Model UN team has achieved unprecedented success, winning many outstanding delegation awards at regional and national conferences.

Students also have numerous opportunities to study abroad through Alma's partnerships with colleges and universities in Australia, Austria, Bolivia, Ecuador, England, France, Germany, India, Italy, New Zealand, Peru, and Scotland.

Great Teaching

Alma College's mission is "to prepare graduates who think critically, serve generously, lead purposefully and live responsibly as stewards of the world they bequeath to future generations." Alma offers more than twenty-five major and preprofessional areas of study to choose from. The most popular majors are business, biology, exercise and health science, and education. Performing arts are also popular, with a strong music program that attracts percussionists. Under Alma's program of emphasis, students can create their own major with committee approval. Most major fields of study require a senior capstone project. Students who pursue high-level scholarship and creative work make presentations on Honors Day, a celebration of scholarly and creative activities in the liberal arts.

Professors at Alma College work with students one-on-one. Student development is viewed as a continuous process, and Alma faculty know their students for more than just a semester or a year—they know their students throughout their college careers. Alma's small average class size of sixteen and low student to faculty ratio of thirteen to one make this individualized approach possible.

At Alma, the culture of connection, emphasizing personalized support and follow-up, helps prepare students to take the next step in their lives.

Vibrant Community

The town of Alma, with ten thousand residents, calls itself Scotland, U.S.A. It is located on the Pine River in the center of Michigan, fifty miles north of Lansing, the state capital.

Detroit is two hours to the southeast, and Chicago is four hours to the southwest. The town is safe, featuring shops about a block away from campus, and many local residents take advantage of campus lectures and athletic events.

In the more than one hundred years since its founding, Alma has stayed true to its roots by keeping its Scottish heritage alive. Alma has its own tartan, members of the marching band wear kilts, and the school features a Highland dance troupe as well as student pipers. Each year, the college and the town of Alma host the Alma Highland Festival and Games, which feature traditional Scottish games and revelry and draw a crowd of more than twenty thousand each year.

Most students at Alma belong to two or more of the ninety-six clubs and organizations on campus, ranging from athletics to choir. In 2006, students participating in the Students in Free Enterprise program placed in the top three in the country for their plan to create a cybercafe in the library, and in addition their award, they were successful in making it happen on campus, giving some of the proceeds back to the library. Alma students are also known for their senses of humor; to raise funds to add trees to the school's campus, students organized a tree-hug-athon, hugging trees all night. Through these activities, Alma students make deeper connections with the college and broaden their own learning experiences beyond the classroom.

Successful Outcomes

Alma College is well-known for its successful placement of premed students: 91 percent of Alma's premed students are accepted at medical schools compared to a national average of 47 percent. The Academic and Career Planning office provides assistance to students and alumni from all fields of study who are engaged in career exploration, facilitating connections between employee and Alma students.

According to the results of the 2006 National Survey of Student Engagement (NSSE), Alma students report a level of interaction with faculty that ranks among the top 5 percent in the nation.

Fast Facts

Alma College is a nationally recognized private liberal arts college that highlights personalized education, social responsibility, and extraordinary achievements.

Web site

http://www.alma.edu/

Location

Alma, Michigan—about 140 miles northwest of Detroit.

Student Profile

1,242 undergraduates (41% male, 59% female); 6% out of state and 1% international; 21 states and 12 foreign countries represented.

Faculty Profile

82 full time faculty. 13:1 student/faculty ratio. Average class size is 16.

Residence Life

Highly residential: 86% of students live on campus.

Athletics

NCAA Division III, Michigan Intercollegiate Athletic Association. 18 varsity sports (9 men's: basketball, swimming and diving, baseball, football, soccer, cross-country, golf, tennis, track & field; 9 women's: basketball, volleyball, swimming and diving, soccer, softball, cross-country, golf, tennis, track & field).

Academic Programs

Majors across four departments. Humanities: American studies; art and design; Christian education; communication; English; general studies; library research; modern languages (French, German, Spanish); new media studies; music; philosophy; religious studies; theatre and dance; women's studies. Natural Sciences: astronomy, athletic training; biochemistry; biology; chemistry; cognitive science; computer science; electronics and computer engineering; environmental studies; exercise and health science; geology; mathematics; physics; psychology; public health. Social Sciences: business administration; economics; education; gerontology; history; political science; public affairs; sociology and anthropology.

Pre-Professional Programs in dentistry, engineering, law, medicine, ministry, nursing, occupational therapy, and physical therapy.

Costs and Aid

2007–08: $31,462 comprehensive ($23,478 tuition). 84% of students receive some financial aid. Average award: $16,163. Average merit-based award: $8,365.

Endowment

$100.4 million.

More Distinctions

• Alma College is one of the 158 colleges named a best midwestern college by the Princeton Review.

• Alma College is profiled in the Princeton Review's book, Colleges with a Conscience: 81 Great Schools with Outstanding Community Involvement.

Hillsdale College

MICHIGAN

Hillsdale College is a liberal arts college with a proud history. It was the second college in the nation to grant four-year, liberal arts degrees to women; it admitted black students to its first classes; and it was a national center for the movement to abolish slavery.

Admissions Contact:

Hillsdale College
33 East College St.
Hillsdale, MI 49242
Ph: (517) 607-2327
Email: admissions@hillsdale.edu
www.hillsdale.edu

The 4 Distinctions

Engaged Students

Hillsdale offers its 1,300 students a number of exciting study-abroad options, including programs at St. Andrews, Scotland; Seville, Spain; University of Oxford, England; Saarbrücken and Würzburg, Germany; Regent's College, London; and Tours, France. Biology majors take advantage of the South Africa Internship Program or a three-week summer course at a marine biology facility in Long Key, Florida. Hillsdale's 685-acre Gordon Biological Research Station, the largest private college biological station in the state, provides students with the opportunity to study the flora and fauna of aquatic and wetland environments.

Domestically, students participate in Hillsdale's many internship programs. Two popular options include the Washington-Hillsdale Internship Program (WHIP), offering students an unparalleled opportunity to work right in the middle of it all in Washington, DC, and the Professional Sales Intern Program, conducted during the college's summer recess months. In addition, the career planning office promotes numerous other internship opportunities.

Most Hillsdale students volunteer in the community, often through organizations and events such as Hillsdale Christian Fellowship, Alpha Omega Crisis Pregnancy Center, Adopt-a-Grandparent, Young Life, Big Brothers/Big Sisters, and Relay for Life.

Great Teaching

Founded to provide "sound learning" in a way to help perpetuate the "inestimable blessings" of "civil and religious liberty and intelligent piety," Hillsdale College prepares students to become leaders worthy of their heritage. Guided by a teaching faculty dedicated to the pursuit of truth, students gain a rich understanding of what freedom means, and what is needed to preserve it.

Classes average around twenty-one students, and the overall student to faculty ratio is ten to one. About 90 percent of faculty hold terminal degrees in their field. The college offers twenty-five majors, seven interdisciplinary

concentrations, and nine preprofessional programs; the most popular programs are business, history, political science, English literature, teacher education, and the sciences. Students at Hillsdale report that they spend a great deal of time studying and engaging in meaningful debate.

All students share the common academic experience of the core curriculum, which requires studies of the United States Constitution, rhetoric, Great Books, and Western and American heritage.

Classes at Hillsdale typically pay special attention to original source documents and embrace the Socratic method of learning, which teaches by asking questions. Students are encouraged to articulate both what they think and why.

Vibrant Community

Hillsdale is proud of its history as the first American college whose charter prohibited discrimination on the basis of race, religion, or gender. Though founded in 1844 by Freewill Baptists, Hillsdale has always been nonsectarian. However, the college makes a point of emphasizing "moral truths that bind all Americans, while recognizing the importance of religion for the maintenance of a free society." The college is committed to the classical liberal arts, Judeo-Christian principles, Greco-Roman heritage, and independence of thought and action.

The student body is self-governed by an honor code that promotes collegiality, passionate and aggressive pursuit of truth, a pledge to live an honorable life, and a commitment to self-governance. The college believes that the honor code contributes to Hillsdale students' reputation for being ferociously independent rather than blind followers.

The college attracts many nationally known speakers to events, both on and off campus, including the National Leadership Seminars, the Churchill Dinner, and events hosted by the Center for Constructive Alternatives. Speakers tend to be of a more conservative stripe than at most colleges, and have included Steve Forbes; conservative radio host Michael Medved; Newt Gingrich; Karl Rove; and

Andrei Illarionov, former chief advisor to the prime minister of the Russian Federation. Hillsdale's distinguished visiting faculty have included Justice Clarence Thomas, historian David McCullough, Sir Martin Gilbert, Mark Helprin, and Victor Davis Hanson.

About 85 percent of students live in campus housing. Dorms are single-sex, with the exception of a new residence hall featuring separate wings for men and women. About one in three students joins a fraternity or sorority, and some choose to live in fraternity or sorority houses.

Varsity athletics are an integral part of the life of the college, and in recent years, some teams—notably, the women's volleyball team—have achieved considerable success at the Division II level.

Successful Outcomes

Hillsdale College continues to carry out its mission today as it has every year since 1844. It teaches its students the skills to be productive citizens and the moral virtues to be good ones. Today this small college continues to "go it alone," to do things its own way, even when that way is neither profitable nor popular, but right. A prayer written in the Bible that was placed inside the 1853 cornerstone reflects a continuing commitment of one-and-a-half centuries: "May earth be better and heaven be richer because of the life and labor of Hillsdale College."

Alumni and parents of current and former students remain fiercely devoted to Hillsdale. Many are actively involved in the recruitment of new students through interviewing, letter writing, phoning, or participating in college fairs in their communities.

According to recent surveys, 99.5 percent of graduated students are employed, enrolled in graduate or professional schools, or obtaining advanced certification within six months of graduation. During the past three years, 46% of Hillsdale graduates have attended graduate school. 85% of Hillsdale's pre-med students gain admission to medical school on their first try. And, 87% of the students applying to law school are admitted after averaging the highest LSAT scores (156.3) in the state of Michigan and ranking among the highest in the country. The college is proud that its graduates are honorable, conscientious citizens who appreciate freedom and live productive lives.

"Students at Hillsdale go into all walks of life. What's important is that they all have something in common: they have learned how to live."

--Hillsdale College President, Larry P. Arnn

Fast Facts

Hillsdale College is an independent, coeducational, residential, nonsectarian, selective, liberal arts college founded in 1844.

Web site

http://www.hillsdale.edu/

Location

Hillsdale, Michigan—90 miles west of Detroit, 70 miles northwest of Toledo, and 200 miles east of Chicago.

Student Profile

1,300 students (48% male, 52% female); 48 states and territories represented; 3% international.

Faculty Profile

110 full-time faculty. 10:1 student/faculty ratio. Average class size is 21.

Residence Life

Highly residential: 85% of students live on campus.

Athletics

NCAA Division II, GLIAC Conference. 13 varsity sports (6 men's: baseball, basketball, indoor track, football, cross-country, track & field; 7 women's: basketball, volleyball, swimming, indoor track, softball, cross-country, track & field), and club and intramural sports.

Academic Programs

Accounting; American studies; art; biology; business; chemistry; Christian studies; classical studies; comparative literature; economics; education; English; European studies; financial management; French; German; history; honors program; international studies in business & foreign language; marketing/management; mathematics; music; off-campus study; philosophy; physical education; physics; political economy; political science; preprofessional; psychology; religion; Spanish; theatre; speech; and Center for Constructive Alternatives.

Costs and Aid

2007–2008: $26,430 comprehensive ($18,600 tuition). Nearly 84% of students receive some financial aid. Average award: $14,000, including self-help.

Endowment

$280 million.

More Distinctions

• Ranked by *U.S. News & World Report* among top 100 of America's Best Colleges.

• Ranked by *Princeton Review* as a "Best 366 College" and 7th among "Best-Value" private colleges.

• ISI's Choosing the Right College lists Hillsdale among the top 134 colleges and an All-American College.

• Listed in *Peterson's guide*: Competitive Colleges—Top Colleges for Top Students.

Lake Superior State University

MICHIGAN

Lake Superior State University (LSSU) is a public school founded in 1946 in Sault Ste. Marie in Michigan's Upper Peninsula, on the international border with Ontario. The school's location makes for an interesting Canadian and American mix, and students at LSSU can easily cross borders.

Admissions Contact:

Lake Superior State University
650 W. Easterday Ave.
Sault Ste. Marie, MI 49783
(888) 800-LSSU
Ph: (906) 632-6841
Fax: (906) 635-2111
Email: admissions@lssu.edu
www.lssu.edu

The 4 Distinctions

Engaged Students

There are approximately three thousand students at LSSU, and almost all of them are undergraduates. On average, 80 percent of LSSU's students come from Michigan, and 10 percent come from Ontario; in-state tuition is offered to both. The remaining students tend to come from Ohio, Illinois, Wisconsin, and Minnesota.

Most programs at LSSU have an intense individual research component. Engineering students, for example, must complete a freshmen and a senior project. Recently, one group of freshmen engineering students developed a submersible robot that could move underwater and perform specific tasks. Senior engineering students are paired with corporate sponsors for their senior projects, and machines they create are ultimately used by those corporations. Students in other majors have conducted water-quality studies; have spoken at conferences on their research findings; and have worked with local, national, and international organizations.

Service learning is gaining momentum at LSSU, especially with a service grant from the state of Michigan. LSSU now features a full-time service-learning coordinator. Nursing majors have service aspects incorporated into their program, and often work with senior citizens during their freshman year. Business students provide free tax preparation service to area senior citizens, and with the aid of a state grant, students in the biology program have helped to install interpretive signs on the city nature trail.

Great Teaching

LSSU's traditional general education requirements focus on writing and composition, and engage students in fulfilling requirements in a variety of courses. LSSU offers a number of opportunities for one-on-one interaction between faculty members and students, especially through research, and all senior students complete a capstone research project or thesis.

Students at LSSU can choose from a variety of academic programs, including the School of Business, which traditionally has a strong enrollment. The fire science program at LSSU is one of a small number of similar programs in the country, and the fire lab on campus allows students to learn how to handle different fires. Fire science students have contributed to the community by creating an emergency response system for the local area, and criminal justice majors gain experience working with local police agencies, as well as with the campus security office.

Fish and wildlife management is a popular major at LSSU, and includes a rare hatchery program for Atlantic salmon and a federally- and state-funded program to conduct research on lake sturgeon in the Saint Marys River.

The geology program features an innovative, field-based curriculum funded by the National Science Foundation. Geology students also benefit from the campus's location in an area surrounded by unique geological formations in both Michigan and Ontario.

LSSU's programs in forensic chemistry and environmental sciences allow students to gain cutting-edge experience in researching, sampling, and testing water quality in the Saint Marys River watershed.

The robotics concentration within the School of Engineering is one of two robotics programs east of the Mississippi River. Students in a number of engineering fields can specialize in robotics and gain hands-on design experience.

Athletic training majors gain experience working directly with LSSU varsity athletics teams, local high school teams, and teams in Ontario. Recently, two students from the athletic training program were selected to work at the 2006 Hula Bowl game.

LSSU students in biology and those with an interest in avian ecology have participated in bird-counting and banding projects at the Vermilion Field Station near the Whitefish Point Bird Observatory, a major pathway on North American bird migration routes.

Vibrant Community

LSSU does not have many commuters; students are required to live on campus the first two years, and after that, many students live close to campus in independently-owned houses and apartment buildings.

Unique LSSU traditions include the burning of a papier-mâché snowman on the first day of spring and the annual word banishment, an event that has drawn over one hundred thousand hits to the LSSU Web site. The school's recent list of banished words includes truthiness, made popular by comedian Stephen Colbert.

Each February, the university celebrates the season by holding a winter carnival with many activities for students, staff, and the community. Students also celebrate the success of the LSSU hockey team, who traditionally ring a ship's bell outside the arena after each victory. Five national championship banners hang from the rafters of Taffy Abel Arena.

The Canadian side of the border offers students a variety of nightlife, arts, and cultural activities. Searchmont Ski Resort is located forty minutes from campus, offering one of the highest vertical drops in the Great Lakes region. In Michigan, the small-town atmosphere offers opportunities for skiing, ice fishing, boating, water-skiing, kayaking, and snowboarding. Many clubs on campus are based around these outdoor activities.

Students are actively involved in theater productions in LSSU's new arts center, staging original and traditional plays. Concerts are also staged in the arts center auditorium on a regular basis. Hunting and fishing are other popular recreational activities. Some dorms even have game rooms on the lower level, where students can clean their catch after a day of hunting or fishing. It isn't unusual for students to have a venison roast or wild-game buffet in the evenings.

The Soo, as Sault Ste. Marie is referred to locally, is conveniently located only forty-five minutes north of Michigan's Mackinac Bridge. One of Michigan's first settlements, Sault Ste. Marie was founded as a fur-trading center in the seventeenth century. Sault Ste. Marie is also home to the Soo Locks, which facilitate all Great Lakes shipping traffic to and from Lake Superior. The historical value of the town of Sault Ste. Marie is an important part of LSSU: the campus is built on the grounds of old Fort Brady, and benches on campus were made of wood from nearby shipwrecks.

Successful Outcomes

LSSU graduates are today's engineers, teachers, lawyers, scientists, and doctors. LSSU offers the unique opportunity to train for a job at a fishery or in the field of wildlife management, to prepare for employment fighting forest fires, or to manage parks and outdoor recreation programs.

Successful alumni include Doug Weight, who currently plays in the NHL; Dr. Richard Gray of the Mayo Clinic; and Mitch Irwin, director of the Michigan Department of Agriculture. On average, 90 percent of students are placed in jobs or graduate programs after graduation from LSSU. The nursing and engineering departments typically boast a 100 percent placement rate for their graduates.

Fast Facts

Lake Superior State University is a public, four-year university founded in 1946.

Web site

http:// www.lssu.edu

Location

Sault Sainte Marie, Michigan—on the St. Mary's River 45 minutes north of the Mackinac Bridge. An international border city linked with Sault Sainte Marie, Ontario by the International Bridge.

Student Profile

2,911 undergraduate students (49 % male, 51 % female); 10% from other states and territories; 10% minority, 10% international.

Faculty Profile

63% hold a terminal degree in their field. 16:1 student/faculty ratio. Average class size is 23.

Residence Life

Moderately residential: 35% of students live on campus. Freshman and sophomore students are required to live on-campus.

Athletics

NCAA Division II, NCAA Division I Hockey, Great Lakes Intercollegiate Athletic Conference (GLIAC). 11 varsity sports (5 men's: hockey, basketball, cross-country, tennis, track & field; 6 women's: basketball, cross-country, softball, tennis, track & field, volleyball), 1 club sport, and 14 intramurals.

Academic Programs

Accounting; athletic training; biology; business administration (business education, international business, legal management, management, marketing); chemistry; clinical laboratory science; communication; computer & mathematical sciences; computer engineering; computer information systems; computer networking; computer science; criminal justice; early childhood education; education (elementary teaching/secondary teaching); electrical engineering; engineering management; English language & literature; environmental chemistry; environmental health; environmental management; environmental science; exercise science; finance & economics; fine arts studies; fire science; fisheries & wildlife management; forensic chemistry; French studies; geology; history; human services; individualized studies; integrated science; legal assistant studies; liberal studies; manufacturing engineering technology; mathematics; mechanical engineering; nursing; parks & recreation; political science; prepharmacy (transfer program); prelaw; psychology; social science; social studies; sociology; Spanish; sport & recreation management.

Costs and Aid

2006–2007: $13,417 comprehensive ($6,558 tuition). 85 % of students receive some financial aid. Average award: $ 8,436.

Lawrence Technological University

MICHIGAN

Lawrence Technological University is a private, accredited university focused on providing superior education through cutting-edge technology, small class sizes, and innovative programs. Lawrence Tech offers over sixty degrees through the Colleges of Architecture and Design, Arts and Sciences, Engineering, and Management, and offers residential and recreational facilities.

Admissions Contact:

Lawrence Technological University
21000 West Ten Mile Road
Southfield, MI 48075-1058
(800) CALL-LTU
Ph: (217) 245-3030
Fax: (217) 245-3034
Email: admissions@ltu.edu
www.ltu.edu

The 4 Distinctions

Engaged Students

The most popular majors at Lawrence Tech are engineering, architecture and design, engineering technology, business and management, and computer science. The College of Architecture and Design is the largest in Michigan and the fifth largest in the nation.

All four colleges offer instruction with a rich blend of theory and practice, in which classroom work and lectures are integrated with hands-on, real-world experience in the lab and/or studio. Leadership, initiative, and innovation are stressed in all programs.

There are many opportunities for students to participate in special competitive projects. Each year, Lawrence Tech students design, build, and race Formula SAE and Baja racing vehicles according to strict specifications. In 2007, Lawrence Tech is one of only twenty U.S. colleges to compete in the Solar Decathlon, in which architecture students design and build a home powered entirely by the sun; the home is being constructed on campus and will then moved to the National Mall in Washington, DC, for the competition. Lawrence Tech is the only U.S. university entered to design, build, and race a hydrogen-fuel-cell, zero-emissions vehicle in the Formula Zero 2008 Student Edition Fuel-Cell Racing Competition. Other projects include the Michigan Zero-Energy-Home Design Competition, in which students design houses that use renewable energy; the American Society of Heating, Refrigeration and Air Conditioning Engineers International Design Competition, which challenges students to design buildings with environmental impact in mind; and the SAE Aero Design Competition, in which students design and build a scale-model cargo plane that is judged by its performance in safely carrying a payload. All these competitive projects provide opportunities for students to apply their learning and gain experience in leadership and group dynamics in preparation for their careers.

Lawrence Tech is involved in a number of innovative applied research partnerships with industry and government. These partnerships offer students remarkable hands-on experience solving real-world problems, even as undergraduates. Numerous co-op jobs and internships give students an extra competitive edge when they graduate, while participation in professional organizations gives students opportunities to network with industry leaders. Because of the university's proximity to the automotive and biotechnology industries as well as many other major businesses, faculty and administration interaction with area companies provides input for academic offerings, sponsored research, and job placement before and after graduation. Over two hundred Fortune 500 corporations have headquarters or major operations within a thirty-mile radius of Lawrence Tech's campus.

Lawrence Tech's Automotive Engineering Institute provides students with the opportunity to conduct sponsored research on a unique four-by-four vehicle chassis dynamometer, which measures several areas of vehicle performance. The university's Lear Entrepreneurial Center teaches engineering students how to create, promote, and bring to market products and services. Lawrence Tech engineering students, through the Global Engineering Program, have opportunities to work and study abroad. Architecture students explore community-based urban design at the university's Detroit Studio, and they can also choose to participate in the Paris Summer Study Abroad Program.

Great Teaching

Lawrence Tech has a strong tradition of utilizing small class sizes and highly skilled, professional instructors. Lawrence Tech has some 445 full- and part-time faculty, and 72 percent of full-time faculty have doctoral degrees. Many faculty have years of successful industrial and professional experience in addition to their academic credentials, or are currently engaged in professional practice in addition to teaching. They've learned what makes professionals successful in the real world, and they pass that experience on to Lawrence Tech students.

The student to faculty ratio is thirteen to one, providing personalized attention that ensures that students are getting the most of their educational experience. Most classes enroll nineteen students or fewer, and all classes and labs are taught by professors, not graduate assistants.

Vibrant Community

Lawrence Tech's modern campus of more than one hundred acres in Southfield provides nearly five thousand enrolled students with a full range of academic, housing, and recreational facilities. The campus provides ample, free parking and is pedestrian friendly with easy access to public transportation. Approximately six hundred students live in two residence halls, and more than fifty student clubs and organizations meet the interests of a diverse student body. These include intramural and club sports, sororities, fraternities, religious organizations, campus publications, student government, and honor and professional societies.

The A. Alfred Taubman Student Services Center serves as a living laboratory of the latest green and energy-efficient building technologies. The building has no boiler, furnace, or even a gas meter, and is heated and cooled entirely by geothermal wells. It also has a multilayer living roof planted with drought-resistant ground covers, an exterior skin designed to reduce heat loss and maximize daylight without succumbing to excessive heat gain, a bioswale, and a water-recycling system. All structural, mechanical, and electrical systems are visible for easy access and study. The design of the Taubman building underscores the university's commitment to sustainable architecture and engineering and the use of renewable resources.

Many activities are open to the students throughout the year. These include Discovery Days for incoming freshmen, Greek Week, concerts, golf scrambles, lectures, community-service opportunities, field trips to other cities, movies, fitness classes, tournaments (basketball, billiards, racquetball, and table tennis), ski outings, comic and dramatic presentations, and much more.

The city of Detroit is fewer than twenty miles away and is easily accessible by driving or public transportation. Detroit professional sports teams include the Tigers baseball team; the Red Wings hockey team; the Pistons basketball team, with an arena in Auburn Hills; and the Lions football team. Rich cultural experiences are available with the Detroit Symphony Orchestra and other musical performers at Orchestra Hall, several playhouses, the Detroit Institute of Arts and other museums, and much more. Interesting communities for dining and entertainment within Detroit include Greektown, Mexicantown, Harmonie Park, and Foxtown. Other vibrant area communities for shopping, dining, and entertainment include Royal Oak, Dearborn, Ferndale, and Birmingham. For outdoor enthusiasts, a number of large parks, lakes, and rivers are within a short driving distance from campus.

Successful Outcomes

Lawrence Tech graduates are ranked well above national norms in salaries and have the reputation for reaching the workplace well prepared and able to do their jobs. The American Society of Employers has ranked Lawrence Tech first among private colleges as a provider of graduates to southeast Michigan employers. Standard and Poor's ranks Lawrence Tech in the top third of colleges nationwide as a provider of leaders for America's most successful corporations. Within one month of graduation, 93 percent of graduates find employment, usually in their field, and many go on to advanced degrees, as well.

Fast Facts

Lawrence Technological University is a private, fully accredited university, founded in 1932, focused on providing superior education through cutting-edge technology, small class sizes, and innovative programs. The University offers more than 60 degree programs at the associate, bachelor's, master's, and doctoral levels through Colleges of Architecture and Design, Arts and Sciences, Engineering, and Management.

Web site

http:// www.ltu.edu

Location

Southfield, Michigan—suburb of Detroit.

Student Profile

2680 undergraduate students (77% male, 23% female); 92% in-state, 8% out-of-state; 38% minority, 2% international.

Faculty Profile

113 full-time faculty. 76% hold a terminal degree in their field. 13:1 student/ faculty ratio.

Residence Life

Moderately residential: 22% of students live on campus.

Athletics

Intramural and club sports.

Academic Programs

Architecture; biomedical engineering; business management; chemical biology; chemistry; civil engineering; computer engineering; computer science; construction management; electrical engineering; engineering technology; environmental chemistry; humanities; digital arts; graphic design; information technology; interior architecture; mathematics; mathematics & computer science; mechanical engineering; media communication; molecular & cell biology; physics; physics & computer science; psychology; transportation design; undergraduate & graduate certificates; master's & doctoral degrees.

Costs and Aid

2006–2007: $19,073 tuition. 70% of students receive some financial aid. Average aAward: $14,255.

Endowment

$31.2 million.

More Distinctions

• Michigan's first wireless campus.

• Among Intel's Top 50 "Unwired" campuses.

University of Detroit Mercy

MICHIGAN

The University of Detroit Mercy (UDM) is the largest and most comprehensive Catholic university in Michigan. UDM's mission is to provide excellent, student-centered education in an urban context. The University seeks to integrate the intellectual, spiritual, ethical, and social development of its students.

Admissions Contact:

University of Detroit Mercy
4001 W. McNichols Road
Detroit, MI 48221-3038
(800) 635-5020
Ph: (313) 993-1245
Email: admissions@udmercy.edu
www.udmercy.edu

The 4 Distinctions

Engaged Students

UDM was formed in1990 by the consolidation of the University of Detroit, founded in 1877 by the Society of Jesus, with Mercy College of Detroit, founded in 1941 by the Religious Sisters of Mercy.

Today, UDM offers about one hundred academic degrees and programs, ranging from architecture and psychology, business and nursing, to teacher education and engineering—as well as some programs that are unique to UDM, such as digital media studies and a five-year physician assistant program. UDM's architecture, science, and dentistry programs are popular and serve as flagship programs for the university as a whole. UDM's business and engineering programs take full advantage of the university's deep connections to local financial and manufacturing firms. Its premed, predental, and prelaw programs provide students with a strong foundation for acceptance into graduate programs. In addition, UDM offers a number of combined undergraduate and master's degree programs for motivated students. UDM also offers a special program for students who have not yet decided on their ultimate field of study. All programs are based on a solid foundation in the liberal arts that hones students' communication and problem-solving skills while giving them the cultural context to thrive in any environment.

UDM offers special opportunities to broaden students' academic experience through study-abroad programs, an honors program that explores the larger world outside the classroom, and opportunities to develop research skills by working with faculty on research projects.

UDM sees Detroit itself as a classroom, making hands-on experiences possible through cooperative learning and internships. UDM's Cooperative Education (co-op) program gives students the opportunity to augment their academic courses with placements or assignments of paid employment in business, industry, and government. The program is considered cutting-edge in some schools, but UDM has been doing it since 1911, offering students who have a clear idea of the career they want to pursue a chance to obtain practical work experience before graduation. The co-op program can

also be a tool for discovery, as well as an opportunity to test students' interests, aptitudes, and abilities. The money earned through co-op can be used to defer some college expenses, and many students become full-time employees of the companies where they did their co-op work.

Service learning is also emphasized in partnership with local agencies and nonprofit organizations. For example, in January 2007, some Detroit Mercy students participated in a citywide program to count the number of unsheltered homeless people, leading to a more accurate gauge of the needs of the chronic homeless in the Detroit area and giving students an opportunity to learn firsthand about the needs of an underserved segment of society.

Great Teaching

UDM's goal is to help students realize their dreams and ambitions. To achieve that goal, UDM offers challenging academic programs taught by talented, committed professors and supplemented by hands-on research, co-op, and internship opportunities.

UDM's professors are endlessly curious about their fields of study, but their true calling is teaching. They share their ideas with students, and expect students to contribute their own. They are always willing to provide students with extra help, whether it's prepping for a test or helping students design a research project that will be an impressive part of a student's application to graduate school.

UDM's thirteen to one student to faculty ratio and small average class size guarantee personalized, one-on-one interaction between students and UDM faculty, who are nationally recognized teachers and scholars. In addition to working with their professors on class assignments, UDM students have direct access to participating in faculty-led research in science, engineering, and architecture.

Vibrant Community

UDM is located in Detroit, one of the world's great commercial and industrial centers, and a learning and cultural center, as well. The many topflight businesses and institutions headquartered in Detroit have offered excellent co-op and internship opportunities to UDM students. Detroit is across the Detroit River from Windsor, Ontario, giving the city a unique, international relationship with Canada.

Students are encouraged to take advantage of the variety of cultural activities, events, and entertainment that Detroit offers, including professional sports, classical and popular music, museums, and the Detroit Zoo.

UDM's student body is a vibrant mix of people with all ranges of talents and interests. Most of its 3,100 undergraduate students come from throughout the state of Michigan, but twenty-six states and fifty-three countries are also represented. About a third are students of color, making UDM the most diverse of the twenty-eight Jesuit colleges and universities. On average, 13 percent of UDM students live in one of the campus's six residence halls.

No matter what interests students may have, they are sure to find friends at UDM who share similar passions. There are more than sixty-five registered organizations on campus that students can join. Students can make a difference through community service; UDM's Student Volunteer Association, the student senate, the JUSTICE organization, and fraternities and sororities are among the many campus groups that provide opportunities for students to give back. Students also enjoy a campus coffeehouse featuring performances by poets and musicians, a fitness center, and NCAA Division I athletics, highlighted by a strong basketball program.

UDM has three campuses in Detroit. The McNichols Campus, located in northwest Detroit, provides academic programs and services to undergraduate and graduate students. The School of Law is located at UDM's Riverfront Campus in downtown Detroit; UDM's School of Dentistry, currently located on the Outer Drive Campus, is scheduled to move to its new location near downtown Detroit on Martin Luther King Jr. Boulevard and I-96 in January 2008.

Successful Outcomes

More than three-quarters of UDM's sixty-eight thousand living alumni remain in the Detroit area, and nearly 90 percent reside in Michigan after graduating. About 8 percent go on to work and live internationally. UDM graduates serve and work in all walks of life, providing a strong network of contacts and mentors to UDM students.

The heterogeneous quality of UDM's student body reflects that of the real world, and employers comment that UDM students are well prepared to succeed in the diverse workforce of the twenty-first century.

Fast Facts

University of Detroit Mercy, Michigan's largest and most comprehensive Catholic university, was founded in 1990 when University of Detroit (founded in 1877) and Mercy College of Detroit (founded in 1941) consolidated.

Web site

http://www.udmercy.edu

Location

Detroit, Michigan—Three campuses are located in northwest and downtown Detroit and another campus is located in downtown Detroit.   City, state—give some other contextual info if possible (15 miles from X, etc.)

Student Profile

3, 141 undergraduate students (40% male, 60% female); 26 states and territories, 53 countries; 29% minority, 8% international.

Faculty Profile

295 full-time faculty. 86% hold a terminal degree in their field. 13:1 student/faculty ratio. Average class size is 20.

Residence Life

Growing residential population: 13% of students live on campus.

Athletics

NCAA Division I, Horizon Conference. 16 varsity sports (7 men's: basketball, cross-country, fencing, golf, soccer, indoor track & field, outdoor track & field; 9 women's: basketball, cross-country, fencing, golf, soccer, softball, tennis, indoor track & field, outdoor track & field), club sports, and 8 intramurals.

Academic Programs

Academic exploration program (for undeclared majors); accounting; addiction studies; African American studies (certificate); architecture (five-year master's program); biochemistry; biology; business administration; Catholic studies (certificate); chemistry; civil engineering; communication studies; computer & information systems; computer science; criminal justice studies; dental hygiene; digital media studies economics; education; electrical engineering; electronic critique; elementary education; English; health services; health services administration; history; human services; language studies (certificate); legal administration; legal studies (certificate); liberal studies; mathematics; mechanical engineering; nursing; philosophy; political science; predentistry; prelaw; premed; prephysician assistant; psychology; religious studies; secondary education; social work; sociology; special education; theatre; women's studies (certificate).

Graduate and doctoral programs are also available.

Costs and Aid

2007–2008: $25,050 annual tuition). $4,470 annual residency fees. Meal plans vary. 82% of students receive some financial aid. Average award: $11,000.

More Distinctions

• Consistently, UDM ranks among the top tier of Midwestern master's universities in U.S.News & World Report's "America's Best Colleges."

• U.S.News & World Report ranks UDM as fifth in the Midwestern category for campus diversity.

Baldwin-Wallace College

OHIO

Baldwin-Wallace College (B-W) is a four-year, private, liberal arts college affiliated with the United Methodist Church. Founded in 1845, BW offers a well-rounded educational learning experience, which focuses on preparing its diverse student population to act and think globally.

Admissions Contact:

Baldwin-Wallace College
Office of Admission
Bonds Hall
275 Eastland Avenue
Berea, OH 44017-2088
Ph: (877) BWAPPLY
Email: admission@bw.edu
www.bw.edu

The 4 Distinctions

Engaged Students

Baldwin-Wallace integrates the hallmarks of a traditional liberal arts education—critical thinking, problem solving, and writing and speaking skills—with an emphasis on professional and career preparation. More than fifty academic majors are available to traditional underclassmen, including nine in the internationally respected Conservatory of Music. Baldwin-Wallace College offers some unique programs in neuroscience, athletic training, sports management, arts management, and criminal justice.

Students participate in many campus activities and organizations, and prepare for life after college through guided career preparation and experiential learning opportunities. The Baldwin-Wallace College Explorations/Study Abroad Center is part of a larger effort to expand students' learning context by linking the curriculum to the world beyond the classroom. While traveling throughout the world, students earn B-W credit for courses, independent-study projects, and/or field experiences. Each year students at B-W study in countries such as Australia, South Korea, Spain, Italy, Iceland, Ecuador, and many more destinations. These learning experiences allow students to engage in social, experiential, and cultural learning, which greatly enhances their knowledge and ability to act and think globally.

Baldwin-Wallace College offers an active, well-established internship program. Students successfully complete approximately four hundred internships for credit each academic year in large and small businesses, nonprofit organizations, and government agencies. Some majors require participation in the internship program, but most students choose to participate voluntarily. Students take advantage of many professional and internship opportunities in and around nearby Cleveland. Current B-W students have participated in internships at some well-known and respected companies and organizations such as the Cleveland Indians, the United States Secret Service, Key Bank Corporation, PPG Industries, Ernst & Young, the Cleveland Clinic, and the Cleveland Metroparks system.

Through the office of community outreach, students are empowered to become contributing, compassionate citizens of an increasingly global society. Each year, B-W students contribute over seven thousand hours of service through programs such as Alternative Spring Break, Project Affinity, Saturday of Service, as well as commitments to organizations such as the Boys & Girls Clubs of America and Big Brothers/Big Sisters.

Great Teaching

Faculty at Baldwin-Wallace College are very accessible, creating a strong bond with the students they teach. Faculty members frequently develop mentoring relationships with students and also serve as academic advisors in their area of expertise. All B-W professors foster a powerful experience of learning that comes from engaging others, tackling tough problems, and being steeped in real professional environments.

In addition to being dedicated teachers, B-W professors are passionate scholars and researchers, actively engaged in creating and discovering. Faculty-Student Collaborative Scholarship (FSCS) is designed to facilitate deep learning as student-faculty teams examine, create, and share new knowledge or works. With generous support from funders, the Summer Scholars research program encourages the development of a community of student and faculty scholars and enables students to pursue research and creative activities under the supervision of a faculty member.

Vibrant Community

Baldwin-Wallace College is located in Berea, Ohio (population nineteen thousand). B-W's tree-lined campus is surrounded by a safe, residential neighborhood. There are many unique shops located within walking distance of campus, along with traditional stores and restaurants. Located less than a mile from campus are the Cleveland Metroparks; here, students take advantage of the extensive bike paths and bridle trails perfect for running, biking, Rollerblading, or simply taking a walk. Known as the Emerald Necklace, it is one of the most attractive, yet peaceful features of Cleveland and its surrounding suburbs.

Cleveland is only fourteen miles away, and provides a number of cultural, recreational, and entertainment opportunities. This all-American city is home to outstanding museums and galleries, theaters, professional sport teams, world-class shops and restaurants, and exciting nightlife. B-W also offers over one hundred clubs and organizations in which students can get involved. These organizations provide a variety of programs for the community.

The Black Student Alliance (BSA), Hispanic American Student Association (HASA), Native American Student Association (NASA), People of Color United (POCU) and Allies are all represented at Baldwin-Wallace College. The B-W chapter of Habitat for Humanity is a team of students committed to building the future by empowering themselves and others to eradicate poverty and provide housing through education and active involvement in the Cleveland area and abroad. Students for Environmental Awareness (SEA) educates B-W and the surrounding community about environmental matters, provides students with information on recycling, cares for the Native Ohio Plant Garden, and volunteers at EarthFest.

Baldwin-Wallace is also part of the Ohio Athletic Conference (OAC), one of the top conferences for Division III athletics. There are twenty-one varsity athletic teams that compete at the highest levels, and more than five hundred Baldwin-Wallace students have been named All-Academic OAC.

Successful Outcomes

More than 90 percent of B-W graduates find employment or go on to the graduate school of their choice within six to nine months of graduation. The office of career services has developed a four-year plan for students that leads to marketable skills and experiences, whether students are deciding on a major, identifying a career path, or already have their sights set on a specific graduate school or career. One-on-one counseling, combined with technology and other resources prepares students with the skills to manage their careers.

Most B-W students participate in at least one internship during their four years. The internship program was established to provide students with meaningful work experiences that directly relate to their career goals while earning academic credit.

In conjunction with a faculty advisor, each student also develops a four-year action plan to identify academic, professional, and experiential opportunities. This plan touches every part of a student's life—courses, projects, leisure activities, even part-time jobs—to bring purpose and coherence to the educational experience. Students create an e-portfolio to store class projects so potential employers can review them later.

Furthermore, many B-W alumni are involved in Career Connections, a resource that students can use to identify and cultivate current or future employment opportunities.

Fast Facts

Baldwin-Wallace College was founded in 1845 and is a four-year, private, liberal arts college affiliated with the United Methodist Church.

Web site

http:// www.bw.edu

Location

Berea, Ohio—an historic community 12 miles southwest of Cleveland.

Student Profile

3,625 undergraduate students (40% male, 60% female); 27 states and territories, 17 countries; 11 % minority

Faculty Profile

164 full-time faculty. 82.3% hold a terminal degree in their field. 15:1 student/faculty ratio. Average class size is 18.

Residence Life

Moderately residential: 55% of students live on campus. There is a two-year residency requirement.

Athletics

NCAA Division III, Ohio Athletic Conference. 21 varsity sports (11 men's: football, basketball, baseball, wrestling, tennis, indoor track & field, outdoor track & field, soccer, cross-country, golf, swimming & diving; 10 women's: volleyball, basketball, baseball, tennis, indoor track & field, outdoor track & field, soccer, cross-country, golf, swimming & diving) 8 club sports, and 20 intramurals.

Academic Programs

Accounting; art history; arts management; art studio; athletic training; biology; broadcasting/mass communication; business; chemistry; communication disorders; computer information systems; computer science; economics; education; English; exercise science; film studies; finance; French; German; health promotion & education; history; human resource management; international studies; management; marketing; mathematical economics; mathematics; medical technology; music composition; music education; music history & literature; music in the liberal arts; music performance; music theater; music theory; music therapy; neuroscience; philosophy; physical education; physics; political science; prephysical therapy; psychology; public relations; religion; sociology/anthropology; Spanish; sport management; theater.

Costs and Aid

2007–2008: $29,762 comprehensive, includes books ($22,404 tuition). 95% of students receive some financial aid. Average award: $17,000

Endowment

$126 million.

More Distinctions

• B-W is one of Princeton Review's best Midwestern colleges.

Defiance College

OHIO

Admissions Contact:

Defiance College
701 N. Clinton Street
Defiance, OH 43512
Ph: (419) 783-2361
Email: msuzo@defiance.edu
www.defiance.edu

Defiance College (DC) is a comprehensive, private, coeducational college affiliated with the United Church of Christ. Founded in 1850, the 150-acre campus is located in northwest Ohio, an area of rolling farmland at the confluence of the Auglaize and Maumee rivers.

The 4 Distinctions

Engaged Students

The Defiance College community of learners is dedicated to nurturing the whole person through the development of the intellectual, emotional, spiritual, social, and physical dimensions of self. The mission of the college is to inspire within students a search for truth, a sensitivity to the world and the diverse cultures within it, the ability to lead in their chosen professions, and a spirit of service. The college's commitment to community service is strong and effective: it was named to the President's Higher Education Community Service Honor Roll with distinction in October 2006 for its ongoing civic engagement and Hurricane Katrina relief efforts, and was ranked as one of the top twenty-five schools in the nation for its service-learning programs by *U.S. News & World Report.*

The National Survey of Student Engagement (NSSE) revealed that Defiance students outpace their peers across the nation in their involvement in community service. More than many students elsewhere, DC students reported that they took part in community-based projects as part of their regular courses and felt they contributed to the welfare of their community.

DC is home to the McMaster School for Advancing Humanity, an innovative research program devoted to teaching, service, scholarship and action to improve the human condition. Unique among colleges and universities across the U.S., the McMaster School utilizes Defiance College's nationally-recognized model of service and civic engagement. Through the McMaster program, students and faculty apply academic expertise in a real-world content in a way that impacts humanity. In recent years participants have developed projects and established partnerships in Belize, Guatemala, Cambodia and Israel with a domestic project in New Orleans. Much of the success of the projects can be credited to learning communities, a component through which groups meet on a regular basis to strategically prepare for their research and travel.

DC programs offer ways for students to explore the educational experience of engagement. The Bonner Leader Program has a service-learning focus. The Carolyn M. Small Honors Program meets weekly and provides research and course-enhancement opportunities for qualified students. The Citizen Leader Program is an intensive campus/community initiative designed to develop citizenship and leadership skills. In addition to structured programs, the campus culture inspires student-led initiatives like the annual Empty Bowls project in which social work students conduct an awareness and fund-raising event with proceeds going to the local homeless shelter.

Great Teaching

Defiance requires students to take courses offered under its general education program, an integrated four-year experience that focuses on global awareness, including compulsory writing projects largely overseen by DC's arts and humanities division. In addition to its interdisciplinary approach to learning about global civilization and issues, general education includes freshman seminars, common readings, physical and social sciences, and English, and religious studies, among other offerings. Every student presents a senior capstone project for his or her major, demonstrating community involvement in tandem with a focus of study.

Defiance's innovative programs and the national recognition the college enjoys are evidence of DC's committed and involved faculty. Like their students, they are engaged in real-world methodologies and operations based on immersion in their fields of expertise. This results in community-based learning and internship opportunities for their students. An example of their global framework includes the WATER (Water Analysis: Targeting Engagement through Research) project, which transferred a successful model of testing from the Maumee watershed to Belize. Locally, students volunteer to interact and work with autistic teen-age students in an on-campus setting as well as at an area residential facility.

Vibrant Community

More than 60 percent of DC's students live on campus. All first-year students live in one residence hall on gender-specific floors. Other students can choose from a variety of options, including apartment-style housing. Many students come from small towns and enjoy the variety of programs and activities sponsored by the office of student life. The staff nurtures the whole person and fosters relationships among the faculty, staff, and students, as well as the wider community. Defiance is a member of the National Association of Campus Activities (NACA), and more than 50 percent of students participate in one of eighteen NCAA Division III sports or intramural programs.

In addition to taking advantage of shopping and entertainment in town, DC students participate in ongoing service-learning projects, further supporting DC's reputation for strong programs of engagement and responsible citizenship.

Historically important as a transportation hub, the town of Defiance served as Johnny Appleseed's principal headquarters from 1811 to 1828. Defiance, population eighteen thousand, offers "big city appeal and small town feel." It is one hour from Toledo, Ohio, and Fort Wayne, Indiana; two hours from Detroit, Michigan; two-and-a-half hours from Columbus, Ohio; three hours from Cleveland, Ohio; and three-and-a-half hours from Chicago, Illinois.

Successful Outcomes

Defiance College students graduate not only with outstanding professional skills but with a sense that they will be contributing to the greater good of society. Defiance students are called upon to think and act within their academic areas, utilizing classroom knowledge to make an impact within their communities and beyond. Such experiences give them the awareness of a diverse world and its needs and the leadership skills to create positive change. Defiance's dedication to engaged learning means students will go beyond books and lectures to opportunities to dig in and learn by doing.

Such experiences provide them with the skills to be better employees, better leaders, and responsible citizens. By the time they graduate, Defiance College students already possess outstanding professional skills that have been tested and polished through engagement with like professionals and real-life experiences.

Education majors who have mentored local at-risk children or who have been involved with a project to provide teachers in Third World countries with much-needed training manuals or course materials leave here with the confidence that they will be better teachers. Criminal justice majors who have formulated a plan to provide the tools for downtrodden Cambodian women to become self-sufficient leave college knowing that they will be better law enforcement officers.

Fast Facts

Defiance College is a four-year, private, coeducational, liberal arts college affiliated with the United Church of Christ, offering associate, bachelors, and master's degrees. The college was founded in 1850.

Web site

http://www.defiance.edu/

Location

Defiance, Ohio.

Student Profile

1,000 students (52% male, 48% female); 35% of students are first-generation college attendees.

Faculty Profile

101 faculty members. 12:1 student/faculty ratio. Average class size is 15.

Residence Life

Moderately residential: over 60% of students live on campus.

Athletics

NCAA Division III, Heartland Collegiate Athletic Conference. 18 varsity sports (9 men's: baseball, basketball, cross-country, football, golf, soccer, tennis, indoor & outdoor track & field; 9 women's: basketball, cross-country, golf, soccer, softball, tennis, indoor & outdoor track & field, volleyball) and numerous intramural sports.

Academic Programs

Accounting; art; arts & humanities; athletic training education; biology; business administration; Christian education; communication arts; computer forensics; criminal justice; education (early childhood, middle childhood, adolescent, multiage); English; forensic science; graphic design; health services management (a completion program for individuals holding an associate's degree in allied heath pending approval by the Ohio Board of Regents); history; international & global studies; management information systems; mathematics; medical technology; molecular biology; organizational leadership & supervision (a completion program for individuals holding an associate's degree); psychology; religious education & design for leadership; religious studies; restoration ecology; social work; sport management; wellness & corporate fitness. Self-designed majors are also available as well as preprofessional programs in dentistry, law, medicine, seminary, & veterinary science.

Costs and Aid

2007–2008: $27,350 comprehensive ($20,120 tuition). 98% of full-time students receive some financial aid.

Endowment

$15.4 million.

More Distinctions

• Ranked in the top tier of comprehensive baccalaureate colleges in the Midwest by U.S. News and World Report."

• The Templeton Foundation Honor Roll for Character Building Colleges recognizes Defiance for encouraging students to "search for truth and develop sensitivity to the world around them through community service and responsible citizenship."

• Defiance College has been named with distinction to the President's Higher Education Community Service Honor Roll for its commitment to community service and Hurricane Katrina relief efforts.

Franciscan University of Steubenville

OHIO

Franciscan University of Steubenville educates its students to be a transforming presence in the Church and the world. Top students are attracted to Franciscan's high-quality academics, its integration of faith and reason in and out of the classroom, and its rich sacramental life, rooted in the teachings of the Catholic Church.

Admissions Contact:

Franciscan University of Steubenville
Ph: (800) 783-6220
Email: admissions@franciscan.edu
www.franciscan.edu

The 4 Distinctions

Engaged Students

Franciscan University is in the top 2 percent of universities in America for the percentage of its students who study abroad. Each semester, about 150 Franciscan sophomores and juniors call the village of Gaming, Austria, home. There, students study and live in a restored fourteenth-century monastery. When not in class, students travel through Europe, visiting religious shrines in France, skiing the Swiss Alps, and taking gondola rides in Venice. Rounding out the students' semester abroad is a class trip to Rome and Assisi that traces the roots of Catholic history and gives students the chance to walk in the footsteps of St. Francis.

Students involved in Missions of Peace travel nationally and internationally to help those who are spiritually or materially impoverished. In greater Steubenville, Works of Mercy teams conduct outreach programs and help the poor through activities such as volunteering in soup kitchens. Past mission destinations have included Hawaii, Florida, Mexico, Honduras, and Russia.

Franciscan students have ample opportunities to apply their knowledge outside the classroom through internships, practicums, cooperative employment, independent study, service learning, and mission trips.

Great Teaching

At Franciscan University of Steubenville, the curriculum offers an integrated academic and spiritual experience unrivaled in the world of higher education. Professors emphasize a personalized approach in their classes. They truly care about each student's educational and individual success, and the student to faculty ratio of fifteen to one provides all students with teachers and faculty advisers who know them on a first-name basis.

In the spirit of Christian humanism, Franciscan strives to educate the whole person. Through classes in history, literature, science, and theology, students come to see not only how all branches of learning relate to one another but also how each gives glory to God.

Franciscan University's honors program challenges students to analyze complex issues and acquire insight into the human experience based on the close reading and vigorous discussion of a Great Books curriculum.

Franciscan University is a teaching institution, which means that classes and labs will never be taught by graduate assistants. Instead, students learn from distinguished, dedicated professors. The faculty at Franciscan do more than just teach in the classroom; they also actively participate in the campus' social and spiritual life, providing guidance for students and serving as role models for successful Catholic living in the larger world.

Vibrant Community

Through the integration of faith and reason, Franciscan University fosters a unique and dynamic campus environment where students grow in mind, body, and spirit. Situated high atop a bluff overlooking the Ohio River Valley, the Franciscan campus is the ideal place for students to study and pray.

The city of Pittsburgh, less than an hour away, offers sporting events, museums, concerts, shopping, and more. Groups of students also travel to support varsity teams at away games and for mission trips, retreats, outreach projects, and prolife activities.

Franciscan's household program offers an innovative social concept in which students discover a family away from home. Households are small groups of students who choose to live as brothers or sisters and openly share ideas, faith, and fun. There are over forty households at Franciscan University, each based on a different Catholic charism and each offering students a unique path to answering the universal call to holiness.

Intramural sports offer opportunities for men and women to compete at an intense level with their peers. On the intercollegiate level, eleven varsity sports are available. Beginning in fall 2007, the university's varsity teams will play their first games under NCAA Division III provisional membership.

Successful Outcomes

As leaders in a number of fields—medicine, business, law, theology, and science—Franciscan graduates are "salt and light" in the Church and the world.

Franciscan is distinct from other orthodox Catholic colleges and universities in that students are not limited to a narrowly defined course of study. Rather, they can choose from thirty-six majors and professional programs, allowing them to develop their God-given talents and interests to the fullest.

With a career planning center dedicated to helping students attain their professional goals, Franciscan students find success after graduation. Companies and organizations employing Franciscan graduates include the United States Department of Justice, the Ford Motor Company, EWTN, the Archdiocese of Atlanta, the Heritage Foundation, St. Jude Children's Hospital, the National Institutes of Health, the Archdiocese of Denver, Northup Grumman Space Technology, the Archdiocese of Washington, and Kimberly-Clark.

Prepared by a challenging liberal arts curriculum, Franciscan students succeed in higher education. Graduate schools attended by recent Franciscan graduates include the University of Notre Dame Law School, the Ohio State University College of Medicine, Catholic University, Yale Law School, Brandeis University, John Paul II Institute, the Angelicum, Loyola University Chicago, and Duquesne University.

"I chose Franciscan University because it was important to me to both get a solid education and live in an environment that could help me grow in my faith. I got what I wanted. From an educational point of view, I was in excellent programs with outstanding and dedicated teachers. On the faith side, Franciscan helped me realize that if one can see something, one can accomplish it, so long as you're following God's will and doing it for his glory. I am so grateful for the opportunities I had at Franciscan University and for the people who invested a significant amount of time in me and my education."

Jason Jones '04
New York City, New York
B.S. Accounting
Investment Banking Analyst, JP Morgan

Fast Facts

Franciscan University of Steubenville is a private, Catholic, Franciscan institution operated by the Franciscan Friars of the Third Order Regular, and founded in 1946.

Web site

http://www.franciscan.edu/

Location

Steubenville, Ohio—40 miles west of Pittsburgh, Pennsylvania.

Student Profile

1,982 undergraduates (40% male, 60% female); 50 states and territories, 12 foreign countries; 7% minority, 1% international.

Faculty Profile

112 full-time faculty, 78 part-time faculty. 15:1 student/faculty ratio.

Residence Life

Moderately residential: 62% of students live on campus.

Athletics

NCAA Division III. 11 varsity sports (6 men's: baseball, basketball, cross-country, rugby, soccer, track; 5 women's: basketball, cross-country, soccer, softball, track, volleyball), and intramural sports offer opportunities for men and women to compete at an intense level in Flag Football, Volleyball, Basketball, and Ultimate Frisbee.

Academic Programs

Costs and Aid

2007-2008 $ 24,550 comprehensive ($ 17,800 tuition); 80% of students receive some financial aid.

Endowment

$26.9 million.

More Distinctions

• America's Best Colleges 2008, published by U.S. News & World Report, ranked Franciscan University in the elite top tier of Midwestern Universities with Master's Programs.

• U.S. News & World Report ranked Franciscan University's study-abroad program, located in a restored medieval monastery in Gaming, Austria, thirty-fifth out of some 1,400 schools with overseas programs.

• Franciscan University was one of 100 colleges and universities recognized for leadership in student character development in The Templeton Guide: Colleges That Encourage Character Development.

• Insight on the News, a national publication of the Washington Times, named Franciscan University as one of the "Top 15 Colleges" in the nation for the school's strong moral development and liberal arts approach to education.

• The Young America's Foundation, an organization that promotes leadership development with a conservative edge, named Franciscan University as one of the top 10 schools in the country for promoting conservative values and beliefs.

Hiram College

OHIO

Admissions Contact:

Hiram College
PO Box 96
Hiram, OH 44234
Ph: (800) 362-5280
Fax: (330) 569-5944
Email: admission@hiram.edu
www.hiram.edu

Hiram College is a liberal arts college with a close-knit, academic community that ensures a student-centered environment. The academic calendar, with long (12-week) and short (3-week) sessions complementing each other, exposes students to learning formats best suited for different subjects.

The 4 Distinctions

Engaged Students

Hiram takes an intensive, systematic approach to its program for new students. Students are introduced to Hiram through a summer orientation event and a three-day New Student Institute that includes workshops, lectures, films, discussions, and essay writing. Students also meet their colloquium professors, as well as the rest of their colloquium class during New Student Institute. Colloquia are intensive first-semester seminars of twelve to fifteen students designed to introduce students to the liberal arts and taught by faculty members from every department. A student's colloquia professor also serves as his or her academic advisor. In their second semester, students take the Spring Semester First Year Seminar, designed to improve students' writing and analytical abilities.

The Hiram Genome Initiative research group led by Professor Brad Goodner is just one example of the many research opportunities open to Hiram students. Professor Goodner has made headlines by leading a team that deciphered the genetic code of agrobacterium, a bacteria that affects plants. Hiram students are working to advance Professor Goodner's research with the goal of improving agriculture and developing a better understanding of certain human ailments. The project is supported by a $1.2 million grant from the Howard Hughes Medical Institute and a one hundred thousand dollar grant from the National Institutes of Health.

In December 2006, Hiram College's Entrepreneurship across the Campus program received a one million dollar grant from the Burton D. Morgan Foundation and the Ewing Marion Kauffman Foundation to more fully integrate entrepreneurship into the liberal arts.

The Center for International Studies coordinates study-abroad opportunities that allow Hiram students to travel with a member of the faculty to destinations on six continents. By planning and managing many of its own programs Hiram is able to more closely tailor study-abroad opportunities to the interests of its students and the requirements of academic programs. Students can also take advantage of exchange opportunities with international universities in Turkey, Japan, and Italy, or arrange their own study-abroad experience. Over 50 percent of Hiram students participate in a study-abroad experience.

Great Teaching

Hiram seeks out faculty members who are committed to working with their students outside of the classroom. Mentoring relationships between students and members of the faculty quickly take hold, creating a rich array of hands-on research opportunities for students. Interaction outside the classroom also greatly enriches both the academic programs and the strong sense of community that prevails on the Hiram campus.

Hiram promotes experiential learning and academic innovation with a unique semester format called the Hiram Plan. Each fifteen-week semester includes a traditional twelve-week period when students take three courses, followed by a three-week period when students are free to take a single course that involves intensive interaction with the professor and may involve international or off-campus study.

The general education program includes an interdisciplinary requirement that may be met by taking an upper-level team-taught collegium course. Collegia are team taught by two or more faculty members from different departments and are designed to develop critical-thinking, writing, and speaking skills. All students are required to produce a capstone project in their majors.

Hiram regularly reviews and assesses every aspect of the academic program, including study-abroad opportunities, in order to ensure that students have the best possible college experience.

Vibrant Community

The experiential orientation of the academic program and the close relationship between members of the faculty and students leads to a strong sense of community, further enhanced by the fact that 91 percent of students live on campus.

With over seventy student clubs and organizations, it's easy for students to find something to do after class. Clubs can be funded through the student senate or created and funded independently. Options include academic groups, student government and media, recreational activities, religious organizations, and special-interest clubs. Students can also join social clubs via the local Greek system, which is governed by the college.

There are eleven residence halls on campus, with construction of a twelfth underway. Each is close to the academic buildings. Living options include twenty-four-hour quiet buildings, substance-free living communities, an international culture hall, a community-service floor, and First Year Experience floors.

Campuswide events like an annual day of community service and social activities, a chili cook-off, and an annual weekend of outdoor music and games called Springfest create a powerful sense of community on the Hiram campus. The Special Events Coordinating Committee greatly enriches campus life with events featuring well-known guests like NPR commentator David Sedaris; Morris Dees, director of the Southern Poverty Law Center; blues performer Robert Jones; and poet Gwendolyn Brooks.

Hiram competes in the NCAA Division III, North Coast Athletic Conference. There are fourteen intercollegiate varsity sports for men and women. Men's sports include baseball, basketball, cross-country, football, golf, soccer, swimming and diving, tennis, and track and field. Women's sports include basketball, cross-country, soccer, softball, swimming and diving, tennis, track and field, and volleyball. The new $12.3 million Les and Kathy Coleman Sports, Recreation, and Fitness Center provides a state-of-the-art facility for all students. Intramural offerings include flag football, ultimate Frisbee, floor hockey, basketball, volleyball, and softball. Hiram also has a club sport program that offers highly competitive opportunities as well as recreational- or instruction-oriented programs. Some of the club sports offered at Hiram include sailing, women's rugby, men's volleyball, cheerleading, equestrian club, archery club, yoga, and martial arts clubs.

Successful Outcomes

On average, 30 percent of Hiram alumni go on to graduate or professional school within nine months of earning their Hiram degree; over 60 percent go on within five years. Institutions attended by recent Hiram graduates include Boston College, Carnegie Mellon University, Case Western Reserve University, College of William & Mary, Cornell University, Duke University, Emory University, Harvard University, Johns Hopkins University, Northwestern University, Penn State University, Princeton University, Rutgers University, University of Chicago, University of Massachusetts, University of Notre Dame, Vanderbilt University, and Washington University.

Prominent Hiram alumni include James A. Garfield, twentieth president of the United States; Vachel Lindsay, poet; Allyn Vine, developer of the minisub Alvin, used for deep ocean research; Bill White, former president of Major League Baseball's National League; Dave Bell Sr., Emmy winner; Dave Bell Jr., a Hollywood writer and producer; Barbara London, video curator at the Museum of Modern Art in New York; Jan Hopkins, former CNN news anchor; and Lance Liotta, chief of pathology at the National Cancer Institute.

Fast Facts

Hiram College is a four-year, residential, liberal arts college founded in 1850.

Web site

http:// www.hiram.edu

Location

Hiram, Ohio—approximately 45 minutes southeast of Cleveland.

Student Profile

1,205 undergraduate students (44% male, 56% female); 30 states and territories, 18 countries; 14% minority, 4% international.

Faculty Profile

73 full-time faculty. 95% hold the Ph.D. or other terminal degree in their field. 13:1 student/faculty ratio. Average class size is 16.

Residence Life

Highly residential: 91% of students live on campus in one of eleven residence halls.

Athletics

NCAA Division III, North Coast Athletic Conference. 14 varsity sports (7 men's: baseball, basketball, cross-country, football, golf, soccer, swimming & diving; 7 women's: basketball, cross-country, golf, soccer, softball, swimming & diving, volleyball). Hiram also offers intramural and club sports.

Academic Programs

Art; art history; biochemistry; biology; biomedical humanities (including accelerated); chemistry; classical studies; communication; computer science; economics; education; English; creative writing; environmental studies; French; history; integrated language arts; integrated social studies; management; mathematics; music; nursing; philosophy; physics; political science; psychobiology; psychology; religious studies; science; sociology/anthropology; Spanish; theatre arts.

Preprofessional programs include: business, dentistry, law, medicine, optometry, podiatry, seminary, and veterinary.

Hiram also offers students the opportunity to create an individualized major that combines coursework from two or more departments.

Costs and Aid

2007–2008: $24,865 comprehensive ($24,250 tuition). 93% of students receive some financial aid. Average award: $14,280.

Endowment

$68 million.

More Distinctions

Hiram College has been recognized by

• The Fiske Guide to Colleges

• Colleges that Change Lives

• The Princeton Review as one of "The Best 331 Schools"

Mount Union College

OHIO

Mount Union College
1972 Clark Ave
Alliance, Ohio 44601
Ph: (800) 334-6682
Email: admission@muc.edu
www.muc.edu

Mount Union College is a private, coeducational, comprehensive, liberal arts college affiliated with the United Methodist Church. Founded in 1846, the college was one of the nation's first coeducational institutions of higher learning.

Admissions Contact:

The 4 Distinctions

Engaged Students

Mount Union focuses on the total experience of each student, not just on academics. Its commitment to providing a liberal arts education affirms the importance of reason, open inquiry, living faith, and individual worth. Service learning is frequently incorporated into Mount Union classes, though it is not required. Some examples include a recent class in international politics, where students invited speakers to campus to talk about AIDS; a concert held on campus to raise funds for a girl in Africa in need of heart surgery; and a class assignment to create a promotional DVD for a day-care facility.

Mount Union students participate in community service outside of the classroom as individuals or as members of groups or Greek organizations. During Make a Difference Week, students can choose from numerous service projects, as well as a fund drive for the United Way. Students have built a labyrinth for a local church and have participated in a Keep Ohio Beautiful campaign by planting flowers. The Kappa Delta Pi (KDP) education honor society collected and donated four hundred pounds of educational materials to grade-school children in Africa.

Overseas experiences are available through study-abroad programs and service groups. Many foreign language students go abroad, and students can also take part in an annual summer trip to Costa Rica and other locations around the world. Recent service-group trips have taken students to Russia and El Salvador. About fifty students study abroad each year as part of programs through the college and its relationship with other universities, offering students study-abroad options at thirty-seven universities in twenty-four countries.

Students also extend the educational experience through research projects both on and off campus and during the summers. Research opportunities for Mount Union students are especially strong in the sciences.

Great Teaching

Mount Union offers forty-seven majors and a variety of preprofessional programs. The most popular majors are education, sport management, and biology for premedical students. The college offers unique programs in biochemistry, cognitive and behavioral neuroscience, media computing, athletic training, and intervention specialist training.

Mount Union's professors are teachers first, and they are committed to helping students become effective communicators and innovative problem solvers who are able to set goals and meet challenges. With a low student to faculty ratio of thirteen to one, Mount Union students enjoy the personal approaches and individualized teaching methods of their highly qualified professors. Students also benefit from the relationship with their academic advisor throughout their years at Mount Union.

The college's general education program presents a broad spectrum of courses, reflecting the strong liberal arts grounding of the college. It establishes a foundation for student inquiry through writing, speaking, and studying religion. The fine arts, natural sciences, writing, and mathematics are considered the contexts for student inquiry, and cross-curricular studies serve as the integration context.

Seniors participate in a Senior Culminating Experience, similar to a senior capstone project. Some Culminating Experiences involve in-depth research, and each gives students an opportunity to pull their studies together in one body of work that can help point toward postgraduate interests.

Vibrant Community

Located in east central Ohio, Alliance has a population of twenty three thousand and is known as the Home of the Scarlet Carnation, Ohio's state flower. The city is twenty miles northeast of Canton, Ohio, and sixty-five miles southeast of Cleveland.

Mount Union's 2,200 undergraduate students come from more than twenty-two states and thirteen countries. About two-thirds live in on-campus housing, including health and wellness, international, honors, and a variety of other theme houses. Mount Union's residential life is developing quickly, with new apartment-style residences scheduled to open in the fall of 2007, and its dining services facility was just renovated.

There are over seventy clubs and organizations Mount Union students can join. Examples include the student senate, professional groups such as the accounting club, and the student activities council, which brings comedians and musicians to perform on campus. There are also a variety of cultural organizations, including the Black Student Union, the Association of International Students, Relay for Life, Environmental Awareness, radio, newspaper, and more.

On-campus events attract members of the wider community, too. They attend Mount Union's lecture series, art galleries and exhibits, homecoming parade and carnival, and cheer at athletic events.

Successful Outcomes

Mount Union's career-development office helps students choose a major, obtain internships and co-op opportunities, and arrange to shadow professionals. The Career Education Professional Development Series, a series of classes that lead students step-by-step through the process of deciding on a career path, won an excellence award in 2005 from the National Association of Colleges & Employers (NACE). In addition to these resources, the alumni network contributes to student success by conducting mock interviews and organizing panels to review student resumes.

Mount Union faculty maintain contacts in their respective fields, providing assistance to students in their postcollege planning, and ensuring that students have the opportunity to gain hands-on learning experience. Recent examples include sport management students who worked with professional organizations and were the subject of a Wall Street Journal article and business students who developed business plans for local businesses.

Some notable Mount Union alumni include Ralph Regula, member of the U.S. House of Representatives; Brian Stafford, director of the United States Secret Service from 1999–2003; Anita Richmond Bunkley, author of African-American romance novels; Vincent G. Marotta, inventor of Mr. Coffee coffeemakers; and Ernest Dominic "Dom" Capers, defensive coordinator of the Miami Dolphins and former head coach of other NFL teams.

Fast Facts

Mount Union College is a private, coeducational, liberal arts college affiliated with the United Methodist church and founded in 1846.

Web site

http://www.muc.edu/

Location

Alliance, Ohio—70 miles from Cleveland and 80 miles from Pittsburgh.

Student Profile

2,200 students (50% male, 50% female); 22 states and territories; 7% minority, 2% international.

Faculty Profile

124 full-time faculty. 13:1 student/faculty ratio. Average class size is 18.

Residence Life

Moderately residential: 70% of students live on campus.

Athletics

NCAA Division III, Ohio Athletic Conference. 21 varsity sports (11 men's: baseball, basketball, cross-country, football, golf, indoor track, outdoor track, soccer, swimming, tennis, wrestling; 10 women's: basketball, cross-country, golf, indoor track, outdoor track, soccer, softball, swimming, tennis, volleyball), club sports, and intramurals.

Academic Programs

Accounting; American studies; art; athletic training; biochemistry; biology; business administration; chemistry; communication studies; computer science; early childhood education; economics; English; environmental biology; exercise science; French; geology; German; health; history; information systems; international business & economics; international studies; intervention specialist (special education); Japanese; mathematics; media computing; media studies; medical technology; middle childhood education; music; music education; music performance, non-Western studies; philosophy; physical education; physics-astronomy; political science; preprofessional programs (prelaw, predentistry, preengineering, premedicine, preministry); psychology; religious studies; self-defined interdisciplinary studies; sociology; Spanish; sport management; theatre; writing. Additional minors: adolescence to young adult education; African-American studies; classics; database management; earth science; gender studies; Internet computing; legal studies; multiage education; public service; Web design.

Costs and Aid

2007–2008: $28,750 comprehensive ($22,050 tuition). 95% of students receive some financial aid. Average Award: $17,370.

Endowment

$130 million.

More Distinctions

• For the thirteenth consecutive year, Mount Union College has been ranked among the top twenty comprehensive colleges in the Midwest region by the editors of U.S. News & World Report.

Ohio Northern University

Admissions Contact:

Ohio Northern University
525 S. Main Street
Ada OH 45810
(888) 408-4668
Ph: (419) 772-2260
Fax: (419) 772-2313
Email: admissions-ug@onu.edu
www.onu.edu

OHIO

Established in 1871, Ohio Northern University (ONU) is a competitive, comprehensive, private, coeducational university affiliated with the United Methodist Church. The university offers abundant learning opportunities, guidance, and a close-knit community that produces individuals prepared to live full and purposeful lives.

The 4 Distinctions

Engaged Students

Motivated students are drawn to ONU, and in this can-do environment, independence, confidence, motivation, and success are the expected outcomes. Northern graduates are balanced individuals who are ready to compete and succeed in a complex and changing world.

Ohio Northern offers hands-on learning that leads to successful outcomes. Internships, clinicals, clerkships, practicums, co-ops, field experiences, student teaching, and field research give students a variety of opportunities to apply their classroom knowledge.

Recent internships and co-ops have included positions with the Hard Rock Cafe, the Indianapolis Indians, Eli Lilly, General Motors, NASA's Johnson Space Center, American University, Mead Corporation, the Columbus Zoo, the Massachusetts Audubon Society, the CIA, and the Florida Department of Environmental Protection.

The international dimensions of Ohio Northern's educational programs seek to develop in students an interest, understanding, and appreciation of other people as well as to cultivate a spirit of world citizenship within the university community. Study-abroad programs include travel to the Netherlands, Korea, Scotland, Finland, Mexico, Spain, Costa Rica, France, and Wales. Some ONU-sponsored programs include travel to Australia, Scotland, and Northern Ireland.

ONU is committed to holistic learning; campus programs help students strengthen their physical, mental, emotional, and spiritual selves. One way students connect spiritually is through religious life at Northern. The university has created a variety of ways for students to express and explore their faiths. Although the school became affiliated with the Methodist Church in the 1890s, religious life programs transcend this Methodist affiliation. They include morning and evening prayer groups, *Chapel Live* on Channel 3, Chapel Band, Chapel Choir, the Worship Design Team, the Fellowship of Christian Athletes, preseminary studies, Christian Pharmacists Fellowship International, as well as missions and volunteer work.

The Office of Multicultural Development at ONU seeks to lead the campus community in a celebration of diversity. This is accomplished through academic and social programming. One of the main purposes of the office is to support the activities of various student organizations, including the Black Student Union, the Black Law Student Association, the Muslim Student Association, the World Student Organization, and the Latino Student Union.

Great Teaching

Ohio Northern's quality education blends the liberal arts with professional programs in its five colleges: Arts & Sciences, Business Administration, Engineering, Pharmacy, and Law. ONU offers its 3,620 students a diverse setting for professional learning in a liberal arts environment. From the start of their first year on campus, students discover the personal attention they receive from faculty and staff—a prominent characteristic of Ohio Northern. The university maintains a thirteen to one student to faculty ratio and an average class size of twenty-four students.

Classroom participation is not only encouraged but expected. The professors at Northern are highly qualified and accessible, and over 80 percent have terminal degrees in their respective fields. At Ohio Northern, students experience a variety of opportunities, grow as individuals, and develop as well-trained professionals in their chosen fields.

ONU faculty do write papers and conduct research, but their focus is on their teaching and the students. Outside the classroom, faculty often tutor students or help students form study groups. Many residence halls include seminar rooms in which faculty can hold meetings and talk with students about special projects. Professors also serve as advisers, helping students develop goals and plan careers. The environment at ONU is one in which students find teachers accessible not only as teachers but as mentors, as well. Many faculty keep in touch with alumni long after graduation.

Vibrant Community

Ohio Northern is located in the friendly, midwestern village of Ada, Ohio. Ada, with a population of five thousand, is an easy drive from several large cities, including Columbus, Dayton, Toledo, and Fort Wayne, Indiana. ONU's beautiful, three-hundred-acre campus boasts thirty-one major buildings with signature red brick and a mingling of the old and new.

Whatever a student's interests are, there is always something to do at ONU. With more than 150 student organizations and honoraries on campus, personal enrichment and leadership opportunities for students are abundant.

Residence life at Northern is a dynamic living-learning environment conducive to student and community development, as well as to individual growth. Athletics and academics go hand in hand, and excellence in both areas has become a standard for the Polar Bears.

The arts are alive and flourishing at ONU, and students from all majors participate in music, art, theater, and broadcasting activities. The department of communication arts presents ten to twelve productions each year, while the department of music offers approximately forty performances. The art department hosts monthly exhibitions of work of Northern students as well as nationally recognized artists. The Headliner Series and the ONU Music Series draw over twenty-five thousand people to campus each year. Such well-known performers include Take 6, Crystal Gayle, Joan Baez, Melba Moore, Carrot Top, the Moscow Boys Choir, Marvin Hamlisch, and Gordon Lightfoot.

Successful Outcomes

In an atmosphere of mutual respect, ONU is a supportive community that fosters, inspires, and champions the success of all its members. Each college has its own career-building programs with emphasis on placing students in their desired careers.

ONU's alumni have a real affinity for the University and are actively engaged in mentoring students, through full-time employment, co-ops or internships. Mentoring has been part of the tradition since the University's founding and spans the student's entire experience at Northern. From guidance provided by admissions counselors to freshman orientation, peer mentoring within the colleges, and through academic advising students receive personal support through every phase of their college experience. Professors help students select courses, offer research opportunities, assist in designing their senior capstone projects and ultimately, shape the course of the student's future.

Fast Facts

Ohio Northern University is a four-year, private, comprehensive, liberal arts university founded in 1871.

Web site

http://www.onu.edu

Location

Ada, Ohio—70 miles south of Toledo, 75 miles northwest of Columbus, 80 miles north of Dayton.

Student Profile

3,300 undergraduates (50% male, 50% female); 37 states and 15 countries; 5.3% minority, 1.3% international.

Faculty Profile

205 full-time faculty. 13:1 student/faculty ratio. Average class size is 25 students.

Residence Life

Mainly residential: 67% of students live on campus.

Athletics

NCAA Division III, Ohio Athletic Conference. 21 varsity sports (11 men's: baseball, basketball, cross-country, football, golf, soccer, swimming & diving, tennis, track & field- indoor & outdoor, wrestling; 10 women's: basketball, cross-country, golf, soccer, softball, swimming & diving, tennis, track & field- indoor & outdoor, volleyball), 7 club sports (men & women's rugby, men's volleyball, men & women's water polo, disc golf, ultimate Frisbee).

Academic Programs

Accounting; art (advertising design, graphic design, studio arts); athletic training; biochemistry; biology; chemistry; civil engineering; clinical laboratory science; communication arts (broadcasting and electronic media, international theatre production, musical theatre, professional and organizational communication, public relations, theatre); computer engineering; computer science; creative writing; criminal justice (administration of justice, behavioral science); education—early childhood; education—middle childhood; electrical engineering; environmental studies; exercise physiology; finance; forensic biology; French; German; health education; history; international business and economics; international studies; journalism; language arts education; literature; management; marketing; mathematics; mathematics/statistics; mechanical engineering; medicinal chemistry; molecular biology; music; music composition; music education; music performance; music with elective studies in business; nursing; pharmaceutical business (economics, management, marketing); pharmacy (doctor of); pharmacy/law; philosophy; philosophy and religion; physical education; physics; political science; professional writing; psychology; religion; social studies; sociology; Spanish; sport management; technology; technology education; youth ministry.

Costs and Aid

2007–2008: $29,400-$33,060 tuition. Over 90% of students receive some type of financial aid. Average award: $23,400.

Endowment

$149.3 million.

More Distinctions

• ONU is ranked #2 among Midwest comprehensive degree-granting colleges in the U.S. News' 2007 edition of "America's Best Colleges".

Ohio Wesleyan University

OHIO

Ohio Wesleyan University (OWU) is a private liberal arts university located on a two-hundred-acre campus in Delaware, Ohio. Founded by Methodists in 1842, the university maintains an active affiliation with the United Methodist Church, but welcomes students of all religious faiths.

Admissions Contact:

Ohio Wesleyan University
61 S. Sandusky St.
Delaware, OH 43015
(800) 922-8953
Ph: (740) 368-3020
Fax: (740) 368-3314
Email: owuadmit@owu.edu
www.owu.edu

The 4 Distinctions

Engaged Students

At Ohio Wesleyan, research, independent study, internships, and service learning are valued as highly as the classroom experience, allowing students to make connections to the real world, find their passions, and seize opportunities to leave positive marks on society. Every faculty member is active in research, and is deeply committed to teaching research techniques and encouraging independent study as early as a student's first year.

Original research options are available in physics, microbiology, premedicine, psychology, astrophysics, zoology, and economics. Students work with state-of-the-art equipment, and, collaborating with professors, OWU students forge new ground, working on projects funded by such agencies as the National Science Foundation and the Howard Hughes Foundation.

In addition, Ohio Wesleyan offers numerous study-abroad options. Semester programs such as the New York Arts Program and Wesleyan in Washington offer students the opportunity to participate in real-world experiences in their areas of academic interest. As freshman, all students are encouraged to plan to participate in these programs.

Ohio Wesleyan's honors program offers students a number of unique opportunities. From the first day of the first semester, honors students work closely with faculty to explore topics of mutual intellectual interest. Courses in a variety of fields help honors scholars develop their considerable abilities through challenging study and rigorous intellectual discussion with faculty and one another. The honors program consists of tutorials, in which students work closely with faculty; honors courses; and advanced sections of existing courses. All honors courses are fully integrated into the university's curriculum; most fulfill distribution requirements as well as major and minor requirements.

Ohio Wesleyan has the longest operating community-service program among universities in the state. True to the university's motto, "Education for leadership and service," over 85 percent of Ohio Wesleyan students participate in some sort of community service. They serve as mentors in middle schools in Columbus, as well as volunteering in the immediate Delaware community, participating in Habitat for Humanity, and joining service-oriented spring-break trips. In 2003, the university was awarded a two million dollar grant from the Lilly Foundation to promote the theological exploration of vocation on campus.

Great Teaching

The core strength of Ohio Wesleyan is the quality of its faculty. Again and again, student surveys show that the high level of teaching is one of the most positive aspects of the undergraduate experience. The faculty are known for their commitment to teaching and to close interaction with students in and out of the classroom or laboratory. Faculty members regularly get together with students in informal settings and engage their students in one-on-one conversations. Small classes afford personalized attention from professors, all of whom hold the PhD or highest degree attainable in their field.

Ohio Wesleyan's faculty number 134, with an additional seven equivalent full-time positions occupied by part-time faculty, who include emeriti faculty and others from the community and nearby Columbus. The faculty is 34 percent female and 66 percent male, with 11 percent from underrepresented groups. The student to faculty ratio is thirteen to one, and the average class size is nineteen.

Undergraduates comment that "while classes can be tough, professors really want you to succeed and truly learn the material." Instructors serve as mentors for students. "Their real reason for being here is to teach," students agree. "They may also do research, but that is secondary, and they always use us (undergraduate students) to assist with any research (which looks great on our resumes)."

Each year, many faculty members receive research grants and fellowships, make presentations at professional meetings, and publish in or serve on editorial boards of prestigious journals, in addition to serving as officers in their professional organizations. Examples of national awards won by the Ohio Wesleyan faculty include National Science Foundation fellowships, National Institutes of Health fellowships, National Endowment for the Humanities fellowships, National Endowment for the Arts fellowships, John Simon Guggenheim fellowships, and Fulbright fellowships.

Vibrant Community

Ohio Wesleyan University is part of the Delaware, Ohio, community. Ohio Wesleyan is situated in a small city that is surrounded by open space and located just outside Columbus, the state capital. Delaware is a vibrant community of twenty-four thousand residents. Tree-lined streets with turn-of-the-century homes set the stage for an historical downtown and an active central business district. Restaurants, shops, movie theaters, and cultural events within walking distance of campus provide entertainment for students, residents, and visitors.

Housing options include six large residence halls with special-interest corridors and a number of smaller special-interest units, ranging from the Creative Arts House to the Peace and Justice House. Ohio Wesleyan also offers a number of substance-free living areas, as well as a variety of sponsored activities that are alcohol free and well attended by students. The campus recently opened a new Wesleyan Student Center that is substance free, and the university sponsors numerous seminars on healthy lifestyles.

The OWU fraternity and sorority system was founded in 1853, and approximately 33 percent of the current student body belong to one of seventeen fraternity and sorority organizations. A number of fraternities have houses on the residential end of the campus. There are no residential sororities. Greek life at OWU is inclusive; all non-Greeks are welcomed to participate in Greek-sponsored activities, and many do. In addition to sponsoring social events, the Greek community is also involved in a wide range of service initiatives.

On campus, students can participate in more than one hundred campus organizations, as well as twenty-three NCAA Division III men's and women's athletic teams. The Ohio Wesleyan Battling Bishops compete in the North Coast Athletic Conference, one of the premier leagues of Division III athletics. Men compete in basketball, tennis, baseball, football, lacrosse, soccer, golf, cross-country, sailing, track and field, swimming, and diving. Women's sports include basketball, tennis, volleyball, field hockey, lacrosse, soccer, cross-country, sailing, track and field, softball, swimming, and diving. On average, 60 to 75 percent of the student body participate in intercollegiate and/or intramural athletics at some point during the school year.

Diversity is an important component of the OWU community. OWU students represent forty-four states and forty-five countries. Individualism is encouraged, and the exploration of cultural boundaries is incorporated into curricular and extracurricular programming. The president's office established the President's Commission on Racial and Cultural Diversity, which issues an annual report about the state of racial and cultural diversity at OWU, and makes recommendations for the university president and others that might improve concerns noted by commission members. This group also annually recognizes outstanding achievements of individuals or organizations with the President's Award for Racial and Cultural Diversity.

Fast Facts

Ohio Wesleyan University is a highly selective, coeducational, residential, privately supported liberal arts college chartered in 1842.

Web site

http://www.owu.edu

Location

Delaware, Ohio.

Student Profile

1,850 undergraduates (48% male, 52% female); 40 states, 45 foreign countries; 8% international, 8% minority. 54% come from Ohio.

Faculty Profile

134 full-time faculty. 100% with terminal degrees in their field. No teaching assistants. 13:1 student/faculty ratio. Average class size is 19.

Residence Life

Highly residential: 84% of students live on campus.

Athletics

NCAA Div III, North Coast Athletic Conference. 23 varsity sports (11 men's: basketball, swimming & diving, indoor track, baseball, football, lacrosse, soccer, cross-country, golf, tennis, track & field. 11 women's: basketball, volleyball, swimming & diving, indoor track, field hockey, lacrosse, soccer, softball, cross-country, tennis, track & field. co-ed: sailing).

Academic Programs

Accounting; ancient studies; anthropology; applied music; art education; art history; astrophysics; biology; biochemistry; Black world studies; botany; chemistry; chemistry; computer science; dance theatre; earth science; East Asian studies; economics; economics management; education; English literature; English creative writing; English nonfiction writing; environmental studies; French; genetics; geology professional; geology general; geography; German literature; German studies; history America; history Europe; history developing world; humanities–classics; international business; international studies general; international studies regional; journalism; Latin American studies; mathematics; mathematics statistics; medieval studies; microbiology; music education; music history & literature; music performance; music theory; neuroscience; philosophy; physical education general; physical education; physics; politics & government; predentistry; preengineering (3-2 program)*; prelaw; premedicine; preoptometry; prephysical therapy; prepublic administration; pretheology; preveterinary medicine; psychology non-quantitative; psychology quantitative; religion; renaissance studies; sociology; Spanish; sports management; sports science; studio art; theatre; theatre education; urban studies; women's & gender studies; zoology general; zoology preprofessional.

* Preengineering 3-2 combined degree options include: biomedical engineering, chemical engineering, computer engineering, electrical engineering, and environmental engineering.

Costs and Aid

2007-2008: $39,960 comprehensive ($31,510 tuition). 98.8% of students receive some financial aid. Average award: $23,802.

Endowment

$176,784,000.

University of Dayton

OHIO

Founded in 1850, the University of Dayton (UD) is a top ten national Catholic university that prepares students for success in their careers and lives. UD's learning environment offers something for everyone: more than seventy academic programs; Division I athletics; over 180 clubs and organizations; and a friendly, welcoming community.

Admissions Contact:

University of Dayton
300 College Park
Dayton, OH 45469-1300
(800) 837-7433
Ph: (937) 229-4411
Email: admission@udayton.edu
www.udayton.edu

The 4 Distinctions

Engaged Students

The University of Dayton emphasizes learning beyond the classroom and offers opportunities for students to apply their knowledge. Recently, UD students have created solar-powered equipment to sterilize medical devices, designed cost-effective cargo planes using new composites, developed fitness programs for grade-schoolers, explored the complexities of urban education, managed and invested nearly seven million dollars of the university's endowment, and organized a GuluWalk.

At UD, students don't have to wait until they graduate to explore a career. While they're in school, they can conduct research with top scientists and engineers at the University of Dayton Research Institute or Wright-Patterson Air Force Base, or gain hands-on work experience through internships and cooperative education. Top companies recruit UD students, including Accenture, General Motors, LexisNexis, and Procter & Gamble.

Opportunities for learning at UD extend beyond campus—and the United States. Approximately 80 percent of students participate in international experiences. Students can earn up to a full semester of credit through UD's summer education-abroad program in sites such as China, England, France, Germany, Greece, Ireland, or Italy. Semester-long exchange programs include travel to China, Finland, France, Germany, Italy, Morocco, and Spain.

UD has been recognized by the Templeton Foundation for providing students with one of the nation's best service-learning programs, encouraging students to contribute and learn through volunteer activity. One of UD's most popular service events is Christmas on Campus, held each year on December 8. UD students decorate the campus and "adopt" area children, treating them to carnival games, candy and cookies, carolers, and a visit with Santa. The university also boasts one of the nation's largest campus ministry programs, which sponsors more than thirty student-run service clubs, retreats, weeklong service trips called BreakOuts, and more.

Great Teaching

The heart of a University of Dayton education is the professors' commitment to teaching undergraduates. With an average class size of twenty-seven and a thirteen to one student to faculty ratio, the university is dedicated to creating an interactive learning environment.

More than eight hundred full-time and part-time faculty make time for students, helping them succeed and develop their potential. In addition to hosting office hours, many professors give out their cell phone numbers and e-mail addresses so students can ask questions—and get answers—at any time.

UD faculty members have been recognized for their excellence by several organizations, including General Motors Corporation, the National Institute of Education, and the National Endowment for the Humanities.

To help students transition to college and maximize resources at the University of Dayton, all first-year students participate in the First-Year Experience (FYE). FYE includes a seminar offering an in-depth look at the university experience, development of a personal portfolio and professional résumé, and access to personal academic advising.

Vibrant Community

UD's 259-acre campus is two miles from downtown Dayton and bordered by a quiet, suburban neighborhood. Students are part of a vibrant community where modern campus housing blurs the line between living and learning.

More than 90 percent of students live in residence halls or the student neighborhood. First-year students live in Founders Hall, Marianist Hall, Marycrest Complex, or Stuart Complex. The student neighborhood—home to upper-level students— features porch-clad houses and ArtStreet, which offers town houses and loft apartments, a student-run café, a recording studio, and visual arts spaces.

The John F. Kennedy Memorial Union, or KU, is one of UD's most popular gathering spaces. KU houses a full-service dining facility; the Galley snack shop; and the Hangar, a game room with pool tables, a video arcade, four bowling lanes, and lounge space.

With so many campus activities, there's never a shortage of things to do. Students can paint themselves red and cheer on the Flyers or join an intramural or club sport team. Approximately 70 percent of UD students participate in intramurals and club sports. Students can also host a show on Flyer TV, build and race a concrete canoe, march with the Pride of Dayton, or join more than 180 clubs and organizations. On-campus entertainment, including comedy troupes, concerts, and movies, and off-campus adventures like white-water rafting, are offered regularly.

There's also plenty to do in the city of Dayton. Located on the edge of campus, Brown Street offers a variety of shops and restaurants, and downtown offers a lively nightlife with coffeehouses, galleries, theater, music, minor league baseball, and a laser-lit riverfront park.

Successful Outcomes

A University of Dayton degree is powerful preparation for whatever comes next: launching a career; gaining admission to graduate, law, or medical school; or spending a year in service.

Employers know that UD graduates have developed the skills and qualities they need to succeed. University of Dayton graduates consistently take jobs with the nation's best firms and are accepted into top graduate programs. Many seniors receive multiple job offers months before graduation.

For students who are thinking about pursuing graduate school, the Center for Graduate Guidance & Post-Baccalaureate Scholarships helps students identify grants and apply to graduate school. Students planning on attending medical school had a 90 percent acceptance rate in 2006, and UD is ranked first in its category for physics and geology graduates who have obtained PhDs in those fields, according to the Baccalaureate Origins of Doctoral Recipients report.

UD helps students prepare for their careers beginning on their first day on campus. From cooperative education and internships to on-campus recruiting, career advising, and job-search strategies, the career services department assists students in exploring career interests, experiencing real work environments, and evolving in their chosen field. Hire-a-Flyer, an online service, connects students, alumni, and employers across the country.

Students can connect with UD alumni through the Alumni Career Network—a searchable database of UD graduates who offer advice about career-related issues, including relocation and the responsibilities of particular jobs.

The university enjoys a growing national reputation for its distinctive approach to education and for the successes of its more than one hundred thousand graduates. Some notable UD alumni include a Nobel prize winner, a NASA scientist and developer of space food, a humor columnist, a coach of the Pittsburgh Steelers, an ESPN anchor, a three-term U.S. congressman from Colorado, and a head coach of the Tampa Bay Buccaneers.

Fast Facts

University of Dayton is a four-year, private, comprehensive, coeducational university affiliated with the Society of Mary (Marianists) of the Roman Catholic Church and founded in 1850.

Web site

http://www.udayton.edu

Location

Dayton, Ohio

Student Profile

7,473 undergraduate students (50% male, 50% female); 34% out-of-state; 7% minority, 1% international.

Faculty Profile

458 full-time faculty. 13:1 student/faculty ratio. Average class size is 27.

Residence Life

Highly residential: 90% of students live on campus.

Athletics

NCAA Division I, Atlantic 10 Conference. 17 varsity sports (7 men's: baseball, basketball, cross-country, football, golf, soccer, tennis; 10 women's: basketball, cross-country, golf, indoor track, outdoor track, rowing, soccer, softball, tennis, volleyball), numerous club and intramural sports.

Academic Programs

Accounting; ADA didactic program in dietetics; adolescence to young adult education; American studies; applied mathematical economics; art education; biochemistry; biology; business economics; Catholic religious studies; chemical engineering; chemistry; civil engineering; communication (communication management, electronic media, journalism, public relations, theatre); computer engineering; computer engineering technology; computer information systems; computer science; criminal justice studies; early childhood education; economics; electrical engineering; electronic engineering technology; English; entrepreneurship; environmental biology; environmental geology; exercise science/fitness & nutrition; exercise science/fitness management; exercise science/prephysical therapy; finance; foreign language education; geology; history; industrial engineering technology; international business; international studies & human rights; intervention specialist (special education); languages (French, German, Spanish); management (leadership); management information systems; manufacturing engineering technology; marketing; mathematics; mechanical engineering; mechanical engineering technology; middle childhood education; music (composition, education, performance, therapy); operations management; philosophy; physical education; physical science; physics; physics—computer science; political science; predentistry; prelaw; premedicine; psychology; religious studies; sociology; sport management; theatre; visual arts (art education, art history, fine arts, photography, visual communication design); women's & gender studies; undeclared arts; undeclared business; undeclared engineering; undeclared engineering technology; undeclared sciences; undeclared teacher education.

Costs and Aid

2007–2008: $34,849 comprehensive ($24,880 tuition); 90% of students receive some financial aid. Average award: $13,930.

The University of Findlay

OHIO

The University of Findlay (UF) is a private, coeducational, comprehensive liberal arts university affiliated with the Church of God. Founded in 1882, the university boasts strong history and traditions, coupled with a desire for innovation. At Findlay, academic programs combine career-focused studies with a solid liberal arts foundation.

Admissions Contact:

The University of Findlay
1000 North Main Street
Findlay, Ohio 45840
(800) 472-9502
Ph: (419) 422-8313
Fax: (419) 434-4822
Email: admissions@findlay.edu
www.findlay.edu

The 4 Distinctions

Engaged Students

UF is a leader in creating entrepreneurial, innovative programs that concentrate on preparing students with the knowledge and skills to compete in the workplace. Strong support is given to the traditional liberal arts philosophy of exposing students to a variety of courses and subjects, including the fine arts, humanities, language and culture, and the social sciences. UF offers more than sixty areas of undergraduate study, and the most popular majors are business, equestrian studies, preveterinary medicine, education, and pharmacy.

The UF honors program provides a challenging educational experience that enriches and accelerates students' academic growth. The program encourages and stimulates students beyond general academic excellence by providing opportunities for independent research, individual guidance, and specially designed projects and seminars. Students design their own honors curriculum based on the projects they develop and the honors classes they choose.

Service learning is an important part of the UF student experience. All first-time students participate in an orientation service project during the weekend before classes begin in the fall, and other students choose to assist with Habitat for Humanity projects or to volunteer with local schools or other local organizations. These experiences help to develop students' citizenship skills and values, encourage collaborative partnerships between campuses and communities, and assist faculty who seek to integrate public and community engagement into their teaching and research.

Innovative opportunities go beyond the classroom. Students at Findlay have traveled and studied all over the globe. During the past two years, Findlay students have studied in Australia, Mexico, Italy, Japan, Ireland, Canada, Costa Rica, and England, and two students have traveled around the world on a cruise ship.

Great Teaching

Professors at UF view teaching as their primary focus, though they also publish articles and textbooks, do research, and are leaders in their professional organizations. Many faculty have worked in business, industry, education, or service areas in their chosen professions, adding a dimension of experience to their perspectives.

The low student to faculty ratio of sixteen to one ensures that UF students have access to their professors. Every club and on-campus organization has a faculty or staff adviser. UF faculty are involved with the students and with campus life because they truly enjoy their teaching role.

Students are encouraged to seriously consider their purposes for coming to the University of Findlay and to design individualized majors in consultation with faculty advisers. The advisers assist in developing programs of study best suited to students' needs, interests, and goals. Degree requirements are focused on the job demands of the twenty-first century. Each student is assigned a faculty adviser to help plan curriculum, to counsel students, and to assist in career preparation.

The Oiler Experience is a program intended to introduce all freshmen to college life at UF. The course is designed and taught by a cadre of student-services professionals whose educational backgrounds and specialized training are focused on helping students to succeed, both in and out of the classroom.

Vibrant Community

UF's seventy-plus-acre main campus is located in Findlay, a city of forty thousand on the banks of the Blanchard River in the northwest corner of Ohio. The city of Findlay has been designated as a "dreamtown" by Demographics Daily, as well as the best micropolitan community in Ohio.

The city of Findlay offers many restaurants and two movie theaters. Toledo is forty-five minutes away, and Columbus is ninety minutes away. The campus features a number of arts events, including concerts, lectures, and ballet and opera performances. Other popular on-campus events include Diversity Week, with speakers and entertainers; appearances by comedians; a coffeehouse series; and a comedy jam featuring three comedians in one night.

On campus, the fine arts flourish with a variety of theater productions, art exhibits, and vocal and instrumental music concerts, which offer creative outlets and training for students, and serve as a source of cultural enrichment for the community.

Residential options at UF are varied. Upper-level students may live in any residence hall, while most freshmen live in traditional college housing. Town houses, cottages, and Greek housing are also available. Themed housing options include an honors house, a pharmacy house, and a prevet/equestrian house. Cultural housing options include two houses for domestic students that focus on cross-cultural experiences: Umoja and Ujima. There is also an international house, which provides a welcoming social atmosphere for students from the U.S. and abroad.

There are more than seventy-five clubs and organizations UF students can join, and it's easy for students to form a new club. The most popular clubs and activities are intramural sports, academic clubs, student government, and the Black Student Union. There are two fraternities and two sororities, each with their own house.

Successful Outcomes

UF has established comprehensive internship and cooperative education programs that enable students to acquire hands-on work experience related to their degree programs and career interests. Work assignments are developed with business, industry, government, and other agencies and organizations. In the past, students have interned at numerous area and regional businesses, restaurants, resorts, theme parks, and radio and television stations, among other organizations.

The office of career services provides comprehensive employment services for undergraduate and graduate students, alumni, and employers. In addition to helping students identify full-time employment, the office offers assistance in résumé writing, cover letter writing, networking, interviewing, job fairs, employment outlook, salary information, and the job-search process.

"My advisor has guided me along and has showed me the possibilities out in the job market by helping me choose certain courses and by presenting me with the opportunities of internships. I really value her genuine concern for my success not just here at Findlay, but in my career when I graduate."

- Chad Benedict, 2007, Computer Science Major

Fast Facts

The University of Findlay, founded in 1882, is a private four-year university affiliated with The Church of God.

Web site

http:// www.findlay.edu

Location

Findlay, Ohio.

Student Profile

3,300 undergraduate students (40% male, 60% female); 78% in-state, 22% out-of-state; 1.7% international, 13% minority.

Faculty Profile

176 full-time faculty. 16:1 student/faculty ratio. Average class size is 20.

Residence Life

Moderately residential: 50% of all undergraduate students live on campus. 80% of first-year freshmen live on campus.

Athletics

NCAA Division II. 22 varsity sports (11 men's: baseball, basketball, cross-country, equestrian (English & Western), football, golf, track & field, soccer, swimming & diving, tennis, wrestling; 11 women's: basketball, cheerleading, cross-country, equestrian (English & Western), golf, track & field, soccer, softball, swimming & diving, tennis, volleyball).

Academic Programs

Accounting; animal science; art; art management; biology; business management; chemistry; children's book illustration; computer science; criminal justice administration; digital media; economics; education (adolescent/young adult, early childhood, intervention specialist, middle childhood & multi-age); English; English as an international language; entrepreneurship; environmental, safety & occupational health management; equestrian studies; equine business management; finance; forensic science; graphic communication; health communication; health education; health science; health studies; history; hospitality management; human resource management; international business; interpersonal communication; Japanese; journalism; law & the liberal arts; marketing; mathematics; medical technology; nuclear medicine technology; operations & logistics; philosophy; physical education; physician assistant; political science; premedicine; preveterinary medicine; psychology; public relations; religious studies; social work; sociology; Spanish; strength & conditioning; studio art; teaching English to speakers of other languages (TESOL); technical communication; theatre.

Costs and Aid

2007–2008: $31,916 average comprehensive ($22,906 tuition). More than 90% of students receive financial aid. Average award: $15,654.

More Distinctions

• Ranked in top tier of *U.S.News & World Report's* "America's Best Colleges" in the Midwest for 2008.

• Named a Best Midwestern College for 2007 by the *Princeton Review*.

Lawrence University

WISCONSIN

Admissions Contact:

Lawrence University
P.O. Box 599
Appleton, WI 54912
Ph: (920) 832-6500
Fax: (920) 832-6782
Email: excel@lawrence.edu
www.lawrence.edu

Attracting students with strong individual drive and diverse interests, Lawrence University might be characterized not so much as a place filled with well-rounded people as a well-rounded community filled with uniquely talented individuals. A third of the students are athletes, while nearly a quarter of the students study music.

The 4 Distinctions

Engaged Students

The heart of the Lawrence program is teaching students to "learn to learn." Faculty help students to understand contexts, to learn problem-posing and problem-solving skills, and to develop the ability to communicate both orally and in writing—all while expanding their knowledge about a broad range of subjects. Rather than major in business, per se, Lawrence students acquire the strategies and abilities that will allow them to efficiently address problems they will encounter in business. For practical experience, Lawrence encourages students to pursue internships.

After building a strong foundation in the liberal arts and sciences, students at Lawrence have extraordinary opportunities for individualized learning. Nearly 90 percent of its graduates have had at least one course—tutorial, independent study, studio classes, and honors projects— where they were the only student in the class.

Interdisciplinary studies allow students to cross departmental or disciplinary boundaries and look at issues from different perspectives. Areas of exploration include biomedical ethics, cognitive science, education, ethnic studies, gender studies, international studies, linguistics, and neuroscience.

Lawrence offers a wide variety of off-campus study programs across the United States and around the world— more than half its students participate before they graduate. Lawrence students study abroad on every continent, save Antarctica. From nation building in Tanzania or Renaissance art in Florence, Italy, to mathematics in Budapest, Hungary, or a music-performance workshop in Vienna, Austria, there's something for everyone to explore.

Great Teaching

Lawrence prepares students for lives of service, achievement, leadership, and personal fulfillment, and is committed to three major tasks: the development of intellect and talent, the acquisition of knowledge and understanding, and the cultivation of judgment and values.

Freshman Studies is the Lawrence student's introduction to liberal learning—a chance to test new ideas and build an intellectual foundation not just for college, but for life. A part of the Lawrence curriculum since 1945, this program brings groups of fifteen students together for two-term, seminar-style courses on common topics from Hamlet to contemporary film. Faculty stretch outside their disciplines—biology professors teach Shakespeare, and English professors teach about "selfish genes." One of the nation's most distinctive programs for first-year students, the program pushes students to increase their reading, writing, and speaking skills as they are introduced to the kind of cross-disciplinary intellectual inquiry that is the core of Lawrence's academic program.

Faculty credentials in the Lawrence Conservatory are first-rate. Professors have performed nationally and internationally with the Atlanta and Milwaukee Symphony Orchestras, the San Francisco Symphony, the Boston and Cincinnati Pops, the Metropolitan and New York City Operas; given recitals in Carnegie Hall and the Kennedy Center; and worked under the direction of Leonard Bernstein and Aaron Copland. They never lose sight of their main goal, though: dedication to the musical, intellectual, and personal growth of their undergraduate students.

Outside of the conservatory, students enjoy similar individual attention with a student to faculty ratio of nine to one and an average class size of fifteen students. Students are virtually guaranteed personal attention as they work toward goals in majors—or often, dual majors—from thirty different areas. Among Lawrence's most popular programs are biology, psychology, music performance, and English.

Vibrant Community

Lawrence is located in the heart of Appleton, Wisconsin, in one of the fastest growing metropolitan areas in the nation. Downtown Appleton offers an eclectic mix of shops, restaurants, coffeehouses, museums, parks, and a new 2,100-seat performing arts center.

One of the key components of a Lawrence education is involvement with the community. LARY (Lawrence Assistance Reaching Youth) links university students with local schools to tutor at-risk children in a variety of subjects. Many music students, particularly those majoring in music education, mentor precollege students in music.

Lawrence students also volunteer in a wide range of other projects, including the American Cancer Society Relay for Life, Big Brothers/Big Sisters, Habitat for Humanity, Oxfam America, Project Home, and the Fox Valley Special Olympics.

The University Convocation Series, open to the Lawrence and Appleton communities, is a long-standing tradition that brings the entire campus community together up to four times a year to learn about and discuss issues. Past speakers have included Joyce Carol Oates, Salman Rushdie, David Sedaris, Maya Angelou, Elie Wiesel, and Lech Walesa.

At Lawrence, student participation in activities like athletics and music are viewed more as important components of cocurricular learning than merely as extracurriculars. That doesn't mean that they don't take sports seriously—the men's basketball team recently went undefeated. And the music program offers concert series that regularly bring major-league musicians, such as Yo-Yo Ma, to campus. In addition, Lawrence students belong to many other groups and organizations; lately, swing dance has been popular.

The university also offers a 425-acre estate on Lake Michigan for educational retreats. Björklunden was bequeathed to Lawrence University by Donald and Winifred Boynton of Highland Park, Illinois, with the understanding that it would be preserved as a place of peace and contemplation. Throughout the academic year, students expand their minds in a magnificent setting with a wide variety of study issues. Each year, Björklunden hosts more than one thousand students in over fifty seminars.

Successful Outcomes

While a large number of Lawrence alumni go on to pursue advanced degrees, Lawrence students can start the path to a graduate degree while they are still undergraduates. Through the cooperative degree program, several professional schools collaborate with Lawrence in programs that let students build a foundation in the liberal arts and then work on specific professional skills. In most cases, students study at Lawrence for three years and then transfer to a professional school for two or more years. Programs include engineering, environmental management/forestry, medical technology/nursing, and occupational therapy.

The university's career center helps students hone their skills through research and decision-making workshops and seminars. The center also brings in visitors to talk about careers in law or art, among other employment paths. Alumni also regularly return to campus for the Following in Their Footsteps forum. The center also helps students arrange internships and summer employment and brings employers to campus to screen candidates for full-time employment, internships, and summer jobs.

Lawrence has one of the highest alumni giving rates in the country—a sure sign that alumni are satisfied with their Lawrence education.

Fast Facts

Lawrence University is a nationally recognized, four-year, undergraduate college of the liberal arts and sciences with a conservatory of music, chartered in 1847.

Web site

http://www.lawrence.edu

Location

Appleton, Wisconsin—a city of 70,000 in the northeastern part of the state.

Student Profile

1,400 undergraduate students; 48 states and over 50 countries.

Faculty Profile

150 full-time faculty. 9:1 student/faculty ratio. Average class size is 15.

Residence Life

Highly residential: Lawrence requires students to live on campus during their education.

Athletics

NCAA Division III, WIAC and Midwest Conference. 23 varsity sports (13 men's: baseball, basketball, cross-country, fencing, football, golf, hockey, soccer, swimming & diving, tennis, indoor & outdoor track, wrestling; 10 women's: basketball, cross-country, fencing, soccer, softball, swimming & diving, tennis, indoor & outdoor track, volleyball) and club and intramural sports.

Academic Programs

Anthropology; art & art history; biology; biomedical ethics; chemistry; Chinese; classics; cognitive science; computer science; East Asian languages & cultures; economics; education; English; environmental studies; ethnic studies; French; gender studies; geology; German; government; history; international studies; Japanese; linguistics; mathematics; music; natural sciences; neuroscience; philosophy; physics; preprofessional programs (business, engineering, forestry & environmental studies, law, medicine, occupational therapy); psychology; religious studies; Russian; Spanish; theatre & drama.

Costs and Aid

2006–2007: $37,660 comprehensive ($29,598 tuition). 90% of students receive some financial aid.

Endowment

$200.4 million.

More Distinctions

• For four years in a row and a fifth time in the last six years, Lawrence University placed in the top tier of U.S. News & World Report's annual America's Best Colleges rankings.

• U.S. News & World Report ranked Lawrence sixteenth nationally, just ahead of Dartmouth College, in its first year experience category, which covers curricular programs that bring small groups of students together with faculty or staff on a regular basis.

Marquette University

Admissions Contact:

Marquette University
Office of Admissions
P.O. Box 1881
Milwaukee, WI 53201
(800) 222-6544
Ph: (414) 288-7302
Fax: (414) 288-3764
Email:
www.marquette.edu

WISCONSIN

Marquette University is a Roman Catholic university of 7,900 undergraduate students in Milwaukee, Wisconsin. Guided by the principles of the Jesuits, Marquette strives to provide an education that not only improves the mind, but also enhances the student's moral and spiritual character.

The 4 Distinctions

Engaged Students

The university's urban location provides numerous opportunities for volunteer service. Each year, Marquette students perform more than one hundred thousand hours of community service in such programs as Big Brothers/Big Sisters, Habitat for Humanity, and the Senior Citizens' Prom. Advertising and public relations students help create information campaigns for nonprofit organizations, and accounting students offer volunteer tax-preparation services. The university offers a service learning program in South Africa, in which students take classes and help community-based organizations to give voice to disadvantaged people. Nursing students take part in Marquette's HIV/AIDS program in Africa.

Marquette students participate in study-abroad programs on six continents, generally during their sophomore or junior year. For those students with language skills, Spain, France, and Mexico are particularly popular destinations. Ireland and Australia are common study-abroad locations for those seeking an English-language experience.

Internships with companies and organizations in Milwaukee play a major role in many Marquette students' education. Dedicated internship coordinators, a comprehensive job database and intensive preparation through the career services center prepare students to discover more about their major, intended field and themselves. In addition, students can earn internship credit toward their degree. The university's downtown location provides for an abundance of internship opportunities within walking distance from the campus.

Marquette's Les Aspin Center for Government began as a single student internship, and has since grown into one of the nation's leading congressional internship programs. Sitting in the shadow of the Capitol Building in Washington, DC, the Aspin Center provides living and classroom space for students interested in government. Students meet and discuss issues with officials from the Pentagon, the Department of State, and the Central Intelligence Agency. Participants have also worked in the White House, the Food and Drug Administration, the Department of Defense, and the Secret Service.

The College of Engineering Cooperative Education (Co-op) Program is one of the first-ever and most renowned programs in the nation. Established in 1919, the Co-op Program integrates classroom work with practical industrial experience. Students alternate semesters of school with semesters of employment for at least three alternating work terms once they have completed their sophomore year. The work is related to some phase of the field of study in which she or he is engaged and is often diversified to afford a wide range of experience. This year the salary for students entering their first Co-op work term ranges from $2400/month to $3400+/month. Upon graduation, many of the corporations hire their Co-op students because of their work experience.

Great Teaching

Drawing on 450 years of Jesuit tradition, Marquette's Core of Common Studies requires students to choose twelve courses from nine different areas, including rhetoric, individual and social behavior, science and nature, literature and performing arts, and diverse cultures.

Marquette's undergraduate business program has received national recognition, and for several years Marquette has been named one of the nation's notable entrepreneurial universities. Using their training in the real world, students from the college of engineering have completed a two-year bridge-building program in Guatemala.

Marquette offers several innovative interdisciplinary majors and minors, including African-American studies, international affairs, and women's studies.

The Manresa Project, established with a grant from the Lilly Foundation, is part of Marquette's commitment to service and learning. This vocational discernment program provides leadership and ministry training for students considering the priesthood or lay ministry. The program also provides workshops on prayerful discernment, hosts alumni speakers, and awards scholarships to qualifying juniors and seniors.

Marquette faculty are known as leaders in research and writing, but also for providing hands-on guidance and advice to their students. The overall student-to-faculty ratio is fifteen to one, and the average class size is twenty-four in the upper division, and thirty-one in the lower division. Marquette offers 113 undergraduate majors.

Vibrant Community

Marquette is located on an eighty-acre campus in an urban setting. With unlimited use of public transportation, Marquette students find it easy to enjoy Milwaukee's cultural, educational, and entertainment opportunities. The Lake Michigan shoreline is just two miles from campus.

Milwaukee is often called a big "small town." Vibrant and cosmopolitan yet accessible and friendly, it offers everything to amp your social life, including cultural activities, dining, sports, music, performance and visual arts.

As it has expanded through the years, Marquette has absorbed several nearby buildings—a hospital, the downtown Milwaukee YMCA, and several hotels—and converted them into attractive residence halls. About 94 percent of students choose to live on campus or adjacent to it. Themed housing options include floors dedicated to engineering, nursing, leadership, and honors scholarship. 12 percent of students join fraternities or sororities, but Greek life is considered to be a relatively minor element in the overall Marquette community.

Marquette has more than 230 student organizations offering cultural, athletic, intellectual, spiritual, and social activities of many different kinds. Through the years, Marquette has been a Division I basketball powerhouse. Marquette students have opportunities to attend numerous basketball games.

Successful Outcomes

A Marquette education is designed to prepare students for their professions, and for life beyond their professions. Marquette's career services department provides students with an extensive database of job listings and search engines, as well as online advice about interviewing, resumes, and networking. These services provide students and alumni with assistance in developing their career paths.

While many Marquette graduates stay in the Milwaukee area, working for multinational firms like GE Medical, the Miller Brewing Company, Harley-Davidson, or Northwestern Mutual, a substantial number of students begin their careers in Chicago; New York; Atlanta; Washington, DC; and Minneapolis-St. Paul. About one in three students continues on to graduate school.

Among Marquette's many notable alumni are Chicago Sun-Times executive editor John Barron; Tony Award-winning actor Anthony Crivello; comedian Chris Farley; Patrick Eugene Haggerty, founder of Texas Instruments; Rudy Perpich, former governor of Minnesota; and Miami Heat basketball player Dwyane Wade. Many other alumni contribute to their communities through their work in politics, medicine, scientific research, nursing, teaching, law, and literature.

Fast Facts

Marquette University is a four-year, comprehensive university affiliated with the Society of Jesus (Jesuits). Marquette University was founded in 1881.

Web site

http://www.marquette.edu

Location

Milwaukee, Wisconsin.

Student Profile

8,040 undergraduate students (46% male, 54% female); 39% in-state students, 61% out-of-state students; 19% minority, 4% international.

Faculty Profile

98% hold a terminal degree in their field. 14:1 student/faculty ratio. Average class size is 31.

Residence Life

Moderately residential: 51% of students live in university housing. 94% of first-year students live on campus. Approximately 95% of undergraduates live within 5 blocks of campus.

Athletics

Division I, Big East Conference. 12 varsity sports (6 men's: basketball, cross-country, golf, soccer, tennis, indoor & outdoor track; 6 women's: basketball, cross-country, soccer, tennis, indoor & outdoor track, volleyball), club sports, and intramurals (badminton, baseball, cheerleading, fencing, football, women's golf, lacrosse, racquetball, rowing, rugby, sailing, skiing, softball, squash, swimming, track & field, water polo, weightlifting).

Academic Programs

Area, ethnic, cultural, & gender studies; arts (visual & performing); biological & biomedical sciences; business, management, & marketing; communications & journalism; computer & information sciences; education; engineering; engineering technologies; English language & literature; foreign language & literature; health professions & clinical sciences; law & legal studies; mathematics; multi/interdisciplinary studies; parks, recreation & fitness; philosophy & religion; physical sciences; psychology; social sciences.

Costs and Aid

2007-2008: $35,000 comprehensive ($26,270 tuition). 78% of students receive some financial aid. Average award: $18,500.

Endowment

Over $300 million.

More Distinctions

• Kiplinger magazine rated Marquette one of the top 50 Best Buys in private education in 2007.

• Marquette was ranked in the Top 100 of Entrepreneur magazine's list of entrepreneurial business college programs in the nation for 2003, 2004 and 2005.

St. Norbert College

WISCONSIN

St. Norbert College was originally founded in 1898 to train young men for the Catholic priesthood. In 1952, St. Norbert College became coeducational. Today, while St. Norbert retains its identity as a Catholic college, its two thousand students study for bachelor's degrees in forty different fields.

Admissions Contact:

St. Norbert College
100 Grant Street
De Pere, WI 54115
Ph: (800) 236-4878
Fax: (920) 403-4072
Email: admit@snc.edu
www.snc.edu

The 4 Distinctions

Engaged Students

St. Norbert is known as one of the best colleges in the northern Midwest, particularly noted for service learning and for its strong international programs. St. Norbert's Center for International Education is dedicated to creating and enhancing international activities. It divides its efforts into four general areas: global education, language and culture, world ecology, and international business. Known for welcoming students from around the world, St. Norbert provides opportunities for students to engage with and learn from students from twenty-eight other countries. In addition, the English as a Second Language Institute attracts large numbers of foreign students who, while learning English on a noncredit basis, become integrated into the college community.

About one in four St. Norbert students participate in study-abroad programs. St. Norbert partners with fifty international institutions of higher learning to offer study-abroad opportunities in eighty locations around the world.

Internships are an important element of many St. Norbert students' undergraduate experiences. Some participate in internships while on study-abroad trips, and others locally or while taking part in the Washington Semester at Catholic University, interning with governmental and nongovernmental organizations in Washington, DC. Internships are available in every academic area; sophomores in the teacher-education program spend considerable time observing in classroom settings, and as seniors they student teach.

Service learning, promoted by the leadership, service, and involvement office, is so deeply ingrained in the culture of St. Norbert that students regularly volunteer their efforts to several major projects every year. One residence hall is devoted especially to service, with each section performing its own year-long project. Fall and Spring Break Alternatives offer many opportunities for involvement beyond the campus, including regular Habitat for Humanity construction projects.

Faculty-student research is common at St. Norbert, with numerous first-year students making two-year research commitments to a particular faculty member through the college's Research Fellows Project.

Great Teaching

St. Norbert ensures that all of its graduates acquire a broad-based liberal education. All students at St. Norbert take a twelve-course general education program that emphasizes critical thinking and writing, providing students with a common basis for intellectual engagement.

The most popular majors are teacher education, business administration, communications, history, and English. All programs at St. Norbert are designed to be completed in four years, rather than the five years that are now typical of many colleges and universities.

Vibrant Community

St. Norbert has a four-year on-campus residence requirement, which the college believes contributes to the students' focus on their education and cocurricular lives, as well as enhancing the overall sense of togetherness among all members of the St. Norbert community. The college offers a wide variety of living options, including all-freshman dorms; an all-women's residence hall; themed housing for students interested in science, service, a particular foreign language, or other specific interests; and townhouses, carriage houses, and apartments for upperclassmen. About 15 percent of students are members of fraternities or sororities.

The religious life of the college is traditionally strong, with a number of student-run groups focused on faith and spirituality. Through worship, prayer, a supportive environment, and faith-centered programs, the college's campus ministry serves students, staff, faculty, and administrators.

Numerous annual events bring the community together, including homecoming, Parents Weekend, and Junior Knights and Days (when the parents of St. Norbert juniors are invited to campus for a dinner and dance, mock classes, and the celebration of Mass). During the summer, the college presents entertainment at the riverfront gazebo every Tuesday evening for the entire De Pere community.

St. Norbert's athletic teams—known as the Green Knights—play a large role in the life of the college, with a special emphasis on the college's successful ice hockey team. St. Norbert has a connection to the National Football League, too, with the Green Bay Packers holding their summer camp on the St. Norbert campus.

Successful Outcomes

St. Norbert students have achieved notable success in many different fields, with teaching being a particularly strong area. Robert John Cornell, a member of the U.S. House of Representatives from Wisconsin, is a St. Norbert graduate.

St. Norbert graduates enjoy a 95 percent placement rate for those seeking full-time employment or admission to graduate school. This success rate is a result of the excellent reputation of St. Norbert graduates in the workplace and in graduate schools. Alumni play a role, too, serving as a reference point for students' networking and placement.

Fast Facts

St. Norbert College is a four-year, Catholic, liberal arts college founded in 1898.

Web site

http://www.snc.edu

Location

De Pere, Wisconsin—a suburb of Green Bay, 90 minutes from Milwaukee.

Student Profile

2,100 students (44% male, 56% female); 27 states and territories; 7% minority, 2% international.

Faculty Profile

153 full- and part-time faculty. 14:1 student/faculty ratio. Average class size is 19.

Residence Life

Highly residential: nearly 100% of students live on campus.

Athletics

NCAA Division III, Midwest Conference. 18 varsity sports (9 men's: baseball, basketball, cross-country, football, golf, soccer, tennis, indoor/outdoor track, ice hockey; 9 women's: basketball, cross-country, golf, soccer, softball, swimming, tennis, indoor/outdoor track, volleyball), 4 club sports, and 9 intramurals.

Academic Programs

American studies; art; biology; business administration; chemistry; communication; computer information systems; computer science; economics; education (elementary/early childhood, elementary/middle, secondary); English; environmental science; French; geology; German; graphic design; history; international business & language area studies; international studies; Japanese; leadership studies; mathematics/computer science; media; music; music education; natural science; nursing; peace & justice; Philippine studies; philosophy; physics; political science; preprofessional programs (predental, prelaw, premedical, preveterinary); psychology; religious studies; sociology; Spanish; theatre arts; women & gender studies.

Costs and Aid

2007–2008: $31,200 comprehensive ($24,253 tuition). 97% of students receive some financial aid. Average award: $17,207.

Endowment

$62.95 million.

More Distinctions

• The 2007 edition of U.S. News & World Report's "America's Best Colleges" ranks St. Norbert as the fourth Best Comprehensive College in the Midwest region. St. Norbert is also ranked third for the highest graduation rate among comprehensive colleges in the Midwest.

• St. Norbert was named to the John Templeton Foundation's Honor Roll for Character-Building Colleges and is included among forty colleges cited for exemplary student leadership programs.

The University of Wisconsin-Superior

WISCONSIN

Admissions Contact:

The University of Wisconsin-Superior
Belknap & Catlin
PO Box 2000
Superior, WI 54880-4500
Ph: 715-394-8230
Fax: 715-394-8407
Email: admissions@uwsuper.edu
www.uwsuper.edu/

The University of Wisconsin-Superior (UW-Superior) is a public liberal arts college founded in 1893. The school began as a school to train teachers. Today, UW-Superior offers more than thirty undergraduate majors, including innovative programs such as legal studies, art therapy, and transportation and logistics management.

The 4 Distinctions

Engaged Students

The university currently enrolls 2,600 undergraduate and three hundred graduate students. On the National Survey of Student Engagement (NSSE), UW-Superior rated well above the national average in internships and field study. Transportation and logistics management majors benefit from Superior's role as a hub for water, rail, truck, pipeline, and air transportation, but also hold internships across the country.

All social-work majors work at least 450 hours in a professional setting. Science students can work alongside scientists at the Lake Superior Research Institute on campus or at state and federal research labs in the Superior-Duluth metro area. Teacher education majors begin working with children on campus and then move into tutoring programs and student teaching in community schools. Music students perform with campus ensembles as well as with the local professional symphony or as freelance musicians.

Each year, students travel to Belize to conduct research on coral reefs and to Bosnia to study the effects of war. Study-abroad opportunities include travel to Scotland, Korea, Costa Rica, China, France, Germany, and other countries. UW-Superior is a member of the National Student Exchange (NSE), enabling students to enroll for up to a year at NSE-member institutions across the United States and Canada.

Great Teaching

The most popular programs at UW-Superior are business, teacher education, sciences, fine arts, and transportation and logistics management. On average, 75 percent of the classes enroll fewer than twenty-five students. UW-Superior prides itself on the personal attention afforded to students, and most professors make sure they know each of their students by name. There are no classes taught by graduate students; all are taught by professors. In many programs, such as biology, chemistry, mathematics, and communicating arts, students have opportunities to work closely with professors on research or special projects. In English, award-winning authors teach advanced writing courses as well as freshman English classes.

Students in the health and human performance program use the new Kessler Exercise Physiology Lab, which provides graduate-school-level equipment to undergraduate students. Students in the legal studies and criminal justice programs often take part in UW-Superior's mock trial teams, which compete in local, regional, and national tournaments.

Student support services provides help with computer software, advice on choosing and scheduling classes, and one-on-one and small-group tutoring in courses at all levels. The writing center is staffed by faculty, staff, and students to help students on individual assignments and to improve their writing skills. Academics are a focus at UW-Superior, which boasts an impressive 88 percent retention rate for varsity athletes.

The Senior Experience enables every student to engage in a significant scholarly or creative work. Students in all majors may present their research projects at the statewide University of Wisconsin System Research Symposium. Science students conducting research projects have the opportunity to present their work at the annual Undergraduate Research Symposium held on campus.

Vibrant Community

Located in Superior, Wisconsin, at the western tip of Lake Superior, UW-Superior boasts the best of both worlds: its campus is situated in a quiet neighborhood, but it's part of the Superior-Duluth metro area, with plenty of internships, jobs, entertainment, and cultural events. Within a twenty-minute drive from campus, students can attend concerts, a professional ballet, and a symphony, as well as enjoy coffeehouses, movie theaters, shopping, Lake Superior beaches, waterfront trails, cross-country and alpine skiing, and a state park.

For students who like the outdoors, UW-Superior is a good fit. The Superior Outdoor Adventure Program (SOAP) offers guided trips in kayaking, canoeing, skiing, and snowboarding. SOAP helps students enjoy the winter with guided snowshoe trips to the ice caves on Lake Superior near the Apostle Islands National Lakeshore and ice-climbing trips to the cliffs of Lake Superior's North Shore. Each year SOAP organizes a spring-break kayak trip to a southern adventure spot. UW-Superior's campus is just ten minutes from alpine skiing, snowboarding, and cross-country skiing at the Spirit Mountain ski area. Outdoor equipment is available to rent seven days a week, and SOAP provides students with a cross-country ski and bike-repair shop. Some outdoor activities that are popular among students are kayaking, cross-country skiing, and mountain biking. The state-of-the-art Health & Wellness Center offers fitness, athletic, and academic facilities that include an indoor track, swimming pool, fitness center, weight room, climbing wall, physiology lab, and training facilities.

Students volunteer in the community by working at children's centers, painting houses, and picking up trash. Each year, the alternative spring break program provides students with the opportunity to travel to a distant area to help local communities build homes or to assist the elderly. Student athletes volunteer at camps and clinics, tutor in local schools, and host Kids' Day Out events.

The UW-Superior campus is fully wired and has wireless network access in many buildings and outdoor areas. Students enjoy online access to the library, course registration, grades, financial accounts, and course management information. Free Internet and cable TV access is available in all residence hall rooms. Students can bring their own computers to connect to the campus network or use the student computer labs found in most academic buildings and all residence halls. All students get a university computer account that includes e-mail and network storage. Specialized labs are available for computer science and geographic information systems, and the technology help desk is available to help students with technical problems.

Successful Outcomes

Because of the close connection with professors at UW-Superior, students are likely to have a good idea of where they will fit in the real world. Alumni stay involved by coming back to speak to students and often hire graduates of UW-Superior. UW-Superior students enjoy a great deal of success in finding jobs after college, and in gaining enrollment to graduate school, medical school, and law school.

Notable alumni include World War II fighter ace Richard Bong; photojournalist Esther Bubley; research psychologist Dr. Oscar Krisen Buros; David DiFrancesco, inventor of some of the processes used in creating animated movies; Donald Schmidt, inventor of the carbon-carbon material that protects spacecraft reentering the earth's atmosphere; outdoors writer Gordon MacQuarrie; Air Force general Charles McDonald; nationally known artist Fritz Scholder; and the current governor of California, Arnold Schwarzenegger.

Fast Facts

The University of Wisconsin-Superior offers a wide range of undergraduate and graduate programs that combine a liberal arts education with top-rate professional training.

Web site

http://www.uwsuper.edu

Location

Superior, Wisconsin—a city of 27,000 at the western tip of Lake Superior.

Student Profile

2,626 undergraduate students (42% male, 58% female); 25 states, 30 countries; 6% minority, 4.4% international.

Faculty Profile

89 of 112 full-time faculty members hold the highest degree available in their field. 18:1 student/faculty ratio. Average class size is 21.

Residence Life

600 students live on campus. Freshmen and sophomores are required to live on campus unless they live within 30 miles of campus or meet other exemptions.

Athletics

NCAA Division III; Wisconsin Intercollegiate Athletic Conference; Northern Collegiate Hockey Association; varsity sports: (Men: baseball, basketball, cross country, hockey, soccer, track. Women: basketball, cross country, golf, hockey, soccer, softball, track, volleyball); intramurals sports.

Academic Programs

Accounting; art (arts administration, art education, art history, art therapy, studio art); biology (cell/molecular biology, ecology, aquatic biology & fishery science, plant sciences); business administration (finance, international business, management, marketing); chemistry; communicating arts (mass communication, speech communication); computer science; economics; elementary education; English; history; individually designed major; legal studies; mathematics (discrete applied mathematics); music (composition, performance); music education (choral music, general music, instrumental); physical education (community health promotion, exercise science, wellness/fitness management); political science; (political science, international peace studies); psychology; secondary education; social work; sociology; theatre; transportation & logistics management.

Costs and Aid

2006–2007: $5,576 in-state tuition & fees; $6,018 Minnesota resident tuition & fees; $7,860 midwest exchange tuition & fees; $13,052 nonresident tuition and fees; $4,576 room and meals. 80% of students receive some financial aid. Average award: $6,809.

Endowment

$7.9 million.

More Distinctions

• Member of the highly selective Council of Public Liberal Arts Colleges.

Colleges of Distinction
Central Region Schools

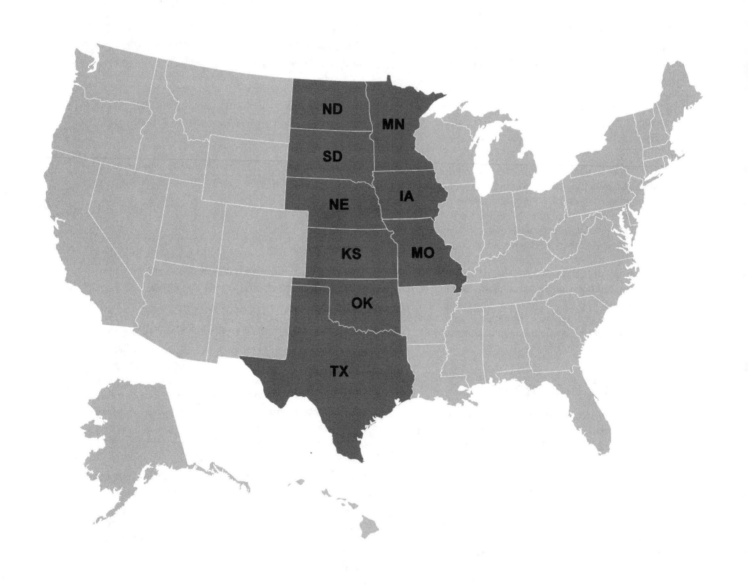

Photo: © iStockphoto.com/lisapics

Notes

_____

_____

_____

_____

_____

_____

_____

_____

_____

_____

Clarke College

IOWA

Clarke College (CC) is a private, Catholic, coeducational liberal arts college. Founded in 1843 by the Sisters of Charity of the Blessed Virgin Mary (BVM), CC offers academic programs in the liberal arts, sciences, fine arts and selected professional and graduate programs.

Admissions Contact:

Clarke College
1550 Clarke Drive
Dubuque, IA 52001
(800) 383-2345
Email:
www.clarke.edu

The 4 Distinctions

Engaged Students

From its beginning, CC has aimed to be "progressive with the times," challenging and supporting students in intellectual and personal growth. Its long tradition of excellence in education is ongoing, maintained and strengthened by today's students, faculty, and staff. Many of its students are first-generation college students.

CC offers more than forty major programs in nearly twenty departments, and the most popular are business administration/management, nursing (offering BSN and MSN degrees), and psychology. A distinctive feature of CC's health-care training is that students are working and learning in hospital settings by their sophomore year. Many students are drawn to CC for its physical training doctorate program.

CC is the only college in its region with a BFA program, and graphic design is one of its strongest majors. The education department includes a Professional Development School (PDS) methodology, which treats local schools as "labs." Clarke faculty have offices in the schools, and CC classes are taught there, too. The primary focus for these lab schools is in art and music.

CC stresses going beyond training and competence in its off-campus educational programs, emphasizing making a positive change, encouraging its students to be kind and caring. PDS, nursing, and physical therapy students offer their skills to benefit the community: for example, physical therapy students help those whose insurance coverage is inadequate for their needs. CC students also can take advantage of Chicago, only about three hours away, for "big city" learning experiences.

At Clarke, students might spend spring break repairing a home for a family in Appalachia, participating in Hunger Clean-Up to help the less-privileged, taking part in the Hesed House Service Trip to reach out to the homeless, or growing spiritually on an Antioch Retreat.

Great Teaching

CC is committed to high-quality instruction: many local residents take classes at Clarke, drawn by the high caliber of the professors and their effective teaching. The student to faculty ratio is eleven to one, and classes are small. Students and faculty are typically on a first-name basis. The faculty also works closely with the student-life staff, developing cocurricular activities and programs to augment their students' academic training. Whatever major students choose, they work with the Clarke faculty and their academic adviser (also a faculty member) to create a personalized education that prepares them for their first job or graduate school.

Faculty from all CC's academic departments teach a cornerstone course for first year students under the aegis of general education. Students are taught speaking, writing, and research skills using common texts. In addition, CC students participate in a traditional senior year capstone experience.

Vibrant Community

Clarke is a Catholic college, which includes the tradition of caring for one another and the challenge to grow spiritually, while welcoming students from all religious backgrounds. The commitment to community, service, and spirituality that started with the BVMs continues to define students' lives at CC today.

About 60 percent of CC's approximately one thousand undergraduate students live on campus in a variety of residential options. There is an all-female dorm and several coed ones. Housing options include apartments for single students, traditional shared rooms, or single rooms. A majority of students are women, reflecting the college's origins, but the gender ratio is becoming more even. Half of the campus buildings were destroyed by a fire in 1984, so many buildings are relatively new, including the library, administration offices, and the Robert and Ruth Kehl Center, the college's athletic facility.

Originally established to educate women, CC became coeducational in 1979, and is the only BVM college in the United States. Politically, the campus is blue, and the Republican Club is a popular student organization. Robert Kennedy Jr. visited campus recently, generating debate.

Students who disagreed with him were encouraged to talk or write about their opinions.

There are forty-eight clubs and organizations CC students can join. The campus ministry is active, and it sponsors many service trips in the Dubuque area. Dubuque, the Masterpiece on the Mississippi is located at the intersection of Iowa, Illinois, and Wisconsin, 150 miles west of Chicago. CC's fifty-five-acre campus is on a bluff overlooking both the city and the Mississippi River. Dubuque has a population of over sixty thousand and is the fastest growing city in Iowa. A heavily Catholic town with five religious congregations, Dubuque is also fine-arts oriented, with a symphony orchestra and a museum of fine arts. Its downtown was renovated recently, and its economy is strong, with job growth in publishing, manufacturing, and tourism.

Whether in the spotlight or in the audience, the arts have a long tradition and an outstanding reputation at CC. Student, alumni and faculty artwork lines the halls of the college and art, drama and music events abound on campus. Each year, the Arts at Clarke Series and the Mackin-Mailander Lecture Series bring internationally known artists, thinkers and performers to campus.

Successful Outcomes

CC graduates are prepared to enter a diverse workforce, and this is exemplified in many individual students, including the art graduate who went on to complete medical school and become a doctor as well as the music student who double-majored in business administration and now works for one of the largest music agencies in the country.

Clarke's mission is to foster, "personal and intellectual growth, global awareness and social responsibility, and spiritual values" in its students. Clarke excels in outcomes for health science careers. Nursing and physical therapy graduates consistently find employment before graduation, and graduates of both programs have tremendously high success rates on licensure exams, going on to have successful careers.

In all of Clarke College's programs, faculty and staff strive to prepare students with the critical thinking and technical skills that enable to students to reach their goals. Across the curriculum, from sciences to fine arts, from humanities to social sciences and everywhere in between, the focus is on the student's future.

Fast Facts

Clarke College is a Catholic, liberal arts institution. Founded in 1843 by Mary Frances Clarke, foundress of the Sisters of Charity of the Blessed Virgin Mary (BVM), it is the only BVM College in the United States.

Web site

http://www.clarke.edu

Location

Dubuque, Iowa—within driving distance of great cities: 3 hours from Chicago, Des Moines and Milwaukee; 4.5 hours from Minneapolis/St. Paul; and 5.5 hours from St. Louis.

Student Profile

1,006 undergraduate students (29% male, 71% female); 23 states and territories, 8 countries.

Faculty Profile

77 full-time faculty. 56% hold a terminal degree in their field. 11:1 student/faculty ratio. Average class size is 15.

Residence Life

Moderately residential: 61% of traditional-age students live on campus.

Athletics

Beginning in 2007-2008, Clarke will compete in the Midwest Collegiate Conference as a member of the NAIA. 16 varsity sports (8 men's: basketball, baseball, cross-country, golf, soccer, tennis, track & field, volleyball; 6 women's: basketball, cross-country, golf, soccer, tennis, track & field, volleyball, softball), a spirit team (cheer and dance) and a wide variety of intramural sports.

Academic Programs

Accounting; art (studio, graphic design, art education K-12); art history; athletic training; biochemistry; bioinformatics; biology; business administration (finance, management, marketing); chemistry; communication (advertising/public relations, journalism); computer information systems; drama and speech; education (secondary, special education); elementary education; English; history; kinesiology; mathematics; music; music education; music ministry; nursing; philosophy; preengineering; prelaw; prephysical therapy; preprofessional health; sciences; psychology; religious studies; social work; Spanish.

Costs and Aid

2007–2008: $27,886 comprehensive ($20,666 tuition). 95% of Clarke's full-time & day-time students receive financial aid in the form of scholarships, grants, loans, and work-study. Average Award: $15,475.

Endowment

$17 million.

Cornell College

IOWA

Recognized as a leading liberal arts college, Cornell College (CC) is also one of the nation's most distinctive colleges. Enabled by an innovative academic schedule called One-Course-At-A-Time (OCAAT), Cornell offers students "one extraordinary experience after another, in the classroom, on campus, and around the world."

Admissions Contact:

Cornell College
600 First Street SW
Mount Vernon, IA 52314-1098
(800) 747-1112
Ph: (319) 895-4477
Email: admission@cornellcollege.edu
www.cornellcollege.edu

The 4 Distinctions

Engaged Students

Founded in 1853, Cornell is an attractively diverse, selective, independent, coeducational, residential college community dedicated to fostering intellectual, moral, and personal growth. Rather than following a traditional semester calendar, Cornell's academic year is comprised of nine terms of three and a half weeks each/ Students take one class per term, or one-course-at-a-time. Also described as the block plan, OCAAT provides Cornell students with optimal focus and flexibility, combined with small classes of about fifteen and never more than twenty-five students. The results are dynamic learning experiences, as well as a myriad of special study opportunities.

Students are able to devote their full attention and best efforts to each and every class. They gain a depth of understanding through an immersion experience in each interactively designed and discussion-rich class. Courses are substantial and are valued at four credit hours.

This innovative system ensures a lively pace throughout the academic year and allows students and teachers to explore unique educational opportunities beyond the classroom. Faculty and students are free to study away from campus in whatever venues best suit the subject. For example, students in the sciences are able to do research with their professors at off-campus locations such as the Mayo Clinic or to participate in a sequence of all-day environmental field studies. Recently, students have traveled to countries such as Australia, Tanzania, Peru, and the Bahamas through the science and psychology programs. Economics and business students have traveled to Chicago and New York City; and English and art and classics students have traveled to England, France, Italy, Mexico, and Greece.

The OCAAT schedule provides many opportunities for students to study abroad, whether for a single term, for multiple terms, or for a traditional semester. Cornell is a member of the Associated Colleges of the Midwest (ACM) and the School for International Training (SIT).

Cornell students also take advantage of the flexible OCAAT schedule to pursue internships and independent studies. Nearly two-thirds of Cornell students have participated in a career-related or professional internship, and two-thirds have completed independent-study courses. Many students complete double majors, if not a major and a minor; others design their own majors. Cornell offers more than forty majors as well as pre-professional programs in architecture, engineering, law, and medicine.

Great Teaching

Mentoring is a valued part of the education at Cornell. Faculty truly know their students and actively cultivate and empower them to pursue their interests, as well as to develop new ones. Since Cornell professors teach only one course at a time, they are able to focus exclusively on the needs of the students in that class, often leading to longer, in-depth discussions not possible within a multiple-class schedule. Many professors feel they are better teachers within the OCAAT schedule because they have the flexibility to concentrate on students' interests, to travel, and to conduct research with their students without the scheduling restrictions of semester-based calendars.

Cornell faculty are active scholars; in part, they are terrific teachers because they include students in their scholarly endeavors. All science professors have research funds devoted to support meaningful research projects with students. The low student to faculty ratio of twelve to one and guaranteed maximum class size of twenty-five also ensure that students receive a high level of attention from their Cornell professors.

Vibrant Community

As one of only two national liberal arts colleges teaching on the block plan, Cornell attracts applicants from all fifty states and dozens of countries. Consequently, it has an attractively diverse student body marked by its openness to individual and cultural differences. At Cornell, students do not wait to be entertained. They create the campus's clear sense of energy and vitality, fully embracing campus life and opportunities for involvement.

The OCAAT program presents opportunities for Cornell's 1,200 students to participate in extracurricular activities in a similarly focused way, and there are over one hundred student clubs and organizations, ranging from performance arts to special-interest groups. More than 90 percent of students live on campus, and about a third are involved in Greek life, belonging to independent fraternities or sororities. The college's beautiful hilltop campus overlooks the Cedar River Valley, and Cornell is proud to have its entire campus listed on the National Register of Historic Places—one of only two schools to receive this honor.

On campus, the Kimmel Theatre provides an outstanding facility for students of drama. Students perform in every type of performance, from musicals to one-act plays, and are able to direct and write, as well as to act. Armstrong Hall, historic King Chapel, and McWethy Hall accommodate Cornell's equally active programs in music and art.

Cornell is a member of the NCAA Division III and ranks among the top fifteen Division III institutions in NCAA postgraduate scholars. Cornell offers nineteen intercollegiate sports and is a member of the nationally competitive Iowa Intercollegiate Athletic Conference (IIAC).

CC's volunteer office provides a variety of outreach programs and other service opportunities for students. These include the Lunch Buddy program, where three hundred students meet regularly with elementary students as tutors and mentors; fund-raising races; issues awareness weeks; adolescent mentoring programs; and an alternative spring-break program, which sends students across the country and even around the world to work on service projects. Living-learning opportunities are also popular residential options.

Between terms, Cornell students enjoy four-and-a-half-day block breaks. These respites provide opportunities for relaxation on campus; road trips to accessible cities such as Chicago, St. Louis, Milwaukee, or Minneapolis; skiing excursions to Utah or Colorado; and camping.

Located in Mount Vernon, Iowa, a rural town of four thousand in eastern Iowa, Cornell is twenty miles southwest of Cedar Rapids and twenty miles north of Iowa City. The Cedar Rapids metro area has a population of two hundred thousand, with urban amenities typical for its size, including Eastern Iowa Airport, and calls itself the City of Five Seasons. Iowa City, home of the University of Iowa, a major national research university with thirty thousand students, has a metro population of one hundred and twenty thousand, and the combined eastern Iowa corridor of Cedar Rapids and Iowa City offers numerous entertainment and cultural options for students.

Successful Outcomes

Cornell is proud that 96 percent of its students graduate within four years, many with double majors. Over 90 percent of Cornell alumni are employed or attending graduate school within three months of graduation. Two-thirds of Cornell alumni continue their studies at the graduate or professional level at some of the nation's finest universities, typically within five years of graduation.

Cornell's Alumni Fellows Network provides students with high-profile internship opportunities, funding, networking, job shadowing, and externships. Alumni return to campus to conduct mock and informational interviews, and to speak about their employment experiences and lines of work. Cornell graduates are prepared for life after college, and feel that their college experiences prepared them to be thorough and efficient.

Fast Facts

Cornell College is a four-year, selective liberal arts college founded in 1853, renowned for its innovative One-Course-At-A-Time (OCAAT) academic calendar.

Web site

http://www.cornellcollege.edu

Location

Mount Vernon, Iowa—30 minutes from Iowa City, 20 minutes from Cedar Rapids, 2 hours from Des Moines, and 3-4 hours from Chicago.

Student Profile

1,154 (43% male, 57% female); 46 states and territories represented; 12% minority, 3% international.

Faculty Profile

92 full-time faculty. 12:1 student/faculty ratio. Average class size is 14.

Residence Life

Highly residential: 91% of students live on campus.

Athletics

NCAA Division III, Iowa Intercollegiate Athletic Conference. 19 varsity sports (10 men's: baseball, football, wrestling, basketball, cross-country, golf, soccer, tennis, indoor track & field, outdoor track & field; 9 women's: volleyball, softball, basketball, cross-country, golf, soccer, tennis, indoor track & field, outdoor track & field), and 40 intramurals.

Academic Programs

Archaeology; art; biochemistry & molecular biology; chemistry; classical studies; computer science; economics & business; education (elementary/secondary); English; environmental studies; ethnic studies; French; geology; German; history; international relations; kinesiology; Latin American studies; mathematics; medieval & early modern studies; music; philosophy; physics; politics; psychology; religion; Russian; Russian studies; sociology; sociology & anthropology; Spanish; theatre; women's studies. Preprofessional programs: architecture; dentistry; engineering; forestry & environmental management; law; medicine; nursing; social work; theology; veterinary medicine.

Costs and Aid

2007–2008: $33,250 comprehensive ($26,100 tuition). 72% of students receive need-based financial aid. Average award: $18,555.

Endowment

$78 million.

More Distinctions

• Cornell College ranks in the top 7% of the nation's 3,600 colleges and universities according to the Carnegie Foundation for the Advancement of Teaching.

• U.S. News & World Report has included Cornell among "America's Best National Liberal Arts Colleges --one of the 164 highly selective national liberal arts colleges" every year since its inception.

• Ranked in top fifteen nationally in NCAA postgraduate scholars among Division III institutions.

• Member of the Associated Colleges of the Midwest (ACM), which includes the University of Chicago, Carleton, Grinnell, Colorado College, and Macalester.

• One of forty colleges featured in Loren Pope's Colleges That Change Lives.

Luther College

IOWA

Admissions Contact:

Luther College
700 College Drive
Decorah, Iowa 52101
(800) 458-8437
Ph: (563) 387-1287
Fax: (563) 387-2159
Email: admissions@luther.edu
www.luther.edu

Luther College (LC) is a coeducational, residential, four-year, liberal arts college affiliated with the Lutheran church (ELCA). Founded in 1861 by Norwegian immigrants, LC sees the connection between faith and learning as central to the education process, teaching students to associate freedom with responsibility and their life's work with service.

The 4 Distinctions

Engaged Students

Luther College offers more than sixty majors, preprofessional programs, and certificate programs. The most popular are biology, education, Spanish, music, and business-related fields such as business administration/management, economics, and accounting.

All LC students are required to take three Paideia Program interdisciplinary courses: a common two-semester sequence for first-year students, and a series of one-semester courses for juniors and seniors. *Paideia* is ancient Greek for "education," implying both formal and informal learning, and the LC Paideia courses include common readings, lectures, and small discussion groups, encouraging strong bonds between students and their professors.

LC students are encouraged to take advantage of off-campus and experiential learning opportunities. Education majors go into actual classrooms to observe, beginning in their first year, and more advanced students can observe in international school settings. With over twenty programs around the world in countries such as Guatemala, China, Japan, Australia, and Norway, about 75 percent of all LC students study abroad at least once, either for a full academic year, a semester, or a January term. All foreign language majors are required to take part in an intensive language immersion program for at least one semester abroad.

Internships in the tristate area of Iowa, Minnesota, and Wisconsin are available to LC students. Students also participate in internships across the country, such as at the Smithsonian Institution, the White House, and the United States Senate in Washington, DC.

Great Teaching

LC's low student to faculty ratio of thirteen to one means classes are small, and professors provide students with extra assistance and guidance. More then 90 percent of the faculty live within five miles of campus and are involved in many college activities, making themselves accessible to students.

In the sciences, a new grant from the National Science Foundation has provided faculty and students with additional sophisticated research equipment for laboratory use. This equipment will allow LC students to engage in collaborative projects with science communities on other college and university campuses. As a result, LC students will benefit from increased opportunities for research internships during the summer months or during the January term. Construction began in May on a new $20 million Science Laboratory and Research Center, which will house the college's biology and chemistry programs. The 64,000 square-foot facility is scheduled to open in the fall of 2008.

LC's Student Academic Support Center (SASC) offers a myriad of services to students, providing them with tools to reach graduation. The services offered range from tutoring to learning-skills workshops to supervised study group sessions.

As a college founded by Norwegian settlers, LC honors its history by offering a Scandinavian studies major. Part of the modern languages and literature department, the Scandinavian studies major gives students the opportunity to learn the Norwegian language while studying Scandinavian culture, history, and economics.

Vibrant Community

LC embraces diversity and challenges its students to learn in community, discern their callings, and serve the common good with distinction. Students, faculty, and staff work together for the development of a living and learning environment that encourages caring relationships and an understanding of the wholeness of life.

LC is located in Decorah, Iowa, in the bluff country, thirty-five miles west of the Mississippi River and fifteen miles south of the Minnesota border. The Upper Iowa River, the only river in Iowa that meets the criteria for wild and scenic river designation, runs through the town and through LC's one-thousand-acre campus. Decorah is home to the Vesterheim Norwegian-American Museum and is known for its well-preserved, representative examples of Midwest architecture from as early as the 1850s. The nearest airport is sixty miles away, in La Crosse, Wisconsin.

The college seeks diversity in its students' upbringing and origin. Luther's 2,500 undergraduate students are from thirty-eight states with 35 percent from Iowa, 4 percent internationals, and 21 percent first-generation college students. Roughly 87 percent of LC students live on campus and 85 percent are there on weekends, attending performances, participating in athletics, or taking part in one of more than 129 registered organizations. With over sixteen music groups on campus, there are many performances to watch or to play in throughout the year.

LC has ten traditional residence halls as well as an apartment-style building for upper-level students, married students, and some faculty. Some residence halls include wellness and chemical-free floors as options. A small percentage of LC students belong to fraternities or sororities.

LC students are involved with their campus and in the wider community. LC's new environmental studies major has raised awareness about and brought attention to environmental issues on campus, leading to the planting of a garden on campus to grow fresh produce for the dining halls. Similarly, a biology professor and students worked together to convert leftover cooking oil from the kitchens into biofuel.

Expressing interest in the local community beyond the campus, LC students, faculty, and staff started a free clinic to meet the need for low cost health care in the area. The clinic provides unique opportunities for premed, nursing, and language students to serve and learn at the same time.

Successful Outcomes

Out of a typical graduating class, approximately 23 percent of LC students go directly to graduate school, and more than 65 percent are employed in a field related to their major within six months of graduation. An additional 7 to 10 percent engage in full-time, post-graduate volunteer service with such organizations as the Peace Corps, Americorps, and several others. Students say their degree from the college provided flexibility and that they learned an appreciation for diversity, effective communication techniques, and the invaluable skills of critical thinking and strong writing.

The college encourages lifelong learning through its annual summer learning program, Lutherlag. Intended for LC alumni, friends, and family, it is a week of courses for adults and teens with numerous outdoor and evening activities, including musical performances. There is also an alumni tours program, offering travel opportunities for LC alumni several times a year to destinations such as Russia, Japan, Australia, New Zealand, Italy, and Norway. In 2007, the tours include a nine-day visit to Vienna and Budapest, and a spring-break trip to the Canary Islands.

Fast Facts

Luther College is an independent, coeducational, residential, liberal arts college affiliated with the Lutheran church (ELCA).

Web site

http:// www.luther.edu

Location

Decorah, Iowa—major cities like Des Moines, the Twin Cities, Chicago, Milwaukee, and Madison are in driving distance.

Student Profile

2476 undergraduate students (43% male, 57% female); 87.5% from MN, IA, WI, and IL; 5.3% domestic students of color; 3.7% international students.

Faculty Profile

181 full-time faculty. 89% hold a terminal degree in their field. 13:1 student/faculty ratio. Average class size is 20.

Residence Life

Highly residential: 87% of students live on campus.

Athletics

NCAA Division III, Iowa Intercollegiate Athletic Conference. 19 varsity sports (10 men's: baseball, basketball, cross-country, football, golf, soccer, swimming & diving, tennis, track & field, wrestling; 9 women's: basketball, cross-country, golf, soccer, softball, swimming & diving, tennis, track & field, volleyball), 4 club sports, and over 50 intramurals.

Academic Programs

Accounting; Africana studies; anthropology; art; athletic training; biblical languages; biology; chemistry; classical studies; classics; communication studies; computer science; economics; elementary education; English; environmental studies; French; German; Greek; health; history; Latin; management; management information systems; mathematics; mathematics/statistics; music; nursing; philosophy; physical education; physics; political science; psychology; religion; Scandinavian studies; social work; sociology; Spanish; speech and theatre; theatre/dance; women's & gender studies. 33 minors. Interdisciplinary minors in athletic training, environmental studies, international studies, museum studies, Russian studies, social welfare, and women's and gender studies; special interdisciplinary programs in international management studies, art management, music management, theatre/dance management, and sports management; preprofessional programs in predentistry, preengineering, prelaw, premedicine, preoptometry, prepharmacy, prephysical therapy, preseminary, preveterinary.

Costs and Aid

2007–2008: $33,500 comprehensive ($28,840 tuition). 98% of students receive some financial aid. Average award: $25,000.

Endowment

$114,000,000.

Mount Mercy College

IOWA

Mount Mercy is a Catholic, coeducational, four-year, baccalaureate institution which was founded as a girls' academy in 1928. Many of Mount Mercy's students are first-generation college students, and the campus atmosphere is active, inclusive, and ecumenical.

Admissions Contact:

Mount Mercy College
1330 Elmhurst Drive NE
Cedar Rapids, IA 52402
(800) 248-4504
Ph: (319) 363-1323
Email: admission@mtmercy.edu
www2.mtmercy.edu

The 4 Distinctions

Engaged Students

Service learning and social-justice work is the backbone of the Mount Mercy experience. Mount Mercy places strong emphasis on service to the common good, and works to promote in its students reflective judgment, purposeful living, strategic communication, and service to those in need. Through the Office of Campus Ministry and volunteerism and as a part of the college's curriculum, Mount Mercy students are heavily engaged in a variety of hands-on service projects. Examples of service-learning opportunities include Spring Community Outreach Day, Alternative Spring Break, and Topics in Social Justice: Appalachia. By traveling to Appalachia in the spring, students help townspeople in schools, learning centers, a clinic, and an ambulance service. Service is so embedded in the culture at Mount Mercy that students themselves have mandated that their clubs and organizations have service requirements.

The College's Emerging Leadership program also promotes service as it takes students off campus to volunteer in the community. Students coach at the YMCA, work at local food pantries, work with women and children in homeless shelters, tutor students, participate in mission trips with local houses of worship, and organize faith retreats.

Students are involved in classroom research and study-abroad options, as well as field research outside the classroom. An interesting opportunity, due to Cedar Rapids's vast Czech heritage, allows Mount Mercy students to participate in a direct exchange program with Palacký University in the Czech Republic. Internship opportunities in Cedar Rapids include an aviation electronics company and international investment firms, among others.

The Mount Mercy Students in Free Enterprise (SIFE) team has won the regional championship for the past ten years, and is a way for students to network in the community. The SIFE team partners with local and state organizations to enhance their business and marketing plans and to ensure that their ventures will become or remain viable in today's marketplace.

Great Teaching

Student life in the classroom revolves around living a life of service, as many core courses entail a service requirement. Nursing, education, social work, criminal justice, and business are among the top majors. Students are more than just a number to the 150 faculty members at Mount Mercy. The student to faculty ratio is thirteen to one, which allows and encourages direct interaction in the classroom. The campus's friendly, relaxed, and welcoming atmosphere allows students, faculty, and staff to interact frequently.

> **"I looked at bigger schools, but I can concentrate better here. And if I want to talk to a professor I just show up."**
>
> -Yesenia Mendoza, Freshman, Administrative Management, Austin, Minnesota

Mount Mercy is home to four Fulbright recipients in the fields of English, art, and education. The college's faculty have also been recognized nationally with prestigious writing awards and for teaching excellence.

Faculty at Mount Mercy continually innovate and update their teaching style to motivate students. Members of the faculty have collaborated on unique course offerings, including a team-taught seminar on the pursuit of happiness and a team-taught honors history course based primarily on role-playing. For first-year students, the Partnership Program offers a transitional classroom experience in which a small group of students and a faculty member explore the content area of the course and discuss first-year issues of concern such as time management, study skills, and career development.

> **"At Mount Mercy, everyone learns to grow in leadership qualities. It's the hidden curriculum."**
>
> -William Mulcahey, Director of Campus Ministries

Vibrant Community

Mount Mercy students can choose to participate in more than thirty clubs and organizations. Campus events and activities include those sponsored by the student programming board and student organizations. Entertainment activities include the Roommate Game and a student version of the hit television show Deal or No Deal. Other popular events include Spring Fling, visits by hypnotists and mentalists, coffeehouse performances, and bingo. There are no fraternities or sororities on campus.

The Mount Mercy cultural affairs committee sponsors a variety of cultural events for students, faculty, staff, and the greater community. Past speakers and presenters include civil-rights leader Julian Bond, former U.S. Poet Laureate Ted Kooser, an annual visit by a Holocaust survivor, and numerous artists and musicians. Faculty members are encouraged to apply to present their research and findings at one of four faculty forums held each year. Off campus, theater and concert tickets are offered at a discounted price for Mount Mercy students.

The college is located in Cedar Rapids, Iowa, and 90 percent of its 1,482 students come from in state. Because of its location in Cedar Rapids, known as the Jewel of the Midwest, Mount Mercy students are able to take advantage of the many events held in the city of 140,000.

Successful Outcomes

Over 96 percent of students report that they are employed or in graduate school within six months of graduation from Mount Mercy College. Over the last five years, those students attending graduate school have ranged from 5 to 14 percent per year.

The alumni participation rate is 21 percent. Mount Mercy alumni serve as resources for current students and are easily accessible, since 73 percent of Mount Mercy graduates choose to stay in Iowa because of the abundance of employment opportunities and the high quality of life. Alumni offer Mount Mercy students internship, job shadowing, and informational interview opportunities, and many alumni participate in the annual Student Alumni Career Ambassadors Networking Event.

Notable alumni include Mary Lacy, district attorney in Boulder, Colorado, who is the lead prosecutor in the ongoing JonBenet Ramsey murder investigation, and Dr. Marita Titler, director of research, quality and outcomes management at the University of Iowa Hospitals and Clinics.

"The real-world opportunities our students experience, like internships, bring the classroom to life and open doors for their futures."

- Deb Brydon, Associate Professor of Criminal Justice and Director of Faculty Development

Fast Facts

Mount Mercy College is a four-year, private, liberal arts college sponsored by the Sisters of Mercy and founded in 1928.

Web site

http://www.mtmercy.edu/

Location

Cedar Rapids, Iowa.

Student Profile

1,482 students (26.9% male; 73.1% female).

Faculty Profile

72 full-time faculty. More than 60% of faculty hold terminal degrees. 13:1 student/faculty ratio. Average class size is 15.

Residence Life

Freshman and sophomore students are required to live on campus. Upper-class students enjoy suite-style and apartment living.

Athletics

NAIA Division II, Midwest Collegiate Conference. 13 varsity sports (6 men's: basketball, baseball, golf, soccer, cross-country, track & field; 7 women's: basketball, softball, volleyball, golf, cross-country, track & field, soccer).

Academic Programs

Accounting; administrative management; applied philosophy; art; biology; business; communication; computer information systems; computer science; criminal justice; elementary education; English; healthcare systems; health services administration; history; interdisciplinary (English/business administration, history/business administration, political science/business administration, psychology/business administration, sociology/business administration, & visual arts/business administration); international studies; marketing; mathematics; medical technology; music; nursing; political science; psychology; religious studies; secondary education with endorsement in biology, business/general, business/marketing, English/language arts, mathematics, music, social science/American government, social science/psychology, & speech communication/theater; social work; sociology; speech/drama; urban & community services.

Costs and Aid

2007–2008: $26,340 comprehensive ($20,070 tuition.) 100% of students receive some financial aid. Average award: $15,663.

Endowment

$22 million.

More Distinctions

• *U.S News & World Report* ranks Mount Mercy College in the top tier of Best Comprehensive Colleges – Bachelor's.

Wartburg College

IOWA

Wartburg College is a nationally recognized, four-year, liberal arts college of the ELCA. It is "dedicated to challenging and nurturing students for lives of leadership and service as a spirited expression of their faith and learning."

Admissions Contact:

Wartburg College
100 Wartburg Blvd
Waverly, IA 50677
(800) 772-2085
Email: admissions@wartburg.edu
www.wartburg.edu

The 4 Distinctions

Engaged Students

Wartburg offers more than fifty academic majors in the liberal arts and professional areas. The top five majors are biology, business administration, communication arts, elementary education, and music education. Wartburg is the only private college in Iowa offering a major in music therapy.

Beginning in their first year, Wartburg students benefit from meaningful research and hands-on learning experiences. Whatever their major or area of interest, students are encouraged to take advantage of experiential learning opportunities on and off campus. Education and social work majors are involved in early field experiences, and communication arts students get hands-on experience through the college television and radio stations, the campus newspaper, and a student-run public relations agency for the campus.

Wartburg West in Denver, Colorado, gives Wartburg students exposure to an urban setting. They spend a term in Denver taking academic courses, pursuing internships or field experiences related to their majors, and experiencing the cultural diversity and resources of a major metropolitan center. Students can also participate in programs offered by the Washington Center for Internships and Academic Seminars in Washington, DC. Wartburg maintains exchange programs with universities in Germany and Japan and offers a wide variety of global and multicultural study programs in countries around the world that challenge students to consider their place in the larger global community and how they might enrich that community.

Great Teaching

A twelve to one student to faculty ratio and an average class size of twenty-one enable close relationships between students and professors. Of the full-time faculty, 94 percent have PhDs or terminal degrees in their field. As one student said, "you get a lot of attention from the teachers, and the quality of the education is amazing."

Faculty members teach unique on-campus courses and accompany students on a variety of trips during Wartburg's one-month May term, an ideal time for off-campus travel and study. As part of May term courses, students travel throughout the world, including China, Germany, Japan, Mexico, the Caribbean, Tanzania, South Africa, Guyana, Alaska, and the Navajo Nation.

More than two hundred students participate in service trips scheduled during fall and winter term breaks and Tour Week. Recent trips have involved work in the areas of AIDS advocacy, poverty and homelessness, hurricane disaster relief, environmental issues, Native American issues, and substance abuse. Faculty members or staff advisors accompany each group.

Vibrant Community

More than 80 percent of Wartburg students live on campus. Accommodations include all-male, all-female, and coed residence halls; small manor units; four-, six-, and eight-person suites; and townhouse-style apartments for senior students. Many of the suites require residents to develop community service or educational projects. Living-learning communities on campus include language suites, where students practice their language skills in German, French, or Spanish and host cultural events for the campus community.

Wartburg students are active in more than one hundred student organizations, including music groups and intercollegiate athletic teams. Approximately 450 students are involved in music organizations, and nearly six hundred students compete in intercollegiate athletics. Wartburg has the highest athletic success rate of any college in the Iowa Conference, winning a national team or individual championship for eleven consecutive years, including five national wrestling titles and a women's outdoor track and field championship.

The Center for Community Engagement (CCE) helps students explore ways to immerse themselves in meaningful community service and internships. The CCE also hosts the Institute for Leadership Education, which coordinates course work and activities for Wartburg's interdisciplinary minor in leadership certification.

Student groups at Wartburg make a meaningful impact on a variety of issues. Mosaico, the Latino student group, targets diversifying enrollment and raising awareness of Hispanic issues around campus. EARTH promotes environmental issues. The International Club encourages interaction among international and American students.

U.S. students of color and international students make up 12 percent of the student body.

Founded in 1852 in Saginaw, Michigan, the college moved several times before establishing a permanent home in Waverly in 1935. It is named after Wartburg Castle, a landmark in Eisenach, Germany, where Martin Luther spent ten months in hiding during the stormy days of the Reformation. Today, Waverly and Eisenach are sister cities, and a formal agreement provides ongoing academic and cultural exchanges between the college and the castle. The Wartburg choir regularly performs at the castle during concert tours of Europe.

Waverly, a northeastern Iowa community of nine thousand residents, is recognized statewide for its progressive businesses and industries. It is twenty minutes north of the Waterloo-Cedar Falls metropolitan area, six hours west of Chicago, five and a half hours north of Kansas City, and three and a half hours southwest of Minneapolis/St. Paul. The Cedar River, a bicycle trail, and two eighteen-hole golf courses provide off-campus recreational outlets. Students find part-time jobs and internships in Waverly, and local residents attend campus events and support college programs.

Successful Outcomes

Approximately 45% of Wartburg graduates will have studied abroad during their college tenure. Students regularly participate in undergraduate research and publication with out faculty. Wartburg's Leadership Certificate program sets our students apart when they interview for positions or apply to graduate and professional schools. More than 40 percent of Wartburg students complete an academic internship (for credit) before they graduate, gaining hands-on experience and valuable connections in their intended careers.

Students can connect with alumni through AlumNet, an online database of graduates willing to serve as career mentors, and the Orange Connection, which provides opportunities for students to job-shadow alumni. The Pathways Center serves as a comprehensive resource for academic advising and career counseling. More than 20 percent of Wartburg students go on to graduate or professional schools, and placement statistics show that seven months after graduation, more than 98 percent of students are employed or continuing their education.

Fast Facts

Wartburg College is a four-year liberal arts college of the ELCA founded in 1852.

Web site

http://www.wartburg.edu

Location

Waverly, Iowa—located just 20 minutes from Waterloo/Cedar Falls, one of the state's largest metropolitan areas.

Student Profile

Approximately 1,800 undergraduate students (47% male, 53% female); 23 states and territories, 36 countries; 7% minority, 5% international.

Faculty Profile

107 full-time faculty. 12:1 student/faculty ratio. Average class size is 21.

Residence Life

Highly residential: 85% of students live on campus.

Athletics

NCAA Division III, Iowa Intercollegiate Athletic Conference. 19 varsity sports (10 men's: baseball, basketball, cross-country, football, golf, soccer, tennis, indoor track & field, outdoor track & field, wrestling; 9 women's: basketball, cross-country, golf, soccer, softball, tennis, volleyball, indoor track & field, outdoor track & field), and a wide variety of intramurals.

Academic Programs

More than 50 majors including: Accounting; art; art education; biochemistry; biology; business administration (finance, international business, management, marketing, sport management); chemistry; church music; communication arts (public relations, electronic media, print, media); communication studies (speech, theatre); communication design; computer information systems; computer science; economics; education (Christian day school, early childhood, elementary, middle, secondary); engineering science; English; fitness management; history; international relations; mathematics; modern languages (French & French studies, German & German studies, Spanish & Spanish studies); music (applied); music education (instrumental, vocal); music performance; music therapy; philosophy; physical education; physics; political science; psychology; religion (camping ministry, parish education; urban ministry; youth & family ministry; social work; sociology (community sociology); writing.

Costs and Aid

2007–2008: $31,285 comprehensive ($23,600 tuition). 98% of students receive some financial aid.

Endowment

$48 million.

More Distinctions

• No. 1 in Iowa, No. 6 in the Midwest in U.S. News & World Report's 2007 ranking of the nation's 320 comprehensive colleges.

Benedictine College

KANSAS

Located in Atchison, Kansas, Benedictine College offers an array of opportunities to enrich one's mind, strengthen one's beliefs, and build the foundations for a successful career. Founded in 1858, the college sees its mission as "the education of men and women within a community of faith and scholarship."

Admissions Contact:

Benedictine College
1020 North Second Street
Atchison, Kansas 6002-1499
(800) 467-5340
Ph: (913) 360-7476
Email: admiss@benedictine.edu
www.benedictine.edu

The 4 Distinctions

Engaged Students

Benedictine College is committed to providing academic excellence to its 1,250 undergraduate students and 350 graduate students. The campus offers nearly forty majors and preprofessional programs, including top programs in business, education, religious studies, and biology. Some uncommon majors offered at Benedictine include astronomy, youth ministry, and criminology. Students can also design a new major unique to their goals.

Benedictine College provides a liberal arts education with a well-rounded core of arts and sciences. This type of education guides students to distinction not only in their majors but in a wide variety of areas needed to succeed in one's professional and personal life. Students are trained to view the world from a variety of academic perspectives and to use the tools of a number of disciplines to understand, analyze, and solve problems.

Benedictine fosters scholarship, independent research, and performance in its students and faculty as a means of participating in and contributing to the broader world of learning. Benedictine College's unique Discovery Program provides the tools and motivation for students to collaborate with faculty on special projects in their areas of interest. The college provides opportunities for financial grants to aid student research, and, while presenting their research during a campuswide day of celebration in the spring, students gain public speaking experience. Benedictine students are encouraged to form the habit of lifelong learning and to apply well-developed ethical standards in every aspect of their lives.

Benedictine College encourages a broad spectrum of learning by offering a variety of study-abroad programs with the aim of providing students with an understanding of other cultures, preparing students to live in a global society, and creating goodwill for the country. The college supports a campus in Florence, Italy, as well as a campus exchange program with 275 colleges and universities in thirty-nine countries.

For those students who wish to continue their education at the postgraduate level, Benedictine College also offers three master's programs: business administration, executive business administration, and a Master of Arts in school leadership, a program that includes a campus in the Kansas City metropolitan area.

Great Teaching

The student-faculty relationships formed at Benedictine College are incomparable to those of many other universities. With a student to teacher ratio of fifteen to one and class sizes ranging from five to thirty students, the Benedictine faculty believe that a personal classroom experience is of the highest importance.

Benedictine College educators are known for their thoughtful and ethical natures, their passion to work with students, and their great distinction within their fields. Faculty truly care that students receive a hands-on education, offering many opportunities for one-on-one assistance outside of the classroom, student study groups, or tutoring. Of the Benedictine College faculty, 77 percent hold a doctorate or a terminal degree, and many faculty members are considered to be some of the best experts within their field. Students are also supported by faculty outside of the classroom. Oftentimes, professors have lunch with students in the cafeteria, develop special-interest extracurricular clubs, attend sporting events, and are among the audience for campus music and theatrical performances.

Vibrant Community

Benedictine College is a beautiful, residential community resting on a bluff that overlooks the Missouri River. The campus offers 110 acres beaming with a rich balance of historical buildings, some dating 150 years, mixed with state-of-the-art, modern facilities for academics, residence, and recreation. Supported by the city of Atchison, Kansas (population twelve thousand), which is located just forty-five miles north of the Kansas City metropolitan area, this midwestern area creates a safe, calm, welcoming environment for Benedictine College students. Benedictine is proud of its Catholic roots within the Benedictine Order, and the nearby sponsoring religious communities of St. Benedict's Abbey and Mount St. Scholastica offer unique opportunities for spiritual connection.

As a residential campus, over 75 percent of students live in comfortable residence halls on campus in order to become immersed in their college experience. Living within this dynamic residential community challenges students to grow in character and as leaders.

Benedictine College offers countless opportunities for extracurricular success, from varsity and intramural athletics; to music, dance, and theatre arts; to student government and political interest organizations; to cultural clubs, community service, and other special-interest groups. Students cannot help but find ways to learn more about themselves and their passions outside of the classroom, equipping them with the skills to nurture and develop the bonds of community.

Finally but possibly most important, Benedictine College students are part of a community that fosters a special connection to one's faith. As a Catholic institution, the college is dedicated to "the ardent search for truth and its unselfish transmission . . . so as to act rightly and to serve humanity better" (Ex Corde Ecclesiae). Students of all faiths are welcomed and encouraged in their quests to grow closer to God, and all students are challenged to put their faith into action.

Successful Outcomes

Over 96 percent of students report that they are emplIn 2004, graduate Dr. Wangari Muta Maathai received the Nobel Peace Prize for environmental work in Kenya. Dr. Maathai is just one fine example of the unique Benedictine education leading students to exceptional futures.

Boasting a well-rounded liberal arts education and a personal residential experience, Benedictine College graduates are of great value. Recent reports show that nearly 95 percent of Benedictine students are placed within a career or graduate school of their choice after receiving their undergraduate degree. Not only does the campus offer an outstanding career services department to prepare graduates for their futures, but proud Raven alumni are often students' greatest resources to pave the way for a successful future. The campus offers career fairs, resume preparation, interview training, graduate school application assistance, and frequent postings for special career and internship opportunities.

"Benedictine College laid the foundation of academic excellence, moral philosophy and lifelong learning that has enabled me to be a successful surgeon, medical educator and Army officer. The Benedictine tradition learned from the monks, nuns, lay faculty and students provides a deep touchstone of strength, purpose and foundation. When I'm faced with highly complex medical, ethical or leadership problems, I consistently return to the strong principles I learned as a Raven."

LTC Thomas K. Curry, MD, FACS '87
Chief of Trauma Surgery, 47th Combat Support Hospital
Operation Iraqi Freedom
Chief of Vascular Surgery, Tripler Army Medical Center
Honolulu, Hawaii

Fast Facts

Benedictine College is a four-year, private, residential, liberal arts institution steeped in Catholic tradition since 1858.

Web site

http://www.benedictine.edu

Location

Atchison, Kansas—an historic town of 12,000 residents located in northeastern Kansas, just 35 miles north of Kansas City

Student Profile

1,229 full-time undergraduate students (49% male, 51% female); 44 states and territories, 21 countries; 18.4% minority

Faculty Profile

67 full-time faculty. 77% hold a terminal degree in their field. 15:1 student/faculty ratio. Average class size is 23.

Residence Life

Highly residential: 72% of students live on campus. As a residential campus, all freshman, sophomore and junior Benedictine College students live in exceptional campus residence halls.

Athletics

NAIA Division II, Heart of America Athletic Conference (HAAC). 17 varsity sports (8 men's: baseball, basketball, cross-country, football, indoor track & field, outdoor track & field, soccer, tennis; 9 women's: basketball, cross-country, indoor track & field, outdoor track & field, soccer, softball, spirit squad—cheer & dance, tennis, volleyball) and multiple club sports and intramurals.

Academic Programs

Accounting; art; astronomy; athletic training; biochemistry; biology; business administration; chemistry; computer science; criminology; economics; education (elementary, secondary, special); English; finance; French; history; liberal studies; mass communications; mathematics; music; music education; natural science; philosophy; physical education; physics; political science; psychology; religious studies; social science; sociology; Spanish; theatre arts; theatre arts management; youth ministry. Preprofessional and graduate programs are also available.

Costs and Aid

2006–2007: $22,538 comprehensive ($16,060 tuition). 95% of students receive some financial aid. Average award: $17,725

Endowment

$10 million.

More Distinctions

• Benedictine is the alma mater of Dr. Wangari Maathai (1964), the 2004 recipient of the Nobel Peace Prize.

• In a 2005 national survey of more than 162,000 students at 472 colleges, Benedictine College scored in the top 5 percent of master's-level institutions for student-faculty interaction, supportive campus environment, and enriching educational experiences.

Bethel College

KANSAS

Bethel College (BC) is a private, coeducational, four-year, liberal arts college affiliated with the Mennonite Church USA. Founded in 1887, BC is the oldest Mennonite college in North America. BC's foundation on the principles of the Menonite Church means that it has high standards for integrity, scholarship, service, and discipleship.

Admissions Contact:

Bethel College
300 East 27th Street
North Newton, KS 67117
(800) 522-1887 ext. 230
Ph: (316) 283-2500
Email: admissions@bethelks.edu
www.bethelks.edu

The 4 Distinctions

Engaged Students

The Bethel experience integrates faith and learning, and includes internships, undergraduate research, and study abroad. With only about five hundred students, BC offers a student-centered education. BC's small size means students are involved, participating in research, performances, and other college-related activities. The college focuses on providing a multiethnic education.

BC students can choose from study-abroad programs at nineteen colleges and universities in fifteen countries, such as France, Germany, Spain, England, China, Japan, India, Ecuador, Mexico, Costa Rica, Australia, Austria, and Northern Ireland. There is a student exchange program with Wuppertal, Germany, and the college offers other interterm travel courses each year.

Service learning is encouraged on the Bethel campus, and a service-learning scholarship is available to students. A concern for the less fortunate is emphasized at BC, in addition to a focus on the pursuit of peace and pacifism. This commitment to give of oneself for the benefit of others is infused through both curricular and extracurricular activities, including an annual service day and spring break service trip.

The campus community gathers regularly for chapels and convocations where speakers discuss issues relevant to the Bethel campus or society at large. BC students are encouraged to engage in intellectual and faithful reflection, asking speakers to elaborate on items that piqued their interest. This integration extends beyond the chapel and even beyond the core class that all Bethel seniors take, Basic Issues of Faith and Life (BIFL). You will be challenged to stretch your mind and heart over a pizza in the residence hall or while serving your local community.

Great Teaching

BC offers academic excellence, opportunities for participation, a caring community, and faith-based values. BC prepares its students to make a difference. The school's mission is "to be a diverse community of learners committed to searching for authentic faith and academic achievement, providing rigorous instruction in the liberal arts and selected professional areas, and inspiring intellectual, cultural, and spiritual leaders for church and society."

BC offers twenty-one degrees in the arts and sciences. The most popular majors are education, business, and nursing. Nursing is BC's largest program. The low student to faculty ratio of ten to one and small average class size of twenty mean that professors work closely with their students to ensure their learning, growth, and development.

BC's academic program and curriculum are focused on helping students develop intellectual, cultural, and spiritual leadership for the church and society. BC's general education curriculum provides a broad understanding of the social and natural world through the perspective of the liberal arts and sciences, and helps students develop basic capacities in essential academic skills. Required courses in Peace, justice, and conflict resolution help enhance ethical perspectives, inspire service, and integrate intellectual and spiritual values.

College issues colloquy, basic issues of faith and life, and convocation are graduation requirements that bring students together in common educational experiences throughout the standard course of study. Many other programs are integrative and interdisciplinary, as well. All major programs demand focused study, leading to intellectual achievement and laying the groundwork for vocational success.

Some programs, like peace, justice, and conflict studies or Bible and religion, reflect a theologically distinctive idea of educational purpose. Others programs, like nursing and social work, express both the values of service and the requirements for licensure in a specific profession.

Vibrant Community

Two-thirds of BC's students live on campus, and 80 percent are there on weekends, participating in some of the more than fifty student organizations and activities available to them, including a full range of academic, social, and athletic opportunities.

The Mennonites trace their origins to the Anabaptist Reformation movement, whose adherents believe that church membership should be a matter of adult decision rather than infant baptism. Though Mennonites represent the largest single denomination at Bethel, more than half of BC's students come from non-Mennonite backgrounds. Spiritual-life activities include Bible-study groups, praise and worship services, hymn sings, and weekly chapel services. The campus pastor is available to all students.

For BC students from outside Kansas, host families provide a home-away-from-home and welcome visiting family members. Host families might also share a family meal, attend a cultural or sporting event, observe holidays, go to movies, or shop together. Activities shared depend on the interests of both the host family and the student. Many BC students develop relationships with their host families that last for years after they graduate.

North Newton is a small city of 1,500 that grew up around the college. It is twenty-eight miles north of Wichita, and 180 miles southwest of Kansas City. North Newton lies in the midst of vast wheat fields and at the edge of the Flint Hills area of Kansas, home to the Tallgrass Prairie National Preserve, only about an hour away from North Newton. BC's distinctive campus includes the college's administration building, listed on the National Register of Historic Places.

Successful Outcomes

BC students find employment after graduation. Bethel College Athletic Training graduates have enjoyed 100 percent job placement in their first year after certification. In the last 24 years, 100 percent of nursing graduates have obtained jobs immediately upon graduation.

In the last 30 years, approximately two-thirds of the graduates of the Bible and religion program have attended graduate school in religion, pastoral ministry, history, law, social work, education or peace studies. Ten percent of Bethel graduates in English since 1995 have opted for some form of graduate education in a variety of fields (e.g., doctoral degrees, law degrees, various master's degrees). Bethel pre-engineering students enjoy 100 percent acceptance into engineering schools

Since 1987, about half of all biology and natural science graduates successfully pursued PhD and/or MD degrees. Overall, about one out of every seventeen Bethel Bachelor of Arts graduates earns a doctoral degree.

Fast Facts

Bethel College is a four-year, liberal arts college affiliated with the Mennonite Church USA, founded in 1887.

Web site

http://www.bethelks.edu/

Location

North Newton, Kansas—28 miles from Wichita and 180 miles from Kansas City.

Student Profile

541 undergraduate students (52% male, 48% female); 22 states, 19 countries.

Faculty Profile

49 full-time faculty, 22 part-time faculty. 9:1 student/faculty ratio.

Athletics

NAIA Division I, Kansas Collegiate Athletic Conference (KCAC). 14 varsity sports (7 men's: cross-country, football, basketball, track & field, golf, soccer, tennis; 7 women's: basketball, cross-country, golf, soccer, tennis, track & field, volleyball) and club and intramural teams.

Academic Programs

Art; athletic training; Bible & religion; biology; business administration; chemistry; communication arts; computer science; elementary education; English; German; health & physical education; history; mathematical sciences; music; natural sciences; nursing; physics; psychology; social work; Spanish.

Costs and Aid

2006–2007: $23,000 comprehensive ($16,700 tuition). 98% of students receive some financial aid. Average award: $7,339.

Endowment

$18,313,665.

More Distinctions

• Listed as the highest-ranked Kansas college in the national liberal arts category of *U.S. News & World Report's* listing of "America's Best Colleges" for 2008.

• Qualified for the American Forensic Association's National Individual Events Tournament every year since the tournament's beginning in 1978.

• A Templeton character-building college.

• Recognized as part of the first-ever President's Higher Education Community Service Honor Roll.

• In 1996, 2003, and 2007, the Howard Hughes Medical Institute (HHMI) has recognized Bethel College for the high number of its science majors who go on to earn M.D. degrees and/or Ph.D. degrees in the sciences.

Augsburg College

MINNESOTA

Founded in 1869, Augsburg College is a liberal arts institution affiliated with the Evangelical Lutheran Church in America. An education at Augsburg prepares students for service in the community and church, and emphasizes practical experience. Set in a metropolitan area, the college has intentionally created a diverse campus community.

Admissions Contact:

Augsburg College
2211 Riverside Avenue South
Minneapolis, Minnesota 55454
(800) 788-5678
Ph: (612) 330-1001
Email: admissions@augsburg.edu
www.augsburg.edu

The 4 Distinctions

Engaged Students

Minneapolis is an unequaled learning laboratory for Augsburg students. One way students can utilize the city to gain experience is through Augsburg's Center for Service, Work, and Learning. Through the center, students are connected with opportunities to conduct internships and perform community service. More than 60 percent of Augsburg students participate in internship and work-learning experiences that combine classroom theory with practice. Students learn about community issues through course-based service learning as well as other service and volunteer opportunities with Twin Cities schools and organizations. Augsburg students must meet experience requirements for graduation, and many of the experiences coordinated through the Center for Service, Work, and Learning meet those requirements.

100 percent of students serve in the community during their time at Augsburg. Students have participated in service and civic engagement activities such as serving food at a homeless shelter, tutoring at a neighborhood school, working with an environmental organization, and encouraging people to vote. Augsburg is the site for one of only ten Campus Kitchens in the country, where student volunteers turn food donations from campus dining operations into meals and then deliver and serve them at neighborhood community service agencies.

Augsburg gives students many options when it comes to studying abroad. Students can participate in study abroad through Augsburg's national, award-winning Center for Global Education (CGE), Augsburg's International Partners (IP), or the Higher Education Consortium for Urban Affairs (HECUA). CGE focuses on social justice issues, and maintains permanent sites with resident adjunct faculty in Mexico, El Salvador, Guatemala, Nicaragua, and Southern Africa. IP allows students to study at partner schools in Norway, Germany, and Finland. HECUA, of which Augsburg is a founding member, offers study programs in Europe and Latin America that emphasize the impact of civil engagement, social change, and cross-cultural factors in the human community.

Students can travel with other Augsburg students and faculty on short-term, faculty-led programs during the summer and May term. Recent programs have included studying Caribbean music in Jamaica; globalization and women's movements in Nicaragua; World War II and its aftermath in Germany, Poland, and the Czech Republic; and exploring the migrant trail in Mexico.

Great Teaching

Faculty at Augsburg are dedicated, supportive, and engaged in students' lives. The small campus promotes a friendly atmosphere between faculty and students. Augsburg's core curriculum gives students a strong base in the liberal arts and is designed to engage students in an inquiry about their faith and calling in life, and to support them as they engage in meaningful experiences outside of the classroom.

There are many components of the core curriculum, including the Augsburg seminar, as well as courses on the search for meaning, engaging Minneapolis, the Augsburg experience, liberal arts foundations, and a senior capstone. The first-year Augsburg seminar helps students make the transition to college in learning communities based on academic interests. The search for meaning courses allow students to reflect on vocation, identity, and Christian faith, as well as non-Christian faiths. Engaging Minneapolis courses introduce students to life in the Twin Cities by exploring the local arts scene, sampling local ethnic cuisine, and more. The Augsburg experience course links academic study in the broader community through study abroad, an internship, research with a professor, community service learning, or an off-campus immersion project.

Vibrant Community

Augsburg offers students a small campus set in the heart of a big city. The campus consists of eighteen major buildings, and is well-known for its accessibility. A skyway, tunnel, and elevator system allows students to access to twelve major buildings without going outside.

There is something for every student on campus. Athletics have a tradition of excellence at Augsburg, with nearly half of all entering students getting involved in sports at either an intercollegiate or intramural level. There are over eighty other clubs and organizations to choose from, including the Augsburg synchronized figure-skating team, the Augsburgian yearbook, the Coalition for Student Activism, and the Goliard Society of Medievalists.

Because of Augsburg's roots in the Lutheran Free Church, the college has a history of welcoming diverse opinions. Many student groups, such as campus ministry and Fellowship of Christian Athletes exist to provide bible study and fellowship for students of Christian faiths. Students of all faiths can connect with a local place of worship through the campus ministry office.

The performing arts also have a tradition of excellence at Augsburg. There are six main stage theater productions each year. Music ensembles such as Gospel Praise, the Augsburg Choir, and the Riverside Singers also perform regularly, with the major ensembles touring nationally and internationally.

Augsburg's campus is just blocks from downtown and across the street from the University of Minnesota. Students can enjoy nearby lakes and parks, or take the light-rail to the Mall of America. From campus, there is easy access to the metro and the bus, so it is easy for students to get to internships, concerts, and shopping in the city. Augsburg is located in the West Bank theater district, which features many restaurants and small shops.

Successful Outcomes

The Center for Service, Work, and Learning offers career assessments and career coaching to help students choose from among career fields or graduate education options, and provides online job and internship search resources. The center also offers career guidance, job search, and graduate school assistance.

There are now over eighteen thousand Augsburg alumni. Notable alumni include Peter Agre, MD, 2003 Nobel Prize winner in chemistry and vice chancellor for science and technology at Duke University School of Medicine; Reverend Mark Hanson, presiding bishop of the Evangelical Lutheran Church in America; Martin Sabo, former U.S. representative; Janet Letnes Martin and Suzann (Johnson) Nelson, authors and winners of a Minnesota Book Award; and Lute Olson, basketball coach at the universities of Iowa and Arizona, who coached Arizona to a national championship.

"I love that Augsburg encourages you to go out into the city and learn."

Shonna Fulford '09
Perham, Minn.

Fast Facts

Augsburg College is a liberal arts college affiliated with the Evangelical Lutheran Church in America, founded in 1869.

Web site

http://www.augsburg.edu

Location

Minneapolis, Minnesota.

Student Profile

3,785 students (51% male, 49% female); 42 states and 40 countries; 11.5% students of color; 2% international; 32% Lutheran.

Faculty Profile

158 full-time faculty, 193 part-time faculty. 74% hold a terminal degree in their field. 14:1 student/faculty ratio. Average class size is 17.

Residence Life

Moderately residential: 54% live on campus (89% of first-year students).

Athletics

NCAA Division III, Minnesota Intercollegiate Athletic Conference. 18 varsity sports (9 men's: baseball, basketball, cross-country, football, golf, hockey, soccer, track & field, wrestling; 9 women's: basketball, cross-country, golf, hockey, soccer, softball, swimming & diving, track & field, volleyball).

Academic Programs

Accounting; American Indian studies; art history; biology (B.A. or B.S.); business administration; chemistry (B.A. or B.S.); communication studies; computational economics; computer science (B.A. or B.S.); economics; education (elementary, secondary, special education); engineering; English; film; finance; health education (B.A. or B.S.); history; international business; international relations; management; management information systems; marketing; mathematics (B.A. or B.S.); medieval studies; metro-urban studies; modern languages; music (music business, education, performance, therapy); Nordic area studies; nursing (B.S.—Weekend College); philosophy; physical education (B.A. or B.S.); physics (B.A. or B.S.); political science; psychology; religion; social work (B.S.); sociology; student-designed; studio art; theatre arts; women's studies; youth & family ministry.

Costs and Aid

2007–2008: $31,461 comprehensive ($24,046 tuition). Over 80% of students receive some financial aid. Average Award: $12,700.

Endowment

$30 million.

More Distinctions

• Recognized by U.S.News & World Report as an outstanding example of first-year experiences and service-learning (America's Best Colleges 2007).

• Named one of 81 "Colleges With a Conscience" by The Princeton Review.

• Named to the President's Higher Education Community Service Honor Roll.

• Ten-time NCAA Division III wrestling national champions.

The College of St. Catherine

MINNESOTA

The College of St. Catherine is the nation's largest undergraduate college for women. Educating women to lead and influence, the college's learning experience promotes personal growth, critical thinking, and leadership development. Based in the liberal arts, the college offers associate through doctoral degrees.

Admissions Contact:

The College of St. Catherine
2004 Randolph Avenue
St. Paul, MN 55105
(800) 656-KATE
Ph: (651) 690-8850
Email: admissions@stkate.edu
www.stkate.edu

The 4 Distinctions

Engaged Students

The College of St. Catherine is committed to offering financial aid and services that assist women—particularly women of color—in attaining higher education. The current student body includes one of the largest numbers of domestic students of color, 22 percent, among Minnesota's private colleges.

Students are drawn to the College of St. Catherine for innovative academic programs, collaborative and supportive faculty, and leadership development opportunities. Highly regarded for its diverse health care and professional programs, St. Kate's engages students from diverse backgrounds in a learning environment uniquely suited to women to prepare them for ethical leadership grounded in social responsibility.

St. Kate's curricula integrate Catholic social teaching with groundbreaking academic programs designed to propel women into leadership positions in their careers and communities. St. Kate's also partners with schools, agencies, and nonprofit organizations for community work and learning opportunities. In these service-learning settings, students apply their education to contribute more fully to their communities and the world.

Global opportunities for community work and learning take students to India to study the social justice aspects of women and work, to South Africa to learn about apartheid, or to Mexico to understand feminism and healing from an indigenous perspective.

St. Kate's growth has come from focusing on the school's vision to educate women to lead and influence, working collaboratively to both serve and learn from communities, and positioning students for future success. The college's exceptional reputation attracts leading companies from across the country to offer students outstanding internship opportunities.

Great Teaching

In 1937, the College of St. Catherine became the first Catholic college in the nation to be granted a chapter of the prestigious Phi Beta Kappa for academic excellence. St. Kate's faculty members are highly regarded in their professional disciplines and more than half—55 percent—are women, while 82 percent of full-time faculty members hold a doctorate or the highest degree in their field.

The student to faculty ratio of eleven to one means that faculty members, not teaching assistants, teach classes at St. Catherine's.

From the core first-year course, The Reflective Woman, to the senior core class, The Global Search for Justice, students learn to understand complex issues, to defend a point of view, to solve problems ethically, and to communicate effectively.

Unique programs include majors in critical studies of race and ethnicity and business-to-business sales, as well as minors in civic engagement and STEM (science, technology, engineering, and math). In addition, St. Kate's was the first college in the upper Midwest to offer Master of Arts programs in Organizational Leadership and Holistic Health. Adapting to the needs of working women, the college was the first in the upper Midwest to offer baccalaureate programs in a weekend college format in 1979.

In 2000, the college formed several centers of excellence, including the Center for Women, Science and Technology, to promote opportunities for students to engage in interdisciplinary collaborations with faculty and community partners. Focusing on issues that face women locally, nationally, and internationally, the centers of excellence support innovative teaching and research in order to broaden understanding, stimulate action, and affect change.

St. Kate's also provides a number of resources to help students achieve their academic potential, including the Abigail Quigley McCarthy Center for Women, which supports spiritual and intellectual development, and the O'Neill Center for Academic Development, which offers programs, services, and facilities promoting academic achievement through a writing and reading center, a math center, and a center of resources for disabilities. In addition, St. Kate's students have access to online databases as well as a traditional library and academic consortium.

Vibrant Community

With beautiful campuses in a dynamic urban setting, St. Catherine's environment is socially engaging and intellectually empowering. The College of St. Catherine has campuses in both Minneapolis and St. Paul, with regular shuttle bus service between campuses. The Minneapolis campus houses many of the college's health care specialties and is adjacent to a major health care system.

The college's St. Paul campus is situated on more than one hundred wooded acres in the heart of Highland Village, one of St. Paul's most welcoming neighborhoods. St. Kate's recently constructed two new residence halls, one of which will house a learning community. In 2004, the college dedicated a new student center and learning commons, Coeur de Catherine.

St. Kate's is home to twenty-four honor societies, three student publications, thirty student groups, an active student government, several musical ensembles, theater productions, and various volunteer projects led and organized by students. Students plan many of the campus events, including karaoke, movies, cultural celebrations, and trips out and about in the Twin Cities.

The college offers nine intercollegiate sports (MIAC and Division III) and a number of intramural activities. The campus features the Aimee and Patrick Butler Center for Sports and Fitness, a state-of-the-art sports, workout, and spa facility.

One of the Twin Cities' premier cultural venues, the O'Shaughnessy is home to the Women of Substance series, celebrating women artists and lecturers. The O'Shaughnessy presents a full season of music, dance, speakers, and more, with substantial discounts for students and college alumni.

Successful Outcomes

With more than forty thousand alumni nationwide, the College of St. Catherine appears on the resumes of notable women in science and health care, business, government, writing, and the arts and education, including U.S. representative Betty McCollum; Weber Shandwick Worldwide managing director Sara Hietpas Gavin; Janet Dolan, former president and CEO of Tennant Company; U.S. ambassador to Moldova, Heather Hodges; and sour-cream-and-onion-flavored potato chips inventor, Emily Niemeyer Anderson.

St. Kate's alumni actively assist students in internship, job shadowing, and networking programs. The college's alumni office offers opportunities to meet, network, and share interests with other Katies across the country.

Career preparation is a vital process throughout the College of St. Catherine learning experience. The college's career development office helps students discover their career interests, develop interviewing skills, and prepare e-portfolios. The office also holds campus job fairs to give students the opportunity to meet recruiters, while a variety of employers interview on campus throughout the academic year.

Approximately 25 percent of St. Kate's graduates go on to complete advanced degrees within five years of completing their bachelor's degrees.

Fast Facts

The College of St. Catherine is a private, non-profit founded by the Sisters of St. Joseph of Carondelet in 1905 and affiliated with the Roman Catholic Church.

Website

http:// www.stkate.edu

Location

Campuses in St. Paul and Minneapolis, Minnesota.

Student Profile

5,246 students (5.9% male, 94.1% female); 37 states and territories; 22.5% minority and international.

Faculty Profile

261 full-time faculty. 11:1 student/faculty ratio. Average class size is 13.

Residence Life

Moderately residential: 37% of students live on campus.

Athletics

NCAA Division III, Minnesota Intercollegiate Athletic Conference (MIAC) Conference. 9 varsity sports: basketball, cross-country, hockey, soccer, softball, swimming & diving, tennis, track & field, volleyball).

Intramural/Recreation: tennis, dodgeball, badminton, floor hockey, kickball, 3 on 3 basketball.

Academic Programs

Accounting; American Sign Language; apparel design; art history; biology; business-to-business sales; chemistry; communication; communication studies; communication arts & literature; critical studies of race & ethnicity; dietetics; economics; education; electronic media studies; English; exercise & sports science; exercise science/nutrition; family & consumer science; fashion merchandising; financial economics; foods & nutrition; foodservice management; French; healthcare management; healthcare sales; history; information systems; international business & economics; international relations; interpreting; marketing & management; mathematics; music; nursing; occupational science; philosophy; political science; psychology; respiratory care; small business/entrepreneurship; social studies; social work; sociology; Spanish; studio art; theater; theology.

Preprofessional: dentistry, engineering, law, medicine, occupational therapy, optometry, pharmacy, physical therapy, veterinary medicine.

Dual-Degree Programs: occupational therapy, physical therapy.

Costs and Aid

2007–2008: $25,664 comprehensive ($802 per credit tuition). 90% of students receive some financial aid. Average award: $10,000.

Endowment

$48,201,758.

More Distinctions

• Largest college for women in the United States.

• First Catholic institution awarded a Phi Beta Kappa Chapter in 1937.

Hamline University

MINNESOTA

A comprehensive university located in Saint Paul, Minnesota, Hamline's schools offer undergraduate, graduate and law degrees.

Admissions Contact:

Hamline University
1536 Hewitt Avenue
Saint Paul, MN 55104-1284
(800) 753-9753
Fax: (651) 523-2458
Email: cla-admis@hamline.edu
www.hamline.edu

The 4 Distinctions

Engaged Students

Hamline has deep roots in Minnesota; the college was founded in 1854 by Methodist pioneers and was the first institute of higher education in the state. Hamline students may choose from a wide variety of majors, and the school excels in many areas, including teaching, research, and scholarship. Hamline's students learn in a diverse community that focuses on the development of values and skills for life after graduation.

Hamline has thirty-seven undergraduate majors, and each line of study places importance on critical thinking and leadership. Hamline's liberal arts education teaches students how to apply practical solutions to their educational foundations and future careers. Students take part in the Hamline Plan, a goal-oriented general education program designed to connect learning and life skills to a liberal arts education. The Hamline Plan focuses on the life skills of writing, speaking, technological competency, critical thinking, formal reasoning, disciplinary breadth, cultural understanding, collaborative and independent learning, internship, and research skills.

In addition to academic pursuits, Hamline's location in the heart of the vibrant, metropolitan area of the Twin Cities provides students with endless cultural, recreational, and professional opportunities. Service learning, volunteerism, student leadership, and participation in a number of organizations are just some of the many cocurricular opportunities students choose from to support their learning.

Hamline also offers a variety of study-abroad programs, and students are permitted to participate in programs of up to one academic year in length. About 35 percent of Hamline's graduating seniors have chosen to study abroad or participate in an overseas intercultural experience in locations all over the world. The university offers shorter study-abroad sessions during the January term and in May as extended spring-term courses.

Hamline students' community involvement pays off. The National Survey of Student Engagement lists Hamline students as more likely than others to think critically and become actively engaged in the classroom. The survey also found that Hamline students are exceptionally involved with their communities.

Great Teaching

The student to faculty ratio at Hamline is thirteen to one, lending a small college feel to a metropolitan university. Almost 94 percent of Hamline's teachers hold the highest degree in their field. Each entering first-year student is required to register for a first-year seminar, which provides students with an introduction to college-level learning in a small-class environment and community. First-year seminars comprise sixteen to eighteen students, and focus on a specific topic that allows the class members to develop reading, thinking, social, and writing skills.

Hamline offers a traditional set of majors and programs, as well as specialized fields of study, such as its 3/3 law program with the Hamline University School of Law; certificate programs in forensic science, international journalism, and conflict studies; and its major in social justice, which focuses on social problems and prepares students for leadership and service positions. The social-justice program teaches students to analyze social problems and discover solutions. Students who choose this major are expected to test their skills off campus and in the community. The social-justice program prepares students for careers in legislative advocacy, social work, and service positions.

Vibrant Community

Hamline's location between the twin cities of Minneapolis and Saint Paul offers students the best of urban and residential life. The university's 60 acre campus includes both modern and traditional buildings with ample outdoor space and convenient entertainment and shopping centers in the community.

Special housing for students includes the first-year experience floors, where first-year students live and are involved in a program designed to assist with the transition into college life. Resident and community advisers on these floors ensure that there are always activities on the schedule both during the week and on weekends.

Hamline students participate in a large variety of extracurricular activities, including nineteen Division III athletic teams in the Minnesota Intercollegiate Athletic Conference. Hamline has had considerable success with its cross-country team, and was one of the first colleges to offer competitive team-oriented basketball, which was brought to the school in 1893; a women's program was organized two years later. Hamline was also host of the first intercollegiate basketball game in history.

The Hamline University Student Congress is a popular organization that allows students to work with the university's staff to plan campuswide events. Hamline also offers students seventy clubs and organizations to choose from. Whether students are interested in art, dance, acting, or the environment, there are many organizations that fit their interests. Hamline also offers several religious organizations, including the gospel choir, InterVarsity Christian Fellowship, Jewish Students Association, Buddhist meditation, Muslim prayer, and the United Methodist Student Movement.

Successful Outcomes

Hamline's Career Development Center (CDC) exists to help students plan their lives after graduation. First-year through senior students receive specialized guidance to help them decide which educational path will lead to a fulfilling career. The CDC also prepares students by having them participate in mock interviews and job shadowing, and by helping students secure internships.

Hamline sends annually one of the largest contingents of undergraduate researchers to the National Conference on Undergraduate Research (NCUR). Students also present their independent research at local, national, and international conferences, distinguishing our graduates as confident leaders in their chosen fields of study.

The Collaborative Research Program funds student research in a variety of academic fields and provides an opportunity to pursue specific, innovative research in close collaboration with faculty members. Students receive a generous stipend that allows them to focus fully on their summer research interests. In addition, students attend weekly seminars with the scholarly community to share their progress. This hands-on approach to research and investigation provides students with opportunities to personalize their education and provide an outstanding preparation for graduate study or their first career.

Fast Facts

Hamline University is a nationally ranked liberal arts university, affiliated with the United Methodist Church and founded in 1854.

Web site

http://www.hamline.edu

Location

Saint Paul, Minnesota.

Student Profile

1,902 undergraduate students (39% male, 61% female); 30 states and 31 countries; 14% minority, 4% international.

Faculty Profile

110 full-time faculty. 94% faculty hold the highest degree in their field. 13:1 student/faculty ratio. Average class size is 18.

Residence Life

Highly residential: 90% of first-year students live on campus.

Athletics

NCAA Division III, Minnesota Intercollegiate Athletic Conference. 19 varsity sports (9 men's: baseball, basketball, cross-country, football, hockey, soccer, swimming & diving, tennis, track & field; 10 women's: basketball, cross-country, fast-pitch softball, gymnastics, hockey, soccer, swimming & diving, tennis, track & field, volleyball). Intramural Sports include: bowling, golf, karate, lacrosse, racquetball, tennis, volleyball, water polo, and weight lifting.

Academic Programs

American law & legal systems; anthropology; art history; art; biochemistry; biology; business management; chemistry; communication studies; criminal justice; East Asian studies; economics; English; environmental studies; exercise and sport science; French; German; global studies; history; international business management; Latin American studies; legal studies; mathematics; music; philosophy; physical education; physics; political science; psychology; religion; social justice; social studies; sociology; Spanish; theater arts; urban studies; women's studies. Preprofessional programs and certificates: dentistry, engineering, law, medicine, physical therapy, veterinary medicine, conflict studies, education (elementary, secondary, K-12), forensic science, international journalism, occupational therapy, paralegal. Dual degree programs: 3/3 law and 3/2 and 4/2 engineering.

Costs and Aid

2007–2008: $35,206 comprehensive ($26,060 tuition). 84% of students receive some financial aid. Average award: $25,932.

Endowment

$66.8 million.

More Distinctions

• Tied to rank ninth out of 141 Midwest comprehensive universities by *U.S.News & World Report* magazine.

• *Peterson's*, and *U.S.News and World Report* list Hamline's liberal arts college in the top ranks for academic excellence.

Avila University

MISSOURI

Avila University (AU) is a Roman Catholic, coeducational, comprehensive, liberal arts and professional university sponsored by the Sisters of St. Joseph of Carondelet. Founded as St. Teresa Junior College in 1916, AU became coeducational in 1969 and a university in 2002.

Admissions Contact:

Avila University
11901 Wornall Road
Kansas City, MO 64145
Ph: (816)942-8400
Email: admission@avila.edu
www.avila.edu

The 4 Distinctions

Engaged Students

AU offers more than thirty-five major fields of study. The most popular majors are nursing, education, business, and psychology. The school's strongest program is nursing, as it has been since AU's founding as a nursing school for women.

Semester study-abroad programs take AU students to Thailand, Spain, England, Switzerland, the Netherlands, Austria, China, and Japan. Service projects also are available, and athletes are required to participate. To help build ties to the community, first-year students take a service class that focuses on efforts such as working at a local food bank.

AU students go into the real world and put their knowledge into action. They come away from an internship, clinical, or practicum with the assurance that the Avila experience has prepared them for success. From the Kansas City Chiefs to Sprint, from St. Joseph Health Center to Hallmark Cards. Kansas City employers appreciate having Avila students working for them in internships - and look for them when they're ready to start their careers.

The focus of the First-Year Seminar at AU is building community. First year students will work with a mentor, learning about and responding to a community need while examining topics important for college success, such as cultural diversity, interpersonal relationships, time-management, health and wellness, and other topics of the students' choosing.

Great Teaching

Throughout its history, AU has maintained its commitment to excellence in teaching and learning in an environment that stresses responsible service to others and respects the uniqueness of each person, including tolerance for a diversity of religious convictions.

AU students work closely with their professors, taking advantage of the low student to faculty ratio of twelve to one and the small class size, typically under twenty. Faculty cultivate and maintain relationships with the wider community to foster internship possibilities, required of all AU students except those in the business program. For example, AU students participate in clinical internships under the nursing and radiological science departments; education majors practice student teaching; and graphic design students and students from other majors work at Hallmark or at local radio stations.

AU's unique radiological science program, one of only thirty-five accredited programs in the country, prepares graduates to be employed as registered technologists in radiology departments. Registered radiographers teach and advise students in clinical sites with student to faculty ratios that never exceed ten to one.

Arts/communications faculty have connections throughout the city, making it possible for their students to participate in course work that is 85 percent hands-on. The students have their own broadcasting studio and perform work for companies in the Kansas City area beyond their in-class assignments.

The political science department also encourages student involvement in off-campus activities, including trips to Washington, DC, to see Congress enact legislation and participation in mock-trial competitions, which are open to all students.

Vibrant Community

AU is "a welcoming community, a university engaged with its neighbors that prepares students to be competent, yet compassionate professionals who work to make a difference." AU's on-campus community is diverse, with 28 percent of its undergraduates representing minorities and one-third of its students coming from out-of-state. In the spring, the university features a monthlong diversity celebration, including a week of food tasting from different cultures. All residence halls are coeducational, and all classes live together. A new suite-style dormitory for juniors and seniors is under construction.

There are more than thirty clubs and organizations for AU students to join, such as the student senate, the Black Student Union, and the campus newspaper, The Talon. Named for AU's mascot, the Eagle, the on-campus Eagles' Nest is a students' lounge with television and air hockey.

AU's forty-eight-acre campus is about ten miles south of downtown Kansas City and is within a half mile of the Kansas state line. Located in an upscale, suburban area, shopping and coffee shops are close by and are especially popular with AU's international students.

Kansas City is called the City of Fountains for the more than two hundred found throughout the city, more than in any city except Rome, Italy. Located at the junction of the Missouri and Kansas Rivers, not far from the geographic and population centers of the United States, Kansas City is the seventh largest city in the Midwest, with wide-ranging and sophisticated urban features such as world-class cultural institutions and events, professional sports, and legendary barbecue.

AU draws neighbors and community residents to its cultural events, such as poetry readings and theatrical performances. In 2007, Sister Helen Prejean gave a sold-out lecture in conjunction with performances of her play, Dead Man Walking.

Successful Outcomes

AU students gain practical experience and develop the professionalism that will set them apart. Starting freshman year, students join a network of highly successful alumni who will help students through the Alumni Mentoring Programs as a student and again through the Alumni Association once they graduate. It's no wonder 96% of Avila's graduates are in career-path jobs or graduate school.

AU students are successful: 95 percent hold jobs or are in graduate school within six months of graduation. Alumni are increasingly active in their support, and an alumni basketball tournament is especially popular. One famous alumnus is Alicia Cabrera-Hill, Miss Kansas USA 2003 and the first AU student to study abroad.

Fast Facts

Avila University is a Catholic, four-year, private, coeducational university by the Sisters of St. Joseph of Carondelet and founded in 1916.

Web site

http:// www.avila.edu

Location

Kansas City, Missouri.

Student Profile

900 full-time undergraduate students (52% male, 48% female); 31% minority, 4% international.

Faculty Profile

65 full-time faculty, 139 part-time faculty. 13:1 student/faculty ratio. Average class size is 18.

Residence Life

25% of students live on campus. Students are required to live on campus for the first two years if they are from outside the Kansas City metro area

Athletics

Member of the NAIA, Heart of America Athletic Conference. 11 varsity sports (4 men's: baseball, basketball, soccer, football; 7 women's: basketball, cheerleading, dance team, soccer, volleyball, golf, softball).

Academic Programs

Accounting; acting; advertising/public relation; art; art education; biochemistry; biology; business; business administration; business education; chemistry; communication; computer science; criminal justice; directing/producing; education (elementary education, middle school education, secondary education, special education); English; film & digital media; finance; general sociology; graphic design; health programs (prechiropractic, predental, premedicine, preoptometry, preosteopathic, prepharmacy, preveterinary); history; human behavior; international business; literature; management; management information systems; marketing; mathematics education; medical technology; music; musical theatre; music education; nursing; occupational therapy; organizational dynamics; physical therapy; piano; political science; preart therapy; prelaw; psychology; radiological science; religious studies; research; social work; sociology; sports science; technical theatre/design; theatre; voice; writing.

Costs and Aid

2007-2008: $18,300 tuition. Average financial aid award: $11,000 ($6,400 in scholarships and grants).

Endowment

$6.7 million.

Saint Louis University

MISSOURI

Saint Louis University (SLU) is a coeducational, Jesuit, Catholic university, founded in 1818. With campuses in Saint Louis, Missouri, and in Madrid, Spain, SLU fosters intellectual and character development among more than 7,400 undergraduate students through teaching, research, health care, and community-service activities.

Admissions Contact:

Saint Louis University
DuBourg Hall, Room 119
221 N. Grand Blvd.
St. Louis, MO 63103-2097
(800) SLU-FOR-U
Ph: (314) 977-2500
Email: admitme@slu.edu
www.slu.edu

The 4 Distinctions

Engaged Students

Known as a place "where knowledge touches lives," Saint Louis University offers students a myriad of ways to learn outside the classroom, including study-abroad programs, service-learning opportunities, internships, and undergraduate research. The university offers more than eighty-five programs of study and 170 student organizations to help students expand their horizons, explore their talents, and make a difference in their communities.

Most Saint Louis University students who study abroad do so during their sophomore or junior years. More than five hundred students study abroad each year, with terms away ranging from a single semester or summer session to a full academic year. In addition to opportunities at the university's Madrid campus, established in 1969 and endorsed as an official foreign university by the Spanish government, Saint Louis University students can also visit countries such as the Netherlands, France, Italy, or Belgium.

Internships and co-op opportunities are widely available, thanks mainly to the university's prominent location near the hub of Saint Louis's multifaceted economy. Most students participate in at least one internship or practicum during their college careers, making experiential learning the norm rather than the exception.

Undergraduate research opportunities at Saint Louis University allow students to develop skills and enhance their academic or professional credentials while learning about a subject from the inside out. One SLU student worked on research projects for NASA, while others assisted with psychology studies and worked in medical research labs on campus.

Service learning opportunities also augment the curriculum at Saint Louis University. One of the most well-known, university-wide activities is SLU's annual Make a Difference Day, during which student volunteers disperse throughout the city to perform community-service projects. Students also perform service work through alternative spring breaks sponsored by campus ministry. Additional service-learning opportunities are available to first-year students through the Micah Program, in which participants share a classroom and residential experience while also tutoring in inner-city schools, rehabilitating underprivileged neighborhoods and participating in service trips to Latin America.

Great Teaching

Saint Louis University offers more than eighty-five undergraduate majors and more than fifty graduate and professional programs, including highly ranked programs in business, law, and engineering. The most popular majors are biology; physical therapy, with a six-year direct-entry doctorate program; psychology; nursing, which takes advantage of three nearby hospitals; and communication, whose versatile offerings reflect the diversity of the local economy. The university also features a medical school and a new eighty-million-dollar medical research building.

The university's low student to faculty ratio of twelve to one and small average class size of twenty-four ensure that students get to know and work closely with their professors. Of SLU's full-time faculty, 99 percent hold a PhD or another terminal degree in their field, meaning that they have completed their education and have a great deal of time to devote to student needs.

First-year students can take advantage of University 101, a course designed to enhance their success in college. Sections of this small, interactive class are limited to twenty students or fewer and are taught by a faculty or staff member and an upper-level student leader. SLU inquiry courses are yet another special offering for first-year students. These small classes of twenty or fewer feature an engaging, discussion-based learning model, helping students to focus on collaborative problem solving and to better connect with their teachers.

At Saint Louis University, the core curriculum requirements vary according to a student's particular program of study. Reflecting the university's Jesuit roots and affiliation, academics are rigorous, and all students take classes in theology and philosophy.

Vibrant Community

On average, 85 percent of Saint Louis University's first-year students live on campus, and most off-campus residents live close by. All first-year students live in one of two complexes. Nine hundred students live in the three-building Griesedieck Complex, and four hundred students live in Reinert Hall. Living together enhances the first-year experience and helps students stay connected to one another and to the university itself. Upper-level students can live in coed residence halls with single-sex floors or in on-campus apartments. SLU's variety of housing options contributes to the overall feeling of community.

SLU offers more than 170 student organizations and clubs, providing many opportunities for students to make connections. The student activities board coordinates most of the concerts, comedians, and other entertainers who visit campus, presenting an array of events that reflects the diversity of students and interests on campus.

Athletics at SLU are strong; the university participates in NCAA Division I athletics as part of the Atlantic 10 Conference, and also offers a wide-range of intramural and club sports. The campus features a newly renovated recreation center, and the Chaifetz Arena, now under construction, will be ready to host Billiken basketball games beginning in March 2008.

Saint Louis University's location in midtown Saint Louis gives it a dynamic, central location in a city of 2.8 million people, well-known for its urban amenities such as great restaurants, top-quality cultural events, major-league sports, and unique neighborhoods.

Saint Louis University students enjoy nearby off-campus dining in the Hill, an Italian neighborhood or coffee shops in the adjacent Central West End area. Saint Louis University students can take advantage of discount tickets to professional music, dance, and theater events at Powell Symphony Hall and the Fabulous Fox Theatre, both of which are located just down the block from campus.

Successful Outcomes

Saint Louis University alumni are employed quickly after graduation. Seniors receive training to help them transition to postcollege life, including interview preparation, etiquette lessons, and resume reviews. In a recent survey of graduates, 94 percent reported that they were either employed or enrolled in graduate or professional school within six months of graduation; 100 percent of physical therapy students had jobs shortly after graduating. SLU also boasts twenty-one alumni clubs across the country, from California to Boston, to help bolster students' connections and networking opportunities.

Fast Facts

Saint Louis University is a research-extensive, coeducational university, affiliated with the Society of Jesus (Jesuits) and founded in 1818, the oldest university west of the Mississippi River.

Web site

http://www.slu.edu

Location

St. Louis, Missouri.

Student Profile

7,479 undergraduate students (42% male, 58% female); from all 50 states and 84 foreign countries; 60% of freshmen come from outside the St. Louis metropolitan area; 72% white/Caucasian, 8% African-American, 5% Asian or Pacific Islander, 2% Hispanic/Latino, 13% other/not specified.

Faculty Profile

12:1 student/faculty ratio. Average class size is 24.

Residence Life

Highly residential.

Athletics

NCAA Division I, Atlantic 10 Conference; 16 varsity sports (7 men's: basketball, baseball, cross-country, soccer, swimming & diving, tennis, track & field; 9 women's: basketball, cross-country, field hockey, soccer, softball, swimming & diving, tennis, volleyball, track & field); 23 club sports and 5 intramurals.

Academic Programs

Accounting; aerospace engineering; aircraft maintenance management; American studies; art history; athletic training; biochemistry; biology; biomedical engineering; chemistry; classical humanities; clinical laboratory science; communication; communication sciences & disorders; computer science; criminal justice; Cytotechnology; economics (arts & sciences); economics (business); education (early childhood, elementary, middle school, secondary, special-behavior disorders, special-early childhood; special-learning disabilities, special-mental handicaps); electrical engineering; electronics engineering technology; English; entrepreneurship; environmental science; finance; flight science; French; geology; geophysics; German; Greek & Latin languages & literature; health information management; history; human resource management; interdisciplinary contract; international business; international studies; investigative & medical sciences; leadership & change management; management information systems; marketing; mathematics; mechanical engineering; mechanical engineering technology; meteorology; modern & classical languages; music; nuclear medicine technology; nursing; nutrition & dietetics; occupational science & occupational therapy; philosophy; physical therapy; physics (arts & sciences); physics (engineering); political science; psychology; radiation therapy; Russian; social work; sociology; Spanish; still deciding; studio art; theatre; theological studies; urban affairs; women's studies. Preprofessional programs in dental, law, medical, optometry, physician assistant, podiatry, and veterinary.

Costs and Aid

2007–2008: $37,030 comprehensive ($28,480 tuition). 90% of students receives some financial aid.

Stephens College

MISSOURI

Admissions Contact:

Stephens College
1200 E. Broadway
Columbia, MO 65215
(800) 876-7207
Ph: (573) 876-7207
Fax: (573) 876-7237
Email: apply@stephens.edu
www.stephens.edu

Stephens College is a private, four-year college in the Midwest. Founded in 1833, Stephens is the second-oldest women's college in the nation, providing an innovative educational experience focused on preprofessional fields and the performing arts, and grounded in the liberal arts.

The 4 Distinctions

Engaged Students

Stephens students learn through experiences beyond the classroom, including study abroad, internships, and hands-on projects. On average, 82 percent of students participate in an internship before graduation, and those who wish to study abroad can choose from numerous programs. Fashion students can take advantage of unique programs in fashion-forward cities and countries such as Paris, New York, and Italy. A special relationship with AOL Corporate Events gives Stephens students the opportunity to intern on teams in the international sector, which has led to permanent employment.

Internships and hands-on projects help students gain practical experience and define their career goals. Depending on their interest area, Stephens students have conducted research at hospitals and laboratories; worked with children in local schools; and interned at Donna Karan and *Women's Wear Daily* in New York City, at equestrian facilities, at the White House, for the Smithsonian Institution, and in network television. Film students have collaborated on projects with visiting filmmakers, completed their own work, and volunteered for credit during Columbia's True/False Film Festival.

Stephens also has one of the leading undergraduate theatre programs in the country. A handful of men are enrolled as apprentice actors in the program. In addition to on-campus opportunities, students spend a summer at the college-owned and professionally operated Okoboji Summer Theatre in the tourist lake region of Iowa. Celebrating fifty years, 'Boji allows students to participate in every facet of commercial theatrical production. The ten-week season usually sells out, and features nine adult plays as well as four plays for children.

Great Teaching

Stephens is committed to its unique array of disciplines. More than 80 percent of students choose to major in a creative field. The School of Performing Arts and the School of Design and Fashion both provide preprofessional training, increasing students' marketability in their fields of interest. Study trips, master classes with visiting professionals, and the chance to work in a student-run theatre or to put on a student-organized fashion show are just a few of the opportunities for students at Stephens.

There are more than fifty undergraduate majors and minors at Stephens. The most popular majors are fashion, theatre/dance, education, psychology, equestrian, and business. Entrepreneurship is growing in popularity and provides solid business training for any major. Students may also design their own majors. Preprofessional study is available in engineering, law, dentistry, medicine, and veterinary medicine.

Most of the Stephens faculty have a Ph.D. or a terminal degree in their field. Faculty are committed to teaching and to women's education. They frequently conduct research (often working with students), publish papers, and present at conferences across the country. Often, students and faculty are on a first-name basis with one another, and faculty and staff can be found at the college's midnight breakfast, serving students a late meal as part of a fun stress reliever before final exams.

The Ten Ideals is a college tradition that originated in 1921, and it continues to function as the core set of values enriching the lives of Stephens women. The entire Stephens community stresses these Ideals (e.g. leadership, independence) and builds them into daily life, making them an integral part of the Stephens College culture.

Vibrant Community

Stephens students live on campus throughout their college experience, housed in close proximity to classes, the dining hall, professors, peers, and campus programming. There are six residence halls; two additional halls have recently undergone historic renovation, and now feature modern amenities. Residence halls, some with hardwood floors and high ceilings, have single rooms on a first-come, first-served basis. New, on-campus apartments are available for upper-level students. A limited number of pet rooms are available for students who want to room with their dog or cat.

In addition to a comprehensive array of extracurricular activities, Stephens offers a full-fledged NAIA athletic program.

The city of Columbia is home to more than ninety thousand residents and two other colleges: the University of Missouri and Columbia College. Stephens women may register for classes at either school at no additional charge—and vice versa—and the schools' central locations make it easy for students to take advantage of the program.

Known as Collegetown, USA, Columbia is located in central Missouri, and ranks high on lists of top cities in the nation. Offering the warm hospitality of the Midwest, Columbia has a good safety record, excellent educational facilities, high-quality health care, strong economic growth, broad cultural opportunities, and a low cost of living, all of which combine to make it an attractive setting for a college as well as for residential living. Columbia's lively downtown—just a few blocks from Stephens—offers restaurants, live music, bookstores, coffeehouses, art galleries, and more. The MKT Nature and Fitness Trail and a myriad of parks are not far away.

Local residents visit the eighty-six-acre Stephens campus for events such as poetry readings, lectures, or for productions or events that allow students to share their work with the public.

Successful Outcomes

Approximately 86 percent of Stephens' graduates are employed within one year of graduating. About 25 percent of students go directly on to graduate or law school. The college's career development office utilizes a variety of venues to connect students and faculty with employers. The Alumnae Career Connection, a database of alumnae contacts, is a resource for students interested in advice or assistance regarding employment.

Stephens women join a supportive and connected network of thirty thousand alumnae across the world, including the late Jeane Jordan Kirkpatrick, first woman to serve as U.S. ambassador to the United Nations; CNN news anchor Paula Zahn; actress Annie Potts; and Alanna Nash, feature writer for *Entertainment Weekly* and the *New York Times*. The Stephens Alumnae Association fosters networking among graduates.

Many Stephens alumnae return to campus to share their knowledge, experience, and connections with students. Annie Potts, star of *Designing Women*, *Ghostbusters*, and the Lifetime network's *Any Day Now*, completed a four-week artist residency on campus, acting alongside students. Anne-Louise Wallace, stage manager for the *Today Show*, *Sesame Street*, and Macy's Thanksgiving Day Parade, spoke at the opening convocation and in Stephens' classes. Fashion experts like Camille Palmer, a Gap Inc. technical designer, whose work has appeared on the cover of *Vogue*, return for the annual fashion show and critique student work.

Fast Facts

Stephens College is a women's college founded in 1833. It is one of the oldest institutions of higher learning for women in the country.

Web site

http://www.stephens.edu

Location

Columbia, Missouri—approximately 120 miles from both Kansas City and St. Louis.

Student Profile

725 residential undergraduates; approximately 50% of students out-of-state; women from nearly every state and several countries outside the U.S.

Faculty Profile

Approximately 50 full-time faculty. 13:1 student/faculty ratio. Average class size is 13.

Residence Life

Highly residential: students are required to live on campus throughout their four years.

Athletics

NAIA Athletics. 6 varsity sports: basketball, swimming, tennis, volleyball, softball, and cross-country.

Academic Programs

Accounting; biology; broadcasting (mass media: TV and radio); business; child development; commercial media writing; creative writing; dance; education (early childhood, elementary education); English; English & women's studies; entrepreneurship & business management; equestrian business management; equestrian science; fashion communication; fashion design & product development; fashion marketing & management; film; graphic design; human development; interior design; journalism (mass media); legal studies; liberal studies; marketing (public relations and advertising); psychology; public relations (mass media); studio art; theatre arts; theatre management; theatrical costume design; writing & language. Partnerships with other institutions allow additional study in animal science, law, occupational therapy, physical therapy and physician assistant studies.

Costs and Aid

2007–2008: $29,970 comprehensive ($21,730 tuition). 95% of students receive financial aid.

Endowment

$20 million.

More Distinctions

• The Princeton Review's Best 361 College Rankings named Stephens 11th in its "Class Discussions Encouraged" category, No. 10 for "Town-Gown Relations are Great" and No. 6 in the nation for "Best College Theatre."

Truman State University

MISSOURI

Admissions Contact:

Truman State University
100 E. Normal
Kirksville, MO 63501
(800) 892-7792
Ph: (660) 785-4114
Email: admissions@truman.edu
www.truman.edu

The Midwest is known for its hospitality and less-hectic pace of living. Truman State University students enjoy both. The university is consistently ranked as one of the Midwest's finest public universities, and the quality of education offered at Truman is worthy of such prestigious rankings.

The 4 Distinctions

Engaged Students

Truman works hard to sustain and support a diverse culture, and more than 9 percent of its student body are African American, Asian, Hispanic, or Native American.

The Truman Study Abroad Program provides students with opportunities to study in over forty countries around the world. Semester, yearlong, and summer programs are available for virtually ever major that Truman offers. About 25 percent of Truman students travel abroad during their college careers to destinations like Austria, Brazil, China, Fiji, France, Germany, Ghana, Korea, Malta, New Zealand, and Thailand.

The Truman in Washington Program offers students the opportunity to experience an internship in the Washington D.C. setting. Internships are available in a wide array of areas including international relations, fine and performing arts, environmental policy, criminal justice, and many other areas. Placement sites have included the U.S. Department of Defense, the Smithsonian, the Heritage Foundation, U.S. senators, and much more.

Part of the liberal arts experience is opening your mind to different cultures and new experiences. Truman's cultural programming facilitates this by hosting speakers and events for all students; a small sample includes *Mythbusters'* Jamie Hyneman and Adam Savage, politician Ralph Nader, and rock band Yellowcard.

Truman's Residential College Program offers all freshman students and many upperclassmen the chance to experience a living/learning community by bringing an academic focus to some of the activities and relationships developed within the residence halls. The Residential College Program facilitates personal engagement in liberal arts learning through small seminars conducted over meals, evenings of Great Conversation, Nights at the University Gallery, and field trips.

Great Teaching

Truman faculty members, all accomplished scholars and professionals in their fields, are eager to share their knowledge with students. Professors are accessible in and out of the classroom to answer questions, give help on an assignment, or discuss the day's events.

The liberal studies program is at the heart of all of Truman's academic majors. This unique program develops and strengthens skills essential to lifelong learning, ranging from writing and speaking to using information technology and solving mathematics-based problems.

The portfolio project at Truman is a great way for students to keep track of their achievements. Students keep an evolving record of projects in several areas, including critical thinking, interdisciplinary thinking, historical analysis, scientific analysis, aesthetic analysis, and their experience at Truman. Students can track how they have grown and developed over the course of their college experience.

All Truman students are eligible for the general honors program. Designed for students who want a greater challenge, the honors program allows students to take advanced, specialized courses in lieu of their general studies requirement.

Truman students don't have to wait until graduate school to conduct groundbreaking research. Each year over one thousand students participate in faculty-supervised research projects.

> **"Professors are generally very down to earth and friendly, not at all intimidating. Most encourage getting to know them personally, which is a great thing because the academics are so challenging."**
>
> **- Truman Student**

Vibrant Community

Truman is located in Kirksville, a town of approximately seventeen thousand, located in the northeast corner of Missouri. The historic downtown area is within walking distance of the Truman campus and provides a connection to the Kirksville community. Citizens of the area offer a variety of cultures, nationalities, interests, talents, abilities, values, and experiences.

With more than 230 student organizations on campus, including service, professional, Greek, religious, political, social, recreational, and honorary influences, Truman students have ample opportunity to get involved.

Cultural events on and off campus offer students the opportunity to broaden their horizons through exposure to new viewpoints. Whether it is a production by the Truman theatre department, a blues festival at the local Round Barn, or a volunteer project within the community, cultural opportunities at Truman abound.

Nearly three thousand students opt to live on campus each year. Truman oversees seven residence halls and three apartment complexes, all of which include modern living facilities and are located within easy walking distance of academic buildings. Within these communities are exciting opportunities for personal, social, educational, physical, and emotional growth.

The Kirksville community has several unique recreational opportunities for active students to enjoy. An indoor/outdoor pool complex offers a variety of activities, classes, and programs designed to appeal to people of all ages, including a six-lane indoor pool perfect for swimming and relaxing. Thousand Hills State Park includes 3,252 acres of beautiful rolling hills and a 573-acre lake. Located ten minutes from the Truman campus, Thousand Hills provides the perfect setting for camping, fishing, swimming, boating, and waterskiing.

Successful Outcomes

Truman graduates are responsible citizens who make significant contributions to their families and their communities. They carry with them the desire to learn for the sake of knowledge, the sensitivity and insight to appreciate cultural diversity, and the ability to think freely and communicate effectively.

Truman is committed to offering students the best possible undergraduate preparation, and over 99 percent of Truman graduates who report their postgraduation plans are placed in professional employment or graduate school within six months of graduation.

Truman graduates have a long tradition of success in a variety of fields. Truman grads work in the U.S. Senate, molecular biology labs at Monsanto, ABC TV Networks, IBM, the Federal Trade Commission, Boeing, the St. Louis Cardinals, and many others.

Many alumni continue their educations at such institutions as the University of Chicago, Harvard University, the University of Notre Dame, Loyola University Medical School, Julliard, Purdue University, Tulane University, and UCLA.

Fast Facts

Truman State University is a four- year, public, liberal arts university founded in 1867.

Web site

http://www.truman.edu

Location

Kirksville, Missouri.

Student Profile

5,762 students (42% male, 58% female); 42 states and territories; 9% minority, 4% international.

Faculty Profile

338 full-time faculty. 16:1 student/faculty ratio. Average class size is 23.

Residence Life

Moderately residential: 48% of students live on campus.

Athletics

NCAA Division II, Mid-American Intercollegiate Conference. 21 varsity sports (11 men's: baseball, basketball, cross-country, football, golf, soccer, swimming, tennis, track & field, wrestling; 10 women's: basketball, cross-country, golf, soccer, softball, track & field, swimming, tennis, volleyball), 37 club and intramural sports.

Academic Programs

Accounting; agricultural science; art; art history; athletic training; biology; business administration; chemistry; classics; communication; communication disorders; computer science; economics; education; English; exercise science; French; German; health science; history; interdisciplinary studies; journalism; justice systems; mathematics; music; nursing; philosophy; physics; political science; predental; preengineering; prelaw; premedical; psychology; romance language; Russian; sociology/anthropology; Spanish; speech; studio art; theatre.

Costs and Aid

2007–2008: $12,247 comprehensive ($6,210 in-state tuition). Over 90% of students receive some financial aid. Average award: $7,546.

Endowment

$18.5 million.

More Distinctions

• Truman is ranked as the number one public university in the Midwest among schools offering bachelor's and master's degrees in *U.S. News & World Report's* America's Best Colleges. Truman has held this ranking for 11 consecutive years.

• Ranked as the second best public college value in the nation by the Princeton Review's *America's Best Value Colleges*, 2008 edition.

• Rated by the *Fiske Guide to Colleges*.

• Included in Kaplan's *Unofficial, Unbiased, Insider's Guide to the 320 Most Interesting Colleges*.

Westminster College

MISSOURI

Admissions Contact:

Westminster College
501 Westminster Avenue
Fulton, MO 65251-1299
(800) 475-3361
Ph: (573) 642-3361
Email: webmaster@westminster-mo.edu
www.westminster-mo.edu

Located in the heart of Missouri, Westminster College is a liberal arts college that strives to provide students with dynamic, hands-on, real-world experiences and seeks to be students' "gateway to the world." Enrolling just one thousand students, Westminster integrates its academics with its student life programs.

The 4 Distinctions

Engaged Students

International students make up 10 percent of the student body, and all students are encouraged to study abroad. England is a particularly popular destination for Westminster students, though students can also choose from a list of more than 150 approved study-abroad programs in more than forty countries around the world.

As part of Westminster's commitment to be students' "gateway to the world," the college hosts frequent lecture series. A recent symposium on democracy featured General David Petraeus, current commander of U.S. forces in Iraq. Other guests have included British Prime Minister Margaret Thatcher, Soviet General Secretary Mikhail Gorbachev, and four American presidents.

With the help of the career services office, many Westminster students undertake internships during their undergraduate years. Each semester, about a dozen students intern in Washington, DC. Students have also interned with legislators and other public officials in Missouri's state capital, Jefferson City. As one Westminster student, a genetic research intern at the Jackson Laboratory in Maine, noted, "This internship allowed me to integrate more possibilities into the path I might take after I graduate."

Students can also gain hands-on experience through their extracurricular activities. Westminster's student-run investment club, the Blue Blazer Club, did so well with their initial investments that the college's board of trustees provided them with two hundred thousand dollars in seed money. Their returns have funded trips for the group's members to New York City.

Great Teaching

Westminster students will tell you they learn more from their classes than just what can be found in lecture materials and textbooks. Professors work hard to make sure their students have a thorough grasp of the material, not just the facts they need to pass a final exam. Faculty teach, advise, and mentor in a personal context.

Westminster offers majors in thirty-six different subject areas, as well as thirty-four minors and twelve preprofessional programs. The college makes it possible for students to design their own majors, and some recent student-designed majors have included advertising, communication, public administration, and sports management. Many students select course work leading to medical school, law school, and doctoral programs.

Westminster's freshmen seminars, with such titles as "Harry Potter" and "Want to Be a President?" provide an opportunity for students to get to know their professors on a personal basis. In these seminars, professors not only teach the subject matter of the course, but important skills, too, such as research options, how to navigate the library system, and personal time management.

The life sciences at Westminster have been greatly enhanced with the addition of the eighteen million dollar Coulter Science Center, featuring biology classrooms, laboratories, research facilities for students and faculty, and new faculty offices.

Vibrant Community

Community service is another important component of life at Westminster. During a recent Into the Streets event, 150 Westminster students cleaned a soup kitchen and a Head Start facility, tended a garden for a domestic violence center, painted park benches, and winterized homes for senior citizens. Last year's summer retreat took a group to New Orleans, where they did residential construction work, helped with cleanup efforts, and passed out food. United Way fund-raising drives are active at Westminster, and the campus schedules regular American Red Cross blood-donation drives. Westminster's international organizations have recently focused their efforts on promoting the use of sustainable products from other countries.

First-year students enjoy suite-style living, and all freshmen sharing a suite take one of the freshman seminars; this tends to create a group of friends with common interests and a healthy support system. Male students further along in their Westminster careers also have the option of living in fraternity houses.

Though Fulton, Missouri, has just twelve thousand residents, it is big enough to offer an eight-screen movie-theatre complex, a new Fulton recreation complex, a new YMCA, a large historic district with beautiful Victorian houses, and many international restaurants.

Westminster College is remembered as the site for Winston Churchill's famous 1946 speech in which he first described the iron curtain falling across the face of Europe. Today's campus features the Winston Churchill Memorial and Library in the U.S.; a sculpture made of eight sections of the Berlin Wall, created by Churchill's granddaughter and dedicated by Ronald Reagan; and a museum in a sixteenth-century English church, bombed during World War II, dismantled, and reassembled at Westminster in 1967.

Westminster supports excellent varsity athletic programs, including a tradition of fine soccer teams and the 2003 and 2004 Division III conference football champions.

Successful Outcomes

The career service office provides comprehensive services to help students develop professional goals and job-seeking skills and to explore graduate school options. Approximately sixty companies come to campus each year to recruit new employees, and 96 percent of students are employed within six months of graduation.

"At Westminster students gain a wide range of skills and knowledge ensuring they will never be limited by a narrow specialized education, but are able to flourish is a nuturing environment of scholars."

-Colleges of Distinction

Fast Facts

Westminster College is a four-year, residential, independent, traditional liberal arts and sciences college founded in 1851.

Web site

http://www.westminster-mo.edu

Location

Fulton, Missouri—located 25 miles from Columbia and Jefferson City, MO, 70 miles from the Lake of the Ozarks, 2 hours from St. Louis, and 3 hours from Kansas City.

Student Profile

960 undergraduate students (55% male, 45% female); 27 states and territories, 55 countries; 10 % minority, 11 % international. Most students enroll from Missouri, Oklahoma, Arkansas, Illinois, Texas & Kansas.

Faculty Profile

95% full-time faculty. 80% hold a terminal degree in their field. 14:1 student/faculty ratio. Average class size is 13; 18 for freshmen.

Residence Life

Highly residential: 90% of students live on campus. All students live in college approved housing unless married, seniors or age 21 or older.

Athletics

NCAA Division III, St. Louis Intercollegiate Athletic Conference. Upper Midwest Athletic Conference for football only. 12 varsity sports (6 men's: football, soccer, basketball, baseball, tennis, golf; 6 women's: volleyball, soccer, basketball, softball, tennis, golf), cheerleading and dance teams and many intramural sports.

Academic Programs

Accounting; biology; business administration; chemistry; computer science; economics; education; English; environmental science/studies; French; history; international business; international studies; management information systems; mathematical sciences; philosophy; physical education; physics; political science; psychology; religious studies; self-designed major; sociology & anthropology; Spanish. Special programs in prelaw, premed, health professions, preengineering, fine arts, speech communications.

Costs and Aid

2007–2008: $22,490 comprehensive ($15,500 tuition). 97% of students receive some financial aid. Average award: $14,000.

Endowment

$50 million.

More Distinctions

• Ranked 4th in Best Value Private College, *Princeton Review.*

• Best Midwestern College, *Princeton Review.*

• Top 160 National Liberal Arts Colleges and Best Buy, *U.S. News and World Report.*

William Jewell College

MISSOURI

Founded in 1849, William Jewell College has earned a respected reputation as one of mid-America's most consistently honored and academically challenging private colleges. At the heart of "The Jewell Journey" is a student-centered model of exploration, creativity and research with strong, one-on-one faculty mentoring.

Admissions Contact:

William Jewell College
(888) 2-JEWELL (253-9355)
Ph: (816) 415-7511
Fax: (816) 415-5040
Email: admission@william.jewell.edu
www.jewell.edu

The 4 Distinctions

Engaged Students

Located twenty minutes north of the heart of Kansas City, Jewell students experience the best of both worlds—access to internship opportunities and cultural and entertainment venues, paired with the serenity of a peaceful hillside campus. William Jewell's national and international reputation is based in part on some of the college's unique programs.

Beginning with the graduating class of 2008, William Jewell will acknowledge completion of the college's thirty eight-hour liberal arts core—plus three applied learning experiences—as a recognized major in applied critical thought and inquiry (ACT-In). The ACT-In major validates a student's learning journey beyond the classroom. Students have the opportunity to officially connect what they learn with what they do.

Jewell's internationally recognized Oxbridge Honors Program—supported by the Hall Family Foundation—combines British tutorial methods of instruction with opportunities for a year of study in Oxford or Cambridge.

The renowned Harriman-Jewell Series is considered the Midwest's premiere program in the performing arts. Luciano Pavarotti made his international solo recital debut as part of the series, and each year's schedule includes the best national and international dance and theater companies, orchestras, ensembles, and recitalists.

The Pryor Leadership Studies Program includes class work, community-service projects, and internships that allow students to enhance their leadership skills in a variety of settings.

Other programs of note include the Undergraduate Research Colloquium, the Tucker Leadership Lab, and an opportunity for freshmen to explore the nature and practice of leadership through the Emerging Leaders Conference.

Great Teaching

With its rigorous academic culture, the college offers students an outstanding liberal arts education with a focus on cultivating leadership, service, and spiritual growth within a community inspired by rigorous intellectual challenges and Christian ideals. Great teaching is also a hallmark at William Jewell, where the student to teacher ratio is fifteen to one and the average class size is seventeen.

William Jewell College has made a major investment in, and commitment to, a liberal arts education that is inter-disciplinary and real-world focused. This unique program takes advantage of rich curricular and diverse co-curricular activities carefully designed to promote the intellectual and personal growth essential for making informed career and life decisions. By enhancing its unique and progressive core curriculum with three active learning experiences, Jewell has created a tightly integrated academic program major with substance, coherence, and intellectual integrity. This new major in Applied Critical Thought and Inquiry (ACT-In) is the only one of its kind in the nation.

Every Jewell student now has the option of completing the core liberal arts ACT-In major in addition to one or more major programs of study, graduating with double or even triple majors in just four years. The skills and abilities developed by the liberal arts ACT-In major are those most highly valued by the nation's business leaders and education experts as vital for career achievement. By the time they graduate, Jewell students will be skilled with deep content knowledge in their majors, practical experience, personal maturity and the intellectual habits of mind for very real career and life successes in a world of accelerating change and challenge.

William Jewell College believes that for an individual to be fully prepared to meet the challenges of today's world, he or she must be capable of placing issues within a larger context rather than isolating them within rigidly defined subject areas. Because of the multidisciplinary philosophy of the school, Jewell's distinctive core curriculum places contemporary issues against a backdrop of relevant historical, cultural, and ethical ideas. The interdisciplinary curriculum is designed for students to consider the social sciences alongside the laws governing the natural world, to study religion in relation to the social settings from which it developed, and to measure technological advances against the ethical dilemmas they sometimes create.

As the only program in the United States offering a full curriculum of tutorial-based instruction in conjunction with a year of study in England, the writing-intensive Oxbridge Honors Program extends over all four years of college. The highly personalized approach to education, with many opportunities for personal connections with faculty members, combines the best of the British and American approaches to education. In addition, international programs allow Jewell students to study at some of the world's great universities in Spain, Italy, Japan, Australia, Hong Kong, and Mexico.

Vibrant Community

Just twenty minutes from downtown Kansas City, the campus is perched above the historic town of Liberty, among the rolling hills of western Missouri. Students enjoy the cultural and professional benefits of a major city, as well as the outdoor recreational opportunities of the beautiful setting.

Seven out of ten students live on campus in one of five residence halls, one sorority complex, or four fraternity houses; all are wired with high-speed Internet access.

William Jewell is home to over sixty student clubs and organizations. Students are involved in a wide range of activities that include Greek organizations, jazz band, the Young Democrats and Republicans, debate team, Amnesty International, Christian Student Ministries, Students in Free Enterprise (SIFE), College Union Activities (CUA), Liberty Symphony Orchestra, and the concert choir. Students also participate in a variety of NAIA varsity and intramural sports.

Successful Outcomes

Within six months of graduation, 98 percent of Jewell students are accepted into graduate school or employed. Graduate schools welcoming Jewell alumni include Yale, Duke, Columbia, and Georgetown.

William Jewell students have recently received numerous national awards, including Goldwater, Marshall, Truman, Fulbright, and *USA Today* fellowships and scholarships. The college's debate team was recently named the nation's best at the National Parliamentary Tournament of Excellence, defeating the top-seeded team from the University of California, Berkeley.

The career services office at William Jewell offers support to students and alumni seeking full-time or part-time employment. In addition, emphasis is placed on career guidance and counseling, and staff members work with individual students to explore career issues.

Fast Facts

William Jewell College, one of the oldest colleges west of the Mississippi, is a private, residential, independent liberal arts college founded in 1849.

Web site

http://www.jewell.edu

Location

Kansas City, Missouri.

Student Profile

1200 undergraduate students (40% male, 60% female); 29 states represented; 10% minority.

Faculty Profile

90% of full-time faculty hold a terminal degree in their field. 15:1 student/faculty ratio. Average class size is 17.

Residence Life

Highly residential: 75% of students live on campus. First-Years - Junior status are required to live on campus unless living with a parent or guardian.

Athletics

NAIA, Heart of America Athletic Conference. 18 varsity sports (9 men's: football, basketball, baseball, soccer, tennis, golf, track, cross-country, spirit team; 9 women's: basketball, softball, volleyball, soccer, tennis, golf, track, cross-country, spirit team).

Academic Programs

Accounting; art; art education; biochemistry; bioethics; biology; biology education; business administration (banking & finance, entrepreneurial leadership, international business French, international business Spanish, marketing); chemistry; chemistry education; clinical lab science; communication; computer science; economics; education/elementary; education/secondary; English; English education; English/Literature; English/Writing; French; French education; history; information systems; international relations; leadership studies; mathematics; mathematics/data processing/ mathematics education; music (church music, composition, education, performance, theory); non-profit leadership; nursing; organizational communication; Oxbridge English language & literature; Oxbridge history; Oxbridge history of ideas; Oxbridge institutions & policy; Oxbridge molecular biology; Oxbridge music; philosophy; physical education; political science; psychology; recreation & sport; religion; science & technology management; social studies education; Spanish; Spanish education; speech education; theatre; theatre education. Preprofessional programs: engineering; forestry & environmental management; journalism; law; medicine (allopathic, osteopathic, dentistry, optometry, veterinary); ministry; occupational therapy; physical therapy.

Costs and Aid

2007–2008: $27,240 comprehensive. 99% of students receive some financial aid. Average award: $19,622.

Endowment

$86,300,000.

More Distinctions

• One of The *Princeton Review's* "Top Ten Best Values" among all private colleges and universities in 2006.
• Listed in 2008 *U.S. News & World Report* top 200 liberal arts colleges nationally.

College of Saint Mary

NEBRASKA

College of Saint Mary, a Catholic university committed to the works, values and aspirations of the Sisters of Mercy, offers undergraduate programs for women and graduate programs in an environment that calls forth potential and fosters leadership.

Admissions Contact:

College of Saint Mary
7000 Mercy Road
Omaha, NE 68106
(800) 926-5534
Ph: (402) 399-2405
Email: enroll@csm.edu
www.csm.edu
www.watchmebloom.com

The 4 Distinctions

Engaged Students

An important focus of College of Saint Mary's curriculum is to provide students with hands-on experience outside of the classroom. These experiences bring valuable insight to classroom lectures.

College of Saint Mary's most popular majors include those focusing on health, business, education, sciences and paralegal studies. CSM is well-known regionally for its nursing program, which features one of the nation's most high-tech learning environments. The school's foundation of support is further exemplified by the Mothers Living and Learning residence hall, designed exclusively for women with children. This special residence hall provides mothers with the opportunity to form support networks that speak to their extra challenges as students. In addition, all of CSM's graduate programs are designed for working professionals by featuring a hybrid delivery format that combines the accessibility of online education with the quality that can only be found in the classroom. Though the undergraduate courses are solely for women, men are granted admission to CSM for graduate and postbaccalaureate programs.

Because of the school's location and reputation, CSM students regularly find a variety of internship opportunities related to their field. Omaha, Nebraska, was recently listed by Newsweek as of the country's most high-tech cities. Each program at College of Saint Mary instills in students the practical abilities and critical thinking skills employers are looking for, with an added emphasis on leadership and teamwork. Outside the classroom, many students are inspired to participate in the annual Spirit of Service Day, which provides as many as twenty regional volunteer efforts. The college also sponsors service-learning trips, which have taken students to New Orleans, Costa Rica, and many other places to perform volunteer work. For students interested in work-study opportunities, there are numerous positions available throughout campus. Though positions vary, most students wishing to obtain a work-study position are likely to find one.

CSM encourages faculty to take an active role in students' development and values this over a focus on faculty research. The College of Saint Mary's Distinguished Scholars program provides upper-level students with a scholarship and the opportunity to work directly with faculty on research projects. Former Distinguished Scholars have been published in academic journals, considered an exceptional honor for undergraduate work. Recently, a group of forensic science students assisted Professor Nicole Wall on a murder case for a study of elder abuse.

College of Saint Mary's business students routinely develop small business plans in conjunction with Nebraska's Rural Services. Marketing students have won their second straight award for excellence in developing a professional advertising campaign. CSM students also compete for the Marie Curie Scholars program, that includes significant financial support for women pursuing degrees in science and mathematics.

Great Teaching

Surveys completed by College of Saint Mary's student body show that one of its strongest features is the relationship between students and teachers. The college's students have reported feeling comfortable with their instructors both inside and outside the classroom. Students feel that their teachers are willing to go the extra mile to ensure students' comprehension and success. The college's women-centered environment provides a cooperative, relaxed environment, where students are able to communicate freely with instructors. At CSM, it is not uncommon to see faculty and students dining together and interacting outside the classroom setting. Students are inspired by faculty members' accomplishments—more than half of CSM instructors have been honored in their respective fields.

College of Saint Mary's tight-knit student body is due in part to small class sizes, with only a few courses of fifty or more students. The average class size is fourteen students. First-year students participate in an introductory seminar and orientation events to help them make the transition to college.

Students aspire to reach their own goals quickly through the college's accelerated programs focusing on women in the workplace, which include the business leadership and Master of Organizational Leadership degrees. Both programs enjoy phenomenal success rates, and the master's program has a career-improvement success rate of 100 percent.

Vibrant Community

CSM's campus is located in the heart of Omaha, a few blocks north of I-80 on Seventy-second Street. Development was recently completed on an entrance and campus park in conjunction with Omaha by Design, a nonprofit group promoting sustainable and engaging city-planning efforts. The campus includes Mercy Hall, home to the bookstore and dining hall; Walsh Hall, which contains the main classroom and office facility; the Hixson-Lied Commons, a brand-new student center with a coffee shop, cafe, counseling center, student organization office and library; the Science Building; Lozier Tower, which joins the campus's two residence halls together; and the Lied Fitness Center, home to the school's athletic teams and exercise facilities. The college campus also includes soccer and softball fields and is adjacent to Omaha's Keystone Trail, a beautiful access point through midtown Omaha.

The college's central location offers students access to part-time jobs, entertainment and outdoor options. Students may choose from a variety of activities. Though there is no Greek life at CSM, thriving student organizations exist, centered on majors, leadership, service and entertainment. The campus is home to one of Omaha's largest art-gallery spaces, which hosts shows throughout the year. College of Saint Mary's Concert Series brings a variety of classical artists to campus each year. Additionally, the college's Irish Heritage Concert Series draws crowds with authentic Irish music performances once or twice a year. Another popular activity on campus is the Great Conversations series, which brings best-selling authors and notable speakers together to discuss topics such as the Da Vinci Code, motherhood in America and female artists.

CSM's students are first and foremost encouraged to be leaders. Students find leadership opportunities through the college's many student groups, which are active in Omaha events and organizations, and CSM provides students with links to career opportunities throughout the Omaha region. The college's Center for Transcultural Learning has become a regional leader in helping to improve the communication skills of the area's increasingly diverse population of health-care providers. College of Saint Mary is routinely the site of professional conferences focusing on everything from obstetrics to health information.

Successful Outcomes

CSM is proud of the strong success rates of its alumni. Graduates entering health professions have extremely high licensure rates for fields including occupational therapy and various types of nursing. The college is considered the foremost source of paralegals, offering the only four-year accredited program in Nebraska.

Overall job placement is high for graduates of CSM. One of the school's most famous alumni is Alex Kava, best-selling mystery author, and many alumni are prominent leaders in health care and business. Students looking for mentors in the region need search no further than the college's board of directors, which is comprised of notable business executives and leaders in the Omaha area. The college's board provides valuable feedback on how to prepare students for the evolving needs of today's workplaces.

Fast Facts

College of Saint Mary is a Catholic university for women serious about attaining high achievement in all aspects of their lives. CSM offers associates', bachelors', masters', and doctoral degrees in a variety of academic fields.

Web site

http://www.csm.edu

Location

Omaha, Nebraska—at the center of commerce, entertainment and opportunity.

Student Profile

960 undergraduate students (100% female); 20 states and territories; 16% minority, 1% international.

Faculty Profile

58 full-time faculty. 48% hold a terminal degree in their field. 9:1 student/faculty ratio. Average class size is 14.

Residence Life

Mildly residential: 15% of students live on campus.

Athletics

NAIA, Midlands Collegiate Athletic Conference. 5 varsity sports (5 women's: cross-country, volleyball, soccer, basketball, softball) and a variety of intramurals.

Academic Programs

Applied psychology & human services; art; biology; business administration; business information systems; business leadership; chemistry; education; engineering; English; general studies; humanities; language arts; mathematics; natural sciences; nursing; occupational therapy; paralegal studies; professional studies; psychology; theology. 5 master's degrees and 1 doctoral degree.

Costs and Aid

2006–2007: $13,115 per semester comprehensive ($9,990 per semester tuition). More than 90% of students receive some financial aid.

More Distinctions

• A practical nursing program created specifically to graduate bilingual (Spanish-English) nurses to serve the growing Spanish-speaking population in Nebraska and surrounding areas.

• An innovative "2+3" engineering program in collaboration with the University of Nebraska College of Engineering and Technology (COET), through which graduates receive two degrees: a bachelor's degree in science or math from CSM, and a bachelor's degree in civil, computer, or electronics engineering or a master's degree in architectural engineering from the Peter Kiewit Institute.

• A masters in leadership programs dedicated to exploring and strengthening the unique leadership qualities of women.

• The region's only four-year paralegal studies program approved by the American Bar Association.

Creighton University

NEBRASKA

Creighton University, a Jesuit Catholic university located just outside Omaha's downtown business district, offers more than fifty majors in the undergraduate divisions of Arts and Sciences, Business Administration, and the School of Nursing, as well as professional and graduate programs in law, business, medicine, dentistry, pharmacy, and physical and occupational therapy.

Admissions Contact:

Creighton University
2500 California Plaza
Omaha NE - 68178
(800) 282-5835
Ph: (402) 280-2703
Email: admissions@creighton.edu
admissions.creighton.edu

The 4 Distinctions

Engaged Students

Currently, Creighton enrolls about four thousand undergraduate and three thousand professional and graduate students. The most popular majors among Creighton students include preprofessional health areas, prelaw, business, nursing, psychology, education, and journalism. Creighton students are offered many different types of internships related to their fields of study. Additionally, about three hundred undergraduate students choose to study abroad each year.

In addition to Creighton's curriculum, there are many chances for students to become involved with community service, which is an essential part of their education. Creighton's mission is not only to prepare students to become leaders in their careers, but to become contributors to the world society. Through Creighton's annual Holiday Spirit community-service event, students provide assistance to Omaha-area shelters and organizations. In past years, faculty, residents, and staff of the pathology/Creighton medical laboratories department have sponsored a single mom with ten children—five biological and five foster. The Holiday Spirit Committee is an opportunity for students to coordinate the outreach service programs of employees and university departments.

The Creighton Center for Service and Justice (CCSJ) is committed to building a community of faith in service for justice. CCSJ members participate in the school's justice and peace studies program. CCSJ also sponsors ongoing disaster relief for organizations like the International Federation of Red Cross and Red Crescent Societies, the American Red Cross, Catholic Charities USA, and Catholic Relief Services.

Every spring, Creighton students of different ages, majors, and faiths come together for spring break service trips. These students devote their entire vacation to visiting different communities, helping the less fortunate, and making a difference in the world. While promoting Jesuit values, students make new friends and experience new cultures. This year, Creighton participants provided over sixty-eight thousand hours of volunteer service in off-campus outreach activities in Omaha and around the world.

Students also participate in the Creighton University Staff Advisory Council, which serves as an advocate for university staff members. The council is committed to fairness, justice, and respect in a quality work environment in accordance with the mission of Creighton University. The council advises Creighton's president in matters affecting the general welfare and working conditions of all members of the staff.

Creighton is in the midst of constructing a dynamic Living Learning Center, which will include a sports cafe, an indoor/outdoor latte bar, a five-hundred-seat multiuse auditorium, ten standard-size classrooms, ten seminar rooms, a bookstore, and a seven-thousand-square-foot exercise space.

Creighton's student body is extremely diverse, and the university enrolls more Hawaiians than any college outside the West Coast. At Creighton, 20 percent of students will become first-generation college graduates. About 20 percent of the student body are from minority groups, and about 62 percent are Catholic.

Great Teaching

Creighton University includes the Creighton University Medical Center, which includes the schools of Medicine, Dentistry, Pharmacy and Health Professions, and Nursing. Also included are a teaching hospital known for its trauma expertise; Creighton's respected Center for Health Policy and Ethics; health-care clinics located throughout the metropolitan area and region; and internationally renowned centers of excellence in cardiac care, hard-tissue research and osteoporosis, hereditary cancer, and patient outcomes research. Creighton offers one of the few accelerated nursing programs in the Midwest, and was one of the first schools to offer entry-level doctoral degrees in occupational therapy, pharmacology, and physical therapy.

At Creighton, academics are taken very seriously. The faculty strive to learn not only where students excel, but more important, who they are and what they care about. The Creighton College of Arts and Sciences is the largest and the oldest program of the university. This school has more than 180 full-time faculty members, each of whom is a productive scholar, talented artist, or respected professional. Each year, these individuals publish groundbreaking books, attract major research grants, and travel to present their work to their peers around the world.

Professors in many fields create opportunities for students to join in respected research projects. Creighton students have the chance to advance their undergraduate studies with enhanced professional opportunities. Research grants are awarded in chemistry, biology, and physics, as well as several other areas of study. Creighton is a leader in cancer research and treatment through the Creighton Cancer Center and the Hereditary Cancer Institute. Headed by world-renowned researcher Henry T. Lynch, MD, the Hereditary Cancer Institute is the nation's only cancer registry that tracks all forms of hereditary cancer.

Vibrant Community

In addition to clubs and organizations, Creighton is well-known for its competitive athletic teams. Creighton has fourteen varsity athletic teams, including women's basketball, crew, cross-country, golf, soccer, softball, tennis, and volleyball, as well as men's basketball, baseball, cross-country, golf, soccer, and tennis. Creighton is the host school for the NCAA Men's College World Series and the Missouri Valley Conference Men's Soccer Tournament. The Creighton's men's soccer team has been one of the top five programs in the NCAA over the past decade. Attendance at basketball games ranks in the top fifteen in the nation.

Omaha is a vibrant city, where Creighton students can enjoy live music and theater, great dining, an active nightlife, and more. The Omaha metropolitan area has a population of more than eight hundred thousand and includes thirty thousand businesses, providing Creighton students with a number of job and internship opportunities. Forbes magazine ranks Omaha as one of the nation's most attractive cities for young professionals.

Local bands often play on the Creighton campus, in addition to their dates at nightspots around the city. Omaha boasts beautiful, tree-covered, rolling hills, and features a lively arts scene, including Saddle Creek Records, which spring boarded the careers of nationally known bands like the Faint and Bright Eyes. The record label is building a new music venue near campus to spotlight local and national music. The Omaha Community Playhouse is the largest and one of the best-endowed community theaters in the United States. The Henry Doorly Zoo is also nationally recognized, and Omaha's downtown area is home to Old Market, which includes a number of shops, restaurants, bars, and art galleries.

Successful Outcomes

More than 97 percent of Creighton graduates are employed, involved in volunteer work, or attending graduate or professional school within six months of graduation. On average, 55 percent of Creighton graduates go on to professional or graduate school.

The Creighton Career Alumni Network (CCAN) is a new alumni mentor program being launched by the career center. The program will provide names and contact information exclusively for Creighton students and alumni. The goal is to provide students with networking opportunities, to educate them about the working world, and to connect them with alumni who are willing to provide advice.

Fast Facts

Creighton University is a national Jesuit Catholic University founded in 1878.

Web site

http://www.creighton.edu

Location

Omaha, Nebraska.

Student Profile

4,000 undergraduate students, 3,000 professional and graduate students (43% male, 57% female); 50 states and territories, 30 countries. 20% minority, 1% international. 70% of freshmen are from out-of-state and 60% come from further than 200 miles from campus.

Faculty Profile

735 full-time faculty. 12:1 student/faculty ratio. Average class size is 24.

Residence Life

Highly residential: 93% of freshmen and sophomores and 50% of juniors and seniors live on campus.

Athletics

NCAA Division I, Missouri Valley Conference. 14 varsity sports (6 men's: baseball, basketball, cross-country, golf, soccer, tennis; 8 women's: basketball, crew, cross-country, golf, soccer, softball, tennis, volleyball); 11 club sports, and 40 intramurals.

Academic Programs

Accounting; American studies; anthropology; art (history, studio); athletic training; atmospheric sciences (applied meteorology, graduate school preparation track); biology; business; business prelaw 3/3; chemistry; chemistry (education); classical & near eastern civilizations; communication studies (interpersonal, human resources, organization, or corporate tracks); computer science; economics; education elementary (k-6, 7-8 middle school, special ed.); education secondary (high school level: specialization, English as a second language, special ed.); emergency medical services; English (creative writing track, Irish Literature, education, general tracks); environmental science (multiple tracks); exercise science; finance; French; German; graphic design; Greek; health administration & policy; history; international business; international relations; journalism (advertising, news, photo journalism, public relations, visual communications tracks); justice & society; Latin; management (human resources, entrepreneurial, business ethics, pre-law, military, standard tracks); management information systems; marketing; mathematics (applied, computing, medical, pure tracks); music; Native American studies; nursing (four-year and one-year accelerated programs); philosophy (additional track in ethics); physics (health sciences, standard tracks); political science (legal studies, public policy, standard tracks); psychology; sociology (applied research, criminal justice, family studies, global health, standard tracks); Spanish; social work; theatre (broadcast performance & production, performance, technical, standard tracks); theology.

Costs and Aid

2007–2008: $34,814 comprehensive ($25,616 tuition). 90% of students receive some financial aid. Average award: $22,500.

Endowment

$450 million.

Doane College

Admissions Contact:

Doane College
1014 Boswell Avenue
Crete, NE 68333
(800) 333-6263
Fax: (402) 826-8600
Email: Admissions@doane.edu
www.doane.edu

NEBRASKA

Founded in 1872 as Nebraska's first liberal arts and sciences college, Doane is a private co-educational liberal arts school. The four pillars at Doane are excellence, empowerment, experience and impact. The school prides itself on graduating leaders from all walks of life.

The 4 Distinctions

Engaged Students

Doane gives students the option to study abroad during their junior or senior years. A special travel scholarship gives four-year students $1000 to participate. One popular option is the semester immersion service-learning experience. These rewarding, semester-long opportunities have taken professors and their students to China and Africa. Study abroad options include trips shorter in length as well. Mexico, Australia and England are only some of the many places to which Doane students have ventured in their studies. Students can also travel inside the United States to New York City and Washington D.C. Internships are available across the country, both in term and during semester breaks.

The Hansen Leadership Program at Doane gets students involved in a comprehensive co-curricular activity that further develops each person's talents and abilities. Students can go on retreats or take an outdoor ropes challenge course. In this program, speakers share their wisdom to inspire students to be leaders in the fields that each wants to pursue. Speakers have included James Earl Jones, Phil Jackson and Susan O'Malley.

Doane students draw practical parallels between the academic and work environments. More than 75 percent of Doane students complete internships. Before a student can participate in an internship, he or she must enroll in a course called Introduction to Field Experience. This 4-week class prepares students for the internship through career research, resume development and orientation to internship procedures. Students may receive academic credit for their internships through their department.

Great Teaching

In Doane's degree and vocational programs, professors, not teaching assistants, lead the instruction. The school's community of learning starts in the classroom and then extends beyond it. Led by a psychology professor, one group of students went to help Hurricane Katrina relief efforts, working on infrastructure development and counseling.

Students can do in-depth research alongside professors as early as sophomore year. During a student's junior and senior years, major-specific research can begin. Environmental studies majors are currently doing research on prairie dog population control in Nebraska.

Doane understands that reflection is a critical component of the educational process. Seniors have the opportunity to reflect at the Senior Capstone Celebration, a forum where students articulate formally the ways in which they have grown since entering college. Conducted during a student's final semester and staged before invited faculty, students and significant others, a capstone celebration involves sharing parts of a student's Achievement Portfolio or Leadership Transcript. Invited guests provide feedback regarding their perception of the student's talents and abilities. The Celebration closes with a discussion of future goals.

Doane is one of only a select few colleges and universities in the nation to offer a four-year guarantee. The college guarantees that its students will graduate within four years, or Doane will pay for additional course expenses.

Vibrant Community

Ninety percent of Doane students live on campus in residence halls or apartments. Not only are there 18 intercollegiate (NAIA) sports teams for men and women, but there is an intramural program for competition, exercise and fun. Doane students prove to be high-spirited supporters of such athletics. Students can participate in academic clubs, the theatre at Doane, choir clubs and spiritual organizations like Campus Crusade for Christ. Both Young Democrats and Young Republicans are represented on campus. Private Greek organizations, to which 40 percent of the student body belongs, are also an option.

Doane has a number of service organizations. It is one of the top five institutions nationwide in raising money for cancer through Relay for Life. Another way Doane ties itself to the community is "Reach Out Day," where students donate their time to Crete's local businesses, schools and community organizations. There is significant interaction between students on campus and the local community. Each first-year class participates in local activities, cementing their relationships with local business owners and citizens.

Doane also offers an extensive intramural sports program for all students. Options throughout the year include coed softball, flag football, tennis, water polo, bowling, ice hockey, floor hockey, Frisbee golf, swimming, sand volleyball, 5-on-5 basketball and coed volleyball.

Successful Outcomes

Year after year, students and alumni continue to make a difference on campus. Students who have a strong interest in being engaged in leadership can be funded through the Hansen Leadership Fund to work as mentors to peers and younger students. These students live together in a leadership hall. Through the Master's Series, Doane alums who have made a notable impact at the local, national or international levels come back to speak and give advice to current students.

Doane has a unique policy in that the college guarantees a four-year graduation. Nearly 100 percent of graduates from the Crete campus are employed or attending graduate school. Alumni success is celebrated and featured in Doane Magazine and on the college's website.

Fast Facts

Doane College is a coeducational four-year, private liberal arts and sciences institution.

Web site

http://www.doane.edu

Location

Crete, Nebraska—approximately 25 miles from Lincoln, the state's capital, and 75 miles from Omaha.

Student Profile

950 students (48% male, 52% female).

Faculty Profile

77 faculty. 65% hold a terminal degree in their field. 13:1 student/faculty ratio. Average class size is 23.

Residence Life

Highly residential. Approximately 90% of students live on-campus.

Athletics

NAIA Division II, Great Plains Athletic Conference. 16 varsity sports (8 men's: basketball, baseball, cross-country, football, golf, soccer, indoor & outdoor track & field, tennis; 8 women's: basketball, cross-country, golf, soccer, softball, indoor & outdoor track & field, tennis, volleyball).

Academics

Accounting; art; biology; business administration; business principles; chemistry; computer science; economics; elementary education; English; English as a second language; English/language arts; environmental studies; French; German; history; honors biology; information systems; international studies; mass communication; mathematics; music; natural science (teaching); organizational communication; philosophy; physical education; physical science; physics; political science; psychology; public administration; religious studies; social sciences (teaching); sociology; Spanish; special education; speech communication; theatre.

Costs and Aid

2007–2008: $18,800 tuition. 98% percent of students receive some financial aid.

Endowment

$73 million.

More Distinctions

• Doane's record of forty-five Fulbright Scholars is higher than any other institution in Nebraska.

• Doane has been named a "hidden treasure" by the Kaplan/Newsweek College Catalog.

• Ranked in the category of great schools at great prices in the 2005 U.S. News & World Report college guide.

Oklahoma City University

OKLAHOMA

Oklahoma City University (OCU) is a small, private, liberal arts and science university of 3,700 students located in Oklahoma's ever-growing capital city. The United Methodist-affiliated university has seven colleges and schools spread over a beautiful, sixty-eight-acre, park-like campus. Oklahoma City University combines a unique blend of tradition, quality, community, and innovation.

Admissions Contact:

Oklahoma City University
2501 North Blackwelder
Oklahoma City, OK 73106-1493
(800) 633-7242
Ph: (405) 208-5000
Email: uadmissions@okcu.edu
www.okcu.edu

The 4 Distinctions

Engaged Students

Founded in 1904, Oklahoma City University embraces the United Methodist tradition of scholarship and service, and welcomes all faiths in a culturally rich community that is dedicated to student welfare and success. Men and women pursue academic excellence through a rigorous curriculum that focuses on students' intellectual, moral, and spiritual development to prepare them to become effective leaders in service to their communities.

Outside of the classroom, OCU students have access to more than fourty social, academic, and service organizations and clubs. Students often find one or two organizations they would like to join. OCU has six national Greek fraternities and sororities, each of which focus on community service, leadership, and personal relationships.

Another national organization on campus is Habitat for Humanity, which is a student-based initiative and extremely popular with Oklahoma City University students. As the voice for campus politics and programs, the student senate is also very popular with OCU students. For students looking for new hobbies or activities, OCU offers a number of extracurricular programs, such as cheerleading, dance groups, dramatics, intramural sports, and student-run publications. Students also have many opportunities to participate in community service throughout the Oklahoma City metro area.

For many students, spiritual life is just as important as academic and social life. Oklahoma City University's religious life council exists to help nurture the personal and communal spiritual life of students during undergraduate and graduate school. The council is committed to providing opportunities for spiritual growth, rewarding friendships, and intellectual inquiry into matters of faith in a supportive environment. The religious life council is pledged to promote the moral and spiritual growth of the Oklahoma City University community; to advocate the university's exercise of free inquiry and its pursuit of the highest standards of intellectual and moral excellence; and to help student, faculty, and staff.

Great Teaching

OCU's administration wants only truly great teachers at the university. The school has an impressive student to faculty ratio of fourteen to one, meaning teachers are very involved with students' academic progress.

Over 70 percent of Oklahoma City University's professors have the highest degrees in their fields, and professors teach all undergraduate classes, as the university has no graduate teaching assistants. OCU provides the benefits of a private university, including small classes, close teacher-student relationships, easily accessible facilities, and the opportunity to work with professors outside of class on special projects.

OCU's most popular majors include performing arts, the sciences, and business. OCU's art department is recognized as one of the most outstanding programs in the region. The classes are informal, yet challenging, and reflect OCU's strong belief in art fundamentals such as the mastery of drawing skills and the elements and principles of design. The university provides students with an understanding of art theory, art history, and contemporary issues, all of which are necessary in the creation of contemporary art. OCU's Meinders School of Business delivers business programs around the world. Faculty prepare students to become socially responsible leaders in a global economy through scholarship in business practice, teaching, learning, and the disciplines.

The moving image arts program at Oklahoma City University is an interdisciplinary program that utilizes the platform of liberal arts study with a strong focus on critical and practical production studies of moving image content.

OCU's Kramer School of Nursing offers the Bachelor of Science in Nursing (BSN) and the Master of Science of Nursing (MSN) degrees. The traditional BSN is a standard four-year undergraduate degree. Students become registered nurses upon completion, and are eligible to apply to take the National Council Licensure Examination (NCLEX) to begin work.

Vibrant Community

As a United Methodist-affiliated institution, the university is committed to helping students of all faiths expand their minds and enrich their souls.

Students in search of entertainment and recreation will enjoy Oklahoma City. There are a wide range of activities around the city, including concerts at the Ford Center, the Civic Center Music Hall, and the Zoo Amphitheatre. Students will also enjoy the performances of the Oklahoma City Philharmonic Orchestra and Ballet Oklahoma, as well as Broadway shows at the Lyric Theatre. Beautiful lakes, parks, championship golf courses, and top-notch tennis facilities also await outdoor enthusiasts. Sports fans will enjoy the Class Triple-A baseball team, the Oklahoma RedHawks, who make their home at the finest Class Triple-A ballpark in the country, and the Oklahoma City Blazers hockey team.

The OCU experience is as much about physical health and fitness as it is about challenging intellectual adventures. OCU offers a wide variety of high-quality athletic programs and facilities to ensure that every day of a student's week is focused on finding new ways to play and have fun. OCU is a member of the Sooner Athletic Conference, and offers students twelve varsity sports, cheerleading, five junior varsity sports, and nine intramurals.

Successful Outcomes

OCU's Career Services Center assists students and alumni in developing and implementing career plans that support their personal and professional objectives by providing a wide range of services. The center provides students with professional job listings for graduating seniors and alumni; an online career job board listing openings in the area and across the country; up-to-date off-campus temporary, part-time, and internship opportunities in the greater Oklahoma City area; interview opportunities with local and national companies; monthly small group seminars on professional job-search techniques; and an annual job fair.

OCU's dance, music, and theater students have appeared in venues all over the nation and the world, building a strong reputation in the performing arts. Some of the brightest stars were in performance ensembles like the Surrey Singers and the American Spirit Dance Company. Three Miss Americas and more than twenty winners of the Miss Oklahoma pageant are graduates of OCU. Alumni include Emmy, Grammy, and Tony award winners.

Other OCU students have become teachers, skilled doctors and nurses, preachers, leading scientists and lawyers, noted public servants, and artists. The OCU campus has been a source of national pride and innovation. Oklahoma City University has seen a variety of distinguished guests visit their beautiful campus, including astronauts and film stars, opera luminaries and foreign dignitaries, bestselling authors and religious leaders, and political and business giants.

Fast Facts

Oklahoma City University is a relatively small private liberal arts and science university founded in 1904.

Web site

http://www.okcu.edu

Location

Oklahoma City, Oklahoma.

Student Profile

Undergraduate population: 1,869 (37% male, 63% female); 48 states, 58 foreign countries; 15% minority, 27% international.

Faculty Profile

167 full-time faculty. 70% of full-time faculty members hold the highest degrees in their fields. 14:1 student/faculty ratio. Average freshmen class size is 16.

Residence Life

All students under age of 21 and not living with a legal guardian must live on campus.

Athletics

NAIA, Sooner Athletic Conference. 12 varsity sports (6 men's: basketball, baseball, crew, golf, soccer, wresting. 6 women's: basketball, crew, golf, soccer, softball, volleyball), cheerleading, 5 JV sports, and 9 intramurals.

Academic Programs

Accounting; advertising; American studies; Asian studies; art; broadcasting; biochemistry; biology; biophysics; business administration; chemistry; computer science; criminal justice; dance management; dance pedagogy; dance performance; early childhood education; economics; elementary education; English; entertainment business; exercise & sports science; film production; film studies; finance; graphic art; history; humanities; information technology; instrumental performance; journalism; marketing; mathematics; modern languages; music; music business; music education; music composition; musical theater; photography; piano pedagogy; public relations; nursing; philosophy; physics; political science; premedicine; preveterinary medicine; prephysical therapy; prepharmacy; psychology; religion & philosophy; religious education; sacred music; secondary education; sociology; studio art; technical theatre; theatre; theatre performance; vocal education; vocal performance; undecided (university studies); youth ministry.

Costs and Aid

2007–2008: $25,000 comprehensive ($19,600 tuition). 55% of students receive some financial aid. Average award: $13,596.

More Distinctions

• Ranked in top tier of Best Universities 2007 (Masters, West) by U.S. News & World Report.

• One of the 122 colleges named a Best Western College by The Princeton Review.

• Designated as one of the best overall bargains - based on cost and financial aid - among the most academically outstanding colleges in the nation.

Oral Roberts University

OKLAHOMA

Oral Roberts University (ORU) is an interdenominational Christian liberal arts university located in Tulsa, Oklahoma. Founded in 1963 by evangelist Oral Roberts, ORU serves students from every state and over sixty countries, offering sixty undergraduate majors, fourteen master's programs, and two doctoral degrees, as well as NCAA Division I athletics.

Admissions Contact:

Oral Roberts University
7777 South Lewis Avenue
Tulsa, OK 74171
(800) 678-8876
Ph: (918) 495-6518
Email: admissions@oru.edu
www.oru.edu

The **4** Distinctions

Engaged Students

ORU prepares its students to be their best in spirit, mind, and body. Through the academic schools and departments, students find unique avenues for service. Numerous departments assist local schools by providing tutoring in subjects such as mathematics, English, reading, and art. The School of Education has adopted an underperforming elementary school, which it provides with tutoring, school supplies, and help for building and grounds improvement. The history, humanities, and government department invites ORU students to help immigrants prepare for U.S. citizenship tests. School of Nursing students distribute information on health care, participate in health fairs, provide health education to Native Americans, and serve in clinics in Mexico. School of Business students conduct case studies of and develop plans for local businesses. Honors program students have taken part in numerous service-learning activities, such as teaching poetry to elementary school students, developing science projects, and providing supplies for animals left homeless after Hurricane Katrina.

Students from a variety of majors, including art, mathematics and computer science, English, communication arts, behavioral sciences, theology, and business take part in internships in the United States and abroad. These internships give students practical experience, teach them how to conduct themselves in the workplace, and allow them to share their skills and talents with their internship sponsors. The School of Theology and Missions sends students to complete local field education practicums as well as internships with missions organizations in countries such as Uganda, Turkey, Jordan, Honduras, India, and Kenya.

The year 2007 marked the fifth anniversary of Ignite, a student-led leadership conference. The conference featured renowned leadership author Dr. John Maxwell. Other speakers included ORU alumni Dr. Tim Elmore and Lynette Troyer Lewis, the Jeff Deyo Band, pastor Terry Henshaw, and former LA Raiders running back-turned-pastor Napoleon Kaufman. The success of Ignite has attracted the attention of other universities who want to offer their students the same opportunities to develop as leaders. In March 2007, Evangel University launched Collision, Ignite's first official offspring.

Great Teaching

When Oral Roberts founded the university, it was with the knowledge that faith in Jesus Christ was only fully realized when it went forth from the chapel into the world, touching and revitalizing lives. In the decades since, thousands of students have felt their spirits soar upon joining ORU's family of faith. Students are asked to sign the honor code, an oath to live by the Christian principles that are the bedrock of ORU.

Instead of a lecture hall filled to capacity, a typical ORU classroom boasts a fourteen to one student to faculty ratio. The smaller class size enables faculty members to give students more of their undivided attention. In the classroom and during regularly scheduled office hours, professors can mentor, advise, and pray with their students. At the head of each class, you're also more likely to find a full-time (and frequently PhD-equipped) professor than a teaching assistant. As for the quality of the ORU faculty, consider psychology professor Terese Hall and her unique educational and career background. Hall is one of only 217 forensic psychologists at the diplomate level in the United States, and one of only thirty-two women in this specialized field.

When it comes to cutting-edge technology and student assessments, ORU is a recognized leader, as one of the first universities in the nation to utilize ePortfolio. Introduced in 2002 and now used across the entire university, ePortfolio is an electronic tool that helps students evaluate their progress and see how their course work is preparing them for real-world situations. It also helps faculty determine whether or not students are achieving ORU's learning outcomes of becoming spiritually alive, intellectually alert, physically disciplined, socially adept, and professionally competent—in other words, whether students are becoming whole people, the goal of ORU's mission to provide a whole-person education.

ORU features a number of notable professors, including Dr. Xiaomin Ma, assistant professor of engineering and physics, and the creator of a unique radar system called ITS (intelligent transport system) that measures the distance between one car and another, as well as relative speed. In an emergency situation, one driver's car sends a signal through wireless communication to warn the other driver of danger. With this early-warning signal, a driver can brake or steer away when he or she is a mere second away from danger. Already, auto manufacturers Ford, GM, and Honda have expressed interest in Dr. Ma's work, and in the not-too-distant future, cars may be equipped with this unique radar system.

Dr. Andrew Lang, another notable ORU professor, recently published an article in the prestigious mathematics journal of the Society for Industrial and Applied Mathematics titled Modeling Basketball Free Throws. Inspired by some of his students, Lang, an associate professor of mathematics, began researching basketball free throws and applying mathematical formulas to them. Through this research, he was able to determine the ideal release angle, according to each player's height, to maximize the players' chances of making a free throw.

Vibrant Community

In keeping with the uniqueness of its faculty, ORU boasts a campus with the world-renowned designs of architect Frank Wallace. Twenty-three major buildings on campus feature his designs. There is symbolism embedded in every building. The most notable is the Prayer Tower, shaped so that a cross is seen from every side, serving as a reminder to visitors that every individual's journey begins and ends at the foot of the cross of Christ. The tower's location at the center of the ORU campus testifies that communion with God must always be the central focus of life. Atop the Prayer Tower, an eternal flame represents the baptism of the Holy Spirit.

Almost all students live on-campus in residence halls. Instead of fraternities or sororities, ORU has brother-sister wings. The students eat in the student cafeteria, the Graduate Center's deli, and the Chick-fil-A restaurant, or enjoy a snack from the Green Cuisine, Hava Java, or the Internet café. Student government, musical and drama performance groups, and over fifty academic and special-interest clubs offer social and leadership development for students. Opportunities to work with the student-run newspaper, yearbook, radio station, and television programs are also available.

Popular spiritual-life activities include chapel services, the community outreach projects, summer and spring-break mission trips, music ministries, wing devotions, retreats, and fall- and spring-break outreaches. Students attend the churches of their choice on Sunday mornings.

Perhaps the most distinctive feature of ORU is its dedication to educating the whole student. Students take a physical education course each semester during which they are enrolled full-time at ORU.

Successful Outcomes

ORU alumni make their marks in literature, scientific research, ministry, technology, art, and entrepreneurship. There's a reason employers have ranked ORU graduates number one in quality among schools in the Tulsa area of Oklahoma, and why corporations like Aetna, Citigroup, and Ernst & Young pursue ORU graduates with such intensity: ORU graduates arrive not just with first-class skills but with bold ideas, commitment, and integrity.

Fast Facts

Oral Roberts University is an interdenominational Christian liberal arts university.

Web site

http://www.oru.edu

Location

Tulsa, Oklahoma.

Student Profile

4,002 undergraduate students (44% male, 56% female); 50 states, 64 countries.

Faculty Profile

198 full-time faculty. 14:1 student/faculty ratio. Average class size is 20.

Residence Life

Highly residential. Students are required to live on campus.

Athletics

NCAA Division I, The Summit League. 16 varsity sports (8 men's: baseball, basketball, cross-country, golf, soccer, tennis, indoor track & field, outdoor track & field; 8 women's: basketball, cross-country, golf, soccer, tennis, indoor track & field, outdoor track & field, volleyball).

Academic Programs

Accounting; art education K-12; Bib. lit./English Bible; Bib. lit./New Testament; Bib. lit./Old Testament; biology; biomedical chemistry; biomedical engineering; business administration; chemistry; computer science; dance performance; drama; drama/television/film performance; early childhood education PK-3; elementary education 1-8; engineering; engineering physics; English literature; finance; French; German; government; graphic design-print; graphic design-video; health & exercise science; health/physical education K-12; history; international business; international community development; international relations; liberal arts; management; management information systems; marketing; mass media communications; mathematics; mathematics secondary education; modern foreign language education K-12; music; music composition; music education K-12; music performance; (music) sacred music; nursing; organizational/interpersonal communication; pastoral Christian ministries; psychology; recreation administration; science secondary education; social studies secondary education; social work; Spanish; special education/mild-moderate disabilities K-12; speech/drama/debate secondary education; studio art; theological/historical studies; worship arts; writing. 14 master's programs and 2 doctoral degrees.

Costs and Aid

2007–2008: $17,000 tuition. 96% of students receive some financial aid. Average award: $17,225.

More Distinctions

• The university has received the 2007 "Award for Institutional Progress in Student Learning Outcomes" from the Council for Higher Education Accreditation (CHEA).

• ORU is listed in The Princeton Review's annual college guide as one of the "Best in the West."

• ORU has also been listed in the Top 50 schools in the Universities-Master's West category for the 2006 edition of America's Best Colleges from U.S. News & World Report.

University of Science and Arts of Oklahoma

OKLAHOMA

The University of Science and Arts of Oklahoma (USAO) is located in Chickasha, a friendly community in southwest Oklahoma, rich in history and culture. USAO is committed to supporting liberally educated men and women to think and act critically, creatively, and humanely.

Admissions Contact:

University of Science and Arts of Oklahoma
1727 West Alabama
Chickasha, Oklahoma USA 73018-5322
(800) 933-8726
Ph: (405) 224-3140
Fax: (405) 574-1220
Email:
www.usao.edu

The 4 Distinctions

Engaged Students

USAO is one of the oldest public liberal arts colleges in America, one of only a few in the nation. Beyond offering career preparation, USAO's unique curriculum enriches the lives of students and strengthens their skills in communication and problem solving. The university's original motto, "Not for livelihood but for life" captures the liberal arts focus still central to the school's mission today.

USAO's unique Interdisciplinary Studies (IDS) is a core curriculum required of all students in every major. More than that, it's a philosophy of learning. Instead of rote memorization, students learn how various perspectives from different fields (such as history, philosophy, math, and others) all relate to one another on a given issue. Service learning is emphasized throughout all majors.

USAO offers twenty-three degree programs across the spectrum, as well as thirteen preprofessional programs such as prelaw and prepharmacy. The most popular majors are elementary education and teaching, art, and psychology.

At the end of the spring semester, there is a five-week independent study period during which students design their own study program sponsored by faculty. Many of these programs of study emphasize service learning, study abroad, and experiential learning. A fully weighted summer term includes unique courses like the history of rock and roll.

Great Teaching

USAO accepts the challenge to provide an academic and social environment that promotes liberal arts learning. The school has a public liberal arts tradition dating back to 1908. Recently, USAO became one of the newest members of the prestigious Council on Public Liberal Arts Colleges (COPLAC) in recognition of the university's strong tradition of liberal arts education.

Beginning in the freshmen year, students are taught by PhDs. Because USAO offers no graduate programs, undergraduate courses are never taught by graduate assistants. Classes are small, and faculty devote themselves

exclusively to providing students with the finest undergraduate learning opportunities anywhere.

The IDS core curriculum differs from other general education programs in several key ways: the breadth and structure of the program, its emphasis on interdisciplinarity, and the use of team teaching. Students commit fifty credit hours to the IDS program over the course of their college careers. This commitment fosters a connection between faculty and students who, unable to completely withdraw into one academic department, interact with a wide range of people, ideas, and viewpoints on a daily basis.

Students from all majors who need a boost in math or science can take advantage of the MAST (Math and Science Tutors) program, offered free to any student who needs assistance in these subjects.

Vibrant Community

USAO has 1,100 students, four-fifths of whom come from Oklahoma. The rest of USAO's students come from twenty-six states and twelve foreign countries. Minorities represent 22 percent of the student body.

USAO's Lawson Court apartments, which opened in fall 2002, are among the most elaborately appointed residence halls in the state, with a fitness center, convenience store, hair and tanning salon, pool, solarium, and movie theater. Sparks Hall reopened in 2000 after a $5.2 million restoration and houses both men and women. A recent $2.3 million renovation of the Student Center makes it a great place for students to eat and to meet friends.

Students at USAO enjoy the greatest access to the Internet of any college campus in Oklahoma—the only totally wireless campus (including parking lots and outdoor spaces) in the state.

Much of campus life occurs outside the classroom. USAO promotes the idea that the total university experience cannot be realized through academic involvement alone, and that if a university education is a rehearsal for one's future, it should include a variety of experiences.

Nash Library serves as the primary research center, but it also is a great place to meet people, read the latest magazines, surf the Internet, and hang out. Computer labs in Austin Hall, Troutt Hall, and Gary Hall also are open to students, and a special Writing Center in Davis Hall (with tutors available) helps students with writing assignments.

Art and music majors will find special computer labs with equipment geared toward their disciplines. The campus also features minilabs designed specifically for various other major degree programs.

At USAO, there are twenty-seven active clubs on campus with a focus on everything from academics and community service to minority culture and fencing. Along with intercollegiate and intramural sports, there are theater, concerts, art exhibitions, and numerous social activities sponsored by the student association.

Chickasha, a small town of seventeen thousand, is thirty-five miles from Oklahoma City's metro area, which features a variety shopping and arts events. The town is the proud home of the internationally recognized Festival of Light, a holiday extravaganza featuring displays with more than 3.2 million Christmas lights, one of the top holiday destinations in America. It draws more than three hundred thousand people to visit Shanoan Springs Park, located just a few blocks from the USAO campus.

Successful Outcomes

USAO students take charge of their lives and develop their unique potentials with reason, imagination, and human concern. Employers everywhere are seeking problem solvers who think critically and logically, the kind of graduates produced by USAO. In fact, USAO matched the highest placement rates of any college in Oklahoma in one recent study.

At USAO, individual students take responsibility for making decisions about their futures, and advisers assist students in choosing courses to complete a degree in their chosen field of study. On campus, the university counselor, student life counselors, the staff of the student services office, resident assistants, and administrators provide students with information, motivation, and career-development opportunities.

"USAO students find jobs: in one recent study, placement rates for USAO graduates were equal with the highest in Oklahoma."

Fast Facts

The University of Science and Arts of Oklahoma is Oklahoma's only public liberal arts college, founded in 1908.

Web site

http://www.usao.edu/

Location

Chickasha, Oklahoma—within 50 minutes of urban shopping and entertainment in three directions.

Student Profile

1,255 undergraduate students (35% male, 65% female); 34% come from the local county, 58% from across Oklahoma, .08% from outside Oklahoma. 26 other states, 12 other countries represented.

Faculty Profile

82% full-time faculty. 93% hold a terminal degree in their field. 18:1 student/faculty ratio. Average class size is 22.

Residence Life

Moderately residential: 42% of students live on campus. Freshmen required to live on campus.

Athletics

NAIA, Sooner Athletic Conference (SAC). 6 varsity sports (3 men's: basketball, soccer, baseball; 3 women's: basketball, soccer, softball), and 5 intramurals.

Academic Programs

23 majors: American Indian studies; art; biology; business; chemistry; communications; computer science; deaf ed; drama; early childhood education; economics; elementary education; English; history; math; music; natural science; physical education; physics; political science; psychology; sociology; speech-language pathology. Preprofessional programs: predental; premed; prenursing; prepharmacy; prephysical therapy; prevet.

Costs and Aid

2007–2008: $9,500 comprehensive ($4,050 in-state tuition, add $5,580 for out-of-state). 87% of students receive some financial aid. Average award: $6,000.

Endowment

$10.5 million.

More Distinctions

• Ranked No. 1 on the list of "Great Schools, Great Prices" among baccalaureate colleges in the western United States by *U.S.News & World Report's America's Best Colleges*, 2008 edition. For the fifth time, USAO is the only public university in Oklahoma on the list.

• Oklahoma's only public liberal arts college, one of the "Seven Sisters of the South," all former women's colleges serving among the few public liberal arts colleges in America.

• Named to exclusive, Council of Public Liberal Arts Colleges (COPLAC), 2006.

• Ranked No. 1 public undergraduate college in the western United States by *U.S. News & World Report America's Best Colleges* five times (from 2001-2005).

The University of Tulsa

OKLAHOMA

As a comprehensive, doctoral-degree granting institution, The University of Tulsa (TU) provides undergraduate, graduate, and professional education in the arts, humanities, sciences, business, education, engineering, law, nursing, and applied health sciences and participates in NCAA Division IA.

Admissions Contact:

The University of Tulsa
600 South College
Tulsa, OK 74104
(800) 331-3050
Ph: (918) 631-2000
Email: admission@utulsa.edu
www.utulsa.edu

The 4 Distinctions

Engaged Students

Tulsa students enjoy the ability to access a variety of unique learning undergraduate research opportunities. The College of Business Administration at TU provides several distinctive learning opportunities. The Williams Risk Management Center allows students to simulate the stock exchange experience and apply risk-theory studies to the trading floor-room technology, complete with real-time data and ticker tape. The student investment fund in the College of Business Administration now exceeds one million dollars and has been used to subsidize scholarships for students the past few years.

The university provides students with a number of resources to make the TU experience rewarding and effective, including Hurricane AdvenTUre, an extensive orientation experience for freshmen. Students can also take advantage of the Center for Student Academic Support, the Math Resource Lab, and the Writing Center and Lab, all of which provide tutorial assistance and guidance.

The Tulsa Undergraduate Research Challenge (TURC) produces scholars and leaders through a fourfold emphasis on advanced study, undergraduate research, community service, and competition for prestigious scholarships.

Since 1995, TU students have won more than one hundred competitive national scholarships and fellowships, including fourty-one Goldwater scholarships, twenty-four awards from the National Science Foundation, eight Truman scholarships, six awards from the Department of Defense, five Udall scholarships, four Fulbright scholarships, four Marshall scholarships, and six Phi Kappa Phi scholarships.

TU is one of the pioneer institutions selected by the National Science Foundation for the Federal Cyber Service Initiative ("Cyber Corps"). Under this program, the TU Center for Information Assurance, which is emerging as a national leader in computer security education and research, trains students for federal careers in computer security.

TU is committed to offering students opportunities to acquire international and cross-cultural experience and to learn a foreign language. Students can choose from several study-abroad options, including summer, semester, and yearlong programs. TU has international exchange partnerships with universities in Austria, Australia, Finland, France, Germany, England, Switzerland, and New Zealand to name a few. The Center for Global Education can also arrange overseas internships for credit.

Great Teaching

The College of Engineering and Natural Sciences provides international visibility for TU, and the university also features the Henry Kendall College of Arts and Sciences, the College of Business Administration, the College of Law, the Graduate School, and the Division of Continuing Education.

TU's academic atmosphere is close-knit and community oriented. Through a wide range of courses and modes of learning, undergraduate education at The University of Tulsa challenges students to develop an appreciation of liberal education, a breadth of knowledge, and the reasoning and communication skills to enhance their ability to participate fully in contemporary society.

Every undergraduate student must fulfill the requirements of Tulsa's core and general curriculum. The core curriculum encompasses requirements in writing, mathematics, and languages and includes the development of fundamental intellectual skills that equip students with basic competencies.

The Honors Program involves a three-year course of study consisting of eighteen hours of academic credit. Students enrolled in the Honors Program explore the moral and political commitments, scientific achievements, and artistic sensibilities that have shaped the modern world. Honors courses feature lively discussion and debate about primary texts.

In addition to conducting research with professors, students have the opportunity to work with faculty outside the classroom. Working together, students and professors have conducted research at NASA and the Department of Homeland Security and have traveled to local water plants in Tulsa to conduct testing.

Most undergraduates at TU complete their course of study with an intensive, semester-long academic experience in the senior year. The nature of this requirement varies by discipline and may be a design project, a recital, an internship, or a specially designed interdisciplinary or major course.

Vibrant Community

The Student Association at TU puts together programming and sponsors over 160 organizations on campus. These include clubs, lectures, varsity and intramural sports, and honors and leadership groups. There are several activities for students to participate in, including festivals such as Fallfest, Springfest, and Oozefest, and the Toilet Bowl, featuring the traditional campus flag football contest complete with the crowning of a queen. Concerts, comedians, and intramural sports provide campus recreation, as well. Students can participate in service activities through The Office of University and Community Service, including lending their time to organizations such as Habitat for Humanity and the United Way. Students also enjoy watching athletic competition.

Extracurricular activities and service learning can be documented through a co-curricular transcript. This official document is a complement to the academic transcript and formally recognizes learning that takes place outside the classroom.

The Donald W. Reynolds Center is home of the Golden Hurricane basketball program and the venue for major campus performances and concerts. Students enjoy working out at the sixty-four thousand-square-foot Collins Fitness Center. Kendall and Tyrrell Hall is home to on-campus musical theatre and theatre performances, and current students and well-known artists utilize the exhibit space found in the Alexandre Hogue Gallery.

Residential life at TU offers a variety of high-quality housing options. Five furnished residence halls and market-quality apartment complexes provide comfortable living. Freshmen can get off to a great start through the First-Year Residential Experience Program.

TU is only a few miles from downtown Tulsa. The city of Tulsa is an important center of commerce and industry with a thriving arts community. Tulsa features more than 1,100 restaurants and several major shopping centers.

Successful Outcomes

TU professors assist students in cultivating connections in their respective areas, and the career services center helps students find and pursue internships and job leads. Over three hundred businesses and industry professionals visit the TU campus to interview students each year for permanent employment and internships.

Alumni stay involved through the alumni association board. This board meets with the student association to coordinate opportunities to connect with current students. Alumni seek employment of new graduates from TU, with especially strong pipelines existing in engineering, business, civic organizations, and the sciences. Some students choose to continue their education at TU by attending graduate school or the law school, and alumni stay connected and build essential networks through a variety of campus events, including homecoming, athletic events, and alumni chapters.

Fast Facts

The University of Tulsa is a private, doctoral-degree granting, accredited, coeducational institution founded in 1894.

Web site

http://www.utulsa.edu

Location

Tulsa, Oklahoma.

Student Profile

2,882 undergraduate students (53% male, 47% female).

Faculty Profile

306 faculty. 96% hold a terminal degree in their field. 11:1 student/faculty ratio. Average class size is 19.

Residence Life

Highly residential: 65% of undergraduates live on campus.

Athletics

NCAA Division I, Conference USA. 18 varsity sports (8 men's: basketball, cross-country, football, golf, indoor track, outdoor track, soccer, tennis; 10 women's: basketball, crew, cross-country, golf, indoor track, outdoor track, soccer, softball, tennis, volleyball) and more than 40 intramurals.

Academic Programs

Accounting; anthropology; art; art history; arts management; athletic training; applied mathematics; biochemistry; biogeosciences; biological science; communication; chemical engineering; chemistry; computer science; deaf education; earth & environmental science; economics; education (elementary & secondary); electrical engineering; energy management; engineering physics; English; environmental policy; exercise & sports science; film studies; finance; French; geology; German; history; information systems technology; international business & languages; management; management information systems; marketing; mathematics; mechanical engineering; music; music education; musical theatre; nursing; organizational studies; petroleum engineering; philosophy; physics; political science; psychology; religion; Russian studies; sociology; Spanish; speech-language pathology; theatre. certificate and preprofessional programs available.

Costs and Aid

2007–2008: $29,699 comprehensive ($21,690 tuition). 90% of students receive some financial aid.

Endowment

$900 million.

More Distinctions

• U.S. News & World Report ranks the University of Tulsa among the top one hundred national universities out of the 1,400 colleges and universities it surveys.

Augustana College

Admissions Contact:

Augustana College
2001 S. Summit Avenue
Sioux Falls, SD 57197
(800) 727-2844
Ph: (605) 274-0770
Email: admission@augie.edu
www.augie.edu

SOUTH DAKOTA

Augustana College (AC) is a private, comprehensive college (liberal arts and professional) affiliated with the Evangelical Lutheran Church in America. Augustana's motto is "enter to learn; leave to serve," and its mission incorporates five shared values: Christian, liberal arts, excellence, community, and service.

The 4 Distinctions

Engaged Students

Rooted in the liberal arts, this nurturing community encourages students to respect diversity, to think for themselves, and to learn from every experience in life. As one dean put it, "You come here to learn to deal with a diverse, complex, demanding world. By the time you leave, you'll be prepared for anything—and everything." Augustana offers more than sixty-five academic programs, many of which can be a major field of study leading to a BA or a preprofessional degree. The most popular majors are nursing, business administration, biology, and elementary education.

Augustana students take part in experiences beyond the classroom early in their college careers to gain an understanding of the fields they may want to pursue. Freshmen education majors, for example, go into local school classrooms to shadow and observe teachers at work.

Many majors require internships, allowing student to gain valuable insights and experience that enhances what they are learning in the classroom. Students in the natural sciences pursue research opportunities, sometimes leading to published results while they are still undergraduates. Augustana's Gilbert Science Center has some of the best facilities in the region, including a three-environment greenhouse and a scanning electron microscope.

Great Teaching

Augustana faculty members are excellent teachers, current in their disciplines, supportive of students, and committed to serving the broader community. Of the 109 full-time faculty, 86 percent possess PhDs or terminal degrees. The low student to faculty ratio of thirteen to one and small average class size of twenty-three students allow professors to know their students and put them first, encouraging student accomplishment and success.

After orientation, freshmen participate in a new-student seminar for the first seven weeks of the fall term. The class size is small—about fifteen students—allowing the students the opportunity to successfully transition to college and make important connections with faculty and student mentors.

Augustana students study abroad, accompanying faculty on academic trips in January or during spring break to locations around the world, including Greece, Spain, Ireland, Norway, and Singapore. Some students also choose to spend a semester or a year abroad. Students can also engage in study programs for a term in Minneapolis and Washington, DC, and take advantage of service-learning programs like Alternative Spring Break, allowing students to travel to build houses for the needy, tutor youth, or participate in other charitable activities.

All students take two religion courses and a senior capstone course in which students wrestle with moral questions from a variety of perspectives. Augustana also has a notable music program and the Center for Western Studies, devoted to the study of the American West, which publishes books, hosts art exhibits, and provides a history of the Great Plains.

Vibrant Community

A majority of Augustana's 1,747 students live on campus, and 80 percent remain on campus on the weekends. Service brings students and members of the community together. Service projects are part of freshmen orientation, and there is a community-service day each spring during which students and faculty work together to serve the local community through the Service and Learning Together (SALT) program. In 2005, SALT provided more than five thousand hours of community service.

There are over sixty organizations and clubs students can choose to participate in, as well as a dynamic athletic program. Augustana participates in NCAA Division II athletics, and is the only private college in the North Central Conference. Another prominent student group is the Augustana Advocacy Group, which spearheads environmental awareness on campus through events and on-campus speakers.

Other extracurricular offerings are academic, such as the Boe Forum on Public Affairs. Since 1995, Boe speakers have included Archbishop Desmond Tutu, former President George Bush, former Vice President Al Gore, former U.S. Secretary of State Colin Powell, and Her Majesty, Queen Noor of Jordan.

Founded in Chicago in 1860, the college's location shifted several times, accompanying the westward population movement following the Civil War. Sioux Falls, South Dakota, has been home to Augustana, familiarly known as "Augie," since 1918, and the college is an acknowledged leader in undergraduate higher education in the northern plains region.

Sioux Falls, Gateway to the Plains, has a population of about 150,000 and is the largest city in South Dakota. Located in the southeastern section of the state, it is about fifteen miles west of the Minnesota border and eight miles northwest of the Iowa border. It is a day's drive to Minneapolis/St. Paul, Kansas City, or Chicago. Sioux Falls, named for the cascading falls of the Big Sioux River, has a regional medical center and ranks first on Forbes list of best small metro areas in which to start a business or career. Its location at a unique juncture of urban and rural cultures has led to a progressive business climate in a vibrant and healthy community. Sioux Falls offers plenty of diversions, with music, cultural events, and many outdoor activities in its sixty parks. In the past, Expansion Management magazine ranked the city number one in the country for "comfortable life," and Forbes put it in the top twenty-five cities for business and careers.

Successful Outcomes

In any given year, 20–25 percent of Augustana's graduates attend graduate and professional schools. Over the past three years, those seeking entrance to medical school have averaged a placement rate of 90 percent.

Many students are ready to begin their careers immediately after graduation and 98 percent obtained positions related to their field of study within eight months. Popular fields include education, business, nursing, and religious service.

Augustana has an outstanding relationship with local schools and hospitals and has served as a conduit for teachers and nurses into the Sioux Falls educational and health systems. The college also has strong ties to the deaf and hard-of-hearing communities, with well respected programs in the education of the deaf and hard of hearing, communication disorders, and a brand new sign language interpreting program.

Augustana alumni provide an important network for our current students and recent graduates. They assist students in finding internships across the nation and help provide students with interview experience. Alumni also return to campus to hold information sessions about their careers, offering advice for students seeking to follow similar paths.

Famous alumni include Dr. Robert Berdahl, chancellor of the University of California, Berkeley; John Hamre, director of the Center for Strategic and International Studies in Washington, DC; Mel Antonen, baseball writer for USA Today; and Mary Hart, co-host for Entertainment Tonight.

Fast Facts

Augustana College is a four-year, private, residential, comprehensive college (liberal arts and professional) founded in 1860 and affiliated with the Evangelical Lutheran Church in America.

Web site

http://www.augie.edu

Location

Sioux Falls, South Dakota—in the southeastern corner of the state, within a day's drive of Minneapolis/St. Paul, Des Moines, Omaha, and Kansas City.

Student Profile

1,747 students (2:1 female-male ratio); 29 states and a number of countries; over 50% from out-of-state; 5% minority/international.

Faculty Profile

134 faculty; 81% full time; 86% hold a terminal degree in their field; 13:1 student/faculty ratio. Average class size is 23.

Residence Life

65% of students live on campus. Students must live on campus for three years from the time of high school graduation.

Athletics

NCAA Division II, North Central Conference. 16 varsity sports (8 men's: baseball, basketball, cross-country, football, golf, tennis, track & field, wrestling; 8 women's: basketball, cross-country, golf, soccer, softball, tennis, track & field, volleyball), 18 intramural and club sports.

Academic Programs

Accountancy (professional); accounting; architecture; art; athletic training; biology; business administration; chemistry; chiropractic medicine; communication; communication/business; communication disorders; computer information systems; dentistry; economics; education (elementary, middle school, secondary); education of the deaf & hard of hearing; engineering; engineering management; engineering physics; English; exercise science; fitness management; French; German; government & international affairs; history; interdepartmental; international studies; journalism; law; mathematics; medical technology; medicine; modern foreign languages; music; nursing; occupational therapy; optometry; parish ministries; pharmacy; philosophy; physical education; physical therapy; physician assistant; physics; psychology; religion; sign language interpreting; sociology; Spanish; special education; sport management; theatre; theology; veterinary science.

Costs and Aid

2007–2008: $27,020 comprehensive ($20,932 tuition). 99% of students receive some financial aid. Average freshman award: $18,800.

Endowment

$50 million

More Distinctions

• Listed as a top ten regional comprehensive college and a best value in U.S. News & World Report..

Abilene Christian University

TEXAS

Outstanding academics and bold Christian faith are the two leading characteristics that define Abilene Christian University (ACU). The university believes that spiritual commitment demands the highest standards of academic excellence, and its Christian values are woven seamlessly throughout its academic programs, campus life, and the whole of the university experience.

Admissions Contact:

Abilene Christian University
ACU Box 29000
Abilene, Texas 79699
(800) 460-6228
Ph: (325) 674-2000
Email: info@admissions.acu.edu
www.acu.edu

The 4 Distinctions

Engaged Students

Welcoming students of character and ability, the university seeks to produce outstanding graduates ready to become values-centered leaders in every field. Most departments at Abilene Christian require some type of internship experience, opportunities that enable students to learn invaluable real-world lessons about their major in a practical setting. Whether the major is journalism, education, business, or premed, students use these experiences to gain excellent practical knowledge outside the classroom.

Through its partnership with the Council for Christian Colleges and Universities, the university is able to give students access to a variety of learning experiences worldwide. Students at Abilene Christian have studied recently in a number of countries, and the university also offers trips by major, where students are accompanied by their professors.

Living/learning communities at Abilene Christian combine groups of students around common academic interests. In one hall, for example, Bible and business majors might live and study with like-minded peers, while elsewhere students with interests in journalism, political science, and history might form their own communities. Students identify issues and questions they want to explore as members of the living/learning communities.

Great Teaching

Abilene Christian's professors foster students' critical thinking skills, connect biblical principles with daily life, and inspire students to the highest standards of conduct and learning. In addition to top-level credentials, scholarship, and research, ACU professors bring real-world experience to the classroom. They teach beyond theory and help students learn how to apply knowledge. This combination, the university believes, gives ACU students an edge as they prepare to become leaders in the world.

ACU professors stress knowledge, competency, and the importance of character. As they teach and mentor, they model a passion for service and leadership, coaching students in how to be Christian leaders in their careers, community, churches, and family.

And while ACU professors excel in the classroom, they also go out of their way to help students in a variety of ways outside the classroom. Recently, for example, physics students have collaborated with their professors on grant-supported research in national nuclear labs in Texas. In psychology, students have given presentations at national conferences along with their professors, based upon research they have conducted together. Medical mission trips with students and professors also take place regularly.

Vibrant Community

In the spirit of service learning and servant leadership, volunteerism is a way of life at ACU. From child care to work with the elderly, from the arts to manual labor, there are plenty of opportunities to be of service to the church, the college, and the community.

Every spring break, students lead campaigns of service in the United States and abroad. Up to six hundred students donate time to these trips each year.

When not playing intramural sports (over half of students do), students are involved in a number of the ninety groups on campus. In 2006, 1,200 students participated in Sing Song, a popular annual student-produced musical with original songs and costumes.

Geographically diverse origins greatly enhance the diversity of the student body. With representation from almost every state and over sixty countries, Abilene Christian is a diverse campus. Some 20 percent of students come from traditionally underrepresented populations.

ACU is particularly proud of its student-run newspaper. Published twice per week, the paper regularly wins honors as the best in higher education in Texas.

Successful Outcomes

Upon graduation, many ACU alumni find meaningful employment in the major cities of Texas. Whether the student stays in Texas or moves away, they often find a job as the direct result of an undergraduate internship, opportunities and experiences that have proven highly marketable for graduates.

ACU graduates are accepted into medical and dental school at a rate approximately double the national average, and the university's Body & Soul program offers exceptional opportunities for pre-med and pre-dental students. ACU has the largest number of youth ministry majors among all U.S. universities with any religious affiliation. ACU's law school acceptance rate consistently tops 90 percent.

Through its mission and everyday activities, the university campus prepares Christian leaders for the world. By promoting a global awareness and a commitment to learning, Abilene Christian instills in its graduates an understanding of how to live. In major national surveys of student satisfaction, Abilene Christian students regularly give very high marks to their university experience and the preparation for life and work they found there.

When alumni return to Abilene Christian, they find an inviting place to renew friendships, to reflect, and to learn. A proposed conference center and other campus facilities will provide year-round learning opportunities for the entire ACU community.

> "In their undergraduate years at ACU, students participate in field experiences, research, service projects, and academic studies that prepare outstanding men and women to enter graduate and professional schools, to begin or enhance their careers, and to serve and lead."
>
> -Colleges of Distinction

Fast Facts

Abilene Christian University is a four-year, private, residential, comprehensive university in the Christian tradition affiliated with the Churches of Christ. It is one of the largest private universities in the Southwest.

Web site

http://www.acu.edu/

Location

Abilene, Texas—about 3 hours west of Dallas.

Student Profile

4,700 undergraduate students (45% male, 55% female); 50 states, 60 countries. 16% minority, 4% international.

Faculty Profile

200 full-time faculty. 95% of the tenure track faculty hold a terminal degree in their field. 17:1 student/faculty ratio. Average class size is 17.

Athletics

NCAA Division II, Lone Star Conference. 16 varsity sports (8 men's: basketball, indoor track, baseball, football, cross-country, tennis, track & field, golf; 8 women's: basketball, volleyball, indoor track, softball, cross-country, tennis, track & field, soccer) and 22 intramural sports.

Academic Programs

Accounting; agribusiness; animal sciences; art; biblical text; biochemistry; biology; chemistry; Christian ministry; communication; communication sciences & disorders; computer information systems; computer science; electronic media; engineering physics; engineering science; English; environmental science; exercise & sport science; exercise science; family studies; financial management; graphic design; history; information technology; instrumental integrated marketing communication; interdisciplinary studies; international studies; journalism; life science teaching; management; marketing; mathematics; ministry to children & families; missions; music; nursing; nutrition; physical education; physics; piano performance; political science; prearchitecture; predental; preengineering; prelaw; premedical technology; premedicine; preoptometry; prepharmacy; preveterinary medicine; psychology; social work; sociology; Spanish; Spanish teaching; teaching (elementary, high school, middle school, social studies); theatre; vocal performance; vocational missions; worship ministry; youth & family ministry.

Costs and Aid

2006–2007: $23,050 comprehensive ($17,509 tuition). 90% of students receive some financial aid. Average award: $12,960.

Endowment

$262 million.

More Distinctions

• ACU has repeatedly been recognized as one of America's Best Colleges by the U.S. News & World Report guidebook.

Hardin-Simmons University

TEXAS

A private university in Abilene, Texas, Hardin-Simmons University (HSU) serves students who seek a Christian, liberal arts education within a supportive community. Founded in 1891, and now home to some 2,400 students in more than fifty majors, HSU distinguishes itself by delivering educational excellence enlightened by Christian faith and values.

Admissions Contact:

Hardin-Simmons University
2200 Hickory
Abilene, Texas, 79698
(877) GO-HSUTX
Ph: (325) 670-1000
Email: enroll@hsutx.edu
www.hsutx.edu

The 4 Distinctions

Engaged Students

Built on a foundation of academics, faith, and fellowship, the Hardin-Simmons student experience offers high-quality academics in the context of a moral, ethical, and spiritual family of faith, complemented by HSU's welcoming and active campus community.

Students in majors throughout the Hardin-Simmons academic program regularly travel outside the classroom to obtain meaningful practical experiences. Education majors, for example, shadow experienced teachers for a set number of hours before they begin to student teach. Students in geology programs go out on digs with professors. Students in physics or astronomy use the campus observatory for research that enriches what they learn in class.

Students studying business at Hardin-Simmons generally take two-week, for-credit, group trips during their May term, during which they typically work with HSU alumni under the supervision of an HSU professor.

The school of business also sponsors an affiliation with Students in Free Enterprise. HSU students are accepted into the program through an application, and compete statewide and nationally against other schools. Students also work with Junior Achievement, striving to teach school-age children about free enterprise and business.

The outdoor education department at Hardin Simmons offers a sports recreation and management trip over May term. Staying in cabins, students learn outdoor safety and other outdoor skills as they participate in rock climbing, canoeing, and related activities.

Several departments offer internships for students, including communications, business, social work, political science, leadership, and criminal justice.

HSU's study-abroad program sends students to Harlaxton College in the United Kingdom, the Salzburg College program in Austria, and the Homerton College program for juniors in Cambridge, England. Several other travel courses are offered through different departments at various times throughout the year.

Great Teaching

HSU's commitment to educational excellence in a nurturing community starts with its faculty. Students at HSU benefit from classes that are kept small and from a student to faculty ratio that is kept low for a reason. HSU faculty practice in a context that enables them to focus clearly on the lives and learning of their students. Professors make time for mentoring and for going the extra mile to help students succeed. In class and across campus, faculty are always available to help students. Off campus, many professors lead study trips to help students gain practical knowledge in their academic areas of interest.

The HSU Leadership Studies Program is devoted to the development of tomorrow's Christian leaders. The program draws students and faculty from all areas of campus. Leadership students pursue a rigorous exploration of leadership theory, organizational psychology, organizational sociology, and administrative theory. They also study communication, critical thinking, and ethics. Then, working with nonprofit organizations, leadership students practice what they've learned by creating and performing service projects that meet real community needs.

The Hardin-Simmons University honors program provide undergraduate students of exceptional promise with an enriched, educational environment designed to address a wide variety of interests and provide students with an enhanced learning opportunity.

Vibrant Community

The Neighborhood Enhancement Program at Hardin-Simmons supports students in community-based service-learning projects. Students in the program work to rebuild houses, literacy, and hope in the neighborhood around campus. Students teach reading and writing to local students, and tutor them in other subjects.

Among other service activities, HSU students have set up a recycling center, worked with Habitat for Humanity, and helped the local community to weatherize houses.

Over 20 percent of the HSU student body participates in some type of service. One day of HSU's first-year orientation is designated for incoming students to complete a community-service project.

Two student organizations unique to HSU are the Six White Horses and the Cowboy Band. The Six White Horses is a group of six female riders who are accepted through tryouts. Riders care for the horses, which are housed right on campus, and lead them in parades nationwide, including gubernatorial and presidential parades. Endowed by a donor, the program includes an associated museum. The Cowboy Band is made up of forty musicians, selected via audition, who accompany the Six White Horses in parades and marches.

Successful Outcomes

Many students attend HSU as undergraduates with an eye toward staying there for graduate school. The university offers nineteen programs of graduate study, including the only Doctor of Physical Therapy degree in Texas. HSU also has the oldest accredited school of music in Texas.

HSU's career services office and alumni office combine to provide students with opportunities as they pursue employment after graduation. An active series of alumni events bring HSU graduates back to campus to assist undergraduates throughout the school year.

HSU graduates' medical and dental school acceptance rates are three times the national average. HSU graduates have a 98 percent first-time success rate on the teacher certification exam, and HSU graduates score in the ninety-fourth percentile of business school graduates across the country.

The HSU Commitment, which ensures that students' rates of tuition won't increase while they are enrolled full time and making satisfactory progress towards their degree, also states that the university will assist students in career planning and a job search, and will provide services for student personal development. What's more, if students want additional instruction after graduation, they're allowed to audit up to twelve semester hours without cost.

Fast Facts

Hardin-Simmons University is a private, coeducational university located in Abilene, Texas. It was established in 1891 and is affiliated with the Baptist General Convention of Texas.

Web site

http://www.hsutx.edu

Location

Abilene, Texas—located near the center of Texas just 150 miles west of the Dallas-Fort Worth metroplex.

Student Profile

2,372 students (55.6% male, 44.4% female); 94% are from Texas. 24 states and five foreign countries represented: 22% minority, 1% international.

Faculty Profile

118 full-time faculty. 75% of faculty members hold the highest possible degree in their field. 14:1 student/faculty ratio. Average class size is 15.

Residence Life

Moderately residential: 44% of students live on campus.

Athletics

NCAA Division III, American Southwest Conference. 12 varsity sports (6 men's: football, baseball, basketball, tennis, soccer and golf, 6 women's: volleyball, basketball, tennis, soccer, softball, and golf); club sports (handball, outdoor club, racquetball, tennis, tae kwon do, gymnastics), and intramurals (football, basketball, soccer, volleyball, tennis, handball, badminton, xbox, racquetball, mini-golf, golf scrambles, pickleball, texas hold'em, chess and more).

Academic Programs

Accounting, art (graphic design, studio, art education); athletic training; Bible; Biblical languages; biochemistry; molecular biology; biology; business administration; chemistry; church music; church ministry (concentrations in missions, music ministry, pastoral ministry, youth ministry); coaching; communications (concentrations in public relations/advertising, telecommunications, speech communications); computer information systems (education); computer science; criminal justice (concentrations in corrections, police science, administration); economics; education; English; English language arts & reading; environmental science; exercise science; fitness & sports science; finance; French; generic special education; general science (education); geology; history; honors; interdisciplinary generalist (education); leadership studies; legal studies; life sciences composite (education); management; marketing; mathematics; music (music with elective studies in business, education, performance, theory & composition); nursing; philosophy; physical education; physics; political science; psychology; religion; social science composite (education); social work; sociology; Spanish; sports, fitness & leisure studies; speech-language pathology; theatre; theology. Preprofessional programs: predental, preengineering, prelaw, premedical, prepharmacy, prephysical therapy.

Houston Baptist University

TEXAS

Admissions Contact:

Houston Baptist University
7502 Fondreu Road
Houston, TX 77074
(800) 969-3210
Ph: (281) 649-3000
Email: admissions@hbu.edu
www.hbu.edu

Houston Baptist University (HBU), founded in 1960, is a coeducational university in an urban setting. HBU prides itself on a diverse student body; an excellent, dedicated faculty; and a strong sense of mission for the community, the world, and Christ.

The 4 Distinctions

Engaged Students

The most popular majors at HBU are business, biological sciences (including premedical studies), psychology, education, and religion. Students majoring in business are afforded extensive internship opportunities in the city of Houston, both during the academic year and during the summer. These internships regularly translate directly into postgraduate employment.

Students in majors other than business also enjoy significant out-of-the-classroom experiences. For example, premed students participate in job shadowing at the Texas Medical Center, and education students gain classroom experience in various types of schools and in all grade levels.

Participation in the Spiritual Life Program (SLP) is required of all students for graduation. The mission of the program is to nurture community, develop student leadership, build moral character, provide an environment for every student to know Christ, and equip students to serve as Christ's ambassadors beyond HBU.

In order to qualify for graduation, all students must earn a specified total number of points during their college careers. Points are earned through convocation, events sponsored by ACTS (Assisting Communities Through Students), service-learning internships, organization-sponsored events, SLP classes and groups, Quest, and other alternatives.

HBU students are active in various community-service activities. Recently, students taught local children about personal safety and used the university's new ID system to photograph local children and provide them with IDs.

Great Teaching

HBU emphasizes applied, hands-on learning. Most classes are small, discussion-based, and personalized. On average, 57 percent of HBU classes have fewer than twenty students enrolled, and all classes are taught by faculty members, not by teaching assistants.

Professors regularly participate in activities outside the classroom. In the nursing program, for example, students and faculty members join together on intramural teams. The Spiritual Life Program features small-group study sessions that take place in professors' homes.

HBU professors accompany groups of students on two-to-three-week trips to domestic and international destinations. The trips, devoted to specific academic subjects, encourage further development of the student-teacher relationship, while allowing both parties to expand their understanding of the subject matter.

Vibrant Community

The HBU campus is home to several museums, including the Bible in America Museum, which features an extensive collection of rare American Bibles available to the public. The Museum of American Architecture and Decorative Arts contains items relating to the social history and material culture of people settling in Texas between 1830 and 1930.

In the spring of 2007, HBU's new Cultural Arts Center will open. This dynamic building will feature a 1,100-seat auditorium and three museums.

There are more than forty-five clubs and organizations on campus for students to choose from, making it easy for HBU students to find a group that fits their interests and enthusiasms. With a campus located near the cultural center of Houston, HBU students have ready access to world-class performances and other events and attractions, including the Houston Symphony, the Houston Grand Opera, the Houston Ballet, as well as exciting sports, great cuisine, and other universities in the city.

HBU's convocation and speaker series bring exciting speakers to campus and provide an opportunity for students and members of the community to interact in a meaningful way. Students of Houston Baptist continually assist the surrounding community. Every Veterans Day, students have the opportunity to interact with the local assisted-living community at an HBU-hosted event.

Successful Outcomes

High-quality academic work and extensive internships lead to workplace success for HBU graduates. Upon graduation, 98 percent of business majors are employed full-time, and they commonly attribute this success to their internship experiences.

At HBU's Enrichment Center, experienced professional counselors help students and alumni explore their personalities, interests, skills, and values to help them make effective career decisions and develop action plans for the future. The Enrichment Center also hosts mock interviews and recruiting events for students throughout the year.

HBU works to provide students with easy access to successful graduates. Alumni and trustees attend Founder's Day every November, an event that offers students the opportunity to network with people who are successful in the students' chosen fields. Each January, HBU's alumni connections workshop assists the entire community with job placement. Throughout the year, students have access to the many alumni who have remained in Houston after graduation.

Fast Facts

Houston Baptist is a four-year, coeducational, independent institution affiliated with the Baptist General Convention of Texas and was founded in 1960.

Web site

http://www.hbu.edu

Location

Houston, Texas.

Student Profile

1,815 undergraduate students (33% male, 67% female); 20 states, 26 countries; 52% minority. 6% international.

Faculty Profile

109 full-time faculty. 15:1 student/faculty ratio. Average class size is 24.

Residence Life

Mildly residential: 37% of students live on campus.

Athletics

NAIA Division I, Red River Athletic Conference. 5 varsity sports (2 men's: basketball, baseball, 3 women's: basketball, volleyball, softball); 11 intramural and club sports.

Academic Programs

Accounting; art; biblical languages; biochemistry-molecular biology; biology; business (BA/BS); business administration (BBA); chemistry; child development; Christianity; computer information systems management; economics; education; English; finance; French; history; international business; kinesiology; management; marketing; mass communication; mathematics; music; nursing (ADN); nursing (BSN); physics; political science; psychology; public policy; sociology; Spanish; speech communication; writing.

Costs and Aid

2007–2008: $22,731 comprehensive ($17,466 tuition only). 89% of students receive some financial aid.

Endowment

$84 Million.

More Distinctions

• For the third consecutive year HBU has been ranked in the top tier among the "Best Universities" offering master's degrees in the Western region by U.S. News & World Report, as reported in America's Best Colleges for 2007.

• Ranked 11th among colleges and universities in its category for best value. These rankings are based on the net cost of attendance for a student who receives the average level of financial aid. The higher the quality of the program and the lower the cost, the better the value.

Howard Payne University

TEXAS

Howard Payne University (HPU) is a private, coeducational, comprehensive institution. Founded as a college in 1889 in the central Texas town of Brownwood and named for an early benefactor, Edward Howard Payne of Missouri, the school was consolidated with Daniel Baker College in 1953 and became a university in 1974.

Admissions Contact:

Howard Payne University
1000 Fisk Street
Brownwood, TX 76801
(800) 880-4HPU
Ph: (325) 649-8020
Email: enroll@hputx.edu
www.hputx.edu

The 4 Distinctions

Engaged Students

HPU offers more than fifty majors, minors, and preprofessional programs. The most popular majors include Christian studies, education, prelaw, criminal justice, and music.

Developing graduates who are innovators and leaders in their fields is the heart of HPU's Douglas MacArthur Academy of Freedom, established in 1962. The academy, HPU's multidisciplinary honors program, of HPU stresses leadership and academic prowess, providing a broad-based, liberal arts education firmly rooted in Christian values. It offers a flexible academic program designed for honors students who want to advance beyond the normal requirements of an undergraduate degree. Almost any major at HPU can be combined with the academy program of study, which provides real-world experiences such as internships in Washington, DC, and Austin, Texas.

Students not affiliated with the academy find opportunities to become leaders in their fields, too. Many work in local churches, at local TV and radio stations, and in the local hospital. Community service is an important component for many on-campus student groups, including serving meals to the needy, participating in Adopt-a-Highway cleanup, and volunteering at the Boys & Girls Clubs of America.

Howard Payne University offers many opportunities for learning outside the classroom. Through university-sponsored programs, students have had the chance to study abroad in such countries as England, Egypt, Turkey, Italy, and Mexico.

Great Teaching

Affiliated with the Baptist General Convention of Texas, HPU's mission is to provide students with exceptional educations, prepare them for meaningful lives, and guide them on their spiritual journeys. Its goal is to produce leaders who see their roles as that of servants.

HPU's motto is: "Believe. Belong. Become.", which underscores its devotion to its Christian heritage, its close-knit community and an emphasis on students becoming all that they were created to be. The school is committed to keeping attendance costs low, maintaining its "best value" ranking, while providing quality educational experiences in the classroom and beyond.

HPU courses are taught by accomplished professors, who challenge their students and give them tools for a lifetime of critical thinking. More than 50 percent of HPU classes have fewer than twenty students, allowing personal teacher/student interaction around academic work.

Students frequently work with faculty members outside of the classroom, performing research, including taking weekend trips to assist in information gathering and analysis. Professional academic advisors are also available to help students assess their strengths and identify areas needing improvement.

Vibrant Community

HPU's residential campus community is intentionally designed to support students and their goals. The school is committed to the idea that a university experience should provide students with a wide range of opportunities for learning beyond the classroom. Residence halls, organizations, activities, and social experiences combine to encourage deeper teaching, learning, and growth in preparation for service.

Howard Payne University is a distinctively Christian university. It sponsors a campuswide prayer ministry, weekly chapel services, and weekday ministry opportunities. Revival services are held each semester, and every spring HPU hosts a Christian music festival on campus. Students across campus participate in spring break mission trips, and more than 120 students serve in ministry positions each summer.

There are more than thirty clubs and organizations on HPU's campus, so students are sure to find a place to belong. Athletics are also strong: almost 30 percent of students are involved in one of the school's twelve NCAA

Division III intercollegiate sports. A coed cheerleading squad, along with energetic student fans make any sporting event exciting and fun.

HPU is recognized favorably by U.S News & World Report for several factors, including its 15 percent Hispanic enrollment and the fact that 39 percent of its undergraduates receive Pell Grants, indicating a large percentage of low-income students. Encouraging diversity on campus mirrors HPU's goal to prepare students for meaningful life.

HPU students take advantage of Brownwood and its location at the northern edge of the Texas Hill Country. Brownwood is 120 miles southwest of Dallas/Fort Worth, 130 miles northwest of Austin, and 190 miles northwest of San Antonio. A town of about twenty thousand, Brownwood "feels like home." Many local businesses and organizations offer employment to HPU students. HPU students, faculty, and staff serve in the community through civic and church activities.

Successful Outcomes

For HPU graduates, graduation is only the beginning. Many of them enter the workforce within the state, across the nation and around the world. Regardless where they find themselves they strive to make their world a better place. Of those who choose to continue their education in graduate studies, a significant number go to a seminary, medical school, law school or pursue advanced learning within the discipline of education.

"At Howard Payne University, students concentrate on their studies and helping those around them. Service plays a prominent role here, allowing students to experience the value of dedicating time and effort to others in need."

-Colleges of Distinction

Fast Facts

Howard Payne University is a Christian, coeducational university of liberal arts and professional studies affiliated with the Baptist General Convention of Texas and founded in 1889.

Web site

http://www.hputx.edu

Location

Brownwood, Texas—within three hours of San Antonio, Dallas/Fort Worth, and Austin.

Student Profile

More than 1300 undergraduate students (51% male, 49% female); 20 states.

Faculty Profile

73 full-time faculty. 62% hold a terminal degree in their field. 12:1 student/faculty ratio.

Residence Life

Moderately residential: more than 50% of students live on campus.

Athletics

NCAA Division III, American Southwest Conference. 12 varsity sports (6 men's: baseball, basketball, football, soccer, tennis, track & field; 6 women's: basketball, soccer, softball, tennis, track & field, volleyball).

Academic Programs

Academy of Freedom Multidisciplinary Honors Program; accounting; art; Bible; Biblical languages; biology; business administration; business management; chemistry; Christian studies; communication; computer information systems; criminal justice; cross cultural studies; education; English; exercise and sport science; family studies; general studies; history; interdisciplinary political science; liberal arts and sciences; mathematics; multimedia communication; music; philosophy; political science; practical theology; psychology; religious education; social work; social studies composite; Spanish; teaching English to speakers of other languages; theatre; youth ministry.

Graduate Program in Youth Ministry is available

Costs and Aid

2007–2008: $20,736 comprehensive ($15,000 tuition). 95% of students receive some financial aid. Average award: $11,516.

Endowment

$ 47,514,360.

More Distinctions

• Consistently ranked as a Top School in the Western Region of the nation, HPU proudly announces recent recognition by *U.S. News & World Report's Best Colleges 2008*. Among Comprehensive Bachelor's Degree-Granting Colleges in the Western Region, HPU was recognized as one of the Best Values (3rd) and ranked 14th overall. Additionally, HPU was recognized for Campus Ethnic Diversity, Economic Diversity, Small Class Size and High Graduation Rates.

Schreiner University

Admissions Contact:

Schreiner University
2100 Memorial Blvd
Kerrville, TX 78028
(830) 896-5411
(800) 343-4919
Email: admissions@schreiner.edu
www.schreiner.edu

TEXAS

Schreiner University is a small university—and they like it that way. With approximately one thousand students and a thirteen to one student to faculty ratio, Schreiner delivers on its promise of personal attention, empowering students and creating a truly personalized learning experience.

The 4 Distinctions

Engaged Students

At Schreiner, students engage with their coursework, teachers, and peers in many interesting programs. The interdisciplinary studies sequence, a required part of the core curriculum, helps students explore key connections among academic disciplines. Directed study helps students create their own courses with the help of a professor. Schreiner's nationally recognized learning support service assists students with learning disabilities.

Many students at Schreiner pursue internships—often in their senior year—that provide practical experience outside the classroom prior to graduation. Recently, a Schreiner student interned in Washington, DC, with the National Federation of Republican Women, and students in a business class conducted viewer research for a local television station. Students have also interned with the Southwest Foundation for Biomedical Research, the Food and Drug Administration, a local VA hospital, and such corporate leaders as Bechtel Corporation and Anderson.

Service is part of the mission at Schreiner. Starting in their first year, students avidly pursue opportunities to volunteer their time and efforts for those in need, particularly among the Kerrville region's nonprofit organizations. Students are active, for example, in Big Brothers/Big Sisters, the Humane Society, local schools, conservation projects, and campus ministry.

Schreiner offers opportunities for study abroad around the world; recently, students have lived in Spain, Mexico, England, Chile, Egypt, Germany, and Japan. Many Schreiner students opt to join interdisciplinary study trips, two-week forays led by professors to destinations all over the world.

As part of its commitment to meet individual student needs, Schreiner will help students design and conduct original undergraduate research, scholarship, and creative projects. Some students, for example, design and run perceptual and cognitive experiments in Schreiner's behavioral psychology lab. With faculty guidance, students can also design their own internships and senior capstone projects.

Reflecting the diversity of student interests, the top five majors at Schreiner are business, teacher education, biology, graphic design, and accounting.

Great Teaching

Affiliated with the Presbyterian Church (U.S.A.), Schreiner dedicates itself to preparing students to live purposeful, humane, and productive lives. Schreiner prides itself on providing classes that are taught by professors, not assistants, which means it's not only possible that students will know their professors well, it's likely—and encouraged. Teachers and administrators know students by name and listen when they have something to say.

The Schreiner Honors Program provides a customized learning environment to meet the needs and interests of academically advanced students. Schreiner's faculty have many traditions that revolve around interaction with students. On the night before final exams, for example, faculty cook breakfast for students, wishing them well for their tests.

Since most Schreiner students declare majors as freshmen, they get a faculty advisor right away, an expert and friend who will help and guide them not just for their last year or two, but for their full four years at the university. To help ensure that students succeed, Schreiner offers free tutoring in any subject, and to accommodate different learning styles, select courses are offered in a self-paced format.

Vibrant Community

Not far from San Antonio and Austin in the beautiful Texas Hill Country, Schreiner is the kind of place where whitetail deer roam the campus, professors often teach under the shade trees, and a host of outdoor activities await outdoor adventurers.

With more than forty student organization on campus, not to mention intramural sports and recreational activities, Schreiner strives to make students' free time as rewarding and as engaging as their experiences in class. Students at Schreiner can start extracurricular groups with ease—a group of students with similar interests need only petition for funding to start their club. Student groups at Schreiner range from the traditional to the more distinctive. Nearly 30 percent of Schreiner's students play on university NCAA Division III athletic teams. On the more unique end of the spectrum, students in the Japanese animation club watch and create original anime movies and share their work with one another. The eco-terra club, another unique group, focuses on bringing environmental interest and awareness to campus, and has implemented comprehensive recycling initiatives.

Each year, Schreiner students form teams and raise funds for the American Cancer Society's Relay for Life, a Schreiner tradition that was started by a student. Students also participate in the Turkey Trot, which involves running while carrying turkeys to raise money for food for local shelters at Thanksgiving. Other students build houses with Habitat for Humanity, raise money for leukemia research, help children with special needs, and take part in scores of other volunteer opportunities.

Spiritual life at Schreiner is vibrant. In its curriculum and extracurricular activities, Schreiner pursues a mission that "holds as sacred the Christian convictions that each student is unique and that the university's reason for being is to empower every student to grow in mind, body, and spirit."

Before their college experience begins, freshmen bond during Schreiner's Mountaineer Days, an orientation tradition that includes river rafting, a ropes course, and team-building activities that help students form relationships that often last well beyond graduation. To help first-year students transition to college, upper-level students are available to help them as peer advisors.

Schreiner's location provides an ideal setting for outdoor fun and adventure. Students get together to swim, fish, canoe, or kayak on the nearby Guadalupe River. Great places for hiking, mountain biking, rock climbing, and camping are also close to campus. The Schreiner Outdoor Adventure Program (SOAP) rents equipment to the campus community and coordinates its own activities, including snow skiing in New Mexico, hiking in Big Bend National Park, and climbing Enchanted Rock.

Successful Outcomes

To help its students achieve career success, the university works closely with each student, helping them to choose a fulfilling major; the university even has a program in which students can tailor a major to meet their future employment goals.

Schreiner alumni have gone on to rewarding careers in business and industry, the arts, education, medicine, and many other professions. To help students find rewarding work after graduation, Schreiner's career services center provides job fairs and assistance and training in resume writing and interviewing.

Schreiner also has an active network of alumni, trustees, and professors who help young graduates land that all-important first job. The Schreiner network brings undergraduates together with all kinds of professionals, especially in the business sector.

Schreiner students often go on to pursue advanced degrees. Professors at Schreiner take pride in writing letters of recommendation for their students and former students, as the many Schreiner graduates who are accepted into their top choices for graduate school will attest. A Schreiner education opens doors: 100 percent of students who have applied to medical school while at Schreiner have been accepted—many to their first choice.

Fast Facts

Schreiner University is a four-year, private, liberal arts, coeducational university affiliated with the Presbyterian Church and founded in 1923.

Web site

http:// www.schreiner.edu

Location

Kerrville, Texas—one hour northwest of San Antonio, 90 minutes west of Austin.

Student Profile

982 students (43% male, 57% female); 26% minority.

Faculty Profile

75% of full-time faculty. 13:1 student/faculty ratio. Average class size is 20.

Residence Life

Primarily residential: 64% of full-time undergraduates live on campus.

Athletics

NCAA Division III, American Southwest Conference. 13 varsity sports (6 men's: baseball, basketball, soccer, tennis, cross-country, golf; 7 women's: basketball, soccer, volleyball, tennis, cross-country, golf, softball); 12 intramurals including basketball, soccer, indoor & grass volleyball, and flag football.

Academic Programs

Areas of Study: Accounting/information systems; biochemistry; biology; business; chemistry; creative arts; English; engineering 3/2; exercise science; finance; general studies; graphic design; history; humanities; international business; management; management information systems; marketing; mathematics; music; political science; psychology; religion; sport management; teacher education; theatre. Preprofessional Programs: Predentistry; premedicine; preoptometry; preveterinary science; prepharmacy; preseminary; prelaw. Graduate Alternative Teacher Certification, Master of Education, Master of Education in Teaching, Principal Certification.

Costs and Aid

2007-08: $16,408 tuition; 98% of freshmen receive financial aid. Average award: more than $12,000 per year.

Endowment

$47 million.

More Distinctions

• Washington Monthly magazine named Schreiner University among its top picks of American liberal arts colleges.

• Schreiner University has joined the Council on Undergraduate Research. The Council and its affiliated colleges, universities, and individuals share a focus on providing undergraduate research opportunities for faculty and students.

Southern Methodist Univeristy

TEXAS

Located in the heart of Dallas, Texas, Southern Methodist University (SMU) is an independent, coeducational, four-year university. The university can be a comfortable fit for the student looking to explore new ideas and experiences while remaining firmly rooted in the American mainstream.

Admissions Contact:

Southern Methodist University
P.O. Box 750181
Dallas, TX 75205
(800) 323-0672
Ph: (214) 768-2000
Email: ugadmission@smu.edu
www.smu.edu

The 4 Distinctions

Engaged Students

Described as "open-minded, outgoing, and friendly," SMU students are known as forward-looking, yet they tend to appreciate traditional values and lifestyles.

According to a survey by *Inc. Magazine*, Dallas is the hub of the country's fastest growing private companies. This gives SMU students tremendous opportunities for internships. For example, 80 percent of School of Engineering graduates complete an internship during their undergraduate careers. Students in the Cox School of Business are offered internship opportunities both locally and nationally with top-ranking companies.

The university provides several opportunities for undergraduates to conduct research. The Richter Fellowship awards grant money to support the costs SMU students incur while researching international or multicultural topics, often in a foreign country. Students studying biomedicine can take advantage of summer research opportunities through the Biomedical Researchers in Training Experience Scholars Program. SMU psychology majors start researching and conducting experiments as early as their sophomore years.

SMU offers twenty-five study-abroad programs in thirteen countries throughout Europe, Asia, Australia, Great Britain, and North America. SMU's campus in northern New Mexico, also known as SMU-in-Taos, offers summer-credit and noncredit courses in disciplines such as anthropology, geology, biology, art history, music, music history, photography, painting, sculpture, literature, and history. Additionally, the program offers a variety of wellness activities, including hiking, biking, river rafting, rock climbing, horseback riding, and fly-fishing.

Great Teaching

SMU offers excellent academic programs and abundant opportunities for students to learn and exercise their leadership abilities. As one professor said, "SMU is large enough that students have almost unlimited opportunities, but small enough that they can get to know individual faculty members very well."

First-year orientation, known as Academic Advising Registration and Orientation (AARO), is held throughout the summer. Here, incoming first-year students learn important SMU traditions and meet their academic advisors to register for classes.

"One-on-one interaction is the heart of an SMU education," says one faculty member. Every first-year student takes a rhetoric class with eighteen or fewer students to ensure that the classroom experience is mutually beneficial for both the students and the professor. The SMU faculty are known for their accessibility to students outside scheduled office hours. Some professors even offer their home or cell phone numbers in case students need assistance after office hours end.

The Altshuler Learning Enhancement Center (A-LEC) offers an array of programs to help student stay on track, including seminars on time and stress management, writing tutorials from full-time faculty, and a course titled ORACLE (Optimum Reading, Attention, Comprehension, and Learning Efficiency). These services are offered to students free of charge Sunday through Friday.

Vibrant Community

Upon first glance, SMU looks like a classic American campus with its beautiful Georgian architecture, perfectly groomed landscape, and smiling students, but the university is definitely a twenty-first-century college. Any student can find their home from one of the several living arrangements, including first-year halls, four-year halls, honors halls, fine-arts communities, and wellness communities.

Honors students have the opportunity to live in special communities. The Hilltop Scholars Program is a live-and-learn community for first-year students. These students live together in Perkins Hall and take up to three classes together. The University Honors Program also offers honors students the option to live in Virginia-Snider, a hall dedicated to the honors community. Students interested in community service can live in the Service House, where their volunteer work and hours help pay for room and board.

SMU is home to over two hundred student organizations and hosts an active intramural athletics program. About 36 percent of SMU students are involved in the fraternity and sorority system. In addition, students can stay active at the new Dedman Recreation Center, which includes a three-thousand-square-foot cardio and weight room, an indoor soccer field, racquetball courts, two sand volleyball courts, and a three-story rock wall. Varsity athletic events also help bring the students together. SMU is a Division I-A school and part of Conference USA. In addition to student clubs and intramurals, the Willis M. Tate Distinguished Lecture Series hosts world famous guests such as Colin Powell, Anderson Cooper, Al Gore, and Barbara Walters.

In addition to all the exciting activities on campus, there's also a lot to do right across the street, and a nearby light-rail system makes the city accessible. There are numerous shops and restaurants within walking distance of the campus. Some of the best shopping and art in the world can be found in Dallas. In fact, SMU's Meadows Museum houses the largest collection of Spanish art outside of Spain. Dallas is also home to several successful professional sports teams like the Dallas Mavericks, Dallas Stars, Texas Rangers, and FC Dallas.

Successful Outcomes

Whether students are planning to attend graduate school or join the workforce, the SMU Hegi Family Career Development Center is prepared to help. The center provides comprehensive testing services, academic guidance, seminars on resume building, and mock interviews. The career center also has a job and internship placement program and is proud to say that there are more internships offered to SMU than students to fill them.

SMU has approximately one hundred thousand alumni worldwide. Alumni continue to show their appreciation for the eduation at SMU by staying connected to the university through donations, guest lectures, and mentoring opportunities.

SMU has approximately one hundred thousand alumni worldwide and around 36,000 SMU alumni live and work in the Dallas-Fort Worth area. Dallas is home to more than six thousand companies and organizations and is consistently ranked as one of the nation's best locations for its thriving environment for commerce. Because of SMU's close ties with the community, area companies, and other organizations, students can gain valuable work experience through internships and part-time jobs. Internships are available in a number of fields, including the humanities. In addition, many top executives serve as student mentors and visit campus for lively exchanges of information and ideas. Alumni continue to show their appreciation for the education at SMU by staying connected to the university through donations, guest lectures, and mentoring opportunities.

Fast Facts

Southern Methodist University is a four-year private university founded in 1911.

Web site

http://smu.edu

Location

University Park—five miles north of downtown Dallas.

Student Profile

6,296 undergraduate students (50 % male, 50 % female); 50 states and territories, 90 countries; 21.6% minority, 9% international.

Faculty Profile

600 full-time faculty. 84% hold a terminal degree in their field.12:1 student/faculty ratio.

Residence Life

Highly residential: All first-year students and approximately 50% of upperclassmen live on campus.

Athletics

NCAA Division I, Conference USA. 16 varsity sports (6 men's: basketball, football, golf, soccer, swimming & diving, tennis; 10 women's: basketball, cross-country, equestrian, golf, rowing, soccer, swimming & diving, tennis, track & field, volleyball), 20 club sports, and 30 intramurals.

Academic Programs

Accounting; advertising; anthropology; art; art history; biochemistry; biological sciences; chemistry; cinema-television; computer engineering; computer science; computer science with biomedical options/premedical options; corporate communications and public affairs; dance; economics; economics with finance applications specialization/systems analysis specialization; electrical engineering; electrical engineering with communications and signal processing specialization/computer specialization or telecommunications specialization; electronic media; English; English with creative writing specialization; environmental chemistry; environmental engineering; environmental geology; environmental science; environmental science with engineering emphasis; ethnic studies; finance; financial consulting; foreign languages and literatures; general business; geology; geophysics; history; individualized studies in the Liberal Arts; international studies; journalism (converged media), Latin American studies, management, management information systems; management science; management science with biomedical options/premedical options; marketing; markets & culture; mathematics; mechanical engineering, medieval studies; music; music composition; music education with Teacher Certification; music performance; music therapy; philosophy; physical therapy certification; physics; political science; predental studies; prelegal Studies; premedical studies; psychology; public policy; real estate finance; religious studies; sociology, statistical science, teacher certification at the elementary and secondary levels; theatre.

Costs and Aid

2007–2008: $42,065 comprehensive ($27,400 tuition). More than 70% of students receive some financial aid.

St. Edward's University

TEXAS

St. Edward's University is a private, Catholic, liberal arts institution located in the vibrant, active city of Austin. Founded by the Congregation of Holy Cross, St. Edward's remains committed to a values-based liberal arts education, preparation for careers, and service to the community.

Admissions Contact:

St. Edward's University
3001 South Congress Avenue
Austin, Texas 78704
(800) 555-0164
Ph: (512) 448-8400
Email: seu.admit@admin.stedwards.edu
www.stedwards.edu

The 4 Distinctions

Engaged Students

St. Edward's University students benefit from unique programs, including a professional writing track in English and a minor in journalism. St. Edward's also offers the only undergraduate theatre program under a U/RTA contract with the Actors' Equity Association. Students who successfully complete the requirements of the Membership Candidate Program are eligible to join Actors' Equity upon graduation.

One strong characteristic of St. Edward's University is the commitment to community service. Each year during the student-led BIG Event, students, faculty, and staff members provide services that benefit the neighbors and neighborhoods that surround the campus. Students pull weeds, plant flowers, wash windows, clean gutters, and repair fences. The university also has an active Alpha Phi Omega chapter, which focuses on principles of leadership, friendship, and service.

Students from every major can benefit from an international experience. Semester-abroad locations include Mexico, Argentina, and Germany. Shorter study-abroad programs are also an option. Faculty-led trips are customized, shorter trips, and have included studying tropical ecology in Panama, marketing in France, and photo communications in China.

Through the campus ministry, students can participate in immersion programs in destinations such as Peru, Ireland, or India. The immersion trips are educational, service oriented, and have a spiritual component. Students have the chance to work on projects that are necessary for the community at that particular time. In addition to serving, students reflect, discuss, and journal on topics such as the economy, church, and political reality.

The annual Symposium on Undergraduate Research and Creative Expression (SOURCE) allows St. Edward's undergraduates to present original research or artistic works to a large audience of faculty and peers.

Great Teaching

The academic experience at St. Edward's is highlighted by small classes. The fourteen to one student to faculty ratio ensures that students receive an abundance of personal attention, and the physical layout of the campus fosters strong student-faculty relationships, with buildings that are close together and numerous public meeting areas. The campus coffee shop, with its laid-back environment, is a popular place for professors to hold office hours.

The honors program at St. Edward's offers even smaller courses with an increased level of participation. Students in the program take a minimum of seven honors seminars and complete an honors senior thesis. The senior thesis gives students an opportunity to complete a project that fits their interests and will benefit them as they go on to graduate school or into a career. Recent examples include an education student who planned and conducted a study for the Austin Independent School District to evaluate athletic programs for girls, a psychology student who researched studies on how memory can be manipulated, and a biology student who explored the politics of reforming the American health-care system.

Through freshman studies, incoming freshmen enroll in a writing class and a team-taught course called introduction to the liberal arts. Each year the program has a common required reading as well as a common theme that extends beyond the classroom. Examples of this have included guest speakers, including the author of the common reading, and a theatre department production examining the common theme. Past themes of freshman studies courses have included Islam and the farmworker rights movement.

Vibrant Community

The 160-acre hilltop campus in Austin is home to half of St. Edward's undergraduate students. Freshmen are required to live on campus. Students enjoy the perks of the campus's urban location. On weekends, students can take advantage of "the live music capital of the world," Austin, Texas. The city is home to more music venues per capita than any other U.S. city.

With 38 percent minority students, St. Edward's serves a culturally diverse student body. There are over sixty student clubs and organizations in areas such as academic and professional, club sports, community service, cultural, honor societies, political, recreational, special interest, and spiritual. On-campus events such as theatre performances and the annual Festival of Lights keep students busy, and the freshman vs. faculty/staff softball game in the spring is a popular event that many students participate in and attend.

St. Edward's offers two living/learning communities: Global Understanding and Service/Social Justice. The Global Understanding community focuses on the principles of American cultures and cultures outside of the United States. As a member of this community, students participate in monthly dinners, weekly chats, and service activities. The Service/Social Justice community is involved in service projects, reflection groups, and monthly dinners served with an interest theme.

Successful Outcomes

St. Edward's is also committed to helping students obtain internships and plan for careers. Students network through their professors and have access to the career planning office's internship database and career library. The annual job and internship fair provides students with opportunities to network with companies such as the Austin American-Statesman, Clear Channel Radio, the FBI, the Round Rock Independent School District, the Texas Department of Public Safety, and the U.S. Army. The career planning department also hosts group workshops and one-on-one sessions on topics such as writing a solid resume and cover letter, interviewing, and networking.

The career planning office can also help students identify appropriate graduate schools, apply for admission, study for entrance exams, and locate financial assistance. St. Edward's University students have an 80 percent acceptance rate into medical school, and 94 percent of graduates are employed within six months of graduation.

Fast Facts

St. Edward's University is an independent, coeducational Catholic university founded in 1885.

Web site

http://www.gotostedwards.com

http://www.stedwards.edu

Location

Austin, Texas.

Student Profile

5,224 students (40% male, 60% female); 3,282 undergraduates; 33 states and 33 countries; 38% minority.

Faculty Profile

192 full-time faculty members. 78% hold a terminal degree in their field. 14:1 student/faculty ratio. Average class size is 20.

Residence Life

Moderately residential: 50% of students live on campus.

Athletics

NCAA Division II, Heartland Conference. 13 varsity sports (6 men's: baseball, basketball, cross-country, golf, soccer, tennis; 7 women's: basketball, cross-country, golf, soccer, softball, tennis, volleyball), and several intramurals, including basketball, co-ed softball, flag football, dodgeball and volleyball.

Academic Programs

Accounting; accounting information technology; art; biochemistry; bioinformatics; biology; business administration; chemistry; communication; computer information science; computer science; criminal justice; criminology; digital media; economics; English/language arts and reading; English literature; English writing and rhetoric; entrepreneurship; environmental chemistry; environmental science and policy; finance; forensic chemistry; forensic science; graphic design; history; international business; international relations; kinesiology; language arts; Latin American studies; liberal studies; management; marketing; mathematics; philosophy; photocommunications; political science; psychology; religious studies; social studies; social work; sociology; Spanish; Spanish/bilingual education; Spanish/international business; theater arts.

Costs and Aid

2006–2007: $29,500 comprehensive ($20,400 tuition). 89% of students receive some financial aid. Average award: $11,010.

Endowment

$59 million.

More Distinctions

• Top 25 Master's-granting institutions in the western region, according to *U.S. News & World Report.*

• Students ranked St. Edward's University above the national average in all categories in the National Survey of Student Engagement.

St. Mary's University

Admissions Contact:

St. Mary's University
One Camino Santa Maria
San Antonio, TX 78228-8503
(800) 367-7868
Ph: (210) 436-3126
Email: uadm@stmarytx.edu
www.stmarytx.edu

TEXAS

Founded in 1852 by the Society of Mary (the Marianists), St. Mary's University is a private, Catholic, coeducational institution. The university's combination of interpersonal relationships, academic excellence, and global perspective results in a community of scholars that crosses generations and cultures.

The 4 Distinctions

Engaged Students

Academic excellence and service are part of St. Mary's educational legacy. Study-abroad programs are designed to stretch the imagination and take experiences to new levels, as well as encourage a global consciousness on the part of both faculty members and students. St. Mary's conducts semester programs in London and Spain, as well as summer study-abroad programs in Asia, the biblical lands of the Middle East, Innsbruck, Mexico, the Southern Cone in Brazil and Chile, and numerous summer immersion trips that combine cultural immersion and community service. The university is also a member of a consortium of U.S. colleges and universities that participate in American University's Washington Semester Program. Partnerships and agreements with institutions in Guadalajara, Mexico; Madrid, Spain; Rome, Italy; and Viña del Mar, Chile, offer students additional opportunities for study abroad and service.

The high degree of personal attention given to students is a major strength of St. Mary's. St. Mary's students have the opportunity to conduct progressive undergraduate research using critically emerging technology in bioengineering and biology. Internships in Texas, around the country, and abroad give students a competitive career edge recognized by top employers.

The Entrepreneur Scholars (E-Scholars) Program in the Bill Greehey School of Business is open to students from all majors across campus. E-Scholars attend classes designed specifically for them, go on domestic and international business trips, receive one-on-one advice, and receive assistance from business mentors while developing and implementing their entrepreneurial ideas. In addition, E-Scholars also have the opportunity to network with successful entrepreneurs and executives from the business community.

St. Mary's students are capable of competing nationally. An international business major won first place in the Elevator Pitch Competition at the National E-Scholar Student Consortium in February 2007. Competitors pitched their ideas for a business concept to two different panels of judges on the first day of competition. The following day, the top ten presenters advanced to another panel of judges, where the St. Mary's student took first place.

The curriculum for St. Mary's honors program spans eight courses, beginning and ending with philosophy, and including courses in the social and natural sciences, aesthetics, and theology. As a capstone project, each honors scholar undertakes a senior thesis, demonstrating the ability to conduct original research at an advanced level. Beyond the curriculum, students find a stimulating variety of activities ranging from plays and concerts to community-service projects and social events, often in collaboration with the student organization, the St. Mary's University Society of Honors Scholars. The majority of honors-program graduates go on to pursue further studies in medicine, law, and other professions.

Great Teaching

St. Mary's challenges students to academic excellence and personal integrity, while educating them for possibilities of greatness in their careers and communities. St. Mary's professors are committed to teaching, and constantly renew their own intellectual perspectives through research, study, and publishing. This spirit of shared learning and a low student to faculty ratio mean that teachers track each of their students, offering personal attention in class, during office hours, or by e-mail. Faculty members take an active interest in students outside the classroom, with many serving as club moderators. Their concern for the individual student is matched by their professional accomplishment—90 percent of the faculty members at St. Mary's have earned a PhD or the highest degree in their field. More than twenty faculty members are Fulbright Scholars or winners of the Piper Professor award for teaching excellence.

It may be unusual for undergraduates at larger universities to do professional-level research, but not for St. Mary's students. For example, biology majors assist Dr. Timothy Raabe, an associate professor of biology studying cell behavior and development that could lead to a better understanding of diabetic neuropathy, a debilitating condition affecting some diabetes patients. Some students are investigating a cell growth factor that could ultimately offer a treatment for multiple sclerosis. Others have worked with Dr. Albert Y.T. Sun, an associate professor of engineering, on the development phases of an innovative hip stem fabrication.

Vibrant Community

Quite possibly one of the friendliest big cities, San Antonio, the seventh-largest city in the United States, offers boundless opportunities for internships and recreation. San Antonio's attractions include the historic Spanish missions, art museums and galleries, Six Flags and SeaWorld theme parks, malls, outlets, and the beautiful Paseo del Rio—a collection of shops, restaurants, and outdoor cafes along the San Antonio River. St. Mary's University offers a 135-acre campus in northwest San Antonio, ten minutes from downtown, where modern and historic buildings provide students with state-of-the-art learning facilities and comfortable living areas.

St. Mary's University students participate in the campus community, exploring interests in academic, political, cultural, social, and community-service activities; university-sponsored clubs; and in programs such as ROTC and the Ethics Bowl. St. Mary's offers exceptional team-sport opportunities in twelve NCAA Division II varsity-level sports, and boasts five national championships.

At St. Mary's University, faith development is a significant and special part of the learning experience. University Ministry, in the Catholic and Marianist traditions, serves St. Mary's by encouraging and promoting personal development, growth in the community, lived faith values, leadership, and service to the university and the world. University ministry provides opportunities for students to enhance their faith lives through worship and retreats. As part of a caring community atmosphere, students from all religious traditions are welcome at St. Mary's.

Successful Outcomes

St. Mary's, cited as a national model for student success by the Education Trust, is among the top ten schools in Texas for high graduation rates. Among St. Mary's alumni are three hundred elected public officials and more than twenty graduates who have earned the rank of general or admiral in the U.S. Armed Forces.

Eleven five-year combined bachelor's and master's degree programs enable students to earn both degrees in the nurturing environment of St. Mary's. Other institutions where students have gained admission to pursue advanced degrees include Dartmouth Medical School, Harvard University, Johns Hopkins University, New York University, Princeton University, Purdue University, the University of Texas, University of Chicago, University of Michigan, and University of Notre Dame, among others.

The career services center ties programming directly to students' needs and interests, and provides a number of resources for successful career development. Among these are a career computer lab, employer files, the job-search database, and an extensive career-services library with close to five hundred titles. Each year, the career services center organizes a number of special programs to prepare students for the career search. Among the most prominent are the resume drive, mock interview day, and the professional etiquette dinner. Students network with potential employers through on-campus interviews, resume referrals, and career fairs.

Fast Facts

St. Mary's University is a four-year liberal arts institution affiliated with Roman Catholic Church. St. Mary's was founded in 1852 by the Society of Mary (Marianists), and is the oldest Catholic university in Texas and the Southwest.

Web site

http://www.stmarytx.edu

Location

San Antonio, Texas—10 minutes from downtown.

Student Profile

2400 undergraduate students (40% male, 60% female); 36 states and territories, 41 countries; recognized Hispanic Serving Institution; 3.5% international.

Faculty Profile

183 full-time faculty; 90% hold a terminal degree in their field; 13:1 student/faculty ratio. Average class size is 20.

Residence Life

Moderately residential: 47% of undergraduate students live on campus; 70% of first-year students live on campus. First-year students are required to live in University housing unless they are local students who remain with their families.

Athletics

NCAA Division II, Heartland Conference. 12 varsity sports (5 men's: baseball, basketball, golf, soccer, tennis, 7 women's: basketball, cross-country, golf, soccer, softball, tennis, volleyball), and 13 intramurals.

Academic Programs

Accounting; biochemistry; biology; chemistry; computer science (computer information systems, computer science, computer science/applications systems); criminal justice; criminology; economics; engineering (computer engineering, electrical engineering, engineering management, engineering science, industrial engineering, software engineering/computer applications); English (English, English communication arts, speech communication); entrepreneurial studies; exercise & sport science; finance (corporate financial management, financial services/risk management); French; general business; history; human resources; information systems management; international business; international relations; marketing; mathematics; multinational organization studies; music; philosophy; physics (applied physics, physics); political science; psychology; sociology; Spanish; teacher education; theology. Pre-professional programs: allied health; dentistry; law; medicine; nursing; pharmacy. Graduate programs and a School of Law are available.

Costs and Aid

2007–2008: $28,308 comprehensive ($20,300 tuition). 84% of students receive some financial aid. Average award: $20,416.

Endowment

$148,719,000.

Stephen F. Austin State University

TEXAS

Stephen F. Austin State University (SFA) is a public, coeducational, comprehensive institution awarding bachelor's, master's, and doctoral degrees. Founded as a teachers' college by the Texas legislature in 1921, it remains an independent, state-supported university not associated with a state university system.

Admissions Contact:

Stephen F. Austin State University
2008 Alumni Drive
Rusk Bldg. Room 206
Nacogdoches TX 75961
Ph: (936) 468-2504
Fax: (936) 468-3849
Email: admissions@sfasu.edu
www.sfasu.edu

The 4 Distinctions

Engaged Students

Named for the man viewed as the founder of Anglo-American Texas, Stephen F. Austin State University is known for its excellence in undergraduate education, its vital community outreach programs, and its advancement of knowledge. Its mission is to provide students with a foundation for success, a passion for learning, and a commitment to responsible global citizenship in a community dedicated to teaching, research, creativity, and service.

Many of the university's 10,100 undergraduate students choose to attend SFA because it combines the feeling of a small college with the advantages of a large campus. Students want the personal experience offered by SFA's faculty and staff rather than the feeling of being treated like a number, as they might expect at larger state schools.

SFA offers eighty majors and 120 study areas. In recent years, students have been drawn to SFA in increasing numbers for its programs in forestry, music, theatre, and the visual arts. Elementary education is the most popular major; one of every six SFA students pursues an elementary education major. Health and physical education and nursing training are popular, as well.

The College of Education draws roughly 30 percent of the student population, followed by the College of Liberal Arts with 26 percent, the College of Business with 16 percent, the College of Sciences and Mathematics with 16 percent, the College of Fine Arts with 7 percent, and the College of Forestry and Agriculture with 5 percent. SFA's School of Forestry is one of only two in Texas.

Nearly a third of SFA's freshmen participate in an experiential leadership program. The students are self-selected and go on an initial three-day trip with the goal of gaining the confidence and perspective to become leaders among their peers. The Freshman Leadership Academy is another program to train students for leadership roles on campus. First-year students who were leaders in high school are selected for the highly competitive, credit-earning program.

SFA 101 is a credit-earning, nonremedial course that helps students establish a solid foundation for a successful college experience, including learning good study habits and how to lead a balanced campus life.

An increasing number of SFA students now participate in study-abroad opportunities. Students have traveled to locations all over the world. The number of international students attending SFA has grown recently, leading to greater diversity on campus.

Great Teaching

SFA prides itself on the faculty's focus on teaching rather than performing research. With a relatively low student to faculty ratio of nineteen to one, professors dedicate themselves to maintaining strong relationships with students, and are accessible outside the classroom. Exceptional students may qualify for SFA's School of Honors, which provides opportunities for one-on-one instruction with professors from different academic disciplines.

Service learning plays an important role at SFA. For example, a music professor created an alliance with local schools where there were no music teachers. As part of the program, SFA music students provide lesson opportunities and teach classes at the schools. In other areas, such as nursing and social work, community-outreach programs developed by SFA faculty provide students with a wide range of hands-on experiences.

Vibrant Community

SFA is located in the town of Nacogdoches, the oldest town in Texas, in the Piney Woods region of deep East Texas. The town has a slow-paced and relaxed atmosphere, and an interesting history. It is about 140 miles northeast of Houston and about 180 miles southeast of Dallas. Shreveport, Louisiana, is located about one hundred miles to the northeast.

Highly residential in nature, campus life at SFA is active, and the atmosphere is inclusive. Five thousand students live on campus in traditional dorms. The university requires students who have earned fewer than a certain number of credit hours to live on campus, and 80 percent of the remainder of SFA students live nearby. An academic excellence dorm, one of two "quiet dorms" on campus, is an option for honors program students with high GPAs in high school and at SFA, and for those who have completed a service-learning requirement.

There are more than 225 clubs for students to join. Greek activities have a big impact on campus, though only 12 percent of SFA students belong to a fraternity or sorority. Service activities are important for all SFA students, and forty thousand hours of community service were completed during the 2005–2006 academic year.

SFA's 360-acre campus is located in the center of Nacogdoches, and it serves as an activity hub for the wider community. The 2007 opening of the Art Center at the Old Opera House created a center for the visual arts serving both the university and the greater East Texas community. In addition, SFA has a six-hundred-plus-acre agricultural research center, roughly eighteen acres of experimental forest, and another twenty-five-acre forestry field station.

Successful Outcomes

SFA alumni are active in university affairs. They participate at homecoming, act as mentors for current students in the Mentor Ring Program, and help SFA students succeed. Notable alumni include national business leaders, government officials, artists, professional athletes, and professional cheerleaders. The latter are graduates of SFA's Spirit Program, with its award-winning cheerleaders and Pompon dance teams.

Notable SFA alumni include business leaders, educators, government officials, artists, professional athletes.

Kim Brimer '67, Texas State Senator; Larry Centers '89, NFL veteran, Top 20 Receivers Pro Football Hall of Fame; Wayne Christian '73, Texas State Representative; Kelvin Davis '88, CNN news executive; Nancy Dickey '72, President, Texas A&M Univ. Health Science Center and Past President of the American Medical Association; Nell Fortner '87, Led Team USA to a Basketball Gold Medal in Summer 2000 Olympic Games; Don Gaston '54, Former General Manager of the Boston Celtics; Jill Grove '90, Opera Singer; Will Jennings '65 & '67, Oscar and Grammy Award-winning songwriter; Joseph W. Kennedy '35, Co-discoverer of plutonium; Brad Maule '74, 14+ years as Dr. Tony Jones on ABC's General Hospital; Mike Moses '74, Former Superintendent of Dallas ISD and Former Texas Commissioner of Education; Bill Owens '73, Former Governor of Colorado; O.A. "Bum" Phillips '50, Former Houston Oilers Head Coach; Mike Quinn '96, Houston Texans, Pittsburg Steelers, Dallas Cowboys, Miami Dolphins; Charles Runnels '48, Chancellor of Pepperdine University; Michael Schneider '65, U.S. District Judge for Eastern District of Texas; Terrance Shaw '94, 2003 Super Bowl runner-up Oakland Raiders, and 2002 Super Bowl champions New England Patriots; Brady Smith '94, TV actor on "Jag," "CSI-Miami" and "ER"; Steve Stagner '91, President, CEO of Mattress Firm; Gen. O.R. "Cotton" Whiddon '55, three-star general, U.S. Army retired.

Fast Facts

Stephen F. Austin State University (SFA) is a 4-year, state-supported, accredited comprehensive university founded in 1923.

Web site

http://www.sfasu.edu

Location

Nacogdoches, Texas —140 miles northeast of Houston and 180 miles southeast of Dallas.

Student Profile

11,756 students (40% male, 60% female); 26.5% minority, 1.3% international.

Faculty Profile

457 full-time faculty. 78% hold a terminal degree in their field. 19:1 student/faculty ratio. Average class size is 28.

Residence Life

Mildly residential: 38% of students live on campus.

Athletics

NCAA Division I, Southland Conference. 14 varsity sports (6 men's: baseball, basketball, cross-country, football, golf, track; 8 women's: basketball, cross country, equestrian, soccer, softball, tennis, track, volleyball).

Academic Programs

Accounting; agribusiness; agricultural development; agricultural development-production; agricultural machinery; agronomy; animal science; applied arts and sciences; art; art history; biochemistry; biology; business economics; chemistry; child development and family living; communication disorders; communication-journalism; communication-radio/TV; communication-speech communication; computer information systems; computer science; creative writing; criminal justice-corrections; criminal justice-law enforcement; criminal justice-legal assistant; dance; deaf and hard of hearing; economics; elementary education; English; environmental science; family and consumer sciences; fashion merchandising; finance; foods and nutrition/dietetics; forest management; forest recreation management; forest wildlife management; forestry; French; general agriculture; general business; geography; geology; gerontology; health science; history; horticulture; hospitality administration; humanities; interdisciplinary studies – education; interior design; interior merchandising; international business; kinesiology; liberal studies; management; marketing; mathematics; military science; music; nursing (generic); nursing (post RN); orientation & mobility; philosophy; physics; physics-engineering; political science; poultry science; prechiropractic; predental hygiene; predentistry; preengineering; prelaw; premedical technology/clinical laboratory sciences; premedicine; preoccupational therapy; preoptometry; prepharmacy; prephysical therapy; prephysician's assistant; preseminary/ministry; preveterinary medicine; psychology; public administration; rehabilitation services; secondary education; social work; sociology; Spanish; special education; theatre.

Costs and Aid

2007–2008: Texas Resident Tuition and Fees (12 semester hours): $2,532; Texas Non-Resident Tuition and Fees: $5,868. During 2005-06, 83% of students received some financial aid. Average Award: $2,642.

Texas Christian University

TEXAS

Texas Christian University (TCU), founded in 1873, delivers a world-class, values-centered university experience, consistently ranking in the top 5 percent of the 3,500 universities and colleges in the nation. TCU has a historic relationship with the Christian Church (Disciples of Christ), and welcomes students of all religious backgrounds and faiths.

Admissions Contact:

Texas Christian University
2800 South University Drive
TCU Box 297013
Fort Worth, TX 76129
Ph: (817) 257-7490
Email: frogmail@tcu.edu
www.tcu.edu

The 4 Distinctions

Engaged Students

TCU students benefit from many of the features found at large universities. They choose from one hundred undergraduate areas of study and participate in innovative programs such as entrepreneurship and nurse anesthesia. TCU professors are leaders in their fields, and academic programs are rigorous. International education is valued, and students have numerous opportunities to study abroad.

TCU annually exceeds enrollment goals, and its $1.1 billion endowment is among the top fifty colleges and universities in the United States. Students flock to TCU because of the experiences offered, starting in the first year. Summer Frog Camp provides new students with a head start on acquiring the skills they need to be successful in college. Frog Camp introduces new students to their classmates, to university history and traditions, and to the concept of ethical leadership and citizenship. First-year students have the additional opportunity to take freshman seminars, taught by TCU's professors, and designed to help students develop a sense of belonging and the skills and self-confidence needed for academic success.

As a major teaching and research university, TCU receives research funding from more than one hundred agencies. The Institute of Behavioral Research is one of the top three drug-related research institutes in the United States. It has had a major influence in national drug policy and treatment for four decades and has expanded its work to the United Kingdom. The Institute for Mathematics, Science and Technology Education brings together researchers from varied disciplines to discover new and innovative ways to teach and learn quantitative skills. Undergraduates have many opportunities to conduct their own research at the Science and Engineering Research Center and to present their findings at the annual Undergraduate Research Day.

The College of Fine Arts provides hands-on learning for its students through public performances and festivals. The biennial Latin American Music Festival draws world-renowned artists, musicians, and composers to the Metroplex, while the TCU choirs have performed at Carnegie Hall

four of the past five years. The school for classical and contemporary dance regularly offers students opportunities to perform internationally. The theatre department often collaborates on productions with professional theaters in Fort Worth, and the art history program offers study at internationally recognized museums such as the Kimbell Art Museum, the Amon Carter Museum, and the Modern Art Museum of Fort Worth.

Great Teaching

With a thirteen to one student to faculty ratio and a teacher-scholar model that results in close mentoring relationships, the university also offers many of the advantages of smaller liberal arts colleges. Consequently, a TCU education is not just the sum of semester hours, but an entire experience that grows from its mission "to educate individuals to think and act as ethical leaders and responsible citizens in the global community."

In recent years, TCU has invested some three hundred million dollars in top-of-the-line facilities and in upgrading residence halls, classrooms, and laboratories, and will invest another $150 million over the next two years. Recent facilities include the Tucker Technology Center, Smith Entrepreneurs Hall, the University Recreation Center, five residential apartment communities, and a number of athletic facilities. High-tech classrooms and wired and wireless networking throughout campus provide easy, secure access to information technology resources.

TCU is made up of seven colleges and schools. The AddRan College of Humanities and Social Sciences is home to the liberal arts, including departments such as philosophy, languages, political science, criminal justice, religion, literature, and history. Internship opportunities abound for AddRan students, and include the London Internship, the Washington Internship program, and numerous local internship programs. The university offers more than thirty opportunities for study abroad through both semester and summer programs.

The Neeley School of Business offers accredited undergraduate and graduate programs in business and entrepreneurship. The Educational Investment Fund provides experience in investments and portfolio management. More than one hundred universities have attempted to replicate this program.

The College of Communication is home to the Schieffer School of Journalism, named for distinguished broadcast journalist Bob Schieffer, class of '59. TCU, one of only eighteen private universities accredited by the Accrediting Council for Education in Journalism and Mass Communication, is recognized for award-winning student publications, the TCU Daily Skiff, and Image magazine. The department of communication studies has two faculty members ranked in the top one hundred of all-time active and prolific scholars in the field, one of whom is ranked in the top ten.

The Harris College of Nursing and Health Sciences offers degrees in speech language pathology and habilitation of the deaf, along with nursing, social work, and kinesiology. The nursing program offers an accelerated track to students with degrees in other fields, allowing them to complete the BSN degree in only fifteen months. Social work students gain intensive practical experience in agencies such as child protective services and senior centers.

The College of Science and Engineering has a yearlong senior interdisciplinary design project for engineering majors. Student teams develop solutions for projects supplied by such organizations as Alcon Laboratories, Lockheed Martin Aeronautics, Bell Helicopter Textron, and the U.S. Army. Students in the prehealth professions program enjoy an acceptance rate to professional schools that is about twice the national average.

Vibrant Community

The campus encompasses 269 acres in a residential neighborhood five miles from the heart of downtown Fort Worth, a welcoming city with a vibrant mix of commerce, culture, and entertainment. The Campus Commons, now under construction, will include the new Brown-Lupton University Union; four new residence halls for students classified as sophomores and above; and a large, open green space that is sure to become the focus of student life.

Successful Outcomes

Over the past eight years, 100 percent of certification graduates from the College of Education have been employed. All teacher education programs at TCU are fully accredited by the state. The pass rate for TCU students on the Texas state exam typically exceeds 98 percent, and in the most recently reported year was 100 percent. With the KinderFrogs School for children with Down Syndrome and the Starpoint School for students with learning differences, TCU is the only school in the nation including two special education laboratory schools, and both schools serve as on-campus training sites for TCU students.

Fast Facts

Texas Christian University is a four-year, independent university affiliated with the Christian Church (Disciples of Christ) founded in 1873.

Web site

http://www.tcu.edu

Location

Fort Worth, Texas—35 miles from Dallas.

Student Profile

7,382 undergraduate students (41% male, 59% female); 51states and territories, more than 80 countries; 19% minority in the freshman class, 4.6% international.

Faculty Profile

465 full-time faculty, more than 90% hold the highest degree in their discipline. 13:1 student/faculty ratio. Average class size is 24.5.

Residence Life

Moderately residential: 60% of students live on-campus.

Athletics

NCAA Division I-A, Mountain West Conference. 18 varsity sports (8 men's: baseball, basketball, cross-country, football, golf, swimming & diving, tennis, track & field; 10 women's: basketball, cross-country, equestrian, golf, rifle, soccer, swimming & diving, tennis, track & field, volleyball). 50% of students participate in intramural sports.

Academic Programs

Accounting; advertising/public relations; aerospace studies; anthropology; art education; art history; Asian studies; astronomy; ballet & modern dance; biochemistry; biology; British & colonial - post-colonial studies; broadcast journalism; chemistry; classical studies; communication studies; computer information science; computer science; criminal justice; early childhood education; economics; education of exceptional children; electronic business; engineering; English; environmental earth resources; environmental science; fashion merchandising; finance; geography; geology; graphic design; habilitation of the deaf; health & fitness; history; interior design; international communications; international economics; management; marketing; mathematics; middle school education; military science; modern languages & literatures; movement science; music; music education; neuroscience; news-editorial journalism; nursing; nutritional sciences; philosophy; physical education; physics; political science; pre-health professions; prelaw, pre-major (undecided); psychology; psychosocial kinesiology; radio-TV-film; ranch management; religion; secondary education; social work; sociology; Spanish & Latin American studies; speech-language pathology; studio art; supply & value chain management; theatre; women's studies.

Costs and Aid

2007–2008: $33,068 comprehensive ($24,868 tuition). 60% of students receive some financial aid. Average award: $17,500.

Endowment

$1.1 billion.

University of St. Thomas

TEXAS

The University of St. Thomas (UST) is a private, Catholic, coeducational, comprehensive, liberal arts university. Since its founding in 1947 by the Basilian Fathers, who stand for education within the Catholic Church's mission of evangelization, UST has adhered to an educational mission "born from the heart of the Church."

Admissions Contact:

University of St. Thomas
3800 Montrose
Houston, Texas 77006
(800) 856-8565
Ph: (713) 525-3500
Email: admissions@stthom.edu
www.stthom.edu

The 4 Distinctions

Engaged Students

UST students can choose from among thirty undergraduate fields of study, seven professional programs, and a strong undergraduate research program. The top majors are premed, business, education, psychology, international studies, and theology. Internships to complement in-class learning can start as early as the freshman year, especially for business students. While not required, internships are encouraged across all fields, taking advantage of the array of opportunities Houston offers.

A unique feature of UST is a living-learning community for twenty-two freshmen students. The group lives together in one hall, takes the same philosophy-based courses, prepares all their own meals, and participates in volunteer work.

UST offers a varied, competitive study-abroad program, ranked sixteenth in the nation by the Institute for International Education in its Open Doors 2006 report. All students are eligible to study abroad, and UTS is constantly increasing the number and types of opportunities it offers, encouraging students to develop a global perspective. Countries where UST students have studied include India, China, Ireland, France, and Mexico.

Great Teaching

UST's philosophy of education is grounded in the Catholic intellectual tradition of dialogue between faith and reason, exemplified by its namesake, St. Thomas Aquinas, the thirteenth-century philosopher and theologian. Today, UST's motto is as modern as its campus architecture: "A balanced education, a bright future." UST programs instill in students the core values of the Basilian Fathers: goodness, discipline, and knowledge. Students of all faiths and from across the country are welcome: in 2005, 62 percent of UST students were Catholic and 90 percent were from Texas.

UST's degree programs provide a variety of opportunities to participate with faculty in shared learning experiences such as conducting and presenting research,

studying and traveling abroad, and completing internships. The highly educated faculty are committed to teaching and helping students prepare for the future. The low student to faculty ratio of fourteen to one, combined with an average class size of twenty, allow strong one-on-one interaction between students and faculty.

Students can assist faculty in their research, especially in psychology and premed, and UST professors are involved with students in academic interest groups such as the French honor society, accounting society, psychology honors, and others. Faculty advise students from their first day on campus and a major-specific advisor is assigned to students once they declare their major at the end of their sophomore year. Faculty also help students find funding and other support for trips and competitions, and write recommendations for graduate school admission.

Vibrant Community

Students are immersed in community service as soon as they arrive on campus: freshman orientation includes a full day of activities designed to make a difference in Houston. Many classes offer service learning as a way to gain practical experience as well as to reach out to the wider community. Some examples include working in local hospitals and nursing homes.

The Student Government Association (SGA) controls the funds generated by the student activity fee paid by all UST students. The SGA is trusted to allocate and disperse the funds responsibly. The six areas to be funded are required to review their past-year spending and forecast their needs for the coming year, providing them with hands-on experience for the future.

UST is located in Houston, the largest city in Texas and the fourth largest city in the nation. Known for its energy—particularly oil—, ship canal, and aeronautics industries, Houston has the official nickname of Space City because it is home to the Lyndon B. Johnson Space Center, where the Mission Control Center is located. Houston also features major sports and other big city attractions, including an active year-round cultural scene. UST's campus is close to the Texas Medical Center and is a gateway to Houston's Museum District, which encompasses sixteen institutions including the zoo.

Successful Outcomes

UST has a strong history of placement for students going to medical school. Its premed program, one of the most rigorous on campus, has a high success rate and has developed a relationship with the Texas Medical Center to provide students with experience and beyond-the-classroom preparation.

The career and counseling centers at UST provide an array of testing and assessments for students. The career center has established contacts all over Houston, as well as in other cities and parts of the country. It also provides a way for employers to connect with St. Thomas students in certain subject areas.

Alumni are also active in promoting student success. Students e-mail or call UST alumni to get opinions and advice while they are in school and after they graduate, and the alumni relations department is developing a mentoring program in which students can interact with alumni as early as their sophomore year.

"As a Catholic Institution in the heart of Houston, the University of St. Thomas lays a unique foundation fashioned with the building blocks of both faith and reason. There, students are prepared to transform their lives, their community, and the world."

-Colleges of Distinction

Fast Facts

University of St. Thomas is a four-year private, co-ed, Catholic university and was founded in 1947.

Web site

http://www.stthom.edu/

Location

Houston, Texas.

Student Profile

1,708 undergraduate students (39% male, 61% female); 33 states and territories, 54 countries; 50% minority, 8% international, 61% Catholic.

Faculty Profile

129 full-time faculty. 13:1 student/faculty ratio. Average class size is 18.

Residence Life

Mildly residential: 15% of undergraduate students live on campus.

Athletics

National Association of Intercollegiate Athletics (NAIA): 2 varsity sports (1 men's: soccer; 1 women's: volleyball), 10 active sport clubs including men's baseball, men's basketball, women's soccer, coed martial arts, men's rugby, and co-ed fencing.

Academic Programs

Accounting; bioinformatics; biology; business administration; Catholic studies; chemistry; communication; drama; education; English; environmental studies (not admitting new students until further notice); finance; fine arts (art history, drama, music, studio art); French; general studies; history; international development; international studies; liberal arts; marketing; mathematics; music; music education; pastoral studies; philosophy; political science; psychology; Spanish; studio arts; theology.

Costs and Aid

2007-2008 $26,370 comprehensive ($19,070 tuition). 42% of students receive some financial aid. Average award: $13,686.

Endowment

$45 million.

More Distinctions

• *Princeton Review:* The Best Western Colleges 2008

• *U.S. News & World Report* consistently names the University of St. Thomas to its top tier of Western Universities.

• Recognized in *Money Magazine* since 1994.

• Ranked 16th in the nation for study abroad by the Institute for International Education in its Open Doors 2006 Report.

Colleges of Distinction
West Region Schools

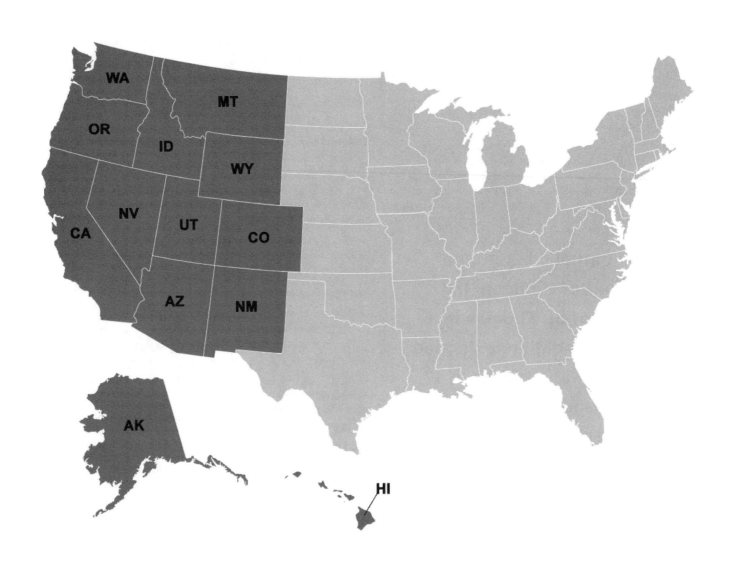

Photo: © iStockphoto.com/lisapics

Notes

_____

_____

_____

_____

_____

_____

_____

_____

_____

_____

_____

_____

Prescott College

ARIZONA

Admissions Contact:

Prescott College
220 Grove Avenue
Prescott, AZ 86301
(877) 350-2100
Email: admissions@prescott.edu
www.prescott.edu

Prescott College is an independent, coeducational, liberal arts college. Tucked into a corner of the central Arizona town of Prescott, Prescott College puts students at the center of its mission and is an evolving experiment in rejecting hierarchical thinking for collaboration and teamwork as the cornerstones of learning.

The 4 Distinctions

Engaged Students

The Southwest is seen as a classroom at Prescott. Students use the region as an educational tool in a number of ways, including participating in expeditionary courses, studying at a field station, and developing community partnerships. Students in all disciplines—arts and letters/humanities, environmental studies, outdoor/adventure education, education, human development, and cultural and regional studies—integrate classroom learning and real-world experience.

The Kino Bay Center for Cultural and Ecological Studies is Prescott College's field station on the shores of the Gulf of California, one of the most remote and unexplored seas in the world today. At the field station, students have quality educational opportunities and engage in cooperative research. Throughout the academic year, courses are held at the Kino Bay Center in academic areas such as marine studies, resource conservation and management, cultural studies, Latin American studies, and writing.

Through the college's partnership with the Northpoint Expeditionary Learning Outward Bound High School, Prescott students can obtain hands-on experience in the field of education. Prescott students assist classroom teachers, design lessons, observe classroom dynamics, and tutor individual students, all while immersed in an active school setting.

The Wilderness Orientation Program—a three-week, backcountry excursion for all incoming students to the Resident Degree Program—welcomes new students to Prescott College, guiding them through the philosophies and processes of the college by using experiential education, community building, and self-direction in the remote, natural environment of the Southwest. On average, 90 percent of first-year and transfer students participate in this program, which builds lifelong friendships. Other options are offered to incoming students who are unable to hike.

Prescott College's Wolfberry Farm is a thirty-acre experimental agroecology farm dedicated to education, demonstration, and research. Located fifteen miles north of Prescott, the farm gives students in agroecology a chance to experiment with water irrigation technologies, drought-tolerant and adapted crops, specialty crops, and fertility-generating rotations.

Great Teaching

Since its founding in 1966, the college has been driven by a philosophy of experiential education and a mission to graduate society's leaders for the twenty-first century, leaders who will be needed to solve the world's growing environmental and social problems. Independent-minded students with a sense of adventure will find that Prescott College offers a uniquely challenging educational experience based on close collaboration with the faculty. At Prescott College the undeniable common denominators that have endured the test of time have been commitments to authentic adventure and travel, field-based activities, and experiential learning in its simplest and purest form: learning by doing.

Students are empowered at Prescott, especially because faculty view students as cocreators of their educational experience rather than as consumers. Prescott stresses self-direction within an interdisciplinary curriculum. Every student collaborates with faculty advisers in the design of their own degree program from the ground up, and in every course, students negotiate a learning contract with their professors, which covers what students expect to learn and how they will be evaluated.

Small class sizes, a student to faculty ratio of seven to one, and a high level of interaction between students and faculty are characteristic of Prescott. Almost every class at Prescott has a strong experiential learning component that takes students out of the classroom, so much so that there are more vans on campus than classrooms.

Every student must complete a senior project/capstone experience. Senior projects have ranged from writing novels to developing classes to starting schools. One student cofounded a nonprofit organization that places the pets of families suffering from domestic violence with specially trained foster families. The Ripple Project helps match student interests with community needs to develop meaningful senior projects, including facilitating collaborations with organizations such as AmeriCorps.

Research often happens under the mentorship of faculty or community experts. For many years now, students have engaged in research on the fire, woodlands, and riparian ecology of the Southwest, working alongside environmental studies faculty members Lisa Floyd-Hanna and David Hanna. Fire ecology classes have worked with Prescott National Forest Service researchers on several projects, including examining core samples of ponderosa pines to understand how local fire cycles changed after settlers populated the region.

Snow and avalanche studies, border studies, and filmmaking for social change are a few of the many interesting subjects students might find themselves studying at Prescott.

Vibrant Community

At Prescott College the combination of field-based and interactive classroom learning encourages a bond between people, and the college places a high value on students being functioning and contributing members of the college community. Students' opinions matter, and there are a number of ways for students to be involved every aspect of running the college.

Surrounded by 1,408,000 acres of national forest and more than 796 miles of trails, Prescott College is a haven of natural beauty. Students can participate in a number of outdoor activities, including rock climbing, hiking, mountain biking, and nearby canoeing, rafting, kayaking, and snow skiing. Students tend to be environmentally conscious and show a deep appreciation for nature.

The Crossroads Center, a twenty-two-thousand-square-foot teaching and learning space on Prescott's campus, is the hub of the campus. The center features a college library that fully integrates technology and research functions, a campus cafe and catering services, a conference facility with an outdoor amphitheatre and a five hundred-person auditorium, social spaces, quiet spaces, and classrooms. The center demonstrates environmental responsibility and economic feasibility with a solar plant on the roof and retaining walls made from recycled concrete.

The college, set in the historic city of Prescott, is located in the Bradshaw Mountains of central Arizona, at an altitude of 5,400 feet. Students will enjoy the area's benevolent climate and interesting geology, highlighted by lakes and granite formations. Prescott began as a mining town in the 1800s and is now a thriving arts community, home to galleries, dance studios, and events such as the Prescott Bluegrass Festival, the Prescott Film Fest, and a folk arts fair.

Successful Outcomes

Prescott alumni go on to exciting and unique careers. Many feel empowered to launch their own businesses. Alumni Kent Madin and Linda Svendsen, founders of Boojum Expeditions, offer "uncommon adventure travel," leading trips in Mongolia, Tibet, China, Argentina, Venezuela, and Yellowstone. Alumnus Dustin Tester started Maui Surfer Girls, an instructional surfing school for girls and women in Hawaii. Kim Reynolds cofounded the dZi Foundation, dedicated to promoting the health, culture, and welfare of indigenous mountain communities.

Fast Facts

Prescott College is a small private liberal arts college with a strong emphasis on experiential education and environmental and social responsibility.

Web site

http://www.prescott.edu/

Location

Prescott, Arizona—set in central Arizona in the historic city of Prescott, 90 miles northwest of Phoenix.

Student Profile

441 undergraduate students (49% male, 51% female); 21 states and territories; 12.6% minority; 96% of students from out-of-state.

Faculty Profile

45 full-time faculty members and 60 adjunct faculty. 10:1 student/faculty ratio; 5:1 student/faculty ratio in field-based classes. Average class size is 10.

Residence Life

Prescott College provides on-campus housing for first-time freshmen; most other students live in the surrounding community.

Academic Programs

Majors: Adventure education; arts and letters; education/teacher certification (elementary, secondary); environmental studies; humanities; cultural & regional studies; human development.

Costs and Aid

2007–2008: $32,500 comprehensive ($19,980 tuition). 66% of students receive some financial aid. Average award: $9,980.

Endowment

$2 million.

More Distinctions

• Prescott College is an evolving experiment in rejecting hierarchical thinking for collaboration and teamwork as the cornerstone of learning. This is an educational institution that puts students at the center in everything it does and is.

• Prescott College is driven by a philosophy of experiential education or "learning by doing" and a mission to graduate society's leaders for the 21st century who will be needed to solve the world's growing environmental and social problems.

• Students are empowered at Prescott, especially because faculty view students as co-creators of their educational experience rather than as consumers.

• At Prescott College the combination of field-based and interactive classroom learning encourages a bond between people and the College places a high value on students being functioning and contributing members of the College community. Students opinions matter and they have many ways to be involved in the life of the College and in every aspect of running the College.

Azusa Pacific University

CALIFORNIA

Azusa Pacific University (APU) originated in 1899 as the Training School for Christian Workers, the first Bible college on the West Coast. Located twenty-six miles northeast of Los Angeles, APU is a comprehensive, Christian, evangelical university that strives to incorporate faith into learning, putting "God first," in keeping with its motto.

Admissions Contact:

Azusa Pacific University
901 E. Alosta Ave
Azusa, CA 91702-7000
(800) TALK-APU
Ph: (626) 812-3016
Fax: (626) 812-3096
Email: admissions@apu.edu
www.apu.edu

The 4 Distinctions

Engaged Students

At APU, students have the opportunity to engage in academia while interweaving the Christian faith into everything they do. With a firm foundation and desire to prepare disciple-scholars for global impact, freshmen at Azusa start out with a solid core of required courses, such as public speaking, writing, and religion. Additionally, all freshmen take a course called Beginnings, a first-year experience course that helps students prepare for college life. Once a major is selected, students at Azusa Pacific become involved in that subject matter in and out of the classroom.

Of the many degree programs APU offers, nursing, premed, education, and communication studies are widely popular among students. The more recently added cinema and broadcast arts program thrives on campus. APU hosts lectures and discussions where producers, actors, directors, writers, and other industry professionals share about the field and how their faith has influenced their work. Through programs like this, APU students explore ways to integrate their beliefs into any industry they chose to enter.

While students have many opportunities to study abroad in places such as China; Oxford, England; and the newly launched South Africa program, another popular program keeps students inside the nation's borders. The High Sierra Semester, located just south of Yosemite National Park, gives students an opportunity to experience the wilderness in a close-knit community while pursuing high academic standards. Students study some of the great works of literature, art, music, philosophy, and theology, taught by APU professors in an integrated format.

In addition, APU students give back to the community by participating in more than thirty community-service programs annually. Beyond local outreach, APU offers missions trips, which attract more than two hundred students each year. Past trips have taken students to India, China, and the Dominican Republic.

Great Teaching

APU offers as many as forty different majors, and maintains a commitment to each student's spiritual development in every major. The university offers more than fifty areas of undergraduate study, twenty-three master's degrees, and seven doctorates to over 8,100 students, 83 percent of whom receive financial aid.

With a fourteen to one student to faculty ratio, students benefit from close interactions with faculty, who often serve as mentors. Professors are accessible and available outside of the classroom and normal office hours. In addition, faculty are involved with students in the community. A professor in the School of Music started a local conservatory for children, a program that enables APU students to gain experience teaching children to play various instruments, while also building relationships with area youth. The program also collects and provides new and used musical instruments for children who cannot afford them.

Vibrant Community

APU is strongly integrated into the surrounding neighborhood and community. Nursing students get involved with the local wellness center and homeless clinic, while business students have conducted an economic study of the city. Students of all majors have volunteered to tutor or read to children at the library. Education majors get involved in local classrooms, gaining experience and contributing to the community. The College Headed and Mighty Proud (CHAMP) program allows fourth-grade students from a traditionally underserved population to learn about college from APU students in hopes of motivating and encouraging children to continue their education through college.

Athletics are also a popular part of APU student life. APU's fourteen intercollegiate sports teams won the Directors' Cup for the third consecutive year in 2006–2007, a recognition of APU as the NAIA's top athletics program in the country. The athletics department is also known for its dedication to character development, striving to educate student-athletes in all areas of their lives. APU athletes are very dedicated, and the fans are equally avid about supporting the teams.

Successful Outcomes

In addition to speakers brought in by the department of theater, film, and television, APU brings a number of guest speakers to campus to allow students to learn about the transition after graduation, and to facilitate networking opportunities. In 2007, VeggieTales creator Phil Vischer spoke at the university's annual Common Day of Learning. Alumni also often speak at such events, allowing them to stay connected to APU and to help inspire students.

The office of career services assists students in their job and internship searches through career fairs, one-on-one resume assistance, and more. These efforts are just a sampling of ways the university strives to set students up for success after college. Distinguished APU alumni include Olympic athletes, Fortune 500 CEOs, teachers of the year, and Fulbright Scholars, not to mention thousands of others making an impact through their chosen vocations.

APU maintains a long-standing reputation for preparing some of the nation's highest-qualified science graduate students, a result of small class sizes, faculty mentoring, quality internships, and hands on learning opportunities, reflecting the faculty's commitment to educating the whole person. The university will soon break ground on a new science center to provide state-of-the-art facilities to further support student learning.

In the past five years, ten APU students have received Fulbright Grants to study abroad, including three APU students who recently received scholarships for 2007-08. Along with one grant awarded in 2006, four APU students are currently making world impact while furthering their education in Bangladesh, Turkey, Indonesia, and Belgium. During the 2007-08 year, APU will also welcome its first Fulbright Visiting Scholar from Korea.

Fast Facts

Azusa Pacific University is a four-year, comprehensive Christian, evangelical university founded in 1899.

Web site

www.apu.edu

Location

Azusa, California—26 miles northeast of Los Angeles in the San Gabriel Valley.

Student Profile

8,128 total students (36% male, 64% female); 4,722 traditional undergraduate students; 50 states, 71 countries; 31% minority, 4% international.

Faculty Profile

352 full-time faculty. 14:1 student/faculty ratio. Average class size is 20-25.

Athletics

NAIA Division I, Golden State Athletic Conference. 14 varsity sports (7 men's: baseball, basketball, cross-country, football, soccer, track & field, tennis; 7 women's: soccer, cross-country, volleyball, basketball, softball, track & field, tennis).

Academic Programs

Accounting; applied health; art; athletic training; biblical studies; biochemistry; biology; business administration; chemistry; Christian ministries; cinema & broadcast arts; communication studies; computer information systems; computer science; English; finance; global studies; graphic design; history; international business; liberal studies; marketing; mathematics; math & physics; music; natural science; nursing; performance; philosophy; physical education; physics; political science; psychology; social science; social work; sociology; Spanish; theater arts; theology; youth ministry.

Costs and Aid

2007–2008: $31,580 comprehensive ($12,215 per semester tuition). 85% of students receive some financial aid.

Endowment

$30,678,068.

More Distinctions

• For the sixth consecutive year, Azusa Pacific University secured a place in this year's Top 25 of the U.S. News & World Report's 2007 America's Best Colleges and Universities, Master's Classification, ranking 15th from among 124 western colleges and universities. Additionally, The Princeton Review designated APU as 1 of 123 colleges in the 2007 Best in the West category.

• APU was recognized for the third year by Diverse Issues in Higher Education as one of the nation's top schools in awarding degrees to minority students. APU ranked among the top 100 in 13 categories, including ranking 10th for awarding Hispanic master's degrees in the education category.

Chapman University

CALIFORNIA

With 3,864 undergraduate and 1,868 graduate and professional students, Chapman University is the largest and oldest independent university in Orange County, California. Originally founded in 1861 by the First Christian Church (Disciples of Christ), Chapman now welcomes students of all religious and nonreligious backgrounds.

Admissions Contact:

Chapman University
One University Avenue
Orange, CA 92866
(888) CU-APPLY
Ph: (714) 997-6711
Fax: (714) 997-6713
Email: admit@chapman.edu
www.chapman.edu

The 4 Distinctions

Engaged Students

Chapman students regularly take advantage of global internships, available during the summer, which allow them to live, study, and work in locations all around the world. The university also offers thirteen different study-abroad programs, lasting for a semester or for the January interterm; these programs are frequently led by Chapman professors.

In close proximity to the heart of Southern California's film and business industries, Chapman students are encouraged to participate in internships with various film companies and Fortune 500 businesses. Though film is a difficult business to break into, Chapman's Dodge College of Film and Media Arts has developed a respected reputation, as well as a number of connections that make film internships possible, thus easing the postgraduate transition into the industry. Chapman's Argyros School of Business features an advisory board made up of the who's who of Orange County business and industry, providing a wide variety of internship and entry-level opportunities for Chapman students and alumni.

Great Teaching

A comprehensive liberal arts and professional sciences university, Chapman's best-known programs include film and television, business administration, psychology, music, theatre, dance, and teacher preparation programs.

Freshman Foundations (FF) courses, taken during students' first semester at Chapman, provide an opportunity for first-year students to get to know their classmates and professors in a small class setting. Each freshman selects an FF class in his or her area of academic interest.

All faculty at Chapman have regular office hours, and they are widely seen to be exceptionally approachable. Many serve as advisers to campus clubs and organizations. Chapman students and faculty also routinely communicate online via Blackboard.

One of Chapman's unique features is the university's relationship with the professional mentoring program known as InsideTrack. In addition to traditionally assigned academic advisers from the various academic disciplines, and tutoring services provided by the Center for Academic Success, each first-year student is also assigned a life coach with whom they meet weekly to develop critical skills, set goals, and address the many challenges that might interfere with their success. Coaching sessions are focused on providing personal development, assistance with planning and organization, and most important, motivation and encouragement. Working in partnership with administrators and faculty, InsideTrack provides an invaluable safety net for students, helping to improve academic preparedness and performance.

On-campus research facilities include the Anderson Center for Economic Research; the Center for Non-Profit Leadership; the Henley Social Science Research Laboratory; the John Fowles Center for Creative Writing; the Hobbs Institute for Real Estate, Law, and Environmental Studies; and the Dodge Institute for Media and Public Interest.

Vibrant Community

Located in the beautiful south coast area between Los Angeles and San Diego, Chapman's suburban, tree-lined residential campus is situated in historic Old Towne Orange. Nearing the end of a several-year-long campus redevelopment program, Chapman has added a number of new residence halls, a second music building, a central library, an interfaith center, a new film and television campus, and an expanded athletics complex, including a new football/soccer/lacrosse stadium and field-turf field, as well as an Olympic pool and stadium.

Over sixty clubs and organizations are available to Chapman students, including twelve nationally chartered fraternities and sororities, each including a mandated community-service/stewardship component built into their programming. Eighteen NCAA Division III athletic teams (eight for men, ten for women) are available, as well as men's lacrosse and men's crew club teams.

The Student L.E.A.D. Center works to foster student growth, leadership, and service learning. Chapman students regularly help to manage and coordinate major Orange County nonprofit events and programming such as the Orange County Marathon, the Relay for Life, and Habitat for Humanity.

Successful Outcomes

Chapman's alumni office schedules regular opportunities for alumni to meet with current students, helping students make valuable connections and gain perspective into real-world circumstances. Chapman's Career Development Center (CDC) helps students cultivate career skills necessary to succeed in a rapidly evolving job market. CDC staff assist students in assessing skills and connecting with prospective employers who come on campus regularly to meet with Chapman students.

Distinguished Chapman alumni include Tony-nominated Broadway star of Showboat, Michel Bell; U.S. Congresswoman Loretta Sanchez; CNBC World anchorwoman Bettina Chua; U.S. Congressman David Bonior; baseball's Cy Young Award winner, Randy Jones; network television executive John David Currey; and philanthropist and U.S. ambassador to Spain, George L. Argyros.

"At Chapman, we aim high. We welcome students who seek challenge; students who will enthusiastically immerse themselves in the search for truth. If you are one of those students, we will offer an academic and social environment that will nurture your creativity and intellectual spirit and help you explore what makes you great."

- James L. Doti

President

Fast Facts

Chapman University is a four-year undergraduate, coeducational university.

Web site

http://www.chapman.edu

Location

Orange, California—a suburban, south coast-area community 34 miles south of Los Angeles.

Student Profile

3,733 undergraduate students (44% male, 56% female), 1,821 graduate and professional school students; 42 states and territories represented; 32% minority, 3% international.

Faculty Profile

222 full-time faculty, 220 part-time faculty. 16:1 student/faculty ratio. Average class size 20.

Residence Life

Moderately residential: 45% of students live on campus. 90% of freshmen live on campus.

Athletics

NCAA Division III, Independent. 18 varsity sports (8 men's: baseball, basketball, cross-country, football, golf, soccer, tennis, water polo; 10 women's: basketball, crew, cross-country, soccer, softball, swimming, tennis, track & field, volleyball, water polo), 3 club sports, including lacrosse, and 19 intramurals.

Academic Programs

Accounting; art; art history; athletic training; biological sciences; business administration; chemistry; communication studies; computer & information systems; computer science; creative writing; dance; dance performance; economics; English; film production; film studies; food science & nutrition; French; history; legal studies; liberal studies; mathematics; music; music composition; music education; music therapy; musical performance; peace studies; philosophy; political science; psychology; public relations & advertising; religious studies; screen writing; sociology; Spanish; studio art; teaching English; television & broadcast journalism; theatre; undecided/undeclared.

Costs and Aid

2006–2007: $40,908 comprehensive ($29,900 tuition). 78% of students receive some form of financial aid or scholarship. Average award: $23,500.

Endowment

$142.6 million.

More Distinctions

• The Argyros School of Business and Economics is accredited by AACSB.

• The School of Music is accredited by NASM.

• The School of Law is accredited by ABA.

California State University, Monterey Bay

CALIFORNIA

California State University, Monterey Bay (CSUMB) is a public, coeducational, comprehensive university. CSUMB was founded in 1994 "to build a multicultural learning community founded on academic excellence from which all partners in the educational process emerge prepared to contribute productively, responsibly, and ethically to California and the global community."

Admissions Contact:

California State University, Monterey Bay
100 Campus Center
Seaside, CA 93955-8001
Ph: (831) 582-5100
Email: admissions@csumb.edu
www.csumb.edu

The 4 Distinctions

Engaged Students

CSUMB values service through high quality education, and required service-learning courses engage students in community service and related classroom learning with the award-winning Service Learning Institute (SLI). An academic resource center as well as an on-campus center for developing community partnerships, the SLI fosters and promotes social justice by cultivating reciprocal service and learning partnerships among CSUMB students, faculty, staff, and the surrounding community.

CSUMB faculty members leverage technology to increase undergraduate student learning by reconfiguring the classroom experience and initiating engaging, innovative, real-world instruction in the earth sciences, social sciences, humanities, kinesiology, foreign language and teacher education fields. Using Tablet PCs, laptops, PDAs, cell phones, digital wireless cameras and printers, and mobile wireless access points, they engage in exciting mobile teaching and learning initiatives both on and off campus. Student-centered projects originate from such diverse remote environments as Elkhorn Slough, the historic California Missions in Carmel and Soledad, Big Sur, Cyberspace, Point Lobos State Park, and the San Francisco Bay.

At Elkhorn Slough, CSUMB faculty and student researchers installed a solar powered transmitter and a wireless mesh network that allow them to conduct wireless interactive web conferences with local K-12 and high school classrooms and teachers by sharing images and data. At the historic California Missions in Carmel and Soledad, satellite uplinks provide real time Internet connectivity between students doing field archaeology and on-campus databases. At Big Sur, students conduct field geology with GPS & GIS equipped Tablet PC's as digital field notebooks. In Cyberspace, a Virtual Language Lab engages peer groups of students at CSUMB and other CSU campuses in critical foreign language learning. At Point Lobos State Park, CSUMB students launch an undersea, video-equipped ROV tethered to a kayak that can be driven by school children to study the kelp forest and sea otters. At the mouth of the San

Francisco Bay, CSUMB students using a towed sonar array and GPS/GIS technologies have discovered and mapped sand wave fields to help fisheries and ocean protection efforts through better understanding of habitats.

Great Teaching

CSUMB offers a curriculum that is "student and society centered and of sufficient breadth and depth to meet statewide and regional needs." CSUMB's programs "strive for distinction, building on regional assets." CSUMB focuses on how people work best together, using technology and reaching out to others. The university also features small classes and emphasizes an interdisciplinary approach to education.

CSUMB offers more than twenty degree programs. The most popular programs are business administration, liberal studies, human communication, earth systems science and policy, and social and behavioral sciences. About 10 percent of CSUMB's students are studying science, and more than half of those are women.

All students must meet the CSUMB language requirement, an important skill in the cultural context of California. There is also a technical skills and knowledge requirement that involves community participation. CSUMB students work in teams to solve the problems of clients such as community groups and schools. The students learn from and give back to the area community at the same time.

Vibrant Community

Two-thirds of CSUMB's full-time undergraduate students live on campus. Students keep busy, participating in more than thirty-five registered student clubs and activities, many of which are outdoor oriented. CSUMB participates in thirteen NCAA Division II sports as part of the California Collegiate Athletic Association. The entire campus is wireless and includes three new buildings: a science center, a housing complex with apartments and suites, and an alumni/visitor center. A new library that incorporates student academic support services will open in fall 2008.

CSUMB's students take advantage of the natural beauty and cultural centers of the Monterey Peninsula and the surrounding area. As part of a recent senior capstone project students painted a scientifically accurate mural of a kelp forest on a wall of CSUMB's Aquatic Center, a piece of artwork inspired by the Monterey Bay's kelp forests and relying on information and resources at the Monterey Bay Aquarium, in addition to those available at CSUMB.

Located on the site of Fort Ord, a military installation closed in 1994, CSUMB overlooks Monterey Bay in the Central Coast area of California, about two hours by car south of San Francisco. The campus is a bit separated from Seaside and other nearby towns, reflecting its origins as an army base. The Monterey Peninsula offers students a number of recreational and sporting opportunities, in addition to charming shops and renowned restaurants.

Successful Outcomes

CSUMB graduates have achieved notable success in a wide variety of careers. Companies hiring CSUMB alumni include Apple; CTB/McGraw-Hill Publishing; Monterey Bay Aquarium Research Institute; and ABC, CBS, and FOX TV networks. CSUMB students also find work in the government and nonprofit sector, with agencies like NOAA, the State of Hawaii Health Department, the Department of Defense, the Coalition of Homeless Services, or the John XXIII AIDS Ministry.

Other students continue their education at graduate schools such as Stanford, San José State, UC Berkeley, San Diego State, Mills College, San Francisco State, Claremont, Antioch, Choevevei Torah, CSU Sacramento, the New College of California School of Law, San Francisco; Boise State, Monterey College of Law, the Monterey Institute of International Studies, and the University of Texas at Austin.

Fast Facts

California State University, Monterey Bay is a four-year, public, liberal arts university founded in 1994.

Web site

CSUMB.EDU

Location

Seaside, California—7 miles from Monterey; 2 hours south of San Francisco.

Student Profile

3,818 undergraduate students (42% male, 58% female); 95% California, 3% other states; 46% minority, 2% international.

Faculty Profile

135 full-time faculty. 77% hold a terminal degree in their field. 23:1 student/faculty ratio. Average class size is 23.

Residence Life

Highly residential: 60-70% of fulltime undergraduates live on campus

Athletics

NCAA Division II, California Collegiate Athletic Association. 13 varsity sports (5 men's: baseball, basketball, cross-country, golf, soccer; 7 women's: basketball, cross-country, golf, soccer, softball, volleyball, water polo; 1 coed: sailing), club sports, and intramurals

Academic Programs

Biology; business Administration; collaborative health & human services; earth systems science & policy; global studies; human communication; human performance & wellness; integrated studies; liberal studies (teaching & liberal learning options); mathematics; music; psychology; social & behavioral sciences; telecommunications, multimedia, & applied computing; teledramatic arts & technology; visual & public art; world languages & cultures.

Learn about graduate programs at CSUMB.EDU/masters and teaching credential options at CSUMB.EDU/teach

Costs and Aid

2007–2008 $2,883 in-state comprehensive ($2,772 tuition); out-of-state: $339 per semester credit, $10,170 maximum. 60-70% of students receive some financial aid

Endowment

$4.2 million (scholarships)

More Distinctions

• USA Today reported that national researchers have recognized CSUMB as one of the top "20 schools that create a campus culture that fosters student success" and for "an unshakable focus on student learning."

• CSUMB was one of only three universities nationwide to receive the President's Award for Excellence in Community Service.

• CSUMB has earned top rankings in U.S. News for both economic and ethnic diversity.

Dominican University of California

CALIFORNIA

Dominican University is an independent college of Catholic heritage. Known for offering high-quality, innovative academic programs, for embracing diversity, for encouraging study and reflection, and for providing opportunities for community service, Dominican has launched a wide range of exciting initiatives that promise to further enhance an excellent, well-deserved reputation.

Admissions Contact:

Dominican University of California
50 Acacia Avenue
San Rafael, CA 94901
(888) 323-6763
Ph: (415) 457-4440
www.dominican.edu

The 4 Distinctions

Engaged Students

Dominican University of California's vision of education encompasses a mission to promote the common good and the values of study, reflection, community service, ethical responsibility, and respect for multiple cultural traditions. These ideals provide a strong foundation for service-learning as a pedagogy that creates intentional links between academic education and community experience, where each strengthens the other. The Dominican Service-Learning Program provides opportunities for students to participate in courses across the majors that integrate academic curriculum with work in the community, encouraging engaged learning and the application of theory to practice. Taking education beyond the classroom, service-learning also promotes value development, social responsibility, and civic awareness as students learn from and contribute to community partner organizations, such as local schools and a wide variety of non-profit organizations and agencies.

Because of Dominican's favorable location in the Bay Area, students have access to a wide range of internship opportunities. Students can also find research and internship opportunities all over the country through the school's Web site. Noteworthy is the Panetta Institute's Congressional Intern Program, which sends a student leader to work for a semester in Washington, DC.

Dominican's Office of International Student Services offers a variety of programs for students to study overseas. Humanities classes have recently traveled to Italy and Greece for interdisciplinary programs in art, language, culture, and economics. Students can also participate in a cultural-learning program that takes students to China. In addition, the ELS Language Centers program, located on the Dominican campus, brings international students to Dominican for intensive instruction in English, helping to create a lively global community at the university.

The North Bay U.S. Export Assistance Center of the U.S. Department of Commerce is located on the Dominican campus, allowing students to acquire hands-on experience in international trade.

Dominican has recently launched a Bachelor of Fine Arts in Dance program. Its participants spend part of their time practicing at Alonzo King's LINES Ballet School in San Francisco.

Great Teaching

With a student to faculty ratio of eleven to one, Dominican successfully blends personal attention and small classes with the academic resources of a larger university. Dominican's focus on interdisciplinary studies offers a challenging academic environment. Humanities students combine intensive study of philosophy, literature, world cultures, and religion with dance and musical performance. Numerous Dominican students participate in sophisticated research projects that lead to presentations at national academic conferences and publication in peer-reviewed journals. Dominican's undergraduate professional programs in business, nursing, and education have strong reputations.

The senior thesis is an intensive research project that gives all Dominican students an opportunity to demonstrate their mastery of their chosen fields of study. Dominican's honors program provides an especially challenging academic experience for highly motivated students. Honors students typically conduct special projects, explore specific topics through honors seminars, or pursue independent research under the guidance of a faculty advisor.

Dominican offers an unusual four-year guarantee: any student who follows a prescribed course load for a major will graduate in four years, or the fifth year will be free.

Vibrant Community

Located in San Rafael, twelve miles north of the Golden Gate Bridge in Marin County, California, Dominican University offers students an exciting location. The campus is within walking distance of San Rafael's town center, and a short car-, ferry-, or bus-ride from San Francisco. In addition to the many sights and activities the city of San Francisco offers, there are dozens of public parks and recreation facilities close by, some on the bay or the ocean, where students can sail, kayak, windsurf, golf, play tennis, go horseback riding, hike, or mountain bike.

Dominican is particularly committed to a diverse student and faculty environment. Over 40 percent of its 1,400 undergraduates are students of color, and around 75 percent are women. Students at Dominican take part in more than sixty clubs and organizations. Several varsity athletes and teams have been very successful recently, competing in the NAIA.

Dominican is committed to developing the bodies, minds, and spirits of its students. Campus ministry offers a variety of programs and activities for students, including Students Promoting Dominican Ideals (SPDI) and Brothers and Sisters in Christ (BASIC). La Bamba, a biannual trip to Mexico, offers students an opportunity to travel to Tijuana to volunteer their time, talent, and heart. Students help in many ways during their trip, performing tasks such as repairing and constructing shelter, cooking and serving food, and visiting local jails and orphanages. The trip also serves to allow Dominican students to unravel stereotypes and challenge injustice.

In the last few years, a variety of construction projects—including the Conlan Recreation Center, a new residence hall, and the recently opened Science Center—have changed the face of the campus.

Successful Outcomes

Several recent surveys have demonstrated that Dominican graduates are highly satisfied with their academic preparation, faculty advising, and mentoring. Dominican's active student-alumni network promotes and fosters connections that help students decide on career paths and find employment. The career services office offers workshops and counseling on career and job-search strategies, resume writing, and interview skills.

Fast Facts

Dominican University of California is an independent, international, learner-centered university of Catholic heritage located in San Rafael, California.

Web site

http:// www.dominican.edu

Location

San Rafael, California—just 12 miles north of San Francisco, the pristine campus is nestled on 80 wooded acres.

Student Profile

1,391 undergraduate students (23% male, 77% female); students come from across the US, although primarily from the Bay Area and Northern California; approximately 40% of undergraduate students are of ALANA heritage (African American, Latino, Asian American or Native American).

Faculty Profile

66 full-time faculty. 11:1 student/faculty ratio. Average class size is 15.

Residence Life

Moderately residential: 49% of students live on campus.

Athletics

National Associate of Intercollegiate Athletics (NAIA), Far West Region Member; California Pacific Conference Intercollegiate Sports: men's and women's soccer, basketball, golf; men's lacrosse; women's volleyball, softball, tennis.

Academic Programs

Art; art history; biological sciences; business administration; communications; dance; digital art; English; English with a writing emphasis; health science; history; humanities & cultural studies; interdisciplinary studies; international studies; Latin American studies; liberal studies/teacher education; music w/ performance concentration; nursing; politics; psychology; religion; sports management; women & gender studies.

Costs and Aid

2007–2008: $$45,590 comprehensive ($30,270 tuition). More than 75% of students at Dominican receive aid to help manage college costs, and more than 90% of undergraduate freshmen receive scholarship or grant aid. Dominican offers hundreds of privately funded merit, athletic, and need-based scholarships and grants each year. Counselors provide expert one-on-one advice on securing federal and state grants and loans.

Endowment

$11.6 million.

Mount St. Mary's College

CALIFORNIA

Offering highly regarded programs in the liberal arts and health-care professions, Mount St. Mary's College (MSMC) is the only Catholic college primarily for women in the western United States. On average, 95 percent of Mount St. Mary's entering undergraduate students are women, and the college reflects Southern California's ethnic diversity.

Admissions Contact:

Mount St. Mary's College
12001 Chalon Rd.
Los Angeles, CA 90049
Ph: (800) 999-9893
Email: mountnews@msmc.la.edu
www.msmc.la.edu/admissions

The 4 Distinctions

Engaged Students

About 60 percent of Mount St. Mary's students are the first in their families to attend college. Many students were involved in community service prior to attending Mount St. Mary's, and two-thirds of them continue to do volunteer work while in college. Mount St. Mary's seeks to integrate out-of-classroom experiences into its students' educations.

In most major programs, senior students are required to conduct an off-campus internship. This encourages students to explore real-world experiences in collaboration with their curriculum. Faculty and staff in the internship and placement office are available to assist students in finding an opportunity to meet their needs.

This year, selected students from a political science and sociology course had the opportunity to participate in the Borders Project. Led by two professors, students spent a weekend camping along the United States/Mexican border. Organized into teams, students assisted with preparing and serving meals, organizing transportation, arranging guest speakers, and creating community connections for future sustainable partnerships. The experience enabled the students to serve border communities while developing an understanding of divisive immigration issues.

All students interested in international travel have the opportunity to participate in the study abroad program, Weekend College Travel. In addition to the traditional study abroad program, the Weekend College offers exciting international travel opportunities. Students participating in the Weekend College program have earned college credit by traveling to places such as Asia, Europe, the British Isles, Russia, South America, the Caribbean, the American South, and Hawaii. These international travel opportunities allow all Mount students to immerse themselves in the cultures and histories of their destinations, while being guided by members of MSMC's dynamic and knowledgeable faculty.

The college's spiritual traditions are steeped in the Catholic intellectual heritage, and approximately 40 percent of the student body is non-Catholic. Students of every faith tradition are welcomed and encouraged to participate in campus ministry programs and to grow as persons of faith whose lives are committed to the service of others and to the unfolding of the mystery of their own purpose and being.

Great Teaching

Mount St. Mary's College students are serious about their education. It has been said that the college's students "know who they are, where they've been, and where they want to go."

Popular majors include, biological sciences, psychology, business, political science and sociology. Mount St. Mary's is well-known for the excellence of its nursing program, which enrolls 20 percent of the college's students. Another notable program includes the degree-granting program in documentary film and social justice, which sponsors an annual Human Rights Film Festival.

Twenty-six Mount St. Mary's students have been awarded the prestigious Rockefeller Brother Fellowship Fund for Aspiring Teachers of Color, more than any other college in the U.S. Mount St. Mary's has also been honored with a National Institutes of Health Minority Access to Research Careers grant to promote research in the sciences by Mount St. Mary's students.

"Real education should educate us out of self into something far finer; into a selflessness which links us to all humanity."

-Lady Nancy Astor

Vibrant Community

Mount St. Mary's College is located on two campuses. The Chalon Campus, located in the Santa Monica mountains and above the J. Paul Getty Museum, houses the baccalaureate degree programs and the Doheny Campus, in the historic West Adams District is home to the Associate of Arts, The Weekend College and The Graduate Programs. On average, 60 percent of students—and 90 percent of freshmen—live on campus.

There are plenty of clubs and organizations for students to join. The Mount's Student Activities and Commuter Services Office helps students connect to activities on campus. Their motto—to enhance personal growth, to encourage community building and leadership development, and to promote social and cultural awareness through meaningful programming and cocurricular involvement—helps to ensure that at MSMC, every student is a leader.

MSMC students can also take advantage of the opportunity to co-register for classes at UCLA, giving Mount students the ability to connect with other students at a larger campus and use of other resources as well. While Mount St. Mary's does not have intercollegiate athletics, many students take part in UCLA's thriving intramural sports programs.

Successful Outcomes

Mount St. Mary's is committed to helping students succeed from the moment they set foot on campus. Students take advantage of services offered by the academic advisement center, where the primary goal is to foster student success and retention by providing comprehensive academic support services and facilitating student transition to the MSMC community.

The staff of the career center assists students with internship placement, resume writing, networking luncheons, and etiquette dinners. Known for their values-based education, Mount St. Mary's students are highly valued by employers and graduate schools.

The college's prelaw program regularly produces award-winning students who go on to study law. In the last few years, MSMC students have been named Best attorney and Best witness twice at the Great Western Regional competition for the American Mock Trial Association.

"The most beautiful thing in the world is precisely, the conjunction of learning and inspiration."

-Wanda Landowska

Fast Facts

Mount St. Mary's College is an independent, Catholic, liberal arts college which offers a values-based education for women, as well as innovative programs for professional men and women on two historical Los Angeles campuses.

Web site

http://www.msmc.la.edu

Location

Los Angeles, California.

Student Profile

1,980 undergraduate students (3% male, 97% female); 21 states and territories; 74% minority, 1% international.

Faculty Profile

72 full-time faculty. 78% hold a terminal degree in their field. 16:1 student/faculty ratio. Average class size is 13.

Residence Life

Moderately residential: 69% of students live on campus.

Athletics

Various Intramurals.

Academic Programs

Bachelor of Arts: American studies; art & graphic design; business administration; English; film & social justice; gerontology; history; language & culture; liberal studies; mathematics; music; nursing; philosophy; religious studies; sociology. Bachelor of Science: biological sciences; biochemistry; business administration; chemistry; education; nursing; political science; psychology; social work.

Costs and Aid

2007–2008: $24,550 tuition. 98% of students receive some financial aid.

Endowment

$71 million.

Point Loma Nazarene University

CALIFORNIA

Point Loma Nazarene University (PLNU), based in San Diego, is a leading Christian liberal arts school with a commitment to educating students as whole people. PLNU prepares graduates for meaningful careers in fields as diverse as medicine, ministry, education, and politics.

Admissions Contact:

Point Loma Nazarene University
3900 Lomaland Drive
San Diego, CA 92106
(800) 733-7770
Email: admissions@pointloma.edu
www.pointloma.edu

The 4 Distinctions

Engaged Students

PLNU's location in San Diego is beneficial to students, as the city is a great resource for internships. Students studying athletic training have the opportunity to intern with both the Padres and the Chargers. Another off-campus opportunity for PLNU students is the study-abroad program; 27 percent of PLNU students participate in the program. Additionally, 90 percent of PLNU students participate in community service of some kind.

PLNU offers students a wide variety of resources to address students' many interests. Some students are interested in exploring the way people worship in foreign countries, while others offer support to families in need. Musically inclined PLNU students often choose to play an instrument in a worship band, while others opt to lead Bible study in the dormitory. PLNU is committed to opening as many doors as possible for its students.

Another specialized program offered by PLNU is the LoveWorks Short Term Mission Program, which functions within the office of spiritual development. The goal of LoveWorks is to allow students to work alongside pastors, missionaries, and congregations who serve Christ in various domestic and international settings. Through LoveWorks, more than two thousand students, faculty, staff, and alumni have traveled to almost sixty world areas in service.

Students also have the opportunity to participate in the CJR Urban Term, a partnership of teaching faculty and community leaders. Every other summer, CJR's director coordinates an intensive cross-cultural immersion program based on a sociological and theological educational curriculum. This curriculum is designed to combine praxis and academic reflection on the complexities of urban life, while students live and serve in City Heights, a diverse, low-income community in San Diego.

PLNU also offers the Entrepreneurial Enrichment Program, which was established to encourage, stimulate, and nourish the entrepreneurial process, in any full- or part-time student, in all academic disciplines at PLNU. This program provides specific personal, business, and professional advice on student-entrepreneur's business plans from recognized industry leaders, entrepreneurs, and financiers.

Great Teaching

Most of PLNU's major areas of study are vocationally oriented, such as business, education, nursing, physics, and communications. The university offers a solid liberal arts program with a strong core of general education courses. Freshmen are eased into college life through an integrated program designed to emphasize critical thinking and practical knowledge. Each PLNU class offers real-world experience and prepares students to become dynamic leaders. Students are encouraged to make their mark in many fields, and in work all over the world. PLNU offers more than fifty specific areas of study and is accredited by the Western Association of Schools and Colleges.

Not only do freshman have a new set of academic challenges, they also are adjusting to a new community and living situation. Within the first few weeks of the school year, the freshman retreat provides students with an opportunity to meet their peers as well as numerous university personnel. Resident assistants make a conscious effort to learn about each freshman student and plan activities throughout the year.

Point Loma Nazarene University's First-Year Experience (FYE) is a comprehensive and cohesive program of academic and personal development activities and services that set the course for students to enter into the community of faithful learners. The goal of Point Loma's FYE is to facilitate the transition to university life by developing in students self-awareness and understanding of others, the enjoyment of a wide variety of services, and the skills to meet the challenges of higher education.

Numerous opportunities for spiritual growth are available to students. Students may participate in worship ministries, small groups, service projects, and community outreach. All of these opportunities are considered to be part of a student's education at Point Loma.

Vibrant Community

PLNU's campus is located near the beach, to which student dormitories have direct access. Of the 2,400 undergraduates at PLNU, 75 percent live on campus and 65 percent come from California.

PLNU offers many recreational activities on and off campus. As part of the After Dark program, students can enjoy drinks and food from the Point Break Cafe while enjoying free musical entertainment by PLNU students and local bands. Musoffee (Music and Coffee) is a campus event that brings students together to share their creative endeavors, such as playing a new composition on an instrument, reading a poem or story, or singing a song.

The PLNU Great Escapes Adventures program exists to provide quality outdoor adventure opportunities for PLNU students and staff through challenging wilderness experiences.

PLNU students participate in chapel three times a week.

Successful Outcomes

Point Loma Nazarene University has over thirty-two thousand alumni worldwide. The university's career services center is devoted to bridging the gap between students and prospective employers. Career services assists current students, prospective students, and PLNU alumni with finding the best job or career for their personality.

The Fermanian Business Center also provides valuable resources to both undergraduate and graduate students. The center offers PLNU students access to an internship and employee database that includes contact information for alumni, corporations, nonprofit organizations, and entrepreneurs who are looking for qualified individuals. PLNU also provides professional development events throughout the year to allow students, faculty, and business professionals to meet, interact, and network. By hosting events such as these, PLNU equips its students for the ever-growing world of business, and helps to establish and cultivate relationships that benefit all participants.

Many of our graduates go straight into the workplace. Currently, PLNU students are working in careers ranging from national presidential campaigns to DreamWorks Studios to Scripps Medical Facilities. Our alumni have proceeded to such prestigious graduate schools as Harvard University, University of California at Berkeley Law, Georgetown and many others.

"The personal attention I received in my education at Point Loma was what really set it apart from the other schools I attended. That one-on-one contact with professors helped me to get a great internship that led to the perfect job for me after I graduated. I still keep in touch with the professors who helped me succeed."

--Jacqueline Serr, 2004 graduate

Fast Facts

Point Loma Nazarene University is a four-year, liberal arts, private Christian university founded in 1902.

Web site

http://www.pointloma.edu

Location

San Diego, California—10 minutes from downtown San Diego, the airport and the train station; beach access on campus.

Student Profile

2400 undergraduate students (41% male, 59% female); 37 states and territories, 17 countries; 35% out-of state.

Faculty Profile

150 full-time faculty. 80% hold a terminal degree in their field. 16:1 student/faculty ratio. Average class size is 20.

Residence Life

Highly residential: 75% of students live on campus.

Athletics

NAIA Division 1, GSAC Conference. 14 varsity sports (7 men's: baseball, basketball, cross-country, golf, soccer, tennis, track & field; 7 women's: basketball, cross-country, soccer, softball, tennis, track & field, volleyball), 3 club sports, and 10 intramurals.

Academic Programs

Accounting; art education; athletic training; biblical studies; biology; biology–chemistry; broadcast journalism; business administration; chemistry; child development; Christian ministry; communication; composition; computer science; consumer & environmental sciences; dietetics; engineering physics; exercise science; family life services; graphic design; history; industrial-organizational psychology; information systems; instrumental performance; international development studies; international studies; journalism; liberal studies; literature; managerial & organizational communication; mathematics; media communication; music; music & ministry; music education; nursing; nutrition & food; philosophy; philosophy & theology; physical education; physics; piano performance; political science; psychology; romance languages; social science; social work; sociology; Spanish; theatre; visual arts; vocal performance.

Costs and Aid

2007–2008: $31,200 comprehensive ($23,200 tuition). 92% of students receive some financial aid. Average award: $13,000.

More Distinctions

• Ranked in U.S. News and World Report's Best Colleges and Universities in the Western Region.

• Ranked in the top ten schools in the U.S. in percentage of students of students to study abroad.

• PLNU's Speech and Debate team finished first in the nation in the 06-07 school year, for both squad and individual team awards.

Saint Mary's College of California

CALIFORNIA

Founded 1863, Saint Mary's College of California is a private, liberal arts college. Based in the Catholic, Lasallian, and liberal arts traditions, Saint Mary's ensures that students develop habits of critical thinking and a desire for lifelong learning.

Admissions Contact:

Saint Mary's College of California
Office of Admissions
PO Box 4800
Moraga, CA 94575
(800) 800-4SMC
Email: smcadmit@stmarys-ca.edu
www.smcadmit.com

The 4 Distinctions

Engaged Students

Saint Mary's offers student a variety of study-abroad options, and approximately 45 percent of students study abroad during their time at Saint Mary's. Programs such as Saint Mary's Study Abroad, the Lasallian Consortium, and Saint Mary's Exchange allow students to continue to utilize their financial aid while studying abroad. Another benefit of these programs is that the college pays half the cost of airfare. Saint Mary's study abroad is available in locations such as Australia, Italy, Mexico, South Africa, England, France, and Spain. The Lasallian International Programs Consortium offers programs in Argentina, Ireland, and South Africa, to name a few. Exchange programs are active in Japan and Mexico.

Students and faculty can take advantage of opportunities for academic exploration and enrichment during the school's January term. Options include travel courses, guided instruction on campus, courses at other 4-1-4 colleges, and independent-study projects.

Internships are available to all students and are coordinated through the career center. San Francisco and Oakland offer opportunities for students to intern in every field, as do the surrounding cities of Walnut Creek and Livermore. Companies frequently come to campus to conduct interviews with students seeking internships.

Saint Mary's students can also participate in service-learning courses. Students enrolled in these courses become volunteers, often for nonprofit agencies. As a result, students gain real-world experience while performing service to the community.

Great Teaching

For over 130 years, Saint Mary's has been guided by the Lasallian Christian Brothers, the Catholic church's oldest order dedicated exclusively to teaching. The most popular majors at Saint Mary's are business, communications, social sciences and history, liberal and civic studies, and psychology. The business program combines theoretical and practical knowledge, and business majors benefit from professors who have experience in their field.

Every student must complete the collegiate seminar program, which introduces students to the works of poets, philosophers, scientists, and historians who have shaped the Western world. Throughout the seminars, students engage in discussion and writing, and are encouraged to read actively, think critically, listen well, converse in a spirit of cooperation, and to reflect upon and refine their ideas and opinions.

With an average class size of twenty students, classes tend to be close-knit and engaged in cooperative learning. One marketing course focuses on cooperative learning by taking on an organization as a client and developing a marketing strategy for them. The class works together to receive a passing grade, which is determined by the organization's acceptance or rejection of the class's proposed marketing strategy. No class has failed yet.

The new science building, Brousseau Hall, is a research and teaching hub with seventeen cutting-edge labs, a seawater tank, and an environmental chamber. The observatory in Galileo Hall includes a sixteen-inch-diameter research telescope, a robotic mount, and a real-time video feed into astronomy labs. Students can perform research with professors during the school year or join summer research programs at colleges and universities across the country.

The inquisitive nature of Saint Mary's students leads to group discussion and friendly debate. There are twenty-six Christian Brother faculty members, and the rest of the faculty are seen as partners in the mission. Because of this, professors not only teach students but also mentor them.

Vibrant Community

Saint Mary's is located in Moraga, twenty miles east of San Francisco, on a 420-acre campus. Students enjoy the moderate climate and take advantage of the hiking and biking trails, several parks, and two shopping centers in Moraga. On campus, the beautiful landscape is highlighted by grassy areas and patios where students get together and study. The campus is self-contained and safe, and students can walk from one end of campus to the other.

Residence options include living-learning communities and themed halls. A science-themed hall and an honors-themed hall are open to freshman, while the Lasallian Community is open to sophomores and juniors. The Lasallian Community lives out the college's commitment to the Lasallian tradition of social justice and outreach. Students in this community learn about faith, prayer, and spiritual practice, and participate in regular community nights and service teams.

Saint Mary's student body is very diverse, and cultural nights are often hosted by clubs such as the Asian Pacific American Student Association, the Black Student Union, and the Latin American Student Association. There are over thirty clubs and organizations on campus. Saint Mary's speech and debate club has won a number of awards and distinctions.

The Saint Mary's College Hearst Art Gallery draws students and members of the surrounding community to its exhibitions throughout the year. Theater performances, athletic events, guest speakers, events in the chapel, and concerts are also hosted on campus.

Successful Outcomes

The career center at Saint Mary's is responsive and available to students from the beginning of their time at college to the end. From offering help with resume building, interview skills, and job searching and tracking, to coordinating a career fair and student interviews with companies, the career center is helpful through the entire employment process. The average starting salary for Saint Mary's grads is forty-four thousand a year. Most alumni find jobs in the local area because of the variety of work options in the Bay Area. Alumni stay active in the college and often attend homecoming as well as an alumni welcoming event for seniors.

Saint Mary's graduates have an outstanding record of admission to graduate and professional schools—including an 80 percent acceptance rate into medical schools—and many alumni have found meaningful work in high technology, advanced research, and health and medicine. Within one year of graduation, 20 percent of Saint Mary's students attend graduate school.

Notable alumni include Laura Garcia-Cannon, anchorwoman for NBC-11; Shirley Griffin, executive vice president of Wells Fargo Bank; Robert Hass, poet laureate of the United States from 1995 to 1997; Harry Hooper, member of the National Baseball Hall of Fame; George P. Miller, member of Congress from California from 1945 to 1973; Nicholas Moore, retired chairman of PricewaterhouseCoopers; Don Perata, majority leader and California State senator; Dr. Carl Wu, cancer researcher, National Institute of Health; Mario Alioto, Senior Vice President, Corporate Marketing, San Francisco Giants.

Fast Facts

Saint Mary's College is a four-year, liberal arts college, affiliated with the Lasallian Christian Brothers, the largest Catholic order dedicated exclusively to teaching, and founded in 1863.

Web site

www.smcadmit.com

Location

Moraga, California—20 miles east of San Francisco.

Student Profile

2,440 students (39% male, 61% female); 23 states and territories, 28 countries; almost 40% minority, 3% international.

Faculty Profile

198 full-time faculty, 90% hold a Ph.D. 12:1 student/faculty ratio. Average class size is 20.

Residence Life

Highly residential: 82% of first-year students live on campus.

Athletics

NCAA Division I, West Coast Conference. 14 varsity sports (6 men's: baseball, basketball, cross-country, golf, soccer, tennis; 8 women's: basketball, cross-country, lacrosse, rowing, soccer, softball, tennis, volleyball); misc. club and intramural sports.

Academic Programs

Accounting; anthropology & sociology; art & art history; biology; business administration; chemistry; classical languages; communication; computer science; cross-cultural studies; economics; education; engineering (3+2); English & drama; environmental science; health science; history; international area studies; kinesiology; liberal & civic studies; math & computer science; modern languages; natural science; nursing; performing arts (dance, music, and theatre); philosophy; physics & astronomy; politics; preprofessional curricula; psychology; religious studies; studies for international students; women's studies.

Costs and Aid

2007–2008: $42,020 comprehensive ($31,090 tuition). 73% of students receive some financial aid. Average award: $23,224.

Endowment

$143 million.

More Distinctions

• St. Mary's has been consistently ranked in the top 10 of *US News and World Report* Top Colleges in the West.

• Ranked in the *Princeton Review Guide to Best Colleges* as one of the top 20 colleges in the nation with the "Best Quality of Life."

University of California - Santa Cruz

CALIFORNIA

Nestled on two thousand acres of redwood-forested hills overlooking the Pacific Ocean and Monterey Bay, University of California, Santa Cruz (UCSC) is one of the University of California's ten campuses.

Admissions Contact:

University of California - Santa Cruz
Office of Admissions - Cook House
1156 High Street
Santa Cruz, CA 95064
Ph: (831) 459-4008
Email: admissions@ucsc.edu
www.ucsc.edu

The 4 Distinctions

Engaged Students

UCSC's location near Monterey Bay makes it ideal for students in the fields of marine biology and marine science. The university's physical and biological sciences programs have exceptional national reputations. In 2001, UCSC was ranked second worldwide for research productivity in the physical sciences by the Institute for Scientific Information. In 2007, the university was ranked first in the nation for research impact in physics by Science Watch, and fifth in the nation for research impact in the space sciences. Many undergraduate students, as well as graduate students, are active in the Institute for Marine Sciences' Long Marine Laboratory, which is located on the bay, just a mile from campus.

UCSC offers students many opportunities to take part in internships and fieldwork. In the health sciences major, for example, internships are an integral part of the program; students are also required to take a course in medical Spanish. All community studies majors undertake a six-month, full-time field study or internship with a community organization or agency for academic credit. With the guidance of a faculty adviser and field study coordinator, community studies students choose field placements related to the issues on which they choose to focus. Internships and field study experiences are also offered by the departments of economics, education, environmental studies, Latin American and Latino studies, and psychology.

Students at UCSC can study for a quarter or a full year in a foreign country as part of the University of California's Education Abroad Program (EAP). Students choose from over 140 host universities in thirty-four countries. Of UC campuses, UCSC has the highest percentage of upper-division students participating in EAP when averaged over the last five years.

Many undergraduate majors at UCSC are in innovative, interdisciplinary fields. UCSC's Jack Baskin School of Engineering offers a major in bioinformatics, which combines biology, chemistry, biochemistry, computer science, mathematics, statistics, bioethics, and specialized bioinformatics classes to develop tools to gain knowledge from biological data. In 2006, the Baskin School of Engineering introduced a new major in computer game design. The first

major of its kind in the UC system, computer game design brings together computer science, computer engineering, art, music, and fiction writing to prepare students to enter the multibillion-dollar computer gaming industry.

UCSC's newest major, which is also overseen by the Baskin School of Engineering, is the bioengineering BS degree. Distinguished by UCSC's strengths in areas such as bioinformatics, molecular biology, and bioelectronics, the major focuses on the application of engineering tools and techniques to the problems of medicine and the biological sciences. Faculty in this program conduct research in areas such as biomolecular sensors, nanoelectronic implants, assistive technologies for the elderly and disabled, bioinformatics, molecular design, and environmental monitoring.

Other innovative majors at UCSC include global economics, in which students study the economics, culture, and language of a country of their choice; history of art and visual culture, which goes beyond the traditional borders of art history to examine visual culture around the globe; and film and digital media, which integrates creative work in film, video, and electronic media with the critical and historical study of film, television, video, and digital media.

Great Teaching

UCSC's 13,900 undergraduate students, known for their diversity, can choose from sixty-one undergraduate majors; the most popular majors are psychology, art, business management economics, literature, and politics. After the initial introductory lecture courses, UCSC offers many small classes, most of which have between ten and twenty-nine students. In addition to letter grades, professors write personalized evaluations for students in their courses.

Opportunities for faculty-student research are abundant. UCSC professors regularly invite undergraduates into their laboratories and studios, and it is common for undergraduates to publish papers in collaboration with professors and researchers.

For students looking for greater challenges, the departments at UCSC offer a variety of intensive programs and tracks. Students may also choose to pursue a combined major or double major, or they may be invited to join one of the many campuswide, national, or international honor societies hosted by UCSC.

Vibrant Community

The university is based on a residential college system. Upon enrollment, whether or not they live on campus, all students join one of ten colleges. Each college provides academic support, organizes student activities, and sponsors events that enhance the intellectual and social life of the campus in addition to housing students in small-scale residential communities. Each college has an academic focus (international relations, environmental studies, etc.), a distinct architectural style, and its own unique atmosphere. Each first-year student takes a core course, with a college-specific curriculum and central theme, in the college. Most faculty members are affiliated with a particular college, providing out-of-classroom opportunities for students and professors to form lasting friendships.

The UCSC community is known as a place where faculty members and fellow students celebrate one another's successes, and where there is very little head-to-head competition. The university offers many academic and support programs to help students with academic and other issues in their lives.

The campus hosts over one hundred student-led organizations, including many ethnic organizations, which stress academic and personal success for their members. UCSC students take part in numerous club and intramural sports, as well as participating in varsity athletics at the NCAA Division III level, though there are no athletic scholarships. Team sports include men's and women's basketball, soccer, swimming and diving, tennis, volleyball, and water polo, as well as women's cross-country and golf. A member of NCAA Division III since 1981, UCSC has already had over 170 all-Americans and 10 National NCAA Championships, and features internationally acclaimed coaches and award-winning programs. In 2007, men's tennis won its sixth national title, and in 2005, the team included winners of both the singles and doubles titles.

The university also sponsors the nationally recognized Shakespeare Santa Cruz festival, which presents plays on campus and is a highly visible presence in the local community.

Successful Outcomes

UCSC's location, just seventy-five miles south of the vibrant San Francisco Bay Area, provides not only opportunities for internships during the undergraduate years, but also a healthy job market for those who seek employment following graduation.

About half of UCSC graduates pursue higher degrees. In a recent survey of elite universities, UCSC ranked fifteenth for the percentage of its graduates who ultimately continue on to earn PhDs. In the University of California system, only UC Berkeley, at fourteenth, ranked higher.

Fast Facts

The University of California, Santa Cruz is a four-year public research university founded in 1965.

Web site

http://www.ucsc.edu

Location

Santa Cruz, California—75 miles south of San Francisco and 30 miles southwest of San Jose.

Student Profile

13,941 undergraduate students (47% male, 53% female); 97% are from the state of California.

Faculty Profile

95% of full-time faculty hold a terminal degree in their field. 19:1 student/faculty ratio.

Residence Life

Moderately residential: 48% of students live on campus. Students are not required to live on campus.

Athletics

NCAA Division III. 14 varsity sports (6 men's: basketball, soccer, swimming & diving, tennis, volleyball, water polo; 8 women's: basketball, soccer, swimming & diving, tennis, volleyball, water polo, cross-country, golf), 17 club sports, and 14 intramurals.

Academic Programs

American studies; anthropology; applied physics; art; biochemistry & molecular biology; bioengineering; bioinformatics; biology; business management economics; chemistry; classical studies; community studies; computer engineering; computer science; computer science: computer game design; earth sciences; earth sciences/anthropology; ecology & evolution; economics; electrical engineering; environmental studies; environmental studies/biology; environmental studies/earth sciences; environmental studies/economics; feminist studies; film & digital media; German studies; global economics; health sciences; history; history of art & visual culture; information systems management; Italian studies; language studies; Latin American & Latino studies; Latin American & Latino studies/global economics; Latin American & Latino studies/literature; Latin American & Latino studies/politics; Latin American & Latino studies/sociology; legal studies; linguistics; literature; marine biology; mathematics; molecular, cell & developmental biology; music; neuroscience & behavior; philosophy; physics; physics (astrophysics); plant sciences; politics; psychology; sociology; theater arts. UCSC also offers graduate programs in 34 academic fields and 46 concentrations.

Costs and Aid

2007–2008: In-state: $23,604; Out-of-state: $43,188. In 2005–2006, UCSC students on financial aid received grants and scholarships averaging $10,340; work-study awards averaging $2,200; and loans averaging $4,895.

More Distinctions

• 2nd worldwide for research productivity in the physical sciences. (2001, Institute for Scientific Information)

• 1st in the nation for research impact in physics. (2007, Science Watch)

• 5th in the nation for research impact in space sciences. (2007, Science Watch)

University of San Francisco

CALIFORNIA

University of San Francisco (USF) is a private, Jesuit, Catholic, university in the heart of vibrant and diverse San Francisco, California. Founded in 1855 as San Francisco's first institution of higher learning, USF has grown dramatically, but continues to fulfill its mission to "educate minds and hearts to change the world."

Admissions Contact:

University of San Francisco
2130 Fulton Street
San Francisco, CA 94117-1080
(800) CALL-USF
Ph: (415) 422-6563
Email: admission@usfca.edu
www.usfca.edu

The 4 Distinctions

Engaged Students

USF prepares students for successful careers without forgetting the need to make a positive difference in the world. Social justice is an important value at USF, and USF's goal is to equip students with the education they need to help them make changes for a more humane and just world.

The top majors at USF are psychology, biology, preprofessional heatlh services, communications, media studies, nursing, and business. All USF students follow the core curriculum, which includes course work in communication, math and science, humanities, social science, visual and performing arts, philosophy, ethics, and theology, as well as service and diversity requirements. The core curriculum supports USF's view that faith and reason should be used as complimentary resources.

USF's location in San Francisco provides students with access to some of the world's most important cultural resources as well as a number of worthwhile internship and service-learning possibilities. The university is a member of the University Career Action Network (UCAN). This consortium of eighteen colleges and universities across the country gives students access to internship opportunities with the nation's top employers, opportunities that enable students to gain experience in their chosen careers.

Integrated learning communities are an important part of the USF campus. The Global Living Community is made up of international and domestic students who gain a global perspective by performing community service, meeting weekly, and attending guest speaker events on global social justice issues. Other learning communities include the Garden Project, centered on global environmental concerns.

The first Jesuit universities were situated in the center of great cities. With more than 150 years in San Francisco, USF carries on the tradition. As San Francisco has grown, so has USF. First serving Irish and Italian immigrants, the university, like the city, has grown, and student names have expanded over the years from Cleary, O'Brien, Pinasco, and Vanzinni, to include Nguyen, Aquino, Takashi, Gonzales and Chang.

Great Teaching

Classes at USF are not taught by teaching assistants, but by faculty members. Of the USF faculty, 92 percent have a PhD or other appropriate terminal degree. USF faculty are recognized for their research as well as for their teaching. After twenty years of research in Antarctica, Deneb Karentz, the chair of the biology department, recently had an Antarctic lake named in her honor.

USF professors often lead immersion experiences in a number of countries. In the past, students have used the winter break to travel to Zambia to build a library. Students in the nursing program have visited Guatemala, and computer science students have traveled to Belize. Students have also traveled to South Africa and India for immersion experiences.

The Honors Program in the Humanities is an intellectually challenging program in which students develop an appreciation for classical expressions of Western civilization. Students in the program take seminars on topics such as renaissance culture, and the origins of Judaism and Christianity, and have the opportunity to complete an independent research project for credit.

Through its twenty-one centers and institutes, including the Leo T. McCarthy Center for Public Service and the Common Good, the Center for Child and Family Development, and the Valery Institute of Poetry and Visual Arts, USF offers its students opportunities for expanded research, internship, travel, and service learning in San Francisco, throughout the U.S., and abroad.

Vibrant Community

Located near Golden Gate Park and only three miles from the Pacific Ocean, USF's fifty-five acre campus is home to 2,200 of the school's 4,200 undergraduates. Known as the Hilltop because of its location on one of San Francisco's major hills, the campus borders three San Francisco neighborhoods: Lone Mountain, the Western Addition, and the Richmond District. This location enables students to easily interact with the city. Students work with St. Anthony's Foundation, a San Francisco nonprofit organization providing shelter, housing, meals, medical care, clothing and furniture, rehabilitation services, and senior services for the needy.

USF is widely recognized as one of the most diverse Jesuit universities, with nonwhite students making up 52 percent of the student body and international students making up 7 percent. USF welcomes students of all faiths, as well as students with no religious beliefs. Currently, half of the student body identifies themselves as Catholic. On average, 63 percent of USF's students are from California, while the other 37 percent come mainly from the Western United States. USF also draws students from urban areas all over the country, and from all fifty states.

On campus, many cultural organizations exist for students, from the Asian Pacific American Student Coalition to the Muslim Student Association. Students of all backgrounds are able to come together in these groups and share their culture with the campus. Clubs such as Amnesty International, Democracy Matters, and Model United Nations also thrive on campus.

Successful Outcomes

USF's focus on integrated learning experiences helps to produce graduates who report being very satisfied with their undergraduate education. Alumni include a justice of the California Supreme Court, a Pulitzer Prize-winning photographer, the former president of Peru, the CEO of Intel, the former chair of Price Waterhouse, and a number of professional athletes.

Academically, the future of education is in the possibilities that the combined study of different subjects create, and what that means to mankind's progress. At USF, exemplar faculty mentor students in research and academic goals that often combine major areas of study, such as computer science and business, biology and technology, preprofessional health studies and communication.

USF"s career services center, in collaboration with the alumni relations office and the Associated Students of the University of San Francisco (ASUSF), gives students an opportunity to connect with alumni to learn about careers during a winter-break externship. The externship, similar to an internship, allows students to shadow an alumni professional over a specified length of time. Students are paired with alumni volunteers based on their interests and availability. During externships, students have the opportunity to observe meetings, ask questions, and network with other professionals.

Fast Facts

University of San Francisco is a Catholic, Jesuit liberal arts university founded in 1855 as the city's first university.

Web site

http://www.usfca.edu

Location

San Francisco, California—located in residential neighborhoods in the heart of the city, three miles from San Francisco Bay and three miles from the Pacific Ocean.

Student Profile

4,200 undergraduate students (39% male, 61% female); 50 states and territories; 52 % minority, 7% international.

Faculty Profile

352 full-time faculty. 93% hold a terminal degree in their field. 15:1 student/ faculty ratio. Average class size is 26.

Residence Life

Moderately residential: 55% of students live on campus. All Freshmen and Sophomores must live on campus.

Athletics

NCAA Division I, Atlantic Coast Conference. 14 varsity sports (7 men's: baseball, basketball, soccer, track & cross-country, golf, tennis; 7 women's: volleyball, basketball, soccer, track & cross-country, golf, tennis), 7 club sports and 4 intramurals.

Academic Programs

College of Arts and Sciences: Architecture & community design; art history/arts management; Asia Pacific studies B.A.-M.A. five year program; biology; chemistry; communication studies; comparative literature; computer science; computer science BS-MS five year program; economics B.A.-M.A. five year program; economics; engineering 3/2; English; environmental studies; environmental science; exercise & sport science; fine arts; French; graphic design; history; international & development economics B.A.-M.A. five year program; international studies; Japanese studies; Latin American studies; mathematics; media studies; performing arts & social justice; philosophy; physics; politics; psychology; sociology; Spanish; theology & religious studies; undeclared arts; undeclared science; visual arts. School of Business and Management: Accounting; business administration; entrepreneurship; finance; hospitality management; international business; management; marketing. School of Nursing: Nursing.

Costs and Aid

2006–2007: $41,180 comprehensive ($26,680 tuition). 67% of students receive some financial aid. Average award: $16,500.

Endowment

$190 million.

More Distinctions

• U.S. News and World Report ranks USF in the top 20 national universities for student ethnic diversity and international student enrollment.

University of the Pacific

Admissions Contact:

University of the Pacific
3601 Pacific Avenue
Stockton, CA 95211
Ph: (209) 946-2211
Fax: (209) 946-2413
Email: admission@pacific.edu
www.pacific.edu/admission

CALIFORNIA

The University of the Pacific is a midsized, private university in northern California. More than six thousand students are enrolled at its campuses in Stockton, Sacramento, and San Francisco. Pacific excels at providing its students with a personalized education while integrating liberal arts and professional education.

The 4 Distinctions

Engaged Students

Pacific's goal is for its students to graduate "practice ready." Through internships, study abroad, research, and volunteer programs, students gain practical experience. In fact, Pacific guarantees that students will have experiential-learning opportunities in every program. The San Francisco Bay Area, the Sacramento metro area, and the Stockton/San Joaquin County areas offer internship opportunities in virtually every field.

Pacific offers students a number of opportunities to participate in overseas study, field studies, and language immersion programs in Africa, the Americas, Asia, Europe, the Middle East, and Oceania. Students who wish to study abroad enroll in a cross-cultural training program required for semester- or year-abroad programs. In this course, students study topics such as U.S. values and assumptions, cross-cultural communication, and cross-cultural adjustment and problems; students also do research on the host country. Upon their return from study abroad, students enroll in cross-cultural training II, which is designed to ease the transition back into the United States and to give students a chance to reflect on, and continue to learn from, their overseas experience. Pacific's School of International Studies is one of six international studies colleges in the nation, and students enrolled in this school are required to study abroad.

Pacific emphasizes the importance of undergraduate research in all disciplines. Undergraduates have participated in a number of research projects in the School of Engineering and Computer Science, including research on predicting landslides, developing efficient and inexpensive solar cooking equipment, and building robotic heads for object recognition and motion tracking. Research is funded by the school, the university, and by grants from the public and private sector.

Great Teaching

For an institution of its size, the university offers an extensive curriculum. Pacific is the only private school in the country with an enrollment of less than ten thousand students to offer as many as eight different professional schools. Classes are kept small, averaging fewer than twenty students per class. These small classes allow for close student-teacher interaction, a hallmark of the Pacific experience. Many students note that what brings them to Pacific and what keeps them there are the faculty.

Unique accelerated programs offer students the chance to obtain a bachelor's degree and an advanced degree in an accelerated time frame. The most popular and most competitive program, prepharmacy, offers an accelerated Doctorate of Pharmacy degree over five, six, or seven years. Other accelerated programs include the eighteen-month MBA; the three-year bachelor's degree in dental hygiene; five-, six-, and seven-year degrees in dentistry; the four-year bachelor's degree in education, including California teaching credential; the five- and six-year bachelor's and doctoral degrees in speech-language pathology; the six-year bachelor's degree and JD in law; and the three-semester master's degree in international relations.

Within the university, the College of the Pacific, the school's liberal arts and sciences branch, offers programs of study leading to exciting careers in the performing and visual arts, the humanities, and the social and natural sciences. The Conservatory of Music at Pacific offers programs in music management and music therapy, as well as vocal and instrumental performance and music education. It is also the home of the Brubeck Institute for Jazz Studies, founded by alumnus and jazz legend, Dave Brubeck.

A unique component of the general education program is the Pacific seminars, the first two taken in the freshman year, and then a third in the senior year. These seminars build a context for what students will do throughout their time at Pacific. The three Pacific seminars focus on the question: What is a good society? The seminars are discussion oriented and writing intensive.

Vibrant Community

Pacific offers students a residential campus, with 58 percent of students living on campus. The traditional brick and ivy buildings give Pacific the feel of a New England school, setting the university apart from the typical California campus.

Greek life plays an important role at University of the Pacific; 20 percent of the student body are involved in Greek organizations. There are thirteen social Greek organizations, including six fraternities and seven sororities. These organizations are committed to service; each house provides support to an organization such as the American Cancer Society or the Delta Blood Bank. When the Greek houses host large events, they donate the proceeds to their designated organization. For students not interested in Greek organizations, Pacific offers over one hundred student organizations and activities, more than almost any university its size.

The Center for Community Involvement connects students to the Stockton community through tutoring, mentoring, community outreach, and environmental education. Pacific maintains a list of eighty community agencies at which students can volunteer. These include teen centers, health agencies, assisted-living facilities, arts organizations and museums, food and shelter agencies, parks and recreation facilities, and more. Pacific students have the chance to interact with kids on Saturdays during Saturday Partners in Education. This program brings kids ages six to twelve to campus with the goal of promoting the idea that college is a possibility for everyone. During the 2005–2006 school year, Pacificans provided nearly ten thousand hours of community service.

Stockton, California, is centrally located on the California Delta in the heart of northern California, close to Lake Tahoe, Yosemite, and the Pacific coast. It is eighty miles east of San Francisco, and forty-five miles south of Sacramento.

Successful Outcomes

Due in part to Pacific's focus on experiential learning, graduates are well prepared for careers and life after college. The career resource center meets the career-related needs of Pacific students and alumni by offering services and programs such as career- and self- assessment, résumé and cover letter assistance, interview preparation assistance, individual counseling, alumni advisers, employment listings, volunteer work, real-world learning, work study, internships, interviewing skills preparation, on-campus interviews, and graduate-school planning. The annual Meet Your Future career fair brings over one hundred employers to campus each spring.

Notable alumni include Dave Brubeck, jazz pianist and founder of the Brubeck Institute; John Doolittle, member of the United States House of Representatives; Jose Hernandez, NASA astronaut; Chris Isaak, actor and musician; Tom Flores, retired Super Bowl-winning coach of the National Football League's Oakland Raiders.

Fast Facts

University of the Pacific is a four-year, independent, university founded in 1851.

Web site

http://www.pacific.edu

Location

Stockton, California—90 miles east of San Francisco.

Student Profile

3,535 undergraduates (44% male, 56% female); 37 states and territories; 50% minority, 4% international.

Faculty Profile

426 full-time faculty, 298 part-time faculty. 13:1 student/faculty ratio. Average class size is 19.

Residence Life

Moderately residential: 58% of students live on campus.

Athletics

NCAA Division I, Big West Conference. 17 varsity sports (7 men's: baseball, basketball, golf, swimming, tennis, volleyball, water polo; 9 women's: basketball, cross-country, field hockey, soccer, softball, swimming, tennis, volleyball, water polo), cheer & dance, 9 club sports, and 21 leagues and tournaments.

Academic Programs

Art; Asian language & studies; biological sciences; business administration; chemistry; communication; computer science; dental hygiene; economics; education; engineering; English; environmental science; environmental studies; gender studies; geosciences; history; international relations & global studies; liberal studies; mathematics; modern language & literature; music; organizational behavior; philosophy; physics; political science; predentistry; prelaw; premedicine; preoccupational therapy; prepharmacy; prephysical therapy; psychology; religious & classical studies; social science; sociology; speech-language pathology; sport sciences; theatre arts.

Costs and Aid

2007–2008: $38,290 comprehensive ($28,480 tuition). 65% of students receive some financial aid. Average award: $20,301.

Endowment

$195.7 million.

More Distinctions

• US News College Guide ranks Pacific in the top 100 national doctoral universities and among the five "best values" in higher education among doctoral level universities on the West Coast and among the top 38 nationally.

• Princeton Review named Pacific as a Best Western College.

Westmont College

CALIFORNIA

Westmont College is a nationally-ranked Christian liberal arts college in the evangelical tradition that remains focused on undergraduate education. One of the most dynamic interdenominational Christian colleges in the country, Westmont combines a world-class liberal arts education with the cultural, educational and recreational resources of an unbeatable Southern California location.

Admissions Contact:

Westmont College
955 La Paz Road
Santa Barbara, CA 93108-1089
Ph: (800) 777-9011
Email: admissions@westmont.edu
www.westmont.edu

The 4 Distinctions

Engaged Students

The five most popular majors at Westmont, each of which offer several different tracks and most of which require an internship, are communication studies, with numerous internship possibilities and tracks in journalism, film, and media; economics/business, with a very successful entrepreneurship program; sciences, the area in which the school has grown most, adding a number of faculty; English, which serves as an entree into future graduate programs; and kinesiology, the study of human movement.

Westmont is proud of the entrepreneurial focus of its programs. Recently, professor David Newton, chairman of the economics and business department, took part in a discussion on CNN featuring colleges with strong entrepreneurial programs. Westmont students take part in the Spirit of Entrepreneurship and Enterprise Development (SEED) Venture Forum, which requires students to create business plans and offers the opportunity for students to receive advice from local businesspeople.

A research assistance program providing students with opportunities to work with faculty members is available during the summer. Students stay on campus for the summer, are paid for assisting faculty members, and then present the research at a symposium.

Service learning is not required, but many students take advantage of the seventy to seventy-five outreach programs. Examples include adopting a grandparent and working with the Special Olympics. Many students find their passion freshman year and stick with it throughout their time at Westmont.

Westmont's study-abroad programs include a semester of travel in Europe and Israel; the England semester, devoted to English literature; an Asian studies summer program led by the economics and business department faculty; the World Vision International Relief and Development Internship program for sociology majors; and the Global Stewardship Study program for biology majors.

Faculty members offer an increasing number of May-term and summer programs with extensive travel, and students can enroll in programs sponsored by the Council for Christian Colleges & Universities (CCCU). Students can also spend a semester in Los Angeles, learning about the film industry through seminars and internships; explore the social, cultural, ethnic, political, and economic aspects of contemporary life while living and working in San Francisco through the college's urban program; or spend a semester in Washington, DC, learning about politics and government.

Great Teaching

Westmont seeks to provide a first-rate liberal arts education to intellectually curious students with a strong sense of faith. Professors are in the classroom all the time, and the average class size is eighteen students. Westmont is adamant about maintaining the college as an exclusively undergraduate institution, which allows faculty to focus on undergraduate students.

Fortysome members of the faculty live along the perimeter of the campus in homes built for them by the college. Students can walk to professors' homes to hang out, and do so all the time.

Many of the off-campus activities are started by faculty. Several competitive and debate programs have been launched by professors, and one of the Europe programs was started by history and art professors to bring together what students learned and to take students abroad.

A number of Westmont students take advantage of the opportunity to build their own majors. Students take a combination of approved programs and prepare a proposal to explain how the programs are related. Proposals are then approved by a council. Many of these student proposals lead to the development of new majors.

Vibrant Community

Set on 133 acres in the foothills of the Santa Ynez Mountains outside Santa Barbara, Westmont's wooded and scenic campus provide an ideal environment for a residential college. The campus includes buildings and land from two former estates and the historic Deane School for Boys. The grounds feature the pathways, stone bridges, and garden atmosphere typical of Montecito, a suburb of Santa Barbara. The campus is located three miles uphill from the ocean, which can be seen from certain spots on campus.

The college will be adding four to five new buildings in the coming years, built along the same theme as existing buildings. These include a chapel, an art center, another residence hall, a second science building, and a new observatory.

Currently, the campus features five residence halls, including two first-year dormitories. Juniors and seniors can opt to live off campus in apartments and houses.

The Christian faith is intertwined into every aspect of the Westmont community. The college encourages and supports the spiritual growth of its students through informal interactions and formal initiatives.

Serving others is an important part of the Westmont experience. Students have countless service opportunities on campus, in the community, and in other countries. Every year, three hundred to four hundred students, along with faculty and staff members travel to Ensenada, Mexico, to work with twenty churches on hundreds of projects, including construction projects, orphanages, medical care, dental work, vocation Bible school programs, and ministry through theater and athletics. Other international ministries have traveled to Costa Rica, India, and Israel.

Westmont and the surrounding community provide students with a wide array of cultural and athletic activities. Nearby Santa Barbara offers numerous cultural activities as well as a supportive community. Many local businesses come to campus to recruit for jobs and internships. There are also several other institutions of higher learning in the area, such as the University of California, Santa Barbara.

Successful Outcomes

Nearly three-quarters of Westmont students go on to graduate school. Westmont students shine, especially in interviews. Their diverse education enables them to converse with ease. A science major, for example, can talk easily about social issues. Students are well prepared, having spent so much time with their professors. Recruiters in the area prefer to hire Westmont students because they know they have received a strong, thorough education.

Since 1990, more than three hundred students have completed Westmont's entrepreneurship courses, and over fifty graduates have successfully launched their own ventures.

Fast Facts

Westmont College is a nationally-ranked liberal arts college rooted in the teachings of Christ.

Web site

http://www.westmont.edu/

Location

Montecito, California—a suburb of Santa Barbara, 90 minutes from Los Angeles.

Student Profile

1,332 undergraduate students (39% male, 61% female); 31 states, 16 countries; 33 religious denominations.

Faculty Profile

90 full-time faculty. 89% hold a terminal degree in their field. 12:1 student/faculty ratio. Average class size is 18.

Residence Life

Highly residential: 80% of students live on campus all four years. Housing is available to all students.

Athletics

National Association of Intercollegiate Athletics (NAIA) and the Golden State Athletic Conference (GSAC). 12 varsity sports (6 men's: baseball, basketball, cross-country, soccer, tennis, track & field; 6 women's: basketball, cross-country, soccer, tennis, track & field, volleyball); 4 club teams and a wide variety of intramural opportunities.

Academic Programs

Alternative major; art; biology; chemistry; communication studies; computer science; economics & business; education program; engineering physics; English; history; European studies; kinesiology; liberal studies; mathematics; modern languages; music; philosophy; physical education; physics; political science; psychology; religious studies; social science; sociology/anthropology; theatre arts.

Costs and Aid

2007–2008: $31,212 (tuition, fees), $9,622 (room, board). 85% of students receive some financial aid. Average award: $20,266.

Endowment

$66 million.

More Distinctions

• Westmont ranks among the nation's finest liberal arts colleges, according to U.S. News & World Report and the Carnegie Foundation.

• Westmont is one of only 13 colleges in California, and the only Christian college among them, cited by "Barron's Best Buys in College Education."

• Entrepreneur magazine ranks Westmont among the "best colleges in America to study entrepreneurship."

Whittier College

CALIFORNIA

Whittier College is a vibrant, residential, four-year liberal arts institution where intellectual inquiry and experiential learning are fostered in a community that promotes respect for diversity of thought and culture. A Whittier College education produces enthusiastic, independent thinkers who flourish in graduate studies, the evolving global workplace, and in life.

Admissions Contact:

Whittier College
13406 E. Philadelphia Street
Whittier, CA 90608
Ph: (562) 907-4238
Fax: (562) 907-4870
Email: admission@whittier.edu
www.whittier.edu

The 4 Distinctions

Engaged Students

While few colleges offer a design-your-own-curriculum option, Whittier College offers the Whittier Scholars Program. This unique option provides students an opportunity to construct a personalized educational program. In addition to seminars with other Whittier Scholars students and classes with professors from across the academic spectrum, the Whittier Scholars program also incorporates off-campus learning opportunities. The goal is the creation of unique and specialized educational programs that succeed in challenging students to become critical thinkers and researchers with specific post-Whittier career skills. Marc Beylerian, class of 1996, designed his own major in international business and now uses his skills to import fabric from Vietnam and China. Oswaldo Rodriguez, class of 1991, used the Whittier Scholars Program to research a particular protein's involvement with Alzheimer's disease, before going on to earn his MD at the Albert Einstein College of Medicine.

Amid its many distinctions, Whittier College is recognized as a Hispanic Serving Institution. Whittier College also offers a number of study-abroad opportunities for students. Traditionally, nearly two-thirds of Whittier students have taken advantage of semester-long programs as part of their four-year curriculum. Study abroad is encouraged for students in a number of majors, and many students choose to participate in the Denmark International Studies International Business Program in Copenhagen, Denmark. Students have also taken advantage of programs in Argentina, Australia, Chile, China, England, France, Germany, Ireland, India, Italy, Japan, Mexico, New Zealand, Poland, Puerto Rico, Russia, Scotland, South Africa, Spain, Sweden, Switzerland, Thailand, and more.

California has always been considered on the edge of social change and innovation, and Whittier College is a vital part of those advances. At the intersection of Los Angeles and Orange counties in Southern California, Whittier is minutes away from the heart of the most dynamic city in the nation, a center of art, commerce, and ideas. Internship options are abundant for Whittier students. Students have interned with New Line Cinema, the J. Paul Getty Museum, Martinsound Studio, Merrill Lynch, Yamaha Instruments, Growthink Research, the American Red Cross, and Valvoline, just to name a few.

Great Teaching

Offering personalized attention for students, Whittier boasts faculty whose commitment to education is paramount. Professors at Whittier are like explorers, leading students on expeditions to discover new worlds each and every day. The student to faculty ratio is twelve to one, while the average class size is nineteen. Perhaps it is because of these small classes, or Whittier's tradition of fostering personal growth in the classroom, or maybe it's a function of who they are, but professors at Whittier College are driven to facilitate the discussion and dissection of ideas. Beyond the classroom, professors are part of the environment in which students live. Some professors supervise living-learning communities—residence halls where students with similar academic interests live together on campus. Others may live at Faculty Masters' houses, where resident professors regularly host one-of-a-kind educational experiences that complement classroom learning. Recent examples of events at Faculty Masters' houses include a visit by Nobel Peace Prize winner Rigoberta Menchú Tum, a Young Hollywood lecture series, henna tattooing, a Valentine's Day card-making party, and more.

Collaborative teaching is common at Whittier. The Whittier experience is rooted in the liberal arts tradition, embracing interdisciplinary understanding at every level. By providing broad educational exposure, Whittier students gain the skills necessary to thrive in an increasingly interconnected world in which disciplines and ideas intersect.

The freshman writing courses offer dynamic classroom discussions on subjects across the academic spectrum. These courses provide fodder both for improving writing skills and creating engaging papers while exposing students to the individual attention and personalized instruction that form the core of the Whittier experience. In Whittier's paired courses, the curriculum links classes from different departments in order to more fully explore a range of thoughts and study, facilitating the application of ideas in new and interesting directions. For example, a biology course and sociology course merge to create a pair called Globalization and the Environment. Not all classes are paired, but those that are stem from a commitment to look beyond a narrow view—to instead see the wider picture.

Vibrant Community

Since its founding in 1887, Whittier College has been a place of academic integrity as well as educational innovation, a community where the exchange of ideas is rigorous and challenging, and where students are given an intellectual grounding that will serve them throughout their lives, as scholars, as professionals, and as responsible world citizens. While Whittier College no longer has a formal affiliation with the Quakers (Whittier became an independent college in the 1930s), many of the traditions and values are evident within the community. The long academic tradition—grounded in the Quaker quest for knowledge and personal growth—aims to foster in students an appreciation for the complexities of the modern world and workplace, while never losing sight of the importance of social responsibility.

With social clubs and service organizations spanning a wide spectrum of interests and pursuits, Whittier students don't just read about places and ideas, they engage at every level. Including athletes and academics, from the city and country, hailing from every part of the country, Whittier is a community of individuals. Numerous clubs and organizations offer an academic outlet, including Whittier's own brand of fraternities and sororities called societies, as well as intramural sports, Division III athletics, and more.

Near to the College, Uptown Whittier offers a historic district full of coffeehouses, boutique shops, restaurants, and movie theaters. For those students who want to escape suburban and city life, the hills behind the college are among the few remaining undeveloped strips of land in Southern California. A corresponding nature corridor runs from campus to the famous beaches that line the Pacific Ocean.

Successful Outcomes

Whittier College has a number of distinguished alumni, including Rhodes Scholars, Fulbright Award recipients, an Academy Award nominee, and even one U.S. president, President Richard M. Nixon (class of 1934).

Fast Facts

Whittier College is a four-year, residential, liberal arts college founded in 1887.

Web site

http://www.whittier.edu/

Location

Whittier, California—at the crossroads of Los Angeles and Orange Counties, 18 miles southeast of downtown Los Angeles.

Student Profile

1,300 students (45% male, 55% female); 34 states and territories, 21 countries; 40% American minority, 5% international.

Faculty Profile

87 full-time faculty. 12:1 student/ faculty ratio. Average class size is 19.

Residence Life

Moderately residential: 60% of students live on campus.

Athletics

NCAA Division III, Southern California Intercollegiate Athletic Conference. 21 varsity sports (11 men's: baseball, basketball, cross-country, football, golf, lacrosse, soccer, swimming, tennis, track & field, water polo; 10 women's: basketball, cross-country, lacrosse, soccer, softball, swimming, tennis, track & field, volleyball, water polo).

Academic Programs

Anthropology; applied philosophy; art; biochemistry; biology; business administration; chemistry; child development; comparative cultures; economics; English; environmental science; French; history; international studies; kinesiology & leisure science; Latin American studies; mathematics; mathematics/business administration; music; philosophy; physics; political science; psychology; religious studies; social work; sociology; Spanish; theater arts; Whittier Scholars Program; women's studies. Preprofessional Studies: Athletic training; dentistry; education; engineering; law; medicine; optometry; pharmacy; physical therapy; social work; veterinary science.

Costs and Aid

2006–2007: $36,416 comprehensive ($27,906 tuition). 80% of qualifying students receive some financial aid.

Endowment

$70 million.

More Distinctions

• Ranked by U.S. News & World Report as the second most diverse liberal arts campus in California with 28% of its student body being Hispanic.

• The Princeton Review ranks Whittier 8th for the quality of its library, 11th for students happy with financial aid and 18th for Intramural sports participation.

• Kaplan Publishing's "The Unofficial, Unbiased Guide to the 328 Most Interesting Colleges, 2004 Edition" recognized Whittier as a "hidden treasure" and dubbed the College "a small school that deserves wider recognition."

• Associate Professor of English Language and Literature David Paddy has been honored as California's Professor of the Year by the Council for the Advancement and Support of Education and the Carnegie Foundation for the Advancement of Teaching.

Fort Lewis College

COLORADO

Fort Lewis College (FLC) is Colorado's public liberal arts college. Named for a former U.S. Army post, Fort Lewis began as an Indian school in 1891. Through the years, the institution has evolved into a high school, a two-year college, and finally the four-year, liberal arts college it is today.

Admissions Contact:

Fort Lewis College
1000 Rim Drive
Durango, Colorado 81301-3999
Ph: (970) 247-7010
Email: admission@fortlewis.edu
www.fortlewis.edu

The 4 Distinctions

Engaged Students

FLC offers more than ninety-six academic options leading to a bachelor's degree. The most popular majors are psychology, business administration, interdisciplinary studies with an elementary education focus, general biology, accounting, and art. In recent years, many new majors, minors, and certificate programs have been developed, especially in career-related fields. Fort Lewis College is accredited by the Higher Learning Commission of the North Central Association of Colleges and Schools, with additional program-level accreditations in music; chemistry; exercise science; accounting, business administration, and economics; education; and engineering physics.

FLC emphasizes hands-on and service-based learning that takes advantage of the opportunities available in the Four Corners region. The FLC curriculum features many programs directly linked to its unique location, including adventure education, American Indian studies, anthropology, biology, environmental studies, geology, mountain studies, and Southwest studies. Service learning is another hallmark of the FLC experience. The Center for Civic Engagement works closely with academic departments to integrate service-learning experiences into the course work in every program.

Great Teaching

The mission of Fort Lewis College is to offer an accessible, high quality, baccalaureate liberal arts education to a diverse student population, preparing citizens for the common good in an increasingly complex world. Part of accomplishing this mission is holding true to the sacred trust, made nearly a century ago, to offer free tuition to any Native American student from a federally recognized tribe.

FLC students report a significantly higher level of interaction with their professors than many other four-year public colleges. While their focus is on teaching and working closely with their students, FLC faculty have also developed national reputations for excellence in teaching, research, and curriculum development.

In addition, faculty members focus their energy and creativity toward the more than twenty learning communities offered each fall for freshmen. Designed around a theme or major, the learning community programs provide opportunities for freshmen to connect with one another as well as with faculty members. In addition, there are five living-learning communities offered to freshmen. These include the Hungry Mind House (the honors hall visited often by a faculty advisor who creates workshops and leads discussions); the Life House (a community concerned with social issues); the Tech Academy (for those interested in computer science and the tech world); two outdoor experience halls (for students who wish to affiliate with the college's Outdoor Pursuits program); and the House of the Round Table (for students with an interest in medieval history).

Another example of FLC's enhanced educational experiences is the Common Reading Experience, through which students and faculty read discuss the same book and the vital, important issues it highlights. Since its creation, the Common Reading Experience has examined such books as Folding Paper Cranes: An Atomic Memoir and Mountains beyond Mountains: The Quest of Dr. Paul Farmer, A Man Who Would Cure the World.

Students can also take advantage of FLC's John F. Reed Honors Program, an academic enrichment program for high-ability and high-achieving students. Honors program students pursue a special curriculum; participate actively in the honors community; and complete their work with the research, writing, and presentation of an honors thesis.

Vibrant Community

Getting an education is a serious endeavor, but it should not be all work and no play. The same diverse environment that affords such outstanding educational experiences also allows students to take part in a great number of outdoor activities.

The Outdoor Pursuits program organizes outdoor adventures for all students of all ability levels, from nature lovers to extreme sports participants. Mountain-climbing students have hiked to the summits of some of the highest mountains in the world, including Mount Kilimanjaro and Mount Elbrus. White-water rafting, snowshoeing, and other more generally accessible sports are also offered. Unlimited access to equipment rental, including tents, skis, and bikes, is available for a nominal fee.

Athletics are also an exciting part of college life. FLC participates at the NCAA Division II level and is a member of the Rocky Mountain Athletic Conference. The college boasts the 2005 NCAA men's soccer national champions, the 2006 Rotary Bowl championship football team, and the 2006 mountain bike and cyclo-cross national championship team. Tom Danielson, a rider on the Discovery Channel Pro Cycling Team, is an FLC alumnus.

Sitting atop a mesa, FLC overlooks the town of Durango, Colorado. With a population of approximately fifteen thousand, Durango is the largest city in southwest Colorado, as well as the cultural hub of the area. Surrounded by the La Plata, San Juan, and Rocky mountains, Durango is less than a day's drive from such major cities as Denver, Albuquerque, Phoenix, and Salt Lake City.

Successful Outcomes

FLC students tend to go on to work rather than pursue graduate studies. For this reason, career advising, internships, and preparation for the job search are important components of the FLC educational experience. Many FLC students begin school without a declared major, so career advising begins in the freshman year. Internships are a required component of many majors. If a major does not require an internship, students may opt to complete an internship through the Cooperative Education Program. FLC students have privileged access to internships in the area, including opportunities at nearby national parks such as Chimney Rock, Crow Canyon, and Mesa Verde National Park. Preparation for the job search, including the annual etiquette dinner, is an emphasis in the senior year. Through an online service and on-campus events, the career services office connects FLC seniors with a variety of professional opportunities.

> "The mission of Fort Lewis College is to offer an accessible, high quality, baccalaureate liberal arts education to a diverse student population, preparing citizens for the common good in an increasingly complex world."
>
> - Colleges of Distinction

Fast Facts

Fort Lewis College is a public, four-year, liberal arts college founded in 1891.

Web site

http://www.fortlewis.edu/

Location

Durango, Colorado.

Student Profile

3,907 undergraduate students (52% male, 48% female); 46 states, 10 countries; 22% minority.

Faculty Profile

201 full-time faculty. 18:1 student/faculty ratio

Athletics

NCAA Division II, Rocky Mountain Athletic Conference. 10 varsity sports (5 men's: basketball, soccer, cross-country, football, golf; 5 women's: basketball, soccer, cross-country, volleyball, softball), 24 club teams, and 16 intramurals.

Academic Programs

Accounting; adventure education; agriculture; American Indian studies; anthropology; art; biology; business administration; chemistry; computer science; economics; engineering; English; environmental studies; exercise science; French; gender & women's studies; geographic information systems; geology; German; history; honors program; humanities; interdisciplinary studies; mathematics; mountain studies; music; philosophy; physics; political science; prehealth; prelaw; psychology; religious studies; sociology/human services; Southwest studies; Spanish; student-constructed major; teacher licensure programs; theatre.

Costs and Aid

$16,212 in-state comprehensive* ($2,650 tuition); $27,892 out-of-state comprehensive ($13,852 tuition). 70% of students receive some financial aid

* Includes fees, room and board, books and supplies, transportation, and miscellaneous personal expenses.

Endowment

$4 million.

More Distinctions

• In 2006 the Princeton Review ranked Fort Lewis College as one of the best universities in the western United States in the first edition of The Best Western Colleges: 121 Great Schools to Consider.

• *U.S. News & World Report's* 2004 issue of America's Best Colleges ranked Fort Lewis College second in the nation in campus diversity for public, bachelor degree-granting liberal arts and sciences colleges.

• Fort Lewis College was listed thirtieth in Outside magazine's "Forty Best College Towns," which appeared in their September 2003 issue.

University of Denver

COLORADO

University of Denver (DU), the oldest independent university in the Rocky Mountain region, enrolls approximately 10,850 students in its undergraduate and graduate programs. DU's location in Denver's university neighborhood offers students a young, vibrant environment; students also benefit from personal attention, small classes, and university-level resources.

Admissions Contact:

University of Denver
Office of Admission
2197 S. University Blvd
Denver, CO 80208
(800) 525-9495
Ph: (303) 871-2036
Email: admission@du.edu
www.du.edu

The 4 Distinctions

Engaged Students

DU strongly encourages all applicants to complete a Hyde Interview- an interview program where students have a conversation with one to three members of DU's community (including faculty, staff and alumni) in more than thirty cities each year. Though grades and test scores play the largest role in admission decisions, the interview helps DU admit students who are motivated, honest, and open to new ideas. The interviews also serve to show prospective students that personal attention is more than a catchphrase at DU—it is a practice.

DU has a strong commitment to internationalizing undergraduate education, sending students abroad to every continent except Antarctica. For qualified students, the Cherrington Global Scholars program offers undergraduates the chance to study abroad in their junior or senior year at no cost above normal DU tuition, room, and board; DU also pays for additional expenses such as transportation costs, visa application fees, mandatory insurance abroad, application fees, programs fees, and the International Student Identity Card. Through this program, students can take courses at one of eighty universities around the globe, and have their credits transferred back to DU. Over 70 percent of students study abroad, ranking DU second out of all doctoral/research institutions for undergraduate participation in study abroad.

Each year, about 1,500 DU students participate in service-learning courses. From courses on philosophy and social justice to intensive Spanish language and Mexican/Mayan cultural immersion, students can choose from a broad range of topics. Some service-learning courses are travel courses, while others serve the city of Denver.

Great Teaching

DU encourages active learning as opposed to the lecture-test format. Group dialogue is encouraged, and professors bring technology into the classroom. All students are required to have a laptop. DU students complete foundational courses, core curriculum requirements, and courses from their chosen major and minor, equipping them with sophisticated thinking skills and cross-disciplinary knowledge.

Undergraduate students benefit from experienced professors who also teach graduate students and do not solely rely on textbooks, but bring their own knowledge and experiences in the field into the classroom. Professors are genuinely involved in students' educations, and are accessible outside of the classroom, often to meet for breakfast or lunch. Some DU professors further extend their accessibility by printing their home phone number on class syllabi.

DU's Partners in Scholarship (PinS) program pairs students with professors on research projects, making the opportunity to perform collaborative research with a faculty partner available to students of all majors. PinS supports undergraduate research, creative projects, and funding for travel by distributing quarterly grants through an application process. Students can also present their work in a symposium held for students; some students are invited to participate in national symposia or to publish their work.

DU faculty have created a digital media studies program, combining communications, computer science, and art. A graduate of this program was hired to do graphics for *The Matrix Reloaded*. Another similar program, animation and game development, is offered through the division of engineering and computer science.

Vibrant Community

Located in a residential community eight miles from downtown, DU offers a 130-acre campus and a scenic view of the mountains. Students can make the fifteen-minute drive downtown, or hop on the light rail, which has a station on campus and is free for DU students and faculty.

Popular for its location and rigorous academics, DU also offers a people-friendly campus and an openly caring environment. Great weather and mild winters draw students to DU. About 55 percent of students come from out of state, providing a variety of perspectives on campus. DU places a strong emphasis on the diversity of its students and the various attributes they bring to campus. Students are required to live on campus during their first two years. Housing options include two residence halls for first-year students. In addition, students can join one of six living and learning communities, dedicated floors where students share common interests and take a number of courses together throughout the year.

Students can also attend or participate in Division I athletics, the school's national championship-caliber hockey program, the performing arts, or any of DU's one hundred clubs and organizations. There are also nine fraternities and six sororities on campus. Around 15 percent of DU students have joined these Greek organizations, and those who have are very involved. Greek life boosts the social scene on campus because events hosted by the Greek organizations are often open to all students. In addition to on-campus activities, some students take advantage of the great Rocky Mountains to bike, hike, ski, or snowboard.

This year, DU will host Project Homeless Connect, a program designed to support the city and county's ten-year plan to end homelessness in the Denver metro area. At Project Homeless Connect, homeless people can access medical care, employment and educational services, legal assistance, permanent housing, hygiene kits, and can apply for Social Security benefits and food stamps. More than sixty organizations from the Denver area provide these services.

Successful Outcomes

Around 70 percent of DU graduates participate in an internship in their years as a student. DU's location provides internship options in a number of disciplines, and the Denver metro area includes thirty-nine thousand DU alumni.

DU offers dual-degree programs in some disciplines, enabling students to earn both a bachelor's and a master's degree in only five years. These programs allow students to carry their undergraduate merit and financial aid awards through their fifth year.

Recent graduates of DU include Rhodes, Truman, Fulbright and Marshall Scholars, and members of the USA Today All-Academic Team. Many DU graduates go on to bright futures in very prolific graduate programs at universities such as Oxford, Stanford, Columbia Harvard, and many challenging and exciting DU graduate programs.

Notable alumni include Condoleezza Rice, U.S. secretary of state; Andy Taylor, CEO of Enterprise Rent-A-Car; Peter Morton, founder of the Hard Rock Cafe; Hao Jiang Tian, opera singer at the Met; Susan Waltz, chair of Amnesty International's international executive committee; Andy Rosenthal, assistant managing editor of the New York Times; James Cox Kennedy, CEO of Cox Communications; Emily Cinader Woods, cofounder of J. Crew; and Gale Norton, former U.S. secretary of the interior.

Fast Facts

University of Denver is a four-year independent, academically challenging university founded in 1864.

Web site

http://www.du.edu

Location

Denver, Colorado.

Student Profile

4,781 undergraduate students (48% male, 52% female); 50 states and territories represented; 14.3% minority, 4.8% international.

Faculty Profile

484 full time faculty. 10:1 student/faculty ratio. Average class size is 20.

Residence life

Moderately residential: 40% of students live on campus.

Athletics

NCAA Division I, Sun Belt Conference. 17 varsity sports (9 men's: basketball, diving, golf, ice hockey, lacrosse, skiing, soccer, swimming, tennis; 10 women's: basketball, diving, golf, gymnastics, lacrosse, skiing, soccer, swimming, tennis, volleyball), 23 club sports, and 18 intramurals.

Academic Programs

Accounting; animal technology; anthropology; applied computing; art history; Asian studies; astronomy; biological sciences; business administration; business economics; business ethics & legal studies; biochemistry; chemistry; cognitive science; communication; computer engineering; computer science; criminology; construction management; creative writing; cultural & critical studies; digital media studies; ecology & biodiversity; biology; economics; electronic media arts designs; electrical engineering; engineering; English; environmental science; finance; finance/marketing; finance/real estate; gender & women's studies; general business; general engineering; geography; history; hotel, restaurant & tourism management; individually structured major; information technology & electronic commerce; integrated science; international business; international studies; journalism studies; languages & literatures; literary studies; management; marketing; mathematics; mechanical engineering; molecular biology; music; philosophy; physics; political science; psychology; public affairs; real estate; religious studies; social science area; sociology; statistics; studio art; textual studies; theatre.

Costs and Aid

2007–2008: $40,929 comprehensive ($31,428 tuition). 77% of students receive some form of financial aid. Average award: $20,603.

More Distinctions

• US News and World Report ranks the University of Denver among the top 100 national universities.

• The 2005 Princeton Review named University of Denver as one of the Best 357 Colleges.

• Open Doors ranked DU 2nd nationally among doctoral and research institutions for percentage of students participating in study abroad programs during their undergraduate careers.

Chaminade University

HAWAII

Admissions Contact:

Chaminade University
3140 Waialae Avenue
Honolulu, HI 96816-1578
(800) 735-3733
Ph: (808) 739-8340
Email:
www.chaminade.edu

Chaminade University is a small, Catholic, comprehensive university located in suburban Honolulu. Offering programs grounded in the liberal arts, Chaminade educates students for life, service, and successful careers, and encourages the development of moral character, personal competencies, and a commitment to building a just and peaceful society.

The 4 Distinctions

Engaged Students

Incoming students are welcomed into the Chaminade community by joining a freshman cohort group. Created by major of interest and level of preparation, the groups give new students a place to learn and grow with a group of peers—soon to be friends—who together take a similar package of introductory courses. There's also a group for students who are still exploring their future paths of study.

Service learning is thoroughly integrated into the Chaminade curriculum in ways that fit students, faculty, and their communities. Many disciplines require course work where students volunteer time and talent in service activities outside the classroom. Through these courses, students can both apply what they've learned in the classroom and gain experience in the real world, where they learn by doing.

Most majors require an internship (paid or otherwise). Internships take place during the semester or the summer and are arranged by the university in a place that's convenient to the student. Recently, fifteen Chaminade premed students interned at prestigious medical schools— programs that culminated in end-of-internship presentations about what students had learned.

Chaminade doesn't offer study abroad directly, but students are able to take advantage of programs through the school's two sister universities, the University of Dayton in Dayton, Ohio, and St. Mary's University in San Antonio, Texas. Chaminade students may also spend a semester at Bay Path College in Longmeadow, Massachusetts. Chaminade has also partnered with the University of Hawaii to provide study-abroad opportunities in England, France, Italy, Spain, Tahiti, and a number of other countries.

With the advantages of an eleven to one student to faculty ratio, Chaminade students and faculty practice the spirit of ohana—a Hawaiian tradition meaning "family" in the extended sense of the term—supporting one another to ensure future success.

In practice, ohana means that students regularly meet their professors outside the classroom, even for lunch. And one of the university's traditions is that faculty and staff invite students to their homes during holidays when students are unable to schedule trips back to their own homes.

In keeping with the Chaminade mission, faculty regularly lead community-service trips, taking students to local areas of Hawaii, as well as to places as far away as India.

Chaminade's Hogan Entrepreneurial Program is a center of activity for students interested in careers in business, government, and nonprofit organizations. One facet of the program is that students can find a mentor among local businesspeople. The program also creates opportunities for study for a semester in places like China or Singapore.

For those students who want to be a real CSI—crime scene investigator—Chaminade offers a highly regarded forensic sciences program that teaches students what it's really like to investigate a crime scene. Lee Goff, chair of Chaminade's forensic sciences program, consults with the CBS's crime drama CSI and its spin-off series. A founder of the American Board of Forensic Entomology, Goff also served as an FBI academy instructor. The author of A Fly for the Prosecution: How Insect Evidence Helps Solve Crimes, Goff participated in the recovery efforts at the site of the World Trade Center following the September 11, 2001, attacks. He also curates a traveling exhibit entitled Crime Scene Insects.

Great Teaching

For Chaminade's 1,200 full-time students, personal interaction with their professors is a major plus in their educational experience. Beyond a couple of introductory courses, no classes have more than twenty-two students.

Vibrant Community

With a campus located on a hillside two miles from Waikiki beach, Chaminade students stay busy even when they aren't consumed in their studies. In addition to traditional activities like student government, student newspaper, and drama, students are involved in an extensive tutoring program with the local community.

Chaminade's intercollegiate athletics department fields ten teams, all with a mission of providing qualified students the opportunity to participate in competitive sports while developing leadership and team skills. Chaminade's basketball team earned worldwide acclaim in 1982 with its seventy-seven to seventy-two victory over number-one ranked University of Virginia, still considered one of the biggest upsets in sports history.

From sailing and camping to paintball and surfing, students can choose from among dozens of campus clubs. Hui Wa'a 'O Kaminaka, the university's canoe club, promotes awareness of Pacific Island cultural activities through outrigger canoeing and Hawaiian cultural practices.

Student volunteer programs include feeding the hungry and homeless on the holidays and cleaning up local rivers and streams.

Successful Outcomes

Many Chaminade graduates have enjoyed successful careers as business leaders, environmental lawyers, translators, ministers, and teachers. A high proportion of students continue their education at Chaminade in a master's degree program or continue their studies at medical or law schools.

Many Chaminade students who intern for local companies return to these organizations after graduation to start their careers. That's especially true for alumni in business, communication, criminology, education, forensic sciences, and interior design.

Chaminade graduated its first four-year class in 1959, when Hawaii became the fiftieth state. Today, with twenty-two major degree programs of study, six master's degree programs, and a variety of professional certificate programs, Chaminade has claimed a unique role as the leader in Catholic liberal arts education in the Pacific Island region.

Fast Facts

Chaminade University is a coed, liberal arts university affiliated with the Marianists, a Roman Catholic religious order, and founded in 1955.

Web site

http://www.chaminade.edu/

Location

Honolulu, Hawaii.

Student Profile

1,112 undergraduate students (31% male, 69% female); 51% of Chaminade students come from outside Hawaii. 45% are Catholic. 3.1% Black Non-Hispanic, 6.9% Hispanic, 63.0% Asian/Pacific Islander, 0.8% Native American Indian, 24.2% White Non-Hispanic, 1.9% non-resident alien.

Faculty Profile

16:1 student/faculty ratio. Average class size is 20.

Athletics

NCAA Division II, Pacific West Conference. 10 varsity sports (4 men's: basketball, cross-country, golf, soccer; women's: basketball, cross-country, soccer, softball, tennis, volleyball).

Academic Programs

Accounting; behavioral sciences; biology/biological sciences; business administration; communication/media; computer & information sciences; computer science; criminology; elementary education; English; environmental studies; forensic sciences; history; humanities; interior design; international studies; marketing; psychology; religious studies.

Costs and Aid

2006–2007: $21,820 comprehensive ($14,820 tuition). 90% of students receive some financial aid. Average freshman institutional gift aid: $5,634.

Endowment

$6.5 million.

More Distinctions

• U.S. News & World Report ranked Chaminade among the top three colleges in the category of diversity.

• Lee Goff, chair of Chaminade's forensic science program, is a consultant for CBS's hit crime drama CSI and its spin-off series. A founder of the American Board of Forensic Entomology, Goff also served as an FBI academy instructor. Goff is also the author of A Fly for the Prosecution: How Insect Evidence Helps Solve Crimes, and he participated in the recovery efforts at the site of the World Trade Center.

• Chaminade operates the Wiegand Observatory, which opened in 2003.

Pacific University

OREGON

Admissions Contact:

Pacific University
2043 College Way
Forest Grove, Oregon 97116
(877) PAC-UNIV
Ph: (503) 352-6151
Email: admissions@pacificu.edu
www.pacificu.edu

With its beginnings as a school serving Native American children and orphans from the Oregon Trail, Pacific University was founded in 1849 and is a small, coeducational, private, liberal arts institution located in Forest Grove, Oregon. Pacific University generates lifelong learners who make valuable contributions to society.

The 4 Distinctions

Engaged Students

Pacific students are intellectual and engaged, both on campus and off. Students motivate and support one another to do well in all aspects of their academic careers, from volunteering to internships to traveling abroad. Internship opportunities at Pacific lead students in many exciting directions. In environmental studies, students use internships to focus on a specific area of interest. Students have recently worked for B-Street Permaculture Farm, which is less than a mile from campus, to look at ways to improve soil nutrients. In computer science, students have used the senior capstone project to develop an adaptive firewall for Internet defense and a 3-D terrain generator that can be used in video-game development. Pacific also supports a burgeoning summer research program for students that provides three thousand dollar stipends and free on-campus housing.

Study-abroad opportunities are possible during January term or for an entire semester. Destinations for these cross-cultural experiences include Russia, India, Zambia, Kenya, Ghana, Costa Rica, Ecuador, Mexico, Belize, Guatemala, Spain, Italy, France, Germany, Austria, England, Wales, Ireland, China, and Japan. One class allowed students to spend a summer on-site at the Chimfunshi Wildlife Orphanage in Zambia to study chimpanzees in conditions that closely resemble the wild. During this course, interaction with the indigenous population sensitized students to cultural topics and issues in Zambia, such as poverty, health, food availability, and deforestation.

The exercise science program draws students to Pacific because of its focus on science, personal instruction, and state-of-the art facilities and equipment. Many students use exercise science, biology, chemistry, psychology, and other disciplines as stepping-stones to health professions careers. Many Pacific undergraduates go on to Pacific's graduate programs in education, physical therapy, occupational therapy, pharmacy, optometry, physician assistant studies, dental health science, and professional psychology.

Pacific also provides excellent work-study options, with approximately 80 percent of students taking advantage of this opportunity. Nearly every office on campus employs students, and many other students earn their work-study hours at local community-service organizations and government agencies or through tutoring in foreign languages, English, math, science, and other disciplines.

Great Teaching

In the summer before freshman year, each student is assigned to an adviser. This allows the student to become familiar with Pacific and enables the formation of a student-professor relationship before the beginning of the school year. Faculty members commonly say that Pacific is where they want to teach because of the emphasis on classroom instruction and because Pacific students love learning. The student to faculty ratio is thirteen to one, resulting in an average class size of twenty. The top majors at Pacific are exercise science, business, psychology, media arts, education, natural sciences, and music.

Professors at Pacific value learning and often venture to other countries and cultures with their students to apply their studies to real communities. Recent sites include Kenya, Ghana, rural Mexico, the Navajo Nation, and the Gulf Coast after Hurricane Katrina. Recently, in the Ecuadorian Amazon, a faculty member took students to work side by side with a family as they planted and harvested crops and erected a building for their community center.

One-on-one attention from faculty gives Pacific undergraduates an edge with collaborative research takes place at the undergraduate level. After developing a research topic, conducting research and interpreting the findings, students share their newfound knowledge with other faculty and their peers. The Senior Capstone research projects culminate on Senior Project Day, an opportunity for researchers to present what they have found. Students are able to use their research as a springboard for graduate research pursuits and employment.

Vibrant Community

For students who enjoy the outdoors, Pacific's outback program takes them away for weekends of kayaking and rock climbing or on extended trips during breaks. On campus, activities such as the annual Hawaiian luau, a lip-sync contest, and Greek Spring Fever Week keep students entertained. There are more than sixty clubs and organizations on campus, from academic interest groups to political clubs to a horseback riding club. Pacific students can live in traditional residence halls or in apartment-style buildings for small groups.

During the year it is common to see boxes all over campus for food and clothing drives, and many campus groups adopt area families in need. Throughout the year, Pacific students can be found tutoring local children, serving as translators, and promoting environmental awareness. Many courses, such as peace and conflict studies classes, integrate this service to the community into their lessons. A number of professional programs at Pacific require students to complete service hours, so service to the community is seen as an educational tradition.

Residential life is lively and exciting at Pacific. Students are required to live on-campus for the first two years and residential options include traditional halls as well as Vandervelden Court, a university-maintained apartment complex. The student-run Residence Housing Association provides programming for campus living.

Successful Outcomes

Undergraduates at Pacific are drawn to the graduate possibilities right on campus. Pacific features the only doctorate in physical therapy in the state of Oregon and also has the only School of Optometry in the Pacific Northwest—one of only seventeen optometry schools in the United States. For those students who don't pursue graduate school immediately, major companies such as Intel and Nike provide internship opportunities for students and often hire them after graduation. Pacific's career center also hosts a number of fairs and speakers throughout the year to put students in touch with companies and professionals in the area.

Pacific holds the record for producing more Fulbright scholars than other institutions of the same size.

Noteworthy alumni include: Shirley Abbot, Ambassador to Lesotho, Africa, Member of the Texas House of Representatives, and winner of the "Cross of Isabella La Catolica" award given by King Juan Carlos of Spain; Steve Boone, Founder of Liquor Barn Division of Safeway Stores, founder of Beverages and More!, and former President of Cost Plus World Market; AC Gilbert, Gold Medallist in pole vault in the 1908 Olympics and inventor of the Erector Set; Lois Larson Allen, the first woman Mayor of Rosenburg, OR; and Michael McCartney, the president and CEO of Hawaii Public Television and a Senator in the Hawaiian State Legislature for 10 years.

Fast Facts

Pacific University is a comprehensive, four-year coeducational institution. It provides degrees in undergraduate and graduate studies.

Web site

http://www.pacificu.edu

Location

Forest Grove, Oregon—25 miles west of Portland and 50 miles east of the Pacific Ocean.

Student Profile

2400 students; 1200 undergraduate and 1200 graduate students. Representing the United States and 28 foreign countries.

Faculty Profile

186 faculty. 96% hold a terminal degree in their field.

Athletics

NCAA Division III, Northwest Conference; 21 varsity sports (9 men's: baseball, basketball, cross-country, golf, soccer, swimming, tennis, track & field, wrestling; 11 women's: basketball, cross-country, golf, lacrosse, soccer, softball, swimming, tennis, volleyball, track & field, wrestling).

Academic Programs

Accounting; biology/biological sciences; bioinformatics; business administration & management; finance; marketing/marketing management; journalism; mass communication/media studies; integrated media; film/video; telecommunications; computer science; art teacher education; education; elementary education; kindergarten/preschool education; music teacher education; secondary education; creative writing; English; literature; Spanish; Chinese; French; German; Japanese; modern languages; international studies; prehealth science; predentistry studies; premedical studies; preveterinary studies; prephysical therapy; preoptometry; history; humanities; liberal arts & sciences/liberal studies; mathematics; environmental studies; kinesiology & exercise science; philosophy; chemistry; biochemistry; physics; applied science; psychology; social work; economics; international relations & affairs; political science & government; prelaw; sociology; anthropology; art; dramatic/theater arts; dance; music; music performance.

Costs and Aid

2007–2008: $26,470 full-time tuition, $580 estimated fees, $700 estimated for books and supplies, and $7,170 approximate room and board includes a University meal plan. 81% of students receive financial aid.

Endowment

$41.9 million.

More Distinctions

• Named a "Best Value" by *U.S.News and World Report*.

• Listed as a "Best Buy" by *Barron's Guide*.

• Named one of "America's 100 Most Wired Colleges" by *Yahoo! Internet Life Magazine*.

University of Portland

OREGON

The University of Portland is renowned for its nationally respected academic programs, dedication to service, award-winning professors committed to teaching, and students who seek to make a difference in the world. Located on a bluff high above the Willamette River, the university is just six miles from vibrant downtown Portland.

Admissions Contact:

University of Portland
5000 N. Willamette Blvd.
Portland, OR 97203-5798
(888) 627-5601
Ph: (503) 943-7147
Email: visit@up.edu
www.up.edu

The 4 Distinctions

Engaged Students

As Oregon's Catholic university, the University of Portland is a place where students of every faith are welcomed, where questions are respected, and where opportunities for spiritual exploration and reflection abound. The University of Portland is home to four professional schools with nationally accredited programs in business, engineering, education, and nursing, and a College of Arts and Science. The university also is well-known for its cutting-edge programs in the sciences, entrepreneurship, theater, music, and more. The University's Core Curriculum forms the heart of an education at the University of Portland. The Core is a selection of thirteen courses from a wide range of disciplines—including philosophy, English, history, and fine arts—that all students take, regardless of major.

All freshmen also take a freshmen seminar, a series of classes led by upper-level students, which help them adjust to college life and the demands of college course work. The seminar is offered through the Shepard Freshman Resource Center, which offers a full slate of programming to help students successfully transition to college.

Since its founding in 1901, the University of Portland has embraced the belief that the mind is little without the heart. Members of the University community believe that what happens outside the classroom is just as important as what is learned during lectures and labs. Through the Moreau Center for Service and Leadership, University students, faculty, and staff together give more than fifty thousand service hours annually. Volunteers feed the homeless and build homes with Habitat for Humanity; they tutor at schools and jails; they volunteer at hospices and participate in environmental cleanup.

The University's Center for Entrepreneurship is an interdisciplinary center that helps students from all majors plan and execute a business venture. The Center sponsors an Entrepreneur Scholars (E-Scholars) program that provides students with local mentors and international travel to explore best business practices throughout the world.

The University's twelve study abroad programs take students to Austria, Australia, England, France, Spain, Mexico, Italy, and Japan. Programs range from five-week summer sessions to full-year opportunities. Programs include language-intensive courses, cultural programs, and special programs just for business or biology majors.

Students leave the university with real-world experience. Social science majors in psychology, sociology, social work, and criminal justice complete a practicum with a local social-service agency; education majors spend more than one thousand hours in classroom settings; nursing majors complete clinical work in small clinics and large hospitals; and many other students seek internships in the metro area with the assistance of well-connected professors and the Office of Career Services.

Great Teaching

There's one faculty member for every twelve students, but what sets the University of Portland apart is the faculty's accessibility. Professors are always willing to meet students one-on-one outside class hours, and can often be found working side by side with students at service events and participating in other university activities.

Portland faculty are accomplished researchers, but their first love is teaching, and they are widely recognized for their outstanding work in the classroom. In recent years, three university professors have been named Oregon's Professor of Year by the national Carnegie Foundation and the Council for Advancement and Support of Education (CASE), including biologists Terry Favero and Becky Houck and education professor Karen Eifler. Spanish professor Kate Regan was recently named a national professor of the year by the Carnegie foundation and CASE.

Vibrant Community

The University of Portland is located in a beautiful residential neighborhood high on a bluff overlooking the Willamette River. About 90 percent of freshmen live on campus in one of eight residence halls just steps way from their classes, the library, computer labs, the dining hall, and recreational facilities.

A steady assortment of interesting guest speakers, fiction and poetry readings, dialogues on faith and justice, theatrical offerings, and other activities fill the campus calendar. Throughout the school year, students actively cheer on their competitive Division I athletic teams.

The university's student activities office oversees the activities of nearly sixty student-led clubs. These range from academic (Student Nurses Association) and athletic (crew, in-line hockey) to multicultural (the Hawaii club) and sociological (the Feminist Discussion Group). Students also participate in the Campus Program Board, which is responsible for bringing entertainment events to campus; student media outlets such as The Beacon student newspaper, The Log yearbook, and KDUP radio station; and the student senate.

Students are rewarded for studying hard with a number of opportunities for recreation. Portland's intramural program offers sports ranging from basketball to ultimate Frisbee, and the Outdoor Pursuits Program takes students cross-country skiing, hiking, and mountain biking. Portland also offers students a number of daily aerobic, step, and yoga classes.

The Office of Campus Ministry offers many programs to help students develop their faith. As a Catholic university, Mass is offered daily in the Chapel of Christ the Teacher and one night a week in each residence hall. About half of Portland's students come from other religious backgrounds, and the campus ministry team helps students find nearby places of worship and faith groups that share their beliefs. The office's services and programs are open to all students, including retreats such as the popular Freshman Escape, which takes students away from campus for a weekend to reflect on their first weeks of college.

Successful Outcomes

Within six months of graduation, 94 percent of graduates hold full-time jobs, are enrolled in graduate school, participating in a service program, or serving in the military.

The Office of Career Services helps students turn their educations into bright futures. From freshman year to graduation and beyond, career services staff provide career counseling, help with resumes, and listings of available job openings for internships or permanent employment. The office also offers workshops and training sessions, including mock interviews, to prepare students for the job market.

The Career Advisory Network, sponsored by the alumni office, matches current students and alumni with alumni working in their intended fields for informational interviews and career advice. The alumni office also sponsors information nights during which students can learn more about various career paths from professional alumni.

The University of Portland is one of the top producers of student Fulbright Award winners among universities of its kind. In recent years, eighteen students have received the award. Recent graduates have also served in the Peace Corps, the Jesuit Volunteer Corps, Holy Cross Associates, and AmeriCorps.

University of Portland graduates continue their tradition of community service long after their college days. Each year, the University organizes a national day of service that brings alumni to work at locations around the country.

Fast Facts

University of Portland is a four-year, liberal arts university affiliated with the Congregation of Holy Cross and founded in 1901.

Web site

http://www.up.edu

Location

Portland, Oregon.

Student Profile

2,849 undergraduate students (37% male, 63% female); 40 states and territories; 15% minority, 1% international.

Faculty Profile

197 full-time faculty, 119 part-time faculty. 12:1 student/faculty ratio. Average class size 25.

Residence Life

Highly residential: 90% of freshmen and half of all students live on campus.

Athletics

NCAA Division I, West Coast Conference. 16 varsity sports (8 men's: baseball, basketball, cross-country, golf, soccer, tennis, indoor & outdoor track; 8 women's: basketball, cross-country, golf, soccer, tennis, indoor & outdoor track, volleyball); misc. club sports, and intramurals.

Academic Programs

College of Arts and Sciences majors include: Biochemistry; biology; chemistry; communication; drama; English; environmental ethics & policy; environmental science; French studies; general studies; German studies; history; life science; mathematics; music; organizational communication; philosophy; physics; political science; sociology/ criminal justice; track; Spanish; theology. Preprofessional Programs: Predentistry study; prelaw study; premedicine study; preoccupational therapy study; prepharmacy study; prephysical therapy study; preveterinary study. School of Business majors include: Accounting; finance; global business; marketing & management. School of Education majors include: Elementary education; music education; secondary education. School of Engineering majors include: Civil & environmental engineering; computer science; electrical & computer engineering; engineering management; mechanical engineering. School of Nursing: Nursing.

Costs and Aid

2007–2008: $35,800 comprehensive ($27,500 tuition). Nearly 94% of students receive some financial aid. Average freshman award: $20,356 in 2005–2006.

Endowment

$90 million.

More Distinctions

• 2002 & 2005 NCAA Division I Women's Soccer National Championships.

• In 2006-2007, ranked second nationally for numbers of Fulbright Scholars among Masters Level institutions; Four recipients of the Carnegie Foundation's Oregon Professor of the Year award since 1997, including National Professor of the Year.

• In 2005, Washington Monthly ranked the University of Portland first among all the nation's colleges and universities for national service.

• Four recipients of the Carnegie Foundation's Oregon Professor of the Year award since 1997, including National Professor of the Year.

Willamette University

OREGON

Willamette University, founded in 1842, is the oldest university west of the Missouri River. Located in Salem, Oregon's capital city, Willamette has been instrumental in pioneering education in the West.

Admissions Contact:

Willamette University
900 State Street
Salem, Oregon 97301
(877) LIBARTS
Ph: (503) 370-6303
Fax: (503) 375-5363
Email: libarts@willamette.edu
www.willamette.edu/admission

The 4 Distinctions

Engaged Students

Willamette students are active; along with local internships and service opportunities, the university maintains a vibrant study-abroad program. On average, 50 percent of students participate in Willamette-sponsored international study programs in forty-one different countries.

Willamette's sister-school arrangement with Tokyo International University of America (TIUA) enables students to pursue related academic goals and further develop intercultural awareness without leaving campus. Cocurricular programs are designed to offer students opportunities to learn through experience about other people and cultures, as well as to reflect upon and share their own cultures. About one hundred Japanese students live on-site in Willamette's residence halls, often with American roommates. Willamette students may also participate in exchange programs to Japan.

Willamette students are involved locally and embody Willamette's motto: "Not unto ourselves alone are we born." Each year, students volunteer more than twenty-three thousand hours through a variety of projects, working with organizations such as Habitat for Humanity and other national and local groups. Additionally, Willamette's unique Take a Break (TaB) alternative spring break program allows students, staff, and faculty to work side by side in the field, learning about contemporary social and environmental issues. TaB is a positive way for students to take leadership positions and facilitate shared learning with different groups, to organize service activities for multiple organizations, and to help develop community-wide discussions of pressing issues.

Academically, Willamette students occupy a wide spectrum of interests. Politics and the social sciences are popular due to the high availability of internships and other interactive programs within these majors, though there are no clearly dominant academic tracks. Interns from any of Willamette's academic departments are regularly placed with agencies of the Oregon state government and the Salem city government; with the Oregon state legislature; and in such facilities as the neighboring Hallie Ford Museum of Art, the Oregon School for the Blind, and Salem public schools. The lab science departments are routinely among the most popular on campus; biology typically resides alongside politics at the top of the major list.

Great Teaching

Freshmen students at Willamette are offered careful guidance while they decide on their ultimate paths of study. The freshman seminar, called college colloquium, is a hybrid academic/advising program designed to enhance traditionally close relationships between students and faculty. The advising function is an important responsibility of every full-time faculty member; students' colloquium professors also serve as their initial academic advisers. Since first-year students are all classified as undecided or undeclared, this initial advising is designed to support progress towards meeting the university's general education requirements and to introduce students to the broadest possible spectrum of choices within the liberal arts curriculum. Once students declare a major, as they must do by the beginning of the junior year, they are expected to select a faculty adviser from the appropriate department.

After fulfilling the requirements for their major course of study, all students are required to complete a senior capstone (thesis) project. Research for such projects is supported on campus through funding and special programs, including the Science Collaborative Research Project (SCRP) program. This program serves up to twenty students and ten instructors each summer, and provides science majors the opportunity to work shoulder to shoulder with a faculty member. The program covers students' housing, travel, and equipment costs, and includes an additional stipend of $3,450. Additionally, Willamette maintains other research programs, such as the Carson Undergraduate Research Grant, which allows nonscience majors to engage in a creative, scholarly, or professional research project during the summer. About ten grants of up to three thousand dollars each are available every year.

Willamette is in the process of hiring an additional twenty-five faculty members by 2010, which will lower the teaching load, allowing more time for research and academic advising. This has already affected the student to faculty ratio; it is currently at ten to one, down from the previous eleven to one, and is predicted to hit nine to one.

Vibrant Community

Willamette's campus is across the street from the Oregon State Capitol, affording students convenient access to internships in the institutions of Oregon government. Salem is a medium-sized city of about one hundred and fifty thousand residents, with restaurants, parks, movie theaters, malls, and shops interspersed among different urban districts. Mountains, the Pacific Ocean, and the city of Portland are all within a short drive from Willamette.

Willamette is a very residential campus. Undergraduate students must live on campus for two years in any of several different arrangements, after which they may move into a private residence or one of the university's apartment complexes. The trend in Willamette's on-campus housing is toward the residential commons model, as opposed to traditional dorms. The residential commons encourages substantially increased student governance, faculty involvement, and themed programming.

Students enjoy the dining-hall food, which was given rave reviews by celebrity chef Rachael Ray. Fittingly, many non-Willamette residents of Salem also come to eat in the campus dining halls, including state officials from the capitol. Faculty members can often be found engaging with students over meals in the cafeterias.

Willamette has three sororities and four fraternities; approximately 27 percent of the student body are involved in Greek life. Greek life is a healthy part of campus life that offers unique leadership opportunities as well as activities that engage students in the community. Additionally, Willamette has more than one hundred student clubs and organizations, and faculty members are encouraged to become involved in this aspect of campus life, as well. Intramural sports garner much attention from students, and these programs are good places for students to look for work as intramural referees, scorekeepers, and timekeepers.

Successful Outcomes

Willamette's emphasis on its motto brings about service as a matter of course. The university has launched the careers of many politicians and elected officials and is ranked in the top ten nationally among small schools for graduates entering the Peace Corps.

The office of career services focuses on many aspects of students' lives after Willamette and helps cement the skills students will need outside the campus limits. The office even offers practical lessons in meal etiquette, assistance with resume writing, and GRE registration, as well as other services. Funding from the Lilly Project, coordinated through the chaplain's office, helps students conduct a wide range of research programs, all centered on the idea of exploring vocation.

Willamette has an extremely strong alumni network, and between 60 and 70 percent of Willamette graduates pursue further education in any of a myriad of fields. Notable alumni include Daryl Chapin, coinventor of the first solar battery; Mark O. Hatfield, former Oregon governor and U.S. senator; Lesil McGuire, member of the Alaska State House of Representatives; and Bob Packwood, former U.S. senator from Oregon.

Fast Facts

Willamette University is a four-year, coeducational university with a strong commitment to the liberal arts.

Web site

http://www.willamette.edu/

Location

Salem, Oregon —the state capital; Portland and Seattle lie to the north; Portland is one hour away and Seattle is four hours away.

Student Profile

1,856 undergraduates (45% male, 55% female); 34 states and territories, 33 countries; 17% minority, 2% international.

Faculty Profile

274 faculty members, 95% hold a Ph.D. 10:1 student/faculty ratio. 68% of classes have fewer than 20 students.

Residence Life

First-year students and sophomores are required to live on campus.

Athletics

NCAA, Division III Northwest Conference (NWC). 20 varsity sports (10 men's: baseball, basketball, cross-country, football, golf, rowing, soccer, swimming, tennis, track & field; 10 women's: basketball, cross-country, golf, rowing, soccer, softball, swimming, tennis, track & field, volleyball.)

Academic Programs

Degrees offered: Bachelor of Arts (B.A.) and Bachelor of Music (B.M.).

American studies; anthropology; art history; art, studio; Asian studies; BA/MBA business management; biology; chemistry; Chinese studies; classical studies; comparative literature & history of ideas; computer science; economics; 3-2 engineering; English; environmental science; exercise science; 3-2 forestry (special program); French; German; history; humanities; international studies; Japanese studies; Latin American studies; mathematics; music; philosophy; physics; politics; prelaw (special program); premedicine (special program); preveterinary medicine (special program); 3-2 public management; psychology; religious studies; rhetoric & media studies; science studies; sociology; Spanish; theatre; women's & gender studies.

Costs and Aid

2007–2008: $41,335 comprehensive ($31,865 tuition). 92% of students receive some financial aid. Average award: $19,784.

Endowment

$248 million.

More Distinctions

• The Washington Post recently recognized Willamette University as "one of the 100 colleges that deserve a bigger reputation" in an article by Washington Post Staff Writer, Jay Mathews. (Washington Post, April 1)

• Of the last 16 Oregon Professors of the Year, as decidedby the Carnegie Foundation for the Advancement of teaching and the Council for Advancement and Support of Education, eight have been Willamette University professors.

Southern Utah University

UTAH

Southern Utah University (SUU) is a public, comprehensive, coeducational, liberal arts and sciences university. SUU's core values are academic excellence, community and social responsibility, and involvement and personal growth. SUU's mission is to provide "an excellent education through a diverse, dynamic and personalized learning environment."

Admissions Contact:

Southern Utah University
351 West University Boulevard
Cedar City, UT 84720
Ph: (435) 586-7700
Fax: (435) 865-8223
Email: adminfo@suu.edu
www.suu.edu

The 4 Distinctions

Engaged Students

SUU has survived against many odds due to the firm commitment of Cedar City's residents. Founded in 1897 as a teacher training school, it grew into the College of Southern Utah in 1953, Southern Utah State College in 1969, and became Southern Utah University in 1991. SUU is committed to preparing "students to be critical thinkers, effective communicators, lifelong learners and individuals who demonstrate integrity and empathy as they pursue their lives' ambitions."

SUU encourages its students to engage in service learning. The university's Service & Learning Center acts as a clearinghouse for student volunteer opportunities. The community agencies and programs included serve the arts and entertainment, children, youth and schools, the environment, literacy, medical and health, and senior citizens. Students can choose from among opportunities to volunteer at cultural and fund-raising events; to teach English as a second language; to work with the terminally ill; to help rescue wildlife; to participate in environmental cleanup work; or to take part in a myriad of social-service programs involving children, teens, and older people. Alternative spring-break programs take students to do service work in Mexico, as well as in locations in the United States.

Great Teaching

The student to faculty ratio of nineteen to one is comparatively low for a university with seven thousand students, and it ensures that students receive personalized attention from their professors in the classroom, regardless of their chosen fields of study.

SUU offers associate's, bachelor's, and master's degrees through six academic colleges: Business; Education; Humanities and Social Sciences; Performing and Visual Arts; Computing, Integrated Engineering and Technology; and Science. The university's education programs are noteworthy, especially in biology, chemistry, and zoology, as is SUU's Rural Health Scholars program. Arts and communications are strong, and the school's theatre program is well respected. Other exciting programs particular to SUU are the outdoor recreation in parks and tourism degree, and the marketable integrated engineering degree.

SUU's general education program requires traditional liberal arts course work, including classes in the humanities, philosophy, social science, arts/fine arts, English, history, mathematics, sciences, and computer literacy. All students take a university seminar in their first year. If they have declared a major, there is a companion general education class dedicated to the major. If they are undecided, there is a wide choice of options. Capstone projects are determined by major.

SUU plans to open a teacher education building in the fall of 2007 and is also planning to build a Center for Hispanic Excellence in Academics.

Vibrant Community

Four-fifths of SUU's students are from Utah; the rest are mostly from Nevada, Arizona and California. Native Americans form a significant group within the student community. A bit more than half of the students are women.

SUU students are active both on and off campus. There are nearly one hundred clubs and organizations they can join. All are student run with faculty advisors. SUU students are active outdoors, taking advantage of the natural resources of the area. The campus also features an outdoor center where students can rent equipment, participate in organized activities, and learn to play a variety of outdoor sports.

Residence hall options range from a traditional dormitory to the Eccles Living Learning Center, which features state-of-the-art apartment-style housing. The campus also includes an honor dormitory. All residence halls have Internet access as well as a variety of spaces for recreational and community activities.

Cedar City is located in southwestern Utah, about two and half hours by car northeast of Las Vegas and three and a half hours south of Salt Lake City. Known as Festival City

USA for its Shakespearean and Neil Simon festivals, Cedar City is located in the midst of several scenic national parks, including Bryce Canyon, Cedar Breaks, Zion, and Kolob Canyons. Brian Head Resort, a recreation area known for its summer mountain biking trails, skiing, and other winter sports, is located nearby.

A city of about thirty thousand, Cedar City is best known for the Utah Shakespearean Festival and Utah Summer Games that take place every summer. Two hundred thousand to three hundred thousand people visit Cedar City each year, drawn to its cultural activities, the nearby ski and mountain biking resort at Brian Head, as well as to the national and state parks in the surrounding area.

Successful Outcomes

SUU graduates enjoy a 94 percent job placement rate, and 87 percent of graduates are working the field of their choice. A high percentage of SUU graduates successfully apply to medical school. SUU career services offers job search workshops to assist students with resume writing and interview skills. The university also includes an alumni mentoring network designed to help SUU students make connections and learn more about the world beyond their campus.

Fast Facts

Southern Utah University is a state-supported, coeducational institution.

Web site

http://www.suu.edu

Location

Cedar City, UT located 2 1/2 hours north of Las Vegas and 3 1/2 hours south of Salt Lake City.

Student Profile

6,465 undergraduate students (43% male, 57% female); 8% transfer students; 14 countries; 0.8% African American, 2% Asian American or Pacific Islander, 2% Hispanic American, 2% Native American, 1% international.

Faculty Profile

274 faculty. 19:1 student/faculty ratio.

Athletics

NCAA Division I except football (Division I-AA). 14 varsity sports (7 men's: baseball, basketball, cross-country, football, golf, soccer, track & field; 7 women's: basketball, cross-country, gymnastics, soccer, softball, tennis, track & field)

Academic Programs

Accounting; agriculture; art; art teacher education; automobile/automotive mechanics technology; biology/biological sciences; botany/plant biology; business administration & management; business teacher education; carpentry; chemistry; child development; computer science; construction engineering technology; criminal justice/law enforcement administration; dance; drafting & design technology; dramatic/theater arts; economics; education; electrical; electronic & communications; elementary education; engineering technology; English; family & community services; family & consumer sciences/home economics teacher education; family & consumer sciences/human sciences; French; geology/earth science; German; history; information science/studies; interior design; mass communication/media; mathematics, music; music teacher education; political science & government; physical education teaching & coaching; physical sciences, preengineering; psychology; secondary education; social sciences; sociology; Spanish; special education; speech & rhetoric; technology education/industrial arts; zoology/animal biology

Costs and Aid

$9,198 in-state comprehensive ($3,274 tuition); $16,728 out-of-state comprehensive ($10,804 tuition).

Endowment

$5.1 million.

More Distinctions

• The National Research Center for College & University Admissions released its annual rankings of Admissions Web sites of more than three thousand postsecondary institutions, and Southern Utah University has been ranked the ninth best Web site in the country.

• In the quest for affordability and value, Southern Utah University has been ranked among America's Best Value Colleges by the Princeton Review for 2007.

• The May/June 2004 issue of Consumers Digest includes its list of Best Values in Colleges and Universities in America, and SUU lands in the top ten on the national ranking.

Westminster College

UTAH

Admissions Contact:

Westminster College
1840 South 1300 East
Salt Lake City, UT 84105
(800) 748-4753
Fax: (801) 823-3101
Email: admission@westminstercollege.edu
www.westminstercollege.edu

Founded in 1875, Westminster College is the only private, comprehensive, liberal arts college or university in the state of Utah. In graduate and undergraduate programs that combine a liberal education with professional studies, students are guaranteed active learning experiences, a dynamic campus community, and real-world opportunities.

The 4 Distinctions

Engaged Students

Westminster College is nationally recognized for its intense focus on individual students and their learning. Students master content-specific material while developing clearly defined skills and attributes critical for success in a rapidly changing world. Students who value learning by doing appreciate Westminster's unique approach to learning. Westminster emphasizes collaboration over competition and active learning over large lectures. Students often work in teams, sharing a variety of perspectives, and faculty members are expert at blending theory and practice. Students take what they learn in the classroom and extend it into a wider arena of hands-on experience through learning communities, service-learning projects, undergraduate research, and May-term classes. As a result, Westminster students are fully engaged in their own learning.

May term, a month-long term at the end of the spring semester, offers students who were enrolled full-time in the fall and spring semesters the opportunity to take four additional credits for free. Students usually take two two-credit courses that allow them to pursue their passions or special areas of interest. Classes include the chemistry and biology of beer; the psychology of yoga; sex in the brain; the statistics of gambling, which includes trips to a casino; and the history of rock and roll, taught by a faculty expert who is also a specialist on the Rolling Stones. Students may also choose from trips to Spain, Italy, Canada, and Mexico.

As an alternative to studying abroad, students from around the country can come to Westminster for a unique winter adventure program called Winter at Westminster. Students learn from winter sports industry leaders and Olympic medalists. Students also receive season passes to two world-class resorts, and have the opportunity to ski or ride at seven other mountain resorts, all within a short distance from campus. Westminster even offers tuition assistance for athletes on the U.S. Ski and Snowboard teams, many of whom attend Westminster because of its proximity to Olympic training facilities.

Westminster offers more then seventy academic programs, including thirty-seven undergraduate majors and nine graduate programs. The school hosts an undergraduate research fair every spring during which students can share their high-level research results with the community. All types of academic interests are represented, including English, history, math, physics, and others. Some students have participated in groundbreaking research on Great Salt Lake, even identifying a new species.

The Center for Civic Engagement involves students in community service throughout the semester by identifying volunteer opportunities, sponsoring service-learning trips to locations such as Native American reservations, and by integrating service-learning opportunities with class work.

Great Teaching

Teachers come to Westminster College because the focus is on students and their learning. While faculty continue their scholarly work, their first priority is always the students.

Of the nearly forty undergraduate majors, the most popular are business, nursing, psychology, and education. One unusual major is aviation. Westminster is one of the few institutions in the country to combine a four-year bachelor's degree with training to be a corporate or commercial airline pilot.

Westminster has recently integrated degree programs that are designed to capitalize on its location, using surrounding areas as an extension of the campus. For example, paleontology is taught by a Harvard-trained geologist who leads students on expeditions to ideal locations in the area.

All freshmen are required to participate in a learning community. These classes are team taught by two professors, each with a different focus, who work together to provide an integrated theme. For example, a course on public interactions and chemical reactions is taught by a professor of speech and a professor of chemistry. Modern war and rhetoric pairs an English professor, who presents the literature revolving around conflicts and a history professor, who discusses the complexities of war. In wilderness, suburbs, and action, students use writing and research skills to explore the natural environment. One recent project encouraged students to create a Thanksgiving dinner using only the farms and natural growth within a ten-mile radius of campus.

Vibrant Community

Set in urban Salt Lake City and just minutes from the Rocky Mountains, Westminster's campus includes twenty-eight buildings on twenty-seven beautifully manicured acres in the city's eclectic Sugar House neighborhood, which features a collection of shops, coffeehouses, restaurants, and cafes. Few schools in the country can boast immediate access to a thriving city and some of the world's best mountain recreation.

Salt Lake City was designated by Outside magazine as its number one "dream town." It's located thirty minutes from skiing and other mountain activities and only a few hours' drive from southern Utah's red rock country, including many parks and rock-climbing sites. Utah also boasts the highest number of national parks in the country.

A campus theme, called Common Ground, is introduced each year to integrate all people, classes, and clubs on campus. The next three years' themes will explore a place. For 2007, the theme is the desert, and all incoming students read Desert Solitaire by Edward Abbey. Activities in and out of the classroom will use the desert as a lens through which to understand learning, life, and the local environment.

About five hundred students live on campus in two traditional residence halls for freshman and three apartment-style residence halls for upper-level students.

A huge number of events are scheduled every week on campus—an average of one event per day for the year—including many lectures, films, art exhibits, musical performances, and athletic events. The student government, ASCW, also sponsors Wild Wednesdays, which include activities such as comedians and cosmic bowling. The college even has a campus concierge desk, similar to the concierge desk at a five-star hotel, to offer assistance with tickets to performances, discount lift tickets, restaurant deals, and access to events all over the city. The new Dolores Dore Eccles Health, Wellness and Athletic Center includes a field house for all athletics and features a three-story rock-climbing wall, a four-lane lap pool, state-of-the-art fitness and weight equipment, and a yoga studio. Student athletes play soccer and lacrosse on the Dumke Field.

Successful Outcomes

One famous Westminster alumnus is William H. Gore, inventor of Gore-Tex. The Bill and Vieve Gore School of Business is named after him and his wife.

About 95 percent of Westminster students go on to graduate school or are employed within six months of graduation. The nursing program boasts a 100 percent placement rate.

A Utah Foundation study found that Westminster graduates have among the highest starting salaries of any university graduates in the state. These high starting salaries were attributed in part to the fact that nearly 70 percent of Westminster students complete an internship before they graduate.

Fast Facts

Westminster College is nationally recognized for its intense focus on individual students and their learning. Students master content specific material while developing clearly defined skills and attributes critical for success in a rapidly changing world. In graduate and undergraduate programs which combine a liberal education with professional studies, students are guaranteed active learning experiences, a dynamic campus community and real world opportunities. Founded in 1875, Westminster is the only private, non-denominational college or university in the state of Utah.

Web site

http://www.westminstercollege.edu/

Location

Salt Lake City, Utah—Westminster is located in the Sugar House neighborhood of Salt Lake, about 10 minutes from the downtown business district and just 30 minutes from seven mountain resorts.

Student Profile

2,500 students (46% male, 54% female); 39 states, 31 countries.

Faculty Profile

119 full-time faculty, 127 part time faculty. 89% hold the highest degree available in their fields. 11:1 student/faculty ratio. Average class size is 17.

Residence Life

Moderately residential: 25% of undergraduate students live on-campus. Freshman can live in traditional residence halls while other students can live in on-campus apartment-style facilities. The college also owns and rents several apartments and students can also find their own places to live throughout the area.

Athletics

NAIA Division I. 10 varsity sports (4 men's: basketball, cross-country, golf, soccer; 5 women's: basketball, cross-country, golf, soccer, volleyball), 4 club sports, including men's lacrosse, and many intramural sports teams.

Academic Programs

Anthropology; accounting; art; arts administration; aviation; biology; business; chemistry; communication; computer science; economics; economics; education; engineering 3-2; English; environmental studies; film studies; finance; financial services; fine arts; French; gender studies; history; information resource management; international business; justice studies; management; marketing; mathematics; music; neuroscience; nursing; paleontology; philosophy; physics; political studies; predental; prelaw; premedicine; preveterinary; psychology; religious studies; social science; sociology; Spanish; special education; theatre arts.

Costs and Aid

2007–2008: $28,728 comprehensive ($22,374 tuition and fees). 98% of students receive some financial aid. Average award: $17,500.

Endowment

$60 million.

More Distinctions

• The Princeton Review's 2007 college rankings names Westminster College as one of the "Best 361 Colleges in America."

Saint Martin's University

WASHINGTON

Founded in 1895, Saint Martin's University is a Catholic, Benedictine university with twenty-one majors, six preprofessional programs, and six graduate programs spanning liberal arts, business, education, and engineering. Saint Martin's strives to inspire students to "Be the Spirit" and lead lives of peace, passion, and purpose.

Admissions Contact:

Saint Martin's University
5300 Pacific Ave SE
Lacey, WA 98503
(800) 368-8803
Ph: (360) 438-4311
Email: admissions@stmartin.edu
www.stmartin.edu

The 4 Distinctions

Engaged Students

Saint Martin's goal is to "prepare students for active, responsible, and productive lives in their professions and as members of the local and global community." To achieve this goal, the university encourages student involvement in internships, study abroad, and community service.

The university's proximity to Olympia gives students opportunities to intern for government offices and agencies in Washington's state capital. Other companies that often hire Saint Martin's students as interns include Microsoft, Intel, and Boeing. Internships are required in the majors of community service, psychology, and education.

Students serve the community in various ways. Recent projects have included working for Habitat for Humanity; traveling to Guatemala, Mexico, and Appalachia to help needy families; raising money for the Saint Agnes Orphanage in Tanzania; and serving dinner once a month at a local homeless shelter. St. Martin's became involved with the orphanage in Tanzania when the university's mechanical engineering students built a desperately needed water purification system for the Saint Agnes Orphanage and school. A Pure Water Concert was put on by students in the music department to raise the money to ship the system. The fundraiser exceeded expectations, raising twice the money necessary, and the extra money was sent to the Saint Agnes Orphanage and school for educational supplies.

Study abroad is available for a semester, a year, or for the summer in locations such as Argentina, Australia, France, Greece, Scotland, and Spain. Summer-abroad programs and study tours are also available. Study tours are short, faculty-led programs lasting one to three weeks. Study tours are an excellent opportunity to explore a new country or culture with a group of Saint Martin's students. Study tour locations change annually, although the China study tour and the Japan cultural exchange tour are offered every year. The Japanese cultural exchange takes students to Tokyo, Osaka, and Kobe. The China study tour takes students to Beijing, Shanghai, and Hong Kong, allowing them to see the Great Wall, Tiananmen Square, and many other famous landmarks.

St. Martin's students are encouraged to explore their spiritual sides. Campus ministry, service projects, and religion courses are just some of the ways they can do so at Saint Martin's.

Great Teaching

Students at Saint Martin's enjoy small classes that allow professors to get to know students individually. Over 89 percent of the classes have fewer than twenty students, and 98 percent have fewer than thirty students. In addition, classes are always taught by professors, not teaching assistants. In some courses, students conduct original research under the guidance of the professor.

The liberal arts experience at Saint Martin's helps students become critical thinkers, effective communicators, problem solvers, compassionate listeners, involved citizens, and openhearted people. Among St. Martin's distinctive programs are elementary education, business, civil engineering, and psychology.

Accredited by the Accreditation Board for Engineering and Technology Inc. (ABET), the civil engineering program provides students with practical training in the creative aspects of engineering design. Students gain hands-on laboratory experience in structures, soils, transportation, hydraulics, and environmental engineering, and enroll in many project-oriented courses.

The criminal justice program provides students with opportunities to intern with criminal justice agencies, law enforcement agencies, adult correction law offices, judges, and the state attorney general's office.

Saint Martin's first-year seminar provides freshmen students with an orientation to university life and study. During the seminar, each class comes up with a community-service component.

Vibrant Community

Students have plenty to do on campus during study breaks and on weekends. The Robert A. Harvie Social

Justice Lecture Series, intended to bring awareness to the community about social justice issues, features four speakers who come to campus to address a variety of issues pertaining to local and national issues. Students and the community can enjoy this series for free. Athletic events, dances, comedy shows, and karaoke nights are also scheduled throughout the year, providing students with a vibrant social life. Saint Martin's offers two dozen clubs and organizations, fifteen NCAA Division II athletic teams, and a variety of intramural sports.

The only Benedictine university west of the Rocky Mountains, Saint Martin's 380-acre campus is set in Lacey, Washington, in the Greater Olympia area. The campus's wooded areas provide students with walking trails and opportunities to observe wildlife. Greater Olympia has plenty of cultural opportunities to complement the university's educational experiences, and well-known entertainers, artists, and musicians often visit the metropolitan area. Saint Martin's is less than an hour from Seattle, thirty minutes from Tacoma, and two hours from Portland, Oregon.

Saint Martin's coed residential village offers both privacy and community. Currently, there are three residential halls in the campus community, including traditional freshmen housing as well as a variety of suite style living for sophomores, juniors and seniors. The newest addition will be Parsons Hall, a freshman and sophomore residence that features an espresso cafe, computer lab, and fitness room. Because Saint Martin's is committed to building and maintaining a strong sense of community in the Benedictine tradition, all single undergraduate students younger than 21 and who have fewer than 60 semester hours are required to live on campus. Exceptions are covered in the University's Housing Exemption Policy.

Successful Outcomes

Within twelve months of graduation, 95 percent of Saint Martin's students have a job in their field or are attending graduate school. Alumni include the first orthopedic surgeon in Hawaii, who is also currently the president of the Hawaii Medical Association; several Major League Baseball draft picks; a King County superior court judge; and a federal public defender.

Saint Martin's alumni have many opportunities to come together throughout the year. Alumni can root for the Seattle Mariners or the Tacoma Rainiers during Saint Martin's baseball nights every summer, or ring in the holidays during the procession of the carols and the annual Christmas cruise. In February, alumni and students show their school pride at the homecoming celebration.

Fast Facts

Saint Martin's University is a private, four-year liberal arts university affiliated with the Benedictine Order of the Roman Catholic Church and founded in 1895.

Web site

http://www.stmartin.edu/

Location

Lacey, Washington—adjacent to the state capitol of Olympia; 60 miles south of Seattle.

Student Profile

1,300 undergraduate students (42% male, 58% female); 16 states and territories, 13 countries; 31% minority.

Faculty Profile

76 full-time faculty. 15:1 student/faculty ratio. Average class size is 15.

Residence Life

Mildly residential: 41% of undergraduates live on campus.

Athletics

NCAA Division II, Great Northwest Athletic Conference. 15 varsity sports (7 men's: baseball, basketball, soccer, golf, indoor & outdoor track, cross-country; 8 women's: basketball, soccer, golf, indoor & outdoor track, cross-country, softball, and volleyball). Ten intramural sports including: basketball, softball, bowling, flag football, golf, kickball, dodgeball, tennis, ultimate frisbee, and volleyball.

Academic Programs

Accounting; biology; business administration; chemistry; civil engineering; community services; computer science; criminal justice; elementary education; English; history; humanities; mathematics; mechanical engineering; music; political science; psychology; religious studies; sociology & cultural anthropology; special education; theatre arts. Preprofessional Programs: dentistry, law, medicine, pharmacy, physical therapy.

Costs and Aid

2007–2008: $33,685 comprehensive ($22,250 tuition). 100% of students receive some form of financial aid. Average award: $21,004.

Endowment

$11,275,848.

More Distinctions

• Ranked as a "top school" in U.S. News Best Colleges – West edition.

• Distinguished as most diverse college in the area according to The Olympian, local newspaper.

University of Puget Sound

WASHINGTON

University of Puget Sound, located in the beautiful Pacific Northwest, is a liberal arts and sciences college that was founded in 1888. While committing itself to excellent teaching and innovative academic programs, the university assists students in developing useful and creative lives.

Admissions Contact:

University of Puget Sound
1500 N. Warner
Tacoma, WA 98416
(800) 396-7191
Ph: (253) 879-3211
Fax: (253) 879-3993
Email: admission@ups.edu
www.ups.edu

The 4 Distinctions

Engaged Students

The university promotes the importance of intercultural understanding; 40 percent of Puget Sound students have studied abroad before they graduate. Programs are available at 150 locations in fifty countries. Typically, Puget Sound students study abroad during their junior year. In their sophomore year, students can use the on-campus study-abroad office as a resource for selecting a program that best fits their academic and personal goals.

The Civic Scholarship Initiative provides unique opportunities for students to work on community problems. Supporting projects that connect the south Puget Sound region and University of Puget Sound faculty and students in areas of mutual concern, the initiative provides real-world laboratories, solves problems, develops policy, and educates the public on significant issues. Faculty and community members suggest and develop ideas. The initiative combines education, service, and research to offer students a productive and meaningful experience. Initiatives include projects such as the Road Home: Homeless Policy for Pierce County, in which the university works with the Pierce County Department of Community Services and the Road Home Leadership Team to reduce the homeless population in Pierce County.

There are many opportunities for students to engage in research, whether in the natural sciences, in the social sciences, in the arts, or in the humanities. Most major programs of study either require or provide the option for a research-based thesis in the senior year. Summer research projects are also available, and many students who choose to perform research over the summer are granted awards.

The university is home to the notable Pacific Rim/Asia Study-Travel (Pac Rim) program. The program sends students from Puget Sound on Pac Rim trips once every three years. These study-travel programs last nine months and offer students rigorous academics and a time of personal inquiry. Visiting eight Asian nations, the group engages in a vast multicultural experience that forces them to confront novel systems of culture, economics, politics, religion, and philosophy. Asian classrooms and hands-on education extend the limits of the regular curriculum taking place on campus in the U.S.

Great Teaching

Boasting an eleven to one student to faculty ratio, classes at Puget Sound are taught by professors, not teaching assistants. The university is home to many distinguished professors, including a Grammy award winner, the recipient of a MacArthur Foundation Genius Award, and a leading expert on the ethics of stem-cell research.

The university has a long tradition of excellence in music. The School of Music offers three professional degrees (Bachelor of Music degrees in performance, music education, and elective studies in music business), a liberal arts degree (Bachelor of Arts), and a music minor.

The international political economy program is popular at Puget Sound, offering a multidisciplinary approach to the study of modern society using the tools and methods of political science, economics, and sociology. The program was designed by Puget Sound professors and has been implemented at other colleges and universities.

Business leadership is also a popular program. Each year, up to twenty-five freshmen are admitted into this intensive four-year program. Not only are students educated in business fundamentals, including finance, accounting, marketing, law, ethics, leadership, and management, but students are also required to apply their knowledge to real-world situations by participating in regional business field trips, an evening leadership speaker series, and a professional internship. Internship opportunities abound in the region, with companies such as Starbucks and Microsoft in Seattle and Tacoma.

Puget Sound is a founding member of the Nationwide Internships Consortium, a group of national liberal arts institutions that share internship resources. This gives Puget Sound students access to thousands of internship opportunities across the county.

Vibrant Community

Nearly 70 percent of students live on Puget Sound's ninety-seven-acre campus. The Tudor-Gothic buildings are set among native fir groves in a residential section in the North End of Tacoma, Washington. With about 75 percent of students coming to the university from out-of-state, Puget Sound has a geographically diverse student body. Students come from forty-nine states and territories and fifteen countries to live and learn at the university.

Puget Sound is a leader in the area of community living. The Freshman Residential Seminar Program allows a group of freshman to live together and take the same first-year seminar. Many themed houses are available for students to live in, each house offering a unique living and learning environment. Honors housing, a social justice residence program, and a languages and culture house are a few of the many living/learning options available. Students develop awareness of their theme throughout the campus by planning educational programs that relate to the theme of the house. Past examples of these activities include wilderness outings hosted by the Outhaus, the Alphabet Music program hosted by the Music House, and hula lessons hosted by the Hawaii House.

Number one in the Northwest, and consistently ranked in the top five in the West Coast, Puget Sound's Division III athletic programs are strong. About 50 percent of students participate in intramurals, and the field house on campus includes six indoor tennis courts and a climbing wall.

Successful Outcomes

Puget Sound prepares students for lives of service and success. Puget Sound is the number one producer nationally of Peace Corps volunteers from small colleges and universities. The university also beats the national average for students accepted to medical school, and is among the top ten schools for producing undergraduates who go on to be Fulbright Scholars.

Business leadership students are paired with regional business leaders, who serve as mentors throughout students' sophomore, junior, and senior years. These volunteer mentors, often Puget Sound alumni, help prepare students for internships and careers by teaching from personal and professional experience.

Career and Employment Services (CES) provides comprehensive resources and counseling for students at every point in their career planning, including part-time, full-time, and work-study employment; internships; and career choices. Faculty also serve as advisers and write recommendations for students. Through the Alumni Sharing Knowledge (ASK) network, students have a valuable career consulting network.

Famous alumni include Deanna Oppenheimer, chief executive of Barclays UK Banking; George Obiozor, Nigerian ambassador to the United States; and Rick Brooks, president and CEO of Zumiez.

Fast Facts

The University of Puget Sound is an independent, liberal arts college with a four-year core and interdisciplinary approach.

Web site

http://www.ups.edu/

Location

Tacoma, Washington—35 miles south of Seattle.

Student Profile

2,576 undergraduate students (42% male, 58% female); 49 states and territories, 15 countries; 16% minority,1% international; 75% of students from out of state.

Faculty Profile

219 full-time faculty. 98% hold a terminal degree in their field. 11:1 student/faculty ratio. Average class size is 18.

Residence Life

Highly residential: 70% of students live on campus.

Athletics

NCAA Division III, Northwest Conference. 23 varsity sports (11 men's: baseball, basketball, crew, cross-country, football, golf, soccer, swimming, tennis, track & field (indoor & outdoor); 12 women's: basketball, crew, cross-country, golf, lacrosse, soccer, softball, swimming, tennis, track & field (indoor & outdoor), volleyball), varied club and intramural sports.

Academic Programs

African American studies; art; Asian studies; biochemistry; biology; business & leadership; chemistry; classics; communication studies; comparative sociology; computer science; connections; dual degree engineering; economics; education; English; environmental studies; exercise science; foreign languages & literature; gender studies; geology; history; honors; humanities; international political economy; Latin American studies; mathematics; molecular & cellular biology; music; natural science; neuroscience; philosophy; physical education (activity courses); physics; politics & government; psychology; religion; science, technology & society; special interdisciplinary major; theatre arts.

Costs and Aid

2007–2008: $40,325 comprehensive ($30,060 tuition). 94% of students receive some form of financial aid, 65% receive need-based assistance. Average award for students with financial need: $22,700.

Endowment

$222.7 million.

More Distinctions

• Puget Sound has been listed in the The Best 361 Colleges, printed by the Princeton Review, for the last 12 years.

• Among colleges and universities with fewer than 5,000 undergraduates, Puget Sound has the most alumni currently serving as Peace Corps Volunteers worldwide.

Whitworth University

WASHINGTON

Founded in 1890, Whitworth University is a private, liberal arts college affiliated with the Presbyterian Church. Whitworth's mission is to provide its students with "an education of the mind and heart, equipping its graduates to honor God, follow Christ, and serve humanity."

Admissions Contact:

Whitworth University
300 W. Hawthorne Road
Spokane, WA 99251
(800) 533-4668
Ph: (509) 777-4786
Email: mhansen@whitworth.edu
www.whitworth.edu

The 4 Distinctions

Engaged Students

Whitworth offers a number of study-abroad options so that all students who wish to study abroad are able to do so. The university offers three long-standing semester study-abroad programs in Central America, France, and the British Isles. In Central America, students study Spanish in Guatemala for four weeks and then travel to the Honduras to work on rural service projects. In France, students earn credits in French language, art, literature, and communication while traveling through France. In the British Isles, students explore British history, literature, and politics as they travel through Great Britain.

More than one-third of Whitworth's 2006 graduating class participated in an off-campus study program during their college years. Most academic disciplines are offered abroad, and there are opportunities for studying in French, Spanish, German, Cantonese, Mandarin, and Japanese. January and May terms offer more than thirty courses that allow students to travel and study abroad with Whitworth faculty members. Topics have included international business in Australia and India, European roots of Christian spirituality in France and Switzerland, and the people and politics of post-Apartheid South Africa.

Whitworth University funds a student leadership position to coordinate service projects on campus and in the local community. Projects include tutoring low-income students weekly through Homework Helpers, and Community Building Day, during which campus is shut down so that faculty, staff, and students can serve in Spokane. In addition, students completed more than 5,500 hours of community service through service-learning courses in spring 2007.

Great Teaching

While some Christian universities limit engagement with certain ideas or secular scholarship on their campuses, Whitworth encourages tough questions and a fearless search for answers wherever they may be found. And though many other institutions deny any role for religion in the pursuit of truth, Whitworth has consistently affirmed Christian conviction and intellectual curiosity as complementary rather than competing values. These dual commitments form a "Grand Paradox" that sets Whitworth University apart in the higher-education landscape.

Whitworth University's faculty members study, research and write. They win prestigious grants and awards. And they display their artistic talents in demanding venues. But they never waver from their primary commitment to teach and mentor students. With a student-faculty ratio of 13-to-1, Whitworth is a place where professors know and are known by their students. Conversations begun in the classroom often carry over into the dining hall or local coffee shops, residence-hall lounges and, even, professors' own homes.

Scholarly activity is viewed at Whitworth as an aid, rather than an obstacle, to great teaching. In fact, many professors engage students fully in the daunting enterprise of discovery and dissemination of new knowledge and in the creation of original contributions to their fields. Students work alongside faculty on research ranging from assessing the impact of micro-lending in low-income neighborhoods and developing countries to exploring the theological insights of early Christian aesthetics and the role particular enzymes play in memory function for treating Alzheimer's patients. Together they face the risks that underlie any research: the risks to follow paths that may lead initially to dead ends, the risks to explore ideas that challenge the prevailing wisdom in a discipline, and the risks inherent in presenting findings for public scrutiny.

Vibrant Community

Whitworth's 200-acre campus of red-brick buildings and tall pines is located seven miles north of downtown Spokane in the beautiful Pacific Northwest. An active campus life offers ten distinct residence halls, dozens of student organizations, abundant opportunities to enjoy fine and performing arts, and a highly successful NCAA Division III athletics program with 20 varsity sports.

Whitworth's student leaders focus on building strong peer relationships and a sense of responsibility around shared values so that students become good decision-makers rather than just good rule-followers. In fact, Whitworth students meet each fall to establish their own residence-area policies for living in community and holding one another accountable to the campus code of conduct.

A national residence life organization recognized Whitworth's student leadership program for involving more students in more diverse roles with more responsibilities than most other colleges and universities. In addition to a relatively high number of resident assistants, each Whitworth residence hall has small-group (ministry) coordinators, medics, and cultural diversity advocates, not to mention dozens of leadership positions in student government. The broad range of leadership positions allows students to receive valuable training and gain experience for careers without crowding out opportunities to participate in other extra-curricular activities. It also expands the network of contact points for engaging students in Whitworth University's active campus life.

As a Christian institution, Whitworth University takes seriously Christ's example of loving across racial, ethnic, gender, socio-economic and religious differences. With such a high standard, Whitworth remains focused on being an inclusive community that seeks out and welcomes people with diverse backgrounds and perspectives who can support our mission. Whitworth partners with the Northwest Leadership Foundation on the innovative Act Six Leadership & Scholarship Initiative that brings 10-12 ethnically and socio-economically diverse students from inner-city Tacoma to Whitworth each year. Whitworth, the first college to join the program, provides training and significant financial aid to student participants.

Successful Outcomes

Whitworth has an excellent track record of preparing students for top graduate schools and successful careers through strong faculty mentoring and a wide range of career exploration, internship and networking resources provided by the Career Services Offices. Just as importantly, Whitworth is committed to helping our students connect their deepest convictions to their work and to other major life decisions.

Whitworth received $2.5 million in grants from the Lilly Endowment for an innovative project focused on "Discerning Vocation: Community, Context and Commitment." Through new course material, co-curricular programs, faculty and staff mentoring, service learning and community engagement projects, students are encouraged to explore ways of connecting their gifts and abilities with the larger needs of society.

Notable alumni include Ross Anderson, a reporter for the Seattle Times who shared the 1990 Pulitzer Prize in journalism for his articles on the Exxon Valdez accident; Frank Hernandez, an internationally recognized opera singer and winner of an ARIA Award, the George London Competition, and the Puccini Competition; Ray Washburn, a former professional baseball pitcher for the St. Louis Cardinals who pitched a no-hitter and won multiple World Series games in his career; Peter Blomquist, the regional director of the CARE Northwest office and former head of the Starbucks Foundation; Desiree DeSoto, a professional long-board surfer who competes internationally; and Marvin Sather, a high school English teacher who received Washington State's Teacher of the Year Award in 1999.

Fast Facts

Whitworth University, founded in 1890, is a private, residential, liberal arts college affiliated with the Presbyterian Church (U.S.A.).

Web site

www.whitworth.edu

Location

Spokane, Washington—200-acre campus located seven miles north of downtown.

Student Profile

2,500 students; 30 states, 17 countries. Non-Caucasian enrollment: 16 percent.

Faculty Profile

125 full-time faculty. 80% hold PhD or terminal degrees. 13:1 student/faculty ratio.

Athletics

NCAA Division III, Northwest Conference. 20 varsity sports (10 men's: baseball, basketball, cross-country, football, golf, soccer, swimming, tennis, indoor/outdoor track & field; 10 women's: basketball, cross-country, golf, soccer, softball, swimming, tennis, indoor/outdoor track and field, volleyball).

Academic Programs

Accounting; American studies; art; art teacher education; arts management; athletic training; biology/biological sciences; business administration & management; chemistry; computer science; dramatic/theater arts; economics; elementary education; English; fine/studio arts; French; history; international business/trade/commerce; international relations & affairs journalism; mass communication/media; mathematics; music; music teacher education; nursing (registered nurse training); peace studies & conflict resolution; philosophy; physical education teaching & coaching; physics; piano & organ; political science & government; predentistry studies; prelaw studies; premedical studies; preveterinary studies; psychology; religious studies; secondary education; sociology; Spanish; special education; speech & rhetoric; voice & opera.

Costs and Aid

2007–08: $25,382 tuition, $7,294 room (double occupancy) and board (full meal plan). More than 95% of Whitworth students receive financial aid; the average scholarship/grant award for 2006 freshmen was $12,450.

Endowment

$72.4 million.

More Distinctions

• In U.S. News & World Report's 2007 America's Best Colleges guide, Whitworth is #3 on the "best values" list and #5 on the "best values" list among 123 master's-level universities in the 15-state Western region.

• Whitworth ranks #32 on Kiplinger's 2007 List of the 50 best values in Private Universities. The California Institute of Technology tops the list followed by Yale, Harvard, Rice, and Duke. West coast schools joining Whitworth (#32) in the top 50 are Stanford (#12), USC (#29), Gonzaga (#42) and Santa Clara (#44).

• Poet Laureate Donald Hall has selected Whitworth poet Professor Laurie Lamon for a Witter Bynner fellowship. In honor of this award Professor Lamon was asked to read from her works at the Library of Congress in March 2007.

Index

Index